READING INSTRUCTION THAT WORKS

Also from the Authors

Learning to Read:
Lessons from Exemplary First-Grade Classrooms
*Michael Pressley, Richard L. Allington,
Ruth Wharton-McDonald, Cathy Collins Block,
and Lesley Mandel Morrow*

Motivating Primary-Grade Students
*Michael Pressley, Sara E. Dolezal Kersey,
Lisa Raphael Bogaert, Lindsey Mohan,
Alysia D. Roehrig, and Kristen Bogner Warzon*

Reading to Learn:
Lessons from Exemplary Fourth-Grade Classrooms
Richard L. Allington and Peter H. Johnston

Shaping Literacy Achievement:
Research We Have, Research We Need
*Edited by Michael Pressley, Alison K. Billman,
Kristen H. Perry, Kelly E. Reffitt,
and Julia Moorhead Reynolds*

READING INSTRUCTION THAT WORKS

The Case for Balanced Teaching

FIFTH EDITION

Tim Pressley
Richard L. Allington
Michael Pressley

THE GUILFORD PRESS
New York   London

Copyright © 2023 The Guilford Press
A Division of Guilford Publications, Inc.
370 Seventh Avenue, Suite 1200, New York, NY 10001
www.guilford.com

Printed in the United States of America

This book is printed on acid-free paper.

Last digit is print number: 9 8 7 6 5 4 3 2 1

Library of Congress Cataloging-in-Publication Data is available
from the publisher.

ISBN 978-1-4625-5184-2 (paperback)   ISBN 978-1-4625-5185-9 (hardcover)

›

About the Authors

Tim Pressley, PhD, is an Associate Professor of Psychology at Christopher Newport University and a faculty member for the university's master's in teaching program and the Center for Education Research and Policy. Prior to receiving his doctorate, Dr. Pressley was an elementary school teacher, which has been a driving force behind his research. His current research focuses on teachers' lives, specifically the impact of COVID-19, teacher effectiveness, and teacher development. He hopes his research gives teachers a voice on aspects affecting their lives.

Richard L. Allington, PhD, is a retired Professor of Literacy Studies in the Department of Theory and Practice in Teacher Education at the University of Tennessee. He has published over 150 articles, chapters, and books, and has twice received the Albert J. Harris Award from the International Literacy Association (ILA) for outstanding contributions to the understanding of the prevention and assessment of reading disabilities. Dr. Allington has served as president of both the ILA and the Literacy Research Association. He is a member of the Reading Hall of Fame.

Michael Pressley, PhD, until his death in 2006, was University Distinguished Professor, Director of the Doctoral Program in Teacher Education, and Director of the Literacy Achievement Research Center at Michigan State University. An expert on effective elementary literacy instruction, he was the author or editor of more than 300 journal articles, chapters, and books. Dr. Pressley was the recipient of the 2004 E. L. Thorndike Award (from Division 15 of the American Psychological Association), the highest award given for career research accomplishment in educational psychology.

Contents

Introduction to the Fifth Edition

Tim Pressley

When Richard Allington and The Guilford Press reached out to me about writing the fifth edition of this book, I knew it was something I could not turn down. I knew Michael Pressley like nobody else in the world. For many, he was a dedicated reading researcher, a mentor, a collaborator, and a friend. But to me, he was Dad. Growing up with a dad that studied effective reading instruction meant there were many books around the house, and he always wanted to know how my teachers were teaching me to read. I have even heard stories of how he made my first-grade teacher cry because she did not know that the whole-language approach she was teaching to my class was not backed by research. He later dropped off a stack of research articles for her to read, so she could learn about a more balanced approach to teaching reading. My first-grade reading experience was just one of the reasons Michael Pressley was so passionate about effective reading instruction. He was also passionate about making sure every child received effective reading instruction. Ultimately, he wanted this book to support preservice teachers and current teachers in their development into highly effective teachers in the subject of reading.

Shortly after Michael Pressley passed away, a close mentor reached out to me and told me, "You will never fill his shoes, but you can follow in his footsteps," and that was my goal with this fifth edition. Let me first state that I am honored to have the opportunity to coauthor a book with my dad. Still, as Richard Allington noted in the Introduction to the Fourth Edition (also included in this volume), I would have much preferred to discuss the latest reading research and the ways teachers can implement such practices in their classrooms with Michael Pressley himself. Throughout this new edition, I preserve a majority of the previous edition's text but update it with more recent research and incorporate application tables for teachers to use when building their lesson plans. These tables may guide teachers in translating the research to classroom practices.

My background is in elementary education. I completed my undergraduate and master's degrees in elementary education and then became a fourth-grade teacher in Crowley, Texas. During my time as a teacher, I realized that I missed conducting research and knew the next step was going for my PhD. I had the honor to work under Michael Pressley's last doctoral student, Alysia Roehrig, who supported me through my PhD in educational psychology. It was an absolute privilege to work with Dr. Roehrig, and I learned from her just as she had from my dad. I am currently a professor in the psychology department and teach classes for the teacher preparation program at Christopher Newport University in Newport News, Virginia. For most of my research career, I have focused on effective teaching and incorporating teacher perspectives into my research. I have used my experiences within the classroom to drive my research and am lucky to have married a teacher. My wife, Stephanie, is entering her 14th year in education and has worked as a classroom teacher, reading interventionist, reading specialist, and assistant principal. Through many conversations with her, I have worked to make the research discussed in this book more applicable to elementary teachers. I cannot thank her enough for her support through this fifth edition and the critical insight she provided into what is going on in today's classrooms.

Currently, in the reading research world, one of the most debated topics is the science of reading (SOR). This debate has split reading researchers on what constitutes SOR based on research designs, instructional focuses, and concepts that make up the reading process. We discuss some of the significant overviews available on the SOR in this new edition. However, before we even arrive at the text, we make it very clear where we stand with SOR. The cover of this book states that the topic is balanced reading instruction, a term that has recently become associated with meaning emphasis or whole-language approaches to teaching reading. I urge readers not to make that assumption, as this book does not fully support meaning-emphasis (whole language) or skills-emphasis instruction (phonics); it rather pulls the research for the many components required of reading and presents the most effective instructional approaches based on reading research. Thus, we believe that this book aligns with SOR because all the components discussed in this book are backed by science and encourage teachers to find the balance between meaning and skill emphasis instruction.

One final addition to this fifth edition is the inclusion of a chapter focused on emergent bilingual (EB) students. As the number of EB students in classrooms increases across the United States, it is critical for teachers to understand how they can support these students in reading. In order to ensure the chapter covered the best science-based approaches for working with EB students, I reached out to an expert in the field to write this new chapter. I am thankful to Ana Taboada Barber for her contribution and believe her chapter provides an excellent research-based resource for teachers working with EB students.

Our ultimate goal for this book is that it will be a resource for preservice and current teachers as they develop their reading instruction. I hope teachers will return to the book as they look to support a struggling reader or put together their lesson plans for the many aspects of reading (e.g., phonics, comprehension, vocabulary). As a recent father to my daughter Ellison, I hope her future teachers use this book as a starting point so that she and other students receive the best reading instruction. In the end, I hope you find this book an excellent resource that helps to develop even more highly effective teachers, just as Michael Pressley would have wanted.

Introduction to the Fourth Edition

Richard L. Allington

I had known Michael Pressley as a casual acquaintance for a number of years before he arrived at the University at Albany, the State University of New York. However, it was during his tenure at UAlbany that Mike and I became friends and collaborating colleagues through the work we did together at the National Research Center on English Learning and Achievement (CELA). It was through the auspices of the CELA that we developed and carried out a national study of exemplary grade 1 and grade 4 teachers. Mike left UAlbany for Notre Dame University as we were beginning the data collection for the grade 4 study, and due to his illness, he turned the project over to me to complete. I then enlisted Peter Johnston, who had just returned from a sabbatical leave spent in his home nation of New Zealand. In the end, the 5 years I spent working with Mike and Peter on the exemplary teacher studies changed my career and my outlook on effective teaching.

For most of my career, I had focused on the intervention efforts that schools engaged in when it came to dealing with struggling readers, both the garden variety struggling readers and those who had been labeled learning-disabled. Generally speaking, though, before the exemplary teacher study I was "burned out" on the topic of struggling readers. Too many years studying efforts that never made much of a difference in the futures of struggling readers had left me wondering why good people so often choose bad designs when it comes to working with struggling readers. What attracted me to the idea of studying exemplary teachers was the fact that I had observed the occasional teacher who solved the problems that struggling readers had and turned them into achieving readers. How they managed to learn how to do that and do it within the confines of school systems that often seemed to be working against them and the struggling readers they served was what interested me.

We learned a lot during that period. Perhaps the most important thing we learned was that the truly effective teachers we were observing in their high-poverty schools really did teach virtually everyone to read. No longer did we have to rely on individual case studies of a single effective teacher because we now had multiple case studies of effective teachers drawn from six states spread geographically about the nation. The second thing we learned was that these teachers taught children differently than did most of their colleagues. In Chapter 10, you will read about these effective teachers and how they taught. You will also read about them in Chapter 11, where the topic is motivation for reading.[1]

The second thing we discovered was that these teachers offered reading instruction that was balanced, with explicit skills instruction embedded in great literary texts with lots of opportunities for students to talk with each other about the reading and the writing they were doing. Those of you who knew Mike know that he was, at least before he began studying effective elementary teachers, a strong proponent of explicit skills instruction. What the effective teachers studies did was to move Mike to a balanced literacy perspective. Out of this work—both data gathering and data interpretation, along with his wide reading and influential discussions—Mike developed his notions of balanced reading lessons. The effective teacher studies simply added more evidence to the case for balanced and effective reading instruction.

Mike wrote the first three editions of this book with no help from me. I am honored to now be his coauthor but would prefer he were still with us so that we could have continued our discussions, which sometimes sounded more like arguments, as this revision was completed. I substantially changed the opening chapter by moving it away from a focus primarily on the weaknesses and the strengths of the whole-language movement such that now the opening chapter is a brief discussion of the skills-emphasis and meaning-emphasis debates that have been recurrent across the past century. I believe that Mike began his shift to balanced literacy instruction after reading the works of Dahl, Freppon, McIntyre, Morrow, Routman, and others. As he noted in the third edition, too often this research has been ignored by the folks pushing for a scientific evidentiary base for beginning reading instruction. The book's other chapters remain largely intact in this fourth edition, but all have been updated to reflect important recent research. I have also decided to retain Mike's Introduction from the third edition (slightly

---

[1]References to chapter numbers have been updated to correspond to the fifth edition.

abridged), which explains the genesis and purpose of the book in a way that no one but Mike could.

For me, the most memorable moment with Mike was a joint presentation he and I did for the Education Writers Association in Washington, DC. We were paired oppositionally with Louisa Moats and Marilyn Adams. They were arguing for explicit decoding instruction and Mike and I were arguing for a less narrow framework that exhibited a far better balance of skills- and meaning-emphasis instruction. Mike suggested that he lead off the presentation, to be followed by Adams, then me, and finally Moats. All I can say is that after he finished his brief talk everyone was largely stymied. He had made such a good case for embedding explicit decoding lessons in rich stories and in invented writing activities that I'm not sure anyone in the audience was really listening to anything the rest of us had to say.

That is another reason I wish Mike were still with us today. I am a poor substitute for his voice on the evidence supporting effective and balanced teaching. Nonetheless, I was the person selected to revise *Reading Instruction That Works: The Case for Balanced Teaching*. I have done so attempting to bring more recent research into the book and to continue to shape the argument Mike began more than a decade ago. I hope you find the book interesting and valuable in creating classrooms where more effective and balanced reading instruction is practiced.

Introduction to the Third Edition

Michael Pressley

This is a book about effective elementary literacy instruction, intended for the many constituencies who have a need to know about what works to develop readers in elementary school. It is intended especially for those who want to form research-based opinions about effective elementary literacy instruction, including reading educators and specialists, staff developers, and in-service professionals who focus on reading, teacher educators, graduate students, policymakers concerned with reading and elementary education, and parents who feel a need to know more about the reading instruction that is occurring and could occur in schools. In short, this volume is aimed at a broad audience that wants an accessible and reader-friendly review of the research evidence pertaining to beginning reading, one that doesn't require them to have technical background knowledge in reading research.

I make the case in this book for a balanced perspective on reading instruction, rather than stressing either a whole-language or skills-first instructional orientation. Balanced-literacy teachers combine the strengths of whole-language and skills instruction and, in so doing, create instruction that is more than the sum of its parts. When the first edition of this book was written in the mid-1990s, taking a balanced approach to literacy instruction was definitely countercultural. There were many who identified strongly with the skills approach or with whole language. Proposing that better instruction entailed both skills instruction and holistic reading and writing experiences irritated both of these warring camps. I have often heard the accusation that the balanced approach is simply whole language in disguise, a criticism offered by some skills enthusiasts. I have just as often heard that the balanced approach is a camouflage for skills instruction, a complaint from some whole-language proponents. Of course, my view is that both of these criticisms distort my position, which is that balanced literacy instruction entails both skills teaching and holistic opportunities. As such, it requires that the well-informed teacher know much about teaching of skills and much about how to structure holistic reading and writing experiences.

Unfortunately, there are now many more ways that a consumer can become misinformed about the nature of balanced literacy instruction than when I wrote the first edition of this book. Look at any internet database of books in print for books on balanced literacy instruction and many titles will appear. My reading of most of these books—and I have read quite a few of them—is that they often are dedicated to either a skills or holistic perspective more than to balance. There has been something of a self-fulfilling prophecy: The claims I heard that balance is a smokescreen for either a skills perspective or whole language seem to have stimulated some authors to construct such smokescreens for their positions. In contrast, I emphasize here that skills and holistic instruction are best when they occur in tandem, with my envisionment of that tandem much better informed as I write in 2005 than when I wrote the first edition 8 years ago or the second edition 4 years ago.

Before you dive into this book, let me offer some advice. Following the first and second editions, I have interacted with many educators who have massively tabbed the book, who have reported to me that they have studied the volume, reading and rereading, and finding new meaning with each pass through the text.

Although the big message of balance comes through loudly and clearly, there are many smaller messages embedded in the text, with my intent to stimulate thinking with respect to a broad range of issues in reading education and research. Based on those previous encounters, be prepared for the possibility that the binding on your copy of the book will give out before you are done studying the volume. I am heartened that it is difficult to find a "clean, tight" copy of the book on any of the used bookseller sites on the web.

Perhaps the most common advice to writers is to "write what you know about." This book is about what I know and believe, based on my interpretation of research on reading and reading instruction, but also my lived experience as a reader and a student as well as by my own research on reading and reading instruction. I overview that life in this Introduction because I think it will help you to understand better the ideas favored in this book.

MY LIFE AS A DEVELOPING READER

Many of the conclusions offered in this book align with the facts of my own life as a student learning to read. I grew up in a home filled with what are now referred to as "emergent literacy experiences," with the early years at my house consistent with the best preschool literacy development practices, covered in Chapter 4 of this volume.

I met Dick, Jane, and Sally as a first-grade student in the fall of 1957. From the earliest days of grade 1, I was learning whole words, consistent with the approach used in the reading series featuring the three children who have become cultural icons representing all that was good and bad about America in the mid-20th century (Kismaric & Heiferman, 1996). In a 1995 letter, my former first-grade teacher, Miss Lindley McKinney, confided to me that she did follow the whole-word approach with a lot of phonics added to the instruction. Her memory jibes well with my own recall of her lessons, in which there was much sounding out of words and much reflection on the sounds in words. I have learned from personal experience that effective instruction need not be entirely consistent with any one perspective, but rather can be a blending of perspectives, a major conclusion of this book.

Although learning to read in the sense of decoding went well for me in grade 1 and after that, I made less certain progress in becoming a good comprehender. For example, in junior high school, my strategy with high school textbook assignments was to read them again and again, which I now know to be a strategy of choice for many high school students (Wood et al., 1998), continuing in many cases into college (Cordón & Day, 1996). That strategy works poorly and demands a great deal of time. As a result, I became exceptionally anxious about school, grades, and exams as a junior high school and senior high school student. For example, during junior year, I was required to read a book a week in the college preparatory English section in which I was enrolled. I always read my book, but I must admit I always had a great deal of fear that I would be quizzed on books read, for I was having difficulty in understanding and remembering much of what was in them.

I was exposed to some comprehension strategies instruction during junior and senior high school through the SQ3R (Survey, Question, Read, Recite, Review) approach (Robinson, 1961), which involves skimming a text first; asking questions about it based on the title, headers, and pictures; and then reading, reciting, and reviewing. It seemed difficult to execute and certainly did not improve my comprehension and memory noticeably. I knew even then that there had to be better strategies. There are, and they will be covered in Chapter 8 of this book.[1]

---

[1]References to chapter numbers have been updated to correspond to the fifth edition.

In college, I learned the value of prior knowledge. My first year at Northwestern University was exceptionally demanding. There was no hope of keeping up with many classmates in some of the subjects I was taking, for they had better background knowledge than I did in those subjects. I was not entirely left out of the prior-knowledge-advantaged club, however, for through some enrichment opportunities in high school, I knew a great deal about chemistry, and thus freshman college chemistry was much easier for me than for other students. By the end of freshman year, I understood very well that background knowledge was critical to understanding and learning, both from when I was disadvantaged in prior knowledge relative to others and when I was advantaged. There will be much about the importance of background knowledge contributing to reading comprehension in the pages of this book.

I started to use reading and study strategies very extensively during college, generally picking them up from classmates. By the late undergraduate years, I was on my way to becoming a strategic reader. It took a while to get to the level of strategy use now evident in my reading, however. At middle age, I can read books very quickly in subject areas in which I possess a great deal of prior knowledge. I have learned to overview books and to skim in order to avoid detailed reading of parts of texts covering material I already know. I attempt to relate what I am reading to my prior knowledge and beliefs, explicitly looking for points of similarity and dissimilarity with other conceptions I have encountered. I pay special attention to and read very carefully those sections of texts that are likely to be useful to me later, sections I want to understand well and remember. At midlife and midcareer, I am a skilled reader who can communicate with confidence the ideas encountered in books. As a scholar studying reading, I also have come to understand that exceptionally strategic reading is rare in college students, requiring years of reading experience to develop. That work is taken up in Chapter 2.

DEVELOPMENT AS A SCHOLAR OF READING AND READING INSTRUCTION

My scholarly experiences had profound effects on the ideas in this book. Specifically, my thinking was influenced by my background in psychology, especially developmental and educational psychologies. This disciplinary preparation in psychology prepared me not only for conducting experimental analyses of reading and reading instruction, but also for adapting my skills and outlooks as new issues in reading have come to the fore. Work from a number of disciplines is reviewed in this book, as is research carried out with a variety of methodologies, consistent with the diversity in my own research.

Education as a Research Psychologist

I majored in psychology at Northwestern between 1969 and 1973. While at Northwestern, I undertook a senior honors thesis that placed me in a number of schools in Evanston, Illinois, for much of my senior year. There was significant innovation going on in the Evanston schools at the time, informed by research and a variety of scholarly perspectives on education. My time spent in the Evanston schools did much to stimulate my career-long interest in how research can inform the education of children.

In August 1973, I drove to Minneapolis to begin a PhD in child psychology at the University of Minnesota. Thanks to a cooperative agreement within the Big Ten, I was able to take some of my doctoral work in the Department of Educational Psychology at the University of Wisconsin–Madison and carried out research there for the concluding 2 years of my graduate program. I emerged in 1977 with a PhD. Since then, I have been involved in a series of interrelated scholarly efforts that prepared me for the task of writing this book.

Research on Human Development and Instruction

During graduate school and the years immediately following completion of the PhD, I conducted much research on natural strategy development and strategy instruction. A major conclusion that followed from this work was that sophisticated intellectual strategies develop over many years. However, I also became aware of much other work supporting the conclusion that even children in the early elementary grades can be taught strategies they would naturally acquire only many years later, if at all. That is, I discovered early in my research career that natural development is often slow and uncertain relative to development via instruction. Since the second edition of this book, I have had a chance to review that work formally (Pressley & Hilden, 2006).

Research on Skilled Reading

Excellent developmental researchers understand that to know development it is essential to know about what is developing. Studies of highly skilled performances can be very informative about factors that should be encouraged during development. In the early 1990s, my students and I carried out a study of exceptionally skilled reading, having university professors think aloud as they read articles in their areas of expertise (Wyatt et al., 1993). The outcomes in that study were consistent with the outcomes in other think-aloud studies that Peter Afflerbach and I reviewed in *Verbal Protocols of Reading: The Nature of Constructively Responsive Reading* (Pressley &

Afflerbach, 1995). The case made in that book and reviewed in Chapter 2 of this volume is that exceptionally skilled reading is very active reading, from before reading begins to after it is concluded. Much of the activity can be described as strategic responses articulated with prior knowledge related to the topical content of what is being read. Pressley and Afflerbach (1995) refer to excellent reading as constructively responsive reading because good readers are continuously attempting to construct meaning. Their meaning-construction activities are consistently in response to ideas encountered in the text, with the responses very much influenced by the reader's prior knowledge that can be related to the text.

This book takes the position that the development of constructively responsive reading is an appropriate goal for reading educators, and one that can begin in the elementary years, in particular, through comprehension strategies instruction (Chapter 8). I came to this position—that comprehension strategies can and should be taught to children—largely through my research on reading instruction. That work has also informed my thinking about beginning reading instruction, including teaching about decoding.

Research on Elementary Reading Instruction

One of my best-known works in reading focused on the development of comprehension skills through strategies instruction. The main research tactic was to study schools where such instruction was making a big impact and to understand the nature of such effective instruction. Many of the insights about comprehension instruction covered in Chapter 8 were developed in this program of research.

This work on comprehension strategies instruction was followed by studies of instruction in primary-level classrooms known to produce high literacy achievement. The work at the primary level is being complemented by research at the middle school level as this revision is being prepared. The research to date on effective primary grade and middle school teaching goes far in informing Chapter 10, which takes up effective teaching in detail.

When I began my studies of excellent teaching, I went in with an open mind. What I have emerged with as a function of those interactions is a well-informed mind about what instruction can look like when it is done well. I am much in admiration of excellent teachers, and I am very grateful that some of them have admitted me into their classroom communities to observe what they do. When I think of my work in excellent classrooms, I am reminded of the motto of Northwestern University, my undergraduate alma mater: "Whatsoever is true, whatsoever is honorable, whatsoever is just, whatsoever is pure, whatsoever is pleasing, whatsoever is commendable, if there is any excellence or anything worthy of praise, think about these things" (Philippians 4:8). That is good advice, especially with respect to the study of teaching. Much more can be learned about teaching by studying good teaching than by lamenting bad teaching. I have done the former, and that goes far in explaining my perspectives on instruction that are detailed in this book.

When reading the descriptions of excellent teaching covered here, give the teachers the credit rather than me. I was privileged to showcase their work with my efforts in collaboration with many graduate students. In particular, Pamela El-Dinary, Rachel Brown, Ruth Wharton-McDonald, Alysia Roehrig, Lisa Raphael, Kristen Bogner, and Sara Dolezal were important colleagues in these research efforts. Together, the outstanding teachers who were studied and these graduate students helped me to shape a more complete perspective on the nature of balanced elementary literacy instruction than existed previously. As effortful as it was to do it, my students and I always found this work interesting and fun, and we were honored that some of the outstanding teachers we observed became our coauthors and friends. I have been privileged to have great people working with me throughout my career.

Integrative Scholarship on Reading Instruction

I have never been a researcher who has carried out his work unaware of related research (Kiewra et al., 1997). Throughout my involvement in reading research, I have studied carefully the major conceptual and empirical works related to reading and reading instruction (e.g., Pressley with McCormick, 1995; Pressley et al., 1995). Those efforts went far in defining the conclusions advanced in the chapters that follow.

Participation in Development of a Reading Instruction Series

In addition to my research and scholarly writing, in 1991 I became part of the author team of an elementary reading program. My interactions with my coauthors, including then Marilyn Adams and still Carl Bereiter, did much to increase my understanding of the nature of reading instruction that makes sense. In particular, this experience sensitized me to many of the issues surrounding decoding instruction, including the tensions that constitute the whole-language versus phonics debate.

HISTORY AND PURPOSE OF THIS BOOK

Much of this book is an expansion of a series of lectures that I gave to many audiences across North America between 1994 and 2004. This was part of my role as a principal investigator at the National Reading Research Center (NRRC) from 1992 through 1997 and the National Center for English Language Arts Achievement (CELA) from 1997 through 2000. The U.S. Department of Education, Office of Educational Research and Improvement (OERI), funded both centers, and I am grateful to OERI for its financial support of my research. I am also grateful to the University of Maryland at College Park (1989–1993) and the University at Albany, State University of New York (1993–1997), the universities at which I was appointed when this book was first conceived and written. The second edition was possible because of the generous support I received from Notre Dame, where I hung my professional hat from 1997 to 2002. Since moving to Michigan State University in 2002, I and my colleagues landed support from the university to fund a Literacy Achievement Research Center (LARC), which hosted me during this second revision effort.

Since this book's first appearance in 1998, many readers have let me know that they found what was in this volume to be credible and helpful. Beyond listening to the praise, however, I have also listened carefully to reservations that were expressed about what I said in the 1998 and 2002 editions and concerns about issues that were not addressed in those versions. My rethinking of those issues in light of the feedback received is reflected in the chapters that follow. I wish that I could have interacted with more people over prior editions, but contending with serious illness prevented me from spending as much time with readers of the book as I would have liked. More personally, their enthusiasm for the balanced perspective intensified my understanding that putting up a fight to remain alive was worthwhile, that I did have a message worth imparting, one that might make an important difference in the literacy education of students. As I pen this third draft, I am enduring treatment for a fourth primary cancer, with the expectation that I will once again survive. I am looking forward to many future exchanges with educators about the ideas in this version of the book.

A positive by-product of being ill is that there is increased opportunity to sit with new books and articles and reflect on them. There have been a lot of papers and articles published about literacy research since the 2002 edition appeared. Thus, there is important updating contained in this edition. One of the more important developments since I wrote the preceding edition was the expanding success of the journal *Scientific Studies of Reading*. Much of my reading of research that enters this edition was in its pages as well as in the pages of the *Journal of Educational Psychology*. As the editor of the latter publication from 1997 to 2002, I was pleased that literacy research increased in prominence during my tenure. Literacy continues to remain a prominent concern under current editor Karen R. Harris.

In short, a lot of good scholarship in literacy education has become available since the 2002 edition was written, and this book continues to be strongly evidence based, including the most recent evidence on literacy and literacy education. Thus, every chapter is updated based on the research published during the past 4–5 years as well as some additional reflection on the research included in the previous editions. Even so, my envisionment of balanced literacy instruction is not something that can be grown only in a university R&D hothouse, but rather something that any teacher could decide to do. Alternatively, any school or school district could decide to promote a balanced approach. The teachers featured in this book all constructed their own balanced instructional worlds, although it is clear that excellent balanced-literacy teachers often go to great lengths to inform themselves about what is research-based best practice in literacy education. Since balanced-literacy instruction is the construction of individual teachers, it is not an instructional package that can be imported, such as many school/classroom reforms that are offered in the marketplace. That said, I am not opposed to widespread reform efforts or even commercial efforts to develop ways to stimulate balanced instruction. Indeed, I am impressed that with every passing year there is additional evidence that some of the most prominent national reform efforts, in fact, are having a positive impact on American students—for example, Reading Recovery, the Perry Preschool Project, the Abecedarian Project, high-quality versions of Head Start and Title 1 early intervention initiatives, and Success for All (e.g., Arnold & Doctoroff, 2003; Borman & Hewes, 2002; D'Agostino & Murphy, 2004; Datnow et al., 2003; Reynolds et al., 2002, 2004; Zigler & Styfco, 2004). Often, the effects of such programs are smaller and more variable than proponents would like, but on the whole there appear to be more positive than negative outcomes for the national reforms that have been in the public eye for some time.

While on the topic of national whole-school efforts, I should mention that since the latest version of this volume I have continued to coauthor a national basal reading series. At every turn, I have done everything possible to encourage users of basals to balance skills instruction and holistic literacy experiences for their students. I urge everyone involved in the development of educational materials and resources to do the same—to do everything they can do to encourage balanced teaching as conceived in this book! Balanced literacy instruction is something that terrific literacy teachers do, but it is also something that terrific curriculum developers and school reformers can promote through their efforts.

A very important direction since the 2002 version of this volume has been the scholarly analyses of the National Reading Panel (2000) report as well as the legislated curricular directions it stimulated (namely, Reading First as part of the No Child Left Behind legislation). The National Reading Panel was narrow methodologically and conceptually. By favoring only true experiments and quasi-experiments, a great deal of excellent literacy scholarship was excluded from its coverage. Even more disturbing was the decision to review instructional research on phonemic awareness, phonics, fluency, vocabulary, and comprehension to the exclusion of many other topics (e.g., writing and its effects on reading; use of literature in reading instruction; and motivation and reading). The result is a national agenda favoring a narrow range of reading skills to the exclusion of much else. Excellent scholars have offered a trenchant critique of these shortcomings of the Panel and the Reading First conceptualization of beginning reading instruction (e.g., Allington, 2002; Cunningham, 2001; Pressley, 2002; Pressley et al., 2004). Reading First as a program is increasingly recognized as the narrow envisionment of a small clique of policymakers rather than the result of deliberate and admirable reflection on what should be emphasized in beginning literacy instruction (Miskel & Song, 2004). Still, the prominence of the National Reading Panel and Reading First forced a change in this book, one that is favorable; the preceding volume covered phonemic awareness, phonics, and comprehension well. This edition now includes chapters dedicated to the two aspects of Reading First that were not covered extensively in prior editions: Chapter 6 takes up fluency and Chapter 7 vocabulary. With these additions, this volume should make sense in many professional development efforts, ranging from those in response to Reading First to conceptually broader undertakings.

Because this book started out as a series of talks and I have talked about the book as often as I could in recent years, the ideas have been tried out on many audiences. I think of the book as being like a Marx Brothers movie. Their zany comedies were funny because they were first tried out on the road as plays. The brothers benefited from audience reactions, only keeping the good stuff in the final film versions. Similarly, I have tried out many ideas about reading and reading instruction on my audiences, who have made very clear which arguments have been more credible to them. Those are the arguments that made it into this book. My goal was to write a book as informative and compelling about reading and reading instruction as Marx Brothers films were entertaining. I leave it to you, the reader, to decide whether I succeeded.

This book can be read alone but will be more useful as a gateway to the literature on reading and reading instruction. There will be some who complain that the parenthetical references in the body of the text interrupt reading and hence distract the reader. I have opted for this approach, however, for I find that alternative referencing systems—for example, using footnotes—do not make as clear who did and claimed what. I have erred on the side of providing more references rather than fewer because my experience is that those interested in elementary reading want a great deal of information, and specifically they want to know where they can go to get more information about points that they consider critical. Thus, I have provided references for each chapter because I am aware that some readers are much more interested in some topics than in others. Each chapter is intended to contribute to the overall book as well as to serve as a stand-alone reference for readers who want information on any of the topics covered in the individual chapters. In closing this Introduction, I want to point out that in the chapters that follow much will be said about reading achievement as defined by objective measures because that is the benchmark of effective instruction for many policymakers and educational administrators. For me, however, there is another way to think about such instruction, a way that brings it to life much better than focusing only on the test scores.

My colleagues and I have been impressed that effective literacy education environments, in which children are learning how to do difficult things and in fact do them well, are also *happy* environments. Most striking, good teachers have far fewer disciplinary encounters with children than do teachers whose literacy instruction is ineffective. Thus, one of the reasons to love effective literacy instruction is the engagement it produces (see Chapter 11), which leads to more harmonious classroom relations. My associates and I frequently have found ourselves wishing that many more children could experience the kinds of classrooms that we have been privileged to study, not simply because the classrooms are good for children's academic development, but also because such classrooms are warm, wonderful places. When instructors become excellent literacy teachers, they also seem to become agents of peace in children's lives.

If you find what follows to be compelling, I'll be pleased. Never forget, however, as you read that much work remains before the ideas detailed in this book are translated as completely as they might be into literacy instruction in elementary schools. There is much more research that can be done and much implementation that needs to occur. More commitment to refine implementation through continuing inquiry also is needed. I expect to revise this book again, perhaps in 5 years or so, and I pray that much revision will then be in order because progress will have been made in the scholarly analysis and dissemination of effective reading instruction, as well as continuing reflective evaluation of literacy development through state-of-the-art teaching.

REFERENCES

Allington, R. L. (2002). *Big brother and the national reading curriculum: How ideology trumped evidence*. Heinemann.

Arnold, D. H., & Doctoroff, G. L. (2003). The early education of socioeconomically disadvantaged children. *Annual Review of Psychology, 54*, 517–545.

Borman, G. D., & Hewes, G. M. (2002). The long-term effects and cost-effectiveness of Success for All. *Educational Evaluation and Policy Analysis, 24*, 243–266.

Cordón, L. A., & Day, J. D. (1996). Strategy use on standardized reading comprehension tests. *Journal of Educational Psychology, 88,* 288–295.

Cunningham, J. (2001). Book review of *The National Reading Panel Report. Reading Research Quarterly, 36,* 326–335.

D'Agostino, J. V., & Murphy, J. A. (2004). A meta-analysis of Reading Recovery in United States schools. *Educational Evaluation and Policy Analysis, 26,* 23–38.

Datnow, A., Borman, G. D., Stringfield, S., Overman, L. T., & Castellano, M. (2003). Comprehensive school reform in culturally and linguistically diverse contexts: Implementation and outcomes from a four-year study. *Educational Evaluation and Policy Analysis, 25,* 143–170.

Kiewra, K. A., Cresswell, J., & Wadkins, T. (1997, March). *Biographical sketches of prolific researchers: R. Anderson, R. Mayer, and M. Pressley.* Paper presented at the annual meeting of the American Educational Research Association, Chicago.

Kismaric, C., & Heiferman, M. (1996). *Growing up with Dick and Jane: Learning and living the American dream.* Scott Foresman.

Miskel, C., & Song, M. (2004). Passing Reading First: Prominence and processes in an elite policy network. *Educational Evaluation and Policy Analysis, 26,* 89–109.

National Reading Panel. (2000). *Teaching children to read: An evidence-based assessment of the scientific research literature on reading and its implications for reading instruction: Reports of the subgroups.* National Institute of Child Health and Human Development.

Pressley, M. (2002). Effective beginning reading instruction: A paper commissioned by the National Reading Conference. *Journal of Literacy Research, 34,* 165–188.

Pressley, M., & Afflerbach, P. (1995). *Verbal protocols of reading: The nature of constructively responsive reading.* Erlbaum.

Pressley, M., Duke, N. K., & Boling, E. C. (2004). The educational science and scientifically-based instruction we need: Lessons from reading research and policy making. *Harvard Educational Review, 74,* 30–61.

Pressley, M., & Hilden, K. R. (2006). Cognitive strategies. In D. Kuhn & R. Siegler (Eds.), W. Damon & R. Lerner (Series Eds.), *Handbook of child psychology: Vol. 2. Cognition, perception, and language* (6th ed., pp. 511–556). Wiley.

Pressley, M., with McCormick, C. B. (1995). *Advanced educational psychology for educators, researchers, and policymakers.* HarperCollins.

Pressley, M., Woloshyn, V. E., & Associates. (1995). *Cognitive strategy instruction that really works with children* (2nd ed.). Brookline Books.

Reynolds, A. J., Ou, S.-R., & Topitzes, J. W. (2004). Paths of effects of early childhood intervention on educational attainment and delinquency: A confirmatory analysis of the Chicago child–parent centers. *Child Development, 75,* 1299–1328.

Reynolds, A. J., Temple, J. A., Robertson, D. L., & Mann, E. A. (2002). Age 21 cost–benefit analysis of the Title I Chicago child–parent centers. *Educational Evaluation and Policy Analysis, 24,* 267–303.

Robinson, F. P. (1961). *Effective study* (2nd ed.). Harper & Row.

Wood, E., Motz, M., & Willoughby, T. (1998). Examining students' retrospective memories of strategy development. *Journal of Educational Psychology, 90,* 698–704.

Wyatt, D., Pressley, M., El-Dinary, P. B., Stein, S., Evans, P., & Brown, R. (1993). Comprehension strategies, worth and credibility monitoring, and evaluations: Cold and hot cognition when experts read professional articles that are important to them. *Learning and Individual Differences, 5,* 49–72.

Zigler, E., & Styfco, S. J. (2004). *The Head Start debates.* Brookes.

1   Skills-Emphasis, Meaning-Emphasis, and Scientifically Based Balanced Reading Instruction

Elementary reading instruction is a topic that has commanded a great deal of attention over the last several decades. A primary reason for this interest is that people are flooded with information and much of that information is in a print version (newspapers, magazines, blog posts, internet sites, etc.). A second reason for the attention is that survival today, in society and in the marketplace, depends heavily upon a literate citizenry. A third and final reason is the international evidence that the rank ordering of American students' academic performance has continually ranked below that of other industrialized nations. This third reason seems to be more related to other nations more rapidly improving the academic performance of their students as compared with American students. This is especially true in reading achievement, especially for the older (12th-grade) students, where performance has largely been stable since 1982.

However, contrary to the opinion of some that reading skills have declined over the past century, the evidence is simply overwhelming that more elementary students read better today than they did at any point in the past and that reported levels of performance on international assessments underestimate the productivity of American schools and teachers (Carnoy & Rothstein, 2013). At the same time, students in some other nations are improving their reading proficiencies at a faster rate than is the case with American students. The task facing American educators is to improve the quality of reading lessons offered in our schools such that virtually all students will attain the proficiencies needed to read almost any text with understanding.

The central message of this text is that we know more about efficient literacy development and more about effective literacy instruction than we ever knew before. In fact, it looks as though we know enough that virtually all students could be reading on grade level, generally by the end of first grade. When the first edition of this book was written, educators were deeply engaged in what were known as the "reading wars." These reading wars looked to oversimplify reading into two "sides." For several years, it appeared that those wars were behind us, but now the "reading wars" seem to have reemerged with the ongoing debate surrounding the use of phonics or skills-emphasis and whole-language or meaning-emphasis approaches to teaching reading. Within this debate, researchers, teachers, and parents have begun to become heavily invested in one approach or another. There remain a handful of folks who continue to argue for their favorite approach to teaching children to read. Some generate personal revenues from the products they tout. Others have invested their careers in promoting an approach and so continue their long-standing advocacy for that approach.

Such debates about the "best" way to teach children to read began more than a century ago, just as universal education opportunities became the norm. Once the vast majority of school-age children began attending school, questions about the preferred method for teaching children to read began to emerge and take the spotlight. The rapid development of commercial reading programs in the 1920s provided educators with various approaches to developing children into readers. The development of these multiple alternative approaches led to debates about which commercial programs were the better fit for the children. Once American schools created a substantial market for commercial reading materials, literally hundreds upon hundreds of reading programs were produced and sold to schools. These reading programs fall along a continuum with meaning-emphasis programs on one end and skills-emphasis programs on the other (see Figure 1.1).

On one side of the argument is the *skills emphasis*, also known as the *bottom-up approach*, or most recently as the *simple view of reading* (SVR) or *phonics-based approach*. From a skills-emphasis framework, teachers must explicitly teach the various skills needed to become a reader. Those who have argued that reading requires a skills emphasis believe that meaning making during reading occurs from the bottom up. For them, reading is about the processing of letters and words. Meaning making is sounding out the words, which are listened to by the mind. Indeed, there is a long history of distinguished research establishing that, even when good readers read

Skills emphasis——Balanced——Meaning emphasis

FIGURE 1.1. Our continuum of approaches to reading.

silently, there is something of a speech process involved. Skills-emphasis folks have a long list of specific skills that will need to be taught if they are to be acquired. Extensive instruction and practice, even in isolation, of these various skills, their argument goes, are needed to foster reading development. In skills-emphasis approaches, it is the skills framework that drives the lessons. More importantly, the various skills are taught separately, rather than in a balanced framework that works together. This is most often seen with a main emphasis on only phonics instruction, rather than a more balanced emphasis on skills such as comprehension, motivation, and fluency.

Sometimes, there is even silent speech (i.e., the reader literally says the words to her- or himself quietly). Sometimes the speech processes are not so complete, but, as words are read, information about the sounds of the words is activated in the mind, which seems to help the reader hold in memory the last few words that were read so that their meanings can be integrated to permit comprehension of the text (Carver, 1990; Perfetti, 1985). The idea that reading involves decoding and listening comprehension, with readers listening to what they have decoded in order to understand the meanings conveyed by the text (Gough, 1984), is a simple view of reading on which much of the *science of reading* (SOR) stances are based.

As seen detailed in the *Reading Research Quarterly* special issues (discussed later in this chapter), a common term teachers and researchers have begun to use is the *science of reading*. Just as in the debate between the skills versus meaning emphasis, the definition of the SOR varies. Many SOR researchers have taken on a view aligned with the SVR, which defines reading as having two basic components: decoding and comprehension. The SVR supporters have particularly latched onto the idea that all research should be backed by science, but only particular research designs should be considered science (e.g., experiments and quasi-experiments with control groups). Although we agree with the idea that reading practices should be backed by science, we feel that this definition of effective reading instruction is much too limited.

We label the other end of the continuum as the *meaning-emphasis approach*, also labeled as a *top-down approach* or *whole-language approach*. The meaning-emphasis approach to literacy education emphasizes natural development of literacy competence. Immersion in real literature and daily writing is favored over explicit teaching of basic reading skills. Skills instruction, when it occurs, appears in wholly committed whole-language classrooms on an as-needed basis only, and then only in the context of reading and writing, rather than as a focal point of instruction (e.g., Smith & Goodman, 1971). Through extensive reading practice coupled with mostly minimal guidance, children become readers, and in the process they acquire the skills proficiencies they need. In the meaning-emphasis framework, it is the text that is to be understood that drives the lesson.

Over the past several decades, a growing body of data addressed what meaning-emphasis whole language can do and what it cannot do. To review, we now know that there are many general points of understanding about reading and writing that are promoted by meaning emphasis. Moreover, literature and writing immersion promote the development of important content knowledge and ability in writing. At least in some whole-language classrooms, phonics is taught, and phonics skills develop. Based on existing comparisons between skills-based and whole-language instruction, however, concerns remain, especially with respect to at-risk students, that learning to read words may not be as certain in meaning-emphasis whole-language classrooms as compared with skills-emphasis code-oriented classrooms (Johnston, 2000).

We want to emphasize that this is not a book about the meaning emphasis versus skills instruction debate. Our view is that the whole-language philosophy has had some profound and very positive effects on elementary literacy instruction and that many of the meaning-emphasis whole-language practices should be part of elementary literacy programs. However, other practices should be there as well, and much space in the chapters that follow is devoted to making a case for a balance of decoding and comprehension skills instruction with meaning-emphasis elements of whole language to create an effective and attractive elementary literacy curriculum.

Getting to a balance of meaning-emphasis and skills-emphasis instruction may require an understanding of meaning emphasis, which can be challenging. Those most strongly identified with meaning emphasis have often resisted attempting to define it precisely in terms of curricular practices, arguing that an approach that is "whole" cannot be easily reduced to "parts." Even so, for many others, including the authors of this book, it is helpful to think in terms of particular instructional practices associated with an educational philosophy.

Between the skills-emphasis approach and meaning emphasis, there is an intermediate position, which includes both in constructing meaning from a text. The case that has been made here is that skilled readers may process every single letter using efficient eye movements that involve fixation on most words. The case has also been made that the reader's mind is very active in constructing hypotheses about what a text might mean, generating inferences, based on prior knowledge, that are necessary in making meaning, and initiating strategies to locate portions of the text that are especially likely to be informative. Bottom-up and top-down processing clearly interact as part of skilled reading. There cannot be one without the other if skilled reading is to occur (Kintsch, 1998; Rumelhart, 1994). They are in balance.

We do not see reading instruction as just skills emphasis or meaning emphasis, but rather believe that teachers should use research-based practices that support all aspects of reading. We place this book at the center because our balanced approach takes the research evidence on the potential of early and explicit decoding instruction and the evidence on explicit comprehension strategies instruction and blends it with the research evidence on the potential of meaning-emphasis instruction for developing vocabulary, comprehension, and motivation to read. Additionally, we do not feel that the science of reading should be limited to just experimental studies, but rather include a more comprehensive look at reading research (Pressley, 2002). In short, we look at research on both sides of the reading argument and present the research for multiple aspects of reading, not just one or two. The scientific evidence overwhelmingly points to the many, many different subprocesses involved in skilled reading that are all amenable to intervention that improves reading comprehension outcomes (phonemic awareness, phonics knowledge, fluency, morphology, vocabulary, comprehension, and cognitive factors like strategic knowledge and executive skills), and it's those scientifically based instructional practices that are the focus of the book.

Does that mean that it will do no good to target educational efforts at either skills-emphasis or meaning-emphasis approaches alone? Not necessarily. In fact, there will be quite a bit of evidence considered in subsequent chapters that makes clear that targeting letter- and word-level processes sometimes can improve reading achievement, as can targeting comprehension strategies. Instruction of particular components can help on the road to skilled reading, which involves bottom-up and top-down thinking in balanced interaction.

REVIEWS OF SCIENTIFIC-BACKED BALANCED READING INSTRUCTION

Over the past several decades, there have been several reports that have reviewed the reading research and provided states, districts, and teachers with guidance on reading instruction. These reports had a goal of sharing the reading research and providing support for reading instruction within the classroom. Below you will find a brief summary of each of these reports.

Becoming a Nation of Readers (Anderson et al., 1985)

One of the first reports on reading instruction, Anderson et al. (1985), summarized the complex nature of reading in *Becoming a Nation of Readers*. The report put together an overview of the reading research and provided guidance based on the research for reading instruction. Specifically,

Anderson and his colleagues presented reading as having five principles that concluded that skilled reading is constructive, fluent, strategic, motivated, and a lifelong pursuit. Anderson et al. (1985) defined reading as "the process of constructing meaning from written texts. It is a complex skill requiring the coordination of a number of interrelated sources of information" (p. 7). Using the analogy of an orchestra, Anderson and his colleagues compare skilled reading to that of a finely tuned orchestra, stating that, just like an orchestra, reading is a holistic act that must be practiced over time and can have multiple interpretations based on a reader's background knowledge and the context of the reading.

Anderson et al. (1985) went on to emphasize the importance of the classroom environment, stating that teachers need to emphasize reading and writing in the classroom with less emphasis on worksheets and standardized test scores (something even today's teachers would most likely support). For instruction, the Nation of Readers report suggested that teachers teach phonics instruction as a way to help students identify words, teach comprehension strategies as a way to help students understand the text, and include discussions of the text that promote students using their background knowledge to grasp an understanding. This comprehensive approach to teaching reading should be done in a stimulating environment that includes texts that students find interesting.

Though the research reviewed by Anderson et al. (1985) is now several decades old, the overall concepts are still true in today's classrooms based on more recent literature and align with the focus of this book. Skilled readers are strong in all aspects of reading and have learned how to integrate the necessary skills to grasp an understanding of a text.

Beginning to Read (Adams, 1990)

Adams's book (1990) laid out what the research tells us about the role played by phonemic segmentation, letter–sound relationships, and orthographic learning in acquiring decoding proficiency. She comes down on the side of skills-emphasis instruction but, like Chall (1983), with some reservations. For instance, she points to a central role for motivation in acquiring decoding proficiency:

> The goal of teaching phonics is to develop students' ability to read connected text independently. For students, however, the strongest functional connection between these two skills may run in the reverse direction. It is only the nature of reading that can make the content of phonic lessons seem sensible; it is only the prospect of reading that can make them seem worthwhile. And, certainly, we hope that such instruction will seem both sensible and worthwhile to students. (p. 272)

She also notes that decoding instruction should play only a small role in reading lessons:

> The extra phonic calories do not enhance growth. They are kept as unnecessary and burdensome tissue or quickly flushed as waste. Worse still, the child may become groggily sated before getting to the other necessary and complementary items on the menu. (p. 51)

In addition, Adams notes that some meaning-based instructional practices provide strong evidence of fostering specific skills development:

> The evidence that inventive spelling activity simultaneously develops phonemic awareness and promotes understanding of the alphabetic principle is extremely promising, especially in view of the difficulty with which children are found to acquire these insights through other methods of teaching. (p. 387)

She writes that "the strongest implication of the theory toward developing solid word recognition skills is that children should read lots and often" (p. 135), and, after reviewing major and competing commercial core reading materials, Adams (1990) concludes that there is no consistency across the materials, even in terms of how many letter–sound relationships should be taught, much less when each should be taught and what method of instruction should be used.

What Adams's book did, however, was move developing decoding proficiencies back into mainstream conversations, something seen as addressing a weakness of the then prominent whole-language approach (and its derivatives). However, the greatest contribution of Adams's book may have been that it began moving the skills-emphasis proponents away from an intense concentration on skills development in isolation (e.g., Flesch, 1955) toward a better balanced discussion of the potential roles of both skills-emphasis and meaning-emphasis approaches, which could and should when joined together provide the most powerful reading lessons possible.

The National Research Council

The National Research Council (NRC) of the National Academies formed a committee of distinguished scholars to review the research on beginning reading. Catherine Snow of Harvard University chaired this committee and served as senior author of the committee's final report. That report, *Preventing Reading Difficulties in Young Children* (Snow, Burns, & Griffin, 1998), synthesized the available research on skills-emphasis and meaning-emphasis programs and concluded that a "balanced" approach that combined the best of our skills-emphasis knowledge about phonemic segmentation and phonics with the best of our meaning-emphasis knowledge on vocabulary, comprehension, and motivation would make for a powerful hybrid approach to developing early literacy proficiencies. They concluded by noting that three factors interfered with the initial acquisition of reading proficiency: (1) problems understanding the alphabetic principle, (2) failure to acquire the verbal knowledge necessary for comprehension, and (3) the absence or loss of motivation to read.

The authors also noted that high-quality lessons in high-motivation classrooms were more likely to be the solution than adhering to any particular approach to teaching children to read. They noted that, in low-achieving schools, both the amount and the use of instructional time needed to be addressed, as did lower levels of student engagement, more frequent external interruptions, and less friendly classroom environments (Snow et al., 1998, p. 129). In other words, their view of the problems that some children had in initial stages of reading acquisition were much broader than the simple question of which reading program the teacher used.

Almost as soon as the NRC report was released, the criticisms began (Snow, 2001), with skills-emphasis proponent Louisa Cook Moats (2000) arguing that the report did not go far enough in addressing systematic phonics and National Institute of Child Health and Human Development division head and presidential education advisor G. Reid Lyon suggesting that the conclusions were too ambiguous (Lyon, 1998). Snow (2001) noted:

> These worries may have strengthened calls for the establishment, in a time period overlapping with the final meetings of the committee, of a federally mandated panel designed to review rigorously the research base on the effectiveness of different instructional techniques. (p. 240)

Thus, shortly after the NRC report was released, congressional action created the NRP to rigorously examine the experimental evidence on skills-emphasis approaches.

The National Reading Panel

The federally funded National Reading Panel (NRP; 2000) conducted meta-analyses on aspects of beginning reading where there were a sufficient number of experimental studies. The three aspects of beginning reading where they found a sufficient supply of experimental studies were phonemic awareness, phonics, and fluency. They reported that phonemic awareness was an essential early literacy proficiency and that it could and should be developed by teachers. They also reported that the meta-analyses indicated that 10 minutes of explicit phonics instruction daily in kindergarten and first grade produced a moderate positive effect size on later decoding but a trivial effect on later comprehension. Increasing the number of minutes did not improve these outcomes. The NRP also reported no positive effects for code-emphasis instruction in grades 2 through 9, even though most of the studies had been conducted with older struggling readers. The NRP also identified repeated readings as an effective strategy for fostering reading fluency.

Alongside the ponderous NRP report was an easily accessible, "plain-language" summary that was much more widely read (Armbruster et al., 2001). This document was much shorter and ignored discussions of the study designs while offering what was supposed to be practical findings for practitioners. One member of the NRP wrote about the summary, noting that it "provides helpful information about instruction and is written in a teacher-friendly way. Sometimes it makes points that are identical to those from the NRP study. Other suggestions are not actually from the NRP report, but are consistent with it" (Shanahan, 2003, p. 647). Shanahan also notes that some recommendations in the summary do not match what the NRP reported. Nonetheless, this summary was widely distributed to states, schools, and colleges of education for dissemination as a reliable summary of the NRP research about beginning reading lessons.

The panel offered some very strong conclusions based on its review of the literature, with the most visible ones being the following:

1. Phonemic awareness instruction is effective in promoting early reading (e.g., word reading, comprehension) and spelling skills. The panel concluded that phonemic awareness instruction is effective with first graders and kindergarten students as well as with students with disabilities who lack phonemic awareness, especially phonemic segmentation, in the later elementary grades.

Systematic phonics instruction improves reading and spelling and, to a lesser extent, comprehension. However, the panel found that systematic phonics only had positive effects when provided in kindergarten and grade 1. That is, code-emphasis reading lessons in grades 2 through 8 did not produce the same positive effects found for early phonics, or code-emphasis, lessons. Even though Chall (1983) had concluded that synthetic phonics (i.e., instruction teaching students explicitly to convert letters into sounds and blend the sounds) is more effective than other forms of systematic phonics instruction, the panel reported no statistically significant advantage for synthetic phonics instruction over other phonics approaches.

2. Guided oral reading (i.e., a teacher listening as a student reads, providing instruction as needed) and repeated reading of texts increase reading fluency during the elementary years. However, more recent research (Kuhn et al., 2006; Schwanenflugel et al., 2009) found that wide reading produced fluency gains faster than did repeated readings.

3. A variety of methods of vocabulary instruction make sense, with vocabulary instruction positively impacting reading comprehension.

4. Comprehension-strategies instruction improves comprehension, with a number of strategies positively affecting understanding of a text, including teaching students to be aware of whether they are comprehending and to deal with miscomprehension when it occurs (e.g., by rereading); using graphic and semantic organizers to represent text; teaching students to attend to story structure (e.g., "who," "what," "where," "when," and "why" information) as they read; question generation and question answering during reading; and summarization. Teaching students to use a small repertoire of effective strategies (e.g., predicting upcoming text content, seeking clarification when confused, asking questions, constructing mental images representing text content, and summarization) was especially strongly endorsed by the NRP. Both direct explanation (Duffy, 2014; Duffy et al., 1987) approaches—starting with teacher modeling and explanation of strategies followed by scaffolding teacher practice of the strategies—and transactional-strategies instruction (i.e., direct explanation with an emphasis on teacher–student and student–student discussions and interpretations of the text during practice of strategies; Brown et al., 1996; Pressley et al., 1992) were supported by the panel.

5. Teacher inservice can change teachers' instruction of reading, with an impact on student achievement, although much more research is needed to identify particular inservice approaches that are helpful.

6. Computer technology has great potential for improving beginning reading achievement, with promising approaches for promoting word recognition, vocabulary development, and comprehension already enjoying some support. However, to date, large-scale studies fail to demonstrate the potential benefits (Cheung & Slavin, 2012; Dynarski, 2007).

However, the NRP also had its critics, as Cunningham (2001) argued, "What are we to make of a report that so boldly lays claim to what science, rigor, and objectivity are in reading research, and first denigrates, then ignores, the preponderance of research literature in our field?" (p. 327). His comments were targeting the choice the NRP made to review only the evidence from experimental studies employing random assignment to treatment or control conditions or quasi-experimental studies with matched treatment and control groups. He pointed out that the very sort of evidence (correlational) used to require warning labels on tobacco products was wholly ignored by the NRP. With such limited standards for inclusion of research, the NRP ignored critical reading research (e.g., Pressley et al., 2003), which led to reading programs like Reading First, discussed in the next section, to be much less research based had the NRP reviewed the broader array of research available (Pressley & Fingeret, 2007). Others criticized the methodology, arguing that using the same set of studies but a different analytical scheme produced "conclusions" different from those the NRP drew (Camilli et al., 2006; Hammill & Swanson, 2006). For instance, Hammill and Swanson (2006), completed a meta-analysis of phonics instruction. The results suggested that the NRP "overestimated the benefits of phonics instruction relative to other approaches" (p. 25). Additionally, Hammill and Swanson (2006) argued that their reanalysis demonstrated that "for all practical purposes, phonics and nonphonics methods are about equally successful in teaching children to read" (p. 25).

The NRP Report and the Reading First Program

Ultimately, the promotional funding to disseminate the plain-language version of the report of the NRP meant that the original report and its recommendations were both largely neglected. Incorporation of the NRP five pillars of reading into the implementation of the Reading First program under the No Child Left Behind Act meant that the NRP report had substantial effects on the design of reading lessons in this nation (Brenner et al., 2009). American primary-grade teachers were flooded with new commercial products with a skills-emphasis focus, including commercial curricula focused on both fostering and assessing phonemic awareness, phonics skills development, and oral reading fluency.

In the end, the federal evaluation of the Reading First program (Gamse et al., 2009) used a regression discontinuity design to establish that, while reading instruction in Reading First schools did increase the use of practices targeted by the program designers and while reading achievement rose in Reading First schools, improvement was no different from the rise in scores in schools not participating in the Reading First program. Additionally, while a small positive effect on reading pseudowords (nonsense words) was observed, that improvement did not lead to improved performances that were different from the improvements observed in nonparticipating schools on the primary assessment, the Stanford Achievement Test–10, at grades 1, 2, or 3. Gamse et al. (2009) reported, "Controlling for the other variables in the model, the regression coefficient between minutes spent teaching the five dimensions of reading . . . is associated with a 0.09 difference in student test scores. This association is not statistically significant ($p = .056$)" (p. 55).

In sum, while the federal Reading First program did result in more schools and classrooms incorporating more skills-emphasis practices during reading instruction, that outcome did not result in reading performance improvements that were different from the improvements observed in nonparticipating schools. That result, along with concerns about violations of the federal prohibitions clause and the influence of some entrepreneurs on the design and the approval of Reading First applications (Harkinson, 2008; Schemo, 2007) resulted in Congress defunding the Reading First program.

Pearson (2010) concluded that, while Reading First was reported to have had a positive effect in some states and in some schools, the overall evaluation indicated that the program failed to accomplish its central goal: improving reading achievement. He hypothesized about the reasons the program did or did not have positive effects in some locations but seemed to produce positive effects in others. While the Reading First program did have a general and broad framework for changing reading lessons, the processes that were initiated by the varying educational authorities were complex and differed from site to site. We would argue that the emphasis that the Reading First program placed on implementing a core reading program with fidelity likely also undermined the quest for improved reading achievement. We argue this because it is clear that commercially available core reading programs rarely provide teachers with the information needed to offer research-based instruction (Dewitz et al., 2009). Thus, the skills-emphasis approach, as implemented through the federal Reading First program, did not produce any significant advantage in fostering reading development.

Reading Research Quarterly Special Issues: The Science of Reading

More recently, the reading debate has resurfaced with the use of the term *science of reading* (SOR), with researchers once again debating the best approaches to teaching reading. To attempt to present both sides of the reading argument, the academic journal *Reading Research Quarterly* published two special issues with articles written by experts in the field of reading. Each author was asked to frame their argument with extensive evidence to support the most effective approaches to reading based on previously published research (Goodwin & Jiménez, 2020, 2021). One clear aspect from these special issues was the inconsistent definition of the SOR. With the inconsistencies across the articles, the journal editors advocated for a broad interpretation of the SOR. Across the 50 articles (several of which we discuss in other chapters), reading researchers argued that the SOR should include many aspects, not just phonics instruction. For example, the SOR should include aspects such as language comprehension, writing, volume of reading, instruction, and background knowledge just to name a few. In short, the special issue looked to unite reading researchers in the idea that reading instruction should be backed by science.

Within the first special issue, there were several key findings across the articles. These key findings included a focus on what some consider the main aspect of the SOR—phonics instruction—and the impact we have seen in classroom instruction. Though several authors specifically focus on phonics instruction, a majority of the articles within the first special issue looks to expand the SOR beyond just phonics. These articles encourage researchers and teachers to think of the SOR as including more than just phonics and comprehension (Goodwin & Jiménez, 2020). As we write this fifth edition, we couldn't agree more. In the second special issue on the SOR, more authors continue to provide evidence and theories for a more expansive view of the SOR beyond just phonics instruction. Additionally, reading researchers express the importance and data supporting reading multiple texts, increasing reading volume, teaching syntax skills, and teaching reading across content areas. Furthermore, the second special issue brings to light the importance of teaching reading across languages and supporting second language reading development (Goodwin & Jiménez, 2021). This is an area that we also believe is important for teachers to gain more understanding of what the research says about teaching children to read. We encourage anyone wanting to learn more about the SOR to take some time to explore the articles in these special issues.

A BALANCED APPROACH TO READING INSTRUCTION

Our best understanding of the research currently available suggests that there are valid aspects of both skills-emphasis and meaning-emphasis approaches to beginning reading. The evidence is quite clear that an early (kindergarten and grade 1), explicit, but modest emphasis on developing phonemic awareness and phonics knowledge (10 minutes per day) leads to readers who can better decode, at least in the short term. At the same time, the research-based advantages of meaning-emphasis approaches include stronger motivation to read and both a better understanding of the reading process and better comprehension after reading. Thus, in our view, the problem may be that American educators place too much emphasis, when either a skills-emphasis or a meaning-emphasis approach is adopted, on one aspect of effective beginning reading instruction, which differs by program emphasis. In other words, both sides in the reading wars are, in part, correct in supporting their preferred emphasis. At the same time, both sides are wrong, in part, because they have elected to ignore the advantages of the opposing camp. Too much of what is marketed as curriculum under the skills-emphasis model ignores the importance of potential tools such as invented spelling and wide independent reading. Too much of what is marketed as curriculum under the meaning-emphasis model ignores the evidence of the importance of accurate reading and developing strong decoding skills.

Our solution is to attempt to integrate the strengths of both the skills-emphasis and the meaning-emphasis approaches, much as the Snow et al. (1998) report suggested. Routman (2002) has already largely followed this path. However, some skills-emphasis proponents (Moats, 2000) have already mischaracterized the balanced approach as yet another variation of the meaning-emphasis approach, in this case whole language.

We will admit that, in our view, beginning reading lessons are more effective when elements of the whole language are integrated into those lessons. At the same time, we believe that the research supports aspects of the skills-emphasis approaches as well. However, as long as the primary advantage of skills-emphasis instruction is improved decoding and little else, it is impossible for us to recommend that approach without some significant modifications, as suggested from the research on the meaning-emphasis approach. The work of Connor and her colleagues (Connor et al., 2004, 2009) supports our point of view while at the same time addressing the complexity of providing high-quality literacy lessons given the commercial materials available in today's market. We can only hope that educators will soon see more balanced curriculum frameworks for beginning reading lessons, but until that time, each individual teacher will have to work to adapt existing commercial programs to better fit a balanced approach to instruction.

We hope that, as you read this text, you come to understand what balanced reading instruction looks and feels like. That, at least, is our primary goal.

SO, WHAT IS READING?

The current reading debate continues to focus on the specific aspects that teachers should emphasize when teaching reading. We believe that reading practices need to be backed by science; however, we fall in line with many researchers in the *Reading Research Quarterly* special issues, who say that the definition of the science of reading is often too limited and must include more than just phonics and comprehension instruction. On the other side, meaning emphasis focuses on using context and student inquiry to drive the reading. This approach has been present in K–12 schools for several decades and has limited success with teaching students to read. One issue is the limited research (limited but not absent) studies or science that supports the use of meaning-emphasis reading instruction. Another major issue: Many teachers do not know that the meaning-emphasis approaches that they are teaching through major reading curriculums are not backed by research.

So where does that lead this book? We believe in a balance between the two approaches—skills emphasis and meaning emphasis. We believe that the skills-emphasis and meaning-emphasis approaches are each too limited to enable a student to become a skilled reader. The fact is that reading is complex and includes multiple skills working together, rather than individual skills working separately. We believe that teachers need to understand and incorporate all aspects of reading to support student learning. There are a lot of reading programs present in today's classrooms that are not backed by any sort of research. It is important for teachers to incorporate reading instruction that is backed by science and not so much by catchy phrases or colorful pictures. We believe that a balanced approach to reading is not focusing on one side or the other (skills emphasis vs. meaning emphasis), but rather incorporating skills backed by research that support the many important aspects of reading, such as decoding, comprehension, fluency, motivation, individual differences, and vocabulary. Thus, throughout this book, we present the research-based approaches for the different components of reading and believe that balancing these components is critical for developing skilled readers.

SUMMARY AND CONCLUDING REFLECTIONS

1. Both skills-emphasis and meaning-emphasis reading instruction have been used in American classrooms for at least a century. Over that period, the reading programs used in American schools have reflected one of these approaches or another, though there has been an abundance of reading programs produced and used that reflect neither stance very well. For at least a century, there have been avid proponents of both approaches. At various times, actual "reading wars" broke out, with one side or the other dominating the nature of reading instruction for a decade or two. Throughout this whole era, publishers have responded to the marketplace by adding and subtracting either skills-emphasis or meaning-emphasis elements from their reading program offerings. Visit any large number of elementary school classrooms today, and you will undoubtedly see remnants of both the skills-emphasis and meaning-emphasis approaches. In some classrooms, you may also see what could be considered pure skills-emphasis or meaning-emphasis approaches.

2. Extensive reviews of the reading literature over the years have found research support for more balanced instructional approaches. Classroom teachers must understand that teaching reading is not a "one or the other" activity (skills emphasis or meaning emphasis). Strong reading incorporates instruction backed by science and understands the complexity that is reading. In order to develop skilled readers, teachers must look for a balanced approach that is supported by reading research.

3. A more recent debate within the field of reading has revolved around the science of reading (SOR). The SOR debate is important for teachers because it is critical for teachers to incorporate reading skills backed by research that supports the many aspects of reading, such as decoding, comprehension, fluency, motivation, individual differences, and vocabulary. In the past, the SOR has often only focused on the NRP report and was often too narrow when examining the reading research. This has led to the simple view of reading that only focuses on phonics and comprehension. Throughout this book, we have reviewed and incorporated research-based reading practices to support teacher development in the different areas of reading instruction. Thus, we frame the SOR for this book as reading practices backed by strong research that incorporates all aspects of reading rather than just one or two aspects.

REFERENCES

Adams, M. (1990). *Beginning to read: Thinking and learning about print.* MIT Press.

Anderson, R. C., Hiebert, E. H., Scott, J. A., & Wilkinson, I. A. G. (1985). *Becoming a nation of readers: The report of the Commission on Reading.*

Armbruster, B., Lehr, F., & Osborn, J. (2001). *Put reading first.* National Institute for Literacy.

Brenner, D., Hiebert, E. H., & Tompkins, R. (2009). How much and what are third graders reading? In E. H. Hiebert (Ed.), *Read more, read better* (pp. 118–140). Guilford Press.

Brown, R., Pressley, M., Van Meter, P., & Schuder, T. (1996). A quasi-experimental validation of transactional strategies instruction with low-achieving second grade readers. *Journal of Educational Psychology, 88,* 18–37.

Camilli, G., Wolfe, P. M., & Smith, M. L. (2006). Meta-analysis and reading policy: Perspectives on teaching children to read. *Elementary School Journal, 107*(1), 27–36.

Carnoy, M., & Rothstein, R. (2013). *What do international tests really show about U.S. student performance?* Economic Policy Institute.

Carver, R. P. (1990). *Reading rate: A review of research and theory.* Academic Press.

Chall, J. S. (1983). *Learning to read: The great debate* (updated ed.). McGraw-Hill.

Cheung, A. C. K., & Slavin, R. E. (2012). The effects of educational technology applications on reading outcomes for struggling readers: A best-evidence synthesis. *Reading Research Quarterly, 48*(3), 277–299.

Connor, C. D., Morrison, F. J., Fishman, B. J., & Ponitz, C. C. (2009). The ISI observation system: Examining the literacy instruction provided to individual students. *Educational Researcher, 38*(2), 85–99.

Connor, C. D., Morrison, F. J., & Katch, L. E. (2004). Beyond the reading wars: Exploring the effect of child-instruction interactions on growth in early reading. *Scientific Studies in Reading, 8,* 305–336.

Cunningham, J. W. (2001). The National Reading Panel report. *Reading Research Quarterly, 30*(3), 326–335.

Dewitz, P., Jones, J., & Leahy, S. (2009). Comprehension strategy instruction in the reading programs. *Reading Research Quarterly, 44*(2), 102–126.

Duffy, G. G. (2014). *Explaining reading: A resource for explicit teaching of the Common Core Standards.* Guilford Publications.

Duffy, G. G., Roehler, L. R., Sivan, E., Rackliffe, G., Book, C., Meloth, M. S., Vavrus, L. G., Wesselman, R., Putnam, J., & Bassiri, D. (1987). Effects of explaining the reasoning associated with using reading strategies. *Reading Research Quarterly*, 347-368.

Dynarski, M. (2007). Effectiveness of reading and mathematics software products: Findings from the first student cohort. Institute for Education Sciences, U.S. Department of Education. Downloaded from *http://ies.ed.gov/ncee/pubs/20074005*.

Flesch, R. (1955). *Why Johnny can't read and what you can do about it.* Harper & Row.

Gamse, B. C., Jacob, R. T., Horst, M., Boulay, B., & Unlu, F. (2009). *Reading First impact study: Final report* (No. NCEE 2009–4038). National Center for Education Evaluation and Regional Assistance, Institute of Education Sciences, U.S. Department of Education.

Goodwin, A. P., & Jiménez, R. T. (2020). The science of reading: Supports, critiques, and questions. *Reading Research Quarterly, 55*, S7–S22.

Goodwin, A. P., & Jiménez, R. T. (2021). The science of reading: Supports, critiques, and questions. *Reading Research Quarterly, 56*, S7–S22.

Gough, P. B. (1984). Word recognition. In P. D. Pearson (ed.), *Handbook of reading research, 1*, 225-253. Longman.

Hammill, D. D., & Swanson, H. L. (2006). The National Reading Panel's meta-analysis of phonics instruction: Another point of view. *Elementary School Journal, 107*(1), 17–26.

Harkinson, J. (2008). Hooked on phonics. *Mother Jones, 33*(5), 58–62.

Johnston, F. R. (2000). Word learning in predictable texts. *Journal of Educational Psychology, 92*, 248–255.

Kintsch, W. (1998). *Comprehension: A paradigm for cognition.* Cambridge University Press.

Kuhn, M. R., Schwanenflugel, P., Morris, R. D., Morrow, L. M., Woo, D., Meisinger, B., et al. (2006). Teaching children to become fluent and automatic readers. *Journal of Literacy Research, 38*(4), 357–388.

Lyon, G. R. (1998, April 28). *Overview of reading and literacy initiatives.* Testimony before the Committee on Labor and Human Resources, Subcommittee on Education Reform, Washington, DC.

Moats, L. C. (2000). *Whole language lives on: The illusion of "balanced" reading instruction.* Thomas Fordham Foundation.

National Reading Panel. (2000). *Teaching children to read: An evidence-based assessment of the scientific research literature on reading and its implications for reading instruction.* Available at *www.nationalreadingpanel.org*.

Pearson, P. D. (2010). Reading First: Hard to live with—or without. *Journal of Literacy Research, 42*(1), 100–108.

Perfetti, C. A. (1985). *Reading ability.* New York: Oxford University Press.

Pressley, M. (2002). What I have learned up until now about research methods in reading education. *51st Yearbook of the National Reading Conference*, pp. 33–43.

Pressley, M., Dolezal, S. E., Raphael, L. M., Mohan, L., Roehrig, A. D., Bogner, K. (2003). *Motivating primary-grade students.* Guilford Press.

Pressley, M., El-Dinary, P. B., Gaskins, I., Schuder, T., Bergman, J. L., Almasi, J., et al. (1992). Beyond direct explanation: Transactional instruction of reading comprehension strategies. *Elementary School Journal, 92*, 511–554.

Pressley, M., & Fingeret, L. (2007). What we have learned since the National Reading Panel: Visions of the next version of Reading First. In M. Pressley, A. K. Billman, K. H. Perry, K. E. Reffitt, & J. M. Reynolds (Eds.), *Shaping literacy achievement: Research we have, research we needed* (pp. 216–245). Guilford Press.

Routman, R. (2002). *Reading essentials: The specifics you need to teach reading well.* Heinemann.

Rumelhart, D. E. (1994). Toward an interactive model of reading. In R. B. Ruddell, M. R.

Ruddell, & H. Singer (Eds.), *Theoretical models and processes of reading* (4th ed., pp. 864–894). International Reading Association.

Schemo, D. (2007, March 9). In a war over teaching: A U.S. vs. local clash. *New York Times*, pp. A1, A14.

Schwanenflugel, P. J., Kuhn, M. R., Morris, R. D., Morrow, L. M., Meisinger, E. B., Woo, D. G., et al. (2009). Insights into fluency instruction: Short- and long-term effects of two reading programs. *Literacy Research and Instruction, 48*(4), 318–336.

Shanahan, T. (2003). Research-based reading instruction: Myths about the National Reading Panel report. *Reading Teacher, 56*(7), 646–655.

Smith, F., & Goodman, K. S. (1971). On the psycholinguistic method of teaching reading. *The Elementary School Journal, 71*(4), 177–181.

Snow, C. E. (2001). Preventing reading difficulties in young children: Precursors and fallout. In T. Loveless (Ed.), *The great curriculum debate* (pp. 229–246). Brookings Institute.

Snow, C. E., Burns, M. S., & Griffin, P. (1998). *Preventing reading difficulties in young children: A report of the National Research Council*. National Academy Press.

2 Skilled Reading

Understanding the nature of skilled reading offers insights about what should be the goal of reading instruction. The analyses summarized in this chapter are among the most important influences on current efforts to develop powerful elementary reading instruction. The information in this chapter is essential for those who wish to understand why many researchers and reading educators are determined to increase the number of decoding and comprehension strategies instruction and increase the volume of reading in the elementary curriculum.

LETTER- AND WORD-LEVEL PROCESSES

Researchers have used a variety of methods to understand how good readers process letters and words. These are discussed in the following subsections.

Eye Movement

When reading at a rate of 200–300 words per minute, good readers appear to process every single letter of the text. One piece of evidence consistent with this point is that the longer a word is, the longer it takes a reader who is reading aloud to begin to pronounce it from the onset of perception of the word. In fact, every additional letter results in about a 10- to 20-millisecond delay in the onset of reading of the word (Samuels, 1994). Another telling piece of evidence about how readers process individual letters is that if text is altered so that individual letters from words are deleted, reading is much slower (Rayner et al., 1981). If you do not believe that single letters can make a difference, try reading an uncorrected letter typed by a pretty good typist in contrast to an uncorrected letter typed by an excellent typist. Midtypes and nissing leters are vert bistracting and skow dowm reeding wuite a dit, dn't they?

It is important to process every single letter during reading because letter-level cues are the primary means of recognizing words. Smith (1979, 2012), on the other hand, has argued that attention to individual letters while reading is unimportant because words can be predicted from the context of the other words in a sentence. However, this point of view simply is not supported by outcomes from eye-movement research. For example, if it were true, then good readers should have a pretty good idea of what the next word in the text is going to be—that is, the word to the right of the word just read. They don't.

When adult readers are reading a text on a computer screen that suddenly goes blank, they can report the last fixated word reliably (McConkie & Hogaboam, 1985) but have a great deal of difficulty guessing the next word in the text, being correct only about a quarter of the time. A skilled adult reader reading a text with content words missing has a very tough time guessing the missing words, doing so correctly with only 10% accuracy (Gough, 1983). Need convincing? Try guessing the correct word that is missing from this sentence:

The lanky ballplayer reached down to pick up a _____ *that had jumped onto the field.* Do you now think that skilled readers guess words on the basis of context cues? If you do, reflect for a moment about how much easier it is to read this: *The lanky ballplayer reached down to pick up a frog that had jumped onto the field.*

Thus, one problem with relying heavily on semantic context cues is that many words will be read incorrectly. That is, the psycholinguistic guesses will be wrong because any of a number of words could fit into the context. Relying heavily on semantic context cues to attempt to determine what the next word may be is a weak strategy—the preferred strategy of weak readers—as a number of investigators (e.g., Share & Stanovich, 1995) have concluded. This point is taken up in greater detail in Chapter 5.

With skilled readers, reading speed varies with the purpose for reading as well as with the type of text being read. Thus, during skimming, reading is faster because many words are skipped by the reader. In contrast, when a reader is attempting to learn what is in the text, reading is a word-by-word affair, with fixations on most of the individual words. For a skilled adult reader who is reading material carefully, each word is typically fixated for about a quarter of a second. That translates to about 200 words per minute when readers are reading to learn material (McConkie et al., 1982). The less the reader is concentrating on learning the ideas in the text, the faster the reading rate. The more familiar the topic of the text being read, the faster a reader reads. Reading at a relaxed pace typically occurs at a rate of between 250 and 300 words per minute, and thus more relaxed reading also is still largely word-by-word reading. Despite claims by speed-reading programs, the fastest that humans can read and comprehend is about 600 words per minute (Carver, 1990).

Finally, eye movements are related to reading proficiency. At fourth grade, the eye movements are still primarily letter by letter. But by 12th grade, eye movements are driven by units larger than the letter but still only rarely is that larger unit the whole word. While reading a 100-word text, first graders fixated approximately 225 times, while 12th graders fixated only 95 times. As reading proficiency develops, fewer fixations are needed because, after many years of successful reading, words and word parts become increasingly familiar. This familiarity means that less visual attention is needed because larger units are being recognized and processed (Samuels et al., 2010).

Decontextualized Word Recognition

The ability to read words quickly and accurately, even when there are no semantic context cues (e.g., on a flash card with only the to-be-read word), is a characteristic of a good reader (Share & Stanovich, 1995). A great deal of research effort has been devoted to determining how good readers recognize words as well as they do. Of course, for good readers, many words are sight words—well known from many past encounters. Recognition of sight words is said to be automatized, for reading these words requires little or no effort and is highly reliable (LaBerge & Samuels, 1974).

For instance, many readers of this chapter have yet to encounter a word that they "sounded out," or decoded with letter-by-letter processing. Some words were decoded using units larger than a letter. Take the word from the last paragraph, *automatized*. The first thing a skilled reader notices is the *auto* segment or the *automa* and the *tized* segment. Very few if any readers actually decoded that word by starting with the *au* segment. But skilled readers have read the *auto* many times and have read the *tized* segment many times, although not very many have read the word *automatized* many times. Using the familiar and larger orthographic units reduces the number of fixations the eye must make and speeds the word recognition process.

Much more telling about the skill of good readers, however, is that they typically can read words that they have never seen before, even words that are really nonsense words or pseudowords, such as *swackle*, *preflob*, and *plithing*. They can do that because they can readily associate letters with their sounds and blend the sounds to pronounce a word. Sounding out is something that good readers do well (Share & Stanovich, 1995). Even here, though, many skilled readers will "see" the *ack/ackle*, the *pre*, and the *ith* along with the familiar consonant blends *sw*, *fl*, and *pl* and see the *ing*. Each of these units is recognized based on previous experiences reading English words. Most readers did not slow down to sound out *s—w*, *f—l*, or *i—n—g*. Instead, much reading practice fostered the development of this fast and accurate decoding.

The process by which such advanced decoding proficiencies are developed has been called the "self-teaching" hypothesis (Share, 2004). To demonstrate that self-teaching is at work when children read, both orally and silently, de Jong and Share (2007) provided third graders with short texts that contained novel words (pseudowords). Several days later, they assessed whether those children "understood" the meaning of those novel words. In fact, they did. They concluded that successfully reading a new word literally prints that word and its constituent parts into a reader's long-term memory. Repeated successful readings of that new word ultimately result in that word being recognized as a word at a glance with minimal, if any, additional processing needed (Adams, 1990; Nation et al., 2007).

Recognition of the common letter combinations in one's native language is automatized in the skilled reader. Good readers can recognize common English-letter combinations, such as *-kle*, *pre-*, and *-ing*, presumably because they have encountered these combinations many times during reading. This permits much more rapid decoding than occurs when an unknown word does not contain familiar letter combinations. Try reading these two words: *retuckable* and *ekuteracbl*. They both contain the same letters, but the first is easier than the second because it is composed of three familiar English-letter combinations, whereas the second word's combinations are less familiar or never occur in English words.

That readers rely more on letter-level cues than semantic–contextual cues to recognize a word does not mean that semantic–contextual cues are not important in processing words. In fact, they can be very important *after the word has been recognized.* Read the following sentence: *The duck could not be stopped from biting the boy, so his mother grabbed the bill!* Now, read this sentence: *The boy could not be stopped from using his money to buy the duck, so his mother grabbed the bill.* How the word *bill* is interpreted depends heavily on semantic–contextual cues in this example (Gough, personal communication, June 1996). Although context does little to facilitate reading a word, it does much to facilitate understanding the meaning of the word once read.

It is largely the use of semantic–contextual cues that drives the process of self-correction when reading. When a word is misread, then the sentence often makes no sense. Take, for instance, the sentence *The goat munched on the grass.* Misread *goat* as *goal* and you get *The goal munched on the grass.* If you have been monitoring the meaning of what you read, then the sentence with the misread word makes no sense. That should cause you to revisit the sentence and try to locate the word that resulted in the nonsensical outcome. This is one characteristic of skilled readers. They do self-correct as they read. In fact, as Clay noted (1969) many years ago, skilled younger readers self-corrected one of every three errors that they made while reading aloud, while the low-progress readers self-corrected on one of every 20 errors. Thus, even young normally developing readers can acquire the basic tools of self-teaching.

One criticism of much of the work on letter-level and word-level processes is that such analyses do not put the focus on the reader as a meaning-maker. That criticism is valid to some extent, as will be made clear as this chapter proceeds, for skilled reading is getting meaning from sentences and paragraphs. Even if we keep in mind the caveat that reading is more than word recognition, however, the active processing of sentences and paragraphs cannot occur unless the reader can recognize individual words reliably and efficiently. That is why learning to decode is so important.

GETTING THE GIST

Every text has many ideas in it (e.g., Clark & Clark, 1977; Kintsch, 1974). Consider the sentence *John carefully nailed down the loose shingles on the roof* (Kintsch, 1982). There are four ideas in it: John nails shingles; nailing is being done carefully; shingles are on the roof; and shingles are loose. When good readers read such a sentence, they understand all of these ideas, although later they may remember only the main idea expressed in the sentence, namely, "John nailed shingles." Unless they have exerted great effort to memorize a text verbatim, people do not remember everything from a text that they read. What people remember is the gist, which comprises the main ideas in the text (Kintsch & van Dijk, 1978; van Dijk & Kintsch, 1983). In long discourse, such as is found in a book, there are layers of main ideas: At the top level, there is an overall summary of the book; then, each chapter in the book has main ideas, as does each paragraph in each chapter. The lower-level main ideas (e.g., at the paragraph level) are integrated by the skilled reader to create the higher-level summaries (e.g., at chapter and then book level; Kintsch, 1988; van Dijk & Kintsch, 1983).

For example, suppose that a reader is beginning to read a paragraph-long text. The first sentence contains a number of ideas, with the reader coding the main idea of the sentence. This idea is held in active memory as the next sentence in the paragraph is read. Attempts are made to link the main idea from the first sentence to the ideas of the second sentence, with another main idea emerging from this synthesis, integrating the meanings expressed in the first two sentences of the paragraph.

Sometimes there will be a need for bridging inferences that reconcile the meaning of the previous sentence with the ideas in a new sentence—that is, to produce coherence between the sentence currently being read and the text read up until this point. These bridging inferences are derived largely from the word knowledge that the reader possesses. For instance, if text about a worker pounding nails never mentions a hammer, the reader may infer "hammer" when the sentence *The head slipped off* is encountered. Perhaps the resulting main idea would be "the hammer broke while being used." By the end of the paragraph, good readers have implicitly generated a summary capturing the gist of the entire paragraph. (I emphasize *implicitly* at this point, for this process occurs automatically and unconsciously in the skilled reader.) Later, if the reader has to recall the paragraph, the most important ideas will be recalled (e.g., Kintsch & Keenan, 1973).

The longer the retention interval between reading and recall, the fewer the details that are remembered (e.g., Kintsch & van Dijk, 1978). The recall data will reflect bridging inferences made during the original reading as well as some inferences made when the text is recalled. Such inferences, again, are based on what the reader already knows; that is, memory for text typically reflects information in the text and the reader's knowledge of the world. For example, when Mike told his son the story of Charles Dickens's *A Christmas Carol*, he told the entire book-length story in about 5 minutes, remembering just about everything he could during that time. What he remembered were the main ideas of the story rather than what specific villagers said, or even the words of the four night visitors.

During his telling of the tale, however, Mike mentioned that Tiny Tim had polio. Mike had to explain to his then 9-year-old son what polio was since the disease is almost never encountered in contemporary America. Later, when his son read the story, he pointed out to Mike that the story actually contained no information about the affliction that put Tiny Tim on crutches. What had occurred was that Mike had inferred at some point, probably during his original reading of the story or during one of the productions of the play that he had seen, that Tiny Tim was a polio victim. Memory of text is very personal because the reader's background knowledge plays a large role in determining the meaning constructed by him or her.

Good readers do not make inferences willy-nilly, however. They do not make associations to prior knowledge that is completely remote from the ideas in the current text. Instead, they make inferences that are needed to understand the text (McKoon & Ratcliff, 1992; van den Broek, 1994). Nonetheless, as good readers read a story, they often create an elaborate understanding of the world in which the story is taking place (e.g., Fletcher, 1994; Kintsch, 1998). One of the important roles of prior knowledge is that it allows people to have a very good understanding of a very large situation, given relatively little information. Even in long novels, the author can describe in writing only the most important features of the story's setting and the most salient characteristics of the characters' personalities, and those readers with extensive prior knowledge are better able to fill in the gaps than those without such knowledge.

Although the model of reading discussed in this subsection has been studied most extensively with respect to narrative texts (i.e., stories), many of its main points apply to various types of expository texts as well (i.e., factual texts; e.g., Britton, 1994; Martin & Duke, 2011).

CONSCIOUS COMPREHENSION: VERBAL PROTOCOLS OF READING

Skilled readers tend to know a lot more about things in general than unskilled readers, resulting in the development of extensive knowledge. Much of this knowledge creation occurs automatically as a function of reading and "gistifying" text. It can also involve more conscious processes, for meaning-making during reading is not just automatic, implicit processing of text—it also involves much conscious, controlled processing.

Much has been learned about conscious, active comprehension processes by having good adult readers think aloud as they read. That is, researchers have asked adults to read text, interrupting them every so often to have them tell exactly what they are thinking and what they are doing as they read. Conscious decision making during reading is more obvious when readers read demanding, difficult texts. Thus, the texts read in verbal protocol studies often have been very demanding, requiring a good deal of thought for readers to understand the messages in them.

Wyatt et al.'s (1993) Study

Because we carried out an ambitious study of skilled reading using verbal protocol methods, we have some firsthand experience in this area (Wyatt et al., 1993). In that investigation, 15 professors from the University of Maryland thought aloud as they read articles that they had selected within their areas of expertise. Although each professor read a different article, and the professors and articles spanned a number of academic disciplines, there were important similarities that could be identified in their reading.

First, all the readers were exceptionally active as they read. Based on information in the article being read and their prior knowledge of the topic of the article, the professors anticipated what might be said later in the article. They were very aware of when their predictions were on target versus when their predictions were in error.

They looked for information that was relevant to their personal interests and personal goals in reading the article. Thus, the professor who was reading the article in preparation for writing a paper looked for information that might be helpful in preparing his or her own paper. Information that was relevant to the professor's personal goal in reading the text was read more slowly than information that was not considered to be as important.

Although the professors generally read the articles from the first page to the last page, they also jumped ahead sometimes to look for information that they thought might be in the article, and sometimes they looked back for additional clarification about a point that seemed confusing at first. Thus, if a sentence that was just read made little sense, they might reread it, and they might look back a few paragraphs to find information (i.e., a critical point that they must have missed previously) that might render the sentence sensible.

The professors explained the ideas in the text to themselves, constructing summaries and reasoning about why what was stated in the text made sense or, in some cases, did not make sense.

The professors monitored their reading a great deal. That is, they were very aware of how difficult or easy the text was to read. They were aware of whether they already knew the ideas stated in the text or the text was covering new territory for them. And, as discussed previously, they were aware of just which portions of the text were most pertinent to their reading goals.

Second, and even more striking than all the activity that occurred during reading, the readers were extremely passionate as they read. They constantly evaluated what they were reading. This was possible because of their extensive prior knowledge. Thus, when the text included ideas near and dear to their hearts, they reacted positively, saying things like "Right on!" or "She's got it!" In contrast were those occasions when text contained ideas that clashed with the reader's thinking. Such ideas were sometimes greeted with exclamations of disgust (including profanity) or nonverbal reactions. Throughout their reading, the readers reported when they were interested and when they were bored. It was very clear that reading was anything but an affectively neutral or passive experience for these readers.

Pressley and Afflerbach's (1995) Analysis of Skilled Reading

This think-aloud study that we conducted is one of more than 60 think-aloud studies that have been published in scientific journals. The exact types of activities reported by readers as they read have varied from study to study, probably reflecting variation in the directions given to participants in different studies as well as the variety of texts read in the various investigations.

Despite the variability across studies in procedures and materials read, when they reviewed all the studies that were published up until 1994, they were able to construct a summary of skilled reading that cut across the various investigations (Pressley & Afflerbach, 1995). The readers whom we studied were not unusual. Active reading is apparent in virtually every verbal protocol study in the research literature. Yes, there is evidence that some readers are much more active than others, but, in general, consciously active reading seems to be common, especially among individuals who are known to be good readers. Moreover, as mature readers become more experienced with a particular type of reading, they often become more sophisticated in how they read the text (Strømsø et al., 2003). Even so, in general, the conscious processing that is skilled reading begins before reading, continues during reading, and persists after reading is completed.

Before reading, good readers make certain that they know why they are reading the text and are clear about what they want to get from it. Rather than simply diving into a text and beginning to read a piece from front to back, good readers often do an overview of the text. During the overview, they are sensitive to the structure of the text, especially noting parts that might contain information that is particularly relevant to their reading goal. Skilled readers make a reading plan in light of the information they obtain during the overview. The information gained during this overview permits the skilled reader to gauge which parts of the text should be read first, which parts of the text should be read more carefully than others, and which ones should not be read at all. The skilled reader begins to relate what is in the text to prior knowledge and to get a summary idea of what is in the text. Sometimes, the overview reveals that the text is entirely irrelevant to the reader's goals. In that case, a skilled reader might decide not to read the text further.

If the reader does think the text is worthwhile based on the overview, he or she begins to read from front to back, varying reading speed from section to section of the text, sometimes skimming and sometimes skipping sections. Sometimes the reader stops and rereads a segment or pauses to think about what was just said. The reader gives greater attention to information that is important relative to her or his reason for reading the text. Earlier predictions based on the overview are updated because of information encountered in the text. New predictions about upcoming content are also made continually as the text is processed. That is, the skilled reader draws conclusions throughout reading, although the conclusions remain tentative, subject to change as reading continues.

Throughout reading, the skilled reader is making conscious inferences as well as inferences that are unconscious and automatic. Skilled readers try to fill in information gaps in the text, attempt to determine the meaning of unknown words, and relate ideas in the text to their prior knowledge (e.g., "That's just like . . . "). They make inferences about the author, such as her or his intentions in writing the text, or the particular sources that the author used. Fiction readers are always making inferences about the intentions of characters in the story. Skilled readers consciously attempt to integrate ideas that are encountered in different parts of a text (e.g., how the actions of characters in a story are related to the larger story). When beginning a work of fiction, they think about the setting and how new characters relate to the setting. The setting is kept in mind as the action proceeds. Skilled readers look for cause-and-effect connections between different parts of the text (e.g., how one character's actions early in a story motivated another character's responses later in the story). In integrating ideas across the text, a skilled reader may review previous text or jump ahead.

Skilled readers make many interpretations as they read. Sometimes this is apparent in paraphrases (e.g., "So this myth is like the exodus story . . . "). They form personal images of the events described in a text. If reading an expository text, they come up with summary comments (e.g., "What the author really wants to say in this chapter is . . . "). In making interpretations, prior knowledge plays a big role. Thus, a gender-stereotyped story written in the early 20th century gets a more sympathetic reading from an ardent feminist reader than a gender-stereotyped story written for the most recent issue of *The New Yorker*.

Processing of text does not conclude when the final word of an article, chapter, or book is read. Rather, the skilled reader sometimes rereads sections or reskims parts that seemed especially important. The skilled reader might try to restate important ideas or construct a summary of the text to make certain the ideas in the text can be recalled later. Sometimes skilled readers make notes. They often continue to reflect on a text and what it might mean long after reading is concluded.

The monitoring processes that we have witnessed in our study of college professors reading articles (Wyatt et al., 1993) were also apparent in many other verbal protocol studies. Readers are consciously aware of many characteristics of a text, from the author's style to the tone of the messages in the text. They are especially aware of whether they are understanding the text and whether such understanding is easy or requires considerable effort. When skilled readers detect problems, whether it is in understanding overall meanings in a text or knowing the meaning of a particular word in it, they do what they can to solve the problem.

Finally, just as evaluations were salient in the verbal protocols collected by Wyatt et al. (1993), they were salient in many other verbal protocol studies. Readers express feelings as they read. They consciously accept or reject the style of the text (e.g., quality of the writing) as well as the ideas expressed in the text.

Analyses of Expert Reading That Leads to Ineffective Educational Interventions

We emphasize at this point that some conspicuous instructional intervention failures have resulted from past conceptions that compared expert reading to weaker reading. (We mention them at this juncture if for no other reason than to get them behind us.) For example, the eye movements of poor readers often differ from the eye movements of good readers, with left-to-right saccadic movement less apparent in poor readers and poor readers less likely to fixate on words than on spaces between words. This deficiency in poor readers has inspired efforts to inculcate more efficient eye movements in poor readers, which sometimes have been successful in modifying fixations and saccades but generally have been unsuccessful in affecting reading. A general conclusion emerging from research on the modification of eye movements is that dysfunctional eye movements do not cause poor reading, but rather are a symptom of poor reading (see Gaddes, 1985; Rayner & Pollatsek, 1989, for reviews).

A second example of ineffective instruction based on a flawed conception of skilled reading is speed-reading instruction. There is no doubt that many readers can be taught to skim rather than read, and this is what speed-reading courses do. The problem is that when readers skim, their comprehension goes down, although not always on the tests used in speed reading courses to prove to clients that they are comprehending. The tests often are very easy, involving questions that could have been answered correctly, even without reading the passage.

In short, there is no credible scientific evidence that teaching people to read quickly can succeed when comprehension is tested with demanding test items (Carver, 1990). This does not negate, however, the point made earlier in this chapter that a state of high prior knowledge often enables skimming with high comprehension and efficient selective reading of text. That is, learning to be a skimmer can be a good thing when there is a need to cover a great deal of material related to areas of high prior knowledge.

THE ROLE OF READING VOLUME

One final characteristic of skilled reading is the substantial volume of reading that skilled readers do. As Anderson et al. (1988) noted in their study of the voluntary out-of-school reading that was accomplished by fifth graders, skilled readers read voluntarily more often and for longer periods of time.

Readers whose reading development placed them at the 90th percentile of proficiency for their grade level engaged in 33 minutes of daily voluntary and independent reading, while readers at the 50th percentile read voluntarily for 9 minutes each day and readers at the 10th percentile of reading performance read but for 1 minute a day. Consider the enormity of those differences. The skilled readers were estimated to have voluntarily read almost 2.5 million words over the school year. The average readers read just over 600,000 words, and the struggling readers read 51,000 words.

Other researchers have made the same observation on the substantial differences in reading volume that exist between readers of differing proficiency levels (e.g., Allington, 2009; Cipielewski & Stanovich, 1992; Guthrie, 2004; Taylor et al., 1990), while others have reported that volume of reading is linked to levels of reading proficiency (Cunningham & Stanovich, 1997). However, the relationship between volume of reading—especially voluntary, independent reading—and improved reading performance has been little studied experimentally. That is, while we have a number of reports that skilled readers do read voluntarily in substantially larger amounts than less-skilled readers, only a few studies have tested whether experimentally increasing reading volume will improve reading performance (Kuhn et al., 2006; Schwanenflugel et al., 2009; Wu & Samuels, 2004).

One of the reasons that reading volume is important is that people who read more are likely to know more—indeed, people who read extensively are more knowledgeable than people who read less (Duke et al., 2011; Stanovich & Cunningham, 1993). The cognitive psychologists interested in how people learn from a text have established how general knowledge of the world changes as a function of reading (e.g., Graesser, 1981; Graesser et al., 1980; Kintsch, 1974; Kintsch & Keenan, 1973; Kintsch et al., 1975). The gist of what has been read is integrated with what the reader knew before reading the text (i.e., prior knowledge) to create new knowledge (e.g., Anderson & Bower, 1973). Thus, if you read a magazine article about the literacy crisis in America, you might implicitly construct a summary that includes the main ideas covered in the article. At a party tomorrow, you could rely on this summary alone to guide partial retelling of the article to a friend who might be interested in the literacy crisis. More importantly, however, your long-term knowledge of literacy might be changed by reading the article. Thus, 6 months from now, when someone makes a claim about literacy that conflicts with what was in the article, you can respond, "But I thought . . . ," going on to relate a general point from the article, perhaps no longer aware of where the information was acquired.

It should not be surprising that the volume of reading a reader engages in is linked to higher levels of reading performance (Allington & McGill-Franzen, 2021). There are compelling reasons to think that the relationship is causal. This is because we do have evidence that skilled readers have larger vocabularies and that reading volume is tied to that performance advantage (Martin-Chang & Gould, 2008). If self-teaching is a potentially powerful factor in skilled reading, and the evidence suggests that it is, then every instance of voluntary reading adds to the reading proficiencies of that voluntary reader. With greater engagement in reading activity comes greater world knowledge as well as increases in both essential aspects of skilled decoding (Share, 1995) and skilled comprehension (Stanovich & Cunningham, 1993) of the texts that have been read.

SUMMARY AND CONCLUDING REFLECTIONS

1. Skilled reading is the effective coordination of higher-order processes (e.g., comprehension) and lower-order processes (e.g., decoding). Getting meaning from a text very much depends on efficient lower-order processing: Skilled readers automatically recognize many words and efficiently decode unfamiliar words that they encounter. Skilled readers process most words in the texts that they read. Indeed, they seem to process most of the individual letters within words. The primary cues used to decode text are the letters and words, not the meaning of the text in which the words are embedded nor the syntactic context in which an unfamiliar word is embedded. The more skilled the reader, the faster and better this interactive process works.

2. When skilled readers read, they abstract the gist from text, getting the big ideas, even though many details may not be recallable. Comprehension involves processing the ideas in the text in light of one's own prior knowledge, with prior knowledge permitting readers to make many inferences as they proceed. One's knowledge, however, often changes as a function of reading.

3. Although much comprehension occurs implicitly, unconsciously, and almost automatically, much of comprehension involves conscious, active processing of the text. The skilled reader can be active before reading (e.g., overviewing the text and making predictions), during reading (e.g., updating predictions, constructing mental images), and after reading (e.g., constructing summaries, thinking about which ideas in the text might be useful later). Skilled readers are both interpretive and evaluative, often reacting to the validity of ideas in the text.

4. Understanding the nature of skilled reading provides perspectives on what reading instruction should accomplish. That expert readers are so proficient at word-level processes provides motivation for instruction that focuses on development of decoding. That skilled reading involves conscious comprehension processes motivates instruction that develops active comprehension habits.

5. That skilled readers do not seem to depend on meaning cues to initially recognize words provides good reason to reject arguments that decoding instruction should emphasize orientation to meaning cues. By the conclusion of this book, it will be clear that advising children to attend first and foremost to meaning cues (e.g., to look at picture cues) to recognize words is very poor and harmful instructional advice. Meaning cues are critical, however, in appraising whether initial word recognition was correct: If the word makes no sense given the context, the skilled reader knows to go back and look at the word again. It is this sort of cross-checking that seems to separate skilled and unskilled beginning readers. Context cues also help the skilled reader to zero in on the intended meaning of words that have more than one definition.

6. Long overlooked in research on skilled reading, the volume of reading in which a reader engages voluntarily is linked to reading proficiency. What we know is that the difference between the volume of voluntary reading that struggling and skilled readers engage in is enormous. It seems that this difference in reading volume explains much of the many differences observed between struggling and skilled readers. However, for voluntary reading volume to play a role, we must consider the potential of self-teaching. That is the sort of learning that occurs while reading voluntarily and independently. The evidence to date is quite strong that reading volume is related to vocabulary size, decoding, fluency, or comprehension development.

7. Those who wish to teach reading well need to understand just what skilled reading is. Reading instruction should be balanced, and the sound teaching of reading should develop readers who read as described in this chapter.

REFERENCES

Adams, M. (1990). Beginning to read: Thinking and learning about print. MIT Press.

Allington, R. L. (2009). If they don't read much . . . 30 years later. In E. H. Hiebert (Ed.), *Reading more, reading better* (pp. 30–54). Guilford Press.

Allington, R. L., & McGill-Franzen, A. (2021) Reading volume and reading achievement: A view of recent research. *Reading Research Quarterly, 56*, S231–S238.

Anderson, J. R., & Bower, G. H. (1973). *Human associative memory.* Wiley.

Anderson, R. C., Wilson, P. T., & Fielding, L. G. (1988). Growth in reading and how children spend their time outside of school. *Reading Research Quarterly, 23*, 285–303.

Britton, B. K. (1994). Understanding expository text: Building mental structures to induce insights. In M. A. Gernsbacher (Ed.), *Handbook of psycholinguistics* (pp. 641–674). Academic Press.

Carver, R. P. (1990). *Reading rate: A review of research and theory.* Academic Press.

Cipielewski, J., & Stanovich, K. E. (1992). Predicting growth in reading ability from children's exposure to print. *Journal of Experimental Child Psychology, 54*(1), 74–89.

Clark, H. H., & Clark, E. V. (1977). *Psychology and language.* Harcourt Brace Jovanovich.

Clay, M. M. (1969). Reading errors and self-correction behaviour. *British Journal of Educational Psychology, 37*, 47–56.

Cunningham, A. E., & Stanovich, K. E. (1997). Early reading acquisition and its relation to reading experience and ability 10 years later. *Developmental Psychology, 33*, 934–945.

de Jong, P. F., & Share, D. L. (2007). Orthographic learning during oral and silent reading. *Scientific Studies of Reading, 11*(1), 55–71.

Duke, N. K., Pearson, P. D., Strachan, S. L., & Billman, A. K. (2011). Essential elements of fostering and teaching reading comprehension. In S. J. Samuels & A. E. Farstrup (Eds.), *What research has to say about reading comprehension* (pp. 51–93). International Reading Association.

Fletcher, C. R. (1994). Levels of representation in memory for discourse. In M. A. Gernsbacher (Ed.), *Handbook of psycholinguistics* (pp. 589–607). Academic Press.

Gaddes, W. H. (1985). *Learning disabilities and brain function* (2nd ed.). Springer-Verlag.

Gough, P. B. (1983). Context, form, and interaction. In K. Rayner (Ed.), *Eye movements in reading* (pp. 203–211). Academic Press.

Graesser, A. C. (1981). *Prose comprehension beyond the word*. Springer-Verlag.

Graesser, A. C., Hoffman, N. L., & Clark, L. F. (1980). Structural components of reading time. *Journal of Verbal Learning and Verbal Behavior, 19*, 135–151.

Guthrie, J. T. (2004). Teaching for literacy engagement. *Journal of Literacy Research, 36*(1), 1–28.

Kintsch, W. (1974). *The representation of meaning in memory*. Erlbaum.

Kintsch, W. (1982). Text representations. In W. Otto & S. White (Eds.), *Reading expository material* (pp. 87–102). Academic Press.

Kintsch, W. (1988). The role of knowledge in discourse comprehension: A construction-integration model. *Psychological Review, 95*, 163–182.

Kintsch, W. (1998). *Comprehension: A paradigm for cognition*. Cambridge University Press.

Kintsch, W., & Keenan, J. M. (1973). Reading rate and retention as a function of the number of propositions in the base structure of sentences. *Cognitive Psychology, 5*, 257–279.

Kintsch, W., Kozminsky, E., Streby, W. J., McKoon, G., & Keenan, J. M. (1975). Comprehension and recall as a function of content variables. *Journal of Verbal Learning and Verbal Behavior, 14*, 196–214.

Kintsch, W., & van Dijk, T. A. (1978). Toward a model of discourse comprehension and production. *Psychological Review, 85*, 363–394.

Kuhn, M. R., Schwanenflugel, P., Morris, R. D., Morrow, L. M., Woo, D., Meisinger, B., et al. (2006). Teaching children to become fluent and automatic readers. *Journal of Literacy Research, 38*(4), 357–388.

LaBerge, D., & Samuels, S. J. (1974). Toward a theory of automatic information processing in reading. *Cognitive Psychology, 6*, 293–323.

Martin, N. M., & Duke, N. K. (2011). Interventions to enhance informational text comprehension. In A. McGill-Franzen & R. L. Allington (Eds.), *Handbook of reading disability research* (pp. 345–363). Routledge.

Martin, N. M., & Duke, N. K. (2011). Interventions to enhance informational text comprehension. In A. McGill-Franzen & R. L. Allington (Eds.), *Handbook of reading disability research* (pp. 345–363). Routledge.

Martin-Chang, S. L., & Gould, O. N. (2008). Revisiting print exposure: Exploring differential links to vocabulary comprehension and reading rate. *Journal of Research in Reading, 31*(3), 273–284.

McConkie, G. W., & Hogaboam, T. W. (1985). Eye position and word identification during reading. In Groner, R., McConkie, G. W. & Menz, C. (Eds.), *Eye movements and information processing* (pp. 159–192). Elsevier.

McConkie, G. W., Zola, D., Blanchard, H. E., & Wolverton, G. S. (1982). Perceiving words during reading: Lack of facilitation from prior peripheral exposure. *Perception and Psychophysics, 32*, 271–281.

McKoon, G., & Ratcliff, R. (1992). Inference during reading. *Psychological Review, 99,* 440–466.

Nation, K., Angella, P., & Castles, A. (2007). Orthographic learning via self-teaching in children learning to read English: Effects of exposure, durability, and context. *Journal of Experimental Child Psychology, 96*(1), 71–84.

Pressley, M., & Afflerbach, P. (1995). *Verbal protocols of reading: The nature of constructively responsive reading.* Erlbaum.

Rayner, K., Inhoff, A. W., Morrison, R. E., Slowiaczek, M. L., & Bertera, J. H. (1981). Masking of foveal and parafoveal vision during eye fixations in reading. *Journal of Experimental Psychology: Human Perception and Performance, 7,* 167–179.

Rayner, K., & Pollatsek, A. (1989). *The psychology of reading.* Prentice-Hall.

Samuels, S. J. (1994). Word recognition. In R. B. Ruddell, M. R. Ruddell, & H. Singer (Eds.), *Theoretical models and processes of reading* (pp. 359–380). International Reading Association.

Samuels, S. J., Hiebert, E. H., & Rasinski, T. V. (2010). Eye movements make reading possible. In E. H. Hiebert & D. R. Reutzel (Eds.), *Revisiting silent reading: New directions for teachers and researchers* (pp. 24–44). International Reading Association.

Schwanenflugel, P. J., Kuhn, M. R., Morris, R. D., Morrow, L. M., Meisinger, E. B., Woo, D. G., et al. (2009). Insights into fluency instruction: Short- and long-term effects of two reading programs. *Literacy Research and Instruction, 48*(4), 318–336.

Share, D. L. (1995). Phonological recoding and self-teaching: Sine qua non of reading acquisition. *Cognition, 55*(2), 151–218.

Share, D. L. (2004). Orthographic learning at a glance: On the time course and development onset of self-teaching. *Journal of Experimental Child Psychology, 87,* 267–298.

Share, D. L., & Stanovich, K. E. (1995). Cognitive processes in early reading development: Accommodating individual differences into a model of acquisition. *Issues in Education: Contributions from Educational Psychology, 1,* 1–57.

Smith, F. (1979). *Reading without nonsense.* Teachers College Press.

Smith, F. (2012). *Understanding reading: A psycholinguistic analysis of reading and learning to read* (6th ed.). Routledge.

Stanovich, K. E., & Cunningham, A. E. (1993). Where does knowledge come from? Specific associations between print exposure and information acquisition. *Journal of Educational Psychology, 85,* 211–229.

Strømsø, H. I., Bräten, I., & Samuelstuen, M. S. (2003). Students' strategic use of multiple sources during expository text reading: A longitudinal think-aloud study. *Cognition and Instruction, 21,* 113–147.

Taylor, B. M., Frye, B. J., & Maruyama, G. M. (1990). Time spent reading and reading growth. *American Educational Research Journal, 27*(2), 351–362.

van den Broek, P. (1994). Comprehension and memory of narrative texts: Inferences and coherence. In M. A. Gernsbacher (Ed.), *Handbook of psycholinguistics* (pp. 539–588). Academic Press.

van Dijk, T. A., & Kintsch, W. (1983). *Strategies of discourse comprehension.* Academic Press.

Wu, Y., & Samuels, S. J. (2004, May). *How the amount of time spent on independent reading affects reading achievement.* Paper presented at the annual meeting of the International Reading Association, Reno, NV.

Wyatt, D., Pressley, M., El-Dinary, P. B., Stein, S., Evans, P., & Brown, R. (1993). Comprehension strategies, worth and credibility monitoring, and evaluations: Cold and hot cognition when experts read professional articles that are important to them. *Learning and Individual Differences, 5,* 49–72.

3 Children Who Experience Problems in Learning To Read

Some primary-grade students of average intelligence experience difficulty in learning to read. Moreover, primary-grade difficulties in learning to read predict to some extent continuing reading difficulties throughout schooling (e.g., Francis et al., 1994; Phillips et al., 2002; Rabiner et al., 2016), with other subjects (e.g., García-Madruga et al., 2014; Morgan et al., 2016), and into adulthood (e.g., Hernandez, 2011; McNulty, 2003; Ransby & Swanson, 2003; Ricketts et al., 2014; Smart et al., 2017).

The most salient problem in learning to read is learning to decode, to recognize words, initially by sounding them out. Problems in this area are probably rooted in other language problems. For example, children with reading disabilities and those at risk for becoming poor readers do not discriminate speech sounds as well as other children (e.g., Bertucci et al., 2003; Breier et al., 2004; Espy et al., 2004; Molfese et al., 2002; Serniclaes et al., 2004). Poor readers and those at risk for becoming poor readers also do not segment words into their constituent sounds as well as other children. They experience a great deal of difficulty hearing and/or saying the sounds represented by the constituent letters of the word and blending the sounds to produce the word. Many analyses have produced outcomes consistent with these conclusions (e.g., Rack et al., 1994; Snowling & Melby-Lervåg, 2016; Troia, 2004; Vellutino et al., 2004).

If struggling readers do not sound out words and blend the sounds specified by letters to produce words, what do such readers do instead? Weaker readers often rely much more on semantic–contextual cues to identify words than do skilled readers. That is, rather than trying to sound out an unfamiliar word, poorer readers rely on textual and picture cues as clues to make a guess about a word's meaning (e.g., Nicholson, 1991;

Schwantes, 1991; Tunmer & Chapman, 2004). Unfortunately, some teachers have been taught that using semantic clues is the best approach to teaching students how to read, thus completely ignoring the data suggesting the importance of letter–sound correspondence (Hanford, 2017, 2018, 2019). Although students who use semantic clues as the primary reading strategy might process the letters somewhat and use some letter-level information in making their guesses (e.g., limiting guesses to words beginning with *p* since the word begins with *p*), their processing of the letter cues is much less complete than it could be, with the picture and semantic–contextual cues given priority.

Strong beginning readers certainly could make use of context cues with respect to decoding, but they do not do so exclusively. For anyone who can analyze words into their sounds and blend them, it makes little sense to rely on the semantic–contextual approach alone for word recognition since there are a number of problems with relying on semantic–contextual cues. One is that the semantic–contextual approach is much less certain to produce accurate pronunciation than is sounding out words: A lot of guesses will be in error. A second problem is that when readers "read" words based on picture and other semantic–contextual cues, they are much less likely to make progress in transforming an unknown word into a sight word (e.g., Samuels, 1970). Thus, use of the semantic–contextual strategy negatively affects future reading by undermining the development of automatic word recognition. A third problem with relying on the semantic–contextual approach to decoding is that it is slow and thus consumes a great deal of short-term cognitive capacity. For the average person, about seven chunks of information can be held in consciousness at any one time (Miller, 1956). Slow decoding eats up much of this short-term capacity, while automatic decoding requires relatively little short-term capacity. When a great deal of capacity is required to decode, little is left over for comprehension, and thus comprehension suffers (Cirino et al., 2013; Clarke et al., 2010, 2013; Elwér et al., 2015; LaBerge & Samuels, 1974; Nation et al., 2010; Samuels et al., 2010).

In the end, attention to the context in which a word appears is one component of what good readers do. Even as early as first grade, children who later are good readers use context cues as tools to cross check the pronunciation produced in decoding a word (Clay, 1969). Self-correction behavior (using context cues) was already established in the first graders who became good readers, while the children who were later poor readers offered little evidence of attention to context as a tool for checking on the identity of the word that was read, use of context then, seems to be a useful skill that needs to be developed and then supported (Weber, 1970).

The reason for reading is not to decode words correctly, but to get meaning from text and self-correction is one early hallmark of a reader developing the proficiency to use contextual cues while reading. Comprehension, however, depends on word recognition skills, and thus this discussion of comprehension begins with word-level comprehension failures in poor readers.

WORD-LEVEL COMPREHENSION FAILURES

Beyond being able to decode words by sounding them out, good readers can read many words without sounding them out. That is, although good readers can sound out unfamiliar words, with additional exposures, unfamiliar words become sight words, ones recognized automatically without the need to effortfully analyze and blend component sounds. Such automaticity is crucial for children if they are to develop into skilled readers (Ehri & Snowling, 2004; Kieffer & Christodoulou, 2020). To be clear, words become sight words not because readers memorize them, but because readers have had repeated opportunities to decode them using their knowledge of letter–sound correspondences, and those repeated opportunities enable decoding processes to become automatic (Miles et al., 2018).

Why does automaticity matter? As discussed earlier, decoding does take place in short-term memory—that very limited capacity that is consciousness. In fact, decoding and comprehension compete for the available short-term capacity (LaBerge & Samuels, 1974). When a reader slowly analyzes a word into component sounds and blends them, a great deal of capacity is consumed, with relatively little left over for comprehension of the word, let alone for understanding the overall meaning of the sentence containing the word and the paragraph containing the sentence. In contrast, automatic word recognition (i.e., recognizing a word that has become a sight word) consumes very little capacity and thus frees short-term capacity for the task of comprehending the word and integrating the meaning of the word with the overall meaning of the sentence, paragraph, and whole text. Consistent with this analysis, uncertain decoders comprehend less than do more rapid, certain decoders (see Perfetti, 1985; Perfetti & Hogaboam, 1975; Perfetti & Lesgold, 1977, 1979). (See Chapter 6 for more discussion of automaticity at the word level.)

Good readers are adept at word-level processing in ways other than rapid and accurate decoding. When a good reader reads a word that has multiple meanings, he or she more quickly zeroes in on the correct meaning of the word in the given context than do weak readers. This is, in part, because good readers more efficiently suppress context-irrelevant meanings than do poor readers (Gernsbacher, 1990; Gernsbacher & Faust, 1990; Gernsbacher et al., 1990; Henderson et al., 2013; Merrill et al., 1981). That is, at the level of meaning, they do use semantic context cues to read the words in the text (Tunmer & Chapman, 2004). For example, the word *rock* differs in meaning depending on the context in which it occurs. When a good reader processes the sentence *The thief lifted the rock from the jewelry case*, he or she understands quickly that *rock* refers to a precious stone rather than to other type of rocks. In contrast, weaker readers are more likely to think about the irrelevant meanings of *rock* when they encounter the word in the sentence. The failure of weaker readers to suppress more familiar but irrelevant meanings of words is consistent with a more general inability of some struggling readers to suppress tangential (often bizarre) associations to material they are reading (McCormick, 1992; Purcell-Gates, 1991; Williams, 1993). The activation of irrelevant information interferes with processing, consuming the limited short-term cognitive capacity. That is, meaning-suppression failures create additional disadvantages for already disadvantaged readers.

FAILURES OF COMPREHENSION ABOVE THE WORD LEVEL

Once poor readers can decode well enough to read texts with accuracy, their problems often continue. Other times, readers learn to decode well, but they fail to comprehend text at a level that would be expected based on their word reading ability (Yuill & Oakhill, 1991). These readers are said to have specific reading comprehension deficits/difficulties (S-RCD; Locascio et al., 2010), and sometimes they are just called poor comprehenders. Students with S-RCD are less likely than good readers to make inferences linking ideas presented in text (Catts et al., 2003; Yuill & Oakhill, 1991). One of the first studies to explore comprehension issues with students able to decode, Yuill and Oakhill (1991, chap. 4) presented skilled and not-so-skilled 7- to 8-year-old readers such passages as the following:

> John had got up early to learn his spellings. He was very tired and decided to take a break. When he opened his eyes again the first thing he noticed was the clock on the chair. It was an hour later and nearly time for school. He picked up his two books, and put them in a bag. He started pedalling to school as fast as he could. However, John ran over some broken bottles and had to walk the rest of the way. By the time he had crossed the bridge and arrived at class, the test was over. (p. 71)

The most important finding in Yuill and Oakhill's work was that poor comprehenders were much less likely to be able to answer inferential questions about such passages than skilled comprehenders, even when the passages remained in front of them so that remembering the information was not a problem. Poor comprehenders had more problems with questions such as these: "How did John travel to school?", "What did John do when he decided to take a break?", "Why did John have to walk some of the way to school?", and "How do you know that John was late for school?" Yuill and Oakhill (1991; see also Cain & Oakhill, 2004; Oakhill & Cain, 2004) reported a number of outcomes consistent with the conclusion that poor and skilled comprehenders differ in their abilities to make inferences.

A number of factors contribute to such inferential failures (Cain & Oakhill, 2004; Oakhill & Cain, 2004). For example, inferential skills depend in part on the possession of prior knowledge related to text. Poor readers are often very deficient in their knowledge of the world relative to good readers—as reflected, for example, in vocabulary differences between good and poor readers (e.g., Ruddell, 1994). Good readers know more, in part, because they read more, and they get more out of each bit of reading they do (Cipielewski & Stanovich, 1992; Stanovich, 1986).

Inferential comprehension also depends, however, on knowing strategies and knowing when to use comprehension strategies (i.e., possessing metacognition about strategies; e.g., Cain, 1999; Cain & Oakhill, 2004; Oakhill & Cain, 2004). With respect to the latter, good emergent readers know more about how to read than do weaker emergent readers. For example, weak emergent readers are less likely than good emergent readers to recognize that they can reread, skim, selectively attend to the text as they read, or test themselves over reading, depending on their purpose (e.g., Forrest-Pressley & Waller, 1984; Garner & Kraus, 1981–1982; Paris & Myers, 1981). Poor readers are less likely than good readers to recognize factors that can undermine their reading comprehension, such as inattention during reading or distraction (Paris & Myers, 1981). Children who are weak readers do not monitor their comprehension as well as do good readers; thus, they are less aware of when they understand and when they do not—and in a worse position than good readers to make decisions about when additional efforts to comprehend are required (e.g., Garner, 1980).

These differences in metacognition are related to strategic differences between weak and strong emergent readers. For example, Owings et al. (1980) observed that weak grade 5 readers were less certain to vary their reading with difficulty of material than good grade 5 readers. Also, weak middle school readers were less likely than good readers to look back in the text for answers to questions that they did not know (Garner & Reis, 1981). In Phillips's (1988) think-aloud study of grade 6 reading, low-proficiency readers were less likely to shift strategies when difficulty in comprehension was encountered, less likely to attempt to verify their emerging interpretations of text meaning, and less likely to empathize with messages in the text. That is, Phillips observed that weak readers are *less active* when they read, leading to reduced comprehension of the material.

It may be that teacher behaviors work to foster the development of the ability to use context to cross-check the pronunciation of a word while reading. That is, teachers generally interact with poor readers differently than they interact with good readers. When good readers make an error while reading aloud, teachers usually draw the good readers' attention to whether the word pronounced makes sense. Good readers then typically self-correct the misread/mispronounced word. Of course, good readers are more likely to spontaneously self-correct an oral reading error without any input from the teacher.

When a poor reader misreads a word in a story, teachers usually draw the poor reader's attention to physical features of the word. Poor readers hear teachers ask, "Does that word begin with a *th*?" Or they hear teachers say, "What sound does *ea* make?" That is, good readers have their attention drawn to sense-making, while poor readers have their attention drawn to letters and sounds. Repetition of meaning versus letter–sound cues occurs every day that teachers ask kids to read aloud. In fact, kids often mimic the teacher's cues and interrupt the reader by asking, "Is that a short vowel, Dick?" The power of hundreds of repetitions of these differing messages means that readers develop different strategies when they encounter or attempt the pronunciation of an unknown word. Good readers learn that a word must make sense in the story being read. Poor readers learn that they should be paying more attention to letters and sounds of the word.

Ultimately, these differences in teacher directions create readers who either attend to whether the word they produced makes sense in the passage read or they attend to physical features (letters and sounds) of the word. Good readers learn to read with self-correction, and poor readers learn to read with paying more attention to letters and sounds. In the end then, we have two types of readers: good readers who use the context of the passage after they have read the word to cross-check whether the word makes sense and poor readers who either attempt to sound the word out again or produce a word that matches some of the target word's letters.

All in all, teachers must teach students to attempt to sound out unknown words, and then, after the child has produced the sounding out, the child cross-checks whether that word makes sense. Because poor readers make so many more reading errors as they read than do good readers, that means poor readers receive a steady diet of directions to attend to letter/sound cues and almost nothing suggesting cross-checking for making sense. Compound this problem with the fact that good readers are more often directed to read the text silently while poor readers are directed to read the text aloud, and two quite different instructional environments are typically created for children who are seen as good versus poor readers. These differences in where the teacher directs the child's attention (to making sense or to making a response to demonstrate the child's attention to letters and sounds) is important if only because children take a teacher's directions quite literally. Cueing the child to make sense on the occasions when a word is misread sends a message that directs the child to pay attention to what the text means (Allington, 2016). We argue that a better balance of teacher directions to children as they read aloud would look much like what teachers currently do when good readers are reading aloud (which is far less often than when poor readers are asked to read aloud). Teachers need first to ensure that children can read the text given the reading skills they have. Then teachers need to ask poor readers to read silently more often than they currently do, perhaps only asking poor readers to read aloud after they have read the text silently. The current classroom environments seem to create two classes of readers: good readers, who use decoding, sight words, and context as they read, and poor readers, who use decoding cues (though often not very well) along with physical features of a word (e.g., word length, beginning letters). That is, kids learn what they are taught, and the two groups of children are taught reading in very different ways. The balanced framework for reading and reading instruction takes advantage of all the cues that are available to the readers.

Another way that children and adolescents with RCD differ from their peers with better reading comprehension is their underlying executive function abilities. Executive function skills are mental processes that underlie goal-directed behaviors and include (at least) three core skills: cognitive flexibility, inhibitory control, and working memory, which underlie more complex skills like planning and monitoring (Diamond, 2013). Readers with S-RCD rank significantly lower than their better-comprehending peers on cognitive flexibility (Cartwright et al., 2017), working memory (Cain, 2006), inhibitory control (Borella et al., 2010), and planning (Locascio et al., 2010). For example, executive function skills support readers' abilities to implement metacognitive comprehension strategies while reading (Gnaedinger et al., 2016). Recent work suggests that executive function intervention may be a useful intervention to support reading comprehension in students with S-RCD (Cartwright et al., 2017).

SUMMARY OF READING DIFFICULTIES

In summary, the most typical difficulty experienced by beginning readers is in learning to recognize words. Poor readers are more likely than good readers to attempt to "read" words by looking at pictures for cues or making a guess based on the meaning of the text. The result is many errors in reading. In addition, poor readers make less certain and rapid progress in developing automatic word recognition skills. They also are less likely to understand individual words because they use capacity-demanding strategies for decoding (e.g., analyzing semantic–contextual cues, sounding out words that are sight words for same-age good readers).

This inability to read text accurately also interferes with strategic functioning above the word level because use of active comprehension strategies requires a great deal of short-term memory capacity. Because reading is difficult and comprehension uncertain for poor decoders, their knowledge base does not expand as dependably through reading as does the knowledge base of good readers. That is, there are strong associations between decoding skills and the knowledge gained through the reading of a text (e.g., Cipielewski & Stanovich, 1992; Stanovich, 1986; Stanovich & Cunningham, 1993). Not learning much content from reading, of course, undermines future comprehension, for facility in comprehension very much depends on prior knowledge—developed, in part, through prior reading.

Above the word level, poor comprehenders are less likely to make inferences and answer inferential questions about a text. In addition, poor comprehenders do not monitor their comprehension and are less likely to be aware of their misunderstanding of a text. Metacognitive theorists explicitly believe that the differences in long-term metacognition and monitoring are causal factors in the use of strategies (Flavell et al., 1993) and thus in comprehension. More recently, researchers have begun to explore the role of executive function and comprehension, with significant findings suggesting that poor comprehenders are more likely to struggle with critical skills for reading such as cognitive flexibility, working memory, inhibitory control, and planning (Borella et al., 2016; Cain, 2006; Cartwright et al., 2017; Locascio et al., 2010). The effect of the steady diet of different text-orienting strategies (decoding, making sense) is little understood but, given the power of consistently different strategies that are recommended to good and poor readers, likely contributes to the differences observed while reading (Allington, 2012).

DYSLEXIA

When a child experiences difficulties learning to read words, it is often tempting to explain it as a biological or neurological problem. Are there normally intelligent children who have neurological differences that make it more difficult or impossible for them to learn to read, even in the context of intensive instruction that would be effective with most students of average or above-average intelligence? The answer seems to be "sometimes." That is, several different research teams have designed and implemented reading intervention programs that dramatically reduce the number of children failing to develop word reading proficiency in the normal grade-level reading range (Mathes et al., 2005; Phillips & Smith, 2010; Vellutino et al.,

1996). In each of these cases, only 1–2% of grade 1 student populations failed to achieve grade-level word reading performances. This suggests that most students struggling to read words are created primarily by lack of access to balanced and appropriate expert and intensive reading instruction.

When most teachers think about students with word reading difficulties, the term *dyslexia* often comes to mind. However, over the past several decades, the definition of dyslexia has varied, with stakeholders debating every aspect of dyslexia. Differences included arguments surrounding the difference (if any) between dyslexia and alternative reasons for reading difficulties, identification of students with dyslexia, and support provided to students who are identified with dyslexia (Allington & Gabriel, in press; Elliott, 2020; Johnston & Scanlon, 2021; Miciak & Fletcher, 2020; Snowling et al., 2020; Worthy et al., 2018). Additionally, parents and educators have actively advocated the prevalence of dyslexia and treatments for dyslexia through phonics instruction (Johnston & Scanlon, 2021) and have had success gaining political support for students labeled with dyslexia (Mather et al., 2020; Zirkel, 2020).

Elliot and Grigorenko (2014) presented four distinct ways of identifying and defining dyslexia across the literature. These four approaches included aspects such as a student being on the lower end of a reading assessment, being poor decoders assessed through cognitive, educational, and neurological assessments, a student who struggles to read after high-quality intervention, and difficulty with memory, organization, and processing speed (Elliot & Grigorenko, 2014). Additionally, they found a wide range of alternative terms aligned with dyslexia, including *specific learning disability, learning disability in reading,* and *reading disorder* (Elliott & Grigerenko, 2014; see Elliott, 2020). However, the disagreement regarding a true definition of dyslexia has also limited the research conducted in the area, as researchers have faced limitations in their criteria for participants and sample size (Allington & Gabriel, in press). Lopes et al. (2020) recently completed a meta-analysis of over 800 studies on dyslexia from the last two decades and found no clear criteria for participation across the 800 studies.

Ultimately, there are many definitions of dyslexia with no consensus between researchers, teachers, practitioners, or parents. This confusion has left teachers and educators struggling to identify students with dyslexia or other learning disabilities and provide appropriate interventions (Worthy et al., 2018). With many definitions of dyslexia in the literature and variations in research on dyslexia, we align with Elliott and Grigorenko (2014) and do not see a reason to prefer one definition over another. However, we believe that dyslexia can describe a student who has difficulty with reading, even after receiving high-quality instruction, but understand that defining high-quality instruction is another gray area of debate.

Dyslexia Versus Other Forms of Poor Reading

If a child of average or superior intelligence receives intensive, high-quality instruction and still fails to learn to read, there is reason to suspect dyslexia (e.g., Harris & Hodges, 1981; There is another type of dyslexia, acquired dyslexia, which refers to difficulty in reading following a brain injury). One hallmark of dyslexia is that the affected individuals experience much more profound problems with reading and closely related language functions than with other academic and cognitive tasks.

Although most of the relevant analyses of dyslexia have been carried out with children, there is a growing body of evidence that many weak adult readers of average intelligence have language problems, with the most salient difficulties associated with decoding print into sound (Bell & Perfetti, 1994; Elbro, Nielsen, & Petersen, 1994; Elliott & Grigorenko, 2014; Greenberg et al., 1997; Swanson et al., 1999). What is particularly important to emphasize in these analyses is that language difficulties related to reading problems at the word level have emerged as a key factor in dyslexia and reading difficulties over a number of other possibilities, including impairments in short-term (working) memory, semantic processing, and syntactic processing skills (Lyon, 1995). For example, de Jong (1998; see also Swanson & Alexander, 1997) provided a compelling demonstration that children's word-reading difficulties really do seem to have less working memory capacity than do normal readers—that is, less ability to process multiple pieces of information concurrently. Since then, multiple analyses have substantiated impaired working memory in children and adults with a reading disability as compared with normal readers and among inefficient readers in general (e.g., Cain et al., 2004; Del Tufo & Earle, 2020; Kibby et al., 2004; Linderholm & van den Broek, 2002; Swanson, 2003).

Also, as important as decoding is in reading, the more the concern is with reading problems above the word level (e.g., miscomprehension), the more factors like executive functions and language difficulties other than phonological problems figure into data-based explanations of reading problems (e.g., Cain & Oakhill, 2004; Hatcher & Hulme, 1999; Nation et al., 1999; Oakhill & Cain, 2004; Swanson, 1999b). Swanson's (1999a) analyses provide particularly compelling support for the hypothesis that high-order reading problems (e.g., comprehension) are determined by a variety of deficiencies, not just phonological processing deficiencies. Regardless of how important basic word recognition is in determining comprehension, it is only one of several factors affecting how well the child understands what is being read (e.g., Zinar, 2000).

It is common for students experiencing severe problems with learning to read to manifest a variety of problems in language functions, from a basic perception of language to memory of language to development of syntax to comprehension skills, with these language deficiencies often apparent from early childhood (e.g., Catts et al., 1999; Elbro & Scarborough, 2004; Katz et al., 1981; Mann & Brady, 1988; Sawyer & Butler, 1991; Stanovich, 1986; Vellutino, 1979). Preschoolers who will later experience severe reading difficulties manifest more differences in their language use than those who will be normal readers: Their utterances are shorter and not as syntactically sophisticated; their pronunciations are not as good; and they understand fewer words. It is harder for the eventually developmentally dyslexic child to label common objects than it is for the eventually normally achieving reader (e.g., Elbro & Scarborough, 2004; Scarborough, 1990).

In contrast to the dyslexic reader is the "garden-variety" poor reader, whose difficulties in learning to read are consistent with other academic difficulties because of his or her generally low intelligence (Stanovich, 1988). The term *garden-variety* emphasizes that poor reading due to generally low intelligence is more prevalent than dyslexia. For Caucasians, about 16% of the population has an IQ less than 85, with many such children experiencing reading difficulties because of low intelligence.

Dyslexia and garden-variety poor reading contrast with poor reading by children of average intelligence and intact biology who are victims of poor instruction or educational neglect. However, it is often difficult or impossible to determine whether a student is developmentally dyslexic, a garden-variety poor reader, or a victim of poor teaching. When it comes to instruction, there should be no difference in whether a student is considered to have dyslexia, is a garden-variety poor reader, or is a victim of previous poor teaching. As schools and teachers attempt to identify students who may fall into one of the three categories of readers, the classification as dyslexic should occur only if it is known that general intelligence is at least average and a variety of expert and intensive approaches to teaching reading have been attempted with the student.

Prevalence of Dyslexia

Throughout the past several decades, researchers have debated the prevalence of dyslexia. The highest estimate that we have encountered is 20% (i.e., 20% of the population suffers from a biological difference that impairs reading; e.g., Shaywitz, 1996), with others citing ranges falling between 5 and 17% (Hoeft et al., 2015; Ozernov-Palchik & Gaab, 2016) or between 3 and 7% (Fletcher et al., 2018; Snowling & Melby-Lervåg, 2016). However, some experts cite much lower figures, with many claiming that 1% or less of normally intelligent children are biologically impaired, with most informed estimates not exceeding 5% of the population (Hynd & Hynd, 1984; Stevenson, 2004). The reason for an elusive agreeable number goes back to how researchers are identifying a cutoff point for reading difficulty to be labeled as dyslexia, how a researcher defines dyslexia, and the use of unreliable identification procedures (Wagner et al., 2020). Thus, after a lot of reflection, our answer when we are asked for prevalence is this: "It is closer to 1% than 20%." Yes, 20–30% of normally intelligent children experience some difficulties in learning to read words, but only a very small fraction of them have biological differences that prevent them from learning to read words when given high-quality and systematic instruction.

An analysis by Frank Vellutino and his associates (Vellutino et al., 1996; see also Scanlon, Vellutino, et al., 2005; Vellutino & Scanlon, 2001; Vellutino et al., 2008) is one of the best bases for making an estimate of prevalence that we have encountered. From a total school population of 827 students in a suburban school district, the 9% who were falling behind the most during the grade 1 year but who were of normal or superior intelligence (i.e., an IQ greater than 90) were enrolled in a daily tutoring program for 30 minutes a day. The tutoring consisted mostly of intensive phonics instruction with substantial time allocated to the actual reading of texts. After one semester of remediation, only 3% of the original sample continued reading below the 30th percentile on a nationally normed test, and only 1.5% of the original sample remained below the 15th percentile. At the end of grade 3, 60% of these formerly at-risk children were still performing at grade level with no additional intervention supports (Vellutino et al., 2007). That is, it was a very small percentage of students who could not learn to read given intense and expert reading instruction. (Vellutino and associates' study, which contained carefully designed control conditions, is but the first of the studies taken up in this book that demonstrate that many children who experience difficulties in learning to read in school can overcome them if given expert and intensive tutoring; see Chapter 5.)

There was a very, very important message in Vellutino et al. (1996): Until there is an intensive effort to teach a child to read using a systematic approach, it is a huge mistake to assume that the child cannot learn to read because of biological differences. This message is especially telling in the context of a nation in which beginning reading instruction often is anything but systematic or intensive with respect to word recognition skills. Vellutino and colleagues' message is that most of the 20–30% of normally intelligent children who experience serious problems with word recognition can be helped with systematic instruction in decoding coupled with extensive text reading. Vellutino and colleagues' perspective is a solidly environmental one: The instructional environment counts for plenty, with the reading achievement of students very much affected by the teaching they experience.

Studies such as Vellutino et al. (1996) have led senior scholars in the fields of learning disabilities and dyslexia to largely reject any idea that there exist very many children who qualify for such labels. As Vellutino et al. (2004) noted, "There is strong evidence that most early reading difficulties are caused primarily by experiential and instructional deficits, rather than basic cognitive deficits associated with neurodevelopmental anomaly" (p. 28). In other words, yes, there may be very few children who exhibit neurodevelopmental differences that make learning to read difficult. At the same time, there are many, many more children, too many of whom are labeled as learning-disabled or dyslexic, who might be better labeled as teacher- or school-disabled simply because few schools are providing them with expert and intensive reading instruction that accelerates their reading growth such that they are no longer struggling readers.

The Vellutino et al. (1996) study provided the impetus for the U.S. Congress to change the way students with learning disabilities would be identified. Under regulations approved in 2004, states were to begin implementing response to instruction (RTI; also called *response to intervention*) to identify pupils with learning disabilities. RTI, as legislated, involves providing struggling readers with increasingly intensive layers of expert and intensive reading instruction. Children who fail to respond to this enhanced reading instruction, then, are candidates for identification as learning-disabled. The background paper behind this law (Lyon et al., 2001) suggests that well-designed RTI interventions might be expected to reduce the identification of children with learning disabilities by 75%.

Interventions for Struggling Readers

While not specified in the federal regulations, most RTI models have adopted three tiers, or three layers, of daily expert reading lessons of increasing intensity. Tier 1 is classroom reading instruction. In this tier, the classroom teacher is charged with providing appropriate daily whole-class and small-group reading lessons. This is important to note because too many reports of classroom teachers failing to provide sufficient reading instruction fill the academic journals (Allington, 2016; Pianta et al., 2007; Vellutino & Fletcher, 2005). Tier 2 is very-small-group reading lessons added to the 90- to 120-minute classroom reading lessons. In many RTI models, the Tier 2 small-group reading lesson is provided by a certified reading specialist. In Tier 3, a daily one-to-one reading tutorial is provided, again usually by a certified reading specialist (Allington, 2009).

Two general models are used in RTI interventions. The first is called the *standard-protocol model* and the second is called the *problem-solving model*. The standard-protocol model assumes that schools would select a research-based commercial reading program and implement it with fidelity. The problem-solving model assumes that schools would create teams of educators to decide what components should comprise each child's intervention plan (Johnston, 2011). In both models, it is the approach to teaching reading that is at essence, while issues such as expertise of intervention teachers, group size, and session scheduling (e.g., daily or three times a week, for 30 minutes or for 45 minutes) are largely ignored. One problem with the standard-protocol model is that little research exists demonstrating the effectiveness of any reading program at fostering reading achievement (visit *http://ies.ed.gov/ncee/wwc* for a review of the effectiveness, or the lack of it, of commercial reading programs). One problem with the problem-solving model is that few educators have any experience working on such teams or the expertise to develop a specific intervention plan based on the available interventions. Nonetheless, in our view, the fundamental lack of research supporting the use of any commercial reading program means that the problem-solving approach is referred.

As discussed earlier in this edition, the reading wars have re-emerged over the most effective way to teach reading. One aspect of the reading wars debate has focused on the most effective approach to providing instruction to struggling readers. Some researchers and practitioners have argued for intense phonics instruction (Buckingham, 2020), while others have argued that struggling readers need a much more balanced approach than just phonics instruction (Allington, 2012, 2013; Fletcher et al., 2018, 2021; Foorman et al., 2016), and still others have argued for a whole-language approach (Bowers, 2020).

Only a few studies have appeared thus far on the effectiveness of various RTI intervention efforts (Bowyer-Crane et al., 2011; Duff & Clarke, 2011; Fuchs & Vaughn, 2012; May et al., 2016; Snowling & Hulme, 2011) and few seem to have evaluated the different progress-monitoring tools that are being used (Schatschneider et al., 2008). That said, the few studies that have been completed have not been able to replicate the success rates evidenced by Vellutino et al. (1996), Mathes et al. (2005), or Phillips and Smith (2010).

It should not be missed, however, that the instruction that worked in Vellutino et al. (1996) was daily one-to-one expert tutoring for a semester or more, consistent with tutorial approaches used with struggling readers in studies that will be cited in the chapters ahead. Such intensity permits careful monitoring of specific difficulties and tailored instruction. That the control in the study was small-group instruction consistent with the school district's normal approach to remediation makes clear that instruction short of intensive one-to-one tutoring is just not as effective. At several points in this book, we'll refer to one-to-one tutoring resources, with a main motivation for doing so being demonstrations like that of Vellutino et al. (1996) that such tutoring can turn struggling readers around.

At the same time, the intervention design used by Mathes et al. (2005) provided intervention teachers with a very small group ($n = 3$) of struggling grade 1 readers with whom to work. This study compared a proactive, or direct, instruction decoding reading program with an embedded, or responsive, decoding program. The proactive treatment had decodable texts and highly scripted lessons, while the responsive treatment had leveled books and embedded phonics and skills in context lessons. At the end of the year-long intervention effort, there were no significant differences between the groups on broad reading achievement measures, although the proactive group had better word-attack performances, while the responsive group had better oral-reading fluency. Perhaps most important, less than 1% of the grade 1 students in the participating districts failed to be reading in the normal achievement range.

More recently, Donegan and Wanzek (2021) completed a meta-analysis of reading intervention studies over the past 30 years that focused on upper elementary struggling readers. Findings suggested small effects for interventions focusing on foundational reading skills and comprehension. Furthermore, the results suggested that interventions should contain multicomponent aspects and that teachers should focus on small-group instruction rather than individual instruction when providing interventions. During the small-group instruction, teachers can provide feedback to students throughout the intervention and allow for conversations to help students learn from others and gather insight into student misunderstandings. Lastly, there was not a significant effect on the length of the interventions; thus, teachers should focus on the type of intervention provided rather than the amount of time for which the student receives an intervention (Donegan & Wanzek, 2021).

It is studies such as these that point out that we could bring virtually every child's reading performance to within the normal achievement range by the end of grade 1. Doing so dramatically reduces the number of children who are identified as learning-disabled or dyslexic. Though there is still a need for more research on effective interventions, it is clear to us that interventions should be tailored to individual students' needs (Connor et al., 2011; Connor et al., 2013; Connor & Morrison, 2016; McDonald, Connor, et al., 2009; Watts-Taffe et al., 2012) and include more than just phonics-based instruction or semantic context instruction—rather, a more balanced approach to supporting struggling readers with the use of decoding strategies, decodable texts, leveled books, comprehension instruction, and, if possible, a small group for intensive instruction (Donegan & Wanzek, 2021; Fletcher et al., 2018; Johnston & Scanlon, 2021; Mathes et al., 2005; NRP, 2000; Petscher et al., 2020; Scammacca et al., 2015; Vellutino et al., 1996). Teachers can tailor instruction based on students' strengths and weaknesses that are determined by formative data (Connor & Morrison, 2016; McDonald Connor et al., 2009; Watts-Taffe et al., 2012).

It is important to note that no single intervention program is going to support every struggling reader. Teachers and stakeholders must have an understanding of each intervention and make decisions on intervention use based on the data collected and revise the plan as necessary (Snowling & Hulme, 2011; Watts-Taffe et al., 2012). More research and development need to be done to support effective RTI as it is implemented in schools. Additionally, more translational research articles are needed to help educators bridge the gap between the research and implementation in the classroom (Petscher et al., 2020).

Summary

It is a tragic mistake to assume that initially poor reading necessarily implies a neurodevelopmental problem. A diagnosis of dyslexia should be reached only after environmental deprivation has been ruled out (i.e., only after it is ensured that the child was provided intensive and expert reading instruction, especially instruction designed to foster the ability to decode, something that is not certain in many contemporary classrooms). The most compelling evidence on this point comes from studies such as the Vellutino and associates (1996), Mathes and associates (2005), and Phillips and Smith (2010) investigations, in which children who were experiencing difficulties with learning to read using normal classroom instruction came up to grade level once expert intensive tutoring began. There will be reference to and discussion of other such investigations in the chapters that follow.

Most children who are experiencing initial reading problems are not developmentally dyslexic. For many, their problem is that they have not been taught how to decode text and/or how to construct meaning from text in ways that are efficient and effective. By the end of this book, we hope to have you convinced that, with most children of average intelligence, both decoding and comprehension are very teachable processes.

READING DIFFICULTIES IN OLDER STUDENTS

What cannot be missed is that reading difficulties that are apparent in the primary grades garner more attention from researchers than do reading problems that become apparent at other age levels. This is so despite the fact that there is a widespread perception that at least some children experience a "fourth-grade slump" (Chall, 1983), exhibiting reading difficulties for the first time at about the fourth-grade level. Because reading demands change in the fourth grade—comprehension is emphasized more, while the amount of informational text reading increases—there are definitely valid reasons to suspect that there might be something to the possibility that some children experience reading difficulties for the first time in the fourth grade.

In an important analysis, Leach et al. (2003) explored this possibility. They studied fourth graders from Philadelphia-area schools, examining their performances in the middle elementary grades and analyzing their reading achievement records before that. The students were drawn from schools serving affluent suburbs as well as more diverse neighborhoods. There were a number of fascinating findings. First, about 31% of the sample were identified as having problems in the primary grades and having those problems persist into grade 3. By contrast, only 8% of the sample were identified as having problems in the primary grades but with remedial services discontinued before third grade—presumably because those students were now reading at an acceptable level. That means that, for every student who responded well to ameliorative efforts, four did not respond well enough to discontinue the intervention. This is a sobering statistic. Getting back on track in public schools is not easy once a reading disability is manifest. Quite honestly, as we contemplate this Leach et al. (2003) statistic through our years of experience around schools, we feel that these researchers' data are accurate: Most troubled readers in the primary grades continue to need more experts and more intensive reading instruction than schools routinely offer.

Considering those students who at grade 4 had a reading disability, which was about 41% of the students studied, there were roughly equal numbers of boys and girls. Of those experiencing difficulties, 42% had a word reading disability only, and 18% had a reading comprehension disability only, while *39% had both word-level and comprehension problems*. If it is safe to worry only about word-level problems in the primary grades, that is definitely not the case by the middle elementary grades. In this sample, at the fourth-grade level, more than half the troubled readers had word-level problems, and more than half had comprehension problems.

However, one of the most important statistics in the analyses was that 47% of those experiencing difficulties in the middle elementary grades did not have difficulties in the primary grades. Notably, these figures are roughly consistent with the proportions of late and early identified problem readers in previous research (Badian, 1999; Shaywitz et al., 1992). Reading problems definitely emerge in the middle elementary grades for some children. Yes, there were some indications that the late-identified troubled readers were not as impaired as the early-identified ones—for example, they read words faster than early-identified disabled readers, but still, they read more slowly than normally achieving readers. Leach et al. (2003) dramatically made the point that there has been too little study of the problems experienced after grade 3.

Not everyone who studies older struggling readers, however, reports findings wholly consistent with Leach et al. (2003). For instance, Buly and Valencia (2002) administered several reading subskills assessments to grade

4 students who had failed their state reading assessment. They used cluster analysis to sort these struggling readers into groups based on similar sub-skills profiles. They found six broad clusters: automatic word callers (18%), with 60% of these students English language learners; struggling word call-ers (15%) who performed better at reading lists than reading text; word stumblers (18%), many of whom self-corrected most of their misreadings, demonstrating much decoding persistence but slow reading of both words in isolation and in texts; slow steady comprehenders (24%) who performed on grade level but read quite slowly; slow word callers (17%) who were not automatic decoders but could decode accurately if slowly; and disabled readers (9%) whose word recognition was at the first-grade performance level and who did not do anything well.

More recently, Torppa et al. (2015) studied four groups of Finnish students from grade 2 to grade 8. The four groups included students with no dyslexia, resolved dyslexia (dyslexia in grade 2, but not in grade 8), late-emerging dyslexia (no dyslexia in grade 2, but yes in grade 8), and dyslexia in both grade 2 and grade 8. They found that students with dyslexia in both grades struggled with language and cognitive deficits throughout their development, while students in the resolving dyslexia group saw a decrease in language and cognitive deficits. Additionally, the late-emerging group struggled with rapid naming, including students naming 30–50 objects as fast as possible. Furthermore, those in the late-emerging group's parents also struggled with rapid naming.

Dennis (2013) conducted a similar study with grades 6, 7, and 8 stu-dents who had failed their state reading assessment. She used factor analysis and cluster analysis to locate four clusters of performance types: slow word callers with high comprehension and poor pseudoword reading perfor-mance; slow word callers with strong but slow decoding skills; automatic word callers with fast and accurate word and pseudoword recognition; and struggling word callers who exhibited a rapid but often inaccurate response to both words and pseudowords along with weak comprehension.

Finally, Hock and Brasseur (2009) studied grade 9 struggling read-ers. Roughly two of three (63%) of these struggling adolescent readers performed at low levels on each of the multiple measures. Overall, these struggling readers scored significantly higher on decoding and word read-ing measures than on fluency, vocabulary, or comprehension and scored significantly lower on all measures than readers judged proficient on the state reading assessment.

These studies suggest that the decoding difficulties that seem to under-lie earlier reading difficulties apparently lessen as struggling readers prog-ress through school. That is, while both Leach et al. (2003) and Buly and Valencia (2002) found substantial deficits in word recognition for most of their grade 4 struggling readers, and at grades 6, 7, and 8 Dennis (2013) found more struggling readers with accurate but slow reading processes,

Hock and Brasseur (2009) found decoding to be the strength of the grade 9 struggling readers they studied. But even though they were better at decoding, they were still performing at a level below their on-level reading peers. These studies were conducted with older struggling readers from three states and multiple schools. Thus, differences in performance may be more related to the reading instruction they were provided than to their ages. At the same time, in each of these analyses, what is clear is that there is no single profile that fits all struggling readers. Some can decode accurately but only very slowly. Others can decode accurately and rapidly but fail to understand much of what they read, and so on. We can only note that it is no wonder that standard protocol models of intervention have too often failed to solve the problems of struggling readers. If only all struggling readers struggled with the same aspects of reading and exhibited similar profiles of strengths and weaknesses, it would be easier to design interventions that might be successful. But since struggling readers fit distinctive profiles, we will be better off if we attempt to identify each struggling reader's profile and then tailor instruction to match the student's needs.

There needs to be serious efforts to determine what can be done at the fourth-grade level and beyond to get the late-emerging problematic readers back on track as well as move those with persistent reading problems as far as they can go. There is no excuse for a national reading agenda targeted only at the primary grades for there remains much reason to remediate reading in the middle elementary grades and beyond. Most struggling primary-grade students will improve if we do a better job of providing expert and intensive reading lessons beginning in kindergarten, but some won't; some who did not struggle in the primary grades will do so in the middle and later grades; and some who did struggle early will continue to do well (see Invernizzi, 2001, and Phillips et al., 2002, for additional supportive data on this point). The nation needs reading agendas that serve all such students well.

SUMMARY AND CONCLUDING REFLECTIONS

1. A salient problem for many poor readers is that they do not decode well. In Chapter 5, more evidence is presented that many children who are experiencing difficulties in learning to read benefit from expert, intensive instruction in decoding, letter–sound associations, and the blending of such sounds to produce words. For many poor readers, their problem may be that they have never received such instruction.

2. Poor readers often rely on semantic–contextual cues in an attempt to decode text. This reliance on semantic cues results in inaccurate decoding. It is also an approach that requires great effort and hence consumes

much short-term memory capacity, leaving little capacity for comprehension of words once they are decoded. Even when struggling readers succeed in decoding a word, they often fail to zero in on one of its several definitions that would make sense in the semantic context in which the word occurs. Poor readers often are confused by irrelevant meanings of words they have decoded.

3. Students can still struggle to comprehend text, even if they can decode well. Poor comprehenders struggle to understand fully the ideas presented in the text, make inferences about the text, and are less likely to monitor their understanding of the text.

4. Defining and identifying dyslexia is an ongoing debate that led to much confusion on the prevalence and use of specific interventions. With a normally intelligent child, dyslexia should not be assumed as an explanation of reading failure until great efforts have been made to teach that student to read. The odds are very great that difficulties in learning to read are not the result of dyslexia, but rather of an environmental failure (poor reading instruction). That is, the child has not experienced reading instruction that is both expert and intensive enough for him or her to learn how to read. Other possible environmental failures, however, will be considered in the next chapter, which takes up development during the preschool years. What happens during the preschool years affects children's subsequent success in learning to read in the primary years.

5. In the past several years, the reading wars debate has heated up on the best instructional approach to support struggling readers. Teachers and reading specialists must be familiar with the interventions they provide to students struggling to read and must have the flexibility to find the proper intervention for each student. Though it has and is currently being debated, we believe the most effective interventions provide phonics instruction and include decoding and comprehension instruction. (Scanlon and colleagues [2005] have done significant research on this topic.) If resources are available, providing intervention instruction in small groups or one on one is best.

6. Reading difficulties are not restricted to the primary grades. Some children who experienced difficulties in the primary grades continue to have difficulties in the upper grades. Some children experience difficulties for the first time *after* the primary grades. And, of course, reading difficulties persist into adulthood. Unfortunately, although there will be much to say about interventions in the elementary years, especially the early elementary years, in the pages ahead, there is disturbingly little intervention work beyond the elementary years. What there is would be for another book, but it would be a short book. Just as we encourage much more support for

intervention research in the middle and later elementary school years, we also encourage much more intervention research beyond those years.

REFERENCES

Allington, R. L. (2009). *What really matters in response to intervention: Research-based designs*. Allyn & Bacon.

Allington, R. L. (2012). *What really matters for struggling readers: Designing research-based programs*. Pearson.

Allington, R. L. (2013). What really matters when working with struggling readers. *Reading Teacher, 66*(7), 4–14.

Allington, R. L. (2016). Reading moves: What not to do. In M. Scherer (Ed.), *On developing readers: Readings from Educational Leadership* (pp. 136–145). ASCD.

Allington, R. L., & Gabriel, R. (in press). The meaning(s) of dyslexia. (Eds.), *International encyclopedia of education* (4th ed.).

Badian, N. A. (1999). Reading disability defined as a discrepancy between listening and reading comprehension: A longitudinal study of stability, gender differences, and prevalence. *Journal of Learning Disabilities, 32*, 138–148.

Bell, L. C., & Perfetti, C. A. (1994). Reading skill: Some adult comparisons. *Journal of Educational Psychology, 86*, 344–355.

Bertucci, C., Hook, P., Haynes, C., Macaruso, P., & Bickley, C. (2003). Vowel perception and production in adolescents with reading disabilities. *Annals of Dyslexia, 53*, 174–200.

Borella, E., Carretti, B., & Pelegrina, S. (2010). The specific role of inhibition in reading comprehension in good and poor comprehenders. *Journal of Learning disabilities, 43*(6), 541–552.

Bowers, J. S. (2020). Reconsidering the evidence that systematic phonics is more effective than alternative methods of reading instruction. *Educational Psychology Review, 32*, 681–705.

Bowyer-Crane, C., Duff, F., Hulme, C., & Snowling, M. J. (2011). The response to intervention of children with SLI and general delay. *Journal of Learning Disabilities, 9*, 107–121.

Breier, J. I., Fletcher, J. M., Denton, C., & Gray, L. C. (2004). Categorical perception of speech stimuli in children at risk for reading difficulty. *Journal of Experimental Child Psychology, 88*, 152–170.

Buckingham, J. (2020). Systematic phonics instruction belongs in evidence-based reading programs: A response to Bowers. *The Educational and Developmental Psychologist, 37*(2), 105–113.

Buly, M. R., & Valencia, S. W. (2002). Below the bar: Profiles of students who fail state reading assessments. *Educational Evaluation and Policy Analysis, 24*(3), 219–239.

Cain, K. (1999). Ways of reading: How knowledge and use of strategies are related to reading comprehension. *British Journal of Developmental Psychology, 17*, 292–312.

Cain, K. (2006). Individual differences in children's memory and reading comprehension: An investigation of semantic and inhibitory deficits. *Memory, 14*(5), 553-569.

Cain, K., & Oakhill, J. (2004). Reading comprehension difficulties. In T. Nunes & P. Bryant (Eds.), *Handbook of children's literacy* (pp. 313–338). Kluwer Academic.

Cain, K., Oakhill, J., & Bryant, P. (2004). Children's reading comprehension ability: Concurrent prediction by working memory, verbal ability, and component skills. *Journal of Educational Psychology, 96*, 31–42.

Cartwright, K. B., Coppage, E. A., Lane, A. B., Singleton, T., Marshall, T. R., & Bentivegna, C. (2017). Cognitive flexibility deficits in children with specific reading comprehension difficulties. *Contemporary Educational Psychology, 50*, 33-44.

Catts, H., Fey, M. E., Zhang, X., & Tomblin, J. B. (1999). Language basis of reading and reading disabilities: Evidence from a longitudinal investigation. *Scientific Studies of Reading*, 3, 331–361.

Catts, H. W., Hogan, T. P., & Fey, M. E. (2003). Subgrouping poor readers on the basis of individual differences in reading-related abilities. *Journal of Learning Disabilities*, 36(2), 151–164.

Chall, J. S. (1983). *Stages of reading development*. McGraw-Hill.

Cipielewski, J., & Stanovich, K. E. (1992). Predicting growth in reading ability from children's exposure to print. *Journal of Experimental Child Psychology*, 54, 74–89.

Cirino, P. T., Romain, M. A., Barth, A. E., Tolar, T. D., Fletcher, J. M., & Vaughn, S. (2013). Reading skill components and impairments in middle school struggling readers. *Reading and Writing*, 26(7), 1059–1086.

Clarke, P. J., Snowling, M. J., Truelove, E., & Hulme, C. (2010). Ameliorating children's reading-comprehension difficulties: A randomized controlled trial. *Psychological Science*, 21(8), 1106–1116.

Clarke, P. J., Truelove, E., Hulme, C., & Snowling, M. J. (2013). *Developing reading comprehension*. John Wiley & Sons.

Clay, M. M. (1969). Reading errors and self-correction behaviour. *British Journal of Educational Psychology*, 39(1), 47–56.

Connor, C. M., & Morrison, F. J. (2016). Individualizing student instruction in reading: Implications for policy and practice. *Policy Insights from the Behavioral and Brain Sciences*, 3(1), 54–61.

Connor, C. M., Morrison, F. J., Fishman, B., Crowe, E. C., Al Otaiba, S., & Schatschneider, C. (2013). A longitudinal cluster-randomized controlled study on the accumulating effects of individualized literacy instruction on students' reading from first through third grade. *Psychological Science*, 24(8), 1408–1419.

Connor, C. M., Morrison, F. J., Fishman, B., Giuliani, S., Luck, M., Underwood, P. S., Bayraktar, A., Crowe, E. C., & Schatschneider, C. (2011). Testing the impact of child characteristicsx instruction interactions on third graders' reading comprehension by differentiating literacy instruction. *Reading Research Quarterly*, 46(3), 189–221.

de Jong, P. F. (1998). Working memory deficits of reading disabled children. *Journal of Experimental Child Psychology*, 70, 75–96.

Del Tufo, S. N., & Earle, F. S. (2020). Skill profiles of college students with a history of developmental language disorder and developmental dyslexia. *Journal of Learning Disabilities*, 53(3), 228–240.

Dennis, D. V. (2013). Heterogeneity or homogeneity: What assessment data reveal about struggling adolescent readers. *Journal of Literacy Research*, 45(1), 1–21.

Diamond, A. (2013). Executive functions. *Annual review of psychology*, 64, 135–168.

Donegan, R.E., Wanzek, J. (2021). Effects of reading interventions implemented for upper elementary struggling readers: A look at recent research. *Reading and Writing*, 34, 1943–1977.

Duff, F. J., & Clarke, P. J. (2011). Practitioner Review: Reading disorders: what are the effective interventions and how should they be implemented and evaluated? *Journal of Child Psychology and Psychiatry*, 52(1), 3–12.

Ehri, L. C., & Snowling, M. J. (2004). Developmental variation in word recognition. In C. A. Stone, E. R. Silliman, B. J. Ehren, & K. Apel (Eds.), *Handbook of language and literacy: Development and disorders* (pp. 433–460). Guilford Press.

Elbro, C., Nielsen, I., & Petersen, D. K. (1994). Dyslexia in adults: Evidence for deficits in non-word reading and in the phonological representation of lexical items. *Annals of Dyslexia*, 44, 205–226.

Elbro, C., & Scarborough, H. S. (2004). Early identification. In T. Nunes & P. Bryant (Eds.), *Handbook of children's literacy* (pp. 339–359). Kluwer Academic.

Elliott, J. G. (2020). It's time to be scientific about dyslexia. *Reading Research Quarterly*, *55*(S1), S61–S75.

Elliott, J. G., & Grigorenko, E. L. (2014). *The dyslexia debate* (No. 14). Cambridge University Press.

Elwér, Å., Gustafson, S., Byrne, B., Olson, R. K., Keenan, J. M., & Samuelsson, S. (2015). A retrospective longitudinal study of cognitive and language skills in poor reading comprehension. *Scandinavian Journal of Psychology*, *56*(2), 157–166.

Espy, K. A., Molfese, D. L., Molfese, V. J., & Modglin, A. (2004). Development of auditory event-related potentials in young children and relations to word-level reading abilities at 8 years. *Annals of Dyslexia*, *54*, 9–38.

Flavell, J. H., Miller, P., & Miller, S. (1993). *Cognitive development* (3rd ed.). Prentice-Hall.

Fletcher, J. M., Lyon, G. R., Fuchs, L. S., & Barnes, M. A. (2018). *Learning disabilities: From identification to intervention*. Guilford Press.

Fletcher, J. M., Savage, R., & Vaughn, S. (2021). A Commentary on Bowers (2020) and the Role of Phonics Instruction in Reading. *Educational Psychology Review*, *33*(3), 1249–1274.

Foorman, B., Beyler, N., Borradaile, K., Coyne, M., Denton, C. A., Dimino, J., et al. (2016). *Foundational Skills to Support Reading for Understanding in Kindergarten through 3rd Grade. Educator's Practice Guide* (NCEE 2016–4008). What Works Clearinghouse.

Forrest-Pressley, D. L., & Waller, T. G. (1984). *Cognition, metacognition, and reading*. Springer-Verlag.

Francis, D. J., Shaywitz, S. E., Stuebing, K. K., & Fletcher, J. M. (1994). The measurement of change: Assessing behavior over time and within a developmental context. In G. R. Lyon (Ed.), *Frames of reference for the assessment of learning disabilities: New views on measurement issues* (pp. 29–58). Brookes.

Fuchs, L. S., & Vaughn, S. (2012). Responsiveness-to-intervention: A decade later. *Journal of Learning Disabilities*, *45*(3), 195–203.

García-Madruga, J. A., Vila, J. O., Gómez-Veiga, I., Duque, G., & Elosúa, M. R. (2014). Executive processes, reading comprehension and academic achievement in 3rd grade primary students. *Learning and Individual Differences*, *35*, 41–48.

Garner, R. (1980). Monitoring of understanding: An investigation of good and poor readers' awareness of induced miscomprehension of text. *Journal of Reading Behavior*, *12*, 55–64.

Garner, R., & Kraus, C. (1981/82). Good and poor comprehenders differences in knowing and regulating reading behaviors. *Educational Research Quarterly*, *6*, 5–12.

Garner, R., & Reis, R. (1981). Monitoring and resolving comprehension obstacles: An investigation of spontaneous text lookbacks among upper-grade good and poor comprehenders. *Reading Research Quarterly*, *16*, 569–582.

Gernsbacher, M. A. (1990). *Language comprehension as structure building*. Erlbaum.

Gernsbacher, M. A., & Faust, M. E. (1990). The role of suppression in sentence comprehension. In G. B. Simpson (Ed.), *Understanding word and sentence* (pp. 97–128). North-Holland.

Gernsbacher, M. A., Varner, K. R., & Faust, M. E. (1990). Investigating differences in general comprehension skill. *Journal of Experimental Psychology: Learning, Memory, and Cognition*, *16*, 430–445.

Gnaedinger, E. K., Hund, A. M., & Hesson-McInnis, M. S. (2016). Reading-specific flexibility moderates the relation between reading strategy use and reading comprehension during the elementary years. *Mind, Brain, and Education*, *10*(4), 233–246.

Greenberg, D., Ehri, L. C., & Perin, D. (1997). Are word reading processes the same or different in adult literacy students and 3rd–5th graders matched for reading level? *Journal of Educational Psychology*, *89*, 262–275.

Hanford, E. (2017, September 11). Hard to read: How American schools fail kids with dyslexia. *APMreports*. Available at *www.apmreports.org/episode/2017/09/11/hard-to-read*.

Hanford, E. (2018, September 10). Hard words: Why aren't kids being taught to read? *APMreports*. Available at *www.apmreports.org/episode/2018/09/10/hard-words-why-american-kids-arent-being-taught-to-read*.

Hanford, E. (2019, August 22). At a loss for words: What's wrong with how schools teach reading. *APMreports*. Available at *www.apmreports.org/episode/2019/08/22/whats-wrong-how-schools-teach-reading*.

Harris, T. L., & Hodges, R. W. (Eds.). (1981). *A dictionary of reading and related terms*: International Reading Association.

Hatcher, P. J., & Hulme, C. (1999). Phonemes, rhymes, and intelligence as predictors of children's responsiveness to remedial reading instruction: Evidence from a longitudinal intervention study. *Journal of Experimental Child Psychology, 72*, 130–153.

Henderson, L., Snowling, M., & Clarke, P. (2013). Accessing, integrating, and inhibiting word meaning in poor comprehenders. *Scientific Studies of Reading, 17*(3), 177–198.

Hernandez, D. J. (2011). *Double jeopardy: How third-grade reading skills and poverty influence high school graduation*. Annie E. Casey Foundation.

Hock, M., & Brasseur, I. (2009). What is the nature of struggling adolescent readers in urban schools? *Learning Disabilities Quarterly, 32*(1), 21–38.

Hoeft, F., McCardle, P., & Pugh, K. (2015). *The myths and truths of dyslexia in different writing systems*. International Dyslexia Association blog.

Hynd, G. W., & Hynd, C. R. (1984). Dyslexia: Neuroanatomical/neurolinguistic perspectives. *Reading Research Quarterly, 19*, 482–498. Invernizzi, M. A. (2001). The complex world of one-to-one tutoring. In S. B. Neuman & D. K. Dickinson (Eds.), *Handbook of early literacy research* (pp. 459–470). Guilford Press.

Johnston, P. (2011). Response to intervention in literacy: Problems and possibilities. *Elementary School Journal, 111*(4), 511–534.

Johnston, P., & Scanlon, D. (2021). An examination of dyslexia research and instruction, with policy implications. *Literacy Research: Theory, Method, and Practice, 70,* 107–128.

Katz, R. B., Shankweiler, D., & Liberman, I. Y. (1981). Memory for item order and phonetic recoding in the beginning reader. *Journal of Experimental Child Psychology, 32*, 474–484.

Kibby, M. Y., Marks, W., Morgan, S., & Long, C. J. (2004). Specific impairment in developmental reading disabilities: A working memory approach. *Journal of Learning Disabilities, 37*, 349–363.

Kieffer, M. J., & Christodoulou, J. A. (2020). Automaticity and control: How do executive functions and reading fluency interact in predicting reading comprehension? *Reading Research Quarterly, 55*(1), 147–166.

LaBerge, D., & Samuels, S. J. (1974). Toward a theory of automatic information processing in reading. *Cognitive Psychology, 6*, 293–323.

Leach, J. M., Scarborough, H. S., & Rescorla, L. (2003). Late-emerging reading disabilities. *Journal of Educational Psychology, 95*, 211–224.

Linderholm, T., & van den Broek, P. (2002). The effects of reading purpose and working memory capacity on the processing of expository texts. *Journal of Educational Psychology, 94*, 778–784.

Locascio, G., Mahone, E. M., Eason, S. H., & Cutting, L. E. (2010). Executive dysfunction among children with reading comprehension deficits. *Journal of Learning Disabilities, 43*(5), 441–454.

Lopes, J. A., Gomes, C., Oliveira, C. R., & Elliott, J. G. (2020). Research studies on dyslexia: Participant inclusion and exclusion criteria. *European Journal of Special Needs Education, 35*(5), 587–602.

Lyon, G. R. (1995). Toward a definition of dyslexia. *Annals of Dyslexia, 45*, 3–27.

Lyon, G. R., Fletcher, J. M., Shaywitz, S. E., Shaywitz, B. A., Torgeson, J. K., Wood, F., et al. (2001). Rethinking learning disabilities. In C. Finn, R. Rotherham, & J. Hokanson (Eds.), *Rethinking special education for a new century* (pp. 259–288). Progressive Policy Institute and the Thomas B. Fordham Foundation.

Mann, V. A., & Brady, S. (1988). Reading disability: The role of language deficiencies. *Journal of Consulting and Clinical Psychology, 56*, 811–816.

Mather, N., White, J., & Youman, M. (2020). Dyslexia around the world: A snapshot. *Learning Disabilities, 25*(1), 1–17.

Mathes, P. G., Denton, C. A., Fletcher, J. M., Anthony, J. L., Francis, D. J., & Schatschneider, C. (2005). The effects of theoretically different instruction and student characteristics on the skills of struggling readers. *Reading Research Quarterly, 40*(2), 148–182.

May, H., Sirinides, P. M., Gray, A., & Goldsworthy, H. (2016). *Reading Recovery: An evaluation of the four-year i3 scale-up.* Consortium for Policy Research in Education.

McCormick, S. (1992). Disabled readers' erroneous responses to inferential comprehension questions: Description and analysis. *Reading Research Quarterly, 27*, 156–176.

McDonald Connor, C., Piasta, S. B., Fishman, B., Glasney, S., Schatschneider, C., Crowe, E., Underwood, P., & Morrison, F. J. (2009). Individualizing student instruction precisely: Effects of child × instruction interactions on first graders' literacy development. *Child Development, 80*(1), 77–100.

McNulty, M. A. (2003). Dyslexia and the life course. *Journal of Learning Disabilities, 36*, 363–381.

Merrill, E. C., Sperber, R. D., & McCauley, C. (1981). Differences in semantic encoding as a function of reading comprehension skill. *Memory and Cognition, 9*, 618–624.

Miciak, J., & Fletcher, J. M. (2020). The critical role of instructional response for identifying dyslexia and other learning disabilities. *Journal of Learning Disabilities, 53*(5), 343–353.

Miles, K. P., Rubin, G. B., & Gonzalez-Frey, S. (2018). Rethinking sight words. *The Reading Teacher, 71*(6), 715–726.

Miller, G. A. (1956). The magical number seven, plus-or-minus two: Some limits on our capacity for processing information. *Psychological Review, 63*, 81–97.

Molfese, D. L., Molfese, V. J., Key, S., Modglin, A., Kelley, S., & Terrell, S. (2002). Reading and cognitive abilities: Longitudinal studies of brain and behavior changes in young children. *Annals of Dyslexia, 52*, 99–119.

Morgan, P. L., Farkas, G., Hillemeier, M. M., & Maczuga, S. (2016). Science achievement gaps begin very early, persist, and are largely explained by modifiable factors. *Educational Researcher, 45*(1), 18–35.

Nation, K., Adams, J. W., Bowyer-Crane, C. A., & Snowling, M. J. (1999). Working memory deficits in poor comprehenders reflect underlying language impairments. *Journal of Experimental Child Psychology, 73*, 139–158.

Nation, K., Cocksey, J., Taylor, J. S., & Bishop, D. V. (2010). A longitudinal investigation of early reading and language skills in children with poor reading comprehension. *Journal of Cchild Psychology and Psychiatry, 51*(9), 1031–1039.

National Reading Panel. (2000). *Teaching children to read: An evidence-based assessment of the scientific research literature on reading and its implications for reading instruction.* National Institute of Child Health and Human Development.

Nicholson, T. (1991). Do children read words better in context or in lists? A classic study revisited. *Journal of Educational Psychology, 83*, 444–450.

Oakhill, J. V., & Cain, K. (2004). The development of comprehension skills. In T. Nunes & P. Bryant (Eds.), *Handbook of children's literacy* (pp. 155–180). Kluwer Academic.

Owings, R. A., Petersen, G. A., Bransford, J. D., Morris, C. D., & Stein, B. S. (1980). Spontaneous monitoring and regulation of learning: A comparison of successful and less successful fifth graders. *Journal of Educational Psychology, 72*, 250–256.

Ozernov-Palchik, O., & Gaab, N. (2016). Tackling the 'dyslexia paradox': Reading brain and behavior for early markers of developmental dyslexia. *Wiley Interdisciplinary Reviews: Cognitive Science, 7*(2), 156–176.

Paris, S. G., & Myers, M. (1981). Comprehension monitoring, memory, and study strategies of good and poor readers. *Journal of Reading Behavior, 13*, 5–22.

Perfetti, C. A. (1985). *Reading ability.* Oxford University Press.

Perfetti, C. A., & Hogaboam, T. (1975). The relationship between single word decoding and reading comprehension skill. *Journal of Educational Psychology, 67*, 461–469.

Perfetti, C. A., & Lesgold, A. M. (1977). Discourse comprehension and sources of individual differences. In M. A. Just & P. A. Carpenter (Eds.), *Cognitive processes in comprehension* (pp. 141–183). Erlbaum.

Perfetti, C. A., & Lesgold, A. M. (1979). Coding and comprehension in skilled reading: Implications for reading instruction. In L. B. Resnick & P. Weaver (Eds.), *Theory and practice of early reading* (Vol. 1, pp. 57–84). Erlbaum.

Petscher, Y., Cabell, S. Q., Catts, H. W., Compton, D. L., Foorman, B. R., Hart, S. A., et al. (2020). How the science of reading informs 21st-century education. *Reading Research Quarterly, 55*, S267–S282.

Phillips, G. E., & Smith, P. E. (2010). Closing the gaps: Literacy for the hardest to teach. In P. Johnston (Ed.), *RTI in literacy: Responsive and comprehensive.* (pp. 219–246). International Reading Association.

Phillips, L. M. (1988). Young readers' inference strategies in reading comprehension. *Cognition and Instruction, 5*, 193–222.

Phillips, L. M., Norris, S. P., Osmond, W. C., & Maynard, A. M. (2002). Relative reading achievement: A longitudinal study of 187 children from first through sixth grades. *Journal of Educational Psychology, 94*, 3–13.

Pianta, R. C., Belsky, J., Houts, R., & Morrison, F. (2007). Opportunities to learn in America's elementary school classroom. *Science, 315*(5820), 1795–1796.

Purcell-Gates, V. (1991). On the outside looking in: A study of remedial readers' meaning-making while reading literature. *Journal of Reading Behavior, 23*, 235–253.

Rabiner, D. L., Godwin, J., & Dodge, K. A. (2016). Predicting academic achievement and attainment: The contribution of early academic skills, attention difficulties, and social competence. *School Psychology Review, 45*(2), 250–267.

Rack, J., Hulme, C., Snowling, M., & Wightman, J. (1994). The role of phonology in young children learning to read words: The direct mapping hypothesis. *Journal of Experimental Child Psychology, 57*, 42–71.

Ransby, M. J., & Swanson, H. L. (2003). Reading comprehension skills of young adults with childhood diagnoses of dyslexia. *Journal of Learning Disabilities, 36*, 538–555.

Ricketts, J., Sperring, R., & Nation, K. (2014). Educational attainment in poor comprehenders. *Frontiers in Psychology, 5*(445), 1–11.

Ruddell, M. R. (1994). Vocabulary knowledge and comprehension: A comprehension–process view of complex literacy relationships. In R. B. Ruddell, M. R. Ruddell, & H. Singer (Eds.), *Theoretical models and processes of reading* (4th ed., pp. 414–447). International Reading Association.

Samuels, S. J. (1970). Effects of pictures on learning to read, comprehension, and attitudes. *Review of Educational Research, 40*, 397–407.

Samuels, S. J., Hiebert, E. H., & Rasinski, T. V. (2010). Eye movements make reading possible. In E. H. Hiebert & D. R. Reutzel (Eds.), *Revisiting silent reading: New directions for teachers and researchers* (pp. 24–44). International Reading Association.

Sawyer, D. J., & Butler, K. (1991). Early language intervention: A deterrent to reading disability. *Annals of Dyslexia, 41*, 55–79.

Scammacca, N. K., Roberts, G., Vaughn, S., & Stuebing, K. K. (2015). A meta-analysis of interventions for struggling readers in grades 4–12: 1980–2011. *Journal of Learning Disabilities, 48*(4), 369–390.

Scanlon, D. M., Vellutino, F. R., Small, S. G., Fanuele, D. P., & Sweeney, J. M. (2005). Severe reading difficulties—Can they be prevented? A comparison of prevention and intervention approaches. *Exceptionality, 13*(4), 209–227.

Scarborough, H. S. (1990). Very early language deficits in dyslexic children. *Child Development, 61*, 1728–1743.

Schatschneider, C., Wagner, R. K., & Crawford, E. C. (2008). The importance of measuring growth in response to intervention models: Testing a core assumption. *Learning and Individual Differences, 18*(3), 308–315.

Schwantes, F. M. (1991). Children's use of semantic and syntactic information for word recognition and determination of sentence meaningfulness. *Journal of Reading Behavior, 23*, 335–350.

Serniclaes, W., Van Heghe, A., Mousty, P., Carré, R., & Sprenger-Charolles, L. (2004). Allophonic mode of speech perception in dyslexia. *Journal of Experimental Child Psychology, 87*, 336–361.

Shaywitz, S. E. (1996). Dyslexia. *Scientific American, 275*(5), 98–104.

Shaywitz, S. E., Escobar, M. D., Shaywitz, B. A., Fletcher, J. M., & Makuch, R. (1992). Evidence that dyslexia may represent the lower tail of a normal distribution of reading ability. *New England Journal of Medicine, 326*, 145–150.

Smart, D., Youssef, G. J., Sanson, A., Prior, M., Toumbourou, J. W., & Olsson, C. A. (2017). Consequences of childhood reading difficulties and behaviour problems for educational achievement and employment in early adulthood. *British Journal of Educational Psychology, 87*(2), 288–308.

Snowling, M. J., & Hulme, C. (2011). Evidence-based interventions for reading and language difficulties: Creating a virtuous circle. *British Journal of Educational Psychology, 81*(1), 1–23.

Snowling, M. J., Hulme, C., & Nation, K. (2020). Defining and understanding dyslexia: Past, present and future. *Oxford Review of Education, 46*(4), 501–513.

Snowling, M. J., & Melby-Lervåg, M. (2016). Oral language deficits in familial dyslexia: A meta-analysis and review. *Psychological Bulletin, 142*(5), 498.

Stanovich, K. E. (1986). Matthew effects in reading: Some consequences of individual differences in the acquisition of literacy. *Reading Research Quarterly, 21*, 360–407.

Stanovich, K. E. (1988). Explaining the differences between the dyslexic and the garden-variety poor reader: The phonological–core variable–difference model. *Journal of Learning Disabilities, 21*, 590–604.

Stanovich, K. E., & Cunningham, A. E. (1993). Where does knowledge come from? Specific associations between print exposure and information acquisition. *Journal of Educational Psychology, 85*, 211–229.

Stevenson, J. (2004). Epidemiology: Genetic and social influences on reading ability. In T. Nunes & P. Bryant (Eds.), *Handbook of children's literacy* (pp. 293–311). Kluwer.

Swanson, H. L. (1999a). *Interventions for students with learning disabilities: A meta-analysis of treatment outcomes.* Guilford Press.

Swanson, H. L. (1999b). Reading comprehension and working memory in learning-disabled readers: Is the phonological loop more important than the executive system? *Journal of Experimental Child Psychology, 72*, 1–31.

Swanson, H. L. (2003). Age-related differences in learning disabled and skilled readers' working memory. *Journal of Experimental Child Psychology, 85*, 1–31.

Swanson, H. L., & Alexander, J. E. (1997). Cognitive processes as predictors of word recognition and reading comprehension in learning-disabled and skilled readers: Revisiting the specificity hypothesis. *Journal of Educational Psychology, 89*, 128–158.

Swanson, H. L., Mink, J., & Bocian, K. M. (1999). Cognitive processing deficits in poor readers with symptoms of reading disabilities and ADHD: More alike than different? *Journal of Educational Psychology, 91*, 321–333.

Torppa, M., Eklund, K., van Bergen, E., & Lyytinen, H. (2015). Late-emerging and resolving dyslexia: A follow-up study from age 3 to 14. *Journal of Abnormal Child Psychology, 43*(7), 1389–1401.

Troia, G. (2004). Phonological processing and its influence on literacy learning. In C. A. Stone, E. R. Silliman, B. J. Ehren, & K. Apel (Eds.), *Handbook of language and literacy: Development and disorders* (pp. 271–301). Guilford Press.

Tunmer, W. E., & Chapman, J. W. (2004). The use of context in learning to read. In T. Nunes & P. Bryant (Eds.), *Handbook of children's literacy* (pp. 199–212). Kluwer Academic.

Vellutino, F. R. (1979). *Dyslexia: Theory and research.* MIT Press.

Vellutino, F. R., & Fletcher, J. M. (2005). Developmental dyslexia. In M. Snowling & C. Hulme (Eds.), *The science of reading: A handbook* (pp. 362–378). Blackwell.

Vellutino, F. R., Fletcher, J. M., Snowling, M. J., & Scanlon, D. M. (2004). Specific reading disability (dyslexia): What have we learned in the past four decades? *Journal of Child Psychology and Psychiatry, 45*(1), 2–40.

Vellutino, F. R., & Scanlon, D. M. (2001). Emergent literacy skills, early instruction, and individual differences as determinants of difficulties in learning to read: The case for early intervention. In S. B. Neuman & D. K. Dickinson (Eds.), *Handbook of early literacy research* (pp. 295–321). Guilford Press.

Vellutino, F. R., Scanlon, D. M., Sipay, E. R., Small, S. G., Pratt, A., Chen, R., et al. (1996). Cognitive profiles of difficult-to-remediate and readily remediated poor readers: Early intervention as a vehicle for distinguishing between cognitive and experiential deficits as a basic cause of specific reading disability. *Journal of Educational Psychology, 88,* 601–638.

Vellutino, F. R., Scanlon, D. M., Small, S. G., Fanuele, D. P., & Sweeney, J. M. (2007). Preventing early reading difficulties through intervention in kindergarten and first grade: A variant on the three tier model. In D. Haager, J. Klingner, & S. Vaughn (Eds.), *Evidence-based reading practices for response to intervention.* Brookes.

Vellutino, F. R., Scanlon, D. M., Zhang, H., & Schatschneider, C. (2008). Using response to kindergarten and first grade intervention to identify children at-risk for long-term reading difficulties. *Reading and Writing, 21*(4), 437–480.

Wagner, R. K., Zirps, F. A., Edwards, A. A., Wood, S. G., Joyner, R. E., Becker, B. J., et al. (2020). The prevalence of dyslexia: A new approach to its estimation. *Journal of Learning Disabilities, 53*(5), 354–365.

Watts-Taffe, S., Laster, B. P., Broach, L., Marinak, B., McDonald Connor, C., & Walker-Dalhouse, D. (2012). Differentiated instruction: Making informed teacher decisions. *The Reading Teacher, 66*(4), 303–314.

Weber, R. M. (1970). First-graders use of grammatical context in reading. In H. Levin & J. P. Williams (Eds.), *Basic studies in reading* (pp. 147–163). Basic Books.

Williams, J. P. (1993). Comprehension of students with and without learning disabilities: Identification of narrative themes and idiosyncratic text representations. *Journal of Educational Psychology, 85,* 631–641.

Worthy, J., Svrcek, N., Daly-Lesch, A., & Tily, S. (2018). "We know for a fact": Dyslexia interventionists and the power of authoritative discourse. *Journal of Literacy Research, 50*(3), 359–382.

Yuill, N. M., & Oakhill, J. V. (1991). *Children's problems in text comprehension: An experimental investigation.* Cambridge University Press.

Zinar, S. (2000). The relative contributions of word identification skill and comprehension-monitoring behavior to reading comprehension ability. *Contemporary Educational Psychology, 25,* 363–377.

Zirkel, P. A. (2020). Legal developments for students with dyslexia. *Learning Disability Quarterly, 43*(3), 127–139.

4   Before Reading Words Begins

Much that is relevant to the development of literacy occurs before a child first passes through school doors. Among literacy researchers, it has become something of a truism to assert that literacy development begins at birth, with many opportunities for events in the home life of preschoolers that have implications for literacy development. That is, there are many opportunities for emergent literacy (Saada-Robert, 2004; Tolchinsky, 2004). These include game and play activities; interactions during meals; media viewed by children and their parents (e.g., watching educational shows); outings (e.g., to the library or zoo); and reading, writing, and drawing (Baker et al., 1994). Such activities can go far in stimulating the development of a child's language, which is critical for subsequent development of reading and writing skills (e.g., Frijters et al., 2000; Leseman & de Jong, 1998). They can also increase a child's knowledge about the conventions of print—for example, understanding that reading in English is from left to right and top to bottom as well as awareness of the difference between pictures and print. Preschool interactions with adults can result in knowledge of the alphabet. In short, the child who experiences rich linguistic interactions with adults during the preschool years is massively advantaged with respect to literacy development relative to the child who has less rich interactions (e.g., McGill-Franzen et al., 2002; Whitehurst & Lonigan, 1998, 2001).

What should be emphasized is that the healthiest environments for the development of literacy during the preschool years are ones in which literate interactions are part of the natural fun of home life. That is, the home that fosters preschooler emergent literacy is not school-like, but rather playful, verbal, and stimulating in ways that are interesting to preschoolers

(Sonnenschein et al., 1996). There are responsive relationships with adults. It is widely accepted by literacy researchers that the environment the preschool child experiences is a critical determinant of reading and writing abilities once formal schooling begins.

Literacy researchers studying the preschool years have been very much influenced by developmental psychology. The first section of this chapter briefly reviews the theory of development proposed by Lev S. Vygotsky, who believed that many of the skills a child acquires reflect internalization of thinking first carried out by the child and adults in interaction. Then, the next section considers emergent literacy skills, which have been studied closely by literacy researchers who are interested in the preschool years. The chapter concludes with coverage of the development of two sets of skills, which seems to be especially important with respect to the development of beginning reading competence—namely, concepts of print (including letter-name knowledge) and the awareness that words are composed of sounds blended together (i.e., phonemic awareness).

VYGOTSKY'S THEORY: INTELLECTUAL DEVELOPMENT THROUGH INTERNALIZATION OF INTERPERSONAL INTERACTION SKILLS

People learn from other people. Many researchers are now studying how interpersonal relationships contribute to the development of thinking and learning skills. Lev S. Vygotsky, who lived during the first third of the 20th century in what became the Soviet Union, has been the most influential theorist in this arena.

Inner Speech and Thought

Vygotsky (1962) believed that, for adults, *inner speech* was an important mechanism involved in thought. Inner speech is very different from outer speech. It is abbreviated and fragmentary, with the meaning of complex thoughts captured in very few words and word fragments. It is speech that supports thought. Some extremely important research in Soviet psychology has focused on when people subvocalize (i.e., use inner speech to mediate performance) and when they do not. Subvocalization occurs when people work on problems that are challenging to them (Sokolov, 1975). For example, Sokolov substantiated the theory that subvocalization occurs during reading, with the intensity of subvocalization varying with the difficulty of the text being read and with the task assigned to the reader (e.g., requiring the reader to attempt to memorize what is being read increases the intensity of subvocalization). Talking to oneself about a task while doing a challenging task is a good thing to do, an essential part of problem solving.

Development of Inner Speech

An important contribution by Vygotsky was a theory about how inner speech develops during childhood. During the first 2 years of life, thought is nonverbal. Speech plays a limited role in thought during the early stages of language development (i.e., beginning at about age 2). Then, children begin to manifest what has been called *egocentric speech* by developmental psychologists. That is, when preschoolers do things, they often talk to themselves about what they are doing. Vygotsky recognized the emergence of egocentric speech as an important intellectual advance, with such speech beginning to influence what the child thinks and does.

How many times does the parent of a preschooler hear "I'm going to play with X" before their child goes and plays with X? How many times does a parent hear "I'm running to X" before the child runs to X? Often, such utterances come when the preschooler is trying to figure out what to do. Vygotsky carried out studies with preschoolers in which the preschoolers were given tasks that were complicated by some obstacle (e.g., when a colored pencil, or paper, or paint that was needed was missing). When difficulties occurred, the amount of egocentric speech was much greater than when preschoolers did the same tasks without obstacles.

Eventually, overt egocentric speech becomes covert and abbreviated. But it can always become overt again if the child encounters a challenging problem. When skilled readers encounter very familiar words, reading of the words is automatic—with little involvement of speech processes; speech processes involving sounding out a word only come into play with difficult words. This is consistent with the general principle that speech is an important part of thinking, especially challenging thinking.

Contemporary literacy researchers are actively studying the development of children's use of speech during thinking. For example, Cox (1994) observed self-regulatory speech in preschoolers as they attempted to construct and dictate a short story to an adult who wrote it down. As the children thought about what might be added next to the story, Cox heard them say things like these: "Now, what did I do then?"; "Think about what you say before you say it"; and "That's it . . . I think that's it." Such an observation is consistent with Vygotsky's and other developmental psychologists' observations (e.g., Kohlberg et al., 1968) that preschoolers use audible speech in order to organize their thinking.

Development of Thought in Social Interactions

The prominence of Vygotsky's thinking with respect to development has soared in the past half-century. In *Mind in Society*, Vygotsky (1978) made the case that interaction with others is a prime mover in the development of children's thinking abilities.

Development of Problem-Solving Skills

Adults often assist children with problems they are confronting. A child might not work through many problems without assistance, but with parental support she or he makes fine progress. What goes on in these interactions is thinking, thinking that involves two heads. Years of participating in such interactions leads to their internalization by the child. That is, thought processes that were once *inter*personal become *intra*personal. The most frequently reprinted Vygotsky (1978) passage captures this developmental progression:

> Any function in the child's cultural development appears twice, or on two planes. First, it appears on the social plane, and then on the psychological plane. First, it appears between people as an inter-psychological category, and then within the child as an intra-psychological category. This is equally true with respect to voluntary attention, logical memory, the formation of concepts, and the development of volition . . . . Social relations or relations among people genetically underlie all higher functions and their relationships . . . . In their private sphere, human beings retain the functions of social interactions. (pp. 163–164)

According to the Vygotskian perspective, cognitive development moves forward most certainly and completely if the child is in a world that provides assistance when the child needs it and can benefit from it. Such a responsive world is not intruding, however; rather, it provides support when the child needs it. When 2- or 3-year-olds can solve a problem themselves, appropriately responsive adults let the 2- and 3-year-olds do so. Any parent of a preschooler knows all too well the phrase "I can do it myself!"; and when the child can, the parent honors that declaration. Of course, there are other tasks that 2- and 3-year-olds cannot perform, no matter how much assistance might be provided. A responsive social environment does not even try to encourage children to do such tasks and, in fact, often discourages attempts at behaviors far outside the range of preschooler competence, as when, for example, a father physically lifts his son from the driver's seat of the car as the youngster urges the father to teach him to drive.

Between the two extremes of tasks, the ones children can do autonomously and those they could not possibly do at their age, critical developmental interactions occur. That is, interactions that facilitate development are most likely to occur with tasks that children can only do with adult help. The responsive social world provides assistance on these tasks that are within the child's *zone of proximal development*, according to Vygotskian theory. In fact, the zone is defined as behaviors beyond a child's level of autonomous functioning but within reach if assistance is provided. Children learn how to perform tasks appropriately within their zone by interacting with more competent and responsive others who provide hints and prompts to the child on an as-needed basis.

Thus, the responsive adult directs a child's attention to important dimensions of a problem if the child seems not to be attending to those dimensions on her or his own. Sometimes the adult suggests a strategy to the child. Through doing the task with support, the child eventually can perform the task without assistance, having internalized the kind of thinking that was previously supported by an adult. Without adult assistance, there are many forms of thinking that the child would not discover, either alone or in interaction with peers.

When adults assist in this fashion, they are said to *scaffold* a child (Wood et al., 1976), a metaphoric reference to the scaffold of a building under construction. It is an appropriate metaphor: The scaffolding on a building under construction provides supports when the new building cannot stand on its own. As the new structure is completed and becomes free-standing, the scaffolding is removed. So, it is with scaffolded adult–child academic interactions. The adult carefully monitors when enough instructional input has been provided to permit the child to make progress toward an academic goal, and thus the adult provides support only when the child needs it. If a child catches on quickly, the adult's responsive instruction will be less detailed than if the child experiences difficulties with a task.

Development of Language Skills

As they use language during the preschool years, some children receive more scaffolding than others. Children from low-income families are less likely than middle- and upper-class children to be immersed in supportive communicative interactions (Bernstein, 1965). This is critical since the development of oral communication skills during the preschool years is logically prerequisite to success in reading and writing (e.g., Snow, 1991). For example, Hart and Risley (1995) documented a correlation between children's language interactions and their subsequent cognitive development. They observed 42 families carefully for 2 years, beginning when a child in the family was 7–9 months of age. During the observations, the researchers attempted to record everything that went on, using tape recorders and notes. The observations then were carefully coded and analyzed for the types of verbal interactions that occurred.

The outcomes in the study were very clear: There were large differences in the quality of language interactions as a function of social class. More high-quality verbal interactions were observed in professional homes than in working-class homes, and more in working-class homes than in welfare homes. The higher the socioeconomic level, the more the parents listened to their children, prompted their children to elaborate their verbalizations, told their children what was worth remembering, and taught them how to cope with difficulties. These differences in the quality and quantity of verbal interactions were observed throughout the 2 years of observations, and they were pronounced: Whereas, on average, a child in a professional family experienced four million verbal utterances a year, a child in a welfare family experienced only 250,000 utterances.

Based on such striking differences in input, it would be expected that there would be differences in outcomes, and there were. By the time the children were 3 years of age, those from professional homes knew much more vocabulary than did the children of working-class parents, who knew more than the children of parents on welfare. However, because there were other differences between the homes of professional, working-class, and welfare families, it was not possible in this study to be certain that the differences in language skills in the children were due to the linguistic interactions they experienced. Nonetheless, when the correlations obtained in this study are combined with evidence from other studies, there is a great deal of support for the conclusion that the quality of a child's verbal interactions is reliably related to linguistic and cognitive development.

Dudley-Marling and Lucas (2009) note, however, that the six poor families studied were all African American families, and none of the parents were well educated. They note that the differences in race, social class, and educational levels between the researchers conducting the observations and those families may have influenced the observed outcomes. In other words, less well-educated African American parents may have felt inhibited by the well-educated observers, and that led to less frequent and less complex interactions with their children. Likewise, the white parents with higher incomes and higher levels of educational attainment may have been influenced to "show off" just how much they interacted with their children. The point that Dudley-Marling and Lucas make is that there were observed differences but that it is difficult to interpret just what the differences mean in terms of parent–child interactions. In any event, they note that differences obviously do exist in the parent–child interactions experienced by any group of emergent readers and that teachers need to design instruction that ameliorates such differences in preschool parental interactions with their children.

Differences in parent–child interactions suggest a strategy that seems too rarely used: supporting all parents of preschool children in rich ways of interacting with their young children. Given the potentially powerful role that experiencing many rich language interactions seems to play in early language development, one could argue that schools should be involved almost as soon as a new baby appears in the school attendance area. By "involved," we mean involved in providing effective parenting classes for the families whose children are likely to attend your school.

Responsive adults spend a great deal of time talking *with* their children about things that happened to the child, assisting the child in learning how to be tellers of their own memories (Nelson & Fivush, 2004). Hudson (1990) analyzed her own daughter Rachel's experiences in talking about the past and how those experiences increased Rachel's ability to describe events in her life. What was particularly critical were her many opportunities to talk about the past with Mom, through extended dialogues about the many things that had happened to Rachel. When Rachel had difficulties in remembering, Mom would prompt her, typically with questions.

Through experiencing such dialogues, Rachel learned how to talk about things that had happened to her. Consistent with the Vygotskian perspective, Hudson (1990) concluded that the important thinking skill of being able to describe events in one's life develops through social interaction. When the child could not structure recall of an event, the mother asked questions, providing a scaffold for the child's recollections. As Rachel became increasingly familiar with what should be told during recall of something that happened in the past and began, in fact, to recall with greater completeness, adult scaffolding in the form of leading questions was reduced. Hudson's description of Rachel's progression from a teller of tales with assistance to an autonomous teller of tales is consistent with a variety of evidence that children's ability to talk about their past depends on dialoguing experiences with supportive adults (Nelson, 1993a, 1993b; Nelson & Fivush, 2004; Pillemer & White, 1989; Ratner, 1984; Reese et al., 1993).

Virtually everyone who thinks about reading believes that success in reading depends on language development (Dickinson et al., 2004). Thus, for the reading-education community, there is obvious significance in the finding that conversational experiences during the preschool years figure greatly in the development of cognitive and communication skills. The work of Hudson and her colleagues seems more significant than that, however. Hudson believes that supportive parent–child dialogic experiences not only promote the development of children's abilities to communicate about the past, but also increase their abilities to organize and understand their previous experiences (Nelson, 1996; Nelson & Fivush, 2004). Prior knowledge based on experience is important in comprehending information presented in texts. Since children who have had rich and supportive dialogic experiences have better organized and more complete prior knowledge, they should be advantaged in comprehending what they read over children who have not had such experiences. Children who live in a richly responsive interpersonal world and who thus learn how to communicate with others are going to be cognitively far ahead of agemates who do not.

Likewise, preschool programs for young children can provide rich language and literacy activity, although the evidence to date suggests that child care and preschool programs vary substantially in this regard. McGill-Franzen et al. (2002) report a qualitative study of such experiences in five urban preschools. These five preschools served children who varied by family income and educational levels. Some preschools served primarily middle-class children, while others served primarily children from low-income families. Some programs were funded by state and federal dollars while in other programs the income was largely fee-based tuition. On every measure—numbers of books available in the classrooms, number of adult read-alouds completed, materials for writing as well as support for initial attempts at writing, and the number of useful adult–child interactions—all were found in far greater numbers in preschools enrolling primarily middle-class children. Only a single religious preschool attended by children from low-income homes and with parents who had attained low levels of education attainment offered a rich language environment. The authors conclude their report with the following summary:

> In income-eligible preschools, curricula and pedagogy reflected a limited view of children as learners. Children had less access to print, fewer opportunities to participate in literacy, and little experience listening to or discussing culturally relevant literature . . . poor children and children of color are socialized to practice a different literacy, one that offers limited experiences with books and is less connected to personal and community identity. If publicly funded early childhood programs, already isolated by class, are to provide an equitable foundation for literacy and schooling for children of low-income families, more challenging curricular and pedagogical frameworks are needed. (p. 443)

EMERGENT LITERACY

For the most part, the discussion in this chapter thus far has emphasized general cognitive and language skills that support the development of literacy, with only limited discussion of research directly tapping the development of literacy skills per se. In fact, a great deal of literacy development occurs during the preschool years—so much so that the preschool years are often referred to as the "period of emergent literacy" by reading theorists and researchers (e.g., Clay, 1966, 1967; Saada-Robert, 2004; Tolchinsky, 2004).

A great deal of research directly focuses on emergent literacy. Literacy development begins before the first birthday through, for example, experiences with plastic "bathtub" books filled with colorful pictures or from mothers and fathers who read nursery rhymes to their children as they rock them to sleep. These early beginnings expand into a rich array of literacy experiences, from scribbling letters to grandma to experiencing stories on grandma's lap. Environments that support emergent literacy include (1) rich interpersonal experiences with parents, brothers and sisters, and others; (2) physical environments that include literacy materials, from magnet plastic refrigerator letters to storybooks to writing materials; and (3) high positive regard by parents and others for literacy and its development in children (Leichter, 1984; McGill-Franzen et al., 2002; Morrow, 2001; Saada-Robert, 2004; Tolchinsky, 2004).

Put more concretely, in homes and early childhood centers in which emergent literacy is fostered, children are exposed to activities, letters, and printed words at an early age. Parents read to their children, and they help children as they attempt to read themselves (e.g., by holding a book upright and pretending to read by recalling the story as they remembered it). Books and other reading materials are prominent in homes and early childhood centers supporting emergent literacy (e.g., Clark, 1976; McGill-Franzen & Jordan, 2012; Morrow, 1983; Neuman & Celano, 2001; Yaden et al., 2000). But there are still homes and early childhood centers where there are few books and little talk with the children. Such homes and preschools are more likely to serve children from low-income families.

Storybook Reading

One activity that has high potential for fostering emergent literacy is storybook reading (Garton & Pratt, 2004; McGill-Franzen & Jordan, 2012; van Kleeck et al., 2003). There are strong and positive correlations between the amount of storybook reading during the preschool years and subsequent vocabulary and language development, children's interest in reading, and early success in reading (Stahl, 2003; Sulzby & Teale, 1991). Given their apparent power in stimulating children's literacy development, caregiver–child interactions during storybook reading have been studied in some detail.

At its best, storybook reading includes rich discussions and animated conversations between the reader and the child. The adult and the child work out the meaning of the text, and they have a lot of fun doing it (Morrow, 2001). There is questioning, both by the adult and the child; there is modeling of dialoguing by the adult, with the child sometimes participating; the adult praises the child's efforts to get meaning from the pictures and print; the adult offers information to the child and responds to the child's reactions to the text; and both the adult and the child relate what is happening in the text to their lives and the world around them (e.g., Applebee & Langer, 1983; Cochran-Smith, 1984; Flood, 1977; Pellegrini et al., 1990; Roser & Martinez, 1985; Taylor & Strickland, 1986). A rich history of such interactions is predictive of subsequent success in literacy acquisition by the child (Stahl, 2003; Sulzby & Teale, 1991).

Scaffolding is prominent when storybook reading is going well—when it is engaging to the youngsters. Parents who are good at storybook reading encourage children to respond to readings and participate as much as possible in reading itself. They provide support as children need it, and provide input that children can understand (e.g., DeLoache & DeMendoza, 1987). With increasing age through the preschool years, children are attentive to longer sections of text (Heath, 1982; Sulzby & Teale, 1987). As they gain experience reading storybooks, adults have more complex discussions with children about the text (Snow, 1983; Sulzby & Teale, 1987). Additionally, storybook read-alouds foster the development of print awareness in young children (Justice et al., 2010). Children who experience a lot of storybook reading are accustomed to interacting with an adult about story content; they are appropriately attentive during storybook reading, much more so than same-age children who have not experienced storybook reading (Bus & van IJzendoorn, 1988).

Some attention has been paid to differences in style of storybook reading and the effects of such variations on cognitive development. Parents who do not put particularly high value on literacy do not engage their children as much as parents who value literacy—for example, they do not prompt their children to think about potential alternative meanings of the text. They do less to make the text fun and understandable for the child (Bus et al., 2000). Children have better vocabulary development when they interact with adults who are skillful at eliciting verbal interactions from them during reading (e.g., Ninio, 1980; Pellegrini et al., 1994). There are also correlations between the degree to which parents elaborate on book content and success in literacy tasks in school (Heath, 1982). In short, not all storybook reading is ideal; the *quality* of the storybook reading very much affects a child's cognitive development (Heath, 2012).

The correlations between quality of storybook reading and literacy development (Sulzby & Teale, 1991) prompted Whitehurst and his colleagues (Whitehurst et al., 1988) to study whether it might be possible to improve parental skills during storybook interactions and thus positively affect the development of emergent literacy in children. The parents of 14 children between 1 year and 3 years of age participated in a 1-month intervention designed to improve interactions between parents and children during storybook reading. Parents were taught to ask more open-ended questions and more questions about the functions and attributes of objects in stories as they read with their preschoolers. The parents were also given instruction about how to respond appropriately to their children's comments during story reading and how to expand on what the children had to say. The parents in the treatment group were also taught to reduce the amount of straight reading that they did, as well as to eliminate questions that the child could answer simply by pointing to something in an illustration. Fifteen other children and their parents, who served as control participants in the study, were encouraged to continue reading storybooks as they normally did with their children.

First, the intervention parents were able to learn to interact differently with their children during storybook reading in ways that increased the quality of interactions between the children and their parents. Although there had been no differences between intervention and control children at the beginning of the study with respect to language variables, there were clear differences favoring the intervention participants at the end of the month of treatment: After the intervention, participants outscored the control subjects on a standardized measure of psycholinguistic ability and on two vocabulary tests. What was most striking in this study was that, when the same measures were repeated 9 months later, the intervention subjects still had an advantage over the control participants, although the differences were not as large.

Unfortunately, storybook reading is not always as interactive and as much fun as it could be and probably needs to be in order to be effective in engaging children (Hammett et al., 2003). High-quality storybook reading especially is less likely in the homes of lower-class and cultural minority children, and when storybook reading does occur, there often is less of the open-ended questioning and fun that seems critical in storybook reading that promotes language development (e.g., Anderson-Yockel & Haynes, 1994; Bergin, 2001; Bus et al., 2000; Hammer, 1999, 2001; van Kleeck, 2004). Notably, and much more positively, Whitehurst's group also has produced positive effects with storybook reading when Hispanic families have been the intervention targets (Valdez-Menchaca & Whitehurst, 1992) and as part of a comprehensive day care/Head Start intervention (Whitehurst et al., 1994, 1999; Whitehurst & Lonigan, 2001). The Whitehurst group has also provided other recent demonstrations that interactive storybook reading promotes the language development of socioeconomically disadvantaged children (e.g., Zevenbergen et al., 2003). There is great potential for storybook reading to contribute to the literacy development of a wide range of children.

Whitehurst and his associates also have made progress in making their approach cost-effective, developing videotapes that teach mothers how to interact with their preschoolers as they read stories (Arnold et al., 1994). Others are also making progress in devising storybook reading interventions. For example, Crain-Thoreson and Dale (1995) taught preschool staff members to interact with children more actively during storybook reading. The targeted students then performed better on a variety of language measures, including a vocabulary test and an analysis of the length and complexity of utterances. Dickinson and Smith (1994) designed a similar intervention that produced similar effects. In short, by actively engaging preschoolers in discussions as part of storybook reading, adults can promote child language development; presumably, the earlier such experience begins, the better (Aram & Biron, 2004; Leyva et al., 2013; Lonigan et al., 1995; Stahl, 2003). However, income-eligible preschool programs will not only need to invest in developing staff competencies in storybook reading, they will also have to invest in expanding the numbers of books available in those child care centers (McGill-Franzen et al., 2002; Neuman, 1999).

Developing Rich Emergent Literacy Knowledge in Preschools

Neuman and Roskos (1997) provided an interesting analysis that made clear just how extensive preschoolers' emergent literacy can be, at least when preschoolers experience an environment rich in emergent literacy learning opportunities. They observed 30 preschoolers over 7 months, who participated in a preschool with three play centers that permitted much emergent literacy activity: a post office, a restaurant, and a doctor's office.

What Neuman and Roskos (1997) found was that children learned the names and functions of a number of literacy objects in the play centers, including the following: envelopes, pencil, letter, mailbox, menu, bill, check, insurance card, and eye chart. The preschoolers also learned how to do many literate things, including the following: getting stamps, putting together a letter, addressing it, mailing it, delivering mail, taking a restaurant order, ordering from a menu, reviewing a restaurant bill, exchanging pleasantries over a meal, taking inventory at the restaurant, taking down information, giving prescriptions, signing in at the doctor's office, and describing medical emergency procedures. Neuman and Roskos (1997) also observed the use of some higher-order strategies similar to those used by older children as they read, write, and do things literate. These include seeking information, correcting and giving feedback to others, self-correcting, checking a literacy product against a standard (e.g., checking whether letters in the post office are sorted the way that they should be sorted), and gathering up resources before beginning a task. In short, much literate behavior can be learned in a preschool classroom designed to foster emergent literacy activities. The teacher who designs her or his classroom to include a library center and a post office has created a setting that can support storybook reading, children's writing, and associated literacy activities (Roskos & Neuman, 2001).

Furthermore, Neuman (2009; also see Koskinen et al., 2000; Leyva et al., 2013; McGill-Franzen et al., 1999) studied one type of item that can be provided to children in preschool settings, one that does much to increase literacy interactions for preschoolers. When books are made available to children and their teachers are provided training in using them, children engage in literacy-promoting activities (e.g., looking at the books, sharing books with other children), with language and literacy skills enhanced. In highlighting the finding that books can make a positive difference when they are in a child's world, Neuman made us aware that the absence of books is a reason for concern. In follow-up work, Neuman and Celano (2001) studied the availability of books in the worlds of middle-income and low-income preschoolers, finding many more books in middle-class schools and communities. Duke (2000a, 2000b) conducted a similar study at the grade 1 level, obtaining a similar finding. One of the ways that middle-class parents and the schools serving their offspring foster emergent literacy in their children is that they provide tangible literature resources at home and during the preschool day.

Interpretational Controversies Regarding Emergent Literacy Experiences

From infancy, there are opportunities for adults and children to interact together with materials and activities related to reading and writing. Some children are more fortunate than others, participating in many more emergent literacy interactions than other children. The lucky children live in families in which literacy experiences are so common that they are family habits that are naturally extended to new family members, beginning shortly after their arrival home from the hospital. That some preschoolers do not have consistent, excellent emergent literacy experiences has stimulated scholars (McGill-Franzen, 2006; Neuman & Roskos, 1993) to begin to study ways of increasing interactions between parents, teachers, and children that promote emergent literacy. Their successes to date fuel enthusiasm for the possibility that many more children could be much better prepared for formal schooling by increasing the quality and quantity of literacy interactions during the preschool years.

In closing this section, however, we must admit that there is some variability in the interpretation of the emergent literacy research. For example, while there is agreement that storybook reading's effects on language and literacy development are not overwhelmingly large, some view the statistical associations produced to date as evidence of the power of storybook reading (Bus et al., 1995; Dunning et al., 1994; Justice et al., 2010; Lonigan, 1994; McGill-Franzen, 2006). That is, despite the many problems of measurement with preschool children (and there are many, not the least of which is the lower reliability of measurements on preschoolers as compared with older children), the lack of statistical power in many studies (which reduces the likelihood of finding significant statistical associations), and the great variability in the procedures from study to study, some researchers are impressed with the consistency of at least positive associations between activities like storybook reading and growth in emergent literacy.

In contrast, other researchers (Scarborough & Dobrich, 1994) have examined exactly the same correlations between storybook reading and emergent literacy and have written them off as small and potentially attributable to other factors, suggesting that perhaps the correlations between storybook reading and language and literacy achievement actually reflect other relationships (e.g., perhaps children more interested in things literate and/or those with higher verbal abilities are more likely to engage in storybook reading than children less interested and/or lower in ability). Our own reading of the evidence is that there is much more reason to believe that children's early literacy interactions are important.

One possibility is that emergent literacy experiences may not be equally positive for all children. For example, in the studies of Bus and van IJzendoorn (e.g., 1988, 1992, 1995), it is striking that, when children interact with parents with whom they are not securely attached, storybook reading is not the happy and engaging event that it can be when securely attached parents and children interact over books. It may very well be that such negative interactions over books may undermine interest in reading (Bus, 1993, 1994). We need to find this out, and then, of course, we must find out how more positive interactions can be encouraged between a preschooler and parent who have yet to develop a trusting relationship, one fostering literacy development.

However positive a child's emergent literacy experiences, they rarely are sufficient for the development of one very important competency associated with successful beginning reading. We take up that competency, phonemic awareness, in the next section.

PHONEMIC AWARENESS AND ITS DEVELOPMENT THROUGH INSTRUCTION

Even though the language competencies developed during the preschool years are insufficient for the child to become a reader, they are nonetheless important. In fact, there are striking correlations between children's language competencies on entry to kindergarten and success in reading during the primary grades (Elbro et al., 1998; Elbro & Scarborough, 2004; Mann, 2003; Muter & Snowling, 1998; Scarborough, 2001). Particularly intense attention has been focused on the finding that kindergarten students who lack the language competency known as phonemic awareness often experience subsequent difficulties in learning to read (e.g., Adams, 1990; Blachman, 2000; Pennington et al., 1993; Stanovich, 1986, 1988), although at-risk kindergarten children often have other problems at the phonological level. For example, Elbro et al. (1998) found that kindergarten children who poorly pronounced common words (i.e., they lacked distinct phonological representations of the words) were at greater risk for reading problems at grade 2.

Phonemic awareness is awareness that words are composed of separable sounds (i.e., phonemes) that are blended to produce words. A number of tasks tap phonemic awareness (Adams, 1990; Anthony & Lonigan, 2004; Slocum et al., 1993; Stahl & Murray, 1994, 1998; Wagner et al., 1993). There are some data-based differences of opinion among the various researchers studying phonemic awareness about whether the particular tasks that reflect less and more advanced forms of phonemic awareness and the various manifestations of phonemic awareness are best thought of as a single competency or as multiple, related competencies (Anthony & Lonigan, 2004; Anthony et al., 2003; Mann & Foy, 2003; Mann & Wimmer, 2002).

Nonetheless, Adams's (1990) conceptualization of phonemic awareness still permits understanding of the various ways phonological awareness can be evident. According to her, the most primitive form is simply having enough of an ear for sounds to remember rhyming words more easily than nonrhyming words. The child with this level of phonemic awareness can recall nursery rhymes with greater ease than the child who lacks this basic form of phonemic awareness (Maclean et al., 1987). At the next level, the child can detect the odd word in a set of words, recognizing, for example, that *sod* is the odd word in the trio *can, dan, sod*. At a still higher level of awareness, the child can blend component sounds to form words—for example, when presented the sounds *m, aah* (i.e., short *a*), and *t*, the child produces the word *mat*. Even more advanced is the ability to segment a word into its sounds; the child at this level of awareness can report that *mat* is composed of the sounds *m, aah*, and *t*. Children at the highest level of awareness can split off individual sounds from intact words—for example, when asked to delete the *m* sound from *mat*, the child says *at*. Thus, phonemic awareness culminates when students can actively manipulate and play around with the sounds that compose words. We emphasize the playfulness in such manipulation, for whenever we have observed classrooms in which children are practicing blending, adding, deleting, and inserting sounds as part of phonemic awareness instruction, they seem to be enjoying themselves. Given the various manifestations of phonemic awareness, it should not be surprising that there are a variety of ways to assess it, both with laboratory tasks and with more standardized assessments (Sodoro et al., 2002).

One study more than any other focused attention on phonemic awareness. Connie Juel (1988) followed children as they progressed from grade 1 through grade 4, collecting a variety of reading and related measures as part of the study. One of the most striking findings in the study concerned continuing underachievement in reading: There was an 88% chance that if a child was having difficulty reading in grade 1, the child would still be having difficulty in grade 4. More importantly in this context, however, was that the best predictor of poor reading achievement in grade 1 was phonemic awareness: The more advanced levels of phonemic awareness discussed earlier were required for a child to score highly in Juel's (1988) study. Especially striking, low phonemic awareness in grade 1 was highly predictive of continuing reading difficulties in grade 4. Since Juel's (1988) study, there have been other early language predictors that are more telling about later reading (namely, rudimentary reading skills and letter identification; see Elbro & Scarborough, 2004; Piasta, Justice, et al., 2012; Scarborough, 2001), although phonemic awareness is a very good predictor of later reading competency averaging across all of the relevant data that are available.

Juel's findings especially stimulated very hard thinking and many additional analyses by a number of researchers about phonemic awareness and how it relates to reading competence. Based on these analyses, it is now known that poor readers at all age levels often are less phonemically aware than same-age good readers (e.g., Pratt & Brady, 1988; Shaywitz, 1996). Children who lack phonemic awareness have a difficult time developing understanding of letter–sound relationships as well as learning to spell (Griffith, 1991; Juel et al., 1986). Since Juel's studies, additional and diverse evidence has been produced to indicate that poor phonemic awareness at 4–6 years of age is predictive, especially of early reading achievement, but also throughout the elementary years (e.g., Badian, 2001; Bowey, 2002; Goswami, 2002b; Hulme et al., 2002; Muter et al., 2004; Speece et al., 2004; Torgesen & Burgess, 1998; Windfuhr & Snowling, 2001). The evidence that phonemic awareness difficulties in the elementary years are associated with reading difficulties has also been established in studies that demonstrate at least as strong relationships between phonemic awareness and reading ability as other potentially important individual differences (i.e., rapid processing and naming of individual letters and numbers; see Cardoso-Martins & Pennington, 2004; Kirby et al., 2003; Parrila et al., 2004; Schatschneider et al., 2004; Sunseth & Bowers, 2002; Swanson et al., 2003; Torgesen et al., 1997) and reading ability. At least in some analyses, more advanced forms of phonemic awareness (i.e., the ability to segment words into component sounds) have been more predictive of reading ability than simpler forms, such as being able to detect rhymes (Nation & Hulme, 1997).

However, the meta-analysis of early training in phonemic awareness by Bus and van IJzendoorn (1999) raises questions about the longer-term advantages of phonemic awareness training in fostering reading development. They highlighted a finding that did not emerge from the NRP analysis: Phonological awareness instruction from ages 5 to 6 had little impact on reading measured several years after the phonological awareness instruction, accounting for less than 1% of the total variability in reading in the middle elementary grades. This is an important finding that raises questions about whether investment in phonemic awareness instruction produces long-term benefits for children, an issue not addressed by the NRP. Once again, more research is needed to clarify what can be expected when preschools and schools engage in developing phonemic awareness in young children.

Gough (1998) suggests that we may be expecting too many benefits from training in phonemic segmentation. He provides an analysis of training teachers to engage their children in Turtle Talk. Gough notes that a key descriptive feature of turtles is that they are slow. Thus, if turtles could talk, they likely would talk slowly, stretching out words phoneme by phoneme. The teacher models how a turtle might talk. As she says words the way a turtle might say them, she asks students, "What word did the turtle just say?" After a bit of practice, the teacher then pairs students together with one identified as the turtle and the other as the person trying to understand the Turtle Talk. After a while the students switch roles. Gough describes a study of Turtle Talk in 48 kindergarten classrooms. Teachers were asked to engage students in Turtle Talk for 10–15 minutes a day for 20 days. Teachers in the Turtle Talk classrooms doubled the number of students able to demonstrate full segmentation of words into their constituent phonemes. The students in 27 control classrooms had more children able to demonstrate full segmentation when the study started, but the Turtle Talk students were significantly better at full segmentation after 4 weeks of Turtle Talk activities. Gough focused on developing the ability to demonstrate full segmentation because it is the most predictive of the tasks that have been created to assess phonemic awareness and because full segmentation is necessary to engage in invented spelling, another activity shown to foster phonemic awareness in emergent readers (Clarke, 1988).

Lack of phonemic awareness seems to be part of a vicious cycle. Children who are exposed to a great deal of language and have well-developed vocabularies early in life have greater phonemic awareness, for a well-developed vocabulary provides many opportunities to discriminate words on the basis of sound differences (Dickinson et al., 2003; Goswami, 2000, 2001; Metsala, 1999). Those with less-rich language experiences know fewer words and are less phonemically aware. Deficiencies in phonemic awareness, in turn, can undermine learning to decode, which in turn undermines reading a wide range of materials and comprehending what is read. The long-term result is less practice in reading and less exposure to information in text, and thus less development of higher-order reading competencies (e.g., ability to make sense of complex syntax) and world knowledge that can mediate understanding of text (Juel, 1988). This is the rich-getting-richer and the poor-getting-poorer story, what Stanovich (1986) referred to as the "Matthew effect" in reading.

For the most advanced levels of phonemic awareness to develop, formal instruction in reading seems essential (i.e., only a very small proportion of preschool children develop the advanced levels of phonemic awareness in the absence of such instruction; e.g., Lundberg, 1991). The one emergent literacy experience that is predictive of phonemic awareness is parental teaching of letters and their sounds (Crain-Thoreson & Dale, 1992). The data from the national Early Childhood Literacy Survey indicated that two-thirds of entering kindergarten students already knew their letter names and one-third already knew most of the consonant sounds (Pearson & Hiebert, 2010). Obviously, many parents and preschool teachers have organized environments for preschoolers that foster this development.

However, one-third of entering kindergartners don't know all of the letter names. As Pearson and Hiebert (2010) noted, it is almost eerie that the same percentage of kids who don't know their letter names upon kindergarten entry matches perfectly with the number of fourth graders who read below the Basic level, and that the one-third of entering kindergartners who knew most consonant sounds matches the one-third of fourth graders who scored at the Proficient level on the National Assessment of Educational Progress. The issue of letter-name knowledge upon entering kindergarten has stimulated research, if only because there is no agreement between state education agencies on just how many letter names should be known. Using a sample of 371 randomly selected students from 85 publicly funded early childhood centers, Piasta, Petscher, et al. (2012) determined that knowing the names of 18 upper-case letters and 15 lower-case letters produced the most reliable predictions of success in developing beginning reading skills in kindergarten and first grade.

Too many parents and too many preschools, however, do not engage in such teaching, so education that impacts both letter-name knowledge and phonemic awareness typically must occur in school. Thus, there is a need to provide both letter-name knowledge and phonemic awareness instruction to kindergarten and grade 1 children if we want to be sure that all children develop these competencies.

Instruction in Letter-Name Knowledge

What we do know is that children who have been read many storybooks, who have access to magnetic letters, say, on the refrigerator, and who have had the opportunity to scribble and scratch while attempting to write a message are the children most likely to enter kindergarten already knowing the letter names (McGill-Franzen, 2006). One absolute essential in kindergarten classes is a display of the upper- and lower-case alphabet letters. Ideally, this would be attached to each student's desk or table. At the very least, every kindergarten classroom needs the alphabet displayed in a location where students can all see the individual letters. Often in the kindergarten classrooms we visit, such a display of the alphabet is located above the chalkboard at the front of the classroom.

McGill-Franzen (2006) provides detailed and research-based discussion of how kindergarten teachers can identify which children know which letters. This is useful if only because, in most classrooms, many children will arrive at kindergarten for the first day of school and already know all the letter names. Effective kindergarten teachers locate what sorts of print awareness each child has and uses that information to create differentiated instructional groups. Some children are more interested in writing than reading when they enter kindergarten and that interest allows us to couple writing and letter-name knowledge together. What better motivation for learning the letter names and shapes than a desire to use those letters when composing your message?

Perhaps because letter names are such a common focus in kindergarten, relatively little research has been done recently on effective instructional routines. Or perhaps it is because almost no kindergartners exit kindergarten without having learned all the letter names and shapes. One thing that is certain, however, is that the letter of the week curriculum plan, which we too often see when visiting kindergarten classrooms, is no longer an acceptable practice.

Alphabet books, those trade books that feature every letter of the alphabet linked to an illustration of that letter at the beginning of a word are one useful tool for developing alphabet knowledge. Some books, such as Mary Jane Martin's (1996) *From Anne to Zach*, feature children's names, with each beginning with a different letter. Johnson's (1999) *Alphabet City* uses objects typically found in urban areas, such as a street light, to represent different letters of the alphabet. Children's names can provide many of the letters to study, and typically each kindergartner is more likely to know the names of the letters in his or her name than the other letters. Since in most kindergarten classrooms each child knows the name of at least one letter, pairing children with different letter-name knowledge as alphabet partners is another useful instructional move.

Using teacher- and class-developed chart stories is another possible avenue for fostering the growth of letter names. This works best when the teacher names the letters as he or she is composing the chart story in front of the children. By this point, you may have decided that we are discussing a meaning-emphasis approach in kindergarten. Well, yes we are, simply because the evidence is quite compelling that meaning-emphasis approaches work well with children, especially children who arrive at kindergarten with few book, print, or letter experiences (Chomsky, 1972; Sacks & Mergendoller, 1997; Stahl et al., 1994; Stahl & Miller, 1989).

More recently, Roberts and colleagues (see Roberts, 2021, for review) completed several small experimental studies with preschoolers to enhance letter learning and letter sound learning. Through these experiments, Roberts and his colleagues found several effective instructional techniques that had positive effects on students learning of letters and letter sounds. For example, when introducing letters and sounds, using a letter embedded as a character with the sound in the name (e.g., Dippy duck or Sam the snake) produced a large effect size (*ES* = 1.31) for learning letter sounds (Roberts, 2021; Roberts & Sadler, 2019) with students learning twice as many sounds as compared with the control group. In a second study, Roberts et al. (2020) found providing preschoolers with more practice seeing and hearing a letter saw students have more success in naming letters, producing letter sounds, and with rapid letter sound as compared with the control group, which received less letter sound instruction. Though these experiments had small sample sizes, the results indicate that preschool teachers should put a greater emphasis on teaching letter names and letter sounds (see Roberts, 2021, for review; Roberts & Sadler, 2019).

Instruction in Phonemic Awareness

Phonemic awareness can be developed through systematic practice in categorizing words on the basis of common beginning, middle, and end sounds. One of the first instructional studies of the development of phonemic awareness, conducted by Lynette Bradley and Peter E. Bryant (1983), continues to be the best known.

An important principle emphasized in Bradley and Bryant's (1983) instruction was that the same word can be categorized in different ways on the basis of sound when it is used in different sets of words. Thus, if *hen* is in a group of words that include *hat, hill, hair,* and *hand,* it would make sense to categorize all of these words together as starting with *h,* especially in contrast to other words starting with another letter (e.g., *b* words such as *bag, band,* and *bat*). If *hen* were on a list with *men* and *sun,* however, these three words could be categorized as ones ending in *n.* If *hen* were on a list of words that included *bed* and *leg,* it would be possible to categorize the words as ones with short *e* in the middle.

The instruction in Bradley and Bryant (1983) took place over forty 10-minute sessions spread out over 2 years. During the first 20 sessions, 5- and 6-year-olds who initially lacked phonemic awareness were taught to categorize words on the basis of common sounds, using pictures of the objects (e.g., pictures of a *hen, men,* and a *leg*). For example, in one lesson, a set of pictures representing the letter *b* was shown to the child, who then named the objects. The child repeated the names, with the teacher urging the child to listen to the sounds. The child then was asked if he or she could hear a sound common to each word. This continued until the child could identify the common sound, with the adult providing help and hints if the child experienced difficulty doing this.

The sound-identification task was repeated a number of times during training, with variations (e.g., presentation of *bus*, with the child required to pick out a picture starting with the same sound from an array of pictures; presentation of *bus*, with the direction to pick out pictures starting with a different sound than the one at the beginning of *bus*). Children were then given sets of pictures, asked to group them together on the basis of common sounds, and then required to justify their classifications. "Odd-one-out" was played, in which the child was required to eliminate a word starting with (or ending with or containing) a sound different from the sounds suggested by the other pictures in a set. Many such exercises were given for each sound (e.g., *b*), with the teacher moving on to a new sound only when the child seemed to be proficient with the sound previously introduced. Of course, as new sounds accumulated, the difficulty of tasks increased.

The 20 sessions with pictures were followed by 20 sessions with words, in which a child was required to determine whether words rhymed or began with the same sound (alliteration). After the child was proficient at this task, there were lessons on end sounds (e.g., odd-one-out exercises requiring elimination of the word ending in a sound different from the others). After the child could manage categorizing on the basis of final sounds, there was instruction of categorization based on middle sounds in words.

Pictures yielded to purely aural presentations in this training. Various discrimination exercises eventually gave way to production exercises so that children had to recall words containing particular sounds in particular positions. In the latter half of the curriculum, children were required to spell words using plastic letters, with the teacher providing help as needed, up to and including spelling the word for the child. Spelling exercises included sets of words sharing common features. Thus, for a set involving *hat*, *cat*, and *rat*, an efficient strategy was simply to change the first plastic letter as each new word was requested. The saliency of many different sound patterns was illustrated with such spelling lists.

This training produced substantial gains in standardized reading performance (i.e., about a year's advantage) relative to a control condition in which children were trained to categorize pictures and words conceptually (e.g., *cat*, *bat*, and *rat* are all animals). The students trained in sound categorization were even further ahead of control participants who had received no supplementary categorization training. Even more striking, however, were the results of a 5-year follow-up. Even though many of the control subjects had received substantial remediation during the 5-year interval following participation in the study, there were still striking reading advantages for students who had experienced the sound categorization training when they were in the primary grades (Bradley, 1989; Bradley & Bryant, 1991).

Since the appearance of the Bradley and Bryant (1983, 1985) studies, there have been a number of well-controlled demonstrations that phonemic awareness can be developed in children with discernible effects on reading and learning to read (Ehri et al., 2001; National Reading Panel, 2000). We review here some of the most noteworthy examples of this research in order to deepen reader understanding of instruction that can promote phonemic awareness. Thus, in Lundberg et al. (1988), classrooms of 6-year-olds were provided with daily phonemic awareness training for 8 months (i.e., rhyming exercises; dividing words into syllables; and identifying phonemes, including segmenting words into phonemes and synthesizing phonemes into words). Control classrooms received no such training. Three years later, students in trained classrooms performed better on reading and spelling tasks than did students in control classrooms.

Similarly, Ball and Blachman (1988) provided instruction to 5-year-olds. In the phoneme awareness condition, kindergarten students met in small groups for 20 minutes, 4 days a week, for 7 weeks. Students moved counters to represent the sounds in words, were exposed to letter names and their associated sounds, and performed categorization tasks like the ones used in Bradley and Bryant's work. In the language activities control condition, students had vocabulary lessons, listened to stories, and practiced semantic categorization activities. They also received instruction in letter names and sounds that was identical to that provided to the phoneme awareness participants. There was also a no-instruction control condition in the study. The phoneme awareness group outperformed the two control groups on a word reading test, even though no word reading had been taught in the phoneme awareness condition. In follow-up studies with kindergarten students, the phoneme awareness treatment again produced superior word recognition and spelling as compared with control performance (Ball & Blachman, 1991; Blachman, 1991; Tangel & Blachman, 1992, 1995).

Lie (1991) taught Norwegian grade 1 students to analyze new words with respect to their phonological structure. This training promoted reading and spelling in grade 2, compared with control students not receiving phonological training. Weaker readers benefited more from the training than did stronger students. Similar findings have come from more recent studies, which have also found positive effects of integrating spelling and reading to promote phonemic awareness and letter learning (e.g., Hofslundsengen et al., 2016; Martins et al., 2016: Møller et al., 2021).

Cunningham (1990) compared two approaches to increasing the

phonemic awareness of kindergarten and grade 1 children. One approach was "skill and drill," with emphasis on segmentation and blending of phonemes. In the second approach, there was discussion of the value of decoding and phonemic awareness and how learning to segment and blend phonemes could be applied in reading. This latter approach was metacognitively very rich, providing children with a great deal of information about when, where, and why to use the knowledge of phonemes they were acquiring. Although both forms of instruction were effective, the metacognitively rich instruction was more effective at the grade 1 level, that is, consistent with the general perspective developed in this volume that instruction that increases children's awareness of when and where to use cognitive skills should result in more general and effective use of cognitive skills.

In more recent work, Roberts et al. (2020) compared two approaches to teaching letters and the impact on letter sound accuracy and phonemic awareness with preschoolers. The first group in this particular study were taught letters within a context such as while reading stories, within words, and within personal names, while the second group received letter instruction in isolation. The isolated instruction included introducing a letter of the day, modeling of letter sounds, repeating the letter name and sound as a group, and connecting the letter to an animal whose name begins with that letter. The results suggested that the group who received the isolated letter instruction saw a larger increase in phonemic awareness and letter sound accuracy; however, there was no difference between the two groups when it came to identifying letter names (Roberts et al., 2020).

We have presented these results of true experimental evaluations of phonemic awareness training in some detail because these studies are very important. In general, regardless of the specific methods used to measure phonemic awareness or the specific comparison conditions (e.g., no-instruction controls or alternative-instruction controls), phonemic awareness instruction has been successful in promoting phonemic awareness (Murray, 1995). But, as just detailed, such instruction does much more, positively affecting early reading achievement.

From those who are opposed to offering instruction aimed specifically at promoting phonemic awareness, we have heard the objection that there is no causal evidence linking phonemic awareness and improved reading. That claim is simply not true. When there is an experimental manipulation of phonemic awareness instruction (i.e., some children receive it and some do not, with recipients determined by random assignment), there is a sound basis for making a causal claim about the effects of phonemic awareness instruction on subsequent reading achievement. In addition to the causal studies already discussed, interested readers should also see the work of Byrne and Fielding-Barnsley (1991, 1993, 1995); Byrne et al., (2000); O'Connor et al. (1995); Vellutino and Scanlon (1987); Vellutino et al. (2008); Williams (1980); and Wise and Olson (1995). When all of the relevant data were considered by the NRP (2000; Adams, 2001; Ehri et al., 2001), the case that developing phonemic awareness between 4 and 6 years of age has powerful positive effects on subsequent reading achievement was clear. The clearest effect of phonemic awareness was displayed on the ability to decode words, although there was even some impact on comprehension. Learning to read is easier and more certain if the child has achieved a high level of phonemic awareness than if the child has not.

Unfortunately, some children do not receive phonemic awareness instruction. Sometimes the argument is made that, because the meaning emphasis involves so much work with poetry, children in such kindergartens receive sufficient exposure to tasks requiring phonemic awareness. Recall, however, that awareness of rhyme, which is the aspect of phonemic awareness that would seem to be most stimulated by poetry experiences, is only one form of phonemic awareness, and one of the easiest of the phonemic awareness tasks at that.

We have also heard the objection that phonemic awareness instruction is boring. However, with an increase of technology, programs and applications are finding ways to make learning experiences more engaging. For example, you might review ABRACADABRA (A Balanced Reading Approach for Canadians Designed to Achieve the Best Results for All), an internet-based reading software program for helping young children learn to read (Abrami et al., 2010). This software was used as a component of classroom reading lessons and produced significantly better performances on phonological blending, phoneme segmentation, and letter–sound knowledge in a large-scale effectiveness study (Savage et al., 2013). The program required little (1 day) training for classroom teachers and yet had a strong positive effect on early reading skills development when compared with the outcomes of students in the control classrooms who did not have access to the software. An ABRACADABRA daily session involved the kindergarten and first-grade children in 10 minutes of word-level work, 10 minutes of text reading, 20 minutes of collaborative work, and 20 minutes of extension activities. Both developing oral reading fluency and the use of comprehension strategies were emphasized. However, at posttest, no differences were found on sight word reading, fluency, or reading comprehension. Thus, the ABRACADABRA software fostered the development of several important prereading skills but had a more limited effect on fostering the later developing skills of oral reading fluency and reading comprehension. Nonetheless, there was high implementation fidelity, especially among first-grade teachers (96%), suggesting that the children in these classrooms found participating in the ABRACADABRA program both interesting and entertaining.

We do caution teachers from relying heavily on prepackaged programs for phonemic awareness instruction. As Brown et al. (2021) found, not all reading programs provide appropriate reading instruction, especially with struggling readers. Brown et al. (2021) specifically found popular reading programs used in Utah kindergarten classrooms were not always developmentally appropriate for students, and struggling readers often did not have the necessary skills in order to have success. Given that some children do not acquire phonemic segmentation proficiencies in kindergarten and grade 1, our hunch is that this occurs because too many teachers still do not know how to develop children's phonemic segmentation. This surmise is based, in part, on the many questions we receive from teachers about what phonemic awareness is and how it can be developed in children. There is also a growing database indicating that teachers lack understanding of phonemic awareness as well as knowledge of how to promote many other beginning reading competencies, with some teachers not aware at all that they are deficient in understanding what should be taught and how to teach it (Bos et al., 2001; Cunningham et al., 2004; Piasta et al., 2009; Spear-Swerling & Brucker, 2003). Not surprisingly, how much the teacher knows about beginning reading makes a difference in what gets taught in the classroom and ultimately in student achievement, although the relationships typically are not particularly strong ones (Hoffman et al., 2003; McCutchen, Abbott, et al., 2002; McCutchen, Harry, et al., 2002; Moats & Foorman, 2003; Piasta et al., 2009).

There is a real need to heighten teachers' awareness about how phonemic awareness and other beginning reading competencies can be fostered in students. For a very good overview of much of the evidence-based knowledge pertaining to beginning reading instruction, we recommend McGill-Franzen's *Kindergarten Literacy* (2006). This book is helpful throughout the primary grades, for the knowledge that teachers need to teach reading shifts dramatically from kindergarten to first grade.

We close this subsection by noting that, despite the evidence that phonemic awareness can be inculcated successfully in isolation, it might be a mistake to do so. Schneider et al. (2000) studied German kindergarten children who were at risk for reading problems because of weak phonological skills. The children subsequently received either instruction in phonemic awareness and letter–sound training or in phonemic awareness alone or in letter sounds alone. When measured in grades 1 and 2, the differences between conditions were not huge, but there were consistent small differences that favored the combined approach. Fuchs et al. (2001) found comparable effects on acquisition of phonemic awareness from phonemic awareness instruction alone and combined with explicit decoding instruction, but with subsequent advantage on decoding favoring the combined training condition. Our intuition is that we need more studies of such combined approaches not only because combined phonemic awareness and phonics instruction might be more powerful (see Bus & van IJzendoorn, 1999), but also because it is more likely to occur in school. Although we have seen many studies of isolated phonemic awareness instruction in the pages of journals, when we see such instruction in school, it is usually occurring with phonics instruction.

Development of Phonemic Awareness through Reading

Just as development of phonemic awareness leads to improved reading, so does reading increase phonemic awareness (e.g., Goswami, 2002a; Goswami & Bryant, 1990), beginning in the preschool years (Burgess & Lonigan, 1998). Among others, Wimmer et al. (1991) and Perfetti (1992; Perfetti et al., 1987; Share, 2008) have presented evidence that phonemic awareness is increased by reading, with the implication that reading-induced increases in phonemic awareness in turn influence subsequent development of reading competence. Again, the rich get richer by reading more (Silven et al., 2004)!

We have heard some folks who are aware that phonemic awareness does increase through reading argue that that is the proof that instruction aimed specifically at the development of phonemic awareness, such as that detailed in the last subsection, is unnecessary. They argue that phonemic awareness will develop from immersing the child in reading. Of course, there is a chicken-and-egg problem here, as the child who is initially low in phonemic awareness experiences more difficulties in learning to decode print (more about this in the next chapter) and hence is less able to read than other children and thus benefits less from reading. We are certain that the phrase is getting boring by now but, again, *the rich get richer*, with children high in phonemic awareness initially learning to read more certainly and thus deriving greater benefits from opportunities to read.

The scientific community has made progress in cracking this chicken-and-egg dilemma, however. The specifics of the analyses are too detailed for presentation here. Suffice it to say that in some analyses phonemic awareness seems to contribute more to learning to read than learning to read contributes to phonemic awareness (Hulme et al., 2002; Nation et al., 2001; Wagner et al., 1994, 1997), and in others it is just the opposite (e.g., Carroll et al., 2003; Goswami, 2002a, 2002b). As we make this point, we must also keep in mind that reading is very good for the young language learner and reader, regardless of whether reading is the chicken or the egg here. Thus, when parents and children read alphabet books together, the child learns about the alphabet and words but also improves in phonemic awareness, and vice versa (Murray et al., 1996). Consistent with the balanced perspective in this book, reading books with children and teaching them skills are complementary activities, with the reciprocity between development of phonemic awareness and reading the best explanation for the patterns of outcomes in at least some studies (e.g., Badian, 2001; Neuhaus & Swank, 2002; Sprenger-Charolles et al., 2003).

There is another set of data devastating to critics of phonemic awareness instruction. When activities that are explicitly intended to increase phonemic awareness are added to meaning-emphasis classrooms, there are discernible benefits. In a study of Australian kindergarten instruction, Castle et al. (1994) manipulated the presence or absence of phonemic awareness instruction for kindergarten students experiencing a meaning-emphasis program. They carried out two studies, one focusing on development of spelling skills and the other on the development of ability to read words not seen previously. The phonemic awareness instruction involved two 20-minute sessions a week for 10 weeks. Control participants received supplementary instruction that involved development of skills not related to phonemic awareness. Although the effects were not large, there were greater gains in spelling skills and reading of pseudowords (i.e., invented words, which ensured that students had not seen them before) in the phonemic awareness training conditions than in the control conditions.

Although Castle et al. (1994) have offered the most carefully controlled insertion of phonemic awareness instruction into what were certainly meaning-emphasis classrooms, there are other studies in which phonemic awareness has been added to classrooms. Thus, Byrne and Fielding-Barnsley (1991, 1993, 1995; Byrne et al., 2000) reported long-term gains from adding phonemic awareness instruction to the preschool experiences of 4-year-olds (i.e., 12 half-hour sessions, once a week). Kindergarten children in a study by Blachman et al. (1994) had previously experienced instruction that was so incomplete with respect to development of skills that the children knew only two letters on average by the middle of the kindergarten year. Adding 11 weeks of systematic phonemic awareness instruction at the end of the year, however, did have an effect on the quality of children's invented spellings, with the trained children producing spellings much closer to the sound pattern of words than did control participants. The trained children were also much more likely than controls to be able to spell words correctly.

In conclusion, when phonemic awareness instruction is added to educational environments in which little skills instruction is occurring, there are clear benefits for the students receiving it. Although the positive effects of phonemic awareness instruction were not large in the Castle et al. (1994) study, they are apparent on several different measures. Moreover, the phonemic awareness instruction in these investigations has been relatively brief as compared with some commercial versions of phonemic awareness instruction, so that detection of effects in that experiment are notable. The phonemic awareness instruction in the studies was brief, but it nonetheless produced positive effects as compared with ongoing instruction that was weak in phonemic awareness training, which further encourages the conclusion that even small amounts of phonemic awareness instruction can be very potent.

Summary

Many kindergarten and grade 1 children lack the awareness that words are streams of sounds that can be disentangled and that sounds can be assembled to produce words. They lack phonemic awareness, a metalinguistic insight that seems to be essential in learning to read, at least in an alphabetic language such as English. Fortunately, phonemic awareness can be developed through instruction, with clear benefits to subsequent acquisition of reading skills. This is an active area of research, with analyses of how teaching students to attend to their articulations of sounds (i.e., mouth movements; Castiglioni-Spalten & Ehri, 2003) improves phonemic awareness and learning to read. There is also assessment of how finger-point reading in kindergarten (i.e., pointing to words as the teacher and group reads them) impacts phonemic awareness and other reading processes (Morris et al., 2003; Uhry, 2002). Not surprisingly, there continues to be research on computer-based approaches to the development of phonemic awareness as well (e.g., Abrami et al., 2010; Cassady & Smith, 2003–2004).

The associations between phonemic awareness and successfully learning to read have prompted much attention to this particular aspect of literacy development. The result has been increased knowledge about phonemic awareness and its development so that clear guidance now can be offered to practicing kindergarten teachers about how to develop phonemic awareness in their students (Table 4.1). Kindergarten is the right time for such instruction since phonemic awareness is an important prerequisite to learning to decode, which is typically a key focus of grade 1 reading instruction.

Frequently, we have heard the claim that phonemic awareness can be developed by having children spend a great deal of time listening to and interacting with books that are filled with playfully varied speech sounds— for example, rhymes and alliterations. Indeed, such language exposure probably does promote phonemic awareness somewhat (Fernandez-Fein & Baker, 1997; Goswami, 2001), and hence it is noteworthy that a list of books that could be used in this fashion has been compiled (e.g., Yopp, 1995). At a minimum, high numbers of such books in kindergarten can provide lots of stimulus for vocabulary development and for students to think about the sounds of words. We also frequently encounter the claim that phonemic awareness will develop if children are allowed to use invented spellings in

TABLE 4.1. Preschool and Kindergarten Strategies

Strategy	Classroom implications
Expose children to text throughout the classroom	Include text in play centers with written letters, envelopes, menus, eye charts, etc.
Have a space for a classroom library	Provide a space for students to engage with texts.
	Teachers should support students' engagement through modeling and showing students how to use books.
Develop centers with literacy in mind	Create centers within the classroom that will expose children to literacy elements, such as a post office or grocery store.
Read to and with students	Storybook reading: Allows adult and child to interact and discuss the story being read. Allows for adult to model reading and scaffolding.
	Expose students to many books
Promote reading at home	Allow students to take books home to read with parents.
	Provide resources to parents for interacting with the text and their child.
Phonemic segmentation of words	Turtle talk: Students say words slowly (as a turtle might say) to draw out the phonemes in each word.
Expose students to letters	Attach sheet with both upper- and lower-case letters to student desks.
	Have alphabet display visible to all students in classroom.
	Have alphabet books available in the classroom.
	Use an alphabet arc to expose and review letter names and sounds.
	Provide activities in the kindergarten class for students to learn about each letter (e.g., a class-developed chart or pairing students with names that begin with different letters).
	Introduce letter sounds, model letter sounds, connect letters to something students know (e.g., animal, character, or toy).
	Most of all, allow for students to practice with letters.
Phonemic awareness instruction	Have students rhyme words, divide words into syllables.
	Integrate spelling and reading together throughout the day.
	Talk through the importance of decoding and support student blending and segmenting of phonemes.

their writings. In fact, there is no doubt that when children invent spellings they are thinking hard about the constituent sounds of words as well as how those constituent sounds can be represented together as the letters in words (Read, 1971; Richgels, 2001). Associations between invented spelling and phonemic awareness have been observed often (Clarke, 1988; Ehri, 1989; Mann et al., 1987; Treiman, 1985). Although we do not think that wordplay and invented spelling will be enough to develop complete phonemic awareness for all children, there are several good reasons to encourage children to engage in wordplay and attempts to write, including that such activities can promote phonemic awareness.

One reaction that we have heard when arguments are made to improve the instruction given to preschoolers is that gains from instruction during preschool are wiped out later—that they are short-term gains. With respect to instruction in phonemic awareness, that is not entirely true. Phonemic awareness instruction can explain about 12% of word recognition performance in the early primary years; although it explains much less of the variance in reading in the later primary and middle elementary years, the effects are still detectable (Bus & van IJzendoorn, 1999). The decline in the importance of phonological awareness with advancing age probably reflects the reality that phonological awareness is more important when developing word recognition is the critical competency emphasized in reading instruction (i.e., during kindergarten and grade 1) than later, when higher-order components of reading (e.g., comprehension) are emphasized more (de Jong & van der Leij, 1999). It also suggests that with more years of schooling most children develop the phonemic awareness proficiencies that would have served them well in kindergarten and first grade.

We are impressed with the evidence that high-quality preschool experiences can have very positive impacts on later reading achievement, including reading achievement measured many years after preschool has been completed (Barnett, 2001; Gorey, 2001; Schweinhart & Weikart, 1997). Given the positive influence of high-quality early childhood education on later academic achievement, why have we not said more about early childhood education in this book?

It is because we do not study early childhood education and do not have the fully informed opinion that we have with respect to elementary schooling, which gets the largest amount of coverage in this volume. That said, when we talk about balanced literacy instruction, we always make the case that the preschool years are critical for literacy development and that educators who wait until kindergarten entrance to intervene in the lives of at-risk children are making a huge mistake. We do know how to design literacy-rich preschool environments that promote children's understanding of print and writing conventions as well as letters and sounds (see Yaden et al., 2000, for a review). Failing to provide rich emergent literacy experiences during the preschool years can leave a child far behind his or her kindergarten classmates; a set of rich emergent literacy experiences, at home and in preschool, can provide long-lasting advantages.

SUMMARY AND CONCLUDING REFLECTIONS

1. Chapters 2 and 3 introduced the phonological processes involved in reading—that is, speech as a mediator of word recognition. The important point at this juncture is that Vygotsky also made the case that the development of problem-solving skills involving speech occurs in interactions with others with problem-solving dialogues internalized by young children and adults. There is very good reason for adults and children to spend time in verbal interaction around problems, including the problems associated with learning about books.

2. At several points in this chapter, research has been reported in which parents are taught how to interact with their children so that parent–child interactions are healthier and more productive. Even brief interventions produce dramatic shifts in these studies. This work makes clear the conclusion that parent–child interactions have a plasticity about them: Parents who are not appropriately responsive to their children can learn to be more responsive. This also anticipates a theme that is reiterated throughout this book: Some adult–child interactions are more likely to promote the cognitive development of children than others. In healthy interactions, the adult does not demand too much or too little, but rather supports the child who is working on new competencies.

3. That natural parent–child interactions alone are typically not enough to prepare the child for success at beginning reading comes through especially clearly in the research on phonemic awareness. More positively, a great deal has been learned about how adults can interact with children in order to develop their phonemic awareness—and it is not by just immersing children in reading and writing and things literate. Rather, it is through instruction that makes sense in light of our understanding of phonemic awareness that has been developed through careful research. However, reports of the quality of literacy lessons in early childhood centers, particularly those targeting children from low-income families, have, at best, a mixed record of attending to the research. While there are reports of high-quality preschools and evidence of the potential long-standing positive effects of such programs, there exists also a set of reports that depict early childhood education for children from low-income families as exhibiting despairingly uneven program qualities (e.g., McGill-Franzen et al., 2002).

4. Whitehurst and Lonigan (1998, 2001) defined "outside-in" literacy components as coming from outside the printed word and developing through informal social processes during the preschool years. These include general language competencies, such as knowledge of concepts and

the words expressing concepts as well as productive use of syntax. Children learn about story structures from such interactions. They acquire an understanding about the conventions of print, including that books are read from left to right and from top to bottom. Developing these understandings are greatly facilitated with the use of big books—books large enough to be displayed in the front of the classroom as the teacher is reading the book aloud.

In contrast are "inside-out" components of literacy, which are sources of information inside the printed word, permitting the translation of words into sounds. These include knowing the names of letters and letter–sound associations, phonological awareness, and understanding that writing of words involves translating sounds into letters. These skills seem to require more explicit teaching than the outside-in competencies.

Children who have preschool experiences promoting a balance of outside-in and inside-out capabilities are better prepared for reading instruction in the primary grades than are children living in a language-impoverished environment (Piasta, Justice, et al., 2012; Whitehurst & Lonigan, 1998, 2001). For example, the child who has been read to frequently develops a number of print concepts useful in beginning reading; the phonemically aware child is prepared to learn how to sound out words; the child whose comprehension of language is well developed through many language interactions during the preschool years readily understands what was read.

Frijters et al. (2000) provided a very nice demonstration of the value of both inside-out and outside-in experiences. They measured the phonemic awareness of kindergarten children and also took measures of how much storybook reading they experienced. What they found was that phonemic awareness predicted letter–sound and letter-name knowledge and storybook reading was linked to vocabulary development. Inside-out and outside-in competencies are both necessary and are complementary to one another in promoting a child's literacy development in school. Children must learn how to read the words and make meaning from those words.

5. It is surprising that very little research attention is being given to technology and its impact on early literacy development. There is the occasional investigation of internet impact (e.g., Karchmer, 2001; Leu, 2002) and various types of interactive media that are computer-driven (e.g., de Jong & Bus, 2002; Ricci & Beal, 2002). The differences produced by these options, as compared with conventional reading, have been rather small (James-Burdumy et al., 2010). The historic success of *Sesame Street* (Ball & Bogatz, 1970; Bogatz & Ball, 1971; Fisch, 2004) has been complemented by evaluations of programs such as *Between the Lions*, with generally modest and somewhat inconsistent effects, although they are positive enough to justify continued support of such programming as supportive of beginning

literacy development (e.g., Linebarger et al., 2004; Savage et al., 2009). Given the expanding presence of electronic products presumably aimed at promoting literacy, there is a great need for additional research in this problem area.

6. Finally, we close this chapter with a reflection on culture and emergent literacy skills. The language experienced by preschoolers in middle-class and working-class homes is typically very different (Gee, 2001; Heath, 1996; Watson, 2001; Wells, 1981). It is rather easy to make the case that the language and parent–child interactions occurring in middle-class, English-first-language American homes is more congruent with the development of both outside-in and inside-out competencies considered in this chapter (Goldenberg, 2001; Goldenberg & Gallimore, 1995; Whitehurst & Lonigan, 1998), although there are surely many children in low-income families who do have high-quality emergent literacy experiences (Anderson & Stokes, 1984; Clark, 1983; Goldenberg & Gallimore, 1995; Goldenberg et al., 1992; Heath, 1996; Paratore et al., 1999; Taylor & Dorsey-Gaines, 1988; Teale, 1986). Nonetheless, students from low-income, English-second-language, and some minority homes are at risk for difficulties in beginning reading, for there are great schisms between the home and school cultures for many of these children (Delpit, 1995; Feagans & Haskins, 1986; Heath, 1996; Ogbu, 1982; Pellegrini, 2001; Steele, 1992; Vernon-Feagans, 1996; Vernon-Feagans et al., 2001). With a growing body of research and number of emergent bilinguals in classrooms, the addition of Chapter 9 provides a more extensive discussion of research based approaches for supporting literacy with emergent bilingual instruction.

Many of the interventions highlighted in this volume have good track records with at-risk populations, which is an important motivation for developing a balanced mix of the types of instruction covered in the various chapters of this book.

REFERENCES

Abrami, P. C., White, B., & Wade, A. (2010). *ABRACADABRA LTK Teachers Guide*. Available at *http://grover.concordia.ca/abracadabra/resources/download/LTKGuide_ABRA_20130327.pdf*.

Adams, M. J. (1990). *Beginning to read*. Harvard University Press.

Adams, M. J. (2001). Alphabetic anxiety and explicit, systematic phonics instruction: A cognitive science perspective. In S. B. Neuman & D. K. Dickinson (Eds.), *Handbook of early literacy research* (pp. 66–80). Guilford Press.

Anderson, A. B., & Stokes, S. J. (1984). Social and institutional influences on the development and practice of literacy. In H. Goelman, A. Oberg, & F. Smith (Eds.), *Awakening to literacy* (pp. 24–37). Heinemann.

Anderson-Yockel, J., & Haynes, W. (1994). Joint picture-book reading strategies in working-class African American and white mother–toddler dyads. *Journal of Speech, Language, and Hearing Research, 37,* 583–593.

Anthony, J. L., & Lonigan, C. J. (2004). The nature of phonological awareness: Converging evidence from four studies of preschool and early grade school children. *Journal of Educational Psychology, 96,* 43–55.

Anthony, J. L., Lonigan, C. J., Driscoll, K., Phillips, B. M., & Burgess, S. R. (2003). Phonological sensitivity: A quasi-parallel progression of word structure units and cognitive operations. *Reading Research Quarterly, 38,* 470–487.

Applebee, A. N., & Langer, J. A. (1983). Instructional scaffolding: Reading and writing as natural language activities. *Language Arts, 60,* 168–175.

Aram, D., & Biron, S. (2004). Joint storybook reading and joint writing interventions among low SES preschoolers: Differential contributions to early literacy. *Early Childhood Research Quarterly, 19,* 588–610.

Arnold, D. H., Lonigan, C. J., Whitehurst, G. J., & Epstein, J. N. (1994). Accelerating language development through picture book reading: Replication and extension to a videotape training format. *Journal of Educational Psychology, 86,* 235–243.

Badian, N. A. (2001). Phonological and orthographic processing: Their roles in reading prediction. *Annals of Dyslexia, 51,* 179–202.

Baker, L., Sonnenschein, S., Serpell, R., Fernandez-Fein, S., & Scher, D. (1994). *Contexts of emergent literacy: Everyday home experiences of urban pre-kindergarten children* (Reading Research Report No. 24). National Reading Research Center.

Ball, E. W., & Blachman, B. A. (1988). Phoneme segmentation training: Effect on reading readiness. *Annals of Dyslexia, 38,* 203–225.

Ball, E. W., & Blachman, B. A. (1991). Does phoneme segmentation training in kindergarten make a difference in early word recognition and developmental spelling? *Reading Research Quarterly, 26,* 49–66.

Ball, S., & Bogatz, G. A. (1970). *The first year of "Sesame Street": An evaluation.* Educational Testing Service.

Barnett, W. S. (2001). Preschool education for economically disadvantaged children: Effects on reading achievement and related outcomes. In S. B. Neuman & D. K. Dickinson (Eds.), *Handbook of early literacy research* (pp. 421–443). Guilford Press.

Bergin, C. (2001). The parent–child relationship during beginning reading. *Journal of Literacy Research, 33,* 681–706.

Bernstein, B. (1965). *Class, codes, and control: Vol. 1. Theoretical studies toward a sociology of language.* Routledge & Kegan Paul.

Blachman, B. A. (1991). Phonological awareness: Implications for prereading and early reading instruction. In S. A. Brady & D. P. Shankweiler (Eds.), *Phonological processes in literacy: A tribute to Isabelle Y. Liberman* (pp. 29–36). Erlbaum.

Blachman, B. A. (2000). Phonological awareness. In M. L. Kamil, P. B. Mosenthal, P. D. Pearson, & R. Barr (Eds.), *Handbook of reading research* (Vol. 3, pp. 483–502). Erlbaum.

Blachman, B. A., Ball, E., Black, R., & Tangel, D. (1994). Kindergarten teachers develop phoneme awareness in low-income, inner-city classrooms: Does it make a difference? *Reading and Writing, 6,* 1–17.

Bogatz, G. A., & Ball, S. (1971). *The second year of "Sesame Street": A continuing evaluation.* Educational Testing Service.

Bos, C., Mather, N., Dickson, S., Podhajski, B., & Chard, D. (2001). Perceptions and knowledge of preservice and inservice educators about early reading instruction. *Annals of Dyslexia, 51,* 97–120.

Bowey, J. A. (2002). Reflections on onset-rime and phoneme sensitivity as predictors of beginning word reading. *Journal of Experimental Child Psychology, 82,* 29–40.

Bradley, L. (1989). Predicting learning disabilities. In J. Dumont & H. Nakken (Eds.), *Learning disabilities: Vol. 2. Cognitive, social, and remedial aspects* (pp. 1–18). Swets & Zeitlinger.

Bradley, L., & Bryant, P. E. (1983). Categorizing sounds and learning to read: A causal connection. *Nature, 301*, 419–421.

Bradley, L., & Bryant, P. E. (1985). *Rhyme and reason in reading and spelling* (International Academy for Research in Learning Disabilities Series). University of Michigan Press.

Bradley, L., & Bryant, P. E. (1991). Phonological skills before and after learning to read. In S. A. Brady & D. P. Shankweiler (Eds.), *Phonological processes in literacy: A tribute to Isabelle Y. Liberman* (pp. 37–45). Erlbaum.

Brown, K. J., Patrick, K. C., Fields, M. K., & Craig, G. T. (2021). Phonological awareness materials in Utah kindergartens: A case study in the science of reading. *Reading Research Quarterly, 56*, S249–S272.

Burgess, S. R., & Lonigan, C. J. (1998). Bidirectional relations of phonological sensitivity and prereading abilities: Evidence from a preschool sample. *Journal of Experimental Child Psychology, 70*, 117–141.

Bus, A. G. (1993). Attachment and emergent literacy. *International Journal of Educational Research, 19*, 573–581.

Bus, A. G. (1994). The role of social context in emergent literacy. In E. M. H. Assink (Ed.), *Literacy acquisition and social context* (pp. 9–24). Harvester Wheatsheaf.

Bus, A. G., Leseman, P. P. M., & Keultjes, P. (2000). Joint book reading across cultures: A comparison of Surinamese–Dutch, Turkish–Dutch, and Dutch parent–child dyads. *Journal of Literacy Research, 32*, 53–76.

Bus, A. G., & van IJzendoorn, M. H. (1988). Mother–child interactions, attachment, and emergent literacy: A cross-sectional study. *Child Development, 59*, 1262–1272.

Bus, A. G., & van IJzendoorn, M. H. (1992). Patterns of attachment in frequently and infrequently reading mother–child dyads. *Journal of Genetic Psychology, 153*, 395–403.

Bus, A. G., & van IJzendoorn, M. H. (1995). Mothers reading to their 3-year-olds: The role of mother–child attachment security in becoming literate. *Reading Research Quarterly, 30*, 998–1015.

Bus, A. G., & van IJzendoorn, M. H. (1999). Phonological awareness and early reading: A meta-analysis of experimental training studies. *Journal of Educational Psychology, 91*, 403–414.

Bus, A. G., van IJzendoorn, M. H., & Pellegrini, A. D. (1995). Joint book reading makes for success in learning to read: A meta-analysis on intergenerational transmission of literacy. *Review of Educational Research, 65*, 1–21.

Byrne, B., & Fielding-Barnsley, R. (1991). Evaluation of a program to teach phonemic awareness to young children. *Journal of Educational Psychology, 83*, 451–455.

Byrne, B., & Fielding-Barnsley, R. (1993). Evaluation of a program to teach phonemic awareness to young children: A 1-year follow-up. *Journal of Educational Psychology, 85*, 104–111.

Byrne, B., & Fielding-Barnsley, R. (1995). Evaluation of a program to teach phonemic awareness to young children: A 2- and 3-year follow-up and a new preschool trial. *Journal of Educational Psychology, 87*, 488–503.

Byrne, B., Fielding-Barnsley, R., & Ashley, L. (2000). Effects of preschool phoneme identity training after six years: Outcome level distinguished from rate of response. *Journal of Educational Psychology, 92*, 659–667.

Cardoso-Martins, C., & Pennington, B. F. (2004). The relationship between phoneme awareness and rapid serial naming skills and literacy acquisition: The role of developmental period and reading ability. *Scientific Studies of Reading, 8*, 27–52.

Carroll, J. M., Snowling, M. J., Hulme, C., & Stevenson, J. (2003). The development of phonological awareness in preschool children. *Developmental Psychology, 39*, 913–923.

Cassady, J. C., & Smith, L. L. (2003–2004). The impact of reading-focused integrated learning system on phonological awareness in kindergarten. *Journal of Literacy Research*, *35*, 947–964.

Castiglioni-Spalten, M. L., & Ehri, L. C. (2003). Phonemic awareness instruction: Contribution of articulatory segmentation to novice beginners' reading and spelling. *Scientific Studies of Reading*, *7*, 25–52.

Castle, J. M., Riach, J., & Nicholson, T. (1994). Getting off to a better start in reading and spelling: The effects of phonemic awareness instruction within a whole language program. *Journal of Educational Psychology*, *86*, 350–359.

Chomsky, C. (1972). Stages in language development and reading exposure. *Harvard Educational Review*, *42*(1), 1–33.

Clark, M. M. (1976). *Young fluent readers: What can they teach us?* Heinemann.

Clark, R. (1983). *Family life and school achievement: Why poor black children succeed or fail.* University of Chicago Press.

Clarke, L. K. (1988). Invented versus traditional spelling in first graders' writings: Effects on learning to spell and read. *Research in the Teaching of English*, *22*, 281–309.

Clay, M. M. (1966). *Emergent reading behavior.* Unpublished doctoral dissertation, University of Auckland, New Zealand.

Clay, M. M. (1967). The reading behavior of five-year-old children: A research report. *New Zealand Journal of Educational Studies*, *2*, 11–31.

Cochran-Smith, M. (1984). *The making of a reader.* Ablex.

Cox, B. E. (1994). Young children's regulatory talk: Evidence of emerging metacognitive control over literary products and processes. In R. B. Ruddell, M. R. Ruddell, & H. Sinder (Eds.), *Theoretical models and processes of reading* (pp. 733–756). International Reading Association.

Crain-Thoreson, C., & Dale, P. S. (1992). Do early talkers become early readers? Linguistic precocity, preschool language, and emergent literacy. *Developmental Psychology*, *28*, 421–429.

Crain-Thoreson, C., & Dale, P. S. (1995, April). *Parent vs. staff storybook reading as an intervention for language delay.* Paper presented at the biennial meeting of the Society for Research in Child Development, Indianapolis, IN.

Cunningham, A. E. (1990). Explicit versus implicit instruction in phonemic awareness. *Journal of Experimental Child Psychology*, *50*, 429–444.

Cunningham, A. E., Perry, K. E., Stanovich, K. E., & Stanovich, P. J. (2004). Disciplinary knowledge of K–3 teachers and their knowledge calibration in the domain of early literacy. *Annals of Dyslexia*, *54*, 139–167.

de Jong, P. F., & Bus, A. G. (2002). Quality of book-reading matters for emergent readers: An experiment with the same book in a regular or electronic format. *Journal of Educational Psychology*, *94*, 145–155.

de Jong, P. F., & van der Leij, A. (1999). Specific contributions of phonological abilities to early reading acquisition: Results from a Dutch latent variable longitudinal study. *Journal of Educational Psychology*, *91*, 450–476.

DeLoache, J. S., & DeMendoza, O. A. P. (1987). Joint picturebook interactions of mothers and 1-year-old children. *British Journal of Developmental Psychology*, *5*, 111–123.

Delpit, L. (1995). *Other people's children: Cultural conflict in the classroom.* New Press.

Dickinson, D. K., McCabe, A., Anastasopoulos, L., Peisner-Feinberg, E. S., & Poe, M. D. (2003). The comprehensive language approach to early literacy: The interrelationships among vocabulary, phonological sensitivity, and prior knowledge among preschool-aged children. *Journal of Educational Psychology*, *95*, 465–481.

Dickinson, D. K., McCabe, A., & Clark-Chiarelli, N. (2004). Preschool-based prevention of reading disability. In C. A. Stone, E. R. Selliman, B. J. Ehren, & K. Apel (Eds.),

Handbook of language and literacy: Development and disorders (pp. 209–227). Guilford Press.

Dickinson, D. K., & Smith, M. W. (1994). Long-term effects of preschool teachers' book readings on low-income children's vocabulary and story comprehension. *Reading Research Quarterly, 29,* 104–122.

Dudley-Marling, C., & Lucas, K. (2009). Pathologizing the language and culture of poor children. *Language Arts, 86(5),* 362–370.

Duke, N. K. (2000a). For the rich it's richer: Print experiences and environments offered to children in very low- and very high-socioeconomic status first-grade classrooms. *American Educational Research Journal, 37,* 441–478.

Duke, N. K. (2000b). Print environments and experiences offered to first-grade students in very-low- and very-high-SES school districts. *Reading Research Quarterly, 35,* 456–457.

Dunning, D. B., Mason, J. M., & Stewart, J. P. (1994). Reading to preschoolers: A response to Scarborough & Dobrich (1994) and recommendations for future research. *Developmental Review, 14,* 324–339.

Ehri, L. C. (1989). Movement into word reading and spelling: How spelling contributes to reading. In J. M. Mason (Ed.), *Reading and writing connections* (pp. 65–81). Allyn & Bacon.

Ehri, L. C., Nunes, S. R., Willows, D. M., Schuster, B. V., Yaghoub-Zadeh, Z., & Shanahan, T. (2001). Phonemic awareness instruction helps children learn to read: Evidence from the National Reading Panel's meta-analysis. *Reading Research Quarterly, 36,* 250–287.

Elbro, C., Borstrøm, I., & Petersen, D. K. (1998). Predicting dyslexia from kindergarten: The importance of distinctiveness of phonological representations of lexical items. *Reading Research Quarterly, 33,* 36–60.

Elbro, C., & Scarborough, H. S. (2004). Early identification. In T. Nunes & P. Bryant (Eds.), *Handbook of children's literacy* (pp. 339–359). Kluwer Academic.

Feagans, L., & Haskins, R. (1986). Neighborhood dialogues of black and white 5-year-olds. *Journal of Applied Developmental Psychology, 7,* 181–200.

Fernandez-Fein, S., & Baker, L. (1997). Rhyme and alliteration sensitivity and relevant experiences among preschoolers from diverse backgrounds. *Journal of Literacy Research, 29,* 433–459.

Fisch, S. M. (2004). *Children's learning from educational television: Sesame Street and beyond.* Erlbaum.

Flood, J. (1977). Parental styles in reading episodes with young children. *Reading Teacher, 30,* 864–867.

Frijters, J. C., Barron, R. W., & Brunello, M. (2000). Direct and mediated influences on home literacy and literacy interest on preschoolers' oral vocabulary and early written language skill. *Journal of Educational Psychology, 92,* 466–477.

Fuchs, D., Fuchs, L. S., Thompson, A., Al Otaiba, S., Yen, L., Yang, N. J., et al. (2001). Is reading important in reading-readiness programs? A randomized field trial with teachers as program implementers. *Journal of Educational Psychology, 93,* 251–267.

Garton, A. F., & Pratt, C. (2004). Reading stories. In T. Nunes & P. Bryant (Eds.), *Handbook of children's literacy* (pp. 213–228). Kluwer Academic.

Gee, J. P. (2001). A sociocultural perspective on early literacy. In S. B. Neuman & D. K. Dickinson (Eds.), *Handbook of early literacy research* (pp. 30–42). Guilford Press.

Goldenberg, C. (2001). Making schools work for low-income families in the 21st century. In S. B. Neuman & D. K. Dickinson (Eds.), *Handbook of early literacy research* (pp. 211–231). Guilford Press.

Goldenberg, C., & Gallimore, R. (1995). Immigrant Latino parents' values and beliefs about their children's education: Continuities and discontinuities across cultures and generations. In P. R. Pintrich & M. Maehr (Eds.), *Advances in motivation and achievement: Culture, ethnicity, and motivation* (Vol. 9, pp. 183–228). JAI Press.

Goldenberg, C., Reese, L., & Gallimore, R. (1992). Effects of school literacy materials on Latino children's home experiences and early reading achievement. *American Journal of Education, 100,* 497–536.

Gorey, K. M. (2001). Early childhood education: A meta-analytic affirmation of the short- and long-term benefits of educational opportunity. *School Psychology Quarterly, 16,* 9–30.

Goswami, U. (2000). Phonological and lexical processes. In M. Kamil, P. B. Mosenthal, P. D. Pearson, & R. Barr (Eds.), *Handbook of reading research* (Vol. 3, pp. 251–267). Erlbaum.

Goswami, U. (2001). Early phonological development and the acquisition of literacy. In S. B. Neuman & D. K. Dickinson (Eds.), *Handbook of early literacy research* (pp. 111–125). Guilford Press.

Goswami, U. (2002a). In the beginning was the rhyme? A reflection on Hulme, Hatcher, Nation, Brown, Adams, and Stuart (2002). *Journal of Experimental Child Psychology, 82,* 47–57.

Goswami, U. (2002b). Phonology, reading development, and dyslexia: A cross-linguistic perspective. *Annals of Dyslexia, 52,* 141–163.

Goswami, U., & Bryant, P. E. (1990). *Phonological skills and learning to read.* Erlbaum.

Gough, P. B. (1998). *Overselling phonemic awareness?* Paper presented at the annual meeting of the National Reading Conference, Austin, Texas.

Griffith, P. L. (1991). Phonemic awareness helps first graders invent spellings and third graders remember correct spellings. *Journal of Reading Behavior, 23,* 215–233.

Hammer, C. S. (1999). Guiding language development: How African American mothers and their infants structure play. *Journal of Speech and Hearing Research, 42,* 1219–1233.

Hammer, C. S. (2001). Come sit down and let mama read: Book reading interactions between African American mothers and their infants. In J. Harris, A. Kamhi, & K. Pollock (Eds.), *Literacy in African American communities* (pp. 21–44). Erlbaum.

Hammett, L. A., van Kleeck, A., & Huberty, C. J. (2003). Patterns of parents' extratextual interactions during book sharing with preschool children: A cluster analysis study. *Reading Research Quarterly, 38,* 442–468.

Hart, B., & Risley, T. R. (1995). *Meaningful differences in the everyday experience of young American children.* Brookes.

Heath, S. B. (1982). What no bedtime story means: Narrative skills at home and school. *Language in Society, 11,* 49–76.

Heath, S. B. (1996). *Ways with words: Language, life, and work in communities and classrooms.* Cambridge University Press.

Heath, S. B. (2012). *Words at work and play: Three decades in family and community life.* Cambridge University Press.

Hoffman, J. V., Roller, C. M., Maloch, B., Sailors, M., & Beretvas, N. (2003). *Prepared to make a difference: Final report of the National Commission on Excellence in Elementary Teacher Preparation for Reading.* International Reading Association.

Hofslundsengen, H., Hagtvet, B. E., & Gustafsson, J.-E. (2016). Immediate and delayed effects of invented writing intervention in preschool. *Reading and Writing: An Interdisciplinary Journal, 29*(7), 1473–1495.

Hudson, J. A. (1990). Constructive processing in children's event memory. *Developmental Psychology, 26,* 180–187.

Hulme, C., Hatcher, P. J., Nation, K., Brown, A., Adams, J., & Stuart, G. (2002). Phoneme awareness is a better predictor of early reading skill than onset-rime awareness. *Journal of Experimental Child Psychology, 82,* 2–28.

James-Burdumy, S., Deke, J., Lugo-Gil, J., Carey, N., Hershey, A., Gersten, R., et al. (2010). *The effectiveness of selected supplemental reading comprehension interventions: Findings from two cohorts* (NCEE 2010-4015). U.S. Department of Education.

Johnson, S. T. (1999). *Alphabet city*. Penguin.

Juel, C. (1988). Learning to read and write: A longitudinal study of 54 children from first through fourth grades. *Journal of Educational Psychology, 80*, 417–447.

Juel, C., Griffith, P. L., & Gough, P. B. (1986). Acquisition of literacy: A longitudinal study of children in first and second grade. *Journal of Educational Psychology, 78*, 243–255.

Justice, L. M., McGinty, A., Piasta, S. B., Kaderavek, J. N., & Fan, X. (2010). Print-focused read-alouds in pre-school classrooms: Intervention effectiveness and moderators of child outcomes. *Language, Speech, and Hearing Services in Schools, 41*, 504–520.

Karchmer, R. A. (2001). The journey ahead: Thirteen teachers report how the Internet influences literacy and literacy instruction in their K–12 classrooms. *Reading Research Quarterly, 36*, 442–466.

Kirby, J. R., Parrila, R. K., & Pfeiffer, S. L. (2003). Naming speed and phonological awareness as predictors of reading development. *Journal of Educational Psychology, 95*, 453–464.

Kohlberg, L., Yaeger, J., & Hjertholm, E. (1968). Private speech: Four studies and a review of theories. *Child Development, 39*, 691–736.

Koskinen, P. S., Blum, I. H., Bisson, S. A., Phillips, S. M., Creamer, T. S., & Baker, T. K. (2000). Book access, shared reading, and audio models: The effects of supporting the literacy learning of linguistically diverse students in school and at home. *Journal of Educational Psychology, 92*, 23–36.

Leichter, H. P. (1984). Families as environments for literacy. In H. Goelman, A. Oberg, & F. Smith (Eds.), *Awakening to literacy* (pp. 38–50). Heinemann.

Leseman, P. P. M., & de Jong, P. F. (1998). Home literacy: Opportunity, instruction, cooperation, and social–emotional quality predicting early reading achievement. *Reading Research Quarterly, 33*, 294–318.

Leu, D. J. (2002). The new literacies: Research on reading with the Internet. In A. Farstrup & S. J. Samuels (Eds.), *What research has to say about reading instruction* (3rd ed., pp. 310–336). International Reading Association.

Leyva, D., Sparks, A., & Reese, E. (2013). The link between preschoolers' phonological awareness and mothers' book-reading and reminiscing practices in low-income families. *Journal of Literacy Research, 44*(4), 426–447.

Lie, A. (1991). Effects of a training program for stimulating skills in word analysis in first-grade children. *Reading Research Quarterly, 26*, 234–250.

Linebarger, D. L., Kosanic, A. Z., Greenwood, C. R., & Doku, N. S. (2004). Effects of viewing the television program *Between the Lions* on the emergent literacy skills of young children. *Journal of Educational Psychology, 96*, 297–308.

Lonigan, C. J. (1994). Reading to preschoolers exposed: Is the emperor really naked? *Developmental Review, 14*, 303–323.

Lonigan, C. J., Anthony, J. L., & Burgess, S. R. (1995, April). *Exposure to print and preschool-age children's interest in literacy*. Paper presented at the biennial meeting of the Society for Research in Child Development, Indianapolis, IN.

Lundberg, I. (1991). Phonemic awareness can be developed without reading instruction. In S. A. Brady & D. P. Shankweiler (Eds.), *Phonological processes in literacy: A tribute to Isabelle Y. Liberman* (pp. 47–53). Erlbaum.

Lundberg, I., Frost, J., & Peterson, O. (1988). Effects of an extensive program for stimulating phonological awareness in preschool children. *Reading Research Quarterly, 23*, 263–284.

Maclean, M., Bryant, P., & Bradley, L. (1987). Rhymes, nursery rhymes, and reading in early childhood. *Merrill–Palmer Quarterly, 33*, 255–281.

Mann, V. A. (2003). Language processes: Keys to reading disability. In H. L. Swanson, K. R. Harris, & S. Graham (Eds.), *Handbook of learning disabilities* (pp. 213–228). Guilford Press.

Mann, V. A., & Foy, J. G. (2003). Phonological awareness, speech development, and letter knowledge in preschool children. *Annals of Dyslexia, 53*, 149–173.

Mann, V., Tobin, P., & Wilson, R. (1987). Measuring phonological awareness through the invented spellings of kindergarten children. *Merrill–Palmer Quarterly, 32*, 310–318.

Mann, V., & Wimmer, H. (2002). Phoneme awareness and pathways into literacy: A comparison of German and American children. *Reading and Writing, 15*, 653–682.

Martin, M. J. (1996). *From Anne to Zach.* Boyd Mills Press.

Martins, M. A., Salvador, L., Albuquerque, A., & Silva, C. (2016). Invented spelling activities in small groups and early spelling and reading. *Educational Psychology, 36*(4), 738–752.

McCutchen, D., Abbott, R. D., Green, L. B., Beretvas, N., Cox, S., Potter, N. S., et al. (2002). Beginning literacy: Links among teacher knowledge, teacher practice, and student learning. *Journal of Learning Disabilities, 35*, 69–86.

McCutchen, D., Harry, D. R., Cunningham, A. E., Cox, S., Sidman, S., & Covill, A. E. (2002). Reading teachers' knowledge of children's literature and English phonology. *Annals of Dyslexia, 52*, 207–228.

McGill-Franzen, A. (2006). *Kindergarten literacy.* Scholastic.

McGill-Franzen, A., Allington, R., Yokoi, L., & Brooks, G. (1999). Putting books in the room seems necessary but not sufficient. *Journal of Educational Research, 93*, 67–74.

McGill-Franzen, A., & Jordan, J. (2012). Emergent literacy. In R. Bean & A. Swan (Eds.), *Best practices of literacy leaders: Keys to school improvement* (pp. 127–146). Guilford Press.

McGill-Franzen, A. M., Lanford, C., & Adams, E. (2002). Learning to be literate: A comparison of five urban early childhood programs. *Journal of Educational Psychology, 94*(3), 443–464.

Metsala, J. L. (1999). Young children's phonological awareness and nonword repetition as a function of vocabulary development. *Journal of Educational Psychology, 91*, 3–19.

Moats, L. C., & Foorman, B. R. (2003). Measuring teachers' content knowledge of language and reading. *Annals of Dyslexia, 53*, 23–45.

Møller, H. L., Mortensen, J. O., & Elbro, C. (2021). Effects of integrated spelling in phonics instruction for at-risk children in kindergarten. *Reading & Writing Quarterly*, 1–16.

Morris, D., Bloodgood, J. W., Lomax, R. G., & Perney, J. (2003). Developmental steps in learning to read: A longitudinal study in kindergarten and first grade. *Reading Research Quarterly, 38*, 302–328.

Morrow, L. M. (1983). Home and school correlates of early interest in literature. *Journal of Educational Research, 76*, 221–230.

Morrow, L. M. (2001). *Literacy development in the early years: Helping children read and write* (4th ed.). Allyn & Bacon.

Murray, B. A. (1995, December). *A meta-analysis of phoneme awareness teaching studies.* Paper presented at the National Reading Conference, New Orleans.

Murray, B. A., Stahl, S. A., & Ivey, G. (1996). Developing phoneme awareness through alphabet books. *Reading and Writing: An Interdisciplinary Journal, 8*, 307–322.

Muter, V., Hulme, C., Snowling, M. J., & Stevenson, J. (2004). Phonemes, rimes, vocabulary, and grammatical skills as foundations of early reading development: Evidence from a longitudinal study. *Developmental Psychology, 40*, 665–681.

Muter, V., & Snowling, M. (1998). Concurrent and longitudinal predictors of reading: The role of metalinguistic and short-term memory skills. *Reading Research Quarterly, 33*, 320–335.

Nation, K., Allen, R., & Hulme, C. (2001). The limitations of orthographic analogy in early reading development: Performance on the clue-word task depends on phonological priming and elementary decoding skill, not the use of orthographic analogy. *Journal of Experimental Child Psychology, 80*, 75–94.

Nation, K., & Hulme, C. (1997). Phonemic segmentation, not onset-rime segmentation, predicts early reading and spelling skills. *Reading Research Quarterly, 32*, 154–167.

National Reading Panel. (2000). *Teaching children to read: An evidence-based assessment of the scientific research literature on reading and its implication for reading instruction—reports of the subgroups*. National Institute of Child Health and Human Development.

Nelson, K. (1993a). Events, narratives, and memory: What develops? In C. A. Nelson (Ed.), *Minnesota Symposium on Child Psychology: Vol. 26. Memory and affect in development* (pp. 1–24). Erlbaum.

Nelson, K. (1993b). Explaining the emergence of autobiographical memory in early childhood. In A. F. Collins, S. E. Gathercole, M. A. Conway, & P. E. Morris (Eds.), *Theories of memory* (pp. 355–385). Erlbaum.

Nelson, K. (1996). *Language in cognitive development: The emergence of the mediated mind*. Cambridge University Press.

Nelson, K., & Fivush, R. (2004). The emergence of autobiographical memory: A social cultural developmental memory. *Psychological Review, 111*, 486–511.

Neuhaus, G. F., & Swank, P. R. (2002). Understanding the relations between RAN letter subtest components and word reading in first-grade students. *Journal of Learning Disabilities, 35*, 158–174.

Neuman, S. B. (1999). Books make a difference: A study of access to literacy. *Reading Research Quarterly, 34*, 286–311.

Neuman, S. B. (2009). *Changing the odds for children at-risk*. Teachers College Press.

Neuman, S. B., & Celano, D. (2001). Access to print in low-income and middle-income communities: An ecological study of four neighborhoods. *Reading Research Quarterly, 36*, 8–26.

Neuman, S. B., & Roskos, K. (1993). Access to print for children of poverty: Differential effects of adult mediation and literacy-enriched play settings on environmental and functional print tasks. *American Educational Research Journal, 30*(1), 95-122.

Neuman, S. B., & Roskos, K. (1997). Literacy knowledge in practice: Contexts of participation for young writers and readers. *Reading Research Quarterly, 32*, 10–32.

Ninio, A. (1980). Picture-book reading in mother–infant dyads belonging to two subgroups in Israel. *Child Development, 51*, 587–590.

O'Connor, R. E., Jenkins, J. R., & Slocum, T. A. (1995). Transfer among phonological tasks in kindergarten: Essential instructional content. *Journal of Educational Psychology, 87*, 202–217.

Ogbu, J. U. (1982). Societal forces as a context of ghetto children's school failure. In L. Feagans & D. C. Farran (Eds.), *The language of children reared in poverty* (pp. 117–138). Academic Press.

Paratore, J., Melzi, G., & Krol-Sinclair, B. (1999). *What should we expect of family literacy? Experiences of Latino children whose parents participate in an intergenerational literacy project*. International Reading Association.

Parrila, R., Kirby, J. R., & McQuarrie, L. (2004). Articulation rate, naming speed, verbal short-term memory, and phonological awareness: Longitudinal predictors of early reading development? *Scientific Studies of Reading, 8*, 3–26.

Pearson, P. D., & Hiebert, E. H. (2010). National reports in literacy: Building a scientific base for practice and policy. *Educational Researcher, 39*(4), 286–294.

Pellegrini, A. D. (2001). Some theoretical and methodological considerations in studying literacy in social context. In S. B. Neuman & D. K. Dickinson (Eds.), *Handbook of early literacy research* (pp. 54–65). Guilford Press.

Pellegrini, A. D., Galda, L., Perlmutter, J., & Jones, I. (1994). *Joint reading between mothers and their Head Start children: Vocabulary development in two text formats* (Reading Research Report No. 13). National Reading Research Center.

Pellegrini, A. D., Perlmutter, J. C., Galda, L., & Brody, G. H. (1990). Joint reading between black Head Start children and their mothers. *Child Development, 61,* 443–453.

Pennington, B. F., Groisser, D., & Welsh, M. C. (1993). Contrasting cognitive deficits in attention deficit hyperactivity disorder versus reading disability. *Developmental Psychology, 29,* 511–523.

Perfetti, C. A. (1992). The representation problem in reading acquisition. In P. B. Gough, L. C. Ehri, & R. Treiman (Eds.), *Reading acquisition* (pp. 145–174). Erlbaum.

Perfetti, C. A., Beck, I., Bell, L., & Hughes, C. (1987). Phonemic knowledge and learning to read are reciprocal: A longitudinal study of first grade children. *Merrill–Palmer Quarterly, 33,* 283–319.

Piasta, S. B., Connor, C. M., Fishman, B. J., & Morrison, F. J. (2009). Teachers' knowledge of literacy concepts, classroom practices, and student reading growth. *Scientific Studies of Reading, 13,* 224–248.

Piasta, S. B., Justice, L. M., McGinty, A. S., & Kaderavek, J. N. (2012). Increasing young children's contact with print during shared reading: Longitudinal effects on literacy achievement. *Child Development, 83*(3), 810–820.

Piasta, S. B., Petscher, Y., & Justice, L. M. (2012). How many letters should preschoolers know? The diagnostic efficiency of various preschool letter-naming benchmarks for predicting first-grade literacy achievement. *Journal of Educational Psychology, 104*(4), 945–958.

Pillemer, D. B., & White, S. H. (1989). Childhood events recalled by children and adults. In H. W. Reese (Ed.), *Advances in child development and behavior* (Vol. 21, pp. 297–340). Academic Press.

Pratt, A. C., & Brady, S. (1988). Relation of phonological awareness to reading disability in children and adults. *Journal of Educational Psychology, 80,* 319–323.

Ratner, H. H. (1984). Memory demands and the development of young children's memory. *Child Development, 55,* 2173–2191.

Read, C. (1971). Pre-school children's knowledge of English phonology. *Harvard Educational Review, 41,* 1–34.

Reese, E., Haden, C., & Fivush, R. (1993). Mother–child conversations about the past: Relations of style and memory over time. *Cognitive Development, 8,* 141–148.

Ricci, C. M., & Beal, C. R. (2002). The effect of interactive media on children's story memory. *Journal of Educational Psychology, 94,* 138–144.

Richgels, D. J. (2001). Invented spelling, phonemic awareness, and reading and writing instruction. In S. B. Neuman & D. K. Dickinson (Eds.), *Handbook of early literacy research* (pp. 142–155). Guilford Press.

Roberts, T. A. (2021). Learning letters: Evidence and questions from a science-of-reading perspective. *Reading Research Quarterly, 56,* S171–S192.

Roberts, T. A., & Sadler, C. D. (2019). Letter sound characters and imaginary narratives: Can they enhance motivation and letter sound learning? *Early Childhood Research Quarterly, 46*(1), 97–111.

Roberts, T. A., Vadasy, P. F., & Sanders, E. A. (2020). Preschool instruction in letter names and sounds: Does contextualized or decontextualized instruction matter? *Reading Research Quarterly, 55*(4), 573–600.

Roser, N., & Martinez, M. (1985). Roles adults play in preschool responses to literature. *Language Arts, 62,* 485–490.

Roskos, K., & Neuman, S. B. (2001). Environment and its influences for early literacy teaching and learning. In S. B. Neuman & D. K. Dickinson (Eds.), *Handbook of early literacy research* (pp. 281–292). Guilford Press.

Saada-Robert, M. (2004). Early emergent literacy. In T. Nunes & P. Bryant (Eds.), *Handbook of children's literacy* (pp. 575–598). Kluwer Academic.

Sacks, C. H., & Mergendoller, J. R. (1997). The relationship between teachers' theoretical orientation toward reading and student outcomes in kindergarten children with different initial reading abilities. *American Educational Research Journal, 34*(4), 721–740.

Savage, R. S., Abrami, P. C., Hipps, G., & Deault, L. (2009). A randomized controlled trial study of the ABRACADABRA reading intervention program in grade 1. *Journal of Educational Psychology, 101,* 590–604.

Savage, R. S., Abrami, P. C., Piquette, N., Wood, E., Deleveaux, G., Sanghera-Sidhu, S., et al. (2013). A (Pan-Canadian) cluster randomized control effectiveness trial of the ABRACADABRA web-based literacy program. *Journal of Educational Psychology, 105*(2), 310–328.

Scarborough, H. S. (2001). Connecting early language and literacy to later reading (dis)abilities: Evidence, theory, and practice. In S. B. Neuman & D. K. Dickinson (Eds.), *Handbook of early literacy research* (pp. 97–110). Guilford Press.

Scarborough, H. S., & Dobrich, W. (1994). On the efficiency of reading to preschoolers. *Developmental Review, 14,* 245–302.

Schatschneider, C., Fletcher, J. M., Francis, D. J., Carlson, C. D., & Foorman, B. R. (2004). Kindergarten prediction of reading skills: A longitudinal comparative analysis. *Journal of Educational Psychology, 96,* 265–282.

Schneider, W., Roth, E., & Ennemoser, M. (2000). Training phonological skills and letter knowledge in children at risk for dyslexia: A comparison of three kindergarten intervention programs. *Journal of Educational Psychology, 92,* 284–295.

Schweinhart, L. J., & Weikart, D. P. (1997). The High/Scope preschool curriculum comparison study through age 23. *Early Childhood Research Quarterly, 12,* 117–143.

Share, D. (2008). Orthographic learning, phonology and the self-teaching hypothesis. In R. Kail (Ed.), *Advances in child development and behavior* (Vol. 36, pp. 31–82). Elsevier.

Shaywitz, S. E. (1996). Dyslexia. *Scientific American, 275*(5), 98–104.

Silven, M., Poskiparta, E., & Niemi, P. (2004). The odds of becoming a precocious reader of Finnish. *Journal of Educational Psychology, 96,* 152–164.

Slocum, T. A., O'Connor, R. E., & Jenkins, J. R. (1993). Transfer among phonological manipulation skills. *Journal of Educational Psychology, 85,* 618–630.

Snow, C. E. (1983). Literacy and language: Relationships during the preschool years. *Harvard Educational Review, 53,* 165–189.

Snow, C. E. (1991). The theoretical basis of the Home–School Study of Language and Literacy Development. *Journal of Research in Childhood Education, 6,* 1–8.

Sodoro, J., Allinder, R. M., & Rankin-Erickson, J. L. (2002). Assessment of phonological awareness: Review of methods and tools. *Educational Psychology Review, 14,* 223–260.

Sokolov, A. N. (1975). *Inner speech and thought.* Plenum Press.

Sonnenschein, S., Baker, L., Serpell, R., Scher, D., Fernandez-Fein, S., & Munsterman, K. A. (1996). *Strands of emergent literacy and their antecedents in the home: Urban preschoolers' early literacy development* (Reading Research Report No. 48). National Reading Research Center.

Spear-Swerling, L., & Brucker, P. O. (2003). Teachers' acquisition of knowledge about English word structure. *Annals of Dyslexia, 53,* 72–103.

Speece, D. L., Ritchey, K. D., Cooper, D. H., Roth, F. P., & Schatschneider, C. (2004). Growth in early reading skills from kindergarten to third grade. *Contemporary Educational Psychology, 29,* 312–332.

Sprenger-Charolles, L., Siegel, L. S., Bechennec, D., & Serniclaes, W. (2003). Development of phonological processing in reading aloud, in silent reading, and in spelling: A four-year longitudinal study. *Journal of Experimental Child Psychology, 84,* 194–217.

Stahl, S. A. (2003). What do we expect storybook reading to do? How storybook reading impacts word recognition. In A. van Kleeck, S. A. Stahl, & E. B. Bauer (Eds.), *On reading books to children: Parents and teachers* (pp. 363–383). Erlbaum.

Stahl, S. A., & McKenna, M. C., & Pagnucco, J. R. (1994). The effects of whole language instruction: An update and reappraisal. *Educational Psychologist, 29*(4), 193–202.

Stahl, S. A., & Miller, P. D. (1989). Whole language and language experience approaches for beginning readers: A quantitative research synthesis. *Review of Educational Research, 59*(1), 87–116.

Stahl, S. A., & Murray, B. A. (1994). Defining phonological awareness and its relationship to early reading. *Journal of Educational Psychology, 86,* 221–234.

Stahl, S. A., & Murray, B. A. (1998). Issues involved in defining phonological awareness and its relation to early reading. In J. Metsala & L. Ehri (Eds.), *Word recognition in beginning reading* (pp. 65–87). Erlbaum.

Stanovich, K. E. (1986). Matthew effects in reading: Some consequences of individual differences in the acquisition of literacy. *Reading Research Quarterly, 21,* 360–407.

Stanovich, K. E. (1988). Explaining the differences between the dyslexic and the garden-variety poor reader: The phonological–core variable–difference model. *Journal of Learning Disabilities, 21,* 590–604.

Steele, C. M. (1992). Race and the schooling of black Americans. *Atlantic Monthly, 269,* 67–78.

Sulzby, E., & Teale, W. (1987). *Young children's storybook reading: Longitudinal study of parent–child instruction and children's independent functioning* (Final Report to the Spencer Foundation). University of Michigan Press.

Sulzby, E., & Teale, W. (1991). Emergent literacy. In R. Barr, M. L. Kamil, P. B. Mosenthal, & P. D. Pearson (Eds.), *Handbook of reading research* (Vol. 2, pp. 727–758). Longman.

Sunseth, K., & Bowers, P. G. (2002). Rapid naming and phonemic awareness: Contributions to reading, spelling, and orthographic knowledge. *Scientific Studies of Reading, 6,* 401–429.

Swanson, H. L., Trainin, G., Necoechea, D. M., & Hammill, D. D. (2003). Rapid naming, phonological awareness, and reading: A meta-analysis of the correlation evidence. *Review of Educational Research, 73,* 407–441.

Tangel, D. M., & Blachman, B. A. (1992). Effect of phoneme awareness instruction on kindergarten children's invented spellings. *Journal of Reading Behavior, 24,* 233–261.

Tangel, D. M., & Blachman, B. A. (1995). Effect of phoneme awareness instruction on the invented spelling of first-grade children: A one-year follow-up. *Journal of Reading Behavior, 27,* 153–185.

Taylor, D., & Dorsey-Gaines, C. (1988). *Growing up literate: Learning from inner-city families.* Heinemann.

Taylor, D., & Strickland, D. (1986). *Family storybook reading.* Heinemann.

Teale, W. H. (1986). Home background and young children's literacy development. In W. H. Teale & E. Sulzby (Eds.), *Emergent literacy: Writing and reading* (pp. 173–206). Ablex.

Tolchinsky, L. (2004). Childhood conceptions of literacy. In T. Nunes & P. Bryant (Eds.), *Handbook of children's literacy* (pp. 11–29). Kluwer Academic.

Torgesen, J. K., & Burgess, S. R. (1998). Consistency of reading-related phonological processes throughout early childhood. In J. Metsala & L. Ehri (Eds.), *Word recognition in beginning reading* (pp. 161–188). Erlbaum.

Torgesen, J. K., Wagner, R. K., Rashotte, C. A., Burgess, S., & Hecht, S. (1997). Contributions of phonological awareness and rapid automatic naming ability to the growth of word-reading skills in second- and fifth-grade children. *Scientific Studies of Reading, 1,* 151–185.

Treiman, R. (1985). Phonemic analysis, spelling, and reading. In T. H. Carr (Ed.), *New directions for child development: The development of reading skills* (pp. 5–18). Jossey-Bass.

Uhry, J. K. (2002). Finger-point reading in kindergarten: The role of phonemic awareness, one-to-one correspondence, and rapid serial naming. *Scientific Studies of Reading, 6,* 319–342.

Valdez-Menchaca, M. C., & Whitehurst, G. J. (1992). Accelerating language development through picture book reading: A systematic extension to Mexican day care. *Developmental Psychology, 28,* 1106–1114.

van Kleeck, A. (2004). Fostering preliteracy development via storybook-sharing interactions: The cultural context of mainstream family practices. In C. A. Stone, E. R. Silliman, B. J. Ehren, & K. Apel (Eds.), *Handbook of language and literacy: Development and disorders* (pp. 175–208). Guilford Press.

van Kleeck, A., Stahl, S. A., & Bauer, E. B. (2003). *On reading books to children: Parents and teachers.* Erlbaum.

Vellutino, F. R., & Scanlon, D. M. (1987). Phonological coding, phonological awareness, and reading ability: Evidence from a longitudinal and experimental study. *Merrill–Palmer Quarterly, 33,* 321–363.

Vellutino, F. R., Scanlon, D. M., Zhang, H., & Schatschneider, C. (2008). Using response to kindergarten and first grade intervention to identify children at-risk for long-term reading difficulties. *Reading and Writing, 21*(4), 437–480.

Vernon-Feagans, L. (1996). *Children's talk in communities and classrooms.* Blackwell.

Vernon-Feagans, L., Hammer, C. S., Miccio, A., & Manlove, E. (2001). Early language and literacy skills in low-income African American and Hispanic children. In S. B. Neuman & D. K. Dickinson (Eds.), *Handbook of early literacy research* (pp. 192–210). Guilford Press.

Vygotsky, L. S. (1962). *Thought and language.* MIT Press.

Vygotsky, L. S. (1978). *Mind in society: The development of higher psychological processes.* Harvard University Press.

Wagner, R. K., Torgesen, J. K., Laughon, P., Simmons, K., & Rashotte, C. A. (1993). Development of young readers' phonological processing abilities. *Journal of Educational Psychology, 85,* 83–103.

Wagner, R. K., Torgesen, J. K., & Rashotte, C. A. (1994). The development of reading-related phonological processing abilities: New evidence of bi-directional causality from a latent variable longitudinal study. *Developmental Psychology, 30,* 73–87.

Wagner, R. K., Torgesen, J. K., Rashotte, C. A., Hecht, S. A., Barker, T. A., Burgess, S. R., et al. (1997). Changing causal relations between phonological processing abilities and word-level reading as children develop from beginning to fluent readers: A five-year longitudinal study. *Developmental Psychology, 33,* 468–479.

Watson, R. (2001). Literacy and oral language: Implications for early literacy acquisition. In S. B. Neuman & D. K. Dickinson (Eds.), *Handbook of early literacy research* (pp. 43–53). Guilford Press.

Wells, G. (1981). *Learning through interaction.* Cambridge University Press.

Whitehurst, G. J., Epstein, J. N., Angell, A. L., Payne, A. C., Crone, D. A., & Fischel, J. E. (1994). Outcomes of an emergent literacy intervention in Head Start. *Journal of Educational Psychology, 86,* 542–555.

Whitehurst, G. J., Falco, F. L., Lonigan, C. J., Fischel, J. E., DeBaryshe, B. D., Valdez-Menchaca, M. C., et al. (1988). Accelerating language development through picturebook reading. *Developmental Psychology, 24,* 552–559.

Whitehurst, G. J., & Lonigan, C. J. (1998). Child development and emergent literacy. *Child Development, 69,* 848–872.

Whitehurst, G. J., & Lonigan, C. J. (2001). Emergent literacy: Development from prereaders to readers. In S. B. Neuman & D. K. Dickinson (Eds.), *Handbook of early literacy research* (pp. 11–29). Guilford Press.

Whitehurst, G. J., Zevenbergen, A. A., Crone, D. A., Schultz, M. D., Velting, O. N., & Fischel, J. E. (1999). Outcomes of an emergent literacy intervention from Head Start through second grade. *Journal of Educational Psychology, 91*, 261–272.

Williams, J. P. (1980). Teaching decoding with an emphasis on phoneme analysis and phoneme blending. *Journal of Educational Psychology, 72*, 1–15.

Wimmer, H., Landerl, K., Linortner, R., & Hummer, P. (1991). The relationship of phonemic awareness to reading acquisition: More consequence than precondition but still important. *Cognition, 40*, 219–249.

Windfuhr, K. L., & Snowling, M. J. (2001). The relationship between paired associate learning and phonological skills in normally developing readers. *Journal of Experimental Child Psychology, 80*, 160–173.

Wise, B. W., & Olson, R. K. (1995). Computer-based phonological awareness and reading instruction. *Annals of Dyslexia, 45*, 99–122.

Wood, S. S., Bruner, J. S., & Ross, G. (1976). The role of tutoring in problem solving. *Journal of Child Psychology and Psychiatry, 17*, 89–100.

Yaden, D. B. Jr., Rowe, D. W., & MacGillivray, L. (2000). Emergent literacy: A matter (polyphony) of perspectives. In M. L. Kamil, P. B. Mosenthal, P. D. Pearson, & R. Barr (Eds.), *Handbook of reading research* (Vol. 3, pp. 425–454). Erlbaum.

Yopp, H. K. (1995). Read-aloud books for developing phonemic awareness: An annotated bibliography. *Reading Teacher, 48*(6), 538–543.

Zevenbergen, A. A., Whitehurst, G. J., & Zevenbergen, J. A. (2003). Effects of a shared-reading intervention on the inclusion of evaluative devices in narratives of children from low-income families. *Journal of Applied Developmental Psychology, 24*, 1–15.

5 | Learning To Recognize Words

In this chapter, we take up a topic that continues to be at the center of the debate about beginning reading instruction, one that has been the focal point of debates about beginning reading for a very long time (Chall, 1967): How should children be taught to recognize words as part of beginning reading instruction? For readers who have read Jeanne S. Chall's classic *Learning to Read: The Great Debate* (1967), there will be a sense of déjà vu about much of this chapter, for in general Chall's conclusions from that book have endured. Today, more than ever, there is strong support for Chall's endorsement of skills-emphasis (i.e., phonics-instructional) approaches to beginning reading over meaning-emphasis approaches that play down the need for explicit decoding instruction. A great deal of research has taken place since Chall's book first appeared in 1967, and even since its update (Chall, 1983), with much of the data supportive of Chall's positions (e.g., recall the word-level research reviewed in Chapter 2, documenting that very good readers sound out words, and the work reviewed in Chapter 3, making clear that for many struggling beginning readers their problem is that they cannot sound out words). New understanding has emerged from research since 1967, but we contend that most of those new findings are compatible with Chall's (1967) conclusions.

Nonetheless, often teachers identifying with the meaning-emphasis approach have resisted explicit, systematic teaching of decoding. A main motivation for this chapter is to inform the teaching community about the types of word recognition instruction that are supported by research evidence.

We first review the progress made in understanding the developmental progression from not being able to read words at all to skillful reading of words. The remainder of the chapter is organized around the two main approaches to teaching word recognition that have been most supported in scientific analyses to date: teaching students to sound out words letter by letter (phonics approach) and teaching them to decode new words by analogy (semantic approach) to words they already know—that is, by using familiar parts of words, parts of words encountered in previously mastered words. We believe that these approaches are complementary. The evidence in support of these two approaches contrasts with the lack of support for word recognition that is focused more on semantic–contextual cues than graphemic–phonemic cues.

Before we move on, it is important to note that these two approaches are quite different. The phonics approach teaches and tests in isolation, while the semantic approach focuses on a child's attempts at decoding contextually, rarely, if ever in isolation. However, when researchers have tested these approaches, students are often asked to read words from lists rather than reading words in the context of a sentence or story. We see this most clearly in studies using nonsense words as a criterion for successful reading. As Walmsley (1978) demonstrated, all students did better when they were reading real, low-frequency words and the most common errors were always on real words, not the nonsense words previously presented to them. Thus, when kids were taught nonsense, phonics did not determine if a student can actually read words within the context of reading.

Chall furthered this argument by challenging the limitations of basal readers, which often focused on one approach to reading. She concluded that basal readers were an impediment to learning effective word recognition skills. She also closed her final chapter of the 1983 book with the following: "I cannot emphasize too strongly that I recommend a code-emphasis only as a beginning reading method, a method to start the child on—and I do not recommend ignoring reading-for-meaning practice—they are developing decoding exercises for upper elementary . . . erroneously assuming that if this approach is good at the beginning, it is also good later on" (p. 307). Additionally, Chall notes that "a beginning code-emphasis program will not cure all reading ills. It cannot guarantee that all children will learn to read easily" (p. 309). Chall concluded that children are individuals and that any proposal to mandate a single approach for teaching beginning readers may result in children not learning to read. We have seen this in action with some of the best teachers (some of which you read about in this book) who do not just use one approach to reading, but use decoding and context cueing to help students make sense of what they read (also see Dahl et al. 1999; McIntyre et al., 2006; McIntyre & Freppon, 1994).

NATURAL DEVELOPMENT OF WORD RECOGNITION SKILLS

There is more than one way to recognize a word, with some more sophisticated than others (see Ehri, 1991, which informs much of what follows, for elaborate discussion of this point; also see Ehri & Snowling, 2004, and Siegel, 2003). In general, the more sophisticated a word recognition process, the later it appears in children's development of word recognition skills.

Logographic Reading

Many American 3-year-olds can "read" the trademark signs for McDonald's, Burger King, and Dunkin' Donuts. They are doing *logographic reading* (sometimes referred to as "visual cue reading"; e.g., Ehri, 1991), which involves using only salient visual characteristics of a display that includes a word to recognize that word rather than relying on letter–sound correspondences. This skill occurs prior to a child receiving any reading instruction and is not a skill teachers should lean on for reading instruction (Chall, 1983; Ehri, 1991). For children using logographic reading there is an association between the distinctive visual cues and the word. Thus, this generation of children often can read the word "Apple" on a computer or the same word on television when the word is shown with the company's apple with a bite out of it; the word *Jell-O* has a memorable shape; *STOP* is read correctly by some children so long as it is in the middle of a red hexagon; many 5-year-olds can read the words *SCHOOL BUS* on the back of a large yellow vehicle; and what 4- to 5-year-old has trouble decoding Walt Disney's signature, even though it is written in script?

Phillip Gough and his colleagues (Gough et al., 1992) presented 4- to 5-year-olds with four words to read, one on each of four flashcards, with a blue thumbprint on one of the flashcards. The participants went through the deck of cards until they could say each word when given its card. Then came the interesting part. Could the children say the word that had been presented with the blue thumbprint if they were shown the word on a clean card devoid of the thumbprint? No. Could they say the word if they were shown just the blue thumbprint? Yes. Gough et al. (1992) refer to this as *selective association*, which is another name for logographic reading or visual cue reading. Regardless of what it is called, it is the same process, and preschoolers typically can do it.

However, while logographic reading is not real reading, it seems to play a role in facilitating real reading later on. Cronin et al. (1995) had children attempt to read logographs in context (e.g., "McDonald's" in the context of its logo, "Stop" on a stop sign). Some logos could be read by the children, whereas other logos could not (e.g., "Zellers" on the Zellers sign). Then, the children were taught the same words as sight words. In general, words that children could read in the context of a logo were learned more quickly than words not read in the context of a logo. There were a variety of controls in the study, which led to the conclusion that learning to read a word in the context of a logo permitted transfer to learning to read the word outside of its logo context. Something was learned by the preschoolers in Cronin et al. (1995) about the words per se on logos!

Alphabetic Reading

Traditional decoding instruction emphasizes sounding out words using letter–sound relations. This mechanism is operative in both reading and writing well before the time when children know *all* of the letter–sound correspondences (e.g., Ehri & Wilce, 1985; Huba, 1984). For example, preschoolers and kindergartners who know some letter–sound correspondences use what they know to attempt invented spellings of familiar words. When readers know some letter–sound relationships, they also are capable of doing what Ehri (1991) refers to as "phonetic cue reading," which is "reading" a word based on only a few of its letters. Ehri (1991) contrasts such phonetic cue reading with logographic reading, using the following example: Logographic readers might remember how to read *yellow* by the "two sticks" in the middle (Seymour & Elder, 1986). In contrast, phonetic cue readers might see the two *l*'s in *yellow*, hear their name in the pronunciation, and use this information to connect the spelling to the word in memory (p. 391).

Certainly, however, such reading has its hazards. If the same letter cues are used for several words or if a cue used to decode some word is experienced in a new word, there may be mix-ups (Allington & Fleming, 1978; Allington et al., 1976). For example, it is not uncommon for a child to misread a word as another similar word sharing common letters that is known to the child (e.g., *yellow* read for *pillow*; see Ehri's [1991] interpretation of Seymour & Elder's [1986] data, and Ehri & Wilce, 1987a, 1987b). And, of course, phonetic cue readers have a devil of a time if asked to learn a set of words that share letters (e.g., *pots, post, spot, stop*; Gilbert et al., 1977).

At some point after phonetic cue reading begins, a child comes to understand the *alphabetic principle*—that "all twenty-six of those strange little symbols that comprise the alphabet are worth learning and discriminating one from the other because [they stand] for . . . the sounds that occur in spoken words" (Adams, 1990, p. 245). Once this realization occurs, the child has to learn a number of specific decoding "rules" if the child is to read using the complete alphabet. Some are easy, for they require learning only one piece of information: The letter *b* is pronounced the same, regardless of context, as are *d, f, l, n, r, v,* and *z*. Some letters are pronounced differently depending on other letters in the word; the most common example is that vowels are long if there is another vowel or a final *e* in a syllable and short if there is not. Another example is that *c* is pronounced differently if followed by an *e* or an *i* than if followed by an *a, o,* or *u* (e.g., compare the pronunciation of the *c* sounds in *celestial, city, cat, cot,* and *cut*). In general, conditional rules (i.e., those involving consideration of more than one letter to determine the sound of a particular letter) are acquired later than rules involving one letter–sound association (e.g., Venezky & Johnson, 1973). Eventually, young readers learn all the letter–sound relationships, although there is much complex information to acquire (e.g., Gough et al., 1992):

> For only a minority of the letters (*b, d, f, l, n, r, v, z*) is it possible to identify the [sound] it represents. For the other 18, at least one additional letter must be identified before the identity of the word's first [sound] can be determined; in some cases, at least four more letters are required (compare *chord* and *chore*). The vast majority of the letter–sound correspondences of . . . English . . . are context dependent. (p. 39)

Not many children acquire all these letter–sound associations through instruction, however. As Adams (1990) points out, there is little consistency among the various reading curricula on how many of these letter–sound relationships need to be taught and perhaps even less agreement about the most appropriate ordering of these relationships for instruction. Some programs teach both long and short vowel patterns at the same time, while others teach the short vowels first and then—after those have been introduced—they teach the long vowel patterns. Some programs teach a handful of letter–sound relationships while others teach a dump truck full. Some programs include decodable texts but others offer no decodable texts. Some emphasize decoding words in isolation, while others focus on decoding words in the context of sentences and stories. Some teach a single letter sound-and-blend strategy and others teach an analogy strategy for decoding words. In other words, the programs used in schools today to foster decoding proficiencies have a variety of unique features. As the National Reading Panel (NRP) noted, there does not seem to be any one "best" way to foster the development of decoding proficiencies, but the NRP also concluded that a focus on developing decoding proficiencies leads to better decoding abilities.

In addition to learning the letter–sound associations, the beginning reader must learn how to use them to decode words, mapping the individual sounds represented by the letters of a word and blending the sounds. At first, such reading is only accomplished with very great effort. Indeed, it is a matter of years before it becomes very fluent and effortless. Long before that, however, individual words can be identified with relatively little effort.

Sight-Word Reading

We doubt that anyone reading this text has had to sound out a single word in this chapter, except perhaps for unfamiliar proper names such as Gough (did you pronounce it to rhyme with *rough* or with *trough*?). Almost every word in this text is in most skilled readers' sight vocabularies. There was a time, however, when you would have sounded out virtually each and every word in this chapter. Conducting many trials of successfully sounding out a word, however, increases the connections between the letter patterns defining the word and the word in memory (Adams, 1990; Ehri, 2014; Ehri et al., 2001). This is one of the primary advantages of being able to sound out words. Learning to sound out words leads to the development of a larger number of words that can be recognized instantly, or sight-word recognition.

Thus, on initial exposure to a word like *frog*, a child sounds the word out. Such sounding out begins a process in which the connections between each letter and adjacent letters are strengthened (e.g., between *fr-* and *-og*), as are connections defining the entire sequence of letters and letter combinations in the word (strengthening of the connection between *fr-* and *-og*). Eventually the spelling is represented in memory as a unit consisting of *frog*. By repeated reading, there is also a strengthening of the connections between this visual stimulus and the conceptual understanding in long-term memory that defines a frog, so that eventually even the briefest exposure to the word *frog* elicits thoughts of a green, jumpy thing. For many beginning readers, there is rapid sight-word development of words commonly encountered while engaged in reading (for more on the development of automatic word recognition, see Chapter 6).

Reading by Analogy to Known Words

After repeated correct readings, letter strings that occur in many different words are perceived as wholes (e.g., repeated co-occurrence of *i*, *n*, and *g* results eventually in *-ing* being perceived as a unit; Stanovich & West, 1989). Prefixes and suffixes are obvious examples, but there are other recurring combinations, many of which are root words (e.g., *-take*, *mal-*, *ben-*, *do-*). When such familiar letter patterns are encountered, it is not necessary to decode alphabetically. Rather, there is a direct connection with the sound sequence in memory. The more developed and practiced the reader becomes, the greater the number of words that he or she can identify at a glance. That is, without decoding the individual letter sounds, the reader can automatically recognize the word.

Many of the highest-frequency words can be decoded by sounding out the letter sounds (*came, can, see*) but many of the words cannot be sounded out because their pronunciation does not follow the typical patterns (*come, was, have*). In most of these words it is the vowel that exhibits a unique pronunciation value; the consonants are often pronounced as they typically are pronounced. Various schemes have been developed over the years to deal with these "exception" words. These range from telling students that the word *was* should be pronounced like *gas* but that we now pronounce it as *wuz*. Other schemes invented new alphabets where every word was pronounced just as it was printed. Thus, *was* was printed as *wuz* and *have* was printed as *hav*. While several of these sorts of phonetic respelling initiatives have come and gone over the past 100 years, we expect that another may appear in the future.

First-grade readers who are developing their reading skills successfully begin to recognize many of the most frequent words in English by midyear. As that reader moves through first and on to second grade, he or she recognizes even more words and fewer and fewer words need to be decoded. But, understand that it is the ability to accurately identify these frequent words that leads to them becoming words recognized at a glance. Some of our readers may be familiar with the Dolch Word List (Dolch, 1936). This list includes the words that appear most frequently in printed English. These are essential words that children need to be able to recognize at a glance. The fastest and easiest method for achieving this goal is to ensure that all beginning readers have texts that they can read accurately. Reading and rereading these early texts develops that small set of high-frequency words as sight words.

When words can be read by sight and recurring letter chunks can be processed as wholes, what LaBerge and Samuels (1974; Samuels et al., 1992) dubbed as "automatic reading," there are tremendous advantages for the reader. According to automaticity theory, two processes must occur for a reader to understand a word: (1) The word must be decoded and (2) what is decoded must be comprehended. Both decoding and comprehension require use of short-term memory, that extremely limited resource that can be thought of as one's conscious attentional capacity. With only 7 ± 2 slots in short-term memory (at best), decoding operations and comprehension processes compete for only a little bit of capacity.

Alphabetic decoding requires a great deal of attention on the part of the reader. Walk into many grade 1 classrooms on any morning, and you will see children during reading group who will have all of their mental energy and attention devoted to the task of sounding out the words when it is their turn to read. If all of their attentional capacity is consumed by decoding, there is nothing left over for comprehension. The result is that words may be pronounced but not understood. One solution for the slow alphabetic decoder might be to decode first and then comprehend. But the cost of this method is enormous: because decoding and comprehending are done in sequence, the phonological representation of the word must be held in short-term memory, which involves further reduction of capacity that is needed for comprehension. No matter how the alphabetic reader approaches the task, he or she places a strain on short-term capacity.

Automatic sight-word reading and automatic recognition of commonly encountered word chunks (e.g., prefixes, suffixes, root words, frequently encountered combinations of letters such as -ake and -op), in contrast, require little effort or attention, and thus there is substantial mental capacity left over for comprehension (e.g., Baron, 1977). Experience in reading promotes faster, more accurate, and less effortful reading (e.g., Horn & Manis, 1987). A paradox of slow, high-effort, alphabetic reading is that it is less certain to result in accurate decoding than fast, low-effort, automatic decoding via sight words and word chunks. It isn't that decoding is unimportant, but that it can acquired through reading, using word chunks, and word partners together. This produces decoding that is both less effortful and guided in part by what makes sense in that spot.

Once readers know a variety of word chunks, they are in a position to exploit the principle that words with the same spelling pattern often sound the same. Thus, a child who knows how to pronounce *beak* could make a good guess at *leak* the first time it is encountered simply by decoding by analogy (i.e., "This is like *beak*, only it starts with a *l*!"). That same *beak*-word knower would have a fighting chance with *bean*, *bead*, and *beat* as well, using the analogy strategy. Adams (1990, pp. 210–211) provides the example of good readers quickly pronouncing the low-frequency word *kale* to rhyme with *ale*, *sale*, *male*, *pale*, *gale*, and *tale*. Each time a word with -ale in it is encountered and pronounced with the long *a* sound, the association between -ale and the long *a* sound is strengthened. Thus, when *kale* is encountered by someone who has had many exposures to the -ale and long *a* association, there can be an automatic activation of *kale* and it is pronounced correctly almost without thinking or pronounced at a glance. It seems unlikely to occur, however, if the child has been taught to read slowly and letter sound by letter sound it is possible.

For the most part, analogy has been considered an advanced strategy used only by adults or by children who have been reading awhile. However, other researchers have demonstrated that emerging readers can be taught to use the analogy strategy effectively to decode most words. Patricia Cunningham (1975, 1992, 2011) and H. G. Marsh and colleagues are especially strong advocates of decoding by analogy (e.g., Marsh et al., 1977; Marsh, Friedman, Desberg, et al., 1981; Marsh, Friedman, Welch, et al., 1981). The case is made later in this chapter (and continued in Chapter 6), however, that children can be profitably taught to decode by analogy well before they might do so on their own.

Summary and Comment

There can be little doubt that, when children are immersed in the world of language and print, they experience some natural development of their word-reading skills. The holistic and insensitive visual pattern matching that is logographic reading only starts the process that becomes the processing of every single letter and the construction of knowledge about commonly occurring letter patterns. The finding that children naturally learn to sound out words and decode by analogy based on frequently encountered word chunks highlights the fact that the instructional recommendations in this chapter only involve systematic elaboration and intensification of powerful natural learning processes. When all of the learning to read is left to children's natural discovery of letter–sound associations and development of knowledge of word chunks, however, reading development is slower and less certain than it can be when children are taught to decode by analogy. That is why the best-informed reading researchers and educators focus so much attention on teaching beginning readers to decode, increasingly using the methods detailed in the remainder of this chapter (see also Gonzalez-Frey & Ehri, 2021; Lovett et al., 2003; McGill-Franzen, 2006; O'Connor & Bell, 2004; Scanlon et al., 2016).

TEACHING STUDENTS TO SOUND OUT WORDS

Many children can be taught to decode words by focusing on the sounds associated with individual letters and letter combinations and blending those sounds to produce a reading of the word. Once the word is read, the child will recognize it. Thus, once a child decodes *cat* by sounding it out, the child recognizes a word he or she has been hearing and using for several years. Since the child who is learning to read knows the meaning of many of the words in books appropriate for beginning readers, understanding of the word once it is decoded is likely.

The criticality of phonemic awareness as a beginning reading competency becomes obvious in the context of the sounding-out strategy. As you will recall from Chapter 4, phonemic awareness is the realization that words are composed of sounds. It would make no sense to a child lacking this insight to attend to the letters of a word and attempt to sound it out! That is, before instruction about sounding out a word can make any sense, it is essential that the child understand that words are amalgams of sounds.

In fact, there is research support for the claim that learning to decode depends on phonemic awareness. One frequently cited study regarding this point observed that first graders who were most certain to make progress in learning to decode were those who possessed phonemic awareness and knew the names of letters (Tunmer et al., 1988). Another frequently cited study making the same point found that 4-year-olds who could segment words into constituent phonemes benefited from decoding instruction involving the segmentation of words into constituent letters, the mapping of letters to sounds, and the blending of sounds. Four-year-olds who could not segment words into constituent phonemes did not benefit from such decoding instruction (Fox & Routh, 1975). It is important to understand that this is not a phonics problem per se, but it is a phonemic awareness problem!

Beyond phonemic awareness, however, the child who is to sound out words needs to know more. A particularly important prerequisite to acquisition of decoding skills is knowledge of the associations between letters and the sounds they make.

Letter-Sound Associations

Much can be taught about letters. In recent generations, something that has been known by many, although not all, young children by the time they enter kindergarten is the names of letters. In part, this is due to intentional educational efforts by our society to teach the alphabet to all preschoolers, perhaps most prominently through *Sesame Street* (e.g., Anderson & Collins, 1988; Bogatz & Ball, 1971; Mielke, 2001; Zill, 2001). *Sesame Street* made contributions to the development of literacy over and above family interactions and other sources of stimulation (e.g., Rice et al., 1990). This television program did much to get preschoolers off to a good start. Perhaps even more impressive, the benefits of watching *Sesame Street* can be detected many years later, when graduates of the *Street* are adolescents (Huston et al., 2001; Wright et al., 2001). Other PBS TV series designed to foster literacy skills of 3- to 7-year-olds include *Between the Lions*, *SuperWhy*, *WordWorld*, and *WordGirl*. We can only hope that these and other literacy based shows produce the same positive effects that have been observed with *Sesame Street*.

Knowing letter names is not sufficient knowledge for learning to decode, however. Learning to analyze a printed word into component sounds followed by blending of those sounds requires knowledge of the letter–sound associations. Young readers need to learn about both the long and the short vowel sounds as well as the sounds associated with the consonants. That is, they need to know various ways that *g* can sound when encountered in a word, as well as all the other consonants of the alphabet. Such instruction highlights the fact that some letters sound the same regardless of the letters around them in a word (i.e., *b*, *d*, *l*, *n*, *r*, *v*, and *z* make the same sound, regardless of the letter context in which they are embedded). Other letters sound different depending on context—for example, *g* is pronounced differently in *gem* than in *get*. Of course, the long vowel sounds typically occur when there is a final silent *e* in a syllable but often are short when there is no final *e*. In addition to teaching the sounds associated with individual letters, good phonics instructors also cover the consonant digraphs (*sh*, *ch*, *th*, and *wh*) and the common consonant blends (e.g., *dr*, *bl*, *sk*, *sch*, and *tw*). In general, a lot of teaching about consonants and vowels and the sounds they make must take place if children are to learn how to decode words. There is some debate about exactly how many sounds there are in English, but a number between 43 and 46 is most typically mentioned.

There is certainly a lot for children to learn when they are acquiring the associations between letters and sounds. The most common way of dealing with the very great memory demand is for the letter–sound associations to be taught over a long period of time, with many repetitions and many examples in the context of exercises and games involving letters and their sounds (Cunningham, 2013, and Fox, 2011, are filled with suggestions about activities that build knowledge of letter–sound associations). Of course, such activities typically take place in the context of real reading and writing, which also permit many opportunities for use and review of the letter–sound associations.

Some researchers and educators who are aware of the memory demands involved in learning the initial letter–sound associations have gone further. Ehri et al. (1984) created a set of pictorial memory aids for learning letter–sound associations (see Figure 5.1). Thus, for each consonant sound, children are presented with a mnemonic picture that integrates the physical letter and a word beginning with the sound associated with the letter. Can you see the *h* in the picture of a house in the top portion of Figure 5.1? How about a *v* in the picture of a vase of flowers? We had a little trouble seeing the *y* in *yak*, but found the picture of a yak with a decidedly *y*-shaped head to be very memorable. The *w* in the wings of the butterfly took us a second to see at first, but now we almost always think of *w* when we see butterfly wings—even on real butterflies! Ditto for the *g* in *glasses*.

Ehri and colleagues' (1984) approach is based on the well-established fact that even very young children can remember picture mnemonics (Pressley, 1977). Rather than simply assuming that this approach is effective because mnemonics generally work for young children, Ehri et al. (1984) conducted a well-controlled experiment demonstrating clearly that picture mnemonics really did increase the rate at which children learned letter–sound associations.

Unfortunately, Ehri et al. (1984) never made their materials available commercially. Thus, individual classroom teachers who wish to use the picture–mnemonic approach are going to have to produce their own picture mnemonics. However, a more recent study (discussed in Chapter 4), Roberts and Sadler (2019) found large effect sizes for teaching letter–sound learning using embedding letters with characters with names beginning with the letter. Though none of the authors have used this method, we have

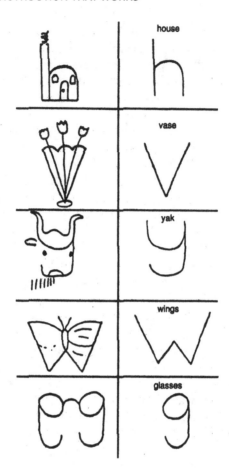

FIGURE 5.1. Mnemonic–pictorial aids for learning letter–sound associations. From Ehri, Deffner, and Wilce (1984). Copyright © 1984 by the American Psychological Association. Reprinted by permission.

talked to teachers who have, and they tell us that with a little imagination it is possible to produce memorable mnemonic pictures for all of the letter-sound associations in English.

Learning the letter–sound associations, which confers some intellectual power, is no small achievement. For example, Byrne and Fielding-Barnsley (1990, 1991) determined that preschoolers with phonemic awareness who also knew the letter–sound associations were very adept at decoding unfamiliar words as compared with other preschoolers. Even so, there is much to be said for also teaching young readers how to blend the sounds of letters.

Blending Letter–Sound Correspondences

We suspect that as long as there have been teachers teaching students to read, there have been teachers teaching students to analyze words into component sounds and to blend the sounds. This instructional approach and its effectiveness is well understood at the beginning of the 21st century largely because of a distinguished mid-20th-century analysis of beginning reading carried out by Jeanne Chall.

Chall's (1967, 1983) Analyses and Summaries

Chall (1967, 1983) provided detailed original analyses and reviews of other analyses of the effectiveness of beginning reading instruction. One of the major conclusions of her review was that programs that included "synthetic phonics" instruction (sometimes referred to as "systematic" or "explicit phonics" instruction), in which the students are systematically taught letter–sound associations and how to blend the sounds made by letters to pronounce and recognize words, were more effective at producing children who scored well when reading word lists. A great diversity of findings supported the conclusion that synthetic phonics instruction was more effective than alternatives.

In reviewing studies dating back to 1912, Chall found evidence that explicit phonics instruction produced word recognition and oral reading during grade 1 superior to look–say approaches, which emphasize students learning words as wholes rather than learning to decode them via phonics (many Americans learned the look–say approach using the popular reading series, *Dick and Jane* readers). Although vocabulary and comprehension tended to be better in early grade 1 with the look–say approach, students receiving synthetic phonics measures did better by the end of grade 2. Although look–say students seemed to read faster than did synthetic phonics students, it was at the price of less accuracy; however, these findings did not align with what other researchers have found (e.g., Freppon & McIntyre, 1999; McIntyre et al., 2006; McIntyre & Freppon, 1994).

Chall also found studies contrasting synthetic phonics instruction with what she termed "intrinsic phonics instruction" (sometimes referred to as "analytic" or "implicit phonics"). Intrinsic phonics teaching involves analyzing the sounds of known sight words, although word analysis is played down in favor of semantic–contextual and picture cues as means for word recognition. (Notably, intrinsic phonics instruction seems to be closest to the phonics instruction often used in meaning-emphasis teaching.) Although these comparisons dated back to 1926, in fact, interest in the issue of whether synthetic or intrinsic phonics produced better readers was especially pronounced in the decade preceding Chall's (1967) text, largely because the most popular reading textbook series of the day used an intrinsic phonics approach. (That is what was going on in many classrooms that used *Dick and Jane* readers: Students learned to read whole words; once the whole words were acquired, they were analyzed into constituent sounds as part of instruction.)

Studies comparing the intrinsic phonics approach with the synthetic phonics approach produced clear results. Oral word recognition was better for students taught with synthetic phonics than for students taught with intrinsic phonics. Spelling tended to be better for students instructed with systematic phonics, with this superiority holding across the elementary grades. Also, at least during the primary grades, the performance of synthetic phonics students on standardized word recognition tests exceeded the performance of intrinsic phonics students. Although not quite as pronounced, the same pattern was observed for standardized comprehension.

In analyzing the studies up through 1965, Chall (1967) found evidence that synthetic phonics was effective relative to alternatives for the broad range of abilities, from low IQ to high IQ. Synthetic phonics seemed to be especially beneficial for low-IQ students, with Chall speculating that approaches that involve a great deal of induction, such as intrinsic phonics, might be too difficult for low-IQ students.

In 1965–1966, the U.S. Office of Education conducted the *First-Grade Comparative Research Studies*, which involved 27 comparative studies of the various methods used to teach grade 1 reading. Several analyses of these data resulted in the conclusion that code-based approaches to beginning reading instruction produced primary-grade reading superior to that produced by other methods, particularly meaning-based methods of the day—the look–say, intrinsic phonics approaches (Chall, 1983; Guthrie & Tyler, 1975). However, the authors of the final report of that large-scale study (Bond & Dykstra, 1967) noted that individual teachers produced larger effects than did any of the reading programs evaluated. They concluded that what should be studied was what it was that different teachers did that made them so successful, almost regardless of which program or type of phonics lessons they offered.

When Head Start was extended into the elementary grades as Follow Through, several Follow Through models were tried. The outcomes produced by them were then contrasted in formal studies. Variations of Follow Through that included systematic phonics instruction (which involved direct instruction of phonics in a basal instructional program) produced a better performance on primary-level standardized tests than did alternative approaches (Abt Associates, 1977; Kennedy, 1978; Stallings, 1975). Chall (1983) interpreted these results as clear evidence favoring systematic phonics for children who are at risk for school failure because they are living in poverty. On the other hand, House et al. (1978) critiqued the various analyses as flawed and noted that none of the various approaches studied actually produced results any different from the control schools that did not use any of the curricula studied. They also noted that size of the differences in achievement outcomes was larger when comparing various sites using a single curriculum than when comparing the varying curricula used.

Beginning in 1967, a number of laboratory studies of phonics instruction were carried out. In general, the critical dependent variable in these studies was the ability to read words not seen before. Both teaching letter–sound associations and teaching of blending proved potent in these comparisons (Chall, 1983, Table I-1, p. 14).

From the appearance of Chall's *Learning to Read: The Great Debate* (1967) through the publication of the updated edition of the book (1983), a number of studies conducted in classrooms explicitly contrasted systematic, direct, synthetic phonics instruction with less systematic, indirect, implicit phonics instruction. Across a variety of measures of word recognition, oral reading, comprehension, vocabulary, and spelling, when there was a difference (and often there was), it favored direct, synthetic phonics instruction over indirect, intrinsic approaches (Chall, 1983, Table I-2, pp. 18–20).

Adams's (1990) Analysis and Summary

The next really important book appraising the effectiveness of systematic or synthetic phonics instruction was Marilyn Adams's (1990) *Beginning to Read*. She reviewed Chall's data analyses and conclusions for a new generation of readers. Beyond that, she also reviewed theory and evidence produced since Chall's book that was supportive of the case for systematic decoding instruction. For example, Adams (1990, chap. 11) reviewed how basal reading programs cover phonics versus how they should do so based on contemporary evidence. She noted that the basal reader series often ignored the accumulating evidence.

Adams also made the case that explicit decoding instruction is now understood to involve a number of different acquisitions:

Adams reviewed the evidence that kindergarten and grade 1 students often need to be taught the alphabetic principle: "One wants the students to understand that all twenty-six of those strange little symbols that comprise the alphabet are worth learning and discriminating one from the other because each stands for one of the sounds that occur in spoken words" (p. 245).

Adams established for her readers that students need to learn the physical representation of each letter. That is, they need to acquire the distinctive features of letters (Gibson et al., 1962; Gibson & Levin, 1975). In doing so, they learn the difference between *P* and *R* as a single feature (i.e., the left-to-right downward diagonal in *R*) as well as the difference between *P* and

B and *R* and *B* as single features (i.e., there is a fat rightward bulge in the bottom half of *B* that does not occur in *P* or *R*).

Adams overviewed why students must learn the specific sounds that are associated with each letter and the common letter combinations in English (see Table 5.1), taking up the pros and cons of various orders of teaching the letter–sound correspondences (e.g., short vs. long vowels first, consonants before vowels).

Adams contended that students need much practice in learning to blend sounds since reading a word consists of both analyzing the letter–sound correspondences and blending those correspondences to pronounce a word.

Adams reviewed as well the case for teaching phonics rules such as these: "When there are two vowels side by side, the long sound of the first one is heard and the second is usually silent"; "Words having double *ee* usually have the long *e* sound"; and "The two letters *ow* make the long *o* sound." She made a compelling case for not relying exclusively on phonics rules: First, none of the rules is entirely reliable. Second, learning the rules in no way can substitute for the complicated network of understandings about letter–sound correspondences that develops through learning the letter–sound correspondences and blending them to sound out words.

Adams was emphatic that beginning reading instruction must involve a great deal of reading words in real texts. Reading of actual texts makes clear to students why they are learning to decode individual words, and it should include many opportunities to apply the decoding skills being learned.

TABLE 5.1. Common Word Families in English

-ab	-amp	-ear (short *e*)	-ick	-it	-ow (*know*)
-ace	-ank	-eat	-id	-ob	-ow (*cow*)
-ack	-ap	-ed	-ide	-ock	-ub
-ad	-ar	-ee	-ies	-od	-uck
-ade	-are	-eed	-ig	-og	-uff
-ag	-ark	-eek	-ight	-oke	-ug
-ail	-ash	-eep	-ile	-old	-um
-ain	-at	-eet	-ill	-one	-ump
-ake	-ate	-ell	-im	-ong	-ung
-ale	-ave	-end	-ime	-oop	-unk
-all	-aw	-ent	-in	-op	-ush
-am	-ay	-ess	-ine	-ope	-ust
-ame	-aze	-est	-ing	-ore	-ut
-an	-eak	-et	-ink	-orn	-y
-ane	-eal	-ew	-int	-ot	
-ang	-eam	-ice	-ip	-out	

Note. Based on List 47 in Fry et al. (1993).

Thus, Adams's (1990) endorsement of the reading of texts from the beginning of reading instruction seems superficially consistent with meaning-emphasis recommendations. The texts Adams favors, however, are ones emphasizing the graphemic–phonemic elements that the child knows at some level already (i.e., through instruction). Reading of such decodable texts is not favored by meaning-emphasis theorists who want children to read authentic children's literature, which often includes many letter–sound combinations unfamiliar to the child. Indeed, the meaning-emphasis advocates succeeded in nearly eradicating decodable texts from American classrooms. Even basal reading programs had far fewer decodable texts during the whole-language era than they did in earlier eras, reflecting the response of many basal publishers to make their materials as consistent as possible with meaning-emphasis principles (Hoffman et al., 1993). However, and perhaps because of the NRP report, basal reading once again included decodable texts in programs produced after 2000 (Hoffman et al., 2002), though there remained substantial diversity on the number of decodable texts made available and the centrality of those texts to the reading lessons offered.

At the same time, research has cast doubts on the efficacy of using decodable texts. The most frequently cited study (Juel & Roper-Schneider, 1985) did find some advantages across the school year for children reading from decodable texts. On the other hand, at the end-of-year reading assessment there were no differences between the groups of children who did or did not have decodable texts to read. The authors conclude their paper with this statement: "The interpretation of the results of this study do not constitute advocacy for any one specific approach to beginning reading instruction" (p. 150).

Jenkins et al. (2004) compared the reading performances of first-grade children enrolled in a supplemental reading intervention. These children attended 11 schools and used five different core reading programs in their classroom reading lessons. Half of the students were randomly assigned to read from decodable texts (85% decodable) during the tutoring sessions and half were selected to read from predictable texts (11% decodable). Tutoring was scripted and was offered 4 days a week over a period of 25 weeks. The tutoring session focused on immersing these children in text-reading activity. The tutored children read or reread texts for half to two-thirds of every intervention lesson. The tutored children outperformed untutored control group children on several measures of reading performance after the tutoring was completed. However, there was no advantage observed for members of the group assigned to reading decodable texts. As the authors noted, "These analyses indicate that regardless of students' entering abilities or response to treatment, no effects emerged for text decodability" (p. 80). In a series of subgroup analyses, they found no group of children who benefited more from reading decodable texts.

This is the same conclusion that Mathes et al. (2005) arrived at when comparing scripted and synthetic phonics approach using decodable texts to an embedded and intrinsic phonics approach using predictable texts. Again, the struggling first-grade readers in both groups engaged in much daily reading in their small intervention groups (one-to-three instruction). At the end of the study, the tutored children read significantly better than the control group who did not participate in the intervention. But again, there were no differences between the explicit and implicit phonics groups of children on end-of-year reading achievement assessment. The explicit phonics group did have better word-reading performances but the intrinsic group had better oral-reading fluency.

The authors conclude by noting that outside the research intervention the four school districts involved in the study provided intensive reading support to the emerging but struggling readers. They also note that offering the intervention teachers the option to choose either the explicit or the implicit approach for developing decoding proficiencies seemed to benefit students if only because intervention teachers were using an approach they believed in. They summed up their argument as follows:

> Perhaps the most important finding of this research is that supplemental intervention derived from different theoretical perspectives were both effective. These findings suggest to us that there is likely not "one best approach" and not one right philosophy or theory for how to best meet the needs of struggling readers. (p. 179)

More recently, Price-Mohr and Price (2020) conducted a study with groups of students reading text with high and low decodablity. This particular study found students had higher levels of comprehension for the group that read the low-decodability-level books. Similar studies have found that decodable texts may be appropriate for beginning readers but provide very little for readers beyond the initial readers due to the lack of exposure to more complex words and sentences (Adams, 2009; Castles et al., 2018; Slavin et al., 2009). Thus, once a student is beyond the initial level of learning to read, it seems that it may be the volume of reading activity that is more important than the type of text (decodable vs. predictable) that is read. It is important to note that decodable texts can provide an unlikely decodability and develop kids' awareness of the central roles that decoding plays in the reading process.

These studies mirror the findings reported by the NRP's (2000) meta-analysis of the research on decoding-emphasis approaches to early reading instruction. First, the NRP reported that very little research had been conducted on the effects of using decodable versus other sorts of texts in beginning reading lessons. Second, the NRP reported that no particular type of decoding instruction was more effective than the other approaches. Explicit, implicit, and analogy-based phonics lessons were found effective when used for 10 minutes daily in kindergarten and first-grade reading lessons. They also found no positive effects for skills-emphasis lessons beyond first grade. Even the effect for the modest amounts of kindergarten and first-grade decoding instruction was observed primarily on later decoding of words in isolation tasks but with only a trivial effect on later comprehension tasks.

Perhaps Adams (2009) summarizes best what we know about the use of decodable texts when she writes that "if there exist data, theory, or cogent argument for extending decodables beyond the very beginning levels of reading, then I am unable to find it" (p. 44). She supports using decodable texts in kindergarten and at the very beginning of grade 1 but not beyond that point. That said, we must note that a variety of decodable texts are available. Some use only a very few words (e.g., *the, was, come*) that are not actually decodable while others use such words more liberally. Some use decodable high-frequency words that are likely already known in the spoken form by young readers, while others use words that may be unfamiliar. In the end, practice in decodable texts may be useful for some children but the evidence to date suggests little advantage for using such texts.

The NRP (2000) concluded that "phonics instruction appears to contribute only weakly, if at all, in helping apply these [decoding skills] to read text and to spell words" (pp. 2–108). In other words, decoding instruction of multiple types was found more useful on measures of decoding proficiency than on measures of oral reading accuracy, oral reading fluency, or text comprehension after reading. We mention these findings primarily because it seems to us that too few educators and researchers have actually read the NRP report. Too many have relied upon a widely distributed shorter and plain-language document entitled *Put Reading First* (Armbruster et al., 2001). That document suggested that explicit synthetic phonics was the most effective approach along with several other assertions that were not supported by the findings of the NRP (Shanahan, 2003).

The misrepresentations of the NRP findings (use explicit synthetic phonics, use decodable texts, don't worry about extended opportunities to engage in reading activity), unfortunately, led to reading instructional designs that too often were not balanced and that were found to be no more effective than the traditional reading lessons primarily offered in schools (Gamse et al., 2009).

Additional Research

Different analyses have confirmed that skilled readers sound out words that they do not know (e.g., Barron, 1986; Patterson & Coltheart, 1987;

Perfetti et al., 1988). The analyses of eye movements produced in the past four decades have made clear that most words are looked at during reading and that the individual letters in the words are processed (McConkie et al., 1982; Rayner et al., 1981; see Chapter 2). Moreover, it is weaker readers rather than good readers who rely on context cues and, in so doing, they often misread words (e.g., Nicholson, 1991; Nicholson et al., 1988; Rayner & Pollatsek, 1989; Stanovich, 1986; Waterman & Lewandowski, 1993).

Four studies (Foorman et al., 1991; Lovett et al., 1989, 1994; Nicholson, 1991) in particular were very telling in turning around thinking about whether decoding skills should be taught.

Nicholson (1991) directly confronted one of the pieces of evidence most frequently cited in support of the meaning-emphasis approach to word recognition. In a study conducted by Goodman (1965), students in grades 1–3 first read lists of words. Then the children were presented the same words to read in meaningful text. The students made many more errors when they read the words out of context (i.e., when the words were in lists) than they did when the words were read in context. This, of course, is consistent with the hypothesis that reading will be facilitated when semantic–contextual and syntactic–contextual cues are present (i.e., when words are read as part of a text) as compared with when words are read devoid of context cues (i.e., when words are read on lists). This finding has been used repeatedly to defend the meaning-emphasis practice of teaching students to recognize words by analyzing syntactic, graphemic–phonemic, and especially semantic cues.

Nicholson (1991) detected several very serious shortcomings in the Goodman (1965) study, however. First, no attention was paid in the Goodman (1965) investigation of the patterns of performance by good and poor readers. In addition, the participants always read the lists followed by reading of the words in context, and thus there was the possibility that the improved performance in moving from list reading to reading in context might reflect some type of practice effect (i.e., the words in context had been seen before, on the lists).

In Nicholson (1991), students once again were asked to process words in lists and in context. In this study, however, the list–context order was manipulated such that some participants read the lists first and others read the words in context first. Moreover, the study included systematic analysis of reading as a function of the grade of participants and their reading abilities relative to other students (i.e., good, average, weak). The outcomes in this study were anything but consistent with Goodman's (1965) results:

- Some readers did benefit from reading the words in the sentence context—namely, poor readers at each age level and average 6- and 7-year-olds.
- In contrast, a positive effect on reading was obtained in sentence

context for good 6-year-old readers and average 8-year-olds only when reading words in sentence contexts followed reading words in lists, consistent with the practice effect explanation of the original Goodman (1965) finding.

- There was no positive effect derived from reading words in context for good 7- and 8-year-old readers. Indeed, when the 8-year-old good readers did sentence-context reading first, they did better on reading of the words in list format.

In short, Nicholson's (1991) results are consistent with the conclusion that semantic contexts aid weaker younger readers but are not particularly helpful for older better readers. Thus, teaching children to attend to semantic–contextual cues for word recognition is teaching them to use an immature strategy associated with poor reading. In contrast, good readers can read based on graphemic–phonemic cues alone.

The other analyses produced in the late 1980s and early 1990s that were considered as supportive of Chall's (1967, 1983) and Adams's (1990) conclusions were instructional studies (e.g., Foorman et al., 1991; Lovett et al., 1989, 1994). These studies provided supportive evidence of the importance of synthetic phonics instruction as conceived of by Chall (1967)—that is, instruction focusing on letter–sound associations and the blending of letters and sounds to produce words while reading instruction remained balanced and attention was paid to using semantic and syntactic cues along with letter sound cues.

Foorman et al. (1991) examined the reading development of grade 1 students enrolled in one of two types of programs: Half the students were experiencing instruction driven by a basal series that emphasized reading words in meaningful context; the meaningful-context cues were emphasized as critical in deciding what an unknown word might be, and relatively little instruction was given in sounding out words in order to recognize them. The other half of the students were enrolled in a program emphasizing letter–sound associations and the blending of sounds to produce whole words. The students experiencing the two programs were matched for socioeconomic status, with the participants all coming from lower-middle-class to middle-class populations in an urban area. By the end of the year, students who were enrolled in the classes experiencing synthetic phonics instruction were reading and spelling words better than the participants in the classrooms emphasizing the use of semantic context cues during decoding.

Complementing Foorman et al. (1991), Foorman et al. (1998) examined three types of instruction delivered to Title I students in grades 1 and 2. One group received a heavy dose of synthetic phonics instruction with lots of practice with decodable texts (i.e., texts written to emphasize practice in sounding-out skills). A second group received synthetic phonics instruction but in the context of a program emphasizing more reading of real literature. A third group received analytic phonics with emphasis on reading of real literature. With respect to word recognition, the best outcomes at the end of a year of instruction were observed in the group receiving synthetic phonics and decodable text. Again, however, no significant differences were found between groups on measures of reading comprehension. This study provides further evidence that systematic phonics instruction produces benefits in reading individual words but has a smaller, or nonexistent, effect on reading comprehension.

Lovett and her associates focused their attention on students experiencing extreme difficulties in learning to read. The participating students in that study were so far behind in reading that they had been referred to the Hospital for Sick Children (in Toronto, Canada), Lovett's home institution, for potential diagnosis and treatment. Lovett et al. (1989) succeeded in improving the decoding of very weak readers between ages 9 and 13 through intensive instruction in letter–sound analyses and blending (i.e., tutoring in very small groups of children), which also improved student performance on a measure of standardized reading comprehension.

Lovett et al. (1994) also succeeded in teaching such students to decode using phonological analysis and blending; again, performance on a standardized comprehension measure showed improvement as compared with a control condition. What is especially impressive in these studies was how well controlled they were, with control participants also enrolled in treatment conditions to evaluate placebo effects. When these results are combined with those of some other analyses (e.g., Francis et al., 1996; Freppon & McIntyre, 1999; McIntyre et al., 2006; McIntyre & Freppon, 1994; Shaywitz et al., 1992), there is substantial evidence that many children who fall behind in beginning reading are not qualitatively different from other readers, but rather require intensive instruction in order to learn to read. Confidence in the instructional conclusions offered by Lovett's group is heightened by the fact that other research teams have also reported that students who experience difficulties in learning to read benefit from intensive systematic phonics instruction (e.g., Blachman et al., 2004, 2014; Johnston & Watson, 1997; Lesaux & Siegel, 2003; McArthur et al., 2018; Torgesen & Burgess, 1998; Torgesen et al., 1999, 2019; Vellutino et al., 1996).

Across these studies several different approaches to developing decoding proficiencies were used. As with the report of the NRP, the fact that diverse approaches to phonics work to improve reading proficiencies increases confidence that one-size-fits-all thinking is not correct with respect to phonics instruction, and that there is room for substantial variation in the way phonics is taught to children, with the caveat that such instruction needs to be extensive and systematic. For teachers this will include a balanced reading approach that does not just focus on phonics instruction, but includes all elements of reading, such as comprehension, vocabulary development, supporting student motivation, and fluency *with* phonics instruction.

We close this section by explicitly addressing a claim we have sometimes heard from opponents of explicit decoding instruction. They say, "All right, so some kids who are experiencing difficulties learning to read do need it, but it really does no good for other students." There are a number of ways to challenge that claim, but we prefer to cite an analysis by Fielding-Barnsley (1997). Her study included 32 children who came to kindergarten extremely well prepared for beginning reading. Their preschool experiences had brought them to a high level of phonemic awareness and high alphabetic knowledge. Half the children in the study were taught 10 words at the beginning of kindergarten, with the instruction emphasizing sounding out the words and highlighting word parts (e.g., the common part of *pam* and *am*). The 10 words were the following: *am, pam, sat, mat, splat, pal, lap, slam, lamp,* and *tam.* The other children learned the words using a whole-word approach. (Remember the approach that predominated in the *Dick and Jane* readers.) In both conditions, the teaching took place over about 6 weeks, with a few minutes a day devoted to teaching of the words.

There were dramatic differences favoring the students who had been taught using decoding as opposed to the whole-word approach. First, the decoding-instructed students read and wrote the taught words better than did the whole-word-instructed students. There were even more dramatic effects, however, with respect to reading novel words that included the letters and word parts of the words taught (e.g., *at, pat, sam, tap*), as well as pseudowords (e.g., *ap, lat, tal*). The students taught using decoding instruction greatly outperformed the whole-word-instructed students. A decoding instruction component prepares students to tackle words they have never seen before, even when they are well prepared for beginning reading.

That said, credible analyses suggest that an emphasis on word-level skills instruction might not be in the best interests of children entering first grade with good skills already in place. For example, they make less progress in the first-grade year than in the kindergarten year, perhaps reflecting that they have already learned what is taught and tested in grade 1 (Leppänen et al., 2004). In addition, there have been several analyses in the United States where students entering first grade with strong word-level skills grew more in their reading if they experienced a curriculum that was richer in the reading of literature and other holistic activities than in explicit decoding instruction (with decoding instruction better suited for readers with weak entering reading skills; Connor, 2009; Connor et al., 2004, 2013; Juel & Minden-Cupp, 2000; McArthur et al., 2018). Based on such analyses, the case for providing extensive and intensive decoding instruction to weaker readers remains intact, but the same instructional recommendation does not necessarily follow for first graders entering with strong word-level skills. These studies and others (Mathes et al., 2005; Price-Mohr & Price, 2017; Vellutino & Scanlon, 2002) also indicate that both groups of children, however, benefit more from reading lessons that involve much text reading or rereading along with effective decoding instruction.

Summary and Comment

A great deal of research in the past several decades has focused on the positive effects of teaching early reading competencies. The case is strong that explicit efforts to teach the alphabet, letter–sound associations, and sounding out of words (i.e., analysis of words into component sounds, which are then blended) make a positive impact on progress in early reading.

The work on phonics instruction conducted throughout the 20th century has succeeded in clarifying what works and what does not work in developing word recognition skills. Every primary teacher and individual responsible for the education of primary-grade children needs to think hard about the research evidence that was covered in this section. As we say that, we also feel some regret that so much of the recent research attention on explicit decoding instruction (often delivered as intensive tutoring) has focused on students experiencing difficulties in learning to read. The good news is that such instruction does improve the reading of many students who have had difficulties learning to read with regular classroom instruction. One piece of bad news is that teaching phonics alone is not enough to support sustained reading success. A much more balanced approach is needed to support students' reading development. Later in this chapter and in Chapter 10, we discuss further how some teachers are balancing explicit skills instruction and immersion in meaning-emphasis activities, such as writing and reading of literature.

We must emphasize, however, that, in fairness as well to Chall (1967, 1983) and Adams (1990), the point must be made that they have been in favor of balanced instruction all along. They made many clear statements in their books about the need for phonics instruction in a much larger program involving a great deal of reading of various types. It was never only skills emphasis *or* only meaning emphasis with either of these careful thinkers. As will become obvious in Chapter 8, there have been many calls for balancing of code-emphasis instruction and meaning-emphasis instruction.

TEACHING STUDENTS TO READ NEW WORDS THROUGH LETTER SOUNDS

As students begin to develop into strong readers, it is important that they begin to make the connection between letters and sounds then move to understanding that sounds put together create words. There is much use of what are known as Elkonin (1973) boxes, with one box for each sound of a word, so that the child puts the letters in the boxes to denote the sounds in a word—for example, the letters *c, a,* and *t* in each of three boxes for the three sounds in *cat* or the letters *k, i, ck* again in three boxes. Another approach, discussed in Chapter 10, is the Reading Recovery program. Reading Recovery teachers have students "make and break" words, using plastic letters to do so. Thus, the word *cat* is broken into *c* and *at,* and then transformed into *bat, fat, mat,* and *rat* (i.e., the student makes these words by adding initial consonants to the -*at* chunk). An important part of Reading Recovery is using letter- and sound-level clues to sound out words during reading; an important part of writing is to "stretch out" their sounds and map letters to the stretched out sounds to write words. Reading Recovery has shown to have some positive effects supporting reading development (e.g., D'Agostino et al., 2017; Holliman & Hurry, 2013; Hurry et al., 2022).

Orthographic Mapping

Skilled readers bring their knowledge of letter sounds to the reading process and must first be able to deconstruct a word down to the letter–sound associations in order to connect the print, sounds, and meanings of the words. "Orthographic mapping (OM) involves the formation of letter–sound connections to bond the spellings, pronunciations, and meanings of specific words in memory" (Ehri, 2014, p. 5). Several recent studies (Austin et al., 2021; Sargiani et al., 2022; Yoncheva et al., 2015) found students who were taught grapheme–phoneme (or letter sounds) rather than chunks of words (i.e., word families) at the beginning of their reading development, led to stronger readers.

For reading instruction, teachers should begin teaching smaller units of sounds rather than larger ones. Once students have mastered individual sounds, teachers can help students begin to blend the sounds and apply them in read words (Ehri, 2014, 2020; Sargiani et al., 2022). Teachers should continue to provide explicit instruction while supporting students ability to decode multisyllable sounds within words (Ehri, 2020). Taking it a step further, Austin et al. (2021) found teaching letters, sounds, and the word meaning during the decoding process was even more effective than just teaching letter sounds, especially with students diagnosed with dyslexia. Thus, when working with struggling readers, teachers may incorporate word meaning into their instruction to better support the decoding process. What Works Clearinghouse (2022) has identified research-based practices for primary-grade teachers to use to support identifying syllables and decoding multisyllabic words.

TEACHING STUDENTS TO READ NEW WORDS BY ANALOGY TO KNOWN WORDS

After a student learns to deconstruct words into grapheme phoneme connections, students can take that knowledge and apply it to words and begin to recognize similar spelling patters produce similar sounds. It is important to note, that reading by analogy is not a substitute for students who struggle with letter sounds to read words. Recall from earlier in this chapter that, as children encounter common root words, prefixes, and suffixes again and again, they come to treat such word parts as wholes, no longer requiring letter-by-letter analysis and sounding out in order to recognize and pronounce them (e.g., Calhoon & Leslie, 2002; Ehri, 2014, 2020; Leslie & Calhoon, 1995). Indeed, even a few exposures to a word chunk are probably enough for beginning readers to begin to learn the chunk as a chunk (Share, 1999)—or perhaps even one exposure will suffice (Share, 2004). This process probably begins in first grade (Savage & Stuart, 1998; Sprenger-Charolles et al., 1998) so that by the middle elementary grades there are clear differences between good and poor readers in their use of word chunks (e.g., Bowey & Hansen, 1994; Bowey & Underwood, 1996; Leslie & Calhoon, 1995). It is likely that good readers process words more at the level of frequently encountered word chunks than as single phonemes much of the time (Booth et al., 1999; Scarborough, 1995) and that poor readers cannot do so, lacking knowledge and awareness of morphemes relative to good readers (Casalis et al., 2004; Nagy et al., 2003). There is even some evidence that there are differences in word-part awareness and knowledge during kindergarten and grade 1 that are predictive of reading competence during the primary and later elementary years (e.g., Badian, 1993, 1995; Carlisle, 1994; Cunningham & Stanovich, 1993). For example, early competence in selecting the exact match of a short word (e.g., *drop*) from among four possibilities (i.e., *droq, drop, borq, brop*) is predictive of reading comprehension in the later elementary grades (Badian, 1995).

That commonly encountered word chunks are used to decode by good readers, and increasingly by children as they improve in reading skill, has suggested to some that word chunks should be highlighted and taught to children in beginning reading. After all, by age 4, children can detect the separate syllables in multisyllable words (Liberman et al., 1974). They can also detect the onsets and rhyming parts (i.e., *rimes*, defined as a vowel with subsequent consonants; e.g., *-at* in *bat*, *cat*, and *hat*) of words. Thus, they can detect the rime *-ealth* in *health*, *stealth*, and *wealth*, identifying as well the onset sounds of *h-*, *st-*, and *w-* (Goswami, 1998). Beyond detecting onsets and rimes, 5- and 6-year-olds can decode new words by analogy to rhyming words, at least when the rhyming relationship is very obvious. Thus, if a 5-year-old sees the word *beak* and hears it pronounced with the word remaining in full view, he or she often can decode words like *peak*, *weak*, and *speak* (Bowey et al., 1998; Goswami, 1986, 1988, 1999; Wang & Gaffney, 1998). As children's reading improves over the course of the first year of reading instruction, they are able to use parts of rhymes (e.g., the *-ea* in *-eak*) in a similar fashion (Cunningham, 2013; Goswami, 1993, 1998).

Decoding by Analogy

Two of the most effective instructional examples for decoding by analogy we have come across come from both Gaskins (Gaskins et al., 1995) and Cunningham (2013). In these two approaches, instruction can be organized to develop proficiencies in decoding by analogy.

One of the best developed decoding-by-analogy programs that we have encountered was developed at Benchmark School, a school serving children who have difficulties in learning to read in the context of regular schooling. The program was devised by the school's instructional leader, Irene W. Gaskins, in collaboration with Professors Linnea C. Ehri (Graduate Center, City University of New York), Patricia M. Cunningham (Wake Forest University), and Richard C. Anderson (University of Illinois). They dubbed their approach the "Word ID" program (Ehri et al., 2009; Gaskins, 1998, 2005; Gaskins et al., 1991, 1992, 1995).

Prior to learning the spelling patterns, students at Benchmark School learn to deconstruct words by letter sounds (Gaskins, et al., 1996). This includes ensuring that Benchmark students have a strong understanding of letter sounds. At the heart of the program are 120 basic words that capture the key spelling patterns associated with the six English-language vowels. In addition, there also are key words for the two sounds of *g* (e.g., *girl*, *giraffe*) and the two sounds of *c* (e.g., *can*, *city*). Some word parts that always sound the same (e.g., *-tion*) are taught as wholes. All of the key words in the program are summarized in Table 5.2.

Thus, to decode the word *dispatcher*, the Word ID user would learn to identify a key word for each syllable of the word. For the first syllable, *dis-*, the key word *this* could be used since the vowel *i* is followed by a consonant. For the second syllable, *-patch-*, the key word could be *cat*, since the *a* in *-patch-* is followed by a consonant. For the final syllable

TABLE 5.2. Benchmark School Word Identification/Vocabulary Development Program: Key Patterns

a	e	i	o	u	y
grab	he	hi	go	club	my
place	speak	mice	boat	truck	baby
black	scream	kick	job	glue	gym
had	year	did	clock	bug	
made	treat	slide	frog	drum	
flag	red	knife	broke	jump	
snail	see	pig	old	fun	
rain	bleed	right	from	skunk	
make	queen	like	on	up	
talk	sleep	smile	phone	us	
all	sweet	will	long	use	
am	tell	swim	zoo	but	
name	them	time	good		
champ	ten	in	food		
can	end	find	look		
and	tent	vine	school		
map	her	king	stop		
car	yes	think	for		
shark	nest	ship	more		
smart	let	squirt	corn		
smash	flew	this	nose		
has		wish	not		
ask		it	could		
cat		write	round		
skate		five	your		
brave		give	scout		
saw			cow		
day			glow		
			down		
			boy		

g		g = i
girl	grab	gym
go	dragon	giraffe
bug	glow	

c = k		c = s	
can	club	city	excitement
corn	discover	princess	centipede

an i mals   drag on
con test   ex cite ment
crea ture   pres i dent
choc o late   ques tion
dis cover   re port
thank ful   un happy
va ca tion

Note. Reprinted by permission of the Benchmark School and Irene Gaskins.

(-*er*), *her* would apply. Thus, the student, who is also learning the simple consonant–sound associations of English plus the digraphs and consonant blends, would know the sequence of vowel sounds and would then be able to sound out the word. Thus, rather than *this-cat-her* being pronounced, the student would sound out the word *dispatcher*.

Because students are taught to self-verbalize their thinking as they apply the strategy, consistent with an approach to strategy teaching that often works with children (Meichenbaum, 1977), you might hear something like the following from a young Benchmark student confronted with a word like *dispatcher*:

> I can tell by looking at this word that it has three vowel sounds, therefore I know it will have three chunks. The three common English parts I see in this word are divided here. The spelling pattern, or the vowel and what comes after it, in the first chunk is *-is*. The word that I know with the same spelling pattern is *this*. The spelling pattern or the vowel and what comes after it in the second chunk is *-at*. The word I know with the same spelling pattern is *cat*. The spelling pattern for the third chunk is *-er* with the word I know with this spelling pattern being *her*. The word is *dispatcher*. (adapted from Gaskins et al., 1995, p. 343)

Similarly, when Benchmark students are presented a word like *caterpillar*, they can sound out an approximate pronunciation through analogy with the component words *cat*, *her*, *will*, and *car*.

The program extends over several years at Benchmark. First, a variety of exercises are used to develop student understanding of the spelling patterns in the key words. Five new key words are introduced at a time, with 5 days of lessons aimed at developing mastery of the words, including practice using the key words to decode other words. After the key words are mastered, lessons in their use continue. During these lessons, teachers model use of the key words to decode. Students review words learned previously in the Word ID program, and they practice decoding new words—with many exercises included in the instruction to produce overlearning of the key words and decoding using them. We have watched many Benchmark students use the Word ID approach: By the middle elementary grades, most of the students can use the memorized key words with ease to decode multisyllable words that they have not encountered previously.

What is especially striking, however, is that, from the introduction of the program to children in their first year at Benchmark, Word ID lessons do much more than teach children to decode. When key words are introduced, children learn the meanings of the key words, which are also used as part of story writing. The lessons include reading of patterned books. Students hear and read good literature every day they are enrolled at Benchmark. The Benchmark approach is anything but a decoding skill-only approach;

rather, Word ID is embedded in ongoing instruction and used to empower children so that they can participate fully in writing and in reading of real literature. More about the Benchmark approach is presented later in Chapter 9.

The development and evaluation of the program has a fascinating history (see Gaskins et al., 1995), beginning with Gaskins's analyses of the particular reading problems of students at the Benchmark School. This led to an initial version of the program, which was tried in a few classrooms at the school. With evidence of improved decoding, spelling, and vocabulary development in those classrooms, the approach was extended. Across-school implementation, however, did not mean that the approach was employed completely and faithfully in every Benchmark classroom. The natural classroom variations in the implementation of the program permitted an important evaluation of it. Richard C. Anderson and his then-student colleague Marlene Schommer analyzed reading achievement as a function of complete implementation of the program and found a striking relationship: The more teachers spent time encouraging and assisting students in the use of the Word ID approach as they read, the better the reading in the classroom. That is, simply providing the Word ID lessons was not as powerful as supplementing the lessons with a great deal of support in applying the lessons. Take note of this finding, for there is plenty of evidence in the chapters that follow that a key ingredient in effective beginning reading instruction is such scaffolding (Wood et al., 1976) of student performance—that teachers who provide support as their students attempt to use skills taught in formal lessons are especially effective teachers.

The Benchmark faculty and the external university faculty monitored difficulties with the program, refining it until it could be taught efficiently in the classroom and be used efficiently by students. The program became especially well known when it was featured in a videotape produced and distributed by the Center for the Study of Reading at the University of Illinois. Although Gaskins and her colleagues never published the program commercially, they have made it available to any school district that wants it for the cost of reproducing the materials. They have had many takers. Regardless of where we talk in the United States, we are frequently asked about the Word ID program.

Such visibility caught the attention of some prominent reading education researchers who were particularly interested in the impact of decoding-by-analogy approaches, especially as compared with synthetic phonics approaches. Greaney et al. (1997) produced evidence that decoding-by-analogy training improved the reading of primary-level struggling readers. Although some short-term comparisons favored sounding out of words over decoding by analogy (Bruck & Treiman, 1992; Wise et al., 1990), in other studies Word ID and synthetic phonics instruction have produced roughly comparable gains in the decoding skills of beginning readers (Dewitz, 1993; Lovett et al., 1994; Walton et al., 2001). Lovett and colleagues' (1994) study was especially notable because it involved teaching students who experienced a great deal of previous difficulties in learning to read—much like Benchmark students. In Walton and associates' (2001) study, although there was little difference between teaching grade 1 children to decode with analogies versus sounding out of words, there were some subtle advantages for students taught to use analogies (e.g., learning to decode with analogies increased sounding-out skills, but learning to sound out did not enhance decoding-by-analogy skills).

In short, the results of decoding by analogy are consistent: Children can do it (see also Ehri & Robbins, 1992; Peterson & Haines, 1992). This holds true even for students who have experienced previous difficulties in reading who now must read long and complex words (e.g., van Daal et al., 1994). In fact, Gaskins (2000) has developed a more advanced version of the Word ID approach. This version is intended for grade 5 and above, with the focus on decoding of longer words. The program includes voluminous direct instruction about many features of words, including accents and common roots.

In closing this discussion of the decoding-by-analogy approach, we emphasize that such instruction at Benchmark occurs in the context of a very balanced literacy instructional program, one filled with reading of fine literature, writing, and comprehension strategies instruction (Chapter 10). Given this balanced mix, Leslie and Allen (1999) offered an interesting analysis. They devised a tutoring approach involving decoding-by-analogy instruction, with the intervention also including instruction in the use of multiple decoding cues, teaching of sight words, comprehension instruction, extensive reading and sharing of reading, and parental involvement in reading instruction. There were clear positive effects with struggling readers, as compared with uninstructed students.

Cunningham and Hall (1998) developed the Four Blocks framework for use in primary-grade classrooms. This balanced approach to reading instruction (see Cunningham & Allington, 2015, for reasonably complete details) offers a working-with-words block every day that occupies roughly one-quarter of the instructional time scheduled for reading instruction. Central to the activities of the word block is decoding by analogy, although synthetic decoding lessons begin the process. The other blocks, each taking roughly one-quarter of the daily reading lesson time, are guided reading block, writing block, and independent reading block. Evaluations of the Four Blocks framework (Cunningham, 2007; Popplewell & Doty, 2001) and the decoding-by-analogy strand (White, 2005) indicate that teaching children to decode using a decoding-by-analogy approach is successful at developing children who can decode words in isolation and read texts with greater accuracy and fluency than was the case for the control children who did not experience the decoding-by-analogy lessons. Balanced literacy mixes that include decoding-by-analogy instruction are defensible based on the available data.

The Need for Decoding-by-Analogy Instruction

If children can learn to read either with synthetic phonics or word analogy, is there really a need for both approaches? For a very long time, reading clinicians have believed that there are some children who experience difficulties with letter-by-letter analysis and blending but who are able to learn whole words and syllables. Indeed, Irene Gaskins's initial motivation for developing the Word ID approach was her perception that many of the Benchmark students really struggled with synthetic phonics. On the other hand, clinicians have also believed that there are children who are quite good at analyzing the individual sounds of words and blending them but who fail to develop word-chunk and sight-word knowledge. Children are better at decoding using a synthetic phonics approach rather than an analogy approach (Berninger, 1995). No one should be surprised that no approach to decoding works equally well with all students.

In support of this possibility, there now is evidence that some primary-level students rely more on synthetic phonics to decode, whereas others are more reliant on a decoding-by-analogy approach (Berninger et al., 1991; Freebody & Byrne, 1988). That is, some weaker readers learn to recognize words more easily if they are presented as wholes without making their phonemic composition salient (Wise, 1992). Others do better with phonics approaches than by using instruction emphasizing analogies (Levy et al., 1999).

Employing only one approach (analogies or sounding out) to the exclusion of the other is probably the wrong way to think about most children's development as readers. Good readers do analyze and blend individual sounds, but they also make use of word chunks (Berninger, 1994, chap. 4; Ehri, 2014, 2020). Although the dynamics are not completely understood, good readers deduce word-chunk regularities as they sound out words; moreover, they learn more about the sounds of individual letters and letter combinations while experiencing those sounds as part of word chunks (e.g., Thompson et al., 1996).

Given all this information, what makes most sense for beginning reading instruction is to encourage children to analyze and blend individual sounds while teaching them to make use of word parts during decoding. Although we have seen very good teachers who take this approach, we must admit that at this time it is not well understood how to obtain the advantages of explicit phonics instruction *and* decoding-by-analogy instruction.

Irene Gaskins and the Benchmark School faculty have adapted their instruction to combine the synthetic phonics and analogy approaches to decoding instruction, consistent with the evidence that decoding by analogy works best when children also can use phonics cues (Ehri, 1998). Likewise, Cunningham (2013) sets forth the detailed plan for the word work, especially decoding-by-analogy, used in her Four Blocks instructional model.

Thus, as Benchmark students learn their key words, they are being taught how to analyze the key words into individual sounds. The key words are used to provide a great deal of instruction about the key letter–sound associations and letter combinations that commonly occur in English. The students spend a great deal of time stretching out the pronunciations of the key words in order to hear their constituent sounds. They are taught to look at the visual patterns in words and to be sensitive that some letter patterns occur in a number of words.

In short, as the Word ID program has matured, it has come to include more about sounding out words, blending the ideas from phonics and decoding-by-analogy approaches (Gaskins et al., 1996).

Our own intuition, consistent with the direction of Gaskins and her Benchmark colleagues and Cunningham and her colleagues, is that decoding instruction will work best combined with flexibility, especially for children who might really have problems with synthetic phonics or with using analogies to decode words. Thus, what we envision in the future is phonics instruction teaching not only analysis and blending of sounds of words and then moving toward teaching students to blend sounds and apply them in read words. Teachers can support students ability to decode multisyllable sounds within words that do not need to be analyzed and blended every time. By providing lots of opportunities for students to experience the major recurring word parts (i.e., frequent letter patterns, such as phonograms, prefixes, and suffixes), they should come to be automatically recognized.

Lovett et al. (2000) provided support for this intuition of ours. The participants in their study were 6- to 13-year-olds with severe reading difficulties. They received 70 hours of intervention. Some received both instruction in the sounding out of words and Word ID-type instruction. Other participants were taught only to sound out words, while others received only Word ID-type instruction. Controls experienced math tutoring with some classroom survival skills training but did not receive any sort of decoding instruction. At the end of instruction, word recognition was clearly better for the participants receiving the combined sounding-out and Word ID-type training. Confidence in Lovett et al.'s (2000) finding is increased by a recent constructive replication study: Walton and Walton (2002) also demonstrated that instruction combining sounding-out and Word ID-type instruction produces superior reading as compared with either type of training alone.

Much more work needs to be done on the effects produced by teaching struggling readers to use both sounding-out strategies and Word ID approaches. If the reading clinicians are right—and we are betting that they are, based on the available evidence—flexibility in decoding instruction is especially important for students who might experience difficulties with either analyzing and blending or decoding analogically using word chunks alone. In short, what is needed is decoding instruction that accommodates individual differences in students rather than one-size-fits-all phonics instruction. Working out the specifics of such instruction is going to be challenging, we suspect, but will pay off in improved beginning reading instruction. That primary-grade classrooms can involve a fluid mixing of diverse approaches to instruction is a point made vividly in the next section.

PHONICS IN WHOLE-LANGUAGE FIRST-GRADE CLASSROOMS

In Chapter 1, we briefly mentioned Dahl et al. (1999), a study that studied phonics in eight grade 1 classrooms, nominated by a whole-language teacher organization in Ohio. We return to that study now to make the point that word recognition skills can be taught explicitly in whole-language classrooms, with many opportunities for that to occur—in other words, that skills and meaning-emphasis approaches can be blended or balanced.

Over the course of a school year, Dahl et al. (1999) made many observations in classrooms, typically during reading and writing. The researchers were particularly focusing on the phonics instruction that occurred in these classes. A first finding was that the researchers observed plenty of phonics instruction. It occurred during read-alouds, with the teacher discussing letter–sound relationships in words the children would encounter in stories they read. Students often made word collections and then grouped the words they knew on the basis of letter–sound features (e.g., same first letter, rhyme). During guided and shared reading, teachers taught strategies for decoding unknown words. Phonics skills instruction was prominent as teachers listened to students read individually. During writing, there was much encouragement of students to sound out words they were writing. There were word analysis games ("I Spy," requiring students to find particular words in a text) and exercises (e.g., sorting word cards on the basis of letter–sound patterns, discussing patterns in dictated words).

A second finding was that the observers saw lots of instruction intended to develop sound- and letter-level skills. They saw much encouragement of phonemic awareness (i.e., teachers prompting students to hear the sounds in words, for example, by stretching the individual sounds of a word out during its pronunciation). There was lots of phonics, focusing on the sounds produced by both vowels and consonants. There was lots of practice blending sounds, too, as well as plenty of attention to root words, affixes, compound words, contractions, and homonyms (Dahl et al., 1999).

A third important finding was that the phonics instruction decidedly focused on teaching students to be strategic, with students encouraged to use a number of decoding strategies in interaction. They were encouraged to use the onset sound of a word to decode as well as to pay attention to the sentence meaning as they attempted to decode. There was much encouragement of stretching out the sounds of words during both reading and writing (i.e., stretching the intended word out and transcribing sound by sound). During writing, students were encouraged to reread what they read, making certain that words as written contained every sound in them. Students were encouraged to look for familiar patterns in words to aid decoding (e.g., vowel digraphs, soft and hard *c* or *g*). The teachers sometimes asked students to focus on how their mouth is shaped when making certain sounds to cue awareness of a letter–sound relationship. Sometimes the teachers encouraged students to point to each sound in a word as the word was read to emphasize how the sounds and letters connected. The teachers pointed out exception words as *come* or *mother*. In addition to these strategies, students were encouraged to use resources available in the room to facilitate decoding (e.g., the word wall, dictionaries, other students).

The teachers were keenly aware of the progress of individual students, with mini-lessons serving a dual purpose of teaching and assessment, so instruction was tailored to students' needs. As teachers sized up the needs of the children, they planned specific lessons for small groups of children and used large groups to make points that needed to be made to all the children. The teachers in this study taught with awareness of their students' needs.

Did the students learn much about reading in these classrooms? They sure did, as documented through several different instruments sensitive to growth of word knowledge. There were substantial gains for readers at all entry levels.

We are impressed with the gains documented in Dahl et al.'s (1999) investigation. We've seen classrooms where skills and holistic literacy experiences intermix well, as will become even more obvious in the chapters ahead. Moreover, there have been very credible indications of real literacy growth in such classrooms, which goes far in motivating this book on balanced literacy instruction. That said, we have also been in classrooms of teachers who identify with meaning-emphasis approaches and who are very resistant to skills instruction, using only a very few of the tactics documented by Dahl et al. (1999). There is real variety out there among teachers who call themselves meaning-emphasis instructors. We think that the teachers described by Dahl et al. (1999) are balanced teachers rather than meaning-emphasis teachers, and we urge the readers of this book to examine this article for a very stimulating review of what balanced grade 1 teaching can be like among teachers who identify themselves as meaning-emphasis teachers.

To the credit of the meaning-emphasis educator community, they have responded to the work of Dahl and her associates and teachers who are attempting to balance skills and whole-language components with significant resources that detail how phonics can be taught in meaning-emphasis classrooms. We urge educators of beginning readers to spend some time with these resources. They include Moustafa's *Beyond Traditional Phonics* (1997) and *Whole to Part Phonics: How Children Learn to Read and Spell* (1998); Dahl et al.'s *Rethinking Phonics: Making the Best Teaching Decisions* (2001); and Pinnell et al.'s *Word Matters: Teaching Phonics and Spelling in the Reading/Writing Classroom* (1998).

CONCLUDING OBSERVATIONS

The goal of reading is not to decode words but to understand the messages conveyed in the text. When readers are not skilled in word recognition, however, comprehension is low. A consistent characteristic of beginning poor readers is that they have difficulties in decoding words, with this factor more than any other accounting for their low comprehension (e.g., Ehrlich et al., 1993). There is very good reason for researcher attention to word-level processes and identification of instructional methods to increase word recognition. Arguments that development of word recognition skills should not be prominent in beginning reading instruction must ignore a great deal of data to the contrary.

Among scholars who have carefully and respectfully studied all of the evidence on early word recognition, there is agreement at least with respect to the key conclusions that are the focus of this chapter. There is a consensus among scientifically oriented reading researchers that teaching children to sound out words and to use commonly encountered word chunks (e.g., root words, prefixes, suffixes) makes more sense than teaching them to orient only to meaning-related cues in order to recognize words.

We like to think about word recognition instruction in Vygotskian terms (Chapter 4). When adults and children work together to sound out words and decode words by recognizing sounds and word chunks, they probably are engaging in the early stages of an internalization process, one in which the child learns how to use speech to decode words. One of Vygotsky's main messages is that the mind develops in interactions with others, interactions involving a lot of dialogue in which adults and children work on problems together. Learning to read should likewise develop in interaction with others, so that reading strategies that the adult scaffolds dialogically, such as those involved in decoding, will potentially be internalized by the child. (The tutoring provided by the likes of Lovett and her associates, Vellutino and Scanlon and their colleagues, and at Benchmark School reveals substantial scaffolding of students in the Vygotskian sense of the term.)

According to Vygotsky and the other researchers, inner speech, including the inner speech that mediates word recognition, has its origins in social interactions between children and adults wherein adults introduce children to the most important problem-solving strategies that they need to acquire. When an adult models the sounding out of words and then assists the child who at first must sound out words with great effort, it is the beginning of an internalization process, one that is decidedly social. In this way, the adult passes on to another generation a powerful set of tools that humans invented in order to read print.

We hope the information presented in this chapter will be translated in general practice, but there are challenges ahead. One of the greatest difficulties is that many primary-grade teachers probably do not understand enough about decoding or commonly encountered word chunks to effectively implement either an explicit phonics program or a decoding-by-analogy approach (Stahl et al., 1998). For example, Scarborough et al. (1998) observed that teachers in training could not reliably identify the phonemes in words, consistent with less-than-complete knowledge about many aspects of beginning reading (Bos et al., 2001; Cunningham et al., 2004; McCutchen, Abbott, et al., 2002; McCutchen, Harry et al., 2002; Moats & Foorman, 2003; Spear-Swerling & Brucker, 2003).

Moreover, Piasta et al. (2009) demonstrated that the effectiveness of primary-grade teachers depended not only on their being more expert about beginning reading, but also on offering larger amounts of useful decoding lessons. As they concluded: "Thus, students who had teachers who were both knowledgeable and devoted more time to explicit decoding instruction made significantly higher gains in word reading" (p. 224). If primary-grade teachers are to develop phonemic awareness and teach phonics to students, they must understand phonemic awareness and phonics well. At present, far too many primary-grade teachers seem to believe that if they simply follow the program manual of any core reading program, they will be effective (Brenner & Hiebert, 2010). Unfortunately, the truth of the matter is that there are no commercial core reading programs that have an actual research base (Dewitz et al., 2009; McGill-Franzen et al., 2006; Schwartz, 2019a, 2019b, 2021; Stevens et al., 2021; What Works Clearinghouse, 2007).

Even when teachers are willing to teach word-level skills, the materials available to them often are not very informative about decoding instruction at its best. Quite frankly, many phonics programs we have seen are dreadful (although there are unambiguous and distinguished exceptions to this general point)—not much more than a collection of worksheets and drills, providing little information to teachers about the skills that should be developed. There are three professional books on the market that we especially like as starting points for the teacher who wants to improve decoding instruction in her or his classroom. Teachers have told us that they have found these three references useful in understanding the word recognition process and how word recognition can be taught: One is Patricia M. Cunningham's *Phonics They Use: Words for Reading and Writing* (2013), Donna Scanlon and colleagues (2016), *Early Intervention for Reading Difficulties: The Interactive Strategies Approach*, and Barbara J. Fox's (2011) *Word Identification Strategies: Building Phonics into a Classroom Reading Program*.

In addition, the best of the tutoring resources also provide a great deal of information about teaching word recognition. These include *The Howard Street Tutoring Manual: Teaching At-Risk Readers in the Primary Grades* by Darrell Morris (2005); *Book Buddies: Guidelines for Volunteer Tutors of Emergent and Early Readers* by Francine R. Johnston and colleagues (1998); and *Word Journeys: Assessment-Guided Phonics, Spelling, and Vocabulary Instruction* by Kathy Ganske (2000). We cannot resist adding at this point that, beyond reading the tutoring manuals, teachers can get involved in such tutoring, and when they do, they can do a lot of good (e.g., Morris et al., 2000; Santa & Høien, 1999). In fact, teachers seem to learn a lot about teaching reading by participating as tutors in programs like *Book Buddies* (Broaddus & Bloodgood, 1999).

Meaning-Emphasis Instruction Today

The case made by opponents of the word recognition instruction summarized in this chapter was that, if children are systematically taught how to recognize words outside the context of reading of real literature, somehow the benefits of meaning-emphasis instruction would be lost. To their credit, some meaning-emphasis proponents offered much advice about how phonics could be taught in the context of experiencing real literature, as determined by the needs of the child, in contrast to being taught as a decontextualized skill in advance of reading of real texts (e.g., Church, 1996; Goodman, 1993; Routman, 1996). These authors did point the way—at least for some teachers—to methods of doing instruction so that effective teaching of phonics and holistic literacy experiences coexist and complement each other. Exceptionally effective primary teachers balance systematic skills instruction, including word recognition, with immersion in real literature and student writing, as described, for example, by Dahl et al. (1999), which was reviewed earlier in this chapter. With every passing year, more and more resources become available about how to create classroom reading lessons that are better balanced, and we urge readers of this book to look for such resources and benefit from them. We urge all teachers to consider as well that, for those children entering first grade with strong beginning reading skills, there is increasing evidence that such an approach promotes their growth as readers better than does an explicit emphasis on decoding (Connor et al., 2004, 2013; Juel & Minden-Cupp, 2000). In most first-grade classrooms, there are children who will benefit more from explicit decoding instruction and others who will benefit more from a high-quality meaning-emphasis approach.

In fact, evidence produced by Connor et al. (2004, 2013) bolsters that last conclusion considerably. They found that students who entered first grade with weak decoding skills, in fact, experienced the most reading growth if they experienced a classroom strong in explicit decoding instruction. In contrast, for students who entered first grade with strong decoding skills, the amount of explicit decoding instruction they received did not seem to matter. For students entering with low knowledge of vocabulary, their decoding improved more in a classroom with greater explicit decoding instruction than in classrooms with less explicit decoding instruction, but they also benefited over the course of a year by increasing their opportunities for holistic reading and writing. Students entering with strong vocabulary skills benefited the most from holistic instruction across the year. In short, students differ with respect to how much explicit decoding instruction they need—with the weaker readers benefiting more from decoding instruction, coupled with opportunities to engage in reading and writing, and the stronger readers benefiting more from holistic reading and writing activities and instruction.

We add, in defense of meaning-emphasis enthusiasts who have consistently feared decontextualized, systematic phonics instruction, that enthusiasm for phonics has often resulted in instruction that only covers lower-order word recognition skills (i.e., in contrast to higher-order comprehension and composition skills), with such instruction differentially aimed at those children who are at risk, including students with disabilities and cultural minority children (Allington, 1991; Au, 2001; Cummins, 2008; Fitzgerald, 1995; Scanlon & Anderson, 2020). Much of the resistance to systematic phonics instruction stems from the fear that such teaching can take over the beginning reading curriculum, with it certainly the case that primary-level classrooms are left with little time in the morning schedule after word-level skills instruction is completed! No one should read this chapter and conclude there is support here for such instruction. This book is about balanced literacy instruction, with such balance including prominent skills instruction and prominent holistic reading and writing experiences for all children, and for some children (i.e., strong beginning readers) probably a mix that is more intensely holistic than aimed at coverage of basic word recognition skills.

The Interactive Strategies Approach

We must also comment on the interactive strategies approach (ISA; Anderson, 2019; Scanlon et al., 2016). This approach to developing early readers emerging literacy skills has garnered six large scale federally funded projects over a 25-year period. We include ISA because it was developed in the series of studies we review here. As the research base expanded, so did the ISA approach. Today, there are two books (Scanlon et al., 2016; Vellutino & Scanlon, 2002) that details the ins and outs of ISA and in providing a detailed description of how ISA was developed and now represents a powerful alternative to traditional beginning reading lessons. The ISA is described as an approach that "involves extensive attention to the development of phonological/phonemic awareness and phonics skills and the application of those skills in combination with the development of strategic word-solving skills in context. In the ISA, substantial emphasis is placed on the interactive and mutually supportive roles of contextual and alphabetic information in the process of word solving. It involves explicit instruction and guidance in the use of word-solving strategies and in the underlying skills and understandings that enable the use of those strategies" (Scanlon & Anderson, 2020, p. 25).

The ISA makes the use of contextual information found in print an essential aspect of the initial stages of literacy development. The ISA counters the argument that the initial stages of literacy acquisition as singular focus on developing decoding proficiencies, arguing that student attention to contextual cues actually develops readers who do not focus on the necessary features of print and that will prevent the students from focusing on print in the ways that are needed to become a skilled reader. While developing decoding proficiencies is important it must be remembered that the written English language is not perfectly decodable (e.g., *have, want, the, they, done, come, shoe, put*). The key seems to be one of teaching children to cross-check the pronunciation to ensure it makes sense in the sentence. As Scanlon and Anderson (2020) have noted, "the ongoing debate around how readers learn to read words, although typically framed around decoding, actually centers on how to help readers build the extensive sight vocabulary they need to become proficient readers. Decoding, of course, plays a critical but not exclusive role" (p. 23).

From the very beginning teachers must make sure that children are not just decoding but decoding and then cross-checking to ensure the word just read makes sense in the story. Ehri (2014) described how children were using context to cross-check their initial decoding and self-correcting their pronunciation when necessary. The role that attention to context plays for young readers matters because it plays a role in the self-teaching process (Share, 1995). The importance of self-teaching in early reading is also a key factor in fostering self-correction, a behavior that separates children who will become proficient readers from the children who won't (Clay, 1969). Young children acquiring literacy need to learn how to use contextual information in the word identification processes. Spontaneous self-correction supports good comprehension an absent component when a child simply misidentifies a word in a text and just carries on seeming not to notice the misreading that has occurred. A common misreading in early literacy lessons is a nonword but a nonword that does follow the phonic rules (e.g., a child has read *fracture* as *frack tour* and continues to read with no attempt at self-correction).

The ISA has available materials to focus children's attention on self-correction as well as a number of other factors. It is just this sort of self-monitoring that enables orthographic mapping that is needed for learning words and to potentially increase a readers familiarity with phonic elements already taught.

The Nature of Excellent Phonics Instruction

That there are only small differences in effectiveness among the various phonics approaches (Ehri et al., 2001; National Reading Panel, 2000; Stahl et al., 1998) does not mean that we do not know what constitutes excellent phonics instruction. After reviewing the literature on phonics instruction, Stahl et al. (1998) developed a sensible set of conclusions about what is part of excellent phonics instruction:

- Good phonics instruction develops the alphabetic principle, the understanding that letters in words represent specific sounds.
- Good phonics instruction develops phonological (phonemic) awareness.
- Good phonics instruction develops a thorough grounding in the letters—that is, automatic recognition of the form of each letter (e.g., there is no confusion between *p* and *q*).
- Good phonics instruction should not emphasize rules (which often are filled with exceptions—e.g., "When two vowels go walking, the first does the talking" works 45% of the time; Clymer, 1963) that depend on worksheets, dominate instruction, or are boring.
- Good phonics instruction involves a great deal of practice in reading words—words in isolation but also in texts—and in writing words.

- Good phonics instruction results in automatic word recognition. Just remember that skilled reading is not sounding out words; it involves recognizing words effortlessly!
- Good phonics instruction is only a small part of reading instruction.

Research To Get Beyond Systematic Phonics and Learning Only about Word Recognition in the Primary Grades

A problem with the list of ideas about developing word recognition just presented, however, is that it is derived mostly from studies of systematic phonics and wholly from studies of primary-grade readers to the exclusion of everyone else (Pianta & Hamre, 2009). Fortunately, since the publication of the NRP (2000) report, there has been research on other methods of phonics instruction and at other age levels, especially through true experimentation, the methodology favored by the panel.

For example, McCandliss et al. (2003) worked with children who had difficulties learning to read in grade 1. The children participated in an intervention called Word Building for twenty 50-minute sessions. (There were also no-intervention control participants.) The centerpiece of Word Building was exercises emphasizing that words change by altering one letter, which also impacts the sound of the word. Thus, *sat* can become *sap* by changing the last letter; *sap* becomes *tap* with a change of the first letter; change the middle letter, and *tap* becomes *top*; add an *s* at the beginning of the word to make *stop*. Such word building was complemented by flashcard reading of the words encountered during Word Building and reading of sentences containing the practiced words, with student–teacher discussions of the meanings of the sentences. The intervention worked well, producing much improved reading of words and even some transfer benefit to a passage comprehension measure. There are many such specific practices that could and should be evaluated in experiments, for they are included in many phonics programs.

Beyond the elementary school, investigators have been studying the effects of word recognition instruction emphasizing sounding out by paying attention to word parts as well as the individual letter sounds in the words and word parts (something akin to the type of instruction studied by Lovett). Such instruction has improved the reading skills, principally word reading, of struggling adolescent readers (Bhattacharya & Ehri, 2004; Kamil et al., 2008; Penney, 2002; Scammacca et al., 2007).

In short, there is a lot of experimentation still occurring with respect to beginning word reading skills and a great deal of work that could be done. Word recognition should be a prominent area of research for some time to come. We would urge educators interested in word recognition to look hard at the interventions now being widely deployed and ask, "What is untested here?" The answer is *much*, which provides great opportunity for more and new inquiry.

SUMMARY AND CONCLUDING REFLECTIONS

1. Ehri (e.g., 1991, 2014) has proposed a general developmental progression in learning to recognize words. Preschoolers can first recognize logographs before they can do alphabetic reading, which begins even before the child knows all the letter–sound associations. Experience in sounding out particular words results in frequently encountered words becoming sight words, no longer requiring alphabetic decoding. Letter strings that occur frequently in words, including root words, phonograms, prefixes, and suffixes, come to be perceived as units, no longer needing to be sounded out when encountered in a new word. At this point, new words can often be decoded by analogy to words known by the reader (e.g., knowing *beak*, the child can read *peak*).

2. There is a great deal of support for the efficacy of systematic phonics instruction. Chall's (1967, 1983) book is a summary of the first wave of evidence, which has continued to accumulate since its publication. Synthetic phonics instruction, the approach most favored by Chall, involves learning the letter–sound associations and blending the sounds specified by a word's letters in order to produce the word. The success in using synthetic phonics to teach beginning readers to recognize words contrasts at least slightly with lower success rates for analytic phonics approaches involving less systematic instruction of phonics (i.e., on an as-needed basis) in some, but not all, studies.

3. It is critical for students to have an understanding of letters and sounds before they begin to blend and learn larger chunks of letters. Students must be able to deconstruct a word to begin to recognize common word chunks.

4. Once students have mastered letters and sounds, an effective approach to teaching common word chunks is to teach students to decode by analogy. This approach requires teaching students a large number of word parts that then can be used to read by analogy. Both the Benchmark School Word ID program (Gaskins, 2005), and the Cunningham (Cunningham, 2013; Cunningham & Allington, 2015; Cunningham & Hall, 1998) Four Blocks model involve decoding by analogy.

5. Good readers decode by analysis and blending and also by analogy, and thus there is hard thinking going on about how to teach beginning readers to use both approaches. A possibility is that each approach is better

for some readers. Effective decoding instruction should be flexible enough to permit students to use the approach or approaches that work for them.

6. In contrast to the substantial database in favor of systematic phonics instruction and the growing database in support of decoding by analogy, there is very little support for teaching students to decode by orienting primarily to semantic–contextual and syntactic–contextual cues, as opposed to graphemic–phonemic cues. However, research does exist demonstrating that good readers use semantic–syntactic information to confirm the word recognition while reading connected texts. That is, when a word is misread good readers notice that the word they produced does not make sense as they continue reading the sentence. Thus, they use semantic–syntactic information as a basis for cross-checking and self-correction, and self-correction is a hallmark of early readers who become proficient readers (Clay, 1969; Scanlon & Anderson, 2020).

7. There are meaning-emphasis teachers who do a great deal of word recognition instruction in context, with documented growth in word recognition skills in their classrooms. In addition, researchers are now using balanced reading models demonstrating the potentially powerful effects of intensive balanced approaches both in the general education classroom and in interventions designed to accelerate the reading development of struggling readers. We now hope that the research base for balanced reading lessons will result in better balance in the reading lessons for all children that offered every day.

8. Research on how to teach decoding has been an extremely active area of research, but, if anything, there is a need for more activity in this area. For example, one important hypothesis that deserves a great deal of attention is that a very effective way to teach decoding is to teach students to attend to letter-level phonological cues first, blending individual letter sounds and word parts, and then to check their decoding by determining its sensibility in light of semantic–contextual and syntactic–contextual cues. The case will be made in the chapters ahead that such teaching can be part of balanced literacy instruction. It provides a place for the skills approach to word recognition and the semantic–contextual ideas favored by the meaning-emphasis theorists. More than that, it provides places for the various components that are sensible, suggesting an articulation that presumably is at the heart of effective word recognition (Gough et al., 1992).

9. The emphasis on letter-, sound-, and word-level approaches in this chapter should not be construed to mean that such instruction would ever be sufficient to produce readers. Rather, word recognition is but one critical component in a complicated mix of components. There is a lot of research

ahead in the chapters that follow on word recognition processes and other processes in reading.

10. One area that is yet largely unresearched in the development of effective decoding proficiencies is the role that reading volume (Allington & McGill-Franzen, 2021) plays in integrating decoding knowledge and fluent reading. There are indications in the research that creating extensive opportunities to engage in reading text enhances decoding proficiencies. The work of David Share (1995, 1999, 2008) provides compelling evidence that children can improve word recognition through engaged reading. Likewise, intervention lessons provided for struggling readers seem more powerful when substantial opportunities to read text are coupled with explicit decoding lessons (e.g., Mathes et al., 2005; Scanlon & Anderson, 2020; Vellutino et al., 1996).

REFERENCES

Abt Associates. (1977). *Education as experimentation: A planned variation model: Vol, IV-B. Effects of follow through models.* Abt Books.

Adams, M. J. (1990). *Beginning to read.* Harvard University Press.

Adams, M. J. (2009). Decodable text: Why, when, and how? In E. H. Hiebert (Ed.), *Finding the right texts: What works for beginning and struggling readers* (pp. 23–46). Guilford Press.

Allington, R. L. (1991). Children who find learning to read difficult: School responses to diversity. In E. H. Hiebert (Ed.), *Literacy for a diverse society: Perspectives, practices, and policies* (pp. 237–252). Teachers College Press.

Allington, R. L., & Fleming, J. T. (1978). The misreading of high-frequency words. *Journal of Special Education, 12*, 417–421.

Allington, R. L., Gormley, K., & Truex, S. (1976). Poor and normal readers' achievement on visual tasks involving high-frequency low-discriminability words. *Journal of Learning Disabilities, 9*, 292–296.

Allington, R. L. & McGill-Franzen, A. (2021). Reading volume and reading achievement: A review of recent research. *Reading Research Quarterly, 56*, S231–S238.

Anderson, D. R., & Collins, P. A. (1988). *The impact on children's education: Television's influence on cognitive development* (Office of Research Working Paper No. 2). U.S. Department of Education, Office of Educational Research and Improvement.

Anderson, K. L. (2019). Explicit instruction for word solving: Scaffolding developing readers' use of code-based and meaning-based strategies. *Preventing School Failure: Alternative Education for Children and Youth, 63*(2), 175–183.

Armbruster, B., Lehr, F., & Osborn, J. (2001). *Put reading first.* National Institute for Literacy.

Au, K. H. (2001). A multicultural perspective on policies for improving literacy achievement: Equity and excellence. In S. B. Neuman & D. K. Dickinson (Eds.), *Handbook of early literacy research* (pp. 835–851). Guilford Press.

Austin, C. R., Vaughn, S., Clemens, N. H., Pustejovsky, J. E., & Boucher, A. N. (2021). The relative effects of instruction linking word reading and word meaning compared to word reading instruction alone on the accuracy, fluency, and word meaning knowledge of 4th–5th grade students with dyslexia. *Scientific Studies of Reading,* 1–19.

Badian, N. A. (1993). Phonemic awareness, naming, visual symbol processing, and reading. *Reading and Writing: An Interdisciplinary Journal, 5,* 87–100.

Badian, N. A. (1995). Predicting reading ability over the long term: The changing roles of letter naming, phonological awareness and orthographic processing. *Annals of Dyslexia, 45,* 79–96.

Baron, J. (1977). Mechanisms for pronouncing printed words: Use and acquisition. In D. LaBerge & S. J. Samuels (Eds.), *Basic processes in reading: Perception and comprehension* (pp. 175–216). Erlbaum.

Barron, R. W. (1986). Word recognition in early reading: A review of the direct and indirect access hypotheses. *Cognition, 24,* 93–119.

Berninger, V. W. (1994). *Reading and writing acquisition: A developmental neuropsychological perspective.* Brown & Benchmark.

Berninger, V. W. (1995). Has the phonological recoding model of reading acquisition and reading disability led us astray? *Issues in Education: Contributions from Educational Psychology, 1,* 59–63.

Berninger, V. W., Yates, C., & Lester, K. (1991). Multiple orthographic codes in reading and writing acquisition. *Reading and Writing: An Interdisciplinary Journal, 3,* 115–149.

Bhattacharya, A., & Ehri, L. C. (2004). Graphosyllabic analysis helps adolescent struggling readers read and spell words. *Journal of Learning Disabilities, 37,* 331–348.

Blachman, B. A., Schatschneider, C., Fletcher, J. M., Francis, D. J., Clonan, S. M., et al. (2004). Effects of intensive reading remediation for second and third graders and a 1-year follow-up. *Journal of Educational Psychology, 96,* 444–461.

Blachman, B. A., Schatschneider, C., Fletcher, J. M., Murray, M. S., Munger, K. A., & Vaughn, M. G. (2014). Intensive reading remediation in grade 2 or 3: Are there effects a decade later? *Journal of Educational Psychology, 106*(1), 46–57.

Bogatz, G. A., & Ball, S. (1971). *The second year of "Sesame Street": A continuing evaluation.* Educational Testing Service.

Bond, G. L., & Dykstra, R. (1967). The cooperative research program in first-grade reading instruction. *Reading Research Quarterly, 2*(4), 5–142.

Booth, J. R., Perfetti, C. A., & MacWhinney, B. (1999). Quick, automatic, and general activation of orthographic and phonological representations in young readers. *Developmental Psychology, 35,* 3–19.

Bos, C., Mather, N., Dickson, S., Podhajski, B., & Chard, D. (2001). Perceptions and knowledge of preservice and inservice educators about early reading instruction. *Annals of Dyslexia, 51,* 97–120.

Bowey, J. A., & Hansen, J. (1994). The development of orthographic rimes as units of word recognition. *Journal of Experimental Child Psychology, 58,* 465–488.

Bowey, J. A., & Underwood, N. (1996). Further evidence that orthographic rime usage in nonword reading increases with word-level reading proficiency. *Journal of Experimental Child Psychology, 63,* 526–562.

Bowey, J. A., Vaughan, L., & Hansen, J. (1998). Beginning readers' use of orthographic analogies in word reading. *Journal of Experimental Child Psychology, 68,* 108–133.

Brenner, D., & Hiebert, E. H. (2010). If I follow the teachers' edition, isn't that enough?: Analyzing reading volume in six core reading programs. *Elementary School Journal, 110*(3), 347–363.

Broaddus, K., & Bloodgood, J. W. (1999). "We're supposed to already know how to teach reading": Teacher change to support struggling readers. *Reading Research Quarterly, 34,* 426–451.

Bruck, M., & Treiman, R. (1992). Learning to pronounce words: The limits of analogies. *Reading Research Quarterly, 27,* 374–398.

Byrne, B., & Fielding-Barnsley, R. (1990). Acquiring the alphabetic principle: A case for teaching recognition of phoneme identity. *Journal of Educational Psychology, 82,* 805–812.

Byrne, B., & Fielding-Barnsley, R. (1991). Evaluation of a program to teach phonemic awareness to young children. *Journal of Educational Psychology, 83,* 451–455.

Calhoon, J. A., & Leslie, L. (2002). A longitudinal study of the effects of word frequency and rime-neighborhood size on beginning readers' rime reading accuracy in words and nonwords. *Journal of Literacy Research, 34,* 39–58.

Carlisle, J. F. (1994). Morphological awareness and early reading achievement. In L. B. Feldman (Ed.), *Morphological aspects of language processing* (pp. 189–209). Erlbaum.

Casalis, S., Colé, P., & Sopo, D. (2004). Morphological awareness in developmental dyslexia. *Annals of Dyslexia, 54,* 114–138.

Castles, A., Rastle, K., & Nation, K. (2018). Ending the reading wars: Reading acquisition from novice to expert. *Psychological Science in the Public Interest, 19*(1), 5–51.

Chall, J. S. (1967). *Learning to read: The great debate.* McGraw-Hill.

Chall, J. S. (1983). *Learning to read: The great debate* (updated ed.). McGraw-Hill.

Church, S. M. (1996). *The future of whole language: Reconstruction or self-destruction?* Heinemann.

Clay, M. M. (1969). Reading errors and self-correction behaviour. *British Journal of Educational Psychology, 37,* 47–56.

Clymer, T. (1963). The utility of phonic generalizations in the primary grades. *The Reading Teacher, 16,* 252–258.

Connor, C. M. (2009). Instruction, student engagement, and reading skill growth in Reading First classrooms. *Elementary School Journal, 109*(3), 221–250.

Connor, C. M., Morrison, F. J., Fishman, B., Crowe, E. C., Al Otaiba, S., & Schatschneider, C. (2013). A longitudinal cluster-randomized control study on the accumulating effects of individualized literacy instruction on students' reading from 1st through 3rd grade. *Psychological Science, 24*(8), 1408–1419.

Connor, C. M., Morrison, F. J., & Katch, L. E. (2004). Beyond the reading wars: Exploring the effect of child–instruction interactions on growth in early reading. *Scientific Studies of Reading, 8,* 305–336.

Cronin, V., Farrell, D., & Delaney, M. (1995, April). *Environmental print facilitates word reading.* Paper presented at the biennial meeting of the Society for Research in Child Development, Indianapolis, IN.

Cummins, J. (2008). Pedagogies for the poor? Realigning reading instruction for low-income students with scientifically based reading research. *Educational Researcher, 36*(9), 564–572.

Cunningham, A. E., Perry, K. E., Stanovich, K. E., & Stanovich, P. J. (2004). Disciplinary knowledge of K–3 teachers and their knowledge calibration in the domain of early literacy. *Annals of Dyslexia, 54,* 139–167.

Cunningham, A. E., & Stanovich, K. E. (1993). Children's literacy environments and early word recognition skills. *Reading and Writing: An Interdisciplinary Journal, 5,* 193–204.

Cunningham, P. M. (1975). Investigating synthesized theory of mediated word recognition. *Reading Research Quarterly, 11*(2), 127–143.

Cunningham, P. M. (1992). What kind of phonics instruction will we have? In C. K. Kinzer & D. Leu (Eds.), *Literacy research, theory, and practice: Views from many perspectives* (pp. 17–31). National Reading Conference.

Cunningham, P. M. (Ed.). (2007). *Six successful high poverty schools: How they beat the odds.* National Reading Conference.

Cunningham, P. M. (2011). Best practices in teaching phonological awareness and phonics. In L. M. Morrow & L. B. Gambrell (Eds.), *Best practices in literacy instruction* (4th ed., pp. 199–223). Guilford Press.

Cunningham, P. M. (2013). *Phonics they use: Words for reading and writing* (6th ed.). Pearson.

Cunningham, P. M., & Allington, R. L. (2015). *Classrooms that work: They can all read and write* (6th ed.). Pearson.

Cunningham, P. M., & Hall, D. (1998). The Four Blocks: A balanced framework for literacy in primary classrooms. In K. Harris, S. Graham, & D. Deshler (Eds.), *Teaching every child every day* (pp. 32–76). Brookline Books.

D'Agostino, J. V., Lose, M. K., & Kelly, R. H. (2017). Examining the sustained effects of Reading Recovery. *Journal of Education for Students Placed at Risk (JESPAR), 22*(2), 116–127.

Dahl, K. L., Scharer, P. L., Lawson, L. L., & Grogan, P. R. (1999). Phonics instruction and student achievement in whole language first-grade classrooms. *Reading Research Quarterly, 34*, 312–341.

Dahl, K. L., Scharer, P. L., Lawson, L. L., & Grogan, P. R. (2001). *Rethinking phonics: Making the best teaching decisions.* Heinemann.

Dewitz, P. (1993, May). *Comparing an analogy and phonics approach to word recognition.* Paper presented at the Edmund Hardcastle Henderson Roundtable in Reading, Charlottesville, Virginia.

Dewitz, P., Jones, J., & Leahy, S. (2009). Comprehension strategy instruction in core reading programs. *Reading Research Quarterly, 44*(2), 102–126.

Dolch, E. W. (1936). A basic sight vocabulary. *Elementary School Journal, 36*, 456–460.

Ehri, L. C. (1991). Development of the ability to read words. In R. Barr, M. L. Kamil, P. B. Mosenthal, & P. D. Pearson (Eds.), *Handbook of reading research* (Vol. 2, pp. 383–417). Longman.

Ehri, L. C. (1998). Grapheme–phoneme knowledge is essential for learning to read words in English. In J. L. Metsala & L. C. Ehri (Eds.), *Word recognition in beginning literacy* (pp. 3–40). Erlbaum.

Ehri, L. C. (2014). Orthographic mapping in the acquisition of sight word reading, spelling memory, and vocabulary learning. *Scientific Studies of Reading, 18*(1), 5–21.

Ehri, L. C. (2020). The science of learning to read words: A case for systematic phonics instruction. *Reading Research Quarterly, 55*, S45–S60.

Ehri, L. C., Deffner, N. D., & Wilce, L. S. (1984). Pictorial mnemonics for phonics. *Journal of Educational Psychology, 76*, 880–893.

Ehri, L. C., Nunes, S. R., Stahl, S. A., & Willows, D. M. (2001). Systematic phonics instruction helps students learn to read: Evidence from the National Reading Panel's meta-analysis. *Review of Educational Research, 71*, 393–448.

Ehri, L. C., & Robbins, C. (1992). Beginners need some decoding skill to read words by analogy. *Reading Research Quarterly, 27*, 12–27.

Ehri, L. C., Satlow, E., & Gaskins, I. (2009). Grapho-phonemic enrichment strengthens keyword analogy instruction for struggling young readers. *Reading and Writing Quarterly, 25*(2–3), 162–191.

Ehri, L. C., & Snowling, M. J. (2004). Developmental variation in word recognition. In C. A. Stone, E. R. Silliman, B. J. Ehren, & K. Apel (Eds.), *Handbook of language and literacy: Development and disorders* (pp. 433–460). Guilford Press.

Ehri, L. C., & Wilce, L. S. (1985). Movement into reading: Is the first stage of printed word learning visual or phonetic? *Reading Research Quarterly, 20*, 163–179.

Ehri, L. C., & Wilce, L. S. (1987a). Cipher versus cue reading: An experiment in decoding acquisition. *Journal of Educational Psychology, 79*, 3–13.

Ehri, L. C., & Wilce, L. S. (1987b). Does learning to spell help beginners learn to read words? *Reading Research Quarterly, 18*, 47–65.

Ehrlich, M.-F., Kurtz-Costes, B., & Loridant, C. (1993). Cognitive and motivational determinants of reading comprehension in good and poor readers. *Journal of Reading Behavior, 25*, 365–381.

Elkonin, D. B. (1973). U.S.S.R in J. Downing (Ed.), *Comparative reading* (pp. 551-579). Macmillian

Fielding-Barnsley, R. (1997). Explicit instruction in decoding benefits children high in phonemic awareness and alphabet knowledge. *Scientific Studies of Reading, 1*, 85–98.

Fitzgerald, J. (1995). English-as-a-second language learners' cognitive reading processes: A review of research. *Journal of Reading Behavior, 27*, 115–152.

Foorman, B. R., Francis, D. J., Fletcher, J. M., & Schatschneider, C. (1998). The role of instruction in learning to read: Preventing reading failure in at-risk children. *Journal of Educational Psychology, 90*, 37–55.

Foorman, B., Francis, D., Novy, D., & Liberman, D. (1991). How letter–sound instruction mediates progress in first-grade reading and spelling. *Journal of Educational Psychology, 83*, 456–469.

Fox, B. J. (2011). *Word identification strategies: Building phonics into a classroom reading program* (5th ed.). Pearson.

Fox, B. J., & Routh, D. K. (1975). Analyzing spoken language into words, syllables, and phonemes: A developmental study. *Journal of Psycholinguistic Research, 4*, 331–342.

Francis, D. J., Shaywitz, S. E., Stuebing, K. K., Shaywitz, B. A., & Fletcher, J. M. (1996). Developmental lag versus deficit models of reading disability: A longitudinal, individual growth curves analysis. *Journal of Educational Psychology, 88*, 3–17.

Freebody, P., & Byrne, B. (1988). Word-reading strategies in elementary school children: Relations to comprehension, reading time, and phonemic awareness. *Reading Research Quarterly, 23*, 441–453.

Freppon, P. A., & McIntyre, E. (1999). A comparison of young children learning to read in different instructional settings. *Journal of Educational Research, 92*(4), 206–217.

Fry, E. B., Kress, J. E., & Fountoukidis, D. L. (1993). *The reading teacher's book of lists*. Prentice-Hall.

Gamse, B. C., Jacob, R. T., Horst, M., Boulay, B., & Unlu, F. (2009). *Reading First impact study: Final report* (NCEE 2009-4038). National Center for Education Evaluation and Regional Assistance, Institute of Education Sciences, U.S. Department of Education.

Ganske, K. (2000). *Word journeys: Assessment-guided phonics, spelling, and vocabulary instruction*. Guilford Press.

Gaskins, I. W. (1998). A beginning literacy program for delayed and at-risk readers. In J. Metsala & L. Ehri (Eds.), *Word recognition in beginning literacy* (pp. 209–232). Erlbaum.

Gaskins, I. W. (2000). *Word detectives program: 5th grade and above*. Benchmark Press.

Gaskins, I. W. (2005). *Success with struggling readers*. Guilford Press.

Gaskins, I. W., Ehri, L. C., Cress, C., O'Hara, C., & Donnelly, K. (1996). Procedures for word learning: Making discoveries about words. *The Reading Teacher, 50*, 312–327.

Gaskins, R. W., Gaskins, I. W., Anderson, R. C., & Schommer, M. (1995). The reciprocal relationship between research and development: An example involving a decoding strand for poor readers. *Journal of Reading Behavior, 27*, 337–377.

Gaskins, R. W., Gaskins, J. C., & Gaskins, I. W. (1991). A decoding program for poor readers—and the rest of the class, too! *Language Arts, 68*, 213–225.

Gaskins, R. W., Gaskins, J. C., & Gaskins, I. W. (1992). Using what you know to figure out what you don't know: An analogy approach to decoding. *Reading and Writing Quarterly, 8*, 197–221.

Gibson, E. J., Gibson, J. J., Pick, A. D., & Osser, H. A. (1962). A developmental study of the discrimination of letter-like forms. *Journal of Comparative and Physiological Psychology, 55*, 897–906.

Gibson, E. J., & Levin, H. (1975). *The psychology of reading.* MIT Press.

Gilbert, N., Spring, C., & Sassenrath, J. (1977). Effects of overlearning and similarity on transfer in word recognition. *Perceptual and Motor Skills, 44,* 591–598.

Gonzalez-Frey, S. M., & Ehri, L. C. (2021). Connected phonation is more effective than segmented phonation for teaching beginning readers to decode unfamiliar words. *Scientific Studies of Reading, 25*(3), 272–285.

Goodman, K. S. (1965). A linguistic study of cues and miscues in reading. *Elementary English, 42,* 639–642.

Goodman, K. S. (1993). *Phonics phacts.* Heinemann.

Goswami, U. (1986). Children's use of analogy in learning to read: A developmental study. *Journal of Experimental Child Psychology, 42,* 73–83.

Goswami, U. (1988). Orthographic analogies and reading development. *Quarterly Journal of Experimental Psychology, 40,* 239–268.

Goswami, U. (1993). Toward an interactive analogy model of reading development: Decoding vowel graphemes in beginning reading. *Journal of Experimental Child Psychology, 56,* 443–475.

Goswami, U. (1998). The role of analogies in the development of word recognition. In J. Metsala & L. Ehri (Eds.), *Word recognition in beginning reading* (pp. 41–63). Erlbaum.

Goswami, U. (1999). Orthographic analogies and phonological priming: A comment on Bowey, Vaughan, & Hansen (1998). *Journal of Experimental Child Psychology, 72,* 210–219.

Gough, P. B., Juel, C., & Griffith, P. L. (1992). Reading, spelling, and the orthographic cipher. In P. B. Gough, L. C. Ehri, & R. Treiman (Eds.), *Reading acquisition* (pp. 35–48). Erlbaum.

Greaney, K. T., Tunmer, W. E., & Chapman, J. W. (1997). Effects of rime-based orthographic analogy training on the word recognition skills of children with reading disability. *Journal of Educational Psychology, 89,* 645–651.

Guthrie, J. T., & Tyler, S. J. (1975). Cognition and instruction of poor readers. *Journal of Reading Behavior, 10,* 57–78.

Hoffman, J. V., McCarthey, S. J., Abbott, J., Christian, C., Corman, L., Curry, C., et al. (1993). *So what's new in the new basals? A focus on first grade* (Reading Research Report No. 6). National Reading Research Center.

Hoffman, J. V., Sailors, M., & Patterson, E. U. (2002). Decodable texts for beginning reading instruction: The year 2000 basals. *Journal of Literacy Research, 34,* 269–298.

Holliman, A. J., & Hurry, J. (2013). The effects of Reading Recovery on children's literacy progress and special educational needs status: a three-year follow-up study. *Educational Psychology, 33*(6), 719–733.

Horn, C. C., & Manis, F. R. (1987). Development of automatic and speeded reading of printed words. *Journal of Experimental Child Psychology, 44,* 92–108.

House, E. R., Glass, G. V., McLean, L., & Walker, D. (1978). No simple answers: Critique of the Follow Through evaluations. *Harvard Educational Review, 48,* 128–160.

Huba, M. E. (1984). The relationship between linguistic awareness in prereaders and two types of experimental instruction. *Reading World, 23,* 347–363.

Hurry, J., Fridkin, L., & Holliman, A. J. (2022). Reading intervention at age 6: Long-term effects of Reading Recovery in the UK on qualifications and support at age 16. *British Educational Research Journal, 48*(1), 5–21.

Huston, A. C., Anderson, D. R., Wright, J. C., Linebarger, D. L., & Schmitt, K. L. (2001). *Sesame Street* viewers as adolescents: The recontact study. In S. M. Fisch & R. T. Truglio (Eds.), *"G" is for growing: Thirty years of research on children and "Sesame Street"* (pp. 131–143). Erlbaum.

Jenkins, J. R., Peyton, J. A., Sanders, E. A., & Vadasy, P. F. (2004). Effects of reading decodable texts in supplemental first-grade tutoring. *Scientific Studies of Reading, 8*, 53–85.

Johnston, F. R., Invernizzi, M., & Juel, C. (1998). *Book buddies: Guidelines for volunteer tutors of emergent and early readers.* Guilford Press.

Johnston, R. S., & Watson, J. (1997). Developing reading, spelling, and phonemic awareness skills in primary school children. *Reading, 31*, 37–40.

Juel, C., & Minden-Cupp, C. (2000). Learning to read words: Linguistic units and instructional strategies. *Reading Research Quarterly, 35*, 458–492.

Juel, C., & Roper-Schneider, D. (1985). The influence of basal readers on first grade reading. *Reading Research Quarterly, 20*, 134–152.

Kamil, M. L., Borman, G. D., Dole, J., Kral, C. C., Salinger, T., & Torgesen, J. (2008). *Improving adolescent literacy: Effective classroom and intervention practices: A practice guide.* Retrieved from *http://ies.ed.gov/ncee/wwc.*

Kennedy, M. M. (1978). Findings from the Follow Through planned variation study. *Educational Researcher, 7*(6), 3–11.

LaBerge, D., & Samuels, S. J. (1974). Toward a theory of automatic information processing in reading. *Cognitive Psychology, 6*, 293–323.

Leppänen, U., Niemi, P., Aunola, K., & Nurmi, J.-E. (2004). Development of reading skills among preschool and primary school pupils. *Reading Research Quarterly, 39*, 72–93.

Lesaux, N. K., & Siegel, L. S. (2003). The development of reading in children who speak English as a second language. *Developmental Psychology, 39*, 1005–1019.

Leslie, L., & Allen, L. (1999). Factors that predict success in an early literacy intervention project. *Reading Research Quarterly, 34*, 404–424.

Leslie, L., & Calhoon, A. (1995). Factors affecting children's reading of rimes: Reading ability, word frequency, and rime-neighborhood size. *Journal of Educational Psychology, 87*, 576–586.

Levy, B. A., Bourassa, D. C., & Horn, C. (1999). Fast and slow namers: Benefits of segmentation and whole word training. *Journal of Experimental Child Psychology, 73*, 115–138.

Liberman, I. Y., Shankweiler, D., Fisher, F. W., & Carter, B. (1974). Reading and the awareness of linguistic segments. *Journal of Experimental Child Psychology, 18*, 201–212.

Lovett, M. W., Barron, R. W., & Benson, N. J. (2003). Effective remediation of word identification and decoding difficulties in school-age children with reading disabilities. In H. L. Swanson, K. R. Harris, & S. Graham (Eds.), *Handbook of learning disabilities* (pp. 273–292). Guilford Press.

Lovett, M. W., Borden, S. L., DeLuca, T., Lacerenza, L., Benson, N. J., & Brackstone, D. (1994). Treating the core deficits of developmental dyslexia: Evidence of transfer of learning after phonologically- and strategy-based reading training programs. *Developmental Psychology, 30*, 805–822.

Lovett, M. W., Lacerenza, L., Borden, S. L., Frijters, J. C., Steinbach, K. A., & De Palma, M. (2000). Components of effective remediation for developmental reading disabilities: Combining phonological and strategy-based instruction to improve outcomes. *Journal of Educational Psychology, 92*, 263–283.

Lovett, M. W., Ransby, M. J., Hardwick, N., Johns, M. S., & Donaldson, S. A. (1989). Can dyslexia be treated? Treatment-specific and generalized treatment effects in dyslexic children's response to remediation. *Brain and Language, 37*, 90–121.

Marsh, H. G., Desberg, P., & Cooper, J. (1977). Developmental strategies in reading. *Journal of Reading Behavior, 9*, 391–394.

Marsh, H. G., Friedman, M., Desberg, P., & Saterdahl, K. (1981). Comparison of reading and spelling strategies in normal and reading-disabled children. In M. P. Friedman, J. P. Das, & N. O'Connor (Eds.), *Intelligence and learning* (pp. 363–367). Plenum Press.

Marsh, H. G., Friedman, M., Welch, V., & Desberg, P. (1981). A cognitive–developmental theory of reading acquisition. In G. E. MacKinnon & T. G. Waller (Eds.), *Reading research: Advances in theory and practice* (Vol. 3, pp. 199–221). Academic Press.

Mathes, P. G., Denton, C. A., Fletcher, J. M., Anthony, J. L., Francis, D. J., & Schatschneider, C. (2005). The effects of theoretically different instruction and student characteristics on the skills of struggling readers. *Reading Research Quarterly, 40*(2), 148–182.

McArthur, G., Sheehan, Y., Badcock, N. A., Francis, D. A., Wang, H. C., Kohnen, S., et al. (2018). Phonics training for English-speaking poor readers. *Cochrane Database of Systematic Reviews, 11,* 1–102.

McCandliss, B., Beck, I. L., Sandak, R., & Perfetti, C. (2003). Focusing attention on decoding for children with poor reading skills: Design and preliminary tests of the word building intervention. *Scientific Studies of Reading, 7,* 75–104.

McConkie, G. W., Zola, D., Blanchard, H. E., & Wolverton, G. S. (1982). Perceiving words during reading: Lack of facilitation from prior peripheral exposure. *Perception and Psychophysics, 32,* 271–281.

McCutchen, D., Abbott, R. D., Green, L. B., Beretvas, N., Cox, S., Potter, N. S., et al. (2002). Beginning literacy: Links among teacher knowledge, teacher practice, and student learning. *Journal of Learning Disabilities, 35,* 69–86.

McCutchen, D., Harry, D. R., Cunningham, A. E., Cox, S., Sidman, S., & Covill, A. E. (2002). Reading teachers' knowledge of children's literature and English phonology. *Annals of Dyslexia, 52,* 207–228.

McGill-Franzen, A. (2006). *Kindergarten literacy.* Scholastic.

McGill-Franzen, A., Zmach, C., Solic, K., & Zeig, J. L. (2006). The confluence of two policy mandates: Core reading programs and third-grade retention in Florida. *Elementary School Journal, 107*(1), 67– 91.

McIntyre, E., & Freppon, P. A. (1994). A comparison of children's development of alphabetic knowledge in a skills-based and a whole language classroom. *Research in the Teaching of English, 28*(4), 391–417.

McIntyre, E., Rightmeyer, E., Powell, R., Powers, S., & Petrosko, J. (2006). How much should young children read? *Literacy Teaching and Learning, 11*(1), 51–72.

Meichenbaum, D. (1977). *Cognitive behavior modification.* Plenum Press.

Mielke, K. W. (2001). A review of research on the educational and social impact of *Sesame Street.* In S. M. Fisch & R. T. Truglio (Eds.), *"G" is for growing: Thirty years of research on children and "Sesame Street"* (pp. 83–95). Erlbaum.

Moats, L. C., & Foorman, B. R. (2003). Measuring teachers' content knowledge of language and reading. *Annals of Dyslexia, 53,* 23–45.

Morris, D. (2005). *The Howard Street tutoring manual: Teaching at-risk readers in the primary grades* (2nd ed.). Guilford Press.

Morris, D., Tyner, B., & Perney, J. (2000). Early steps: Replicating the effects of a first-grade reading intervention program. *Journal of Educational Psychology, 92,* 681–693.

Moustafa, M. (1997). *Beyond traditional phonics.* Heinemann.

Moustafa, M. (1998). *Whole to part phonics: How children learn to read and spell.* Heinemann.

Nagy, W., Berninger, V., Abbott, R., Vaughan, K., & Vermeulen, K. (2003). Relationship of morphology and other language skills to literacy skills in at-risk second-grade readers and at-risk fourth-grade writers. *Journal of Educational Psychology, 95,* 730–742.

National Reading Panel. (2000). *Teaching children to read: An evidence-based assessment of the scientific research literature on reading and its implications for reading instruction.* National Institute of Child Health and Human Development.

Nicholson, T. (1991). Do children read words better in context or in lists? A classic study revisited. *Journal of Educational Psychology, 83,* 444–450.

Nicholson, T., Lillas, C., & Rzoska, M. A. (1988). Have we been misled by miscues? *The Reading Teacher, 42*(1), 6-10.

O'Connor, R. E., & Bell, K. M. (2004). Teaching students with reading disability to read words. In C. A. Stone, E. R. Silliman, B. J. Ehren, & K. Apel (Eds.), *Handbook of language and literacy: Development and disorders* (pp. 481–498). Guilford Press.

Patterson, K. E., & Coltheart, V. (1987). Phonological processes in reading: A tutorial review. In M. Coltheart (Ed.), *Attention and performance XII: The psychology of reading* (pp. 421–447). Erlbaum.

Penney, C. G. (2002). Teaching decoding skills to poor readers in high school. *Journal of Literacy Research, 34,* 99–118.

Perfetti, C. A., Bell, L. C., & Delaney, S. M. (1988). Automatical (prelexical) phonetic activation in silent word reading: Evidence from backward masking. *Journal of Memory and Language, 27,* 1–22.

Peterson, M. E., & Haines, L. P. (1992). Orthographic analogy training with kindergarten children: Effects of analogy use, phonemic segmentation, and letter–sound knowledge. *Journal of Reading Behavior, 24,* 109–127.

Pianta, R. C., & Hamre, B. K. (2009). Conceptualization, measurement, and improvement of classroom processes: Standardized observation can leverage capacity. *Educational Researcher, 38*(2), 109–119.

Piasta, S. B., Connor, C. M., Fishman, B. J., & Morrison, F. J. (2009). Teachers' knowledge of literacy concepts, classroom practices, and student reading growth. *Scientific Studies of Reading, 13,* 224–248.

Pinnell, G. S., Fountas, I. C., Giacobbe, M. E., & Fountas, A. C. (1998). *Word matters: Teaching phonics and spelling in the reading/writing classroom.* Heinemann.

Popplewell, S. R., & Doty, D. E. (2001). Classroom instruction and reading comprehension: A comparison of one basal reader approach and the Four Blocks framework. *Reading Psychology, 22*(2), 83–94.

Pressley, M. (1977). Imagery and children's learning: Putting the picture in developmental perspective. *Review of Educational Research, 47,* 586–622.

Price-Mohr, R., & Price, C. (2017). Gender differences in early reading strategies: A comparison of synthetic phonics only with a mixed approach to teaching reading to 4–5 year-old children. *Early Childhood Education Journal, 45*(5), 613–620.

Price-Mohr, R., & Price, C. (2020). A comparison of children aged 4–5 years learning to read through instructional texts containing either a high or a low proportion of phonically-decodable words. *Early Childhood Education Journal, 48*(1), 39–47.

Rayner, K., Inhoff, A. W., Morrison, R. E., Slowiaczek, M. L., & Bertera, J. H. (1981). Masking of foveal and parafoveal vision during eye fixations in reading. *Journal of Experimental Psychology: Human Perception and Performance, 7,* 167–179.

Rayner, K., & Pollatsek, A. (1989). *The psychology of reading.* Prentice-Hall.

Rice, M. L., Huston, A. C., Truglio, R., & Wright, J. (1990). Words from "Sesame Street": Learning vocabulary from viewing. *Developmental Psychology, 26,* 421–428.

Roberts, T. A., & Sadler, C. D. (2019). Letter sound characters and imaginary narratives: Can they enhance motivation and letter sound learning? *Early Childhood Research Quarterly, 46,* 97–111.

Routman, R. (1996). *Literacy at the crossroads.* Heinemann.

Samuels, S. J., Schermer, N., & Reinking, D. (1992). Reading fluency: Techniques for making decoding automatic. In S. J. Samuels & A. E. Farstrup (Eds.), *What research has to say about reading instruction* (pp. 124–144). International Reading Association.

Santa, C. M., & Høien, T. (1999). The assessment of Early Steps: A program for early intervention of reading problems. *Reading Research Quarterly, 34,* 54–79.

Sargiani, R. D. A., Ehri, L. C., & Maluf, M. R. (2022). Teaching beginners to decode consonant–vowel syllables using grapheme–phoneme subunits facilitates reading and spelling as compared with teaching whole-syllable decoding. *Reading Research Quarterly, 57*(2), 629–648.

Savage, R., & Stuart, M. (1998). Sub-lexical inferences in beginning reading: Medial vowel digraphs as functional units of transfer. *Journal of Experimental Child Psychology, 69,* 85–108.

Scammacca, N., Roberts, G., Vaughn, S., Edmonds, M., Wexler, J., Reutebuch, C. K., et al. (2007). *Interventions for adolescent struggling readers: A meta-analysis with implications for practice.* RMC Research Corporation, Center on Instruction.

Scanlon, D. M., & Anderson, K. L. (2020) Using context as an assist in word solving: The contributions of 25 years of research on the interactive strategies approach. *Reading Research Quarterly, 55,* S19-S34.

Scanlon, D. M., Anderson, K. L., & Sweeney, J. M. (2016). *Early intervention for reading difficulties: The interactive strategies approach.* Guilford Press.

Scarborough, H. S. (1995, April). *The fate of phonemic awareness beyond the elementary school years.* Paper presented at the biennial meeting of the Society for Research in Child Development, Indianapolis, IN.

Scarborough, H. S., Ehri, L. C., Olson, R. K., & Fowler, A. E. (1998). The fate of phonemic awareness beyond the elementary school years. *Scientific Studies of Reading, 2,* 115–142.

Schwartz, S. (2019a). The most popular reading programs aren't backed by science. *Education Week.* Retrieved from *www.edweek.org/teaching-learning/the-most-popular-reading-programs-arent-backed-by-science/2019/12.*

Schwartz, S. (2019b). New curriculum review gives failing marks to two popular reading programs. *Education Week.* Retrieved from *www.edweek.org/teaching-learning/new-curriculum-review-gives-failing-marks-to-popular-early-reading-programs/2021/11.*

Seymour, P. H. K., & Elder, L. (1986). Beginning reading without phonology. *Cognitive Neuropsychology, 3,* 1–36.

Shanahan, T. (2003). Research-based reading instruction: Myths about the National Reading Panel report. *The Reading Teacher, 56*(7), 646–655.

Share, D. L. (1995). Phonological recoding and self-teaching: Sine qua non of reading acquisition. *Cognition, 55*(2), 151–218.

Share, D. L. (1999). Phonological recoding and orthographic learning: A direct test of the self-teaching hypothesis. *Journal of Experimental Child Psychology, 72,* 95–129.

Share, D. L. (2004). Orthographic learning at a glance: On the time course and developmental onset of self-teaching. *Journal of Experimental Child Psychology, 87,* 267–298.

Share, D. L. (2008). Orthographic learning, phonology and the self-teaching hypothesis. In R. Kail (Ed.), *Advances in Child Development and Behavior, 36,* 31–82.

Shaywitz, S. E., Escobar, M. D., Shaywitz, B. A., Fletcher, J. M., & Makuch, R. (1992). Evidence that dyslexia may represent the lower tail of a normal distribution of reading ability. *New England Journal of Medicine, 326,* 145–150.

Siegel, L. S. (2003). Basic cognitive processes and reading disabilities. In H. L. Swanson, K. R. Harris, & S. Graham (Eds.), *Handbook of learning disabilities* (pp. 158–181). Guilford Press.

Slavin, R. E., Lake, C., Chambers, B., Cheung, A., & Davis, S. (2009). Effective reading programs for the elementary grades: A best-evidence synthesis. *Review of Educational Research, 79*(4), 1391–1466.

Spear-Swerling, L., & Brucker, P. O. (2003). Teachers' acquisition of knowledge about English word structure. *Annals of Dyslexia, 53,* 72–103.

Sprenger-Charolles, L., Siegel, L. S., & Bonnet, P. (1998). Reading and spelling acquisition in French: The role of phonological mediation and orthographic factors. *Journal of Experimental Child Psychology, 68*, 134–165.

Stahl, S. A., Duffy-Hester, A. M., & Stahl, K. A. D. (1998). Everything you wanted to know about phonics (but were afraid to ask). *Reading Research Quarterly, 33*, 338–355.

Stallings, J. (1975). Implementation and child effects of teaching practices in Follow Through classrooms. *Monographs of the Society for Research in Child Development, 40*(7–8, Serial No. 163).

Stanovich, K. E. (1986). Matthew effects in reading: Some consequences of individual differences in the acquisition of literacy. *Reading Research Quarterly, 21*, 360–407.

Stanovich, K. E., & West, R. F. (1989). Exposure to print and orthographic processing. *Reading Research Quarterly, 24*, 402–433.

Stevens, E. A., Austin, C., Moore, C., Scammacca, N., Boucher, A. N., & Vaughn, S. (2021). Current state of the evidence: Examining the effects of Orton-Gillingham reading interventions for students with or at risk for word-level reading disabilities. *Exceptional Children, 87*(4), 397–417.

Thompson, G. B., Cottrell, D. S., & Fletcher-Flinn, C. M. (1996). Sublexical orthographic-phonological relations early in the acquisition of reading: The knowledge sources account. *Journal of Experimental Child Psychology, 62*, 190–222.

Torgerson, C., Brooks, G., Gascoine, L., & Higgins, S. (2019). Phonics: Reading policy and the evidence of effectiveness from a systematic 'tertiary' review. *Research Papers in Education, 34*(2), 208–238.

Torgesen, J. K., & Burgess, S. R. (1998). Consistency of reading-related phonological processes throughout early childhood. In J. Metsala & L. Ehri (Eds.), *Word recognition in beginning reading* (pp. 161–188). Erlbaum.

Torgesen, J. K., Wagner, R. K., Rashotte, C. A., Rose, E., Lindamood, P., Conway, T., et al. (1999). Preventing reading failure in young children with phonological processing disabilities: Group and individual responses to instruction. *Journal of Educational Psychology, 91*, 579–593.

Tunmer, W. E., Herriman, M. L., & Nesdale, A. R. (1988). Metalinguistic abilities and beginning reading. *Reading Research Quarterly, 23*, 134–158.

van Daal, V. H. P., Reitsma, P., & van der Leu, A. (1994). Processing units in word reading by disabled readers. *Journal of Experimental Child Psychology, 57*, 180–210.

Vellutino, F. R., & Scanlon, D. M. (2002). The Interactive Strategies Approach to reading intervention. *Contemporary Educational Psychology, 27*(4), 573–635.

Vellutino, F. R., Scanlon, D. M., Sipay, E. R., Small, E. G., Pratt, A., Chen, R., et al. (1996). Cognitive profiles of difficult-to-remediate and readily remediated readers: Early intervention as a vehicle for distinguishing between cognitive and experiential deficits as basic causes of a specific reading disability. *Journal of Educational Psychology, 88*(4), 601–638.

Venezky, R. L., & Johnson, D. (1973). Development of two letter–sound patterns in grade one through three. *Journal of Educational Psychology, 64*, 109–115.

Walmsley, S. A. (1978). The criterion referenced measurement of an early reading behavior. *Reading Research Quarterly*, 574-604.

Walton, P. D., & Walton, L. M. (2002). Beginning reading by teaching in rime analogy: Effects on phonological skills, letter-sound knowledge, working memory, and word-reading strategies. *Scientific Studies of Reading, 6*, 79–115.

Walton, P. D., Walton, L. M., & Felton, K. (2001). Teaching rime analogy or letter recoding reading strategies to prereaders: Effects on prereading skills and word reading. *Journal of Educational Psychology, 93*, 160–180.

Wang, C. C., & Gaffney, J. S. (1998). First graders' use of analogy in word reading. *Journal of Literacy Research, 30*, 389–403.

Waterman, B., & Lewandowski, L. (1993). Phonologic and semantic processing in reading-disabled and nondisabled males at two age levels. *Journal of Experimental Child Psychology, 55,* 87–103.

What Works Clearinghouse. (2007). *Beginning reading.* Retrieved from *http://ies.ed.gov/ncee/wwc/publications_reviews.aspx.*

What Works Clearinghouse. (2022). Providing reading interventions for students in grades 4–9. Retrieved from *https://ies.ed.gov/ncee/wwc/PracticeGuide/29.*

White, T. G. (2005). Effects of systematic and strategic analogy-based phonics on grade 2 students' word reading and comprehension. *Reading Research Quarterly, 40(2),* 234–255.

Wise, B. W. (1992). Whole words and decoding for short-term learning: Comparisons on a "talking-computer" system. *Journal of Experimental Child Psychology, 54,* 147–167.

Wise, B. W., Olson, R. K., & Treiman, R. (1990). Subsyllabic units in computerized reading instruction: Onset–rime versus postvowel segmentation. *Journal of Experimental Child Psychology, 49,* 1–19.

Wood, S. S., Bruner, J. S., & Ross, G. (1976). The role of tutoring in problem solving. *Journal of Child Psychology and Psychiatry, 17,* 89–100.

Wright, J. C., Huston, A. C., Scantlin, R., & Kotler, J. (2001). The Early Window Project: *Sesame Street* prepares children for school. In S. M. Fisch & R. T. Truglio (Eds.), *"G" is for growing: Thirty years of research on children and "Sesame Street"* (pp. 97–114). Erlbaum.

Yoncheva, Y. N., Wise, J., & McCandliss, B. (2015). Hemispheric specialization for visual words is shaped by attention to sublexical units during initial learning. *Brain and Language, 145,* 23–33.

Zill, N. (2001). Does *Sesame Street* enhance school readiness? Evidence from a national survey of children. In S. M. Fisch & R. T. Truglio (Eds.), *"G" is for growing: Thirty years of research on children and "Sesame Street"* (pp. 115–130). Erlbaum.

6 Fluency

Fluent reading refers to accurate and fast reading at the word level, with good prosody (i.e., the reading has expression consistent with mature reading; Stahl, 2004). What we emphasize, however, is that by far the most important function of reading, in our view, is comprehension. Accurate, fast, and even prosodic reading that does not result in the reader's understanding the text is not good enough, though in some cases such word-level fluency may be necessary for attaining comprehension.

Commercially available assessments of fluency often involve asking readers to read a passage for a set period of time, usually aloud, perhaps for a minute or so. Fluent readers read quickly and with few accuracy errors. When we have administered such measures, we often notice that readers do not pause to think about what they are reading. In fact, the only activity they exhibit is reading the words quickly and accurately, and, although rarely scored on fluency measures, we feel better if the reading is carried out with good expression (i.e., is prosodic).

Such an emphasis on fluent reading bothers us, for we know, based on many studies of good comprehenders, that the best readers do not read texts straight through, but rather are very reflective as they read (Almasi et al., 2011; Pressley & Afflerbach, 1995). Excellent comprehenders overview text and scan it. They relate their prior knowledge to ideas in the text. They notice when they are confused or need to reread, and do so. They construct images in their mind's eye reflecting the content of the text. Good readers summarize, and they interpret, often with intense feeling, rejecting or embracing the ideas of an author. Such reflective reading, actually, can be pretty slow.

Nevertheless, fluency at the word level, as operationalized as reading accurately and quickly, is necessary so that the reader can choose to slow down and employ the comprehension strategies described above (i.e., there is enough available cognitive capacity when word-level reading is fluent to permit the decision to use the comprehension strategies and execute them). The criterion we should want in reading education is readers who are fluent at the word level but who constructively respond to text, building meaning and reacting to text all along the way, which involves skillful use of the comprehension strategies used by the best readers (Pressley & Afflerbach, 1995) and consistent relating of relevant prior knowledge to the ideas in the text (Anderson & Pearson, 1984). Such reading is slower than racing through a text, an assessment sometimes accepted as evidence of fluent reading, but the slowness is due to thinking about the ideas in the text, with our view that *truly* fluent readers can and do think hard about what they are reading (Newkirk, 2012).

In this chapter, we discuss the theory, research, and classroom practices that should be on the mind of the researcher community and educators as we attempt to better understand the nature of fluent reading, how it can be promoted, and whether fluent reading is a realistic, or even necessary, possibility for all readers (Newkirk, 2012). In the end, however, we will come back to a strong pitch for comprehension to be the measure that matters most in reading.

A FLURRY OF THEORIES, DATA, AND INSTRUCTIONAL PRACTICES

At this point, we must provide a warning. What follows is a flurry of individual theoretical, research, and practice directions that we have on our mind as we think about fluency. The work should be on the minds of everyone concerned with the development of fluent reading. As a flurry, at times you might feel lost in a snowstorm. In the concluding section of the chapter, we survey the landscape, present how the various bits and pieces fit together and, to continue the analogy, try to begin to clear a path to instructional practices educators can implement with regularly developing and struggling readers, as well as our thinking about where researchers interested in fluency could and should focus.

We enter the flurry discussing an article that many describe as without a doubt, the most influential theoretical perspective on fluency ever produced and continues to be cited in virtually every scholarly paper on fluency. It was published at a time when thinking about reading was shifting, with the article becoming a primary causal force in the shift.

LaBerge and Samuels (1974)

LaBerge and Samuels (1974) appeared at a time when George Miller's (1956) insight that human consciousness has limited attentional capacity was finally being fully appreciated as pertaining to all conscious life, not just the laboratory-list learning tasks that had spawned it. Scholars interested in human attention, in particular, realized that what people could attend to at any one moment was very limited (Kahnemann, 1973). A complex activity like reading has to be accomplished within the limits of such limited attention, meaning that picking up information from the letters of words to recognizing the parts of words sufficiently to sound out the whole word to comprehending the word all must happen within limited attentional capacity. The only way a word can be comprehended, given this limitation, was that some parts of the task had to be automatic. So, according to LaBerge and Samuels (1974), the mature reader automatically recognizes letters and whole words (i.e., sight words) and even makes associations from the sounded-out words to their meanings with little attention expended.

Less mature readers expend much capacity. For the prereading child, all the attentional capacity might be consumed discriminating one letter from another. For the child who has mastered the letters and their sound associations to the point of automaticity, blending the sounds might take up a great deal of capacity, with the result that the child might read all the words in a sentence and still have no idea what the sentence means. The transition from effortful to effortless, error-free, automatic performance at each stage depends on practice in doing the task. Practice does make perfect from this perspective, in the sense that both accuracy and speed increase and attentional capacity demands decrease. Consistent with the basic learning analyses of the time, LaBerge and Samuels (1974) posited that distributed practice (i.e., practice of a task over days and weeks and over various texts and tasks) was better than massed practice (i.e., much drilling in a short period of time with a specific type of text). LaBerge and Samuels appreciated that feedback during practice helped learning, that affirmations of correct responses would strengthen associations (e.g., between a letter and its sound, between a root word as a visual stimulus and its correct pronunciation), and that negative feedback could weaken errant responses. Because of practice, letter features came to be recognized as whole letters among prereaders; root words composed of individual letters came to be recognized as wholes in grade 1; root words sounded out with effort in grade 1 came to be recognized at first glance by grade 2; meanings of words that are first brought to mind by the reader sounding out the word (i.e., the meaning of *boat* comes to mind after the young reader says "boat") eventually come to mind from simply seeing the word, even in the absence of a conscious articulation of the meaning. In short, throughout learning to read, effortful and inaccurate processes are replaced with almost effortless and more accurate processes. As that occurs, preschoolers who could not recognize a single letter will, over time, become fluent readers of whole words and eventually longer texts.

Overall, LaBerge and Samuels's (1974) work represented a brilliant integration of the theoretical perspectives of the time, resulting in a series of experiments, briefly summarized in the article, that supported their framework. Reading the piece today, there is only one really strange component and one possible concern. The paper paid significant attention to visual analysis and perceptual learning of letters, mirroring the psychology of the day, as reflected in the most visible psychology of reading published in the 1970s (Gibson & Levin, 1975). At the same time, a series of analyses were being conducted in other places to evaluate the role of visual versus verbal factors in reading disability. At the end of the decade, Vellutino (1979) would summarize the evidence, making the case that the assumption of many that reading disabilities represented a visual–perceptual impairment was wrong. Reading disabilities were much more about verbal impairments. Ever since publication of Vellutino's book, that perspective has prevailed, a central by-product being that understanding the psychology of language, especially at the word level, is the key to understanding reading, both disabled reading and skilled reading. In the next section, we turn our attention to that overarching perspective, which must be understood to encompass much of contemporary thinking about fluency.

Before we do that, however, we feel compelled to mention another possible problem with LaBerge and Samuels, one already touched upon in the introduction that we will revisit at length later in the chapter. The goal of reading is comprehension, and fluency, at best, can be valued only as a means to that end. When LaBerge and Samuels developed their theory of automatic information processing, or "automaticity theory," they *placed* a premium on speed (and accuracy) in oral reading that may have extended beyond the natural pace characteristic of effortless reading. It is possible that this has led to a widespread overemphasis on oral reading speed in instruction and assessment, to the potential detriment of comprehension. As we conduct oral reading assessments on young readers, for example, we notice that many read as quickly as possible with little attention to detail. This is so common among young readers that it seems entirely likely that an implicit, if not also explicit, goal of early reading instruction is to get children to read rapidly, while probably ignoring comprehension measures. As we move further away from a simple view of reading (e.g., Gough & Tunmer, 1986), which would have children learn to read rapidly, so they can hear and then understand what they are reading, we may begin to question the extent to which we should be emphasizing the goal of speed in our instruction and assessments at all. Instead, we wonder if focusing more on comprehension strategies, even at a young age, would help to decrease the phenomenon of children reading as fast as they can to finish a passage. This issue should not be confused with problems some children have with speed of processing, which will be addressed later in the chapter, and at this time we present this theory only as another addition to the flurry of possibilities for further inquiry.

Reading Is About Verbal Processing—in Particular, Phonological Processing of Words

You already have read about the contributions that Jeanne Chall and Marilyn Adams made to reading instruction, primarily by emphasizing phonemic awareness and phonics (Chapter 5). Chall and Adams's phonics-based approach to reading instruction emerged as the dominant approach, especially as the National Institute of Child Health and Human Development (NICHD) became interested in this research and began to fund it heavily. The result of this interest from the NICHD was a substantial body of work in the next few years in which struggling beginning readers were provided several years of intensive, explicit, systematic phonics instruction.

Such instruction did increase these children's word recognition abilities (i.e., their accuracy), putting them within sight of the decoding accuracy of the general population of readers by the late elementary grades. But it did not produce fluent reading (see Torgesen, 2004, for a review; also see Torgesen & Hudson, 2006), with these students reading much more slowly in the later elementary grades than the general population of readers. More positively, however, when students who are at risk for reading failure but who have not yet exhibited any deficit are provided with systematic phonics instruction in kindergarten and grade 1, the result in the later elementary grades for these students is reading that is almost as fluent (i.e., fast) as the general population of late elementary readers (Torgesen, 2004). There seem to be two important implications here.

There is nothing in these data to suggest that for most readers phonologically based instruction in kindergarten and grade 1 somehow interferes with the development of fluency. That said, for really troubled beginning readers, phonics is not going to be enough to assure fluent reading. To its credit, based on research, the NICHD has concluded that more than phonics is required for fluency to develop. This was made clear in the fluency section of the NRP (2000) report. First, however, NICHD-sponsored work has provided some strong hints about why the most troubled readers do not become fluent readers.

Brain Imagery Research

The NICHD has been a major sponsor of research intended to map brain functioning in both normal and dyslexic child and adult readers. Today's brain-imaging techniques permit the detection of more and less active areas of the brain as people read words. (See Shaywitz & Shaywitz, 2004, for a review, which is the basis for this subsection; also see Goswami, 2004, for an overview of neuroimaging research conducted in the area of language and comprehension over the past 25 years. See Gernsbacher & Kaschak, 2003, and for a more critical view of such research, see Hruby & Goswami, 2011.)

One important finding is that normal mature readers, especially, activate a set of three sites on the left side of the brain more reliably than readers with dyslexia (Shaywitz et al., 2002). One area that is especially active is the parieto-temporal region, with healthy functioning of this region associated with the ability to phonologically analyze words (i.e., sound out words). This region is about three-quarters of the way toward the back of the brain and two-thirds of the way toward the top of the brain. A second very active region in normal functioning is the occipito-temporal region, which is near the back of the brain and the bottom of the cortex. The healthy functioning of this region is important in recognizing words as wholes—that is, as sight words—rather than sounding them out. The third region, Broca's area, is closer to the front of the brain and functions in the analysis of spoken words. In good readers, these three areas work well in coordination, with the result that readers recognize familiar words automatically without sounding them out and can quickly and accurately sound out unfamiliar words.

Good readers probably are not born with these left-brain areas especially active during verbal processing. For example, Turkelbaum et al. (2003) reported in a cross-sectional developmental study that activity in these areas increased with age—that is, as children learned to read. What was also very interesting was that, with development, activation of areas on the right side of the brain decreased. Keller and Just (2009) studied the effects of 100 hours of intensive reading remediation on the microstructure of the white matter in readers' brains. The white matter in our brains supports the various parts of the brain working together. Brain imaging indicated that prior to the intervention the white matter in struggling reader brains was of "lower structural quality" than that in better readers. After 100 hours of remediation, including lots of text reading and rereading, the structure of the white matter was improved. White matter structural changes predicted improved reading abilities. This indicates that brain activation in response to words changes as people learn to read.

In general, the left-brain functioning of readers with severe reading difficulties is different. The parieto-temporal region, in particular, seems impaired. Often, Broca's area (and some other areas) will be more active in such readers, suggesting that these regions are somehow compensating for the lack of function in the parieto-temporal region, but since these regions are not quite matched to task, word recognition is slow at best and less accurate than in normal readers. Some adults who were dyslexic as children have, somehow, somewhat compensated for it as adults (Fink, 1998; Shaywitz et al., 2003). They recognize familiar words well. Interestingly, these compensating readers have more pronounced activity in the occipito-temporal region than do adults with dyslexia who do not recognize familiar words. Because these compensated readers also seem to have more connection between the functioning of the occipito-temporal region and regions of the brain responsible for short-term memory than other readers (including normal readers), it seems likely that they have somehow memorized the sight words. In contrast, in normal readers, there are stronger connections between the parieto-temporal and occipito-temporal regions, suggesting that the fluent reading of familiar words in normal individuals may be caused by repeated sounding out of words rather than rote memorization (Table 6.1). The normal reader first sounds out the word and over repeated encounters comes to recognize the word as a sight word. There is some evidence in young readers of active functioning of the parieto-temporal region preceding the active functioning of the occipito-temporal region, as beginning readers who are good at sounding out begin to develop sight vocabulary as a result of their repeated correct pronunciations of the new words they encounter. Of course, typically developing readers read much more text than do early struggling readers. The role of the volume of reading in reading development has been largely ignored (Allington & McGill-Franzen, 2021), and even now there seems to be little interest in developing a clearer understanding of how reading volume impact the ability to read generally and learn to read fluently.

Consider additionally the childhood dyslexics who seem to compensate as adults. Their reading is still not fluent because they have trouble with unfamiliar words. They still cannot sound out words, with the brain imagery data confirming that there is less than optimal functioning in their parieto-temporal regions (see Shaywitz et al., 2003, for the original data on this fascinating study, which we consider potentially very

TABLE 6.1. Differences in Brain Functioning Normal Readers versus Readers with Dyslexia

Normal readers	Readers with dyslexia/struggling readers

• Activated regions include parieto-temporal (supports sounding out words), occipito-temporal (supports recognizing sight words), and Broca's area (analysis of spoken words)
• Strong connections between parieto-temporal and occipito-temporal regions
  • Suggest repeated sounding out words
	• Lower structural quality of white matter (supports parts of brain working together)
	  • Remediation of text reading and rereading may improve white matter
	• Parieto-temporal region is impaired, while Broca's region is more active
	  • Suggest memorization of words → leading to trouble with unfamiliar words

important as thinking about reading education proceeds; Compton et al., 2004).

Not surprisingly, the NICHD scientists doing brain imagery work are interested in phonologically based reading interventions—specifically, whether experiencing these interventions produces changes in brain activation in areas associated with normal reading. Shaywitz et al. (2004) reported an interesting initial study supportive of the possibility that the phonologically based interventions favored by NICHD, in fact, stimulate the development of the brain regions associated with skilled reading. That is, they asked whether brain activation in the left-side areas associated with skilled reading was more likely in students receiving such instruction than those not receiving such instruction. Children who, at the end of first or second grade, were performing below the 25th percentile on standardized tests of word recognition and word attack skills were the participants in the study. Students receiving the phonologically based intervention received systematic phonics instruction for the school year, including reading of decodable books, complemented by reading of trade books as decoding skill increased. Other students who were below the 25th percentile on word-level skills experienced the regular school reading curriculum in grade 2 or 3, which varied from school to school, but did not focus on phonological skills. After the year of intervention, the students who received the phonological intervention were reading better than those who did not receive the intervention, with better word recognition and slightly faster reading as well as very slightly better comprehension. That said, the phonological students remained far behind same-age normal readers.

Brain images during reading were also recorded at the beginning and end of the year of the intervention. The most striking result by the end of the year of intervention was that the phonologically treated students had brain images resembling nonimpaired agemates. In particular, there was normal activation in the areas of the brain associated with sounding out words. The disabled readers receiving regular reading instruction had less pronounced brain activation in the areas associated with skilled reading. Brain-imaging data were also collected on participants receiving the phonological intervention a year after intervention concluded.

Encouragingly, there was now more activity in the occipito-temporal region, the area that appears to mediate recognition of words as wholes. The hypothesis that phonologically based interventions may have effects beyond teaching students how to sound out words gains additional credence with the results of this study, although much additional study still needs to occur. In the past few years, more research has provided support for an increase in brain functioning following reading interventions, especially with struggling readers (Nugiel et al., 2019; Partanen et al., 2019,

2021) The idea that phonologically based interventions may have effects beyond teaching to sound out words is exciting! Seeing as this research is still limited, researchers need to continue to investigate the long-term effects of phonologically based interventions, balanced literacy instruction, and extensive engagement in the primary grades, on both behavioral data (i.e., volume of reading activity, accuracy of reading words, reading fluency, and reading comprehension) and brain functioning.

Of course, as this discussion continues, it will be clear that there is a need for much more research with respect to fluency, even with respect to interventions that have been around a long time. That is clear from reviewing the outcomes reported in the NRP report (2000).

Executive Function and Fluency

A more recent area of research on brain function and reading has focused on executive functions (EF; e.g., Kieffer & Christodoulou, 2020; Welsh et al., 2010). EF includes three core skills of working memory, attention shifting, and inhibitory control, which influence key behaviors of self-regulation, such as planning and monitoring (Friedman & Miyake, 2017; Miyake et al., 2000). Specifically, researchers have explored the role of EF in word reading, reading fluency, and reading comprehension for students in elementary and middle school and in adulthood (Arrington et al., 2014; Best & Miller, 2010; Cartwright, 2015, 2017, 2019; Cartwright, Lee, et al., 2020; Cutting et al., 2009; Jacobson et al., 2011; Kieffer & Christodoulou, 2020; Lipka, 2017; Zelazo et al., 2016). Though the area of EF and reading fluency is still relatively new, researchers have begun to find that EF and reading fluency predict reading comprehension for low-achieving readers in samples in primary elementary students (Cartwright et al., 2019), upper elementary students (Cutting et al., 2009), and middle school students (Jacobson et al., 2011; Kieffer & Christodoulou, 2020).

Though previous studies have found EF deficits in struggling readers; EF also influences typically developing readers (Cartwright et al., 2019; Lipka, 2017; Nyguen et al., 2020). For example, Cartwright et al. (2019) found cognitive flexibility, such as being able to switch from phonological and semantic aspects while reading, influenced typically developing readers and struggling readers. Not only that, but EF intervention that teaches such flexibility improves reading fluency (Cartwright et al., 2019) and reading comprehension (Cartwright 2002; Cartwright et al., 2017; Cartwright, Bock, et al., 2020). Additionally, Nyguen et al. (2020) sampled a range of skilled readers and found EF influenced the mistakes made during oral reading fluency and also impacted students' ability to self-correct fluency mistakes. Specifically, students with better EF skills were more able to monitor their oral reading and self-correct when necessary to preserve meaning.

Thus, teachers need to understand that EF can influence a reader's fluency, whether they are strong or weak readers.

There is still much research that needs to be done when it comes to EF and reading. However, we believe it is an important area as recent studies have provided critical information on how parts of the brain influence both reading fluency and reading comprehension, specifically noting differences between struggling and typically developing readers. Continued research on EF and fluency is key to continue moving forward developing effective readers in today's classrooms. Additionally, we believe the current research on EF and reading strengthens our argument that reading instruction should be taught collectively rather than compartmentalized.

The NRP Report (2000)

We have already examined the NRP report and its findings in the areas of phonemic awareness and phonics (NRP, 2000). But what about fluency? The NRP found clear support for the conclusion that reading fluency can be increased through repeated oral reading with feedback and guidance. That is, both accuracy in reading and speed of reading can be increased. The procedures for doing so are a real "mulligan stew," however, as described by Stahl (2004). They vary in how much repeated reading occurs in the intervention as well as according to whether an adult assists reading, an adult tutors the child, or the child reads along with audiotapes. Moreover, the NRP did not attempt to differentiate among the alternative procedures for increasing fluency in respect to their relative efficaciousness.

Kuhn and Stahl (2003) looked again at the studies included in the NRP report and broadened the criteria a bit so that more than just experimental and quasi-experimental studies were considered. Their analyses of the studies examined by the NRP and the additional investigations highlighted some important points.

1. Adult assistance was quite important with respect to increasing fluency, with simple repeated reading by the child much less certain to produce a positive outcome as compared with repeated reading with adult assistance.
2. There was no difference in fluency or other reading outcomes between repeated reading of the same text and the same amount of time spent reading a variety of texts (Homan et al., 1993; Mathes & Fuchs, 1993; Rashotte & Torgesen, 1985; von Bon et al., 1991). This finding led to a series of studies with comparisons between repeated reading of texts and extended time actually reading texts, discussed below.

3. Assistance during repeated reading promoted both fluency and comprehension.
4. There was more evidence in favor of having readers confront somewhat challenging rather than easy texts as they experience fluency instruction.
5. Although most of the research on fluency instruction has been carried out with one-to-one tutoring, there are promising whole-group approaches (Rasinski et al., 1994; Stahl et al. 1997) that deserve closer evaluation.
6. All that said, the fluency instruction evaluated to date certainly is not enabling weak readers to catch up to regularly achieving readers in terms of fluency!

The second finding stimulated large-scale and longer-term studies of the roles of repeated-reading and extended-reading activities. Kuhn (2005) initially compared repeated reading with both a wide-reading and a listening-only treatment with a second-grade low-achievement population of students. She found that both repeated readings and wide-reading groups outperformed the listening group on increases in word recognition, words correct per minute, and prosody. In addition, the wide-reading group outperformed the repeated reading and the listening groups of growth in reading comprehension.

The advantage demonstrated by the wide-reading group prompted further studies. Kuhn et al. (2006) compared repeated reading with a wide-reading treatment as well as with a control group that engaged students in neither. The classroom texts used were all grade-level texts, even though many of the students were reading below grade level. Total volume of reading practice was comparable between the repeated-reading and wide-reading groups across the treatment period. The repeated-reading group read and reread the same texts multiple times each week. The wide-reading group initially engaged in rereading a text read aloud by their teacher, then reread that text with a partner. The wide-reading students then engaged in a choral reading of the text with classmates and wrote something related to that text. On the final 2 days of the week, the wide-reading students did echo reading and partner reading of new texts. Thus, over the course of a week, the wide-reading students did some repeated readings but then went on to read new texts. The authors concluded:

> By the end of the school year, FORI [repeated-reading group] and wide-reading approaches showed similar benefits for standardized measures of word reading efficiency and reading comprehension compared to the control approaches, although the benefits of the wide-reading approach emerged earlier and included oral text reading fluency skill. (p. 358)

Both treatment groups exhibited better sight word reading performances and better reading comprehension than the control group, but only the wide-reading group exhibited better oral reading fluency than the control group children.

Schwanenflugel et al. (2009) examined the longer-term effects of these two approaches to fostering reading fluency and reading achievement of second-grade students in two states. Neither treatment had better fluency or sight-word performances than the control group students. However, both produced better comprehension performances when compared with the control group. The authors indicated:

> The conclusion that we draw from this picture is that having children read a wide variety of challenging connected text with some minimal repetition but in a manner that supports their decoding needs is more consistently effective than asking them to carry out repeated reading on the same text over and over again. (p. 333)

In short, these studies suggest that repeated readings, while useful, may not be the most powerful tool for fostering either reading fluency or reading comprehension. The original report of Kuhn and Stahl (2003) noted that it was difficult to sort out whether it was the repeated reading texts or simply the additional text reading opportunities that led to improved fluency. These later studies suggest that a mix of a little repeated reading practice along with lots of reading of new texts works to foster both better fluency development and better reading comprehension than relying on repeated reading tasks alone.

In brief, there is support for developing phonemic awareness, teaching phonics, and encouraging fluency through both repeated reading with guidance and feedback and wide reading of texts. At the same time, involving dysfluent readers in more actual reading activity and less involvement in repeated readings offers more promise for fostering reading development. As additional analyses on these topics are occurring, it seems likely that, based on evidence, more can probably be done to improve reading and fluency than the NRP concluded. In general, a broad instructional agenda incorporating wide-reading experiences makes sense with respect to increasing fluency and comprehension in struggling readers (Allington, 2009).

Developing Sight-Word and Vocabulary Knowledge

Given the emphasis on reading at the word level in the most popular conceptions of fluent reading, it makes sense to us for all concerned with reading education to be thinking about what words students are learning to read. Returning to LaBerge and Samuels's (1974) framework, it is essential that readers both decode words automatically and access the meanings of the words automatically (i.e., once the word is read, they know what it means). Considering the millions of words in the English language—the unabridged *Oxford English Dictionary* (Simpson & Weiner, 1989), for example, taking up some 20 volumes—how can this happen? It can happen because readers do not need to know all of the words in the dictionary!

Consider first a historically prominent reading fluency intervention. Dolch (1939/1945, 1941/1951/1960) believed that children should be taught the words most often encountered in text as sight words, words they should recognize automatically. Through his research, he identified 220 words that made up between 50 and 75% of words that children read, with most being function words (e.g., *the, a*), conjunctions, pronouns, prepositions, and common verbs. He also identified 95 nouns that commonly occurred in texts read by children. Both of these lists were part of a larger list of the 1,000 most commonly encountered words.

Dolch had a view of reading and reading instruction that was far ahead of his time (see Pressley, 2005)—here, we can cover only those elements most pertinent to our discussion. Although he believed that much learning of sight words could occur in a decontextualized fashion, Dolch also developed many literary stories to enable students to encounter the selected words in context. For struggling readers, in particular, Dolch felt that these stories should be read orally by students with substantial feedback from the teacher, including feedback about how to sound out the words (i.e., the stories contained related words that could be comprehended through phonics skills, which Dolch believed in teaching explicitly). Dolch was emphatic that reading stories was not about reading words but rather about getting meaning from text, often very personalized meanings informed by students' prior knowledge. Dolch's approach emphasized motivation and was filled with practices that are now known to motivate students, based on substantial research (see Pintrich & Schunk, 2002). He advocated texts that were somewhat challenging and believed in providing lots of praise, practicing reading skills in the context of games, and maintaining cooperative classrooms rather than ones emphasizing competition among students.

Dolch lived in an era when experimental research was relatively uncommon and little understood as a means of evaluating curriculum. Thus, Dolch's ideas about instruction have never been subjected to widespread evaluation. What *has* been studied is whether intensive, short-term teaching of sight words in a decontextualized fashion, in fact, improves subsequent reading of text containing those words. Although the data are mixed on that subject (Fleisher et al., 1979; Levy et al., 1997), what Dolch actually proposed was the *long-term* teaching of sight words and the reading of real stories containing the words, which, for the 220 most common words and 95 most common nouns, was easily accomplished. Such learning of words and reading of text should occur in a very balanced reading instructional program that extends across the school day, according to Dolch.

Dolch's idea of making certain that students know a core set of commonly encountered words makes even more sense today in light of some recent research. Much is now being learned about just what words K–12 students really need to know, the basic vocabulary of children and adolescents.

Biemiller and Slonim (2001) provided useful input in this effort. They performed analyses to identify words understood by 80% of children at each grade level (i.e., most children know the meanings of these words). Very importantly, they were focusing on root words (e.g., *fish*, from which *fishing*, *fishy*, and *fished* are derived). By the end of grade 2, children know about 5,000 root words. After that, through grade 12, students gain about 1,000 words a year to a total of about 15,000 words. In short, Biemiller and Slonim (2001) have identified the words that children at each grade level need to understand. While certainly more than Dolch's basic 1,000 words, their list stops short of being an overwhelming number of words. Since many of these words are not especially high-frequency words in English or in texts children encounter, teachers can prioritize further which words should be targeted for sight-word development and students' ready access to their meanings. Biemiller and Boote (2006) even developed a strategy that allowed teachers to quite effectively foster growth in recognizing these words. Biemiller and Boote found elementary teachers who taught vocabulary words with repeated readings saw an increase of 21–24% words learned. It is important to note that teachers taught different vocabulary words each time the story was read aloud (for a total of 8–12 words a week) and students repeated the readings two to four times with more words learned the more the story was read. Similarly, Coyne et al. (2009) found students had even more success learning new vocabulary words when given the opportunity to interact outside of the story context.

It is a truism that reading is not just about decoding words. Even the simplest view of reading (e.g., Gough & Tunmer, 1986) posits that reading involves decoding the words and then comprehending them, largely by listening to one's own interpretation of the words. Hence, reading comprehension is viewed as determined by a combination of word recognition skills and listening comprehension abilities. In an important study, Catts et al. (2003) assessed the word recognition, listening comprehension, and reading comprehension skills of a group of students, who ranged widely in reading ability, when they were in second, fourth, and eighth grades. Word recognition was much more predictive of reading comprehension at grade 2 than at grade 4, and again more predictive at grade 4 than at grade 8, where it accounted for a *negligible* portion of the variance in reading comprehension. The researchers also examined the weakest readers at each of the grade levels. Word recognition difficulties were more prominently associated with poor reading when students were younger than when they were older. With increasing age, listening comprehension problems became progressively more prominent in students' reading problems. Based on these data, there is more reason to be concerned about word recognition with younger as compared with older students, but for poor readers word recognition problems are still obvious in grade 8. At all grade levels, however, reading comprehension reflected a balancing of word recognition and listening comprehension skills. The need for balanced development of skills was apparent in these analyses, consistent with the message in research of the past decade that a balancing of factors is essential in effective reading instruction.

Another important hypothesis is that developing word recognition skills to the point of fluency should increase comprehension, although comprehension gains are not always obtained when readers learn new words to the point of automatic recognition of them (e.g., Fleisher et al., 1979; Samuels et al., 1974; Yuill & Oakhill, 1988, 1991). Tan and Nicholson (1997) offered an especially important set of data, however, in support of the position that word recognition fluency improves comprehension.

The participants in Tan and Nicholson's (1997) study were 7- to 10-year-old weaker readers. In the critical training condition of the study, participants practiced recognizing target words until they could read each word without hesitation. As word recognition fluency was developed, there was also some attention to the meaning of the trained words. In contrast, in the control condition, training focused on word meanings rather than on word recognition and consisted of discussions between the experimenter and the student about the meanings of target words. In fact, in this control condition, the students did not even see the words during training but only heard them.

Following training, all participants in the Tan and Nicholson (1997) study read a passage containing the target words, with 12 comprehension questions following the reading. There were both literal questions and ones requiring readers to make inferences in order to respond to them. The most important result was that the trained participants answered more comprehension questions than did control participants, despite the fact that, if anything, the control condition developed understanding of the target words better. Breznitz (1997a, 1997b) provided another set of analyses confirming that more rapid automatic decoding improves comprehension, probably by freeing up short-term capacity for comprehension.

Prosody

Although fluent reading is characterized as fast, accurate, and prosodic, there has been relatively little attention paid to the role of prosody in fluent reading. On the one hand, reading prosody may be a by-product of fluent, skilled reading, naturally resulting once decoding becomes automatic enough to free up sufficient attention to permit reasonably good comprehension of what is read (Gough & Tunmer, 1986; Kuhn & Stahl, 2003: Kuhn et al., 2010). On the other hand, it could be that prosody increases reading skill—for example, comprehension—in which case it should be taught to readers like other skills that increase understanding of text. So far, however, although rereading tends to produce increases in prosody, other approaches (e.g., prosodic modeling by a teacher) have not had much impact on prosodic reading (see especially Young et al., 1996).

Schwanenflugel et al. (2004) provided an especially analytical evaluation of reading fluency and prosodic issues in the reading of second- and third-grade students. What they found was that the automatic decoding of words was strongly related to prosody and comprehension. In contrast, prosody was not powerfully related to comprehension, as either a cause or effect of understanding what had been read (although there was a slight positive relationship between prosody and comprehension, consistent with other data; e.g., Kitzen, 2001). The most likely hypothesis based on these data was that for many children prosodic reading was a by-product of becoming fluent at the word level (see also Bear, 1992) but was not strongly associated with comprehension either as a cause or an effect.

From an instructional standpoint, though, we do not believe teachers should solely focus on prosody instruction, as Schwanenflugel et al. (2015) recently explored an instructional method to increase student prosody while reading. The researchers included two groups of third-grade students who were provided short reading passages. One group received a marked passage and the other an unmarked passage. The marked passage highlighted contrastive stress, exclamation, and direct quotations within the text, while the unmarked passage had no such markings. The results found students with the marked passages read the highlighted texts with a higher pitch and contrastive stress and exclamation with greater intensity than students with unmarked passages.

To help educators assess prosody, Benjamin et al. (2013) developed an instrument that assesses two dimensions of oral reading: automaticity (rate and accuracy) and prosody (intonation and pausing data analyzed through spectrographic analyses of the reading performance). Benjamin et al.'s new fluency procedure is called the Comprehensive Oral Reading Fluency Scale (CORFS). Benjamin et al. (2013) used a two-study framework for studying the CORFS. The first study collected oral reading from 90 second-grade students. The CORFS was then minimally modified based on expert use and critiques. The second study used 120 third-grade students in two states to further evaluate the CORFS. In study 2, correlations between CORFS Total Expression score and scores on three assessments

(QRI-5 Fluency, TOWRE-SWE, and WIAT-RC) were examined. Correlations between CORFS and these measures were all statistically significant at the p = .01 level. What this study suggests is that neither reading rate nor prosody measured alone is nearly as good at predicting which students can read effectively and efficiently as measuring reading rate, accuracy, *and* prosodic performance.

We are also aware that some common instructional practices may also be implicated in oral reading dysfluency. The first factor that must be considered is text difficulty. In American classrooms, it is the better readers who are most likely to read fluently from their classroom texts. But those students are typically reading from texts well below their reading level. Thus, daily they practice reading texts that are easy for them to read. Struggling readers, on the other hand, spend most of their school days with texts that are written at a level considerably above their current reading level (Allington, 1983). Second, because teachers (and other students) are likely to interrupt at the misreading of a word, struggling readers are more likely to be interrupted while reading aloud than are better readers (Allington, 1980). Thus, two quite different reading environments are typically created for readers of differing levels of proficiency.

Our hunch is that many reading behaviors are induced by environmental factors (Allington, 2009). Thus, if we change the instructional environment in certain ways we can reduce the incidence of certain behaviors. Based primarily on our clinical work, we have found that two changes to the instructional environment can be made that foster improved reading fluency. The first change is to ensure that the reader has in his or her hands a text that he or she can read with a high level of accuracy. The second change involves just listening to the struggling reader and neither offering nor allowing any interruptions. It is fine to jump in, say, at the end of a page to ask the reader about a misreading that occurred (especially an uncorrected misreading). But even at the end of a page it might be more helpful to simply ask the reader to reread the sentence where the misreading occurred rather than to identify the word that was misread.

Torgesen and Hudson (2006) review a series of studies demonstrating that improving word reading proficiencies, usually with intensive decoding lessons, had little effect on improving reading rate, a central aspect of reading fluency. Students who improved from the 2nd to the 39th percentile on decoding words showed almost no improvement in reading rate (moving from the 3rd percentile to the 5th percentile). They conclude that, at least with older struggling readers,

> The most important factor appears to involve difficulties in making up for the huge deficits in accurate reading practice the older children have accumulated by the time they reach later elementary school.... One of the major results of

> this lack of reading practice is a severe limitation in the number of words the children with reading disabilities can recognize automatically, or at a single glance . . . . Such "catching up" would seem to require an extensive period of time in which the reading practice of the previously disabled children was actually greater than that of their peers. Even if word reading accuracy is dramatically increased through more efficient use of analytical word-reading processes, reliance on analytic processes will not produce the kind of fluent reading that results when most words in a passage can be recognized at a single glance. (p. 147–148)

The goal in such extended reading activity is stimulating self-regulating behaviors. Prosody reflects reading with understanding and seems related to a reader's level of self-regulation. Similar to self-correction of oral reading errors, readers can learn to self-regulate their prosody while reading. But they will acquire this self-regulating strategy only if the teacher or other students do not consistently interrupt them as every word is misread. In the common case of much teacher interruption, we see the development of what has been dubbed "learned helplessness." Most poor readers exhibit learned helplessness when they wait for the teacher or someone else to correct their error (Johnston & Winograd, 1985). What Clay (1969) reported, though, was that emergent readers who became good readers self-corrected one of every three errors while the low-progress readers self-corrected only one of every 20 oral reading errors.

What concerns us is that, if low-progress readers actually decide to wait for someone else to correct their errors, they will never be either fluent or proficient readers. Unfortunately, most struggling readers find themselves in instructional environments that do little to foster either fluency or self-regulation. Thus, they read in a herky-jerky manner with little prosody and often with many misreadings. However, our clinical work suggests that, by selecting texts that the reader can read with a high degree of accuracy and then limiting the interruptions to the end of the page and there focusing on having the reader reread the misread text, then progress toward both fluency and understanding will be made.

Assessment

Fluent reading is most often measured in terms of the number of words read accurately in a set period of time. Although there are ways to measure prosody (Benjamin et al., 2013; Schwanenflugel et al., 2004), far less attention has been paid to its assessment. In the past several years, a set of measures known as the Dynamic Indicators of Basic Early Literacy Skills (DIBELS; see *dibels.uoregon.edu*) has been widely deployed at the primary-grade levels and now at the upper elementary level.

Basically, this is a measure that involves computing the speed of accurate reading (i.e., how many words of grade-level text can be read in a minute). Since the development, researchers have found mixed results on the effectiveness of DIBELS to predict student comprehension (Carlisle et al., 2004; Mathson et al., 2006; Pressley, Hilden, et al., 2006; Roehrig et al., 2008; Shelton et al., 2009).

For example, Pressley, Hilden, et al. (2006) analyzed data on the third-grade version of DIBELS. One very important finding in this investigation, as noted earlier, is that children often can read with great speed and accuracy and yet recall few of the ideas in the text they have read. Furthermore, the DIBELS performances only weakly correlated with the scores on the Terranova, a standardized reading achievement test. Likewise, Carlisle et al. (2004), Shelton et al. (2009), and Mathson et al. (2006) each found DIBELS scores to be less predictive of comprehension than one might hope for and echo the Pressley, Hilden, et al. (2006) argument that fast reading is not a useful goal, especially in the absence of understanding what was read. However, Roehrig et al. (2008) found moderate to strong positive correlations between DIBELS and comprehension achievement with the Florida statewide reading assessment and SAT-10. It is important to note that these results were collected throughout the third grade year and the strongest correlations appeared approximately two-thirds (February/March) of the way through the school year.

With such mixed results, it is concerning the emphasis schools put on DIBELS assessments in today's classrooms. Nobody should be interested in or promoting fast reading with low comprehension (Samuels, 2007). Yet, given the emphasis on DIBELS testing in many schools, there is reason to continually examine the validity of this assessment with respect to skilled reading. We emphasize that we do not endorse assessments that reward fast reading without regard to comprehension.

Comprehension Strategies Instruction

Weak readers can become better readers through the teaching of comprehension strategies. The work of Brown et al. (1996) and Anderson (1992) is especially powerful evidence of this reality. In the former study, weak second-grade readers were taught a small repertoire of comprehension strategies over the course of a school year of instruction, with huge gains in reading achievement at the end of the year. In the latter study, weak readers in grades 6 through 9 were provided similar instruction, with similar large gains in reading achievement. In both studies, there were positive effects across a variety of measures. Many of the children in both of these studies were far from being fluent readers at the word level. Using the comprehension strategies very much seemed to make up for the lack of fluency.

Of course, there is also a bonus in learning to use comprehension strategies. Students get more out of reading, which, if they are reading quality material, increases their knowledge of the world, with such richer world knowledge empowering future comprehension of topically related texts (Anderson & Pearson, 1984). So, by teaching comprehension strategies that permit students to read books with worthwhile content, there is the potential to do much for literacy development, even of students who are not as fluent as their classmates (see Chapter 8).

Summary and Comment

So, what can be made from this flurry of theory, research, and practices with respect to developing fluent readers as well as considering future research on fluency? First of all, the case does seem strong that, for some readers, explicit teaching of word recognition skills through phonics instruction works to inculcate sounding-out capabilities and is a stepping stone to fluent reading. For some children, however, phonics instruction either is not successful or produces only slow decoding of words. When it is not successful at all, comprehension almost certainly is undermined. You cannot get above-word-level meaning from text without reading the words. For the slow decoders, sounding out words takes up so much cognitive capacity that little is left over for higher-order comprehension, consistent with LaBerge and Samuels's (1974) conception of short-term memory as a potential bottleneck in the cognitive system supporting reading.

Once again, we will remind readers that it has been rare for educators to examine instructional practices as a source of ineffective reading performances. As was noted above with the interrupting behaviors of teachers while poor readers are reading aloud, slow decoding may also be instructionally induced. As Johnston and Allington (1990) noted regarding the multisensory Orton–Gillingham phonics program:

> Seemingly it did not seem to occur to Gillingham that the laborious decoding emphasis in the instruction may have actually produced the continuing slow reading, or that the displeasure created in reading by the instruction may have severely reduced the amount and frequency of actual reading that the child might do, and hence, [reduced the likelihood of] the automation of word recognition. (p. 999)

As Barr (1975) and Cohen (1974) both report, the type of beginning reading instruction experienced did influence the types of errors that readers made. Thus, it seems consistent, at least, that the instruction would influence just how the reader attempted to decode unknown words. If most of the instructional attention is paid to sounding out words letter by letter (or phoneme by phoneme), then at least some students may adhere to this method, even when a more rapid pace of word recognition is possible.

The reports of compensating readers who seem to learn high-frequency words so they can recognize them immediately prompts us to think that for some readers something other than phonics is needed. Better reading in such students, if not fully fluent reading, might be produced by assuring that students who experience great difficulties in learning to sound out words might be able to learn sight words as unanalyzed wholes. This, in fact, is an idea that has been around for a long time, most prominently in the work of Dolch. Research on that approach to teaching reading should be a high priority, especially with students who do not become proficient in phonics after great efforts are made to teach them how to sound out words. We emphasize that, in arguing for more work on Dolch's approach, we favor the broad and balanced approach to teaching detailed in Dolch's writing. We do not advocate just a flashcard approach, but rather instruction that provides many opportunities for students to practice reading, including the Dolch words in meaningful, connected text. That would include much opportunity for the student to experience oral reading of texts with teacher guidance and feedback. In doing research on the hypothesis that some dysfluent readers would benefit from the teaching of whole words, that work should probably get beyond the original Dolch words. We know more than ever before what words students of various grade levels should be acquiring, with high-frequency words that age- and grade-mates are acquiring potentially serving as a very good guide for choosing words to develop as sight words in struggling beginning readers (Hiebert & Martin, 2009).

There is much more work on fluency as fast and accurate decoding than there is work on prosody. That prosody is modestly correlated with comprehension suggests that developing prosody should not be a priority element of instruction. That said, because prosody is a hallmark of skilled reading, some attention should be paid to it in readers who do not read with expression.

We remain committed to the hypothesis that skills such as fluency are best developed through instruction that balances skills instruction and balanced reading and writing instruction. Overly focusing on just a few skills (e.g., phonological decoding instruction, fast and accurate decoding to the point of fluency at the word level) was never observed in the very best elementary classrooms we have studied. We firmly believe that teachers must teach reading as a whole rather than separate pieces.

To return to where we began, the major goal of reading is to understand. Reading fast and accurately means little if comprehension remains low. Future research on the development of fluency should always include assessments of comprehension. There should be a lot of research ahead—if for no other reason than that the connections between fluency and comprehension hypothesized by LaBerge and Samuels (1974) some 50 years ago have not been explored in depth. Indeed, far too few of the studies that were read to inform this chapter did not even include measures of comprehension! We need to continue progressing research on fluency in general as well as more encompassing work including more expanded work connecting fluency with comprehension (Cartwright et al., 2019; Kieffer & Christodoulou, 2020; Kim, 2015; Samuels, 2007; Valencia et al., 2010).

Finally, what should each reading practitioner do on Monday morning? Pressley, Gaskins, Solic, and Collins (2006) provide a study of the Benchmark School, one of the premier schools in the world in terms of evidence-based instruction for students with reading disabilities. Students enter the school after a year or two of reading failure. After 4–7 years at the school, most students leave as competent readers, although many are not fluent in the sense of being able to read all the words in the text with high speed and accuracy.

How is this improvement accomplished? Yes, there is systematic teaching of decoding, lots of repeated oral reading, lots of independent reading, and lots of emphasis on sight vocabulary. The particular mix a student receives depends largely on how he or she responds to instruction. That level of customization can happen because of the close monitoring that occurs at the school. In addition, the school never loses track of the goal that students should understand what they read in text and should use text productively in higher-order literacy tasks, such as composing written work. There is much teaching of comprehension strategies and writing strategies. By the end of the middle school years at the school, many Benchmark students are very strategic and constructively responsive as they read, even if they can't sound out every word quickly. They get much from the text and can use what they get. Thus, the Benchmark students are proof positive that fully fluent reading in the sense of every word being read accurately and quickly is not absolutely necessary. Even if word-level fluency is beyond the capacities of some children, there remains the hope that they can learn to get much out of text and be functionally literate through the teaching of higher-order literacy competencies, beginning with comprehension strategies. And, of course, the more they comprehend, the more they will develop prior knowledge that will permit them to better understand topically related texts in the future. So, what should reading practitioners be doing on Monday mornings? The answer is balancing instruction in all the components that contribute to skilled reading. As preservice teachers and classroom teachers begin to develop balanced instruction, we encourage them to reference the strategies in Table 6.2 and those presented in other chapters to help build balanced reading lessons.

TABLE 6.2. Strategies for Teaching Fluency

Supporting fluency development	Instructional practice
Provide systematic phonics instruction in grade 1—phonologically based intervention	• Include reading of decodable books (in Kindergarten and the beginning of 1st grade), complemented by reading of trade books as decoding skills increase, and natural language books. ○ Students need to read many types of text, including decodable texts, predictable texts, high frequency word texts, and natural language texts. • See Chapter 5 for more details. • Know that this approach may *not* be enough for all readers.
Support students' sight words	• Expose students to new words with similar patterns through text, across content areas, and through engaging lessons to build sight word knowledge.
Wide reading	• Students participate in rereading of text with the teacher and then with a partner, engage in a choral reading with classmates, write about the text. • In the final 2 days of the week, students do echo reading and partner reading of new texts. • Teachers can teach important vocabulary words during each rereading of a text to build student vocabulary. • Though similar to repeated reading, there are mixed results with repeated readings. It is important to note that there is no difference when students read the same text multiple times compared with reading a variety of texts for the same amount of time; thus, we advise exposing students to multiple texts.
Build a supportive reading environment	• Ensure that all students are reading a text that they can read with high levels of accuracy. • Don't interrupt or allow for interruptions of struggling readers. Rather, wait until the end of the page to ask about misreading or to ask the reader to reread the sentence where misreading occurred.
Develop prosody	• Highlight important features within the text to scaffold students to change pitch or stress while reading certain aspects of the text (e.g., exclamation marks, commas, or direct quotes).
Read, read, read, and read some more!	• Read aloud to students. • Allow students extensive time to read individually, with partners, with adults, in small groups, etc. • Motivate and engage with students about their reading.

Note: Teachers must incorporate all aspects of reading into lessons and remember not all strategies will work with every student.

IMPLICATIONS AND CONCLUDING REFLECTIONS

1. Fluency research and practice remain a flurry of theories rather than one cohesive picture about what fluency is and how we should be teaching it in classrooms.

2. LaBerge and Samuels's 1974 article explained the importance of automaticity for emergent readers. Until immature readers become able to recognize and decode words effortlessly, much of their cognition is tied to identifying words; as word recognition becomes effortless, their attention becomes freed up for comprehension.

3. Systematic phonics instruction can be helpful in promoting fluency in some at-risk readers but is often insufficient. It should not be viewed as a panacea for all struggling readers.

4. There has been a lot of activity in the area of brain-imaging research recently, and it has yielded some interesting findings. Normal mature readers utilize three regions on the left side of the brain, the parieto-temporal region, the occipito-temporal region, and Broca's area. We also know that extensive reading activity produces improved structure in the white matter aspect of the brain. This improved structure is linked to improved reading performances.

5. A slow speed in verbal processing can impair fluency for some readers. This process impairs the speed of decoding, even though it is not rooted in phonological ability.

6. Fluency can be developed in the classroom with repeated readings and with a wide reading design that emphasizes lots of independent reading of texts of an appropriate level of difficulty. In effective primary-level classrooms (Pressley et al., 2003), a main approach to fluency is to give struggling readers ample opportunity to read with support from teachers.

7. An important area for future research and possibly instruction is developing sight-word recognition and vocabulary knowledge. Edward Dolch, a true visionary in reading instruction, developed a system of sight-word instruction embedded in a holistic reading program that should be further explored through experimental research. Additionally, we have a clearer sense than ever of which vocabulary words young children should know, owing to the work of Biemiller and Slonim (2001), and teachers can support students learning of sight words by exposing students to words through text and beyond the context of the book (Biemiller & Boote, 2006).

8. Prosodic reading is most likely a by-product of becoming fluent. At the same time, instructional environments seem to play a role in whether

readers develop prosodic reading proficiencies. Both the nature of the word recognition instruction and the nature of the interactions that occur while students are orally reading seem to influence the strategies readers use when reading aloud.

9. As always, comprehension is the chief goal in reading instruction, while fluency may be merely one means to that end. Teachers should not focus solely on fluency strategies, but rather incorporate strategies for all aspects of reading into their instruction. As such, teaching comprehension strategies can help students to make gains in comprehension, even when they are dysfluent readers (Anderson, 1992; Brown et al., 1996).

10. Finally, build a supportive environment in which students can have success with reading and give students the opportunity to read a lot.

REFERENCES

Allington, R. L. (1980). Teacher interruption behaviors during primary grade oral reading. *Journal of Educational Psychology, 72,* 371–377.

Allington, R. L. (1983). The reading instruction provided readers of differing abilities. *Elementary School Journal, 83,* 548–559.

Allington, R. L. (2009). *What really matters in fluency: From research to practice.* Pearson.

Allington, R. L., & McGill-Franzen, A. M. (2021). Reading volume and reading achievement: A review of recent research. *Reading Research Quarterly, 56,* S231-S238.

Almasi, J. F., Palmer, B. M., Madden, A., & Hart, S. (2011). Interventions to enhance narrative comprehension. In A. McGill-Franzen & R. L. Allington (Eds.), *Handbook of reading disability research* (pp. 329–344). Routledge.

Anderson, R. C., & Pearson, P. D. (1984). A schema-theoretic view of basic processes in reading. In P. D. Pearson (Ed.), *Handbook of reading research* (pp. 255–291). Longman.

Anderson, V. (1992). A teacher development project in transactional strategy instruction for teachers of severely reading-disabled adolescents. *Teaching and Teacher Education, 8,* 391–403.

Arrington, C. N., Kulesz, P. A., Francis, D. J., Fletcher, J. M., & Barnes, M. A. (2014). The contribution of attentional control and working memory to reading comprehension and decoding. *Scientific Studies of Reading, 18*(5), 325–346.

Barr, R. (1975). Influence of reading materials on response to printed words. *Journal of Reading Behavior, 7,* 123–135.

Bear, D. R. (1992). The prosody of oral reading and stages of word knowledge. In D. R. Bear & S. Templeton (Eds.), *Development of orthographic knowledge and the foundations of literacy: A memorial festschrift for Edmund H. Henderson* (pp. 137–189). Erlbaum.

Benjamin, R. G., Schwanenflugel, P. J., Meisenger, E. B., Groff, C., Kuhn, M. R., & Steiner, L. (2013). A spectrographically grounded scale for evaluating reading expressiveness. *Reading Research Quarterly, 48*(2), 105–133.

Best, J. R., & Miller, P. H. (2010). A developmental perspective on executive function. *Child Development, 81*(6), 1641–1660.

Biemiller, A., & Boote, C. (2006). An effective method for building meaning vocabulary in primary grades. *Journal of Educational Psychology, 98*(1), 44–62.

Biemiller, A., & Slonim, N. (2001). Estimating root word vocabulary growth in normative and advantaged populations: Evidence for a common sequence of vocabulary acquisition. *Journal of Educational Psychology, 93*, 498–520.

Breznitz, Z. (1997a). Effects of accelerated reading rate on memory for text among dyslexic readers. *Journal of Educational Psychology, 89*, 289–297.

Breznitz, Z. (1997b). Enhancing the reading of dyslexic children by reading acceleration and auditory masking. *Journal of Educational Psychology, 89*, 103–113.

Brown, R., Pressley, M., Van Meter, P., & Schuder, T. (1996). A quasi-experimental validation of transactional strategies instruction with low-achieving second grade readers. *Journal of Educational Psychology, 88*, 18–37.

Carlisle, J. F., Schilling, S. G., Scott, S. E., & Zeng, J. (2004). *Do fluency measures predict reading achievement? Results from the 2002–2003 school year in Michigan's Reading First schools* (Technical Report No. 1). University of Michigan.

Cartwright, K. B. (2002). Cognitive development and reading: The relation of reading-specific multiple classification skill to reading comprehension in elementary school children. *Journal of Educational Psychology, 94*, 56–63.

Cartwright, K. B. (2015). *Executive skills and reading comprehension: A guide for educators.* Guilford Press.

Cartwright, K. B., Bock, A. M., Clause, J. H., Coppage August, E. A., Saunders, H. G., & Schmidt, K. J. (2020). Near- and far-transfer effects of an executive function intervention for 2nd to 5th grade struggling readers. *Cognitive Development, 56*, 1–11.

Cartwright, K. B., Coppage, E. A., Lane, A. B., Singleton, T., Marshall, T. R., & Bentivegna, C. (2017). Cognitive flexibility deficits in children with specific reading comprehension difficulties. *Contemporary Educational Psychology, 50*, 33–44.

Cartwright, K. B., Lee, S. A., Taboada Barber, A., DeWyngaert, L. U., Lane, A. B., & Singleton, T. (2020). Contribution of executive function and intrinsic motivation to university students' reading comprehension. *Reading Research Quarterly, 55*(3), 345–369.

Cartwright, K. B., Marshall, T. R., Huemer, C. M., & Payne, J. B. (2019). Executive function in the classroom: Cognitive flexibility supports reading fluency for typical readers and teacher-identified low-achieving readers. *Research in Developmental Disabilities, 88*, 42–52.

Catts, H. W., Hogan, T. P., Adlof, S. M., & Barth, A. E. (2003, June 14). *The simple view of reading: Changes over time.* Presented at the annual meeting of the Society for the Scientific Study of Reading, Boulder, CO.

Clay, M. M. (1969). Reading errors and self-correction behaviour. *British Journal of Educational Psychology, 37*, 47–56.

Cohen, A. S. (1974). Oral reading errors of first grade children taught by a code-emphasis approach. *Reading Research Quarterly, 10*, 616–650.

Compton, D. L., Appleton, A. C., & Hosp, M. K. (2004). Exploring the relationship between text-leveling systems and reading accuracy and fluency in second-grade students who are average and poor decoders. *Learning Disabilities Research and Practice, 19*, 176–184.

Coyne, M. D., McCoach, D. B., Loftus, S., Zipoli Jr., R., & Kapp, S. (2009). Direct vocabulary instruction in kindergarten: Teaching for breadth versus depth. *The Elementary School Journal, 110*(1), 1–18.

Cutting, L. E., Materek, A., Cole, C. A., Levine, T. M., & Mahone, E. M. (2009). Effects of fluency, oral language, and executive function on reading comprehension performance. *Annals of Dyslexia, 59*(1), 34–54.

Dolch, E. W. (1939/1945). *A manual for remedial reading* (1st and 2nd eds.). Garrard Press.

Dolch, E. W. (1941/1951/1960). *Teaching primary reading* (1st, 2nd, and 3rd eds.). Garrard Press.

Fink, R. (1998). Literacy development in successful men and women with dyslexia. *Annals of Dyslexia, 48*, 311–346.

Fleisher, L. S., Jenkins, J. R., & Pany, D. (1979). Effects on poor readers comprehension of training in rapid decoding. *Reading Research Quarterly, 15*, 30–48.

Friedman, N. P., & Miyake, A. (2017). Unity and diversity of executive functions: Individual differences as a window on cognitive structure. *Cortex, 86*, 186–204.

Gernsbacher, M. A., & Kaschak, M. P. (2003). Neuroimaging studies of language and comprehension. *Annual Review of Psychology, 54*, 91–114.

Gibson, E. J., & Levin, H. (1975). *The psychology of reading.* MIT Press.

Goswami, U. (2004). Neuroscience and education. *British Journal of Educational Psychology, 74*, 1–14.

Gough, P. B., & Tunmer, W. E. (1986). Decoding, reading, and reading disability. *Remedial and Special Education, 7*, 6–10.

Hiebert, E. H., & Martin, L. A. (2009). Repetition of words: The forgotten variable in texts for beginning and struggling readers. In E. H. Hiebert & M. Sailors (Eds.), *Finding the right texts: What works for beginning and struggling readers* (pp. 47–69). Guilford Press.

Homan, S., Klesius, P., & Hite, S. (1993). Effects of repeated readings and non-repetitive strategies on students: Fluency and comprehension. *Journal of Educational Research, 87*, 94–99.

Hruby, G. G., & Goswami, U. (2011). Neuroscience and reading: A review for reading education researchers. *Reading Research Quarterly, 46*(2), 156–172.

Jacobson, L. A., Ryan, M., Martin, R. B., Ewen, J., Mostofsky, S. H., Denckla, M. B., & Mahone, E. M. (2011). Working memory influences processing speed and reading fluency in ADHD. *Child Neuropsychology, 17*(3), 209–224.

Johnston, P. H., & Winograd, P. (1985). Passive failure in reading. *Journal of Reading Behavior, 17*, 279–301.

Johnston, P. H., & Allington, R. L. (1990). Remediation. In P. D. Pearson (Ed.), *Handbook of reading research* (Vol. II, pp. 984–1012). Longman.

Kahnemann, D. (1973). *Attention and effort.* Prentice-Hall.

Keller, T. A., & Just, M. A. (2009). Altering cortical activity: Remediation-induced changes in the white matter of poor readers. *Neuron, 64*(5), 624–631.

Kieffer, M. J., & Christodoulou, J. A. (2020). Automaticity and control: How do executive functions and reading fluency interact in predicting reading comprehension? *Reading Research Quarterly, 55*(1), 147–166.

Kim, Y. S. G. (2015). Developmental, component-based model of reading fluency: An investigation of predictors of word-reading fluency, text-reading fluency, and reading comprehension. *Reading Research Quarterly, 50*(4), 459–481.

Kitzen, K. R. (2001). Prosodic sensitivity, morphological ability, and reading ability in young adults without childhood histories of reading difficulty. *Dissertation Abstracts International, 62*(2-A), 460.

Kuhn, M. R. (2005). A comparative study of small group fluency instruction. *Reading Psychology, 26*(2), 127–146.

Kuhn, M. R., Schwanenflugel, P. J., & Meisinger, E. B. (2010). Aligning theory and assessment of reading fluency: Automaticity, prosody, and definitions of fluency. *Reading Research Quarterly, 45*(2), 230–251.

Kuhn, M. R., Schwanenflugel, P., Morris, R. D., Morrow, L. M., Woo, D., Meisinger, B., et al. (2006). Teaching children to become fluent and automatic readers. *Journal of Literacy Research, 38*(4), 357–388.

Kuhn, M. R., & Stahl, S. A. (2003). Fluency: A review of developmental and remedial practices. *Journal of Educational Psychology, 95*, 3–21.

LaBerge, D., & Samuels, S. J. (1974). Toward a theory of automatic information processing in reading. *Cognitive Psychology, 6,* 293–323.

Levy, B. A., Abello, B., & Lysynchuk, L. (1997). Transfer from word training to reading in context: Gains in reading fluency and comprehension. *Learning Disabilities Quarterly, 20,* 173–188.

Lipka, O. (2017). Reading fluency from grade 2–6: A longitudinal examination. *Reading and Writing, 30*(6), 1361–1375.

Mathes, P. G., & Fuchs, L. S. (1993). Peer-mediated reading instruction on special education resource rooms. *Learning Disabilities Research and Practice, 8,* 233–243.

Mathson, D., Solic, K., & Allington, R. L. (2006). Hijacking fluency and instructionally informative assessment. In T. Rasinski, C. Blachowicz, & K. Lems (Eds.), *Fluency instruction: Research-based best practice* (pp. 106–119). Guilford Press.

Miller, G. A. (1956). The magical number seven, plus-or-minus two: Some limits on our capacity for processing information. *Psychological Review, 63,* 81–97.

Miyake, A., Friedman, N. P., Emerson, M. J., Witzki, A. H., Howerter, A., & Wager, T. D. (2000). The unity and diversity of executive functions and their contributions to complex "frontal lobe" tasks: A latent variable analysis. *Cognitive Psychology, 41*(1), 49-100.

National Reading Panel. (2000). *Report of the National Reading Panel: Teaching children to read: An evidence-based assessment of the scientific research literature on reading and its implications for reading instruction: Reports of the subgroups.* National Institute of Child Health and Human Development, National Institutes of Health.

Newkirk, T. (2012). *The art of slow reading.* Heinemann.

Nguyen, T. Q., Pickren, S. E., Saha, N. M., & Cutting, L. E. (2020). Executive functions and components of oral reading fluency through the lens of text complexity. *Reading and Writing,* 1–37.

Nugiel, T., Roe, M. A., Taylor, W. P., Cirino, P. T., Vaughn, S. R., Fletcher, J. M., et al. (2019). Brain activity in struggling readers before intervention relates to future reading gains. *Cortex, 111,* 286–302.

Partanen, M., Kim, D. H., Rauscher, A., Siegel, L. S., & Giaschi, D. E. (2021). White matter but not grey matter predicts change in reading skills after intervention. *Dyslexia, 27*(2), 224–244.

Partanen, M., Siegel, L. S., & Giaschi, D. E. (2019). Effect of reading intervention and task difficulty on orthographic and phonological reading systems in the brain. *Neuropsychologia, 130,* 13–25.

Pintrich, P. R., & Schunk, D. H. (2002). *Motivation in education: Theory, research, and applications* (2nd ed.). Prentice-Hall.

Pressley, M. (2005). *Dolch professional development guide.* SRA.

Pressley, M., & Afflerbach, P. (1995). *Verbal protocols of reading: The nature of constructively responsive reading.* Erlbaum.

Pressley, M., Gaskins, I. W., Solic, K., & Collins, S. (2006). A portrait of the Benchmark School: How a school produces high-achievement in students who previously failed. *Journal of Educational Psychology, 98*(2), 282–306.

Pressley, M., Hilden, K., & Shankland, R. (2006). *An evaluation of end-of-grade 3 Dynamic Indicators of Basic Early Literacy Skills (DIBELS): Speed reading without comprehension, predicting little.* Literacy Achievement Research Center, Michigan State University.

Pressley, M., Roehrig, A., Raphael, L., Dolezal, S., Bohn, K., Mohan, L., et al. (2003). Teaching processes in elementary and secondary education. In W. M. Reynolds & G. E. Miller (Eds.), *Handbook of psychology: Vol. 7. Educational psychology* (pp. 153–175). Wiley.

Rashotte, C. A., & Torgesen, J. K. (1985). Repeated reading and reading fluency in learning disabled children. *Reading Research Quarterly, 20*, 180–188.

Rasinski, T. V., Padak, N., Linek, W., & Sturtevant, B. (1994). Effects of fluency development on urban second-grade readers. *Journal of Educational Research, 87*, 158–165.

Roehrig, A. D., Petscher, Y., Nettles, S. M., Hudson, R. F., & Torgesen, J. K. (2008). Accuracy of the DIBELS oral reading fluency measure for predicting third grade reading comprehension outcomes. *Journal of School Psychology, 46*(3), 343–366.

Samuels, S. J. (2007). The DIBELS tests: Is speed of barking at print what we mean by reading fluency? *Reading Research Quarterly, 42*(4), 563–566.

Samuels, S. J., Dahl, P., & Archwamety, T. (1974). Effect of hypothesis/test training on reading skill. *Journal of Educational Psychology, 66*, 835–844.

Schwanenflugel, P. J., Hamilton, A. M., Kuhn, M. R., Wisenbaker, J. M., & Stahl, S. A. (2004). Becoming a fluent reader: Reading skill and prosodic features in the oral reading of young readers. *Journal of Educational Psychology, 96*, 119–129.

Schwanenflugel, P. J., Kuhn, M. R., Morris, R. D., Morrow, L. M., Meisinger, E. B., Woo, D. G., et al. (2009). Insights into fluency instruction: Short- and long-term effects of two reading programs. *Literacy Research and Instruction, 48*(4), 318–336.

Schwanenflugel, P. J., Westmoreland, M. R., & Benjamin, R. G. (2015). Reading fluency skill and the prosodic marking of linguistic focus. *Reading and Writing, 28*(1), 9–30.

Shaywitz, B. A., Shaywitz, S. E., Blachman, B. A., Pugh, K. R., Fulbright, R. K., Skudlarski, P., et al. (2004). Development of left occipitotemporal systems for skilled reading in children after a phonologically-based intervention. *Biological Psychiatry, 55*, 926–933.

Shaywitz, B. A., Shaywitz, S. E., Pugh, K. R., Mencl, W. E., Fulbright, R. K., Skudlarski, P., et al. (2002). Disruption of posterior brain systems for reading in children with developmental dyslexia. *Biological Psychiatry, 52*, 101–110.

Shaywitz, S. E., & Shaywitz, B. A. (2004). Neurobiologic basis for reading and reading disability. In P. McCardle & V. Chhabra (Eds.), *The voice of evidence in reading research* (pp. 417–442). Brookes.

Shaywitz, S. E., Shaywitz, B. A., Fulbright, R. K., Skudlarski, P., Mencl, W. E., Constable, R. T., et al. (2003). Neural systems for compensation and persistence: Young adult outcome of childhood reading disability. *Biological Psychiatry, 54*, 25–33.

Shelton, N. R., Altwerger, B., & Jordan, N. (2009). Does DIBELS put reading first? *Literacy Research and Instruction, 48*(2), 137–148.

Simpson, J. A., & Weiner, E. S. (Eds.). (1989). *The Oxford English dictionary* (2nd ed.). Oxford University Press.

Stahl, S. A. (2004). What do we know about fluency? Findings of the National Reading Panel. In P. McCardle & V. Chhabra (Eds.), *The voice of evidence in reading research* (pp. 187–211). Brookes.

Stahl, S., Heubach, K., & Cramond, B. (1997). *Fluency-oriented reading instruction.* National Reading Research Center and U.S. Department of Education, Office of Educational Research and Improvement, Educational Resources Information Center.

Tan, A., & Nicholson, T. (1997). Flashcards revisited: Training poor readers to read words faster improves their comprehension of text. *Journal of Educational Psychology, 89*, 276–288.

Torgesen, J. K. (2004). Lessons learning from research on interventions for students who have difficulties learning to read. In P. McCardle & V. Chhabra (Eds.), *The voice of evidence in reading research* (pp. 355–382). Brookes.

Torgesen, J. K., & Hudson, R. F. (2006). Reading fluency: Critical issues for struggling readers. In S. J. Samuels & A. E. Farstrup (Eds.), *Reading fluency: The forgotten dimension of reading success* (pp. 130–158). International Reading Association.

Turkelbaum, P. E., Gareau, L., Flowers, D. L., Zeffiro, T. A., & Eden, G. F. (2003). Development of neural mechanisms in reading. *Nature Neuroscience, 6,* 767–773.

Valencia, S. W., Smith, A. T., Reece, A. M., Li, M., Wixson, K. K., & Newman, H. (2010). Oral reading fluency assessment: Issues of construct, criterion, and consequential validity. *Reading Research Quarterly, 45*(3), 279–291.

Vellutino, F. R. (1979). *Dyslexia: Theory and research.* MIT Press.

von Bon, W. H. J., Boksebeld, L. M., Font Freide, T. A. M., & van den Hurk, A. J. M. (1991). A comparison of three methods of reading-while-listening. *Journal of Learning Disabilities, 24,* 471–476.

Welsh, J. A., Nix, R. L., Blair, C., Bierman, K. L., & Nelson, K. E. (2010). The development of cognitive skills and gains in academic school readiness for children from low-income families. *Journal of educational psychology, 102*(1), 43–53.

Young, A. R., Bowers, P. G., & MacKinnon, G. E. (1996). Effects of prosodic modeling and repeated reading on poor readers' fluency and comprehension. *Applied Psycholinguistics, 17,* 49–84.

Yuill, N., & Oakhill, J. (1988). Effects of inference awareness training on poor comprehension. *Applied Cognitive Psychology, 2,* 23–45.

Yuill, N., & Oakhill, J. (1991). *Children's problems in reading comprehension.* Cambridge University Press.

Zelazo, P. D., Blair, C. B., & Willoughby, M. T. (2016). Executive function: Implications for education. NCER 2017-2000. *National Center for Education Research.*

7 Vocabulary

This chapter takes up how children naturalistically learn vocabulary and how they can be taught other vocabulary that they do not learn naturalistically. Since the publication of the National Reading Panel (NRP; 2000) report, the teaching of vocabulary has been much on the minds of educators because it is one of the five elements of evidence-based reading instruction, along with phonemic awareness, phonics, fluency, and comprehension. There is one consistent relationship in the research literature pertaining to vocabulary that suggests its importance in understanding reading acquisition: People with larger vocabularies tend to comprehend better (Cunningham & Stanovich, 1997; Davis, 1944, 1968; Singer, 1965; Spearitt, 1972; Thurstone, 1946). Bear in mind that just teaching vocabulary is insufficient for improving comprehension if only because there are so many words in the English language.

NATURALISTIC LEARNING OF VOCABULARY

By early adulthood, many individuals have learned 15,000 or more root words (i.e., words that are the bases for families of words, such as *child*, which is the root word for *children*, *childlike*, and *childish*; Biemiller & Slonim, 2001). Most vocabulary words are learned incidentally in context (Sternberg, 1987). Given that only a few hundred words a year appear to be taught directly in school, the only way to explain the learning of so many words is that people acquire them by interacting with others, listening to radio and television, and by reading—acquiring words' meanings incidentally as they do other tasks. There have been a number of analyses of such contextual learning in the past quarter-century, with the naturalistic acquisition of vocabulary now reasonably well understood (McGregor, 2004).

Family Conversations

Without a doubt, one of the most talked about correlational studies having anything to do with vocabulary acquisition was Hart and Risley's (1995) *Meaningful Differences in the Everyday Experience of Young American Children*. The authors observed 42 families for over 2 years, beginning when each participating child was 6–9 months old. The sample included families from upper, middle, and lower socioeconomic classes. A major interest was the language the children experienced at home, with the most prominent finding being that the amount and quality of language the child experienced varied dramatically as a function of social class. The less affluent the family, the less that was said to the child. The less affluent the family, the less complex was the language directed at the child. The less affluent the family, the more discouraging were the messages the child received (i.e., lower-class children heard a higher proportion of prohibitions relative to more socioeconomically advantaged children). Very importantly, there was a clear relationship between the quantity and quality of input and the child's vocabulary development.

At 3 years of age, the upper-class children had much more extensive vocabularies than the middle- and lower-class children. For example, the upper-class child with the smallest vocabulary knew more words than the lower-class child with the best-developed vocabulary. As you would expect, the children who experienced the most language in the first 3 years of life were, with the parents' language interactive style, the very strongest predictor of later reading achievement (i.e., accounting for 59% of the variance).

There are other strong correlations in the research literature between amount and quality of language experienced early in life and language development in general as well as vocabulary development in particular (Dickinson & Porche, 2011; Huttenlocher et al., 2001; Pace et al., 2017; Pearson et al., 1997; Romeo et al., 2018). A reasonable possibility is that early language interactions are causally important in vocabulary development and subsequent reading achievement. From 2 to 3 years of age, children can import words into their language when they experience them, with incidental learning more likely when children experience a word (in both print and orally) multiple times and over several days (Schwartz & Terrell, 1983).

Such repetition can occur when children engage in consistent, extensive, and rich verbal interactions with more linguistically mature people or listening to someone else read. The correlational data on conversations provide strong impetus for encouraging parents to surround their children with language, although admittedly these are only correlational data. Additionally, providing environments that encourage children to read or allow for opportunities for children to listen to adults read can support vocabulary development.

Fast Mapping

One of the most powerful demonstrations of children's readiness to acquire language is their "fast mapping" of meanings of words encountered in language. Carey and Bartlett (1978) asked some preschoolers to do them a favor—"Bring me the chromium tray; not the blue one, the chromium one"—with the request in the context of two available trays, one blue and the other olive. Tested 1 week and 6 weeks later, some of the children receiving this request knew that chromium was a color (i.e., when given a group of names and asked to identify the colors, *chromium* was identified as a color), and others even knew it was olive. They had learned something about the meaning of the word through just one incidental learning opportunity. Moreover, when preschoolers learn a new term via fast mapping, they generalize the term. For example, they recognize another instance of the object, even if it differs in irrelevant features (e.g., size; Behrend et al., 2001; Kleinknecht et al., 1999; Waxman & Booth, 2000).

Perhaps the most dramatic demonstrations of fast mapping have been with 2-year-olds who sometimes fast-map vocabulary meanings (Heibeck & Markman, 1987; Kalashnikova et al., 2018; Markson, 1999;) and with demonstration that incidental fast mapping impacts vocabulary learning as much as attempts to teach meanings directly to young children (Jaswal & Markman, 2003). Although others had previously noted the power of single or a few incidental learning opportunities on children's vocabulary acquisition (e.g., Brown, 1957), Carey and Bartlett's (1978) conceptualization and description of such learning as fast mapping focused attention on this phenomenon more than earlier demonstrations of it. Although there is far from complete understanding of fast mapping (Bloom, P., 2000), that fast mapping occurs makes obvious the fact that incidental learning is a powerful mechanism in vocabulary development. Rich vocabulary environments permit many fast-mapping opportunities as well as opportunities to think about repeated words multiple times.

Children Drawing Attention to Objects That Can Be Named

Lois Bloom and her colleagues have provided evidence that children very much are determinants of what gets talked about when young word learners and adults interact. Caregivers tend to name and talk about objects that children are attending to, with the children definitely making clear to caregivers what it is in the environment that interests them and commands their attention. That is, they let adults know what they want to talk about. In turn, what caregivers talk about influences the words that children learn (Bloom et al., 1996; Bloom, L., 2000; Bloom & Tinker, 2001).

If you would like to see the differences in the way different caregivers interact with children, just visit any supermarket and observe the interactions that occur between caregivers and small children. Some caregivers speak almost constantly to the child with them. They say, "OK, we need to get two cans of peas. Can you help me find the cans of peas? Remember, peas are green. [showing a can of corn] Are these peas? No, those are yellow. How about these? [showing a can of carrots] No, these are orange. How about these, is this a can of peas? [showing a can of peas] Yes, we've found the cans of peas we need!"

Other caregivers say little other than criticizing a child's behavior. In these cases, the interactions go something like this: "Keep your hands down . . . . Don't bother me. I'm getting food for supper . . . . No, you cannot have one of those . . . . Sit still and keep your hands down."

You will observe positive and negative, continual and sporadic, praising and criticizing interactions. All this will occur in one visit to a supermarket. Consider how the differences in the interactions you observed impact vocabulary learning. Consider the reality that some children will have a childhood full of rich verbal interactions with caregivers and other children will live childhoods where verbal interactions with adults are scarce and many that are encountered will do little to foster the development of cognition, much less vocabulary. It is these childhood differences, often found among children enrolled in the same classroom, that make effective teaching complex but rewarding.

Reservations about Incidental Vocabulary Learning from Context

When Sternberg (1987) offered the conclusion that most vocabulary is learned from context, there were definitely data that made clear that learning from context was anything but certain. For example, it was known that often learners failed to correctly infer the meanings of novel words encountered in texts (e.g., Daalen-Kapteijns & Elshout-Mohr, 1981; McKeown, 1985; Nicholson & Whyte, 1992; Schatz & Baldwin, 1986). Even so, Sternberg (1987) inspired additional evaluations of incidental vocabulary learning from context. Swanborn and de Glopper (1999) reviewed these evaluations and concluded that readers often do learn vocabulary from context, but such learning is anything but certain. They estimated that about 15% of novel vocabulary encountered in text is learned to some extent with a single exposure. Maybe readers do not get the whole meaning, but they get at least some of it, just as fast-mapping preschoolers do not get the whole meaning of words they hear one or two times, but fast-map some of the meaning (Carey & Bartlett, 1978). At a 15% rate, children require seven or so encounters with a word for there to be a high probability of learning the word from context.

However, there are enormous differences in the volume of reading that different children engage in. The classic study in this area was an analysis of out-of-school reading conducted by Anderson et al. (1988). This study used fifth-grade students who logged their out-of-school reading every day over 8 to 26 weeks. The amount of time children spent reading was widely variable and highly correlated with gains in reading achievement between second and fifth grade. Students at the 50th percentile in reading achievement read voluntarily about 10 minutes a day out of school, but students scoring at the 80th percentile read for roughly a half hour each day, and those students at the 98th percentile of reading achievement engaged in out-of-school reading for more than 1 hour each day. Volume of out-of-school reading dropped as reading performance dropped so that children scoring at the 30th percentile read roughly half as much as those at the 50th percentile and one-tenth as much as those at the 80th percentile.

Thus, regardless of how many exposures to a word might be required for acquiring the meaning of the new word, some children are far more likely to read sufficiently large amounts of texts to foster such development. At the same time, other children will read so little text that one might expect that almost no new vocabulary will be acquired incidentally while reading.

Even more negatively, research now makes it clear that when readers attempt to derive the meanings of words that are encountered in context (i.e., in sentences, paragraphs, stories), they often get them wrong (for a review, see Fukkink & de Glopper, 1998). Why? Sometimes the reader lacks enough prior knowledge to make sense of the clues to a word's meaning that are in a text. In addition, verbal contexts surrounding vocabulary words can be rich in clues to meaning or sparse in them, and such variations make a difference in whether people learn the meanings of unfamiliar words and use them sensibly (see Nist & Olejnik, 1995, for a telling empirical analysis). Unfortunately, we do not yet know how to determine which contexts have enough information for most learners to be able to figure out the meaning of a word versus not being able to interpret the words.

What we do know, however, is that different contexts provide richer and poorer bases for fostering incidental acquisition of vocabulary. Hayes and Ahrens (1988) analyzed different contexts on the frequency of rare word occurrences. They found children's books to be a relatively rich source of such words (31), at least when compared with children's television programs (2) or the speech of two college-educated adults engaged in a conversation (17). Children's books even had more rare words than primetime adult television shows (23).

We understand that young children will watch television, but it is important to understand that the type of television will impact their vocabulary development. Children can watch *Sesame Street* and other informative television (i.e., the stuff on PBS and other educationally oriented channels), or they can watch a steady diet of cartoons, situation comedies, and other mainstays of commercial television. Watching more informational television as compared with entertainment television can lead to more extensive vocabulary development. A secondary benefit is that children who get hooked on informational television during the early preschool years are more likely to choose to view better programming during the later preschool years (Wright et al., 2001).

Even with potential benefits of informational television, the data supporting reading over television viewing are a main reason that parents are told to restrict young children's television viewing and promote reading of books instead. Given that reading a child a children's book exposes a child to more than 10 times as many new words as watching a children's television program, you can see why children who have been read 1,000 books before they start school really do have a head start for school when compared with children who have watched a lot of television but read only 100 books. And some children begin school having never been read a single book!

Children Participate in High-Quality Lessons

Although there has been a great deal of attention to vocabulary learning in context during the preschool years, vocabulary learning continues throughout childhood (Biemiller & Slonim, 2001). One way that vocabulary learning can occur is through high-quality curricular instruction, even when it is not the main focus of the lesson. Consider what happened when Carlisle et al. (2000) provided a high-quality science unit, although vocabulary learning definitely was not the focal point of the study unit, but rather an incidental outcome of students participating in the unit. Carlisle et al. (2000), in fact, found some incidental acquisition of words covered in the unit. (There were control conditions to assess whether learning of words pertaining to the science unit exceeded acquisition of new words in general over a month, which it did.) Even so, there was certainly room for more learning, with knowledge of the vocabulary in the unit far from perfect at the end of the unit of study.

Carlisle et al. (2000) included lots of interesting additional assessments—for instance, establishing that students who began the unit with greater understanding of vocabulary pertaining to the topic of the unit learned more vocabulary incidentally during instruction than students who started the unit with little prior knowledge. What vocabulary a student learns incidentally during content instruction depends both on exposure to vocabulary and the student's previous knowledge about the topic of instruction.

More generally, over the past several decades, all the authors of this book and other researchers have studied the characteristics of very effective and less effective primary-grade teachers (e.g., Bogner et al., 2002; Dolezal et al., 2003; Morrow et al., 1999; Pressley, Wharton-McDonald, & Mistretta, 1998; Pressley, Allington, et al., 2001; Pressley, Wharton-McDonald, Allington, et al., 2001; ressley, Dolezal, et al., 2003; Pressley, Roehrig, et al., 2003; Pressley, Wharton-McDonald, Raphael, et al., 2001; Wharton-McDonald et al., 1998; also see Chapter 10 of this volume) and upper elementary grade and middle school teachers (Allington & Johnston, 2002; Allington et al., 2002; Gabriel et al., 2011; Johnston, 2004; Pressley et al., 1997, 2020; Pressley, Wharton-McDonald, Mistretta-Hampston, et al., 1998; Stronge, 2018).

Excellent teachers teach vocabulary opportunistically and frequently. When a word comes up that is an important word for students to know and the teacher knows that the students do not know it, that becomes a teachable moment for excellent teachers. We have noted as well that excellent teachers do not talk down to their classes but, rather, consistently use mature vocabulary, providing opportunities for students to experience incidental learning of mature vocabulary in context. High-quality lessons include many opportunities for student vocabulary development.

One might think that these effective teachers more often used the guidance provided with their curriculum materials to design these powerful opportunities for developing vocabulary knowledge than did the less effective teachers. Unfortunately, that was virtually never the case. It seems that vocabulary development lessons provided in core reading programs rarely reflect much of what we know about the most effective ways to foster vocabulary growth. Recently, Graves et al. (2019) and Fitzgerald et al. (2021) analyzed several reading programs used in today's primary and upper elementary classrooms. Though these analyses saw an increase in the number of words presented within the reading programs as compared with previous reading programs, the amount was not considered a significant increase (Fitzgerald et al., 2021). Furthermore Graves et al. (2019) suggested that stakeholders using such reading programs should also consider "students' word knowledge, the importance of the words in the selections students are reading, and the importance of the words to the major themes and topics students are studying" (p. 407) when selecting vocabulary for lessons. Though reading programs are improving, in many respects current instructional materials for developing vocabulary seem as inept as the reading comprehension components of those materials (Dewitz et al., 2009; Fitzgerald et al., 2021; Graves et al., 2019; Maniates & Pearson, 2008). In other words, the suggested instructional activities rarely provide multiple exposures to new vocabulary words and rich contexts for facilitating the acquisition of the new words' meaning(s).

However, research has demonstrated that curriculum materials vary substantially both on the numbers of vocabulary words introduced and on the quality of the instruction provided. Consider the findings of Wright and Neuman (2013), who conducted a document analysis on 12 weeks of lessons offered in the four most widely used kindergarten curricula. Substantial differences in the number of vocabulary words targeted for instruction were found, with some programs focusing on developing the meanings of two words each week and others focused on developing the meanings of 20 words each week! How words were selected for inclusion in the lesson design was not obvious, with some programs focusing on words the researchers deemed likely to be familiar. Finally, the instructional activities recommended rarely had much support in the research on teaching vocabulary. Wright and Neuman (2013) conclude, "These results suggest that instruction in kindergarten core curricula does not reflect the current research base for vocabulary development and may not be systematic enough to influence children's vocabulary learning trajectories" (p. 286).

A few researchers have reported on the nature of vocabulary development lessons in elementary classrooms, with both Lloyd (1995) and Scott et al. (2003) noting that vocabulary was typically taught through decontextualized word-level activities—often with emphasis on pronunciation rather than meaning. Similarly, Dickinson (2011) reported that, in first-grade classrooms, teachers spend 60 minutes per day engaging children in decoding lessons (far more than has been recommended) but only spend 5 minutes a day on engaging children in activities to develop their language or vocabulary (far less than what has been recommended). These various studies suggest that few elementary children experience rich vocabulary development lessons in their classrooms.

Academic Vocabulary

Most research on vocabulary acquisition has focused on learning words that are part of our general word knowledge, the sorts of words we might use in nonacademic conversations or compositions. However, central to the goal of schooling is developing students' understanding of key academic vocabulary. Every science, mathematics, social studies, music, or art class develops students' understanding of words linked primarily, and often only, to the field of study. Outside of scientists talking or writing, the number of citizens who use words such as *organism, physiology, mitosis,* or *bilirubin* in daily conversations, text messages, letters, or email messages to friends is small—infinitesimally small. Nonetheless, prompting development of the meaning of such words is what science teachers must do every day. There is a second and smaller set of studies focused on understanding both the effects of knowing these word meanings and how teachers might effectively develop this vocabulary with their students. Much of this work is recent and has illustrated why academic vocabulary learning is important.

Townsend et al. (2012) studied the knowledge that ethnically diverse middle school students from low-income families had of key academic vocabulary. Low-income students performed worse than middle-income students on all tasks, and native English speakers performed better than English language learners on all tasks. An examination of the relationship between knowledge of academic vocabulary and achievement in four other subjects found that academic vocabulary knowledge explained significant and considerable variance in academic achievement.

Lesaux et al. (2010) reported on their study of academic vocabulary knowledge among struggling sixth-grade readers from 26 multi-ethnic and high-poverty urban schools. Over two-thirds of the subjects were English language learners. Decoding was the overall strength of three-quarters of these struggling readers. What the struggling readers had most in common was low meaning vocabulary knowledge, including low academic vocabulary knowledge. English language learner status did not predict membership in any of the three profiles (slow word callers, automatic word callers, or globally impaired readers). The authors conclude:

> Struggling readers in middle schools overwhelmingly receive intervention targeted at word-level reading skills, especially reading fluency (Deshler et al., 2007). These interventions are characterized by such practices as repeated reading of books with low vocabulary to promote automaticity skills and phonics activities with the intention of developing what is presumed to be a weak understanding of foundational letter–sound correspondences. For the majority of struggling readers in this study, and consistent with the findings from a study conducted with a similarly urban population of fourth graders (i.e., Buly & Valencia, 2002), our data suggest that efforts focused on word reading fluency would be misplaced and unnecessary. (p. 622)

In other words, what the available research suggests is to place a far greater emphasis on fostering growth in the number of words that students know the meanings of. What most older struggling readers seem to have learned is how to decode unknown words, which is not surprising given the amount of attention that decoding lessons have received in remedial and special education interventions. However, the primary problem facing older struggling readers, including English language learners, is their lack of knowledge of the meaning of many, many words that achieving readers know, especially the meanings of key academic vocabulary. The good news is that we know quite a bit about developing meaning vocabulary. The unfortunate news is that too few classrooms or intervention efforts provide any of the effective vocabulary development activities (Deshler et al., 2007).

Fortunately, intentional approaches to teaching vocabulary result more certainly in vocabulary being learned than incidental learning approaches. Intentional approaches to vocabulary instruction are the focus of the remainder of this chapter.

HOW CAN VOCABULARY BE TAUGHT?

There are a variety of ways to teach vocabulary, some incredibly simple and others more complicated. In general, this discussion will proceed from the simpler approaches to ones that are more encompassing. For greater in-depth coverage of many of these topics, see in particular Baumann and Kame'enui (2004) or Cunningham (2008).

Providing Definitions

In a study by Pany et al. (1982), a range of children were asked to learn the meanings of vocabulary words—from average grade 4 children, to students in grades 4 and 5 described as learning-disabled, to grade 4 students who were considered at risk because of their family's low socioeconomic status. The participants in the study were to learn the meanings of vocabulary words, with the words presented and then memory of meanings tested a few minutes later. There were recall measures in the study, recognition of synonyms from distractors (i.e., multiple-choice questions), and items requiring that the learner determine whether the taught words were used correctly in context.

The key independent variable in the study was how the vocabulary words were presented. In the *meanings from context* condition, the vocabulary words appeared in a two-sentence context from which the meaning of the target word could be inferred. In the *meanings given* condition, the student read a sentence containing the word, and then the experimenter told the student the meaning of the word and provided another sentence example in which the word was used. In the *meanings practiced* condition, the experimenter provided a synonym for the target word and the student repeated the synonyms twice. Then there was an undemanding control condition. Participants in that condition were presented only with the vocabulary words—they were not provided the meanings of the words during study. As undemanding as it was, that control condition permitted an important conclusion. Just providing a definition of a word improves learning, for performances in both the *meanings given* and the *meanings practiced* conditions were much better than in this undemanding control condition.

Another very important finding, however, was that performances in the *meanings from context* condition were generally not much better than in the undemanding no meaning exposure control condition, consistent with a main conclusion of the first section of this chapter: Learning vocabulary meanings incidentally from context is anything but certain. That was despite the fact that the contexts were rigged in Pany et al. (1982) so that inferring the meanings should have been easy (i.e., the first sentence contained the target vocabulary word and the second contained an explicit synonym). Even though children can learn word meanings from context, as they seem to do when they fast-map, such learning was not as certain or great as when the meaning was provided in the Pany et al. (1982) study.

Since Pany et al. (1982), there have been several studies in which the meanings of unfamiliar words were explained when the words were encountered, with performance in such conditions contrasted with reading of the text in the absence of vocabulary explanations. Providing explanations has produced generally large effects on vocabulary learning (Brabham & Lynch-Brown, 2002; Brett et al., 1996; Elley, 1989; Penno et al., 2002). That said, providing definitions to students does not guarantee that they will really understand completely the meanings of the words defined.

Hence, as long as there have been dictionaries, teachers have been sending students to them to look up the meanings of words. Confidence that this practice produces understanding of the words looked up was shattered by Miller and Gildea's (1987) article. They asked children in grades 5 and 6 to read dictionary definitions for words they did not know and then write meaningful sentences containing the words. The children wrote many sentences that those authors referred to as mystifying, including the following examples (Miller & Gildea, 1987, p. 98):

Me and my parents *correlate*, because without them, I wouldn't be here.
I was *meticulous* about falling off the cliff.
The *redress* for getting well when you're sick is to stay in bed.
I *relegated* my pen pal's letter to her house.
That news is very *tenet*.

Moreover, it did not help if the definition was accompanied by a model sentence. Consider *usurp*, which loosely means *take*, accompanied by the illustrative sentence "The king's brother tried to *usurp* the throne." Children's own sentences for *usurp* still missed the meaning, however. In all of the following children's generated sentences, the word *take* or a variation of it would make sense, but not the word *usurp*:

The blue chair was *usurped* from the room.
Don't try to *usurp* the tape from the store.
The thief tried to *usurp* the money from the safe.

Yes, like the participants in Pany et al. (1982) who were provided the definitions of new words, Miller and Gildea's (1987) participants got something out of the definitional information. But the bottom line from Miller and Gildea (1987) was that providing definitions alone or with examples of words used in context is a teaching strategy fraught with difficulties. Since these studies from the 1980s, there is almost no evidence that looking words up in a dictionary is actually helpful in the development of a more extensive vocabulary.

There are better and worse dictionary definitions (i.e., clearer and more complete definitions vs. more vague and incomplete definitions). There needs to be systematic study about what difference the quality of a dictionary definition makes (although see Scott & Nagy, 1997), for dictionaries seem omnipresent in reading instruction. It is high time that we find out whether and which dictionaries result in the most certain learning for students.

Teaching Students To Make Intentional Contextual Analyses of Unfamiliar Words in Text

In the studies of learning in context considered thus far, students have been left to their own devices to figure out the words. Students can be taught to make contextual analyses, however. Sternberg (1987) and his colleagues recognized two types of contextual clues that could facilitate vocabulary learning that learners could be taught to analyze. One was external context cues (i.e., meaning cues in the text surrounding a new vocabulary word). The second was internal context clues—prefixes, suffixes, and stems (Sternberg & Powell, 1983; Sternberg et al., 1983). Sternberg's theoretical analysis of vocabulary learning from contexts stimulated researchers to study such teaching.

Kuhn and Stahl (1998) identified 14 studies in which students had been taught to use external semantic context clues, with clear evidence that, as compared with no-instruction controls, students taught to use external semantic contexts, in fact, are better at figuring out the definitions of words. (See also Fukkink & de Glopper, 1998, who also meta-analyzed the studies in which students were taught to use context clues, concluding that such instruction had a moderate impact on students' abilities to figure out meanings.) That said, Kuhn and Stahl (1998) detected an interesting twist that is very important. In four of the studies, control participants simply practiced figuring out the meanings of words in text in the absence of instruction. They improved as much as participants taught specific context analysis strategies. Just being prompted to figure out the meanings of words in context and given a little practice at it is as powerful as much more elaborate instruction (i.e., instruction providing detailed information about the various types of semantic context cues).

What about analysis of internal context clues (i.e., word parts)? The clearly interpretable database on the value of teaching internal clue analysis is thin and equivocal (see Baumann, Kame'enui, et al., 2003, for a review). That said, Levin et al. (1988) demonstrated that if undergraduates are taught word components (i.e., the meanings of prefixes, suffixes, stems), they can use them to figure out the meanings of previously unknown words. The effects in that study were clear and large, although the conditions in the study were such that it was saliently obvious to apply the root word knowledge that was just taught. Graves and Hammond (1980) reported a similar finding with grade 7 students, demonstrating that seventh graders could generalize knowledge of prefixes taught in the context of one set of vocabulary words to new vocabulary words that included the prefixes. Wysocki and Jenkins (1987) found that fourth-, sixth-, and eighth-grade students could transfer knowledge of suffixes to new lists, although the effects were only large with generously liberal scoring of the inferred definitions by the students. In short, there is at least some evidence that teaching morphemes (i.e., the smallest units of meaning: prefixes, suffixes, root words) can improve children's and adults' skills at inferring the meanings of words. That said, we have yet to see a study where this effect is general—that is, obtained when it was not fairly obvious that what was previously learned could and should be used to infer the meanings of new words. Thus, there is need for more study of teaching students to use internal context clues to infer meanings of words, with enough positive data to encourage the hypothesis that such teaching can increase the learning of vocabulary.

One set of investigations of intentional contextual analyses caught our attention more than others as we reviewed this literature. Baumann and his associates (Baumann et al., 2002; Baumann, Edwards, et al., 2003) studied the effects of teaching morphemic (i.e., internal) and semantic contextual (i.e., external) analyses to grade 5 students. In one study, instruction occurred over 2 months; in the other, there were more than twelve 50-minute lessons. In the most ambitious instructional conditions of the experiments, students were taught to use both the morphemic analysis procedures and the semantic contextual analysis procedures. The morphemic lessons focused on teaching students to use root words, prefixes, and suffixes to learn the meanings of new vocabulary words encountered in readings, with 15 specific prefixes and five specific suffixes taught. The semantic context instruction emphasized reading carefully the sentences around a novel word to determine the word's meaning, with instruction about how context sometimes includes definitional clues, actual synonyms for novel words, information about the opposite meaning of the word, and examples if the novel word is a general concept. The participants were taught that clues to meaning are often spread over several surrounding sentences.

In general, the lessons were well planned, including a lot of practice in using the morphemic and semantic context strategies. The participants were also provided an overarching scheme for applying the morphemic and semantic context strategies they had learned, one emphasizing the critical metacognitive information about when and where the morphemic and semantic context strategies should be used. The fifth graders were explicitly instructed to do as detailed below.

When you come to a word and you don't know what it means, use:

1. CONTEXT CLUES: Read the sentences around the word to see if there are clues to its meaning.
2. WORD-PART CLUES: See if you can break the word into a root word, prefix, or suffix to help figure out its meaning.
3. CONTEXT CLUES: Read the sentences around the word again to see if you have figured out its meaning. (Edwards et al., 2004, p. 170)

There were some clear effects among the specific findings in these studies. Teaching the morphemic and semantic context strategies promoted learning of the words in the texts that were read by the students during the study (see also Tomesen & Aarnoutse, 1998). Also, there was some evidence that the fifth graders were able to transfer the skills they learned to determine the meanings of words in novel texts, although the effects were moderate-sized at best and more often small to nonexistent. There was no evidence, however, that the teaching of these skills increased comprehension of what was read. Teaching ways to enhance vocabulary acquisition does not guarantee more general effects on reading.

Additionally, Bowers and Kirby (2010) supported the use of morphological analysis with upper elementary students. Providing 20 mini-lesson interventions for students in grades 4 and 5, Bowers and Kirby found students were able to increase their vocabulary beyond the words taught using parts of the word to determine meaning. Throughout the mini-lessons, students were taught different morphemes and practiced identifying and understanding words with the taught pattern. Throughout the mini-lessons, students worked as word detectives using dictionaries and discussion to determine morpheme meaning. It is important to note that the learning of words was limited to the morphologies taught to the students. More recently, Gellert et al. (2021) found positive short and long term effects of morphological interventions with grade 5 Danish students and vocabulary acquisition.

Furthermore, Joanne Carlisle (2010) provided an integrative review of 13 experimental studies of instruction in morphological awareness. She notes that the studies available differed substantially in the age of subjects with whom they worked, in the native language of the subjects (e.g.,

Chinese, French), and in research methodology. Thus, Carlisle provides an integrative review of this research rather than a meta-analysis. The primary finding was that 12 of 13 experimental studies improved participants' performance on morphological measures when compared with nonparticipating control group peers. More recently, Graves et al. (2018) found positive effects of teaching students strategies for using internal and external context clues when encountering unknown words. Though the three experiments had small samples, Graves and colleagues (2018) found positive results as compared with the control groups.

Overall, the findings of these studies focused on morphological analysis and meaning vocabulary and reading comprehension suggest that students generally do become more able to infer the meanings of unfamiliar words after receiving instruction in morphological analysis; however, to date, there is little evidence that learning to apply morphological analysis contributes to improved reading comprehension. Carlisle reports a correlation of .91 between morphological awareness and vocabulary knowledge and a correlation of .86 with reading comprehension. She concludes that further study is needed of both the roles morphological awareness plays in reading development and the effects of instruction on morphological analysis.

Repeating To-Be-Learned Words and Their Meanings

A final finding in Pany et al.'s (1982) study (i.e., the study with the very undemanding control) that deserves mention is that if practicing the word and its meaning does not make definition learning perfect, it makes it better as compared with a single presentation of the meaning. The general point that frequency of exposure to specific vocabulary words increased the learning of them was definitely clear by the mid-1980s (Stahl & Fairbanks, 1986). Moreover, there continued to be demonstrations that repeated presentations of vocabulary improves acquisition relative to a single presentation (e.g., Leung, 1992; Penno et al., 2002; Senechal, 1997), with repetition most effective if the reencounters are spread over a period of time (e.g., days rather than all within 1 day; Childers & Tomasello, 2002). That is, Thorndike's (1911) views on repetition—that learning increases with repeated exposure—are valid with respect to learning vocabulary meanings.

Talking with Children about Objects That Interest Them

Valdez-Menchaca and Whitehurst (1988) studied a second-language learning situation, with English-speaking children learning Spanish. In the experimental situation, adults labeled a toy in Spanish when the child expressed interest in it. Controls heard the same labels, but not at a time when they seemed to be intrigued by the toy. The children who heard the labels when they were interested in particular toys were more likely to use the words in their later speech, although both groups of children learned the meanings of the words. In matters of vocabulary acquisition, as in many aspects of learning, children's interest matters, with learning more certain when teachers teach to children's interests (Hidi, 1990). Student interest is especially true for supporting English language learners, as Lee and Pulido (2017) found that children's interests played a positive role in developing student vocabulary.

Reading with Children

Parents and teachers can increase children's vocabulary by reading with them. The more that parents interact with children over books, the better developed is children's language (e.g., Mol & Bus, 2011; Payne et al., 1994; for reviews, see Bus et al., 1995, and Scarborough & Dobrich, 1994). Most impressive, there are some very well controlled experimental evaluations that parents and teachers of preschool and primary-grade children can be taught to interact with children over picture books in ways that increase emergent language skills, including vocabulary development (e.g., Baker et al., 2013; Brabham & Lynch-Brown, 2002; Leung, 1992; Lonigan & Whitehurst, 1998; Robbins & Ehri, 1994; Valdez-Menchaca & Whitehurst, 1992; Whitehurst et al., 1999; Whitehurst, Arnold, et al., 1994; Whitehurst, Epstein, et al., 1994; Zevenbergen et al., 2003). For example, teachers might provide explicit instruction that includes multiple texts that incorporate specific vocabulary across subjects (Baker et al., 2013), focus instruction on specific vocabulary while incorporating rereading of text throughout the week that includes discussion of vocabulary during the reading lesson (Brabham & Lynch-Brown, 2002), or provide interactive small reading groups (three to five times a week) and have students reread the same book at home with a parent or older sibling (Whitehurst, Arnold, et al., 1994; Whitehurst, Esptein, et al., 1994, 1999). In short, high-quality book reading by adults and children causes increases in children's language competence, including their vocabulary development.

Wide Reading and Vocabulary Development

As was noted earlier, engaging in much voluntary reading is linked to both vocabulary and reading development. While the incidental acquisition of new word meanings while reading is fraught with perils, engaging in voluntary reading also offers much promise. Krashen (2006, 2011) is probably the strongest advocate for supporting wide and voluntary reading (he calls it free, voluntary reading [FVR]). His book sets out the evidence, both correlational and experimental, on the effects of stimulating wide voluntary reading.

Given the evidence (Brenner & Hiebert, 2010) that core reading programs provide an average of only 15 minutes of daily reading activity, it becomes clearer that far too many children read too little to foster much reading or vocabulary growth. Ask any athlete or chess grand master whether a person can become a talented athlete or chess player if he or she practices only 15 minutes every day. What we know from Ericsson et al.'s (1993) analysis of expert activity is that really exceptional performers differ from less talented individuals primarily on the extent of "deliberate practice" they engage in. Deliberate practice involves voluntarily electing to engage in practice activity. Sometimes that activity is narrow (practice shooting foul shots or practice reversing direction while skating) and at other times deliberate practice is just playing the game (basketball, chess, fencing) while trying to incorporate the new moves you've been working on into your play. Elite pianists engage in 10 times as much practice activity as do amateur pianists. Ericsson et al.'s (1993) article drives home the truth that every athlete or musician has heard, "Practice makes perfect."

Cunningham and Stanovich (1991, 1997, 1998) argue that a variety of data demonstrate that reading volume predicts not just vocabulary size but also reading proficiency. Cunningham and Stanovich (1991) demonstrated that the quantity of students' reading significantly contributed to their verbal abilities, including growth in both vocabulary and overall knowledge. This finding held true even when researchers controlled for general ability and phonological coding skill as possible contributing factors and removed them from the analysis. Cunnningham and Stanovich (1997) concluded that "individual differences in exposure to print can predict differences in growth in reading comprehension ability throughout the elementary grades and thereafter" (p. 940). Furthermore, they argued that the evidence indicates that fostering more extensive voluntary reading "becomes doubly imperative for precisely those children whose verbal abilities are most in need of bolstering, for it is the very act of reading that can build those capacities" (p. 7).

As long as children from low-income families live in homes and neighborhoods where few books are available and attend schools where books are less plentiful than in schools serving nonpoor children, we will be forced to continue waiting to understand what role wide reading plays in fostering vocabulary and comprehension development. The current situation in America is that children from low-income families have limited access to books. This is not to say that there are no books available in the schools they attend; it is just that those schools have fewer books (Allington et al., 1995; Duke, 2000; Neuman & Celano, 2001; Neuman & Moland, 2019). If we wanted a recipe for ensuring that children from low-income families *never* challenged children from more affluent families academically, the current situation is a good one.

So how can teachers help buck this trend? First, teachers need to allow time for students to engage in reading a wide variety of texts. This might include working with the librarian to bring more books into the classroom or providing time for students to visit the school library as necessary. To help develop vocabulary, students need to read fiction and nonfiction books, students need to read books across subject areas, and on their interests. Students need practice reading and exposing them to more books will expose them to new vocabulary opportunities. Teachers can also use this as an opportunity to build relationships with their students by learning more about student interests, engage in discussions about meanings of words in texts, and have students practice finding internal and external clues to determine meaning.

Providing Rich Vocabulary Instruction

Beck et al. (1982) and McKeown et al. (1983) taught about 100 vocabulary words to elementary students over a semester. These words were taught using what Beck and her colleagues refer to as a "rich instructional approach" (Beck et al., 1987; Dole et al., 1995; McKeown & Beck, 2004). Such an approach requires the learners to use and think about the to-be-learned vocabulary in many ways—for example, by making decisions about whether and when a word is used in a context correctly and making decisions requiring students to make distinctions about subsets of the words that were related in meaning. There were many encounters with each taught word over the months of instruction, with McKeown et al. (1985) providing a very analytical demonstration that more frequent encounters with a vocabulary word as part of rich instruction definitely make a difference in how well vocabulary is learned. Also, as part of the Beck and McKeown approach, students often were required to explain their thinking as they worked with the words they were learning. In short, Beck and McKeown emphasized long-term instruction of vocabulary that stimulated student thoughtfulness. Carlo et al. (2004) also provided a demonstration that similarly rich vocabulary instruction can benefit English language learners who are learning English vocabulary and to about the same extent as English native speakers.

Beck, McKeown, and their associates provided the most visible studies confirming that rich teaching of vocabulary increases comprehension of text containing taught vocabulary, with more general effects on comprehension smaller (for a review, see Stahl & Fairbanks, 1986; also see Wixson, 1986). Their work permitted an optimist to see the glass as half full (see also Kame'enui et al., 1982)—at least comprehension improved if the texts contained the words taught—or a pessimist to see the glass as half-empty—comprehension did not improve much more generally from teaching vocabulary words, most emphatically on standardized assessments of comprehension. In the four decades since Beck's research, we are aware of no work that changes that two-edged conclusion.

One tactic to take, given the classic Beck and McKeown outcome, is to teach words that students will encounter in text. Given that only a few hundred vocabulary words can be taught in school each year, the question arises: Which words should be taught? Beck et al. (2002) have proposed an intriguing hypothesis that takes into account the theory that children should be taught words they will encounter and the number of words they can be taught is limited. First, do not worry about teaching the words that children know already as a function of living in the world (e.g., *car, baby, happy, dog, funny*). Also, do not bother teaching words that have a very low frequency in the language, perhaps because they are very domain-specific (e.g., *isotope*, unless, of course, you are teaching chemistry). What should be taught are high-frequency words that occur across a number of domains but are not known by many students (e.g., at the elementary level, teach *coincidence, absurd, industrious, flounder, fortunate*). Beck et al. (2002) refer to these as Tier 2 words, referring to well-known words as Tier 1 and low-frequency words as Tier 3. As far as we know, however, Beck et al.'s (2002) position is an untested hypothesis, although one that seems testable to us and should be tested. See as well the earlier discussion of Biemiller and Slonim's (2001) work. They have identified the 15,000 or so root words that should be known by the end of high school, with that group developing normative data for the entire period of K–12 schooling, which should permit more intelligent decision making in the near future about which words to emphasize for vocabulary instruction at particular grade levels. Additionally, as teachers begin to select vocabulary words from the text, it is important that they do not rely too heavily on a core reading program to provide appropriate and challenging words, which often provide more common, less challenging words that most students already know (Hiebert et al., 2019).

More recently, August et al. (2021) reported positive effects of using multiple strategies for teaching grade 2 English language learners. Strategies included shared reading with teachers summarizing the text, modeling use of the vocabulary word, and discussing word meanings with students. Additionally, teachers used picture cards for more abstract words with definitions in English and Spanish on the back of the card to support teaching of the word. Lastly, students engaged in interactive lessons that had them engage in peer talks, class discussions, and individual and partner writing using the new vocabulary.

Emergent bilinguals are a large pool of students in today's elementary schools, accounting for one-quarter of all students. It surprises many people to learn that American schools now enroll more Hispanic students than African American students. We will later go into a more comprehensive discussion of the recent research supporting emergent bilinguals (Chapter 9).

Benchmark School

As discussed in other chapters of this edition, Benchmark School is a school in which we have observed highly effective reading instruction and have noted reading success with struggling readers (Pressley et al., 1991, 2006). To support student learning of vocabulary, Benchmark teachers have incorporated a rich vocabulary instruction approach within each reading lesson. For instance, Benchmark teachers identify important vocabulary prior to presenting the text to students. The selected vocabulary words (three to four key words from the text) are presented to students on flashcards that provide the word, the decoding of the word (see Chapter 5), and a sentence from the text with the vocabulary word. Prior to reading the story, the Benchmark teachers present the vocabulary words and discuss possible meanings based on the decoding and sentence provided. Teachers and students then discuss how the vocabulary might appear within the text. The teaching of vocabulary does not stop there! While reading the selected story, teachers will stop when the group comes across the new vocabulary to have more discussions of the word meaning within the text. New vocabulary is reviewed after reading and throughout the week to help solidify the learning of the new vocabulary.

IMPLICATIONS AND CONCLUDING REFLECTIONS

1. To increase vocabulary development, surround the child with vocabulary-rich language. That metamessage comes through repeatedly in this chapter. Read to a child and talk with the child during storybook reading and during formal vocabulary instruction, prompting the child to think about the to-be-learned vocabulary words in many, many ways. Flood the classroom with vocabulary-rich talk during formal lessons and informal interactions. The talk and the vocabulary in the world that the child experiences matters most to the development of a broader vocabulary.

2. If you accept the goal proposed by Biemiller and Slonim (2001) of 15,000 root words known by the end of high school, many of which are learned naturalistically, the task of vocabulary instruction can seem manageable. Our calculation is that perhaps 5,000 or so root words (and certainly not as many as 10,000 root words) require formal instruction,

assuming the child has reasonably rich language interactions during the schooling years (i.e., many of the root words are learned incidentally through verbal interactions and encounters). That 5,000 figure translates to teaching two to four root words a school day, a goal that should be within the reach of most teachers. Educators need to pay much attention in the near future to the specific words that need to be taught and make certain that students are acquiring the vocabulary that occurs most frequently in the world. Biemiller and Slonim (2001) and Beck et al. (2002) are pointing to an important research direction.

3. As we urge more systematic attention to and teaching of vocabulary, we also note that, in the analyses to date, when vocabulary acquisition has generally had an impact on reading (e.g., through increased reading comprehension), the impact has not been large. Passages containing words taught are understood a little better; other impacts are often quite small, often not detectable—or at least not detected in the studies we reviewed in writing this chapter. One possibility is that in the research to date there has not been extensive consideration of the many ways that knowing vocabulary can improve literacy, with comprehension most frequently studied as an indicator of the general impact of learning vocabulary. For example, more extensive vocabulary impact might occur in and be detected in students' writing and speaking.

Vocabulary acquisition might also influence aspects of comprehension besides text comprehension—for example, in understanding comments in conversations or on television. In short, we do not believe that researchers have exhaustively considered the benefits of vocabulary acquisition on literacy. Until there is a lot more evidence that vocabulary has only modest impact on literacy, we remain optimistic that there might be future evaluations that will substantiate that vocabulary teaching makes differences that are worth the instructional investment. We will urge that students be taught to pay attention to unfamiliar vocabulary words when they encounter them and to try to figure out what the words mean. We know, based on the research reviewed here, that students can learn to do that, and now is the time to figure out what happens when students do, in fact, pay attention to novel words and try to figure them out—especially when they are provided many opportunities to experience high-quality talk and texts, talk and texts filled with the words that literate folks know.

4. Most vocabulary is learned in context, either encountered in written text or in oral interactions. Thus, although we applaud the efforts of individuals such as Andy Biemiller (e.g., 2005), who is attempting to identify the words that children at various age levels need to know (i.e., the words that most kids will have learned) as part of determining what words should be taught in school, we are not optimistic that it is ever going to be the case

TABLE 7.1. Teaching Vocabulary Strategies

Promoting new vocabulary strategies	What the strategy looks like in the classroom
Day-to-day discussions with students	Engage with students using mature vocabulary and provide students opportunities to learn from mature vocabulary in context.
Student inquiry of new vocabulary	Use as a teachable moment. Engage students in conversation about possible meanings, talk through meaning of word, and support learning within context of text and outside of text.
More than the definition	Teachers need to provide explanations of words to students. Having students look up definitions in a dictionary does not lead to vocabulary learned.
Provide instruction on using external semantic clues (i.e., meaning cues in the text surrounding new vocabulary word)	Model and use think-aloud strategy to help students learn how to use clues from the text to figure out an unknown word's meaning.
	For example, teach students to look for context clues in sentences around the unknown word. Discuss possible meanings of new word based on clues found in text.
	Take the opportunity to teach multiple meaning words and how context is an important tool to determine meaning.
	Note: Using only external semantic clues *does not* lead to greater text comprehension.
Provide instruction on using internal context clues	Help students use word parts (prefixes, suffixes, and affixes) to determine meaning of words.
	For example, teach students to break word into parts (i.e., root, prefix, or suffix). Discuss meanings of each word part with students to determine meaning of new word.
	Note: Research has yet to demonstrate that using only internal context clues leads to greater text comprehension.
Repetition of new vocabulary	Present new vocabulary in multiple settings over multiple days. Review previously learned vocabulary from earlier in the week or earlier in the unit. Don't focus on teaching vocabulary for one day and move to the next word.
Read with students	Read more challenging texts aloud or with scaffolding.
Give students time to read	Allow students to engage in wide reading of different texts and genres (Chapter 6) by providing a variety of texts (fiction/nonfiction) in a classroom library.
Provide rich vocabulary instruction	Teach high-frequency words that students will experience across subjects, but not known to students (Tier 2 words).
	Provide students many opportunities to encounter new vocabulary.
	Have students explain their thinking as they learned new words.

that most vocabulary words are taught through reading lessons. Even a very vocabulary-ambitious elementary reading program only attempts to teach 1,000 words a year, with 400 learned considered a success (Biemiller & Boote, 2006). Even if lower-boundary estimates of vocabulary size are closer to accurate than upper-boundary estimates (i.e., high school graduates know 15,000–20,000 root words; Biemiller & Slonim, 2001), learning 400 words a year would not keep pace (Pressley, 2006, p. 14).

5. We have evidence that teachers can develop students' proficiencies at deriving word meanings from the context, in this case the print context, that surrounds the unknown word. Given that there is virtually unanimous agreement that wide reading accounts for a major segment of words adults know, it would seem sensible to ensure that all children are provided such strategy lessons and time to engage in wide reading, beginning in the primary grades.

6. Teachers play an important role in helping develop students' vocabulary, especially with emergent bilinguals and at-risk populations (August et al., 2021; Chapter 9). Teachers should develop lessons with vocabulary words that will challenge students, students will come across in the text, and expose students to the vocabulary across multiple subjects. We encourage teachers to use multiple strategies found in Table 7.1 to support student learning of vocabulary rather than just homing in on one strategy.

REFERENCES

Allington, R. L., Guice, S., Baker, K., Michelson, N., & Li, S. (1995). Access to books: Variations in schools and classrooms. *Language and Literacy Spectrum, 5*, 23–25.

Allington, R. L., & Johnston, P. H. (Eds.). (2002). *Reading to learn: Lessons from exemplary 4th grade classrooms.* Guilford Press.

Allington, R. L., Johnston, P. H., & Day, J. P. (2002). Exemplary fourth-grade teachers. *Language Arts, 79*(6), 462–466.

Anderson, R. C., Wilson, P. T., & Fielding, L. G. (1988). Growth in reading and how children spend their time outside of school. *Reading Research Quarterly, 23*, 285–303.

August, D., Uccelli, P., Artzi, L., Barr, C., & Francis, D. J. (2021). English learners' acquisition of academic vocabulary: Instruction matters, but so do word characteristics. *Reading Research Quarterly, 56*(3), 559–582.

Baker, S. K., Santoro, L. E., Chard, D. J., Fien, H., Park, Y., & Otterstedt, J. (2013). An evaluation of an explicit read aloud intervention taught in whole-classroom formats in first grade. *Elementary School Journal, 113*(3), 331–358.

Baumann, J. F., Edwards, E. C., Boland, E. M., Olejnik, S., & Kame'enui, E. J. (2003). Vocabulary tricks: Effects of instruction in morphology on fifth-grade students' ability to derive and infer word meanings. *American Educational Research Journal, 40*, 447–494.

Baumann, J. F., Edwards, E. C., Font, G., Tereshinski, C. A., Kame'enui, E. J., & Olejnik, S. F. (2002). Teaching morphemic and contextual analysis to fifth-grade students. *Reading Research Quarterly, 37*, 150–176.

Baumann, J. F., & Kame'enui, E. (Eds.). (2004). *Vocabulary instruction: Research to practice*. Guilford Press.

Baumann, J. F., Kame'enui, E. J., & Ash, G. E. (2003). Research on vocabulary instruction: Voltaire redux. In J. Flood, D. Lapp, J. R. Squire, & J. M. Jensen (Eds.), *Handbook of research on teaching the English language arts* (pp. 752–785). Erlbaum.

Beck, I. L., McKeown, M. G., & Kucan, L. (2002). *Bringing words to life: Robust vocabulary instruction*. Guilford Press.

Beck, I. L., McKeown, M. G., & Omanson, R. C. (1987). The effects and uses of diverse vocabulary instructional techniques. In M. G. McKeown & M. E. Curtis (Eds.), *The nature of vocabulary acquisition* (pp. 147–163). Erlbaum.

Beck, I. L., Perfetti, C. A., & McKeown, M. G. (1982). Effects of long-term vocabulary instruction on lexical access and reading comprehension. *Journal of Educational Psychology, 74*, 506–521.

Behrend, D. A., Scofield, J., & Kleinknecht, E. E. (2001). Beyond fast mapping: Young children's extensions of novel words and novel facts. *Developmental Psychology, 37*, 698–705.

Biemiller, A. (2005). Size and sequence in vocabulary development: Implications for choosing words for primary grade vocabulary instruction. In A. Hiebert & M. Kamil (Eds.), *Teaching and learning vocabulary: Bringing research to practice* (pp. 223–242). Erlbaum.

Biemiller, A., & Boote, C. (2006). An effective method for building meaning vocabulary in primary grades. *Journal of Educational Psychology, 98*(1), 44–62.

Biemiller, A., & Slonim, N. (2001). Estimating root word vocabulary growth in normative and advantaged populations: Evidence for a common sequence of vocabulary acquisition. *Journal of Educational Psychology, 93*, 498–520.

Bloom, L. (2000). The intentionality model of word learning: How to learn a word, any word. In R. M. Golinkoff, K. Hirsh-Pasek, L. Bloom, L. B. Smith, A. L. Woodward, N. Akhtar, et al. (Eds.), *Becoming a word learner: A debate on lexical acquisition* (pp. 19–50). Oxford University Press.

Bloom, L., Margulis, C., Tinker, E., & Fujita, N. (1996). Early conversations and word learning: Contributions from child and adult. *Child Development, 67*, 3154–3175.

Bloom, L., & Tinker, E. (2001). The intentionality model and language acquisition. *Monographs of the Society for Research in Child Development, 66*(Serial No. 267), i–viii, 1–91.

Bloom, P. (2000). *How children learn the meanings of words*. MIT Press.

Bogner, K., Raphael, L. M., & Pressley, M. (2002). How grade-1 teachers motivate literate activity by their students. *Scientific Studies of Reading, 6*, 135–165.

Bowers, P. N., & Kirby, J. R. (2010). Effects of morphological instruction on vocabulary acquisition. *Reading and Writing, 23*(5), 515–537.

Brabham, E. G., & Lynch-Brown, C. (2002). Effect of teachers' reading-aloud styles on vocabulary acquisition and comprehension of students in the early elementary grades. *Journal of Educational Psychology, 94*, 465–473.

Brenner, D., & Hiebert, E. H. (2010). If I follow the teachers' editions, isn't that enough? Analyzing reading volume in six core reading programs. *Elementary School Journal, 110*(3), 347–363.

Brett, A., Rothlein, L., & Hurley, M. (1996). Vocabulary acquisition from listening to stories and explanations of target words. *Elementary School Journal, 96*, 415–422.

Brown, R. W. (1957). Linguistic determinism and the parts of speech. *Journal of Abnormal and Social Psychology, 55*, 1–5.

Buly, M. R., & Valencia, S. W. (2002). Below the bar: Profiles of students who fail state reading assessments. *Educational Evaluation and Policy Analysis, 24*(3), 219–239.

Bus, A. G., van IJzendoorn, M. H., & Pellegrini, A. D. (1995). Joint book reading makes for success in learning to read: A meta-analysis on intergenerational transmission of literacy. *Review of Educational Research, 65,* 1–21.

Carey, S., & Bartlett, E. (1978). Acquiring a single new word. *Papers and Reports on Child Language Development, 15,* 17–29.

Carlisle, J. F. (2010). Effects of instruction in morphological awareness on literacy achievement: An integrative review. *Reading Research Quarterly, 45*(4), 464–487.

Carlisle, J. F., Fleming, J. E., & Gudbrandsen, B. (2000). Incidental word learning in science classes. *Contemporary Educational Psychology, 25,* 184–211.

Carlo, M. S., August, D., McLaughlin, B., Snow, C. E., Dressler, C., Lippman, D. N., et al. (2004). Closing the gap: Addressing the vocabulary needs of English-language learners in bilingual and mainstream classrooms. *Reading Research Quarterly, 39,* 188–215.

Childers, J. B., & Tomasello, M. (2002). Two-year-olds learn novel nouns, verbs, and conventional actions from massed or distributed exposures. *Developmental Psychology, 38,* 967–978.

Cunningham, A. E., & Stanovich, K. E. (1991). Tracking the unique effects of print exposure in children: Associations with vocabulary, general knowledge, and spelling. *Journal of Educational Psychology, 83*(2), 264–274.

Cunningham, A. E., & Stanovich, K. E. (1997). Early reading acquisition and its relation to reading experience and ability 10 years later. *Developmental Psychology, 33,* 934–945.

Cunningham, A. E., & Stanovich, K. E. (1998). What reading does for the mind. *American Educator, 22*(1), 8–17.

Cunningham, P. M. (2008). *What really matters in vocabulary: Research-based practices across the curriculum.* Allyn & Bacon.

Davis, F. B. (1944). Fundamental factors in reading comprehension. *Psychometrica, 9,* 185–197.

Davis, F. B. (1968). Research in comprehension in reading. *Reading Research Quarterly, 3,* 499–545.

Deshler, D. D., Palincsar, A. S., Biancarosa, G., & Nair, M. (2007). *Informed choices for struggling adolescent readers: A research-based guide to instructional programs and practices.* International Reading Association.

Dewitz, P., Jones, J., & Leahy, S. (2009). Comprehension strategy instruction in core reading programs. *Reading Research Quarterly, 44*(2), 102–126.

Dickinson, D. K. (2011). Teachers' language practices and academic outcomes of preschool children. *Science, 333,* 964–967.

Dickinson, D. K., & Porche, M. V. (2011). Relation between language experiences in preschool classrooms and children's kindergarten and fourth-grade language and reading abilities. *Child Development, 82*(3), 870–886.

Dole, J. A., Sloan, C., & Trathen, W. (1995). Teaching vocabulary within the context of literature. *Journal of Reading, 38,* 452–460.

Dolezal, S. E., Welsh, L. M., Pressley, M., & Vincent, M. (2003). How nine third-grade teachers motivate student academic engagement. *Elementary School Journal, 103,* 239–267.

Duke, N. K. (2000). For the rich it's richer: Print experiences and environments offered to children in very low- and very high-socioeconomic status first-grade classrooms. *American Educational Research Journal, 37*(2), 441–478.

Edwards, E. C., Font, G., Baumann, J. F., & Boland, E. (2004). Unlocking word meanings: Strategies and guidelines for teaching morphemic and contextual analysis. In J. F. Baumann & E. J. Kame'enui (Eds.), *Vocabulary instruction: Research to practice* (pp. 159–176). Guilford Press.

Elley, W. B. (1989). Vocabulary acquisition from listening to stories. *Reading Research Quarterly, 24,* 174–187.

Ericsson, K. A., Krampe, R. T., & Tesch-Romer, C. (1993). The role of deliberate practice in the acquisition of expert performance. *Psychological Review, 100*(3), 363–406.

Fitzgerald, J., Relyea, J. E., Elmore, J., & Hiebert, E. H. (2021). Has the presence of first-grade core reading program academic vocabulary changed across six decades? *Reading Research Quarterly, 56*(4) 737–759.

Fukkink, R. G., & de Glopper, K. (1998). Effects of instruction in deriving word meaning from context: A meta-analysis. *Review of Educational Research, 68,* 450–469.

Gabriel, R., Day, J. P., & Allington, R. L. (2011). Exemplary teacher voices on their own development. *Phi Delta Kappan, 92*(8), 37–41.

Gellert, A. S., Arnbak, E., Wischmann, S., & Elbro, C. (2021). Morphological intervention for students with limited vocabulary knowledge: Short-and long-term transfer effects. *Reading Research Quarterly, 56*(3), 583–601.

Graves, M. F., Elmore, J., & Fitzgerald, J. (2019). The vocabulary of core reading programs. *Elementary School Journal, 119*(3), 386–416.

Graves, M. F., & Hammond, H. K. (1980). A validated procedure for teaching prefixes and its effect on students' ability to assign meaning to novel words. In M. L. Kamil & J. Moe (Eds.), *Perspective on reading research and instruction: Twenty-ninth yearbook of the National Reading Conference* (Vol. 29, pp. 184–188). National Reading Conference.

Graves, M. F., Ringstaff, C., Li, L., & Flynn, K. (2018). Effects of teaching upper elementary grade students to use word learning strategies. *Reading Psychology, 39*(6), 602–622.

Hart, B., & Risley, T. R. (1995). *Meaningful differences in the everyday experience of young American children.* Brookes.

Hayes, D. P., & Ahrens, M. (1988). Vocabulary simplification for children: A special case of "motherese." *Journal of Child Language, 15,* 395–410.

Heibeck, T. H., & Markman, E. M. (1987). Word learning in children: An examination of fast mapping. *Child Development, 58,* 1021–1034.

Hidi, S. (1990). Interest and its contribution as a mental resource for learning. *Review of Educational Research, 60,* 549–571.

Hiebert, E. H., Scott, J. A., Castaneda, R., & Spichtig, A. (2019). An analysis of the features of words that influence vocabulary difficulty. *Education Sciences, 9*(8), 1–24.

Huttenlocher, J., Vasilyeva, M., Cymerman, E., & Levine, S. (2001). Language input and child syntax. *Cognitive Psychology, 45,* 337–374.

Jaswal, V. K., & Markman, E. M. (2003). The relative strengths of indirect and direct word learning. *Developmental Psychology, 39,* 745–760.

Johnston, P. H. (2004). *Choice words: How our language affects children's learning.* Stenhouse.

Kalashnikova, M., Escudero, P., & Kidd, E. (2018). The development of fast-mapping and novel word retention strategies in monolingual and bilingual infants. *Developmental Science, 21*(6), 1–11.

Kame'enui, E., Carnine, D., & Freschli, R. (1982). Effects of text construction and instructional procedures for teaching word meanings on comprehension and recall. *Reading Research Quarterly, 17,* 367–388.

Kleinknecht, E. E., Behrend, D. A., & Scofield, J. M. (1999, March). *What's so special about word learning, anyway?* Paper presented at the biennial meeting of the Society for Research in Child Development, Albuquerque, NM.

Krashen, S. (2006). Free reading: Is it the only way to make kids more literate? *School Library Journal, 52*(9), 42–45.

Krashen, S. (2011). *Free voluntary reading.* Libraries Unlimited.

Kuhn, M. R., & Stahl, S. A. (1998). Teaching children to learn word meanings from context: A synthesis and some questions. *Journal of Literacy Research, 30,* 119–138.

Lee, S., & Pulido, D. (2017). The impact of topic interest, L2 proficiency, and gender on EFL incidental vocabulary acquisition through reading. *Language Teaching Research, 21*(1), 118–135.

Lesaux, N. K., Kieffer, M. J., Faller, S. E., & Kelley, J. G. (2010). The effectiveness and ease of implementation of an academic vocabulary intervention for linguistically diverse students in urban middle schools. *Reading Research Quarterly, 45*(2), 196–228.

Leung, C. B. (1992). Effects of word-related variables on vocabulary growth through repeated read-aloud events. In C. K. Kinzer & D. J. Leu (Eds.), *Literacy research, theory, and practice: Views from many perspectives: Forty-first yearbook of the National Reading Conference* (Vol. 41, pp. 491–498). National Reading Conference.

Levin, J. R., Carney, R. N., & Pressley, M. (1988). Facilitating vocabulary inferring through root word instruction. *Contemporary Educational Psychology, 13*, 316–322.

Lloyd, C. V. (1995). How teachers teach reading comprehension: An examination of four categories of reading comprehension instruction. *Reading Research and Instruction, 35*(2), 171–185.

Lonigan, C. J., & Whitehurst, G. J. (1998). Relative efficacy of parent and teacher involvement in a shared-reading intervention for preschool children from low-income backgrounds. *Early Childhood Research Quarterly, 13*, 263–290.

Maniates, H., & Pearson, P. D. (2008). The curricularization of comprehension strategies instruction: A conspiracy of good intentions. In Y. Kim, V. J. Risko, D. L. Compton, D. K. Dickinson, M. K. Hundley, R. T. Jimenez, et al. (Eds.), *57th yearbook of the National Reading Conference* (pp. 271–282). National Reading Conference.

Markson, L. (1999). *Mechanisms of word learning in children: Insights from fast mapping.* Unpublished doctoral dissertation, University of Arizona, Tucson.

McGregor, K. K. (2004). Developmental dependencies between lexical semantics and reading. In C. A. Stone, E. R. Silliman, B. J. Ehren, & K. Apel (Eds.), *Handbook of language and literacy: Development and disorders* (pp. 302–317). Guilford Press.

McKeown, M. G. (1985). The acquisition of word meaning from context by children of high and low ability. *Reading Research Quarterly, 20*, 482–496.

McKeown, M. G., & Beck, I. L. (2004). Direct and rich vocabulary instruction. In J. F. Baumann & E. J. Kame'enui (Eds.), *Vocabulary instruction: Research to practice* (pp. 13–27). Guilford Press.

McKeown, M. G., Beck, I. L., Omanson, R. C., & Perfetti, C. A. (1983). The effects of long-term vocabulary instruction on reading comprehension: A replication. *Journal of Reading Behavior, 15*, 3–18.

McKeown, M. G., Beck, I. L., Omanson, R. C., & Pople, M. T. (1985). Some effects on the nature and frequency of vocabulary instruction on the knowledge and use of words. *Reading Research Quarterly, 20*, 522–535.

Miller, G. A., & Gildea, P. M. (1987). How children learn words. *Scientific American, 252*(3), 94–99.

Mol, S. E., & Bus, A. G. (2011). To read or not to read: A meta-analysis of print exposure from infancy to early adulthood. *Psychological Bulletin, 137*(2), 267–296.

Morrow, L. M., Tracey, D. H., Woo, D. G., & Pressley, M. (1999). Characteristics of exemplary first-grade literacy instruction. *Reading Teacher, 52*, 462–476.

National Reading Panel. (2000). *Teaching children to read: An evidence-based assessment of the scientific research literature on reading and its implications for reading instruction: Reports of the subgroups.* National Institute of Child Health and Human Development.

Neuman, S., & Celano, D. (2001). Access to print in low-income and middle-income communities. *Reading Research Quarterly, 36*(1), 8–26.

Neuman, S.B., & Moland, N. (2019). Book deserts: The consequences of income segregation on children's access to print. *Urban Education, 54*(1), 126–147.

Nicholson, T., & Whyte, B. (1992). Matthew effects in learning new words while listening to stories. In C. K. Kinzer & D. J. Leu (Eds.), *Literacy research, theory, and practice: Views from many perspectives: Forty-first yearbook of the National Reading Conference* (Vol. 41, pp. 499–503). Chicago: National Reading Conference.

Nist, S. L., & Olejnik, S. (1995). The role of context and dictionary definitions on varying levels of word knowledge. *Reading Research Quarterly, 30,* 172–193.

Pace, A., Luo, R., Hirsh-Pasek, K., & Golinkoff, R. M. (2017). Identifying pathways between socioeconomic status and language development. *Annual Review of Linguistics, 3,* 285–308.

Pany, D., Jenkins, J. R., & Schreck, J. (1982). Vocabulary instruction: Effects on word knowledge and reading comprehension. *Learning Disability Quarterly, 5,* 202–215.

Payne, A. C., Whitehurst, G. J., & Angell, A. L. (1994). The role of home literacy environment in the development of language ability in preschool children from low-income families. *Early Childhood Research Quarterly, 9,* 427–440.

Pearson, B. Z., Fernandez, S. C., Lewedeg, V., & Oller, D. K. (1997). The relation of input factors to lexical learning by bilingual infants. *Applied Psycholinguistics, 18,* 41–58.

Penno, J. F., Wilkinson, I. A. G., & Moore, D. W. (2002). Vocabulary acquisition from teacher explanation and repeated listening to stories: Do they overcome the Matthew effect? *Journal of Educational Psychology, 94,* 23–33.

Pressley, M. (2006, April 29). *What the future of reading research could be.* Paper presented at the annual meeting of the International Reading Association, Chicago.

Pressley, M., Allington, R., Wharton-McDonald, R., Block, C. C., & Morrow, L.M. (2001). *Learning to read: Lessons from exemplary first grades.* Guilford Press.

Pressley, M., Dolezal, S. E., Raphael, L. M., Welsh, L. M., Roehrig, A. D., & Bogner, K. (2003). *Motivating primary-grade students.* Guilford Press.

Pressley, M., Gaskins, I. W., Cunicelli, E. A., Burdick, N. J., Schaub-Matt, M., Lee, D. S., et al. (1991). Strategy instruction at Benchmark School: A faculty interview study. *Learning Disability Quarterly, 14,* 19–48.

Pressley, M., Gaskins, I. W., Solic, K., & Collins, S. (2006). A portrait of the Benchmark School: How a school produces high-achievement in students who previously failed. *Journal of Educational Psychology, 98*(2), 282–306.

Pressley, M., Roehrig, A., Raphael, L., Dolezal, S., Bohn, K., Mohan, L., et al. (2003). Teaching processes in elementary and secondary education. In W. M. Reynolds & G. E. Miller (Eds.), *Comprehensive handbook of psychology: Vol. 7. Educational psychology* (pp. 153–175). Wiley.

Pressley, M., Wharton-McDonald, R., Allington, R., Block, C. C., Morrow, L., Tracey, D., et al. (2001). A study of effective grade-1 literacy instruction. *Scientific Studies of Reading, 5,* 35–58.

Pressley, M., Wharton-McDonald, R., & Mistretta, J. (1998). Effective beginning literacy instruction: Dialectical, scaffolded, and contextualized. In J. L. Metsala & L. C. Ehri (Eds.), *Word recognition in beginning literacy* (pp. 357–373). Erlbaum.

Pressley, M., Wharton-McDonald, R., Mistretta-Hampston, J., & Echevarria, M. (1998). Literacy instruction in 10 fourth- and fifth-grade classrooms in upstate New York. *Scientific Studies of Reading, 2*(2), 159–194.

Pressley, M., Wharton-McDonald, R., Raphael, L. M., Bogner, K., & Roehrig, A. D. (2001). Exemplary first grade teaching. In B. M Taylor & P. D. Pearson (Eds.), *Teaching reading: Effective schools and accomplished teachers* (pp. 73–88). Erlbaum.

Pressley, M., Yokoi, L., Rankin, J., Wharton-McDonald, R., & Mistretta, J. (1997). A survey of the instructional practices of Grade 5 teachers nominated as effective in promoting literacy. *Scientific Studies of Reading, 1*(2), 145–160.

Pressley, T., Isom, R., Johnson, C., Barnes, A., & McAuliffe, L. (2020). Becoming a highly effective teacher and how to support teachers' development. *Journal of Educational Leadership in Action, 7*(1).

Robbins, C., & Ehri, L. C. (1994). Reading storybooks to kindergartners helps them learn new vocabulary words. *Journal of Educational Psychology, 86,* 54–64.

Romeo, R. R., Leonard, J. A., Robinson, S. T., West, M. R., Mackey, A. P., Rowe, M. L., et al. (2018). Beyond the 30-million-word gap: Children's conversational exposure is associated with language-related brain function. *Psychological Science, 29*(5), 700–710.

Scarborough, H. S., & Dobrich, W. (1994). On the efficiency of reading to preschoolers. *Developmental Review, 14,* 245–302.

Schatz, E. K., & Baldwin, R. S. (1986). Context clues are unreliable predictors of word meanings. *Reading Research Quarterly, 21,* 439–453.

Schwartz, R. G., & Terrell, B. Y. (1983). The role of input frequency in lexical acquisition. *Journal of Child Language, 10,* 57–64.

Scott, J. A., Jamieson-Noel, D., & Asselin, M. (2003). Vocabulary instruction throughout the day in twenty-three Canadian upper-elementary classrooms. *Elementary School Journal, 102*(3), 269–312.

Scott, J., & Nagy, W. (1997). Understanding the definitions of unfamiliar verbs. *Reading Research Quarterly, 32,* 184–200.

Senechal, M. (1997). The differential effect of storybook reading on preschoolers' acquisition of expressive and receptive vocabulary. *Journal of Child Language, 24,* 123–138.

Singer, H. A. (1965). A developmental model of speed of reading in grades 3 through 6. *Reading Research Quarterly, 1,* 29–49.

Spearitt, D. (1972). Identification of subskills of reading comprehension by maximum likelihood factor analysis. *Reading Research Quarterly, 8,* 92–111.

Stahl, S. A., & Fairbanks, M. M. (1986). The effects of vocabulary instruction: A model-based meta-analysis. *Review of Educational Research, 56,* 72–110.

Sternberg, R. J. (1987). Most vocabulary is learned from context. In M. G. McKeown & M. E. Curtis (Eds.), *The nature of vocabulary acquisition* (pp. 89–105). Erlbaum.

Sternberg, R. J., & Powell, J. S. (1983). Comprehending verbal comprehension. *American Psychologist, 38,* 878–893.

Sternberg, R. J., Powell, J. S., & Kaye, D. B. (1983). Teaching vocabulary-building skills: A contextual approach. In A. C. Wilkinson (Ed.), *Classroom computers and cognitive science* (pp. 121–143). Academic Press.

Stronge, J. H. (2018). *Qualities of effective teachers.* ASCD.

Swanborn, M. S. L., & de Glopper, K. (1999). Incidental word learning while reading: A meta-analysis. *Review of Educational Research, 69,* 261–285.

Thorndike, E. L. (1911). *Animal intelligence.* Macmillan.

Thurstone, L. L. (1946). A note on a reanalysis of Davis' reading texts. *Psychometrica, 11,* 185–188.

Tomesen, M., & Aarnoutse, C. (1998). Effects of an instructional programme for deriving word meanings. *Educational Studies, 24,* 107–128.

Townsend, D., Filippini, A., Collins, P., & Biancarosa, G. (2012). Evidence for the importance of academic word knowledge for the academic achievement of diverse middle school students. *Elementary School Journal, 112*(3), 497–518.

Valdez-Menchaca, M. C., & Whitehurst, G. J. (1988). The effects of incidental teaching on vocabulary acquisition by young children. *Child Development, 59,* 1451–1459.

Valdez-Menchaca, M. C., & Whitehurst, G. J. (1992). Accelerating language development through picture book reading: A systematic extension to Mexican day care. *Developmental Psychology, 28,* 1106–1114.

van Daalen-Kapteijns, M. M., & Elshout-Mohr, M. (1981). The acquisition of word meanings as a cognitive verbal process. *Journal of Verbal Learning and Verbal Behavior, 20,* 386–399.

Waxman, S. R., & Booth, A. E. (2000). Principles that are invoked in the acquisition of words, but not facts. *Cognition, 77,* B33–B43.

Wharton-McDonald, R., Pressley, M., & Hampston, J. M. (1998). Literacy instruction in nine first-grade classrooms: Teacher characteristics and student achievement. *Elementary School Journal, 99,* 101–128.

Whitehurst, G. J., Arnold, D. S., Epstein, J. N., Angel, A. L., Smith, M., & Fischel, J. E. (1994). A picture book reading intervention in day care and home for children from low-income families. *Developmental Psychology, 30,* 679–689.

Whitehurst, G. J., Epstein, J. N., Angel, A. L., Payne, A. C., Crone, D. A., & Fischel, J. E. (1994). Outcomes of an emergent literacy intervention in Head Start. *Journal of Educational Psychology, 86,* 542–555.

Whitehurst, G. J., Zevenbergen, A. A., Crone, D. A., Schultz, M. D., Velting, O. N., & Fischel, J. E. (1999). Outcomes of an emergent literacy intervention from Head Start through second grade. *Journal of Educational Psychology, 91,* 261–272.

Wixson, K. K. (1986). Vocabulary instruction and children's comprehension of basal stories. *Reading Research Quarterly, 21,* 317–329.

Wright, J. C., Huston, A. C., Murphy, K. C., St. Peters, M., Piaton, M., Santlin, R., et al. (2001). The relations of early television viewing to school readiness and vocabulary of children from low-income families: The Early Window Project. *Child Development, 72,* 1347–1366.

Wright, T. S., & Neuman, S. B. (2013). Vocabulary instruction in commonly used kindergarten core reading curricula. *Elementary School Journal, 113*(3), 386–408.

Wysocki, K., & Jenkins, J. R. (1987). Deriving word meanings through morphological generalization. *Reading Research Quarterly, 22,* 66–81.

Zevenbergen, A. A., Whitehurst, G. J., & Zevenbergen, J. A. (2003). Effects of a shared-reading intervention on the inclusion of evaluative devices in narratives of children from low-income families. *Journal of Applied Developmental Psychology, 24,* 1–15.

8 The Need for Increased Comprehension Instruction

Some readers might be wondering how they could be so far along in a book dedicated to elementary literacy instruction but find so little written yet about anything beyond grade 3. Intense researcher interest in emergent literacy and the renewed great debates about the nature of beginning reading have led to much more research attention paid to the preschool and primary grades in recent years. Nonetheless, there is good reason to think about the upper elementary grades and to worry about the instruction that is occurring there. In particular, much more could be done to promote comprehension abilities in elementary students, with that often thought of as more of an upper elementary goal than a primary grades goal. By the end of this chapter, we hope it is clear to you that we do not agree that comprehension as a reading goal should be put off until the middle and upper elementary grades, but we recognize that it often is, and thus we begin this chapter with a discussion of what goes on in the upper elementary grades.

THE NATURE OF LITERACY INSTRUCTION IN FOURTH AND FIFTH GRADES

In 1996, Pressley and some of his colleagues (Pressley et al., 1998) decided to study the nature of literacy instruction in fourth and fifth grades because they are often the final 2 years of elementary school. We carried out the fourth- and fifth-grade study much as we had conducted the observational study of first-grade instruction reported in Chapter 10. We observed 10 classrooms in upstate New York over the course of a year, all of which were selected by the participating school districts as very solid classrooms. In addition to the observations, we conducted two in-depth interviews with each teacher to clarify the instruction that we observed and to gain understanding of the teacher's intentions in teaching the way she or he did.

Background

We expected to find quite complex instruction in the upper grades:

1. The first-grade study had made it clear that literacy teaching is a complex articulation of components. It made sense that instruction at the upper end of the elementary years would be at least as complex.
2. In addition, however, we had conducted a survey of fifth-grade teachers from across the nation who had been nominated as outstanding in the promotion of literacy achievement in their classrooms (Pressley et al., 1997). The methodology for that survey was much like the methodology in the primary-grade survey: The teachers first responded to a few open-ended questions about the elements of their teaching, and then the elements mentioned by the teachers were examined in a questionnaire requiring teachers to indicate the frequency of each element of instruction in their classroom.

Consistent with the results obtained at the primary level, the sample of nominated outstanding fifth-grade teachers reported that their instruction balanced many components, including meaning-emphasis and skills-emphasis instruction. The various components that entered into the instructional mix included the following:

- Extensive reading at the heart of language arts instruction
- Diverse grouping patterns (e.g., whole-class instruction, small-group instruction, cooperative learning experiences, individual reading)
- Teaching of both word-level and higher-order (e.g., comprehension, critical thinking) skills and processes
- Development of student background knowledge
- Regular instruction in writing, including lower-order mechanical skills and higher-order composition skills (e.g., planning, drafting, revising as a process)
- Extensive evaluation of literacy competencies, using diverse assessments
- Integration of literacy and content-area instruction
- Efforts to promote student motivation for reading and writing

As was the case at the primary level, we felt that, even though the survey was informative about some of the diversity of experience in the upper elementary grades, it did not provide the type of in-depth understanding that comes from getting to know a number of individual classrooms. It did, however, sensitize us somewhat to what we should be looking for in the classrooms in the observational study.

Results of the Observational Study

What emerged from the initial observational study (Pressley et al., 1998) was a much more complicated set of results than came out of the survey research. Basically, we observed some practices that were common across classrooms, but we also observed many dimensions of difference. In what follows, we detail both and comment on several other findings that were very important and somewhat unexpected.

Commonalities across Classrooms

We observed some instructional practices in at least eight of 10 classrooms. Because virtually all of these practices were also represented on the survey of exceptionally strong fifth-grade teachers from across the nation, we were not surprised that the following might be found in some way, shape, or form in most fourth- and fifth-grade classrooms in the United States:

- Some class discussions driven by teacher questioning, with student responses evaluated by the teacher
- Literature-driven reading instruction
- Direct instruction in specific skills
- One-to-one miniconferences with students
- Reading of trade books—in particular, novels
- Opportunities for students to select reading materials
- Teacher read-alouds
- Expressed belief in the importance of reading comprehension at this level of instruction
- Teacher activation of students' prior knowledge
- Exercises emphasizing reading comprehension
- Independent reading time
- Writing of connected text on at least a weekly basis
- Use of the writing process model and instruction in its components (i.e., planning, drafting, and revising long compositions)
- Connections between reading, writing, and content-area coverage (e.g., readings related to a social studies theme inspiring writing of stories related to the theme)

- Use of procedural facilitators for writing assignments (e.g., worksheets reminding students of the parts of a story)
- Teaching of writing mechanics
- Use of computers for writing of final drafts
- Worksheets (both teacher-made and commercial)
- Book projects
- Spelling exercises and tests
- Explicit vocabulary instruction
- Homework

In short, in keeping with the fifth-grade survey, which reported a balancing of meaning-emphasis (i.e., reading of literature, writing) and skills-emphasis instruction components, we observed such balancing in the classrooms in upstate New York. Even so, our sense as we watched these classrooms was that they were very different from one another, with the differences at the fourth- and fifth-grade levels much more pronounced than the differences we had observed in primary-level classrooms.

Dimensions of Difference

Because we became aware very early in the study that the classrooms we were watching differed dramatically from one another, we were sensitive throughout most of the study to the many differences that existed. In the end, the differences could be clustered into five groups, pertaining to differences in classroom management, reading, writing, word-level skills, and student academic engagement.

The teachers varied tremendously in their *class management*. For example, in some classes, every day was pretty much the same, whereas there was much day-to-day and week-to-week variability at the other extreme. Some teachers used classic behavior management tactics well, and others used them hardly at all. Grouping varied from predominantly whole-class to predominantly individualized instruction, with just about everything in between also observed. An exceptionally important dimension of difference among classrooms was the extent to which student progress was monitored and responded to in an appropriate fashion. Some teachers were very aware of their students and provided assignments that matched student needs and competencies, whereas others were less concerned with such monitoring and tailoring of work. The classrooms also varied in the extent to which they were driven by concern with external standards (e.g., preparing for state tests) versus concern for student improvement. In addition, whereas some classrooms included a high density of activity, others were relaxed. Homework varied from skills practice to authentic reading and writing.

There were substantial differences in the *amount of reading* in each class and *variability in types of reading*, although much reading of novels was observed. There were many different ways that reading could connect with the content-area curriculum, from well-planned literature-based units relating to important curricular themes to generally haphazard comments made by the teacher relating ideas in current readings to social studies and science concepts.

There was great variability as to how much *writing* occurred, from being the focus of literacy instruction to being quite a small part of it. Students in most classes did narrative writing. Although planning, drafting, and revising occurred in all classes, the classes varied in the extent of their commitment to the process, from consistent use of and great reflection on planning, drafting, and revising to much more implicit use of the writing process. There were differences in how mechanics were covered as well, from substantial reflection on rhetorical devices used by authors of works the students were reading to coverage of mechanics on worksheets.

There was great variation between classrooms in the extent to which *word-level skills* were emphasized. The amount of vocabulary instruction varied from class to class (e.g., in some classes there were published lists with tests, whereas others focused on discussion of words encountered in readings). Spelling instruction and tests occurred in all classrooms, although the sources of the words varied (e.g., published lists, words encountered in reading), as did the amount of drilling and the extent to which spelling and vocabulary instruction were connected (i.e., from being completely independent to vocabulary words being the spelling words).

Student engagement varied considerably from classroom to classroom, as defined by the percentage of students typically involved in academic activities. In some classes, engagement was usually high. In others, it was much more variable.

Different Core Emphases

Each classroom had at its core some particular emphases around which the curriculum was organized and presented. These core sets of activities, while observed in every classroom, differed somewhat from one classroom to the next. The most common emphases included reading of trade books and writing, which were related through thematic connections, although (as summarized in Table 8.1) each classroom really did have a unique orientation.

Instruction That Was Not Happening

In some classrooms, there were aspects of the instruction that we found to be very disturbing. For example, we observed explicit comprehension

TABLE 8.1. Central Emphases for Each Classroom in the Pressley et al. (1998) Study of Fourth- and Fifth-Grade Classrooms

1. Trade book reading and process writing, with thematic connections; reader response to literature; encourages self-regulation including thorough use of modified reciprocal teaching as students respond to literature in small groups.

2. Reader response to novels consistent with a current theme; writing process instruction with emphasis on self-regulated writing, reading, and studying.

3. Reading of trade books, with connections to writing; heavy emphasis on process writing and self-regulation of reading, writing, and behavior.

4. Basal reading and teacher question-driven discussion of basal selections; isolated skills instruction; quiet seatwork.

5. Content strongly emphasized, including current events; heavy emphasis on vocabulary acquisition and acquisition of factual knowledge; process writing; explicit skills instruction; whole-group teacher question-driven discussions and individual seatwork.

6. Cooperative exploration; theme-driven instruction; lots of reading of trade books; skills instruction, which is not tied to current theme or readings.

7. Reading–writing–content integration, with many activities relating to trade books currently being read by class; extensive discussions driven by teacher questions.

8. Reading trade books; skills instruction with worksheets.

9. Process writing; reading of trade books; reading–writing–content instruction connections.

10. Teacher reading of literature to class; student reading of trade books; writing with process instruction and teaching of mechanics; clear reading–writing–content connections.

---

instruction only rarely, despite a great deal of research in the past several decades on how to promote children's comprehension of what they read (Almasi & Fullerton, 2013; Applebee et al., 2003; Blachowicz & Ogle, 2008; Gersten et al., 2001; Pearson & Fielding, 1991). Indeed, the situation seemed to be much as Durkin (1978–1979) described it more than 40 years ago, with a great deal of *testing* of comprehension but very little *teaching* of it.

A twist on this situation, however, was that the comprehension tasks now being given to students did seem to be informed by the comprehension process research of the past two decades. It was common, for example, for students to be asked to respond to short-answer questions requiring them to summarize what they had read, identify confusing points in a text, construct questions pertaining to a text, or predict what might be next in a text. That is, they were asked to respond to questions constructed around the cognitive processes involved in skilled comprehension (i.e., summarizing, monitoring confusion, self-questioning, predicting based on prior knowledge). However, there was little evidence that students were being taught to self-regulate comprehension processes *as* they read, and in some classrooms there was no evidence at all that they were being taught the active comprehension processes validated in the past two decades—for example, being asked to write down images that occurred to them as they read a story without a hint to the students that they could actively generate images as they read as a comprehension strategy. More generally, students were prompted to generate the types of ideas that might occur to strategic readers as they read, but they were not actually taught the strategies themselves, how to use them, or the utility of the strategies.

It also was striking how little teaching of self-regulation occurred. Rather than teaching students how to become self-regulated learners, the teachers seemed to expect that the behaviors would develop naturally if students were given enough assignments (e.g., work sheets) that prompted them to generate the kinds of thoughts nurtured by strategic readers as they read (i.e., that required them to report questions, images, or summaries that occurred to them as they read). There is, of course, no evidence that we are aware of that such prompting leads to anything like active, self-regulated use of comprehension strategies.

A National Observational Study of Effective Fourth-Grade Teachers

The observational study of fourth- and fifth-grade teachers in upstate New York (Pressley et al., 1998) led to development of a larger and broader study of effective fourth-grade teachers (Allington & Johnston, 2002). The 30 effective teachers in this later study were drawn from six states (two textbook adoption states and four states with no state textbook adoption process) after a snowball nomination process. The two types of states allowed us to observe effective teachers in school systems with very different schemes for fostering effective reading instruction as well as providing for a national set of data (California, Texas, New Hampshire, New Jersey, New York, and Wisconsin). Two full weeks (one in the fall, the other in the spring) of full-day observations of classroom lessons allowed us to gain a good sense of just how reading instruction was offered. This qualitative study produced daily field notes that described the teachers' activities and the sorts of tasks and interactions that occurred with the teacher. These field notes along with our interviews with each teacher were used to develop thick case studies of each classroom. Case studies of six of these effective teachers are the central feature of the book-length manuscript (Allington & Johnston, 2002).

Our findings were described broadly in terms of six T's (Allington, 2002): *time, texts, tasks, talk, teaching,* and *test.* These effective fourth-grade teachers allocated large and consistent blocks of *time* to reading instruction. They had more time in large part because they were such effective classroom managers. Large blocks of uninterrupted instructional time were the norm in these classrooms. These effective teachers made less use of commercial reading programs, even in the textbook adoption states. In the place of textbooks students read trade books, typically trade books the student had selected herself. Much like the upper elementary teachers observed in Pressley et al. (1998), then, the type of texts that students were engaged with differed from the *texts* more typically used. Similarly, and perhaps because of the two aspects described just above, the nature of the *tasks* that students completed also differed from typical practice. That is, students completing worksheets, especially everyone doing the same worksheet, was a relatively rare event in these classrooms. Instead, students developed individual projects, often around a central science or social studies theme (sea life, insects, weather, mission life, Spanish influences on California life, etc.). Students in these classrooms of effective teachers also wrote much more frequently than is the norm. They wrote short responses and reactions as well as summaries and research papers. Linked to these different tasks students were assigned was the relative frequency (Nystrand, 2006) of classroom discussions, both whole-class discussions and pair and share peer-led discussions. Thus, these classrooms differed from the more typical classrooms in that student *talk* featured prominently across the school day. This was productive talk about both content and reading strategies in use (Johnston, 2004). These effective teachers were continually *teaching*—teaching the whole class, small groups, pairs, and individuals. Central to this teaching was developing self-regulation skills in students—self-regulation of classroom behavior and self-regulation while both reading and writing. In this case, these effective teachers seemed to differ from those observed by Pressley and colleagues (1998). However, what was observed was teachers developing self-regulation as opposed to teaching self-regulation directly.

While there were fewer direct explanations of strategies that students could be using (Duffy, 2014), strategy lessons were being offered through teacher modeling and scaffolding of student reading experiences. The final *T* was *test* because these teachers knew much more about individual students as learners than is commonly found in less effective teacher classrooms. These effective teachers knew their students as developing readers and could provide instruction that fostered further development of reading proficiency. Most of what these teachers knew about their students was not derived from any sort of formal testing, however. Instead, their expertise was gathered via conversations with students and observations of students working in their classrooms. Thus, less time was spent on testing in these classrooms.

While we have described the similarities of these teachers, do not be lulled into thinking that their classrooms or their instruction looked and sounded similar. Some of these fourth-grade teachers had more rigid classroom management routines than others. Some made greater use of the core curriculum materials that had been provided by the schools. Some were "touchy-feely" personalities who were big on hugs for children. Other teachers were more formal and reserved. At the same time, in both studies, while teachers varied, there were a number of similarities across the instruction they provided.

It seems important to also note that these teachers described their initial teaching experiences as far more traditional than the instruction we observed (Gabriel et al., 2011), suggesting that, as Duffy (2004) asserted, "Effective teachers are developed not born." In fact, these effective teachers described a process of becoming the teachers they were when we observed them. The process was primarily one of first learning how to manage a classroom and then acquiring the skills needed to manage an *effective* classroom. Far more of these effective teachers pointed to a colleague who mentored them as they became effective teachers than pointed to the more formal activities generally thought of when developing teacher expertise (e.g., university classes, district professional development). These effective teachers argued that it was access to mentoring colleagues, administrative trust, and autonomy, along with a deep personal desire to always be improving, that led them to develop as effective teachers.

Both of these studies demonstrate what effective upper elementary-grade classrooms might look like: engaged students, high-level reading and writing tasks, and high levels of achievement that included but went beyond high test scores. Our effective fourth-grade teachers looked very much like the teachers that produced high levels of reading achievement in the Taylor et al. (2003) study. In both studies the most effective upper elementary-grade teachers provided a balanced approach to acquiring reading proficiencies in their classrooms.

Summary

The 10 fourth- and fifth-grade classrooms observed by Pressley et al. (1998) and the 30 fourth-grade classrooms observed by Allington and Johnston (2002) and their colleagues varied greatly. In general, the teachers heading these classrooms tended to emphasize a few aspects of literacy development in their classroom, with the core instructional emphases varying from classroom to classroom. Despite the great variability between classrooms, it was possible to find commonalities. An important commonality was a mixture of literature and writing experiences and skills instruction, consistent with the balanced model developed in this book. Additionally, that there was balance is not to say that we felt the instruction we observed was always as good as it could be. Specifically, self-regulation was actively encouraged in many of the classrooms, but there was too little explicit instruction on how to acquire self-regulation skills.

Similar to Pressley et al. (1998) and Allington and Johnston (2002), today's classrooms vary in classroom management, instruction, and student self-regulation skills. However, what hasn't changed is the approaches effective teachers put into action within the classroom. Effective teachers build effective classroom management through relationships with students and promote intrinsic motivators. Additionally, effective teachers discuss academic progress with students, encourage students to take risks within the classroom, and self-regulate (Pressley, Croyle, et al., 2020; Pressley, Isom, et al., 2020; Roehrig et al., 2012).

When it comes to reading instruction, specifically reading comprehension, many teachers have centered their instruction around developed reading programs and supplement reading instruction with a novel or alternative texts (Davis et al., 2015; Dewitz & Graves, 2021; Ness, 2011). Reading program texts often include brief texts with very little background information about the text, author, or other critical information (Davis et al., 2015). Davis et al. used video data from the Measure of Effective Teaching Study (MET) to complete observations of 63 fourth- through eighth-grade teachers and found reading instruction teacher dominated and focused on implementing a specific strategy. Reading comprehension was limited as most texts were used to learn about implementation of a strategy such as identifying cause and effect within a story or using a specific strategy while reading rather than constructing new knowledge or gaining a new perspective on a topic. Lastly, teachers encouraged students to use reading strategies, but rather than discussion why and when to use a strategy, teachers often cued students to use a single strategy, thus missing an opportunity to promote self-regulation (Davis et al., 2015).

Across the decades, one striking concern commonly found within upper elementary classrooms is the lack of comprehension strategy instruction, especially given the widespread assumption that development of comprehension skills should be a key activity in the upper elementary grades (e.g., Chall, 1983). On the other hand, the presence of substantial amounts of literate conversations and discussions in these classrooms created an interactional environment that was far more likely to stimulate the development of effective strategy use. As Ivey and Johnston (2013) have argued:

> Strategic behavior . . . appeared to be less the result of strategy instruction than a response to [the students'] own need to make sense. Their reading processes suggest that although it is possible to teach particular strategies, instructional time might be better spent supporting engaged reading, a context in which students are more likely to actually become strategic. (p. 48)

We have a hunch that actively engaging in peer-led and teacher-led discussions is more powerful than has been generally believed. To date there are only a handful of studies, almost all done with older students, demonstrating the potential of classroom discussion in developing higher-order reading comprehension (Almasi et al., 2001; Applebee et al., 2003; Ivey & Johnston, 2013; Malloy & Gambrell, 2011; Nystrand & Gamoran, 1991; Wolf et al., 2005). For now, though, we will have to wait while additional research studies are done.

FOUNDATIONS OF MODERN COMPREHENSION INSTRUCTION

Since 1990, when Marilyn J. Adams's *Beginning to Read* reviewed in detail the letter-level and word-level processing skills that young readers must acquire, reading researchers and educators have focused much of their attention on the processes surrounding children's acquisition of decoding skills. One reason for this focus was that the dominant approach to beginning reading education in the United States in the 1990s (e.g., Weaver, 1994) had been suspected of not developing decoding skills in students (Rayner et al., 2002; Seidenberg, 2013). Even so, regardless of whether instructional orientation is meaning emphasis or skills emphasis, there is a broad base of agreement that the most important goal of reading education should be to develop readers who can *derive meaning* from texts. One of the reasons that researchers have focused on word recognition is because of the belief of some reading researchers and educators that word decoding is *the* bottleneck in the meaning-getting process. Of course, when children cannot decode at all, there is no chance of comprehension. When they can decode only with effort, decoding competes with comprehension efforts for the limited attention capacity available for the processing of text (i.e., the 7 ± 2 chunks of short-term memory; Miller, 1956) so that effortful decoding consumes capacity that might otherwise be used to understand text. With increasing automaticity of decoding, there is a freeing-up of capacity, which permits greater comprehension of what is being read (LaBerge & Samuels, 1974). According to the LaBerge and Samuels model, if decoding is automatized, comprehension at the word level is more or less taken care of (Chapter 6). Although we agree that word-level comprehension is facilitated by automatic decoding, there is no doubt that comprehension of texts requires much, much more.

A great deal of research in the past four decades has focused on how to increase the reading comprehension of elementary-level students, selectively discussed below. Most of this work is concerned with teaching students to use comprehension strategies. In the following subsections we explore the various reasons that researchers focused on the teaching of comprehension strategies as a means to improve comprehension. This work on strategies instruction did not occur in a vacuum; rather, it reflected many converging efforts (see Pressley & Hilden, 2006).

Awareness of the Need for Comprehension Instruction

In a landmark study, Dolores Durkin (1978–1979) raised the consciousness of the reading education community about the need for reading comprehension instruction. She observed third- through sixth-grade classrooms and students, watching for comprehension instruction during reading and social studies lessons, but seeing little of it. Instead of teaching students how to comprehend, teachers were assessing comprehension, asking students questions about material they had just read, or assigning workbook pages to be completed. The teachers also "mentioned" useful strategies for fostering comprehension but rarely provided any instruction on the strategy or on its use. Durkin's study did much to stimulate researchers to study comprehension as a process and identify ways to increase it.

More recently, Dewitz et al. (2009) analyzed leading core reading programs to evaluate how nearly these materials represented evidence-based reading comprehension strategy instruction. What they found was disturbing. Teacher questions dominate advice offered in the teaching manuals, with over 50% of all recommended instructional moves being questions during and following reading in three of the five core programs. They also noted:

> Looking across these five programs, we noted that direct explanation, discussion, and questioning are more common than modeling, skill explanations, or guided practice. The manuals provide little support for learning these skills and strategies while students are reading. (p. 116)

In other words, the reading instructional materials used in many American elementary school classrooms provide lessons targeting a huge number of comprehension skills and strategies but offer the teacher almost no useful information on modeling such skills and strategies for students, little in the way of supported practice in acquiring them, and virtually never engage in the gradual release of responsibility in using the targeted strategies. The authors conclude that faithfully implementing these flawed reading programs cannot be considered either effective instruction or virtuous.

Study Skills Instruction as the Norm

In the 1970s, the conventional way of thinking about increasing comprehension was through study skills instruction. Such instruction often boiled down to the teaching of strategies, such as reflecting on prior knowledge related to a reading, or restudying difficult portions of passages, visualizing, and summarizing (Forrest-Pressley & Gilles, 1983). One of the most systematic and well-known approaches was the SQ3R approach (Robinson, 1946), involving survey of the text, question generation in advance of reading based on text headers, reading, reciting the text, and reviewing. The problem with all of the study skills approaches was that there was little or no evidence that they really worked (e.g., Tierney et al., 1980). That is, there was no convincing proof that the great effort required to execute SQ3R paid off in equivalent benefits (Johns & McNamara, 1980). Although the study skills developers had not done the research and development required to hone their procedures so that they worked well (i.e., provided substantial benefits for the effort expended), the study strategies approaches made it sensible to think about teaching strategies as a way to increase comprehension.

Theories of Meaning Representation That Stimulated Research on Specific Types of Strategies Instruction

In the late 1970s and early 1980s, there was much new theorizing about how meaning is represented in the mind and how mental representations of meaning determine comprehension of complex ideas such as those represented in text. The various representational theories stimulated hypotheses about the nature of effective comprehension strategies instruction.

For example, Kintsch and van Dijk (1978; also see van Dijk & Kintsch, 1983) developed a theory about how skilled readers construct representations of the main ideas of text (*macropropositions*, to use their terminology). Their work inspired studies on teaching students how to summarize texts in order to make them more memorable, producing quite a bit of evidence that elementary students could generate good summaries (e.g., Doctorow et al., 1978; Taylor, 1982).

Canadian cognitive psychologist Allan Paivio (e.g., 1971, 1986; Clark & Paivio, 1991) proposed that knowledge is composed of complex associative networks of verbal and imaginal representations. This speculation led to work on how children could be induced to construct mental images that would increase their memories of text content through dual imagery and verbal coding (Levin, 1973; Pressley, 1976). In general, when children were taught to construct mental images representing the content of texts, they demonstrated increased memory (e.g., as tested by literal, short-answer questions) and understanding (e.g., as tested by questions tapping inferences that could be made during reading of the text), as compared with when same-age students read as usual (Pressley, 1977).

Several theorists proposed that stories have conventional structures: a beginning, including information about the time, setting, and characters in the story; an initiating event, setting a goal or leading to a problem; a series of attempts to achieve the goal or overcome the problem; achievement of the goal or resolution of the problem; and character reactions to the resolution (e.g., Mandler, 1984; Stein & Glenn, 1979). Children, especially weak readers, can be taught to attend to story grammar elements as they read, leading to improved comprehension and memory of stories (e.g., Short & Ryan, 1984).

Without a doubt, the most prominent representational theory among reading researchers and educators during the late 1970s and early 1980s was schema theory, as specified by Richard Anderson and David Pearson (1984) at the Center for the Study of Reading. A schema integrates a number of commonly co-occurring concepts into an orderly representation. For example, the schema for the christening of a ship includes its ultimate purpose—to bless the ship. It includes information about where it is done (i.e., in dry dock), by whom (i.e., a celebrity), and when it occurs (i.e., just before the launching of a new ship). The christening action is also represented (i.e., breaking a bottle of champagne that is suspended from a rope). Schema activation can dramatically affect comprehension, inferences, attention allocation, and memory of what is read. Thus, schema theorists advocated encouraging students to activate, in several ways, their prior knowledge while reading by making predictions about text content before reading, relating information encountered in text to prior knowledge, and asking themselves questions about the reasons for the relations specified in text (Anderson & Pearson, 1984).

In summary, representational theorists in the 1970s and early 1980s believed that, if children failed to understand and remember text, the problem might have been that they were not constructing complete representations of the ideas coded in the text. Their solution was to encourage students to construct fuller representations through instruction, using strategies for enhancing mental representations of texts—strategies that could be applied before, during, and after reading (Levin & Pressley, 1981) to construct summaries, images, story grammar representations, and specific instantiations of schemata capturing the ideas in text.

Verbal Protocols of Skilled Reading

As discussed in Chapter 2, many verbal protocol studies of reading were carried out in the 1970s and 1980s. It became apparent in these think-aloud studies that skilled readers used cognitive strategies as they read, including strategies favored by the representational theories—summarizing, constructing images, attending to story grammar elements, and relating to prior knowledge including schematic knowledge (Pressley &

Afflerbach, 1995). This work made apparent the fact that teaching students to use comprehension strategies was to teach them to read as exceptionally skilled readers do.

The Emergence of Metacognitive Theory

An approach known as metacognitive theory was also developed in the 1970s. *Metacognition* is cognition about cognition (Flavell, 1977). It plays an important regulatory role in cognition: Knowing that one can retain more of what one reads by creating a summary of it is important metacognitive knowledge—conditional knowledge (Paris et al., 1983) about summarization. Such knowledge can inform a student about how to proceed when confronted with a text containing ideas that must be remembered. That is, metacognition increases the likelihood of long-term appropriate use of strategies (for reviews, see Johnston & Winograd, 1985; Pressley et al., 1984, 1985).

Both Flavell (1977) and Flavell and Wellman (1977) offered analyses of how metacognition might regulate cognitive strategies in various task situations. That many strategies were definitely teachable became well established during this era as well (Pressley et al., 1982), although it also became obvious that long-term use of taught strategies only occurred when strategies instruction was metacognitively embellished (e.g., information about the usefulness of a trained strategy was included in instruction; see Borkowski et al., 1976; Cavanaugh & Borkowski, 1979; Kennedy & Miller, 1976). Metacognitive theory, implicating strategies as critical in effective thinking, was thriving, borne out by the first analyses and tests of it.

Vygotskian Theories about the Development of Internalized Cognitive Competence

Lev S. Vygotsky's (1978) theory of cognitive development became prominent in the late 1970s and early 1980s. Recall from earlier chapters that Vygotsky's view that interactions between adults and children that are critical to cognitive development occur with tasks that are within the child's *zone of proximal development*, tasks that the child can do only with assistance. Vygotsky's perspective on this zone did much to stimulate developmentally oriented researchers and educators to embrace the teaching of cognitive skills that are not fully developed in children but that could develop with adult support—such as comprehension strategies. In particular, developmentalists felt that development of cognitive skills might be consistent with Vygotsky's (1962) theory that skills once acquired from others and used come to be internalized as self-directed inner speech.

One prominent developmentalist who promoted this theory was Donald Meichenbaum (e.g., 1977), who formulated a position about how adults could interact with children to encourage their acquisition and autonomous use of new cognitive skills. Like Vygotsky (1962), Meichenbaum believed that self-speech began as interpersonal overt speech between adults and children, with the adult role being highly directive at first but gradually fading as children increasingly internalized directive speech. By the mid-1970s, a number of American analyses suggested that the development of self-directive speech plays an important role in the development of children's self-regulation (e.g., Johnston & Winograd, 1985: Kohlberg et al., 1968; Patterson & Mischel, 1976; Wozniak, 1972).

Thus, in the late 1960s and early 1970s, Meichenbaum hypothesized that children could learn a variety of cognitive skills if they were taught simultaneously to use self-speech to direct their use of the cognitive skills they were acquiring (e.g., Meichenbaum & Goodman, 1969). Meichenbaum's general approach can be illustrated by a study conducted by Bommarito and Meichenbaum (reported by Meichenbaum & Asarnow, 1979). They taught comprehension strategies to middle school students who could decode but were experiencing difficulties understanding what they read.

Instruction began with an adult modeling self-verbalized regulation of comprehension strategies: looking for the main idea, attending to the sequence of important events in a story, and attending to how characters in a story feel and why they feel the way they do, among other components. The students saw the adult read and heard the following verbalizations:

> Well, I've learned three big things to keep in mind before I read a story and while I read it. One is to ask myself what the main idea of the story is. What is the story about? A second is to learn important details of the story as I go along. The order of the main events or their sequence is an especially important detail. A third is to know how the characters feel and why. So, get the main idea. Watch sequences. And learn how the characters feel and why . . . . While I'm reading I should pause now and then. I should think of what I'm doing. And I should listen to what I'm saying to myself. Am I saying the right things? Remember, don't worry about mistakes. Just try again. Keep cool, calm, and relaxed. Be proud of yourself when you succeed. Have a blast. (Meichenbaum & Asarnow, 1979, pp. 17–18)

By the end of six training sessions, the students were self-verbalizing covertly, as control was gradually transferred to them over the course of the sessions. Did the self-verbalization instruction affect reading comprehension? Yes: There was greater pretest-to-posttest gain on a standardized comprehension test among these students than for control condition participants. That is, the researchers concluded that adults could advance the cognitive development of children through scaffolded teaching of important cognitive processes.

Reader-Response Theory

Thus far, we have made the case that in the late 1970s and early 1980s lots of pieces of cognitive psychology supported the teaching of comprehension strategies. For comprehension instruction to make sense and be acceptable to the reading education community, most of whom do not identify principally with cognitive psychology, it had to be consistent with traditions embraced by reading educators. As it turned out, the teaching of comprehension strategies was consistent with an exceptionally important language arts perspective.

Language arts educator Louise M. Rosenblatt (1938) made the then-radical proposal that the meaning of a text will vary somewhat from reader to reader. Like Vygotsky, Rosenblatt would be discovered anew in the late 1970s, in her case with the 1978 publication of her book *The Reader, the Text, the Poem.* The reader-response theory defined by that book had an enormous impact on the language arts education community. It legitimized the teaching of active and interpretive reading.

According to reader-response theory, interpretive variability occurs because the meaning of a text involves a transaction between a reader, who has particular perspectives and prior knowledge, and a text, which can affect different readers in different ways (e.g., Beach & Hynds, 1991; Rosenblatt, 1978). Readers sometimes form impressions of characters in stories and frequently relate their personal and cultural experiences to events encountered in the text. As part of responding to the text, readers sometimes explain events in a text to themselves. Often, they form vivid images. In short, language arts theorists and educators viewed as reader responses the processes that psychologists considered to be comprehension strategies. Reader-response theory has been acceptable to the language arts community since the late 1970s. This means that the cognitive psychologists and the language arts specialists had the same idea of prompting student readers to be more active as they read.

Reciprocal Teaching

By the late 1970s and early 1980s, the stage was set for research on teaching elementary students to use comprehension strategies as they read. The diverse elements in this mixture came together at the University of Illinois, Center for the Study of Reading. The center was the intellectual home of Dolores Durkin, whose work established the need for comprehension strategies instruction. A great deal of important work was carried out there.

Several scholars at the center would put together a summary of study skills (Tierney et al., 1980). Important work on individual comprehension strategies was conducted there, including work on summarization (Brown & Day, 1983), imagery (Anderson & Hidde, 1971), and prior knowledge activation (Anderson & Pearson, 1984).

The landmark study of reciprocal teaching (1984) had a major impact on interest in comprehension strategies instruction. *Reciprocal teaching* (Palincsar & Brown, 1984) involves teaching comprehension strategies in the context of a reading group. Students are taught to make predictions when reading, question themselves about the ideas in the text, seek clarifications when confused, and summarize content. The adult teacher initially explains and models these strategies for students but quickly transfers responsibility to the members of the group, with individual students taking turns leading the reading group.

During a reciprocal teaching lesson, one student is assigned the role of group leader, supervising the group's generation of predictions, questions, and summaries as reading proceeds. The group leader also solicits points that need to be clarified and either provides clarifications him- or herself or elicits them from other group members. The group interactions are cooperative, and the adult teacher provides support on an as-needed basis only. That is, the adult teacher provides scaffolding: enough support so that the group makes progress, but not so much support as to stifle students' active self-direction of their reading and comprehension.

Brown and Palincsar (1989) summarized a typical discussion of a text in a reciprocal teaching group:

> The dialogue leader begins the discussion by asking a question on the main content and ends by summarizing the gist. If there is disagreement, the group rereads and discusses potential candidates for question and summary statements until they reach consensus. Summarizing provides a means by which the group can monitor its progress, noting points of agreement and disagreement. Particularly valuable is the fact that summarizing at the end of a period of discussion helps students establish where they are for tackling a new segment of text. Attempts to clarify any comprehension problems that might arise are also an integral part of the discussion. And, finally, the leader asks for predictions about future content. Throughout, the adult teacher provides guidance and feedback tailored to the needs of the current discussion and his or her respondents. (p. 413)

Reciprocal teaching is chock-full of good things, according to cognitive views of learning and development (Brown & Palincsar, 1989; Palincsar, 2007). First of all, students are presented with multiple models of cognitive processing. The teacher models and explains. Every day, the group comes together and executes a sequence of strategies well matched to the processes required to understand text; thus, peers in the group are continually modeling reasoning about text. With respect to the learning of content, students are led to make the types of elaborations and inferences that should facilitate learning of the text—that is, predictions, inferences required as part of question generation and elaboration, and summarization. The discussions permit various points of view to be aired and require students to justify and back up their claims. These discussions permit review and commentary about the strategies being learned and the content being covered. Thus, reciprocal teaching offers opportunities both to learn new content and to learn how to process new content.

A major assumption of reciprocal teaching is that, through participation, students eventually internalize use of the four strategies practiced in the group. That is, the processing that was once carried out between persons in the group will come to be carried out within the individual students, consistent with the Vygotskian perspective that individual cognitive development develops from participation in social groups (Oczkus, 2010).

Reciprocal teaching has shortcomings, however (Hacker & Tenent, 2002; Marks et al., 1993). Many reciprocal teaching lessons involve a preponderance of literal questions and little in the way of evidence that students are monitoring their comprehension. This is obvious from a lack of clarification questions in many reciprocal teaching lessons. Because reciprocal teaching emphasizes a gradual reduction of teacher support, there are often long pauses in lessons, with students fumbling because the teacher is uncertain whether to enter into the conversation and provide input. With respect to performance on standardized comprehension tests, the effects of reciprocal teaching are not particularly striking, with an average effect size of 0.3 SD, although it is more successful when reciprocal teaching includes more direct instruction of the four comprehension strategies (Rosenshine & Meister, 1994). More recently, Lee and Tsai (2017) conducted a meta-analysis of comprehension interventions for students with specific poor comprehension skills. The six reviewed reciprocal teaching studies showed students who received reciprocal teaching instruction improved their comprehension as compared with the control groups with a large effect size of 0.856.

The Role of Discussion in Developing Reading Comprehension

Perhaps because reciprocal teaching involves students engaging in short, peer-managed discussions, recent research has focused on the potential of peer-led discussions in fostering improved understanding of texts read. Nystrand (2006) provides a review of early studies of discussion, noting that longer periods of discussion, proportion of authentic questions asked, and proportion of uptake (follow-up questions asked) result in better student understanding of texts read and of course content. Nystrand also notes that discussion is rarely observed in classrooms. That is, only a minority of classroom teachers ever engage their students in discussions. When discussion is observed it is almost always teacher led discussion with student to student discussion rarely available. Murphy et al. (2009) conducted a meta-analysis on 42 studies of nine discussion-based programs designed to improve students' understanding of texts they had read. Overall, discussion-based instructional approaches led to stronger gains in student learning than conventional approaches used in control or comparison groups. In addition, these approaches had stronger effects on students of below-average achievement. However, while the meta-analysis found stronger literal and inferential text comprehension among discussion-based participants, no such evidence was observed for critical reasoning about texts read.

Almasi et al. (2011) again reviewed the research on discussion as an instructional event and concluded:

> Interventions that provided space for students to engage in dialogic peer discussions of text provided a different space for students to participate actively in meaning construction. These contexts required students to engage in social and cognitive processes in which they asked thoughtful, meaningful questions, and brought up issues they felt would help them understand the text better. This process requires students to actively think about the text, identify those aspects that do not make sense, and work collaboratively to understand the text. These are the same self-regulatory processes involved in comprehension-strategies instruction—recognizing and resolving comprehension difficulties. (p. 340)

Discussion not only buoys reading comprehension, but also enhances written composition. Reznitskaya et al. (2001) studied the effects of a small-group discussion technique called "collaborative reasoning." Groups of six to eight students met twice weekly for 5 weeks in sessions lasting 15–20 minutes, where the students discussed controversial issues raised in a set of stories selected by the authors. Students in the control classrooms received their regular language arts instruction during the study.

Part of the teacher's role was to model, prompt, or encourage students to use information from the stories to support their arguments. Teachers also directly taught students how to think of counterarguments to a position being taken by another student.

Students who participated in the collaborative reasoning groups performed significantly better on their essays on a number of dimensions than did students in the control group. They wrote more arguments, counterarguments, and rebuttals, and they showed greater use of text information to support their arguments than did students in the control classrooms. Overall, the study provides evidence that reasoning skills acquired in one context (oral discussion) can generalize to another literacy context (persuasive writing).

In the past decade, the Institute of Education Sciences released an evidence-based practice guide for improving reading comprehension in the early elementary school years (Shanahan et al., 2010). Concerning the potential role of a greater use of classroom discussion, Shanahan et al. asserted:

> The panel recommends that teachers lead their students through focused, high-quality discussions in order to help them develop a deeper understanding of what they read. Such discussions among students or between the students and the teacher go beyond simply asking and answering surface-level questions to a more thoughtful exploration of the text. Through this type of exploration, students learn how to argue for or against points raised in the discussion, resolve ambiguities in the text, and draw conclusions or inferences about the text. (p. 23)

While small-group, peer-led discussion has demonstrated its potential as an instructional routine, few teachers seem well prepared to manage such groups. Kucan et al. (2011) studied 60 upper elementary–grade teachers (fourth and fifth grade) who completed an assessment of comprehension-related knowledge including analysis of passages and specialized knowledge for fostering reading comprehension particularly through discussion. They found that only one-third of teachers could engage in the integration and inferencing required to provide coherent statements about the most important ideas in the texts. Too often, teachers used very general probes and exhibited a willingness to allow students to focus on tangential ideas rather than important ideas found in the text. Perhaps reflecting years of experience with core reading programs,

> Teacher responses across all the responding-to-students tasks revealed that teachers did not offer the specific kinds of support that students needed in order to explain text information, and instead relied on general probes for more information and rereading. Their responses were more routinized than flexible and opportunistic. (Kucan et al., 2011, p. 75)

This study may provide us with the answer as to why discussion is seldom observed in classrooms. Since core reading programs rarely mention discussion, as Dewitz and colleagues (2009) observed, and since most teachers seem never to have acquired the expertise needed to effectively organize and manage these discussions, it seems only logical that effective discussions would be rare.

DIRECT EXPLANATION OF COMPREHENSION STRATEGIES AND MORE: TRANSACTIONAL COMPREHENSION STRATEGIES INSTRUCTION

In 1981, researchers Gerald G. Duffy and Laura Roehler proposed an important model of teaching that begins with teacher explanations. At the heart of this proposal is a process that they referred to as "mental modeling," which is showing students what a strategy is and how to apply a strategy by thinking aloud (Duffy & Roehler, 1989). For example, the teacher introducing mental imagery as a comprehension strategy using Duffy and Roehler's (1981) approach might tell students about how good readers sometimes make pictures in their heads that are consistent with the ideas in a story. Then the teacher might begin to read a story aloud to the students, stopping from time to time to explain the images she or he is constructing of what is going on in the story. Students would then try the strategy, monitored by the teacher, who would provide additional explanations and modeling as needed. Feedback and instruction are reduced as students become more and more comfortable with the strategic process being taught. The information provided to students during practice depends very much on the particular problems the students encounter and the particular ways that their understanding is deficient. Reinstruction and re-explanations occur, as well as follow-up mental modeling. The teacher responds to specific student needs, sometimes offering an elaboration of student understanding up until that point. That is, instruction is scaffolded, according to the Duffy and Roehler approach.

Duffy et al. (1987) produced an extremely well-designed study of the effects of direct-explanation strategy instruction on third-grade reading, with 10 groups of weak readers assigned randomly to the direct explanation condition and 10 control groups receiving their usual instruction. Duffy et al. (1987) taught grade 3 teachers to explain directly the strategies, skills, and processes that are part of skilled third-grade reading as the study continued over the course of an entire academic year. The teachers were taught first to explain a strategy, skill, or process and then to mentally model use of it for their students. Then came guided student practice, in which the students initially carried out the processing overtly so that the teacher could monitor their use of the new strategy. Assistance was reduced as students became more proficient. Teachers encouraged transfer of strategies by reviewing when and where the strategies being learned might be used. Teachers cued use of the new strategies when students encountered situations where the strategies might be applied profitably, regardless of when these occasions arose (i.e., scaffolding continued throughout the school day). Cuing and prompting continued until students autonomously applied the strategies they were taught.

By the end of the year, students in the direct-explanation condition outperformed control students on standardized measures of reading, including a measure of reading achievement given the year after the intervention had been administered. These results had a profound effect on the reading education community. Direct explanation as defined by Duffy et al. (1987) was subsequently used by many educators as a starting point as they implemented comprehension strategies instruction in their own schools. Direct explanation continues to this day to be an important model of reading skills instruction, including of comprehension skills (Duffy, 2014).

Descriptive Studies of Transactional Comprehension Strategies Instruction

The Pressley research group studied several places where teaching of comprehension strategies was developed and implemented in light of the Duffy and Roehler (1981) model. Because the instruction we studied involved so much more than direct explanation, a different term was needed to describe it, one more inclusive of all that occurs during such teaching. In particular, we wanted a summary term that better captured the dynamic give-and-take between teachers and students that typifies classrooms employing strategies instruction. The descriptive label *transactional strategies instruction* thus seemed appropriate from three different perspectives.

Recall Rosenblatt's (1978) reader-response position that meaning is not in the text alone or in the reader's head alone but rather is constructed by readers as they consider text content in light of their previous knowledge and experiences. Such meaning construction, termed "transactional" by Rosenblatt, was certainly emphasized in the instruction described here, as students were encouraged to use strategies such as prediction, visualization, and summarization to create personalized interpretations and understanding of text.

The term *transactional* was also appropriate for a second reason. Most comprehension strategies instruction occurred in small reading groups involving a teacher and students reading texts together, applying comprehension strategies as they did so. In the developmental psychology literature (e.g., Bell, 1968), *transactional* refers to interactions in which the child's actions in part determine the behaviors of adults in the child's world. Consistent with that use of the term, teachers' reactions in the instruction detailed here were determined largely by the reactions of the students. Teachers responded to student interpretations and difficulties: If a student offered a good summary, the teacher might prompt elaboration of the summary. If the student's summary was difficult for the teacher to understand, she or he might prompt rereading or reconsideration of the text. What happened in transactional strategies instructional groups was determined largely by the reactions of students to teachers and to other students. Such conversations about literature make a great deal of sense, for children's comprehension of ideas in a text increases when they have conversations about literature with peers and teachers (Applebee et al., 2003; Van den Branden, 2000).

The strategies instruction described in what follows was transactional in yet a third sense. Organizational psychologists (e.g., Hutchins, 1991) in particular have been concerned with the types of solutions produced during group problem solving as compared with individual problem solving: Groups invariably produce interpretations that no one individual in the group would have produced by him- or herself. Group interpretations following this pattern were prominent during the comprehension strategies instruction we observed. The group used the strategies they were learning as interpretational tools, producing impressive interpretations of texts.

To summarize, there were three senses in which the classroom strategies instruction we observed was transactional:

1. Meaning was determined by employing strategies as readers processed the text.
2. How one reader reacted was largely determined by what other readers in the group were doing, thinking, and saying.
3. The meaning that emerged as teachers and students together used strategies to read and comprehend a text was the product of all of the individuals in the group.

Instruction was transactional in all of these senses largely because of extremely effective teacher assistance to students during strategies instruction and practice. That is, direct explanation of strategies and teacher modeling were followed by sensitive teacher scaffolding of strategies use as students worked in small groups.

Example Schools With Highly Effective Comprehension Instruction

Benchmark School Studies

Michael Pressley's initial studies on comprehension strategies instruction were conducted at the Benchmark School in Media, Pennsylvania, which is dedicated to the education of high-ability students who experience difficulties learning to read during the first 2 years of schooling. Even though the Benchmark students are at great risk for long-term school failure, most emerge after 4–7 years well prepared to return to regular education. Virtually all Benchmark graduates complete high school, and most attend college. Because much of the Benchmark approach involves teaching students to use cognitive strategies to accomplish reading and other literacy tasks, the school seemed like a perfect place to carry out an initial investigation of effective strategies instruction: reading strategies are taught in primary through middle school, with students encouraged to use them across the curriculum.

One study was an interview study of the faculty (Pressley, Gaskins, Cunicelli, et al., 1991). The 31 teachers at Benchmark were asked 150 questions about their instruction, each requiring an objective answer but also permitting any additional input the responding teacher might wish to provide. The questions had been generated after extensive observations at the school and were intended to tap the most important instructional issues surrounding the comprehension strategies instruction being offered at the school. Up to 5 hours of face-to-face interviews permitted ample opportunity for teachers to provide detailed explanations, based on their extensive experience, of what they believed about strategies instruction as well as why they believed it.

Generalizing across the 31 teachers, we found that there were many points of agreement, including the following:

The Benchmark teachers strongly endorsed direct explanation and modeling as essential components of effective strategies instruction. Many observations at Benchmark confirmed that such explanations were used during small- and large-group instruction and as part of one-to-one tutoring and reinstruction. Teachers reported that their initial explanations and modeling were more complete than later explanations and modeling, although the faculty members, especially the more experienced ones, were emphatic that explanations and modeling should continue for a long time after introduction of strategies.

Extensive practice in use of strategies was endorsed by the teachers, as was extensive guidance and feedback in response to student needs during such practice. Even so, the teachers admitted that it is often difficult to diagnose the specific problems experienced by students, and it is a challenge to devise remediation. The teachers were aware that students did not learn strategies quickly: Facile use of strategies across a wide range of tasks and materials occurred only after extensive practice, which included struggling to adapt strategies to a wide range of academic problems.

Teaching of strategies and their application was reported as occurring across the curriculum, consistent with our frequent observations of Benchmark teachers encouraging use of strategies in many different contexts. The teachers considered it essential to provide extensive information to students about when and where to apply the strategies they were learning, as well as information about the learning benefits produced by use of strategies.

The teachers recognized that transfer of the newly acquired strategies to new academic tasks and contents was anything but automatic; rather, it required extensive teaching about when strategies might be applied as well as practice applying strategies across a number of situations.

The teachers were emphatic that only a few strategies could be introduced at a time. In accordance with this belief, in-depth instruction of strategies over months and years was the preferred approach to teaching at Benchmark. The teachers' view was that students developed strategic repertoires over the course of their years in the school—strategies instruction was definitely not seen as a quick fix. This is, of course, far removed from "the strategy of the week," the lesson planning model common to core reading programs (Dewtiz et al., 2009).

Although cognitive in their orientation, the teachers also recognized the need for explicit reinforcement of student efforts and successes in applying strategies and accomplishing difficult academic tasks. Feedback to students was considered essential. It was seen as especially important to follow students' success with positive feedback as a means of keeping them motivated. The teachers were well aware that their students had already experienced several years of school failure and believed that Benchmark students' successes needed to be rewarded in order to offset the damage produced by the previous failures (Gaskins, 2005).

Pressley, Gaskins, Cunicelli, et al. (1991) presented the same questions that had been given to the Benchmark teachers to a sample of nine nationally known researchers in strategies instruction, distinguished investigators who had extensive hands-on experience in implementing long-term strategies instruction at their home institutions. What was striking was the high congruence between the responses of the Benchmark teachers and the researcher sample. Extensive experience with strategies instruction seems to produce perceptions of it that are consistent with the thinking of the Benchmark teachers.

Three additional studies at the school provided even more detailed understanding of how Benchmark teachers do what they do. One was a case study of the instruction in one Benchmark classroom during the spring semester of 1990 (Pressley, Wile, et al., 1991). The focal strategy taught there was the generation of an outline of the major ideas in each text, which would include information about causes and effects coded in the text, temporal sequences, comparative and contrasting information, and simple descriptions. Teaching of these strategies was thoroughly integrated with the teaching of content, with focal strategies instruction occurring during reading, writing, and social studies as teachers and students interacted to create maps. For example, semantic maps were generated by students as they planned writing assignments as part of social studies. Social studies homework often required semantic mapping.

Consistent with teachers' claims in the interview study, explanations and modeling of the semantic-mapping strategy were more extensive and explicit early in the instruction. After several months, given a one-line direction from the teacher (e.g., "Make a map of what's in this text"), students often began to map the meaning of a text. The teachers provided assistance to students on an as-needed basis, often giving gentle hints about how specific relationships in a text might be represented in a semantic map.

Instruction in other strategies did not stop when semantic mapping was introduced. Rather, teachers modeled and explained the use of semantic mapping in conjunction with other strategies. For example, the strategies of activating prior knowledge, predicting, seeking clarification, and summarizing were all prompted frequently during lessons intended primarily to provide new information about semantic mapping as a strategy.

We had an important insight at Benchmark School that cognitive strategies were being taught as methods to encourage interpretations, which we define as the construction of personally significant understanding. For example, the teachers observed in the Pressley, Wile, et al. (1991) case study taught their students that no two semantic maps should be alike and that each student's map should reflect reactions to the content of the text. The information was seen as important, if only because most school assignments require similar responses from the variety of students who attend to lessons in that classroom daily. Because individual students have different life experiences, expecting a single common "answer" makes no sense. But after several years of schooling, students may have adopted the common but mistaken notion that everyone comprehends a text in the same manner. Helping students develop a more accurate idea of what it means to comprehend a text seems an important outcome of such activity.

Interpretive activities were especially apparent in analyses of Benchmark classroom dialogues produced by Gaskins et al. (1993), who studied the strategy instruction lessons of six teachers at Benchmark. Three lessons were analyzed for each teacher, one when a new focal strategy was introduced, the second somewhat later, and a third considerably later than that. The discourse in these classrooms was markedly different from the discourse in conventional classrooms in typical schools: Many repeated cycles consisting of a teacher asking a question, a student responding to it, and the teacher evaluating the response ordinarily observed in many classroom studies (see Cazden, 1988; Durkin, 1978–1979; Mehan, 1979) were not found in the Benchmark data. Instead, the teachers engaged in interactive dialogues with their students 88% of the time in what Gaskins et al. (1993) referred to as "process–content" cycles: The teacher used content as a vehicle to stimulate application and discussion of strategies. When students made comments during discussions, Benchmark teachers did not attempt to evaluate their responses, but rather encouraged the students to elaborate on them—encouraging students to process the content further using strategies. The goal was to encourage student understanding of content through strategic processing. Thus, a teacher might ask a student to summarize a passage. Then the teacher might ask the student if any images came to mind while he or she was reading the text, or encourage the student to liven up the summary by relating it to prior knowledge (e.g., "Do you think most people would ask Bob Cratchet to work on Christmas Eve?"; "Do your parents have to work on Christmas Eve?").

The personalization of the instruction offered at Benchmark was another feature documented in the Pressley et al. (2006) case study of the school and its operations. An extremely important finding in this study and in the earlier study (Gaskins et al., 1993) was the identification of events that occurred often in many lessons:

- Students were provided instruction about how to carry out the strategies.
- Teachers modeled the focal strategies (and sometimes use of other strategies as well).
- Students practiced strategies, with teacher guidance and assistance provided on an as-needed basis.
- The focal strategy for a lesson and the focal curriculum content for the day were identified for students early in the lesson.
- Information was presented about why the focal strategy (and sometimes nonfocal strategies as well) was important; often, teachers provided anecdotal information about how strategies had helped them.
- Information about when and where strategies apply was conveyed to students.

In summary, Benchmark teachers provided direct explanations about and modeling of strategies, followed by student practice that was guided and assisted by teachers, who carefully monitored student attempts to use strategies, offering help when needed. It also seems important to note that elementary content coverage was not displaced in favor of strategies instruction; rather, strategies were applied as students learned elementary content.

A Comprehension Strategies Instructional Program in a Maryland County

As it turned out, the Benchmark School was not the only place where such instruction took place. We extensively studied comprehension strategies programs that were developed and implemented in one Maryland countywide school district. The comprehension instruction in that county occurred around high-quality texts, often in reading groups small enough to encourage exchanges between all students about interpretations of text, imaginal reactions to content, and summaries. When strategies were initially introduced (i.e., in grade 1 or 2), lessons often focused on individual strategies. For example, there were several weeks of students making predictions, predictions, and more predictions followed by weeks of students visualizing, visualizing, and visualizing. Once again, this instruction was far more extensive than the instructional guidance provided in commercial core reading programs. We will suggest that this greater extensivity of the strategies instruction was central to its success.

Once students were familiar with the strategies, the lessons emphasized coordinated use of strategies, although this required a great deal of teacher prompting, which continued for months and sometimes years. Eventually, by the third year of participation in such instruction, students could meet in groups and carry out strategic processes in a self-directed fashion—that is, teacher prompting and cuing were much less pronounced than they had been in previous years (El-Dinary et al., 1992; Pressley, El-Dinary, et al., 1992). We summarized the comprehension instruction that was observed in this Maryland school district:

- Students were provided instruction about how to carry out the strategies emphasized in the curriculum. Usually, this was re-explanation of strategic processes that were somewhat familiar to the students, amounting to a recasting of the strategies in new terms.
- Teachers modeled use of the comprehension strategies that were taught.
- Students practiced strategies, with teacher guidance and assistance provided on an as-needed basis. Prompts were often in the form of questions suggesting additional strategic processing or possible ways to extend or expand an interpretation.
- Information was presented about why the focal strategy (and sometimes nonfocal strategies as well) was important. Teachers often provided anecdotal information about how strategies had helped them.
- Students were often required to model and explain use of the comprehension strategies.
- Information about when and where strategies could be applied was conveyed to students. The positive effects of strategies were continually pointed out to them.
- Sophisticated processing vocabulary (e.g., terms like "predictions," "clarifications," "validation of predictions," and "summaries") was used frequently.
- Flexibility in strategy use was apparent, with teachers emphasizing how different students might apply strategies in different ways to the same content.
- Teachers sent the message that student thought processes mattered.

Comment

Both school settings had developed strategies instruction involving a great deal of direct explanation and mental modeling, consistent with Duffy and Roehler's (1981) recommendations. In both settings, students and teachers talked aloud a great deal about their thinking processes (i.e., did mental modeling). They shared their interpretations of texts in an open and generally relaxed group context. Coordination of strategies was emphasized in both programs, with students engaging in years of practice in such coordination.

Explaining strategies to students, showing them how to use strategies, and helping them as they attempt to apply strategies as part of in-school practice seemed sensible to these educators. The transactional strategies instruction described here evolved as teachers worked with them. Credit the educators with this intervention, which really does affect student achievement, although previous basic and applied theory and research provided great impetus for and guidance during its development.

Validation of Transactional Strategies Instruction

Three studies have been conducted in which transactional strategies instruction has been evaluated in a carefully controlled fashion. Taken together, their outcomes support the conclusion that transactional strategies instruction can promote reading instruction beginning in grade 2 and continuing into high school.

Brown, Pressley, Van Meter, and Schuder (1996)

The study of Brown et al. (1996) was a year-long quasi-experimental investigation of the effects of transactional strategies instruction on grade 2 children's reading. Five grade 2 classrooms receiving transactional strategies instruction were matched with grade 2 classrooms taught by teachers who were well regarded as language arts teachers but who were not using a strategies instruction approach. In each classroom, a group of readers who were low achieving at the beginning of grade 2 was identified.

In the fall, the weak readers in the strategies instruction classrooms and the weak readers in the control classrooms did not differ on standardized measures of reading comprehension and word attack skills. By the spring, however, there were clear differences on these measures, favoring the transactional strategies instruction classrooms. In addition, there were differences favoring the strategies-instructed students on strategies-use measures as well as interpretive measures (i.e., strategies-instructed students made more diverse and richer interpretations of what they read than did controls).

One of the most compelling differences between Brown and colleagues' (1996) transactional strategies-instructed students and control students was a demonstration that the students who had learned strategies acquired more content from their daily lessons. We emphasize as well that it was not that the control students did not improve over the course of the year; they did, but students experiencing transactional strategies instruction improved significantly more.

Cathy Collins (1991)

Cathy Collins (1991) improved comprehension in grade 5 and 6 students by providing a semester (3 days a week) of comprehension strategies lessons. Her students were taught to predict what will happen in the story, seek clarification when uncertain, look for patterns and principles in arguments presented in the text, analyze decision making that occurs during text processing, solve problems (including the use of backward reasoning and visualization), summarize, adapt ideas in the text (including rearranging parts of ideas in it), and negotiate interpretations of texts in groups. Although the strategies-instructed students did not differ from controls before the intervention with respect to standardized comprehension performance, there was a 3 standard deviation difference between students in the treated and control conditions on the posttest, a very large effect for the treatment.

Valerie Anderson (1992)

Valerie Anderson (1992; see also Anderson & Roit, 1993) conducted a 3-month experimental investigation of the effects of transactional strategies instruction on reading-disabled students in grades 6 through 11. Students were taught comprehension strategies in small groups, with nine groups of transactional strategies students and seven control groups. Although both strategies-instructed and control students made gains on standardized comprehension measures during the study, the gains were greater in the trained group. Anderson (1992) also collected a variety of qualitative data supporting the conclusion that reading for meaning improved in the strategies-instructed condition. For example, strategies instruction increased students' willingness to read and attempt to understand difficult material, collaborate with classmates to discover meanings in text, and react to and elaborate upon text.

Comment

Doing research on long-term interventions such as transactional strategies instruction is very difficult, requiring researchers to make careful measurements in a number of classrooms over a long period of time. As far as policymakers are concerned, the gold standard is that an educational intervention makes a difference with respect to performance on standardized tests. What was striking in these validations was that a semester to a year of transactional-strategies instruction made a definitive positive impact on standardized tests performances and also made differences that were captured by other measures. What is also striking is that others besides the originators of transactional strategies instruction approaches are finding ways to adapt the procedures to new contexts and contents with clear improvements in student comprehension, although not always as striking as in the original validation studies (e.g., Klingner et al., 1998, 2004; Mason, 2004; Vaughn et al., 2011).

Transactional Strategies in the Classroom

Having spent a great deal of time in classrooms in which transactional strategies instruction occurs, and in many other classrooms as well, we can say without hesitation that daily life is very different in classrooms based on the transactional-strategies instruction model than it is in other classrooms. Most noticeable is that there is really intelligent discussion of readings occurring in the transactional-strategies instruction classes, with the students using the strategies they are learning in conversations about readings. In these conversations, they make predictions about what will happen in the story. They talk about the parts of readings that are confusing and about ways to overcome those confusions. The children offer summaries of what they read, permitting differences in interpretation. The students in these classrooms have come to expect differences, since they know that the meaning of a text is a function of both what is in the text and what the reader knew before reading the text.

In the typical classroom, one that does not include strategy instruction, most talk occurs in a participation structure in which the teacher asks questions and the students answer them (e.g., Durkin, 1978–1979; Mehan, 1979). In transactional-strategies instruction classrooms, the students have learned how to talk about a text without being prompted by the teacher to do so. The teacher never prompts students by saying, "Now, it's time for a prediction," or "Can someone think of a good question to ask about this part of the story?" Rather, if the teacher needs to prompt at all, he or she merely prompts the students to be active, asking students to decide for themselves what they should be doing to understand the text. Prompts like "What might you do here?" or "I was wondering how you were thinking about this portion of the text" are common. The teacher prompts students to choose to think, with the students learning that thinking about text involves making predictions based on prior knowledge and what has happened so far in the text, constructing mental images, generating questions and looking for answers, seeking clarifications when confused, and constructing summaries and interpretations about the ideas in the text. There is considerable evidence that the opportunities to participate in such student-driven dialogues are highly motivating to students, enabling them to think of plenty of questions to ask about the text and plenty of ways to relate to one another about the ideas in texts being read (e.g., Almasi & Gambrell, 1994). Such discussions about the content of the text—that is, negotiations about text meanings—have great potential for increasing the comprehension of the individuals in the group (Almasi & Garas-York, 2009; Applebee et al., 2003; Nystrand, 2006; Van den Branden, 2000).

Transactional-strategies instruction is about the development of self-regulation, developing students who, on their own, use the comprehension strategies that excellent readers use. Return to Chapter 2 and review the comprehension processes used by excellent readers. Those processes—prediction, questioning, making images, seeking clarification, and constructing summaries—are exactly the processes that are taught as strategies by transactional-strategies instruction teachers. Exceptionally skilled readers use these aids on their own, and thus the transactional-strategies instruction teacher does not want to be cuing students to use any specific strategy. Rather, the transactional-strategies instruction teacher consistently sends the message that students should be active during reading, choosing their own activities and strategies. If self-regulation is anything, it is choosing to be cognitively active, and transactional-strategies instruction is all about teaching students to choose active reading over passive reading and to decide for themselves which strategy to use when they confront challenging texts.

Before leaving this discussion of transactional strategies instruction, we feel that we must reflect a bit more on its predecessor, reciprocal teaching, covered earlier. When teachers try to implement reciprocal teaching, they often transform it dramatically—to the point that it looks like transactional-strategies instruction (Hacker & Tenent, 2002; Marks et al., 1993), with an entire volume summary now available about how reciprocal teaching can be used flexibly in the classroom (Oczkus, 2010). Thus, one route to transactional-strategies instruction can be by starting with reciprocal teaching of prediction, clarification, questioning, and summarization, with the goal of flexible use of these strategies by students kept in the forefront of the implementing teacher's mind.

Concerning the way strategies instruction stimulates cognitive activity, we cannot resist the temptation to point out that even when very insensitive analyses are employed, as when national databases of questionnaire data are analyzed, there are clear relationships between cognitive-strategies instruction and the reported frequency of reading (Guthrie et al., 1993). Even more intriguing is evidence in the Guthrie et al. (1993) analysis that part of the reason for the increased reading when comprehension strategies are taught is that it leads to more dialogue about what was read. There is plenty of reason to teach comprehension strategies in elementary school, and we suspect that there will be more evidence documenting that students receiving such instruction read better, read more, talk more, and talk more intelligently about what they read.

BALANCED COMPREHENSION INSTRUCTION IS MORE THAN COMPREHENSION STRATEGIES

This chapter has focused on comprehension strategies instruction because a great deal of comprehension-instructional work has been about strategies. Certainly, comprehension strategies are important. However, balanced comprehension instruction is much more, with comprehension instruction not beginning in the middle and upper elementary grades, but much earlier. Yes, there is probably going to be more comprehension instruction in the middle and upper elementary grades, as implied up until this point in the chapter, but that is not to say that concerns about developing comprehension should be absent from the primary grades.

One other debated strategy is the idea of "close reading" (e.g., Boyles & Sherer, 2012; Snow & O'Connor, 2016). Close reading requires students to deal with the ideas expressed in the read text, thus focuses on what the text says, not how it is interpreted. In other words, close reading focuses just on the facts rather than the ideas presented. Researchers who support close reading believe it allows all students to have success because questions can be answered by referencing the text (Snow & O'Connor, 2016). Additionally, supporters of close reading argue that it provides English language learners the opportunity to engage with complex texts (Fillmore, 2014). However, others argue that close reading ignores crucial aspects of comprehension such as ignoring student background knowledge, decreases student motivation to read, and limits classroom discussions about the text (Fisher & Frey, 2012; Murphy et al., 2009; Snow & O'Connor, 2016). We believe teachers should be aware of the strengths and limitations of close reading instruction when it comes to student comprehension. There are still limited empirical evidence on the effectiveness of close reading with elementary students and we encourage future research on the topic of close reading.

Decoding With Fluency and Comprehension

There are those who assume that, if children can decode words in the books they are reading, that will go far in permitting understanding of the messages in texts (Gough & Tunmer, 1986). From this perspective, word-level decoding is a critical bottleneck in the comprehension process: If the reader cannot decode a word, she or he cannot comprehend it (e.g., Adams, 1990; Metsala & Ehri, 1998). Of course, there is some truth to this position. Not being able to read words at all seriously impairs comprehension! Indeed, not being able to decode fluently (Chapter 6) impairs comprehension, for both word recognition and comprehension occur within short-term memory (i.e., consciousness), which is limited in its capacity (Miller, 1956). Hence, word recognition and higher-order comprehension processes compete for the short-term capacity that is available during reading. The more effort required to decode a word, the less capacity that is left over to comprehend it and the larger messages in the text (LaBerge & Samuels, 1974). In general, the more completely developed decoding processes are during the elementary years, the better the understanding of words and connected text (Gough & Tunmer, 1986; Rupley et al., 1998; Shankweiler et al., 1999).

When teachers develop word recognition fluency, they are teaching students to improve comprehension. In fact, this is the main motivation for emphasizing fluency as the goal of word recognition instruction. Much has been said in this book about the teaching of word recognition processes as part of balanced literacy instruction, with the point made emphatically that many struggling readers can learn to recognize words through explicit decoding instruction. A critical research issue is to determine whether struggling readers can learn to recognize words to the point of fluency. In most studies of word recognition considered in this book, the criterion was word recognition accuracy rather than fluency. Yes, struggling readers can be taught to sound out words, but such sounding out is effortful. Being able to sound out words with effort will not produce fluent readers who have high comprehension. Every primary-level teacher has experienced the child who can sound out word after word, sentence after sentence and paragraph after paragraph, but has no clue at the end of a reading about what was read. Those children are accurate decoders. Comprehension requires more. It requires word recognition fluency. Developing such fluency seems to depend on both effective decoding instruction and extensive high-accuracy reading activity. In other words, developing fluent decoding proficiencies depends on engaging in much reading—more reading than most struggling readers seem to do (Torgesen & Hudson, 2006).

To support fluency and comprehension, teachers can implement several research-based strategies within their reading lessons—strategies such as choral, echo, and partner reading, which focus on the fluency of reading—but also have success in increasing student comprehension of complex texts (Ellis, 2009; Kuhn, 2020; Paige, 2011). When implementing these strategies, teachers should use choral, echo, and partner reading with the same reading over the course of multiple days with support from the teacher when needed (Ellis, 2009; Kuhn, 2020). This support may include scaffolding, posing discussion, questioning, and summary of the reading selection (Kuhn, 2020).

Good readers not only understand what they read, they also know when they are *not understanding what they read*—that is, they monitor their comprehension. Comprehension monitoring is critical, for awareness of a failure to understand prompts the good reader to reread the text and try to make sense out of it. An important finding in recent years is that with increasing skill in decoding the comprehension monitoring of grade 1 students improves as well (Kinnunen et al., 1998). Skilled decoding goes far in promoting skilled reading.

Using Semantic Context Cues To Understand Word Meanings

Relying on semantic context cues (e.g., pictures, overall meaning of a text) as primary in word recognition is a mistake. Good readers rely on the letters of a word and word parts to recognize a word! Once the word is recognized, it is important for readers to use picture and semantic context cues to determine the meaning of the decoded word, however. In English, as in most languages, most words have multiple meanings. The only way to know which one applies when a word is sounded out is to pay attention to context cues (Gough, 1983, 1984; Isakson & Miller, 1976). Thus, when a good reader reads "I'll stamp at the post office," she or he gets a mental image of someone placing postage stamps on letters rather than an image of a person stamping feet in a public place. Such a good reader would get a very different image for the sentence "I'll stamp at the pep rally." Context determines the meaning of particular words. This is the reason that many approaches aimed at the improvement of beginning reading, such as Reading Recovery, teach students to pay attention to whether the word that has been sounded out makes sense in the context being read (Clay, 1991). An important component in balanced comprehension instruction is teaching students to pay attention to semantic context cues to help understand what they read, including making decisions about the particular meaning of a word intended by the author of a text. Though we must stress, that good readers use context cues as a cross-checking mechanism as they read, while poor readers too often use context cues as an initial strategy when encountering words they do not know while reading. Thus, context cues are used differently by good and poor readers, with good readers using context cues effectively.

Vocabulary

There has been some debate about whether it makes sense to teach vocabulary explicitly, although there is a very clear and positive association between the extent of a reader's vocabulary and his or her comprehension skills (e.g., Anderson & Freebody, 1981; Blachowicz & Fisher, 2000; Elleman et al. 2009; Nagy et al., 1987). The main argument against teaching vocabulary is that the task is overwhelming. That is, a good reader knows more than 100,000 words, and there is no way so many words can be taught (Nagy & Anderson, 1984). Recall from Chapter 7, however, that by the end of high school a student should be expected to know only about 15,000 root words, which certainly is a more manageable number than 100,000 words (i.e., many of the remaining 85,000 are derived from the root words; e.g., Biemiller & Slonim, 2001; d'Anna et al., 1991; Swanborn & DeGlopper, 1999). Another concern is that, because children often do not understand the meaning of words fully from exposure to their formal definitions in the dictionary (Chapter 7), much of their meaning can be acquired only by encountering words in rich contexts (Miller & Gildea, 1987).

Those holding the view that explicit teaching of vocabulary is futile take comfort in the fact that humans seem to have considerable capacity to acquire vocabulary incidentally (i.e., from encountering words in speech and reading; Nagy & Scott, 2000; Sternberg, 1987; also see Chapter 7). Leaving vocabulary development to incidental learning, however, is leaving much to chance. When readers encounter a new word in the text, often they do not infer its meaning correctly (Miller & Gildea, 1987; again, see Chapter 7). For example, Harmon (1998) observed that the fourth graders in his study were about as likely to infer a word's meaning from the context as to make an *incorrect* inference. At best, learning vocabulary meanings from text encounters is a slow and uncertain process for elementary students (Schwanenflugel et al., 1997). This is because inferring word meanings from context depends on extensive knowledge of language as well as understanding of the situation being described in the text and coordination of a number of strategies (Harmon, 1998; Nagy & Scott, 2000). Such a result also depends on prior knowledge, for children who know a lot about a topic are more likely than less knowledgeable children to infer the meaning of unfamiliar words related to the topic when they are encountered in context (Carlisle et al., 2000). As always, the rich are more likely to get richer!

The main reason to teach vocabulary to children, however, is that when children are taught vocabulary their comprehension does increase, at least of passages containing the taught words (e.g., Beck et al., 1982; Elleman et al., 2009; McKeown et al., 1983, 1985). Hence, we emphasize in this volume that a comprehension development program should include the teaching of the words that students most need to know. An adequate vocabulary is only some of the knowledge a young reader needs, however.

World Knowledge

During the late 1970s and early 1980s, a group spearheaded research on the criticality of background knowledge to reading comprehension (e.g.,

Anderson & Pearson, 1984). Specifically, they found that what readers knew about the topic of a text before reading it very much influenced the messages they took away from reading that text. An important hypothesis emerging from this work is that students' reading comprehension can be improved by developing their world knowledge (Hirsch, 1987).

Hirsch and his associates have developed an entire elementary curriculum based on their conception of core knowledge, with the curriculum specifying knowledge that should be acquired in each of the elementary grades. Although the evaluations of it are not as complete or analytical as we would like, in initial evaluations the core knowledge approach has been boosting language arts performance in schools where it has been tried (Datnow et al., 2000). Of course, if we go back to the Center for the Study of Reading theory and data, it makes a great deal of sense that developing world knowledge should increase comprehension. From this perspective, teachers should be doing everything possible to make certain that students not only read extensively, but also read material filled with worthwhile information.

Beyond having world knowledge, students need to be taught to use the knowledge they possess as they try to make sense of newly encountered texts. One of the really important findings produced by reading researchers in recent years is that skilled thinkers often do not make inferences unless understanding of the text demands them (McKoon & Ratcliff, 1992). That is, when reading a text, good readers typically make prior-knowledge-based inferences only when they are absolutely required to understand the ideas in the text. Another important discovery in the past three decades, however, is that if readers are encouraged to relate what they already know about a topic to a new reading about that topic, their understanding and memory of the text can improve dramatically.

In particular, one way to encourage readers to relate their world knowledge to what they read is to teach them to ask "why" questions as they go through a text. That is, fact-filled text can be rendered much more memorable by encouraging students to ask themselves why the facts in the text make sense. Wood et al. (1990, Experiment 2) provided a clear demonstration that children in grades 4–8 can benefit from asking themselves "why" questions about facts presented in a connected text. The children studied in Wood et al. (1990, Experiment 2) were asked to learn elementary science content pertaining to different types of animals. For each animal, they read a paragraph specifying the physical characteristics of the animal's home as well as its diet, sleeping habits, preferred habitat, and predators. Some students were instructed to ask themselves why each fact in the text made sense (e.g., for the facts related to skunks, "Why do skunks eat corn?"; "Why do owls prey on skunks?"; "Why is the skunk away from 3 A.M. until dawn?") and to attempt to answer such "why" questions based on prior knowledge as they read. These students remembered much more of what was presented in the text than did control students, who read and studied the text as they normally would.

Such "why" questioning produces large effects on learning and can be used profitably by elementary and middle school students to learn material in factually dense text (Pressley, Wood, et al., 1992). It does so by orienting readers to prior knowledge that can render the facts in a text more sensible, and hence more comprehensible and memorable (Martin & Pressley, 1991). We think it is worthwhile to teach students to get in the habit of trying to figure out why new ideas presented in a text make sense.

Although relating one's prior knowledge to the ideas in a text can increase comprehension, it also has the potential sometimes to undermine comprehension. In fact, one of the ways that weak readers undermine their comprehension is by relating prior knowledge to texts they are reading that is not directly relevant to the most important ideas in the text, making unwarranted and unnecessary inferences as they do so (e.g., Williams, 1993, 2002).

Several studies (Williams, 2002, 2003) have preliminary data about a teaching approach intended to encourage readers with learning disabilities to relate relevant prior knowledge to what they read. The students experience a series of lessons involving activities that make salient that attending to the ideas actually presented in a text is what reading for understanding is about. During each lesson, there is a discussion about a text that will be read during the session, with the teacher talking extensively with the students about the theme of the upcoming story and the importance of the theme in understanding a story. Then, the teacher and students read the story aloud, with the teacher asking questions during the reading intended to orient the students to the thematic ideas of the story. These are questions requiring students to use their prior knowledge—for example, to make predictions about what is going to happen next in a story and to explain the basis for those predictions. After reading the story, there is a discussion involving five main questions, each of which requires processing of the main ideas in the story that was read: Who is the main character? What did he or she do? What happened? Was this good or bad? Why was this good or bad? The students learn to state the main theme of a story in a standard form: "The (main character) should (should not) have _____."
For example, "Goldilocks should not have made herself so much at home in the bears' house." Students are then asked to think about when the theme of the story would apply, answering these questions: "To whom would this theme apply?" and "When would it apply?" Students with learning disabilities do, in fact, orient more to the big ideas of stories after experiencing this training, using appropriate prior knowledge to understand what they are reading, with some evidence that this type of training can be effective with

at-risk students as early as grades 2 and 3 (Wilder & Williams, 2001; Williams et al., 2002). In summary, it makes sense to do everything possible to encourage students to develop worthwhile world knowledge through reading and other experiences.

Contemporary core reading series typically include stories and expository texts that are chosen to include material that is worthwhile for the child to read, reflecting the understanding that an important shortcoming of the old-style *Dick and Jane* approach is that the stories did not expose children to information they could subsequently use to understand other texts and situations that might be encountered. Having knowledge is one thing; using it is another. We always tell audiences that, if they are considering a reading series, look at the themes for the units and the readings within units. If the themes are not about important literary topics, science, social studies, or values, reject the series categorically. With more and more of the elementary school day being ceded to language arts, it is more essential now than ever that language arts thematic units cover important content.

That readers often do not relate what they are reading to what they already know has prompted research about how to encourage more extensive use of prior knowledge by young readers. One way of doing so is to encourage readers to be asking themselves why the ideas in a text are sensible and to figure out why what is being presented in that text makes sense based on what the reader already knows. With children who have learning disabilities, more complete instruction might be necessary, such as the teaching devised by Williams (2002, 2003), which involves a teacher modeling, explaining, and supporting orientation to the major thematic messages in texts. Such instruction demands that readers make predictions as they read, with predicting always requiring that readers relate what they have encountered in the text with what they already know in order to gauge what might happen next in the reading.

Processing Diverse Texts

Elementary reading instruction is filled with the disproportionate reading of stories, relative to other types of text. For example, Duke (2000a, 2000b) found first-grade instruction flooded with narratives, with only 3.6 minutes per day of exposure to informational texts on average and half that amount in schools serving students from low-income families! In contrast, balanced reading instruction should involve substantial exposure to a variety of texts. Because so much of secondary content reading is expository, it makes sense to make certain that elementary students practice comprehension strategies with nonfiction informational texts (Almasi & Fullerton, 2013; Ogle & Blachowicz, 2002). The number of texts now available on the internet allows for students to access a variety of text within seconds. At a minimum, elementary school students need to have practice working with such texts, although much research is required before the unique comprehension demands of such electric texts are understood (Chiong et al., 2012; Spires & Estes, 2002).

Diverse Text Tasks

The prototypical text task for elementary students is to read a selection so that they can answer questions about it. Sometimes the questions are printed after the text and require a written response. Sometimes teachers ask the questions. Balanced comprehension instruction is going to include asking students to do more than answer questions after reading. There are many other ways to assess comprehension, including ones that require readers to use the ideas encountered in text (e.g., "Write an essay integrating ideas in the text"; Flower et al., 1990). Balanced comprehension instruction will include teaching students how to find information they want in a text (Dreher, 2002; Reynolds & Symons, 2001; Symons et al., 2001) and using that information once found.

Reader-response theory (Rosenblatt, 1978) had made us very much aware that people read not simply to be informed, but also for enjoyment. Good readers often respond affectively to texts (Pressley & Afflerbach, 1995). A strength of the transactional strategies instructional approach favored in this chapter is that teachers do model their affective responses to what they read, and students share with one another their interpretations and responses to texts. Balanced reading instruction should be aimed at developing not only readers who learn from a text, but readers who interpret and respond to the messages in that text. Good readers must learn how to do diverse things with text and react in diverse ways.

Summary

Balanced reading comprehension instruction involves multiple components, as does all balanced reading instruction. Students' word-level processes must be honed, with word recognition developed to the point of fluency and development of extensive vocabulary.

Extensive reading of worthwhile books is a critical part of balanced reading instruction (e.g., Guthrie et al., 1999). Extensive reading is not a common feature in the lives of children today. A typical third-grade reading lesson allocates less than a quarter of a daily 90-minute reading period to actually reading (Hiebert & Martin, 2009b). Our point here is that currently schools are not typically a site where children read extensively. Given the power of simply expanding the amount of time a child engages in reading is a simple but powerful condition for enhancing reading achievement (Allington, 2014). Consider that, while 90 minutes daily is allocated to reading instruction in most elementary classrooms, American children spend only 15 minutes of that 90-minute period engaged in reading. While 15 minutes is better than 5 or 10 minutes of reading activity, few adults would consider 15 minutes a day sufficient reading activity to foster higher levels of achievement. From our perspective, and from the research evidence available, 60 to 75 minutes of actual reading each day could be considered sufficient. But that would entail teachers deciding to ignore large segments of the daily lesson plan found in commercial reading programs. The first activity we would recommend be scuttled are the workbook pages that accompany all commercial programs. Producing workbook pages is an inexpensive activity, but workbooks produce huge profits for the companies that purchase a basal reader series. Thus, we do not believe that we will live to see the day when children are not assigned to waste a lot of time completing workbook pages. We say "wasting time" because the only evidence on the role that time spent on workbook activities has on reading achievement is evidence that most of the time currently allocated to workbook page completion could and should be eliminated so as to create time for children to experience extensive reading activity.

Wide reading works as well or better than repeated reading in fostering oral reading fluency (Kuhn, 2005) and promotes growth of vocabulary and other world knowledge. Readers are most likely to get the most out of the good stuff if they use sophisticated comprehension strategies as they read. A main message of this chapter is that such comprehension strategies can be taught, with the new twist in this section being that one strategy that should be included in the mix is relating what is being read to prior knowledge.

Often, reading educators do not worry much about comprehension in kindergarten and grade 1, focusing instead on word recognition. Balanced comprehension instruction can and should begin in the early primary years (Duke et al., 2011; Pressley, El-Dinary, et al., 1992), with development of word recognition skills as part of the comprehension instructional balance. That many college students do not use the most sophisticated of comprehension strategies (e.g., Cordón & Day, 1996), however, makes obvious the reality that there needs to be much thinking about how comprehension instruction can be more universal and more effective elementary schools.

We very much believe that educating teachers about the nature of reading comprehension is critical if better comprehension instruction is to occur in schools, and hence the next section is concerned with an important hypothesis about how to jump-start the teaching of comprehension in elementary schools, one that begins with professional development of the teachers themselves.

MOSAIC OF THOUGHT AND TEACHERS REFLECTING ON THEIR OWN COMPREHENSION

Ellin O. Keene and Susan Zimmermann (1997) in their book, *Mosaic of Thought: Teaching Comprehension in a Reader's Workshop*, took an interesting perspective. They felt that an important first step to being a good teacher of comprehension strategies is to become a user of comprehension strategies! They argued that teachers benefit from learning about comprehension strategies and attempting to use the strategies in their own reading. In particular, by using comprehension strategies, the teachers come to understand the positive effects of using comprehension strategies.

We think that this is an important insight because teachers often resist teaching comprehension strategies. A particularly illuminating analysis was provided by Pamela Beard El-Dinary in her dissertation study (Pressley & El-Dinary, 1997). She studied seven teachers as they attempted to become transactional-strategies instruction teachers over the course of a school year. What became apparent early in the year was that learning to be a strategies instruction teacher was very challenging. For example, some of the teachers felt that transactional-strategies instruction conflicted with their own beliefs about reading and the teaching of reading. Some felt that it conflicted with the whole-language methods they learned in their teacher education courses (i.e., strategies instruction seemed too teacher directed). Some teachers felt that comprehension strategies instruction and use of comprehension strategies during reading-group sessions took too much time, with the result that students were not reading nearly as many books and stories in reading groups. Also, there were teachers who had problems with the many interpretations emanating from reading-group discussions that were strategies-driven: Some permitted any interpretation that emerged, regardless of whether it seemed consistent with the reading, and others seemed uncomfortable with anything except standard interpretations. By the end of the year of observations, only two of the seven teachers were committed comprehension strategies instruction teachers. Pressley and El-Dinary's (1997) work made clear that comprehension strategies instruction, or at least the transactional-strategies instructional approach, is not for every teacher.

In a similar vein, Kucan et al. (2011) noted that two-thirds of the teachers they studied did not have sufficient expertise to manage an effective classroom discussion. They involved 60 upper elementary–grade teachers (fourth and fifth grade) who were assessed on their specialized knowledge for fostering reading comprehension particularly through discussion as well as their analysis of passages and which structural features of the passage would likely pose problems for students.

They found that only one-third of teachers could engage in the integration and inferencing required to provide coherent statements about the most important ideas in the texts. Only 15% "were able to specify the possible difficulties posed by the texts at a useful level of detail" (p. 71). The teachers' responses to questions focused on responding to student queries indicated that few had developed any repertoire of responses that actually addressed the problem posed.

It is obvious to us, based on more recent work, that learning to be a comprehension strategies instruction teacher is painfully difficult for many teachers. Hilden and Pressley (2007) studied two middle school groups as teachers attempted to improve their reading comprehension instruction through professional development (monthly or more frequent meetings, book groups, and coaching by staff members). While many teachers improved their instruction over the course of a year, each teacher had a set of challenges. For example, some struggled with classroom management issues when working with small groups that they had not previously faced when teaching whole-class lessons. Also, many of the teachers had to radically change the way they thought about reading comprehension before they could even begin to teach it differently! That is, comprehension strategies instruction was difficult for some teachers to understand, as it was very different from anything they had taught previously.

Many teachers were not confident that they could teach comprehension strategies. These teachers often worried that they would fail and had difficulty seeing how the approach would fit with the rest of the curriculum. In contrast, some teachers dropped out of the professional development program within the first month at one site because they felt that they already knew enough about how to teach reading comprehension effectively in their classrooms, even though observations of their teaching did not confirm this confidence. Finally, some teachers saw the students as a challenge. At one of the middle schools, the teachers complained that their students thought the goal of reading was only to read fast rather than to understand and appreciate a piece of literature, whereas other teachers feared that their weaker students would not be able to carry out the strategies. However daunting these challenges, many of the teachers felt that the goal of improving comprehension instruction was well worth their time, effort, and thought. We note that other researchers have also reported considerable challenges in coaching teachers to undertake competent and confident teaching of comprehension strategies (e.g., Deshler & Schumaker, 1993; Klingner et al., 1999, 2004; Pressley & El-Dinary, 1997). As Dewitz and Graves (2021) stated, "For teachers to learn how to skillfully and appropriately model strategies, scaffold students' efforts, and release responsibility requires years of experience" (p. S137), and we could not agree more. Becoming a highly effective teacher who can implement research-based strategies takes time and practice.

Since the first edition of this volume, several other valuable resources for teachers who wish to improve their comprehension instruction have appeared. Miller's *Reading with Meaning: Teaching Comprehension in the Primary Grades* (2013), Blachowicz and Ogle's *Reading Comprehension: Strategies for Independent Learners* (2008), Nichols's *Comprehension through Conversation: The Power of Purposeful Talk in the Reading Workshop* (2007), and Tovani's *I Read It, but I Don't Get It: Comprehension Strategies for Adolescent Readers* (2000). More recently, Duke et al. (2021) released science based comprehension practices, which includes a layered model for comprehension instruction. All deserve serious study by any teacher who wants to teach comprehension strategies.

As we recommend such resources, we also point out that the effective strategies instruction that has been validated (and reviewed in this chapter) is pretty simple—direct teacher explanations and modeling followed by scaffolding of a few strategies. Such instruction typically has not included all the bells and whistles showing up in the many how-to-do-comprehension-strategies-instruction manuals entering the marketplace, bells and whistles inferred from teacher experiences by the authors of these manuals. Our predilection is for teachers to try the simple version and look to these volumes for suggestions very selectively—remembering always that comprehension strategies instruction is about students using strategies on their own, not about the completion of worksheets or worksheet proxies of any kind (e.g., written reports of predictions, images, questions, clarifications, summaries occurring during reading). Such proxies fill these manuals! Make your comprehension instruction about students practicing the strategies as mental processes, modeling for other students as they do so, talking together about the strategies being used during actual reading.

WHAT SHOULD STUDENTS BE READING?

We have little doubt about what students should be reading. Beginning reading students should be reading real literature and informational texts, along with some decodable texts in the earliest stages of reading acquisition. Whenever we visit classrooms where achievement is clearly high, the students often are reading authentic books consistent with the meaning-emphasis perspective that literature-based instruction is best (Morrow & Gambrell, 2000, 2001). Nonetheless, many schools still use commercial core reading programs, but today's core programs are filled with excerpts drawn from real literature and informational readings.

These core resources also come with decodable books. Indeed, it is very hard to be in a primary-grade classroom where students are not reading a mix of trade books, basals, and decodables, with the decodables rather quickly fading into the background as students become better at recognizing words.

We note especially that some contemporary primary classrooms have bins and bins of books that are rated using a scheme from Reading Recovery or another text-leveling system. Good teachers everywhere are encouraging students to move through the bins to progressively more complex books. What an absolutely great way to assure that all the children in a primary classroom are reading within their own zone of proximal development!

The various types of books that can be included in the primary-level classroom are inspiring new debates (Hiebert & Martin, 2001), however. For example, how many times must a child encounter a word in order to learn it as a sight word? Assuming that the answer is somewhere between five and 50, doesn't that mean that the child should be reading quite a few books filled with repeated words—quite a few leveled books? Does it make sense to ask a child to read a book containing words that include sounds not already covered during systematic phonics instruction—a trade book? That said, there are reasons for concern about reading so many decodables (Adams, 2009). If the child came away with little worthwhile world knowledge from reading about Dick and Jane's neighborhood, think about the little bit of knowledge that follows from reading about how "Pat and Mat sat on a fat cat" and about why "Ted's bed is red." So, there is a probable downside. In addition, since the goal is reading real books—not decodables—shouldn't students be spending time working on decoding words in real texts?

Although we agree with others (Hiebert & Martin, 2001, 2009a) who believe that there is a need for a great deal of research on the consequences of various mixes of text types, we have been impressed that the best controlled test to date of the effects of reading decodables versus other types of texts on young children's reading found no difference in reading outcomes as a function of the type of text read (Jenkins et al., 2004). Their finding of no significant differences in the reading achievement of students who read decodables as compared with students who read predictable texts mirrors the findings of Juel and Roper-Schneider (1985), who also reported no significant end-of-year differences on two reading assessments between students using decodable texts and students who did not have access to decodable texts. Reading of both real literature and not-so-real literature (Hiebert & Martin, 2001, 2009a) is an American tradition, regardless of the supposed reading program emphasis. We expect primary students to continue to read a mix of book types for the foreseeable future.

Volume of Reading

As noted, classrooms with bins and bins of books for students to read is great for several reasons when it comes to reading comprehension. It can also encourage students to read more. For many years, the practice of sustained silent reading was incorporated into elementary classrooms as a way to increase the volume of reading and provide teachers an opportunity to work with individual or groups of students. This approach, however, lacked empirical evidence for supporting reading achievement (Stahl, 2004). To improve on this approach, Reutzel et al. (2008) developed scaffolded silent reading, which they found to have similar effects as guided oral reading instruction. To help teachers monitor student progress, scaffolded silent reading provides teachers time to meet with individual students while promoting reading with the whole class. Scaffolded silent reading includes teacher instruction in strategies to select books and individual reading conferences with students. Students learn strategies to select from a wide variety of book genres for their reading level. During individual conferences, students read aloud, answer questions about the text, and set goals for the text (Reutzel et al., 2008).

Student reading does not have to be limited to just within the classroom. Several studies have found positive effects on reading comprehension promoting summer reading activities (e.g., Allington, 2014; Allington & McGill-Franzen, 2021). In these cases, students were simply given the opportunity to attend a book fair and there to self-select a number of books they wanted to read (McGill-Franzen et al., 2020). The children in the control group had no such opportunities. After three consecutive summer book summers, the books group read almost a year better than the children in the no summer books group. The reading achievement gains of the summer books children matched or exceeded the gains of children enrolled in summer school programs. Additionally, summer reading programs such as *Freedom Schools* have seen positive results with reading scores for students coming from high poverty areas (Mesa et al., 2021; Watson, 2014).

SUMMARY AND IMPLICATIONS

1. Similar to the primary grades, instruction in the fourth and fifth grades involves a balancing of skills instruction and more authentic reading and writing. Although there are many commonalities across fourth- and fifth-grade classrooms, there are also many optional emphases, with each classroom seeming to have a core of practices that define its emphasis. More recently, instruction is driven by reading programs and state standards. Requirements may bind teachers to these, but it is important for teachers to bring in other texts and implement balanced instruction to promote comprehension of read texts (Table 8.2).

TABLE 8.2. Classroom Application of Comprehension Strategies

Comprehension strategy	What the strategy looks like in the classroom
Reciprocal teaching	• Ask students to make predictions before reading, ask questions about the text, seek clarification through rereading when confused, and summarize what they read.
Discussion	• Pose questions to students to begin discussion of the text, but then allow students to ask meaningful questions and bring up issues that would help them understand the text. • Teachers can also allow for peer-led discussions between pairs or small groups of students. This can also allow for students to collaborate to discover meanings of texts. • Collaborative reasoning: Within small groups, students analyze a controversial issue raised by the author. Teachers can model, prompt, and encourage students to use the text to support arguments. Teachers can help students develop counterarguments based on information in the text. • Encourage students to elaborate on responses and process the content further (e.g., ask students if images came to mind while reading or connect to prior knowledge). • With all discussions, teachers must go beyond surface-level questions and develop higher level cognitive questions. Teachers must be prepared to offer specific support when needed or scaffold students to focus on content rather than tangential ideas.
Semantic mapping	• Early in instruction, teachers can introduce and model for students how to develop an outline of the major ideas in each text, which includes information about causes and effects coded in the text, order of events, comparative and contrasting information, and simple descriptions. Remember that each semantic map will be different because it reflects each student's reaction to the text.
Independent and guided reading	• Encourage students to activate prior knowledge. • Predict what will happen in the text before reading. • Seek clarification when confused. • Look for patterns and principles of arguments presented in the text. • Analyze decision making that occurs during text processing. • Use backward reasoning and/or visualization to identify student misconceptions about the text. • Summarize the text. • Discuss student interpretations of texts in groups.
Choral, echo, and partner reading	• Using the same text, the teacher reads the text on day 1, has students repeat reading after teacher on day 2, and has students read text with a partner on day 3. The teacher will scaffold, pose questions, and have students summarize text on each day.
Semantic context	• Once students recognize the word, students can use the context and pictures as clues to determine word meaning.
Teach important vocabulary	• Before reading a text, teachers can select important words students must know before reading the text. This would include words that students will see across multiple text, but not used often in spoken language, and technical vocabulary that is content specific. • Before reading, teachers can discuss the meaning of each word by discussing parts of the word, definition, and context within the text with students.

(continued)

TABLE 8.2. (*continued*)

Comprehension strategy	What the strategy looks like in the classroom
"Why" questions	• Teach students to ask "why" when reading a nonfiction text.
Scaffolded silent reading	• Teachers teach students strategies for selecting books from a variety of genres. Teachers can meet with students individually to discuss books, pose questions, and set goals.

2. Although development of comprehension ability is a widely agreed-upon goal of literacy instruction, it rarely is offered as systematically as it could be in the elementary grades. This is especially striking in the early 21st century, given the many different lines of evidence that support the teaching of comprehension strategies to elementary students. Parallel to this lack of powerful comprehension strategies instruction is the finding that commercial core reading programs provide little advice to teachers of students that reflects much of what research has confirmed is effective comprehension instruction.

3. Reciprocal teaching is perhaps the best known of the comprehension-instructional efforts developed and evaluated by researchers. This approach consists of students learning to use predicting, questioning, seeking clarification, and summarization by working in small groups, with the members of the group taking turns leading the group through the strategic processes. We think reciprocal teaching was an important first step in teaching students a repertoire of comprehension strategies, but it was no more than that, as more flexible long-term teaching has now been developed and validated by educators and researchers.

4. Transactional-strategies instruction begins with teacher explanations and modeling of strategies, modeling think-aloud, and with scaffolded student practice in strategies application following over a long period of time. To date, the consistently positive effects of transactional-strategies instruction demonstrated in validations are consistent with the interpretation that such instruction is producing such internalization. The record of the positive effects of transactional-strategies instruction on standardized tests in well-controlled studies is quite striking, but so are other qualitative benefits produced by such instruction.

5. Much of the practice takes place in small reading groups, which involve a great deal of student conversations, rich in student reports of how they are applying strategies in their interpretations of texts being read by the group. Long-term participation in such groups is intended to

produce internalization of the strategic processes. The most common strategies included are (a) predicting, (b) questioning, (c) constructing mental images representing text content, (d) seeking clarifications, (e) responding to the text based on prior knowledge, (f) summarizing, and (g) interpreting. Young readers who participate in such instruction are being taught to use the comprehension processes reported by exceptionally skilled readers.

6. Balanced reading instruction is also balanced comprehension instruction. It involves the development of word recognition skills, vocabulary, world knowledge (e.g., through extensive reading), and the teaching of comprehension strategies—including strategies that encourage use of prior knowledge, the reading of diverse types of text, and diverse tasks. Although those interested in comprehension have focused more on comprehension strategies instruction than on other ways of developing comprehension competence, good comprehension instruction is much, much more than the teaching of comprehension strategies. There is much more that can be done to increase students' comprehension than what many teachers are now doing.

7. An interesting contemporary hypothesis is that an important first step in becoming a good teacher of comprehension is to become a good comprehender by learning to use the strategies that good comprehenders use. Thus, teachers need to practice what they teach to students and understand that mastery takes time, it is not a skill learned overnight.

8. Young children read diverse text types as part of beginning reading instruction, typically a mix of real literature, predictable texts, and decodables. This is a good thing. Reading lots of texts across the school years is also a necessary goal. Additionally, increasing student reading in an out-of-school environment can also support comprehension. Within the classroom, teachers can scaffold student reading by incorporating scaffolded silent reading or scaffolding student reading of books based on student interest. Outside of the classroom, summer reading programs have shown success for fostering student comprehension. However, too few schools have the resources (books) needed to ensure all children have easy access to books they want to read.

9. Few classrooms provide students with opportunities to engage in either teacher-led or peer-led discussions. Teachers can incorporate a variety of discussion approaches, including having students question the author's purpose, posing questions through inquiry learning, and having student-led discussions through instructional conversations and Socratic seminars. Given the evidence of the potential for discussion to foster the development of student reading comprehension, we would expect a greater emphasis on managing discussion in teacher education programs. We call for more emphasis because we have evidence that far too many teachers are truly unskilled in developing and managing discussion in their classrooms.

CONCLUDING REFLECTIONS

We have spent a great deal of time in elementary classrooms during the past 30 years. Most classrooms we have seen have included a great deal of teacher direction and student passivity. There is very little teaching of students to be self-regulated comprehenders. There is a great deal of worksheet doing and a great deal of responding to low-level literal questions about the story that was read, the implicit theory being that if children do enough worksheets and answer enough questions they will become skilled comprehenders. The problem remains, as Durkin (1978–1979) described it, that there is much emphasis on assessment and a bit of mentioning of comprehension skills but almost a total absence of effective comprehension instruction and classroom discussions. Perhaps relatedly, as Dewitz and colleagues (2009) report, current core reading curriculum materials reflect little of what we know about effective comprehension development.

Good comprehension is not just word-level processing. It involves abstracting the big ideas in a text—the "macrostructure" (Kintsch & van Dijk, 1978). Sometimes good readers construct images capturing the big ideas expressed in a text as well as the critical details. The ideas expressed in the text are understood in terms of and related to prior knowledge by the skilled reader. There is no reason to believe that elementary students naturally discover that they should use such processes to understand a text. Indeed, quite the contrary: There is substantial evidence that many students can make it to college without learning the active comprehension processes used by skilled readers (Pressley & Afflerbach, 1995). More positively, there is substantial evidence that elementary students can learn to comprehend actively: They can learn to predict, question, make mental images, seek to clarify confusions, and summarize as they read.

There is a real excitement in classes in which comprehension processing is being taught. By the end of the year, small groups of children will be using the strategies while they do paired reading. When individual children retell stories they have read, it is not just a spitting back of information in the text; rather, it is interpretive, reflecting the cognitive activity that occurred during reading.

Why is such instruction not more common? For one thing, many teachers do not understand comprehension as active reading—nor as active predicting, questioning, imagining, seeking clarifications, summarizing, and interpreting. One of the most interesting reflections that we have heard again and again from teachers who have become teachers of comprehension strategies is that they did not really know how to read actively until they learned about the comprehension strategies model and began to teach students to use such comprehension strategies.

Another reason that this form of teaching is not more common is that it leads to classroom interactions that are very different from the norm.

In typical classrooms, teachers control most interactions, asking questions that students then answer. The goal with comprehension strategies instruction, however, is to teach students to take over their own reading and thinking. When teachers and students read texts together, the teacher is not asking questions but rather participating in a real conversation. The students make predictions, talk about the questions that occur to them as they read, report the images they get during reading, discuss parts of the text that are hard to understand, and generate interpretations, including summary interpretations. After the early stages of comprehension strategies instruction—that is, after the teacher is no longer introducing the strategies—the teacher's role in the conversation is limited to prompting students to be active in deciding how they might process the text at this point. Throughout classroom life, the teacher is also supposed to model strategies use to make clear to students how the comprehension strategies the students are learning can be usefully adapted across many different types of reading. Such mental modeling is not always easy for many teachers (e.g., Hilden & Pressley, 2007; Pressley & El-Dinary, 1997).

A final reason that comprehension strategies teaching is not more widespread is that constructivist educators send the message that processes that are taught rather than discovered are not natural strategies. Our reply is that the explanations and mental modeling the teacher provides are just a starting point, and that students actively discover much about the usefulness and adaptability of comprehension strategies as they attempt to use them. From our perspective, good teaching is constructivist in that it sets students to exploring in productive directions. As students in transactional strategies instruction classrooms use strategies together, there is plenty of constructive discovery going on (Pressley, Harris, et al., 1992). Long-term strategies use seems to result in individual students internalizing active cognitive processing during reading; the proof in the pudding is better reading when measured in a number of ways across studies. There is much to be said for encouraging many more teachers to define their elementary classrooms as ones in which students learn to use comprehension strategies constructively, practicing them with other students with the many types of reading that can be encountered in the elementary curriculum.

Despite the reluctance of many educators explicitly to teach strategies, researchers continue to explore the value of teaching strategies to students, with, for example, basic research efforts to understand the benefits of teaching young children to construct mental images as they process text (Glenberg et al., 2004). In addition, given that, with increasing age during the elementary years, there is increasing emphasis on learning from informational texts, it is heartening that there are renewed efforts to determine how to teach students to get the most out of informational texts (Cervetti ct al., 2012; Meyer et al., 2002). In particular, Meyer is exploring how to teach students to analyze expository text over the web, a potentially important direction in figuring out how to teach students to do something we have known to be powerful for some time—that is, to use graphic organizers to organize information in an exposition, to pay attention to sequences of events, to make comparisons, to isolate causes and effects, and to analyze problem-and-solution approaches (see, e.g., Almasi & Fullerton, 2013, chap. 5).

Cervetti et al. (2012) evaluated the efficacy of a curriculum-based approach to science-literacy integration that engaged students in reading text, writing notes and reports, conducting firsthand investigations, and discussing key concepts and processes in comparison with a "business-as-usual" approach in 94 fourth-grade classrooms. Results indicated promising, occasionally robust, trends in science and literacy outcomes. In short, researchers are turning their attention to ever more powerful ways to teach the basic comprehension processes, and that probably will permit more powerful insights in the near future about how to teach students to use comprehension strategies more completely.

At this point in the lecture that inspired this book, Michael Pressley would always ask the audience to think back to the expert reading described in Chapter 2 and ask them, "Isn't that what you want for your students?" He would continue:

"If you start to teach your students to read that way, something wonderful is going to happen to you. You are going to become a more active reader yourself. But there's more! As you read great stories and books with your students, you are going to experience myriad student responses that you never dreamed possible. If you do not believe it, read an article by Rachel Brown and Lynn Coy-Ogan (1993) that discusses the differing interpretations of Maurice Sendak's *Where the Wild Things Are* (1963) offered by three different groups of students in Lynn's classes. Your classroom is going to become more interesting for everyone in it, including you."

REFERENCES

Adams, M. J. (1990). *Beginning to read*. Harvard University Press.

Adams, M. J. (2009). Decodable text: Why, when, and how? In E. H. Hiebert (Ed.), *Finding the right texts: What works for beginning and struggling readers* (pp. 23–46). Guilford Press.

Allington, R. L. (2002). What I've learned about effective reading instruction from a decade of studying exemplary elementary classroom teachers. *Phi Delta Kappan*, 83(10), 740–747.

Allington, R. L. (2014) How reading volume affects both reading fluency and reading achievement. *International Electronic Journal of Elementary Education*, 7(1), 13–26.

Allington, R. L., & Johnston, P. H. (Eds.). (2002). *Reading to learn: Lessons from exemplary 4th grade classrooms*. Guilford Press.

Allington, R. L., & McGill-Franzen, A. M. (2021). Reading volume and reading achievement: A review of recent research. *Reading Research Quarterly*, 56(S1), S231–S238.

Almasi, J. F., & Fullerton, S. K. (2013). *Teaching strategic processes in reading* (2nd ed.). Guilford Press.

Almasi, J. F., & Gambrell, L. B. (1994). *Sociocognitive conflict in peer-led and teacher-led discussions of literature* (Reading Research Report No. 12). National Reading Research Center.

Almasi, J. F., & Garas-York, K. (2009). Comprehension and peer discussion. In S. Israel & G. G. Duffy (Eds.), *Handbook of research on reading comprehension* (pp. 470–493). Erlbaum.

Almasi, J. F., O'Flahavan, J. F., & Arya, P. (2001). A comprehensive analysis of student and teacher development in more and less proficient discussions of literature. *Reading Research Quarterly, 36,* 96–121.

Almasi, J. F., Palmer, B. M., Madden, A., & Hart, S. (2011). Interventions to enhance narrative comprehension. In A. McGill-Franzen & R. L. Allington (Eds.), *Handbook of reading disability research* (pp. 329–344). Routledge.

Anderson, R. C., & Freebody, P. (1981). Vocabulary knowledge. In J. T. Guthrie (Ed.), *Comprehension and teaching: Research reviews* (pp. 77–117). International Reading Association.

Anderson, R. C., & Hidde, J. L. (1971). Imagery and sentence learning. *Journal of Educational Psychology, 62,* 526–530.

Anderson, R. C., & Pearson, P. D. (1984). A schema-theoretic view of basic processes in reading. In P. D. Pearson, R. Barr, M. Kamil, & P. Mosenthal (Eds.), *Handbook of reading research* (pp. 255–291). Longman.

Anderson, V. (1992). A teacher development project in transactional strategy instruction for teachers of severely reading-disabled adolescents. *Teaching and Teacher Education, 8,* 391–403.

Anderson, V., & Roit, M. (1993). Planning and implementing collaborative strategy instruction for delayed readers in grades 6–10. *Elementary School Journal, 94,* 121–137.

Applebee, A. N., Langer, J. A., Nystrand, M., & Gamoran, A. (2003). Discussion-based approaches to developing understanding: Classroom instruction and student performance in middle and high school English. *American Educational Research Journal, 40,* 685–730.

Beach, R., & Hynds, S. (1991). Research on response to literature. In R. Barr, M. L. Kamil, P. Mosenthal, & P. D. Pearson (Eds.), *Handbook of reading research* (Vol. 2, pp. 453–489). Longman.

Beck, I. L., Perfetti, C. A., & McKeown, M. G. (1982). Effects of long-term vocabulary instruction on lexical access and reading comprehension. *Journal of Educational Psychology, 74,* 506–521.

Bell, R. Q. (1968). A reinterpretation of the direction of effects in studies of socialization. *Psychological Review, 75,* 81–95.

Biemiller, A., & Slonim, N. (2001). Estimating root word vocabulary growth in normative and advantaged populations: Evidence for a common sequence of vocabulary acquisition. *Journal of Educational Psychology, 93,* 498–520.

Blachowicz, C. L. Z., & Fisher, P. (2000). Vocabulary instruction. In M. L. Kamil, P. B. Mosenthal, P. D. Pearson, & R. Barr (Eds.), *Handbook of reading research* (Vol. 3, pp. 503–523). Erlbaum.

Blachowicz, C., & Ogle. D. (2008). *Reading comprehension: Strategies for independent learners* (2nd ed.). Guilford Press.

Borkowski, J. G., Levers, S., & Gruenenfelder, T. M. (1976). Transfer of mediational strategies in children: The role of activity and awareness during strategy acquisition. *Child Development, 47,* 779–786.

Boyles, N., & Scherer, M. (2012). Closing in on close reading. *On Developing Readers: Readings from Educational Leadership, EL Essentials,* 89–99.

Brown, A. L., & Day, J. D. (1983). Macrorules for summarizing texts: The development of expertise. *Journal of Verbal Learning and Verbal Behavior, 22*, 1–14.

Brown, A. L., & Palincsar, A. S. (1989). Guided, cooperative learning and individual knowledge acquisition. In L. B. Resnick (Ed.), *Knowing, learning, and instruction: Essays in honor of Robert Glaser* (pp. 393–451). Erlbaum.

Brown, R., & Coy-Ogan, L. (1993). The evolution of transactional strategies instruction in one teacher's classroom. *Elementary School Journal, 94*, 221–233.

Brown, R., Pressley, M., Van Meter, P., & Schuder, T. (1996). A quasi-experimental validation of transactional strategies instruction with low-achieving second grade readers. *Journal of Educational Psychology, 88*, 18–37.

Carlisle, J. F., Fleming, J. E., & Gudbrandsen, B. (2000). Incidental word learning in science classes. *Contemporary Educational Psychology, 25*, 184–211.

Cavanaugh, J. C., & Borkowski, J. G. (1979). The metamemory–memory "connection": Effects of strategy training and maintenance. *Journal of General Psychology, 101*, 161–174.

Cazden, C. B. (1988). *Classroom discourse: The language of teaching and learning*. Heinemann.

Cervetti, G. N., Barber, J., Dorph, R., Pearson, P. D., & Goldschmidt, P. G. (2012). The impact of an integrated approach to science and literacy in elementary school classrooms. *Journal of Research in Science Teaching, 49*(5), 631–658.

Chall, J. S. (1983). *Stages of reading development*. McGraw-Hill.

Chiong, C., Ree, J., & Takeuchi, L. (2012). *Print books vs. e-books*. Joan Ganz Cooney Center.

Clark, J. M., & Paivio, A. (1991). Dual coding theory and education. *Educational Psychology Review, 3*, 149–210.

Clay, M. M. (1991). *Becoming literate: The construction of inner control*. Heinemann.

Collins, C. (1991). Reading instruction that increases thinking abilities. *Journal of Reading, 34*, 510–516.

Cordón, L. A., & Day, J. D. (1996). Strategy use on standardized reading comprehension tests. *Journal of Educational Psychology, 88*, 288–295.

d'Anna, C. A., Zechmeister, E. B., & Hall, J. W. (1991). Toward a meaningful definition of vocabulary size. *Journal of Reading Behavior, 23*, 109–122.

Datnow, A., Borman, G., & Stringfield, S. (2000). School reform through a highly specified curriculum: Implementation and effects of the core knowledge sequence. *Elementary School Journal, 101*, 167–191.

Davis, D. S., Bippert, K., & Villarreal, L. (2015). Instructional tendencies in the teaching of reading comprehension: A portrait of practice in the Measures of Effective Teaching (MET) database. *Literacy Research: Theory, Method, and Practice, 64*(1), 285–306.

Deshler, D. D., & Schumaker, J. B. (1993). Strategy mastery by at-risk students: Not a simple matter. *Elementary School Journal, 94*, 153–167.

Dewitz, P., & Graves, M. F. (2021). The science of reading: Four forces that modified, distorted, or ignored the research finding on reading comprehension. *Reading Research Quarterly, 56*, S131–S144.

Dewitz, P., Jones, J., & Leahy, S. (2009). Comprehension strategy instruction in core reading programs. *Reading Research Quarterly, 44*(2), 102–126.

Doctorow, M., Wittrock, M. C., & Marks, C. (1978). Generative processes in reading comprehension. *Journal of Educational Psychology, 70*, 109–118.

Dreher, M. J. (2002). Children searching and using information text: A critical part of comprehension. In C. C. Block & M. Pressley (Eds.), *Comprehension instruction: Research-based best practices* (pp. 289–304). Guilford Press.

Duffy, G. G. (2004). Teachers who improve reading achievement: What research says about what they do and how to develop them. In D. Strickland & M. Kamil (Eds.), *Improving reading achievement through professional development*. Christopher-Gordon.

Duffy, G. G. (2014). *Explaining reading: A resource for explicit teaching of the Common Core standards* (3rd ed.). Guilford Press.

Duffy, G. G., & Roehler, L. R. (1981). Classroom teaching is more than opportunity to learn. *Journal of Teacher Education, 32*(1), 7–13.

Duffy, G. G., & Roehler, L. R. (1989). Why strategy instruction is so difficult and what we need to do about it. In C. B. McCormick, G. Miller, & M. Pressley (Eds.), *Cognitive strategy research: From basic research to educational applications* (pp. 133–154). Springer-Verlag.

Duffy, G. G., Roehler, L. R., Sivan, E., Rackliffe, G., Book, C., Meloth, M., et al. (1987). Effects of explaining the reasoning associated with using reading strategies. *Reading Research Quarterly, 22,* 347–368.

Duke, N. K. (2000a). 3.6 minutes per day: The scarcity of informational texts in first grade. *Reading Research Quarterly, 35,* 202–224.

Duke, N. K. (2000b). For the rich it's richer: Print experiences and environments offered to children in very low- and very-high-socioeconomic status first-grade classrooms. *American Educational Research Journal, 37*(2), 441–478.

Duke, N. K., Pearson, P. D., Strachan, S. L., & Billman, A. K. (2011). Essential elements of fostering and teaching reading comprehension. In S. J. Samuels & A. E. Farstrup (Eds.), *What research has to say about reading instruction* (4th ed., pp. 51–93). International Reading Association.

Duke, N. K., Ward, A. E., & Pearson, P. D. (2021). The science of reading comprehension instruction. *The Reading Teacher, 74*(6), 663–672.

Durkin, D. (1978–1979). What classroom observations reveal about reading comprehension instruction. *Reading Research Quarterly, 15,* 481–533.

El-Dinary, P. B., Pressley, M., & Schuder, T. (1992). Becoming a strategies teacher: An observational and interview study of three teachers learning transactional strategies instruction. In C. Kinzer & D. Leu (Eds.), *Literacy research: Theory and practice: Views from many perspectives. Forty-first yearbook of the National Reading Conference* (Vol. 41, pp. 453–462). National Reading Conference.

Elleman, A. M., Lindo, E. J., Morphy, P., & Compton, D. L. (2009). The impact of vocabulary instruction on passage-level comprehension of school-age children: A meta-analysis. *Journal of Research on Educational Effectiveness, 2*(1), 1–44.

Ellis, W. A. (2009). *The impact of C-PEP (Choral reading, Partner reading, Echo reading, and Performance of text) on third grade fluency and comprehension development.* Doctoral dissertation, University of Memphis.

Fillmore, L. W. (2014). English language learners at the crossroads of educational reform. *TESOL Quarterly, 48*(3), 624–632.

Fisher, D., & Frey, N. (2012). Close reading in elementary schools. *The Reading Teacher, 66*(3), 179–188.

Flavell, J. H. (1977). *Cognitive development.* Prentice–Hall.

Flavell, J. H., & Wellman, H. M. (1977). Metamemory. In R. V. Kail & J. W. Hagen (Eds.), *Perspectives on the development of memory and cognition* (pp. 3–33). Erlbaum.

Flower, L., Stein, V., Ackerman, J., Kantz, M. J., McCormick, K., & Peck, W. C. (1990). *Reading to write: Exploring a cognitive and social process.* Oxford University Press.

Forrest-Pressley, D. L., & Gilles, L. A. (1983). Children's flexible use of strategies during reading. In M. Pressley & J. R. Levin (Eds.), *Cognitive strategy research: Educational applications* (pp. 133–156). Springer-Verlag.

Gabriel, R., Pereira, J. D., & Allington, R. L. (2011). Exemplary teacher voices on their own development. *Phi Delta Kappan, 92*(8), 37–41.

Gaskins, I. W. (2005). *Success with struggling readers: The Benchmark School approach.* Guilford Press.

Gaskins, I. W., Anderson, R. C., Pressley, M., Cunicelli, E. A., & Satlow, E. (1993). Six teachers' dialogue during cognitive process instruction. *Elementary School Journal*, 93, 277–304.

Gersten, R., Fuchs, L. S., Williams, J. P., & Baker, S. (2001). Teaching reading comprehension strategies to students with learning disabilities. *Review of Educational Research*, 71, 279–320.

Glenberg, A. M., Gutierrez, T., Levin, J. R., Japuntich, A., & Kaschak, M. P. (2004). Activity and imagined activity can enhance young children's reading comprehension. *Journal of Educational Psychology*, 96, 424–436.

Gough, P. B. (1983). Context, form, and interaction. In K. Rayner (Ed.), *Eye movements in reading* (pp. 203–211). Academic Press.

Gough, P. B. (1984). Word recognition. In P. D. Pearson (Ed.), *Handbook of reading research* (pp. 225–254). Longman.

Gough, P. B., & Tunmer, W. E. (1986). Decoding, reading, and reading disability. *Remedial and Special Education*, 7, 6–10.

Guthrie, J. T., Schafer, W., Wang, Y. Y., & Afflerbach, P. (1993). *Influences of instruction on amount of reading: An empirical exploration of social, cognitive, and instructional indicators* (Reading Research Report No. 3). National Reading Research Center.

Guthrie, J. T., Wigfield, A., Metsala, J. L., & Cox, K. E. (1999). Motivational and cognitive predictors of text comprehension and reading amount. *Scientific Studies of Reading*, 3, 231–256.

Hacker, D. J., & Tenent, A. (2002). Implementing reciprocal teaching in the classroom: Overcoming obstacles and making modifications. *Journal of Educational Psychology*, 94, 699–718.

Harmon, J. M. (1998). Constructing word meanings: Strategies and perceptions of four middle school learners. *Journal of Literacy Research*, 30, 561–599.

Hiebert, E. H., & Martin, L. A. (2001). The texts of beginning reading instruction. In S. B. Neuman & D. K. Dickinson (Eds.), *Handbook of early literacy research* (pp. 361–376). Guilford Press.

Hiebert, E. H., & Martin, L. A. (2009a). Repetition of words: The forgotten variable in texts for beginning and struggling readers. In E. H. Hiebert & M. Sailors (Eds.), *Finding the right texts: What works for beginning and struggling readers* (pp. 47–69). Guilford Press.

Hiebert, E. H., & Martin, L. A. (2009b). Opportunity to read: A critical but neglected construct in reading instruction. In E. H. Hiebert (Ed.), *Reading more, reading better* (pp. 3–29). Guilford Press.

Hilden, K. R., & Pressley, M. (2007). Stories of obstacles and success: Teachers' experiences in professional development of reading comprehension instruction. *Reading and Writing Quarterly*, 23(1), 51–75.

Hirsch, E. D., Jr. (1987). *Cultural literacy: What every American needs to know*. Houghton Mifflin.

Hutchins, E. (1991). The social organization of distributed cognition. In L. Resnick, J. M. Levine, & S. D. Teasley (Eds.), *Perspectives on socially shared cognition* (pp. 283–307). American Psychological Association.

Isakson, R. L., & Miller, J. W. (1976). Sensitivity to syntactic and semantic cues in good and poor comprehenders. *Journal of Educational Psychology*, 68, 787–792.

Ivey, G., & Johnston, P. H. (2013). Engagement with young adult literature: Outcomes and processes. *Reading Research Quarterly*, 48(3), 255–275.

Jenkins, J. R., Peyton, J. A., Sanders, E. A., & Vadasy, P. F. (2004). Effects of reading decodable texts in supplemental first-grade tutoring. *Scientific Studies of Reading*, 8, 53–85.

Johns, J. C., & McNamara, L. P. (1980). The SQ3R study technique: A forgotten research target. *Journal of Reading*, 23, 705–708.

Johnston, P. H. (2004). *Choice words: How our language affects children's learning.* Stenhouse.

Johnston, P. H., & Winograd, P. (1985). Passive failure in reading. *Journal of Reading Behavior, 17,* 279–301.

Juel, C., & Roper-Schneider, D. (1985). The influence of basal readers on first grade reading. *Reading Research Quarterly, 20*(2), 134–152.

Keene, E. L., & Zimmerman, S. (1997). *Mosaic of thought: Teaching comprehension readers workshop.* Heinemann.

Kennedy, B. A., & Miller, D. J. (1976). Persistent use of verbal rehearsal as a function of information about its value. *Child Development, 47,* 566–569.

Kinnunen, R., Vaurus, M., & Niemi, P. (1998). Comprehension monitoring in beginning readers. *Scientific Studies in Reading, 2,* 353–375.

Kintsch, W., & van Dijk, T. A. (1978). Toward a model of discourse comprehension and production. *Psychological Review, 85,* 363–394.

Klingner, J. K., Vaughn, S., Arguelles, M. E., Hughes, M. T., & Leftwich, S. A. (2004). Collaborative strategic reading: "Real-world" lessons from classroom teachers. *Remedial and Special Education, 25,* 291–302.

Klingner, J. K., Vaughn, S., Hughes, M. T., & Arguelles, M. E. (1999). Sustaining research-based practices in reading: A 3–year follow-up. *Remedial and Special Education, 20,* 263–274.

Klingner, J. K., Vaughn, S., & Schumm, J. S. (1998). Collaborative strategic reading during social studies in heterogeneous fourth-grade classrooms. *Elementary School Journal, 99,* 3–22.

Kohlberg, L., Yaeger, J., & Hjertholm, E. (1968). Private speech: Four studies and a review of theories. *Child Development, 39,* 691–736.

Kucan, L., Hapgood, S., & Palincsar, A. S. (2011). Teachers specialized knowledge for supporting student comprehension in text-based discussions. *Elementary School Journal, 112*(1), 61–82.

Kuhn, M. R. (2005). A comparative study of small group fluency instruction. *Reading Psychology, 26*(2), 127–146.

Kuhn, M. R. (2020). Whole class or small group fluency instruction: A tutorial of four effective approaches. *Education Sciences, 10*(5), 145–156.

LaBerge, D., & Samuels, S. J. (1974). Toward a theory of automatic information processing in reading. *Cognitive Psychology, 6,* 293–323.

Lee, S. H., & Tsai, S. F. (2017). Experimental intervention research on students with specific poor comprehension: a systematic review of treatment outcomes. *Reading and Writing, 30*(4), 917–943.

Levin, J. R. (1973). Inducing comprehension in poor readers: A test of a recent model. *Journal of Educational Psychology, 65,* 19–24.

Levin, J. R., & Pressley, M. (1981). Improving children's prose comprehension: Selected strategies that seem to succeed. In C. M. Santa & B. L. Hayes (Eds.), *Children's prose comprehension: Research and practice* (pp. 44–71). International Reading Association.

Malloy, J. A., & Gambrell, L. B. (2011). The contribution of discussion to reading comprehension and critical thinking. In A. McGill-Franzen & R. Allington (Eds.), *The handbook of reading disability research* (pp. 253–261). Routledge.

Mandler, J. M. (1984). *Stories, scripts, and scenes: Aspects of schema theory.* Erlbaum.

Marks, M., Pressley, M., in collaboration with Coley, J. D., Craig, S., Gardner, R., Rose, W., & DePinto, T. (1993). Teachers' adaptations of reciprocal teaching: Progress toward a classroom-compatible version of reciprocal teaching. *Elementary School Journal, 94,* 267–283.

Martin, V. L., & Pressley, M. (1991). Elaborative-interrogation effects depend on the nature of the question. *Journal of Educational Psychology, 83,* 113–119.

Mason, L. H. (2004). Explicit self-regulated strategy development versus reciprocal questioning: Effects on expository reading comprehension among struggling readers. *Journal of Educational Psychology, 96,* 283–296.

McGill-Franzen, A.M., Allington, R.L., & Ward, N. (2020). Low-cost annual book fairs to mitigate summer reading loss in high poverty communities: Two-state RCT studies in the U.S. Paper presented at the 4th Baltic Sea Conference on Literacy, Tallinn, Estonia.

McKeown, M. G., Beck, I. L., Omanson, R. C., & Perfetti, C. A. (1983). The effects of long-term vocabulary instruction on reading comprehension: A replication. *Journal of Reading Behavior, 15,* 3–18.

McKeown, M. G., Beck, I. L., Omanson, R. C., & Pople, M. T. (1985). Some effects of the nature and frequency of vocabulary instruction on the knowledge and use of words. *Reading Research Quarterly, 20,* 522–535.

McKoon, G., & Ratcliff, R. (1992). Inference during reading. *Psychological Review, 99,* 440–466.

Mehan, H. (1979). *Social organization in the classroom.* Harvard University Press.

Meichenbaum, D. (1977). *Cognitive behavior modification.* Plenum Press.

Meichenbaum, D., & Asarnow, J. (1979). Cognitive–behavioral modification and metacognitive development: Implications for the classroom. In P. C. Kendall & S. D. Hollon (Eds.), *Cognitive–behavioral interventions* (pp. 11–35). Academic Press.

Meichenbaum, D., & Goodman, J. (1969). Reflection-impulsivity and verbal control of motor behavior. *Child Development, 40,* 785–797.

Mesa, M. P., Roehrig, A., Funari, C., Durtschi, S., Ha, C., Rawls, E., & Davis, C. (2021). Young African American scholars make reading gains at literacy-focused, culturally relevant summer camp that combats summer reading loss. *Florida Journal of Educational Research, 59*(1), 252–267.

Metsala, J., & Ehri, L. (Eds.). (1998). *Word recognition in beginning reading.* Erlbaum.

Meyer, J. F., Middlemiss, W., Theodorou, E., Brezinski, K. L., McDougall, J., & Bartlett, B. J. (2002). Effects of structure strategy instruction delivered to fifth grade children using the Internet with and without the aid of older adult tutors. *Journal of Educational Psychology, 94,* 486–519.

Miller, D. (2013). *Reading with meaning: Teaching comprehension in the primary grades* (2nd ed.). Stenhouse.

Miller, G. A. (1956). The magical number seven, plus-or-minus two: Some limits on our capacity for processing information. *Psychological Review, 63,* 81–97.

Miller, G. A., & Gildea, P. (1987). How children learn words. *Scientific American, 257*(3), 94–99.

Morrow, L. M., & Gambrell, L. B. (2000). Literature-based reading instruction. In M. L. Kamil, P. B. Mosenthal, P. D. Pearson, & R. Barr (Eds.), *Handbook of reading research* (Vol. 3, pp. 563–586). Erlbaum.

Morrow, L. M., & Gambrell, L. B. (2001). Literature-based instruction in the early years. In S. B. Neuman & D. K. Dickinson (Eds.), *Handbook of early literacy research* (pp. 348–360). Guilford Press.

Murphy, P. K., Wilkinson, I. A., Soter, A. O., Hennessey, M. N., & Alexander, J. F. (2009). Examining the effects of classroom discussion on students' comprehension of text: A meta-analysis. *Journal of Educational Psychology, 101*(3), 740–764.

Nagy, W. E., & Anderson, R. (1984). How many words are there in printed school English? *Reading Research Quarterly, 19,* 304–330.

Nagy, W. E., Anderson, R., & Herman, P. (1987). Learning word meanings from context during normal reading. *American Educational Research Journal, 24,* 237–270.

Nagy, W. E., & Scott, J. A. (2000). Vocabulary processes. In M. Kamil, P. B. Mosenthal, P. D. Pearson, & R. Barr (Eds.), *Handbook of reading research* (Vol. 3, pp. 269–284). Erlbaum.

Ness, M. (2011). Explicit reading comprehension instruction in elementary classrooms:

Teacher use of reading comprehension strategies. *Journal of Research in Childhood Education, 25*(1), 98–117.

Nichols, M. (2007). *Comprehension through conversation: The power of purposeful talk in the reading workshop.* Heinemann.

Nystrand, M. (2006). Research on the role of classroom discourse as it affects reading comprehension. *Research in the Teaching of English, 40,* 392–412.

Nystrand, M., & Gamoran, A. (1991). Instructional discourse, student engagement, and literature achievement. *Research in the Teaching of English, 25,* 261–290.

Oczkus, L. D. (2010). *Reciprocal teaching at work: Strategies for improving reading comprehension* (2nd ed.). International Reading Association.

Ogle, D., & Blachowicz, C. L. Z. (2002). Beyond literature circles: Helping students to comprehend informational texts. In C. C. Block & M. Pressley (Eds.), *Comprehension instruction: Research-based best practices* (pp. 259–274). Guilford Press.

Paige, D. D. (2011). "That sounded good!" Using whole-class choral reading to improve fluency. *The Reading Teacher, 64*(6), 435–438.

Paivio, A. (1971). *Imagery and verbal processes.* Holt, Rinehart & Winston.

Paivio, A. (1986). *Mental representations: A dual-coding approach.* Oxford University Press.

Palincsar, A. S. (2007). Reciprocal teaching 1982 to 2006: The role of research, theory, and representation in the transformation of instructional research. In D. W. Rowe, R. T. Jimenez, D. L. Compton, Y. Kim, K. M. Leander, & V. J. Risko (Eds.), *56th yearbook of the National Reading Conference.* National Reading Conference.

Palincsar, A. S., & Brown, A. L. (1984). Reciprocal teaching of comprehension-fostering and monitoring activities. *Cognition and Instruction, 1,* 117–175.

Paris, S. G., Lipson, M. Y., & Wixson, K. K. (1983). Becoming a strategic reader. *Contemporary Educational Psychology, 8,* 293–316.

Patterson, C. J., & Mischel, W. (1976). Effects of temptation-inhibiting and task-facilitating plans on self-control. *Journal of Personality and Social Psychology, 33,* 209–217.

Pearson, P. D., & Fielding, L. (1991). Comprehension instruction. In R. Barr, M. L. Kamil, P. B. Mosenthal, & P. D. Pearson (Eds.), *Handbook of reading research* (Vol. 2, pp. 815–860). Longman.

Pressley, M. (1976). Mental imagery helps eight-year-olds remember what they read. *Journal of Educational Psychology, 68,* 355–359.

Pressley, M. (1977). Imagery and children's learning: Putting the picture in developmental perspective. *Review of Educational Research, 47,* 586–622.

Pressley, M., & Afflerbach, P. (1995). *Verbal protocols of reading: The nature of constructively responsive reading.* Erlbaum.

Pressley, M., Borkowski, J. G., & O'Sullivan, J. T. (1984). Memory strategy instruction is made of this: Metamemory and durable strategy use. *Educational Psychologist, 19,* 94–107.

Pressley, M., Borkowski, J. G., & O'Sullivan, J. T. (1985). Children's metamemory and the teaching of memory strategies. In D. L. Forrest-Pressley, G. E. MacKinnon, & T. G. Waller (Eds.), *Metacognition, cognition, and human performance* (pp. 111–153). Academic Press.

Pressley, M., & El-Dinary, P. B. (1997). What we know about translating comprehension-strategies instruction research into practice. *Journal of Learning Disabilities, 30,* 486–488.

Pressley, M., El-Dinary, P. B., Gaskins, I., Schuder, T., Bergman, J., Almasi, L., et al. (1992). Beyond direct explanation: Transactional instruction of reading comprehension strategies. *Elementary School Journal, 92,* 511–554.

Pressley, M., Gaskins, I. W., Cunicelli, E. A., Burdick, N. J., Schaub-Matt, M., Lee, D. S., et al. (1991). Strategy instruction at Benchmark School: A faculty interview study. *Learning Disability Quarterly, 14,* 19–48.

Pressley, M., Gaskins, I. W., Solic, K., & Collins, S. (2006). A portrait of the Benchmark School: How a school produces high-achievement in students who previously failed. *Journal of Educational Psychology, 98*(2), 282–306.

Pressley, M., Gaskins, I. W., Wile, D., Cunicelli, B., & Sheridan, J. (1991). Teaching literacy strategies across the curriculum: A case study at Benchmark School. In J. Zutell & S. McCormick (Eds.), *Learner factors/teacher factors: Issues in literacy research and instruction: Fortieth yearbook of the National Reading Conference* (Vol. 40, pp. 219–228). National Reading Conference.

Pressley, M., Harris, K. R., & Marks, M. B. (1992). But good strategy instructors are constructivists! *Educational Psychology Review, 4*, 1–32.

Pressley, M., Heisel, B. E., McCormick, C. G., & Nakamura, G. V. (1982). Memory strategy instruction with children. In C. J. Brainerd & M. Pressley (Eds.), *Progress in cognitive development research: Vol. 2. Verbal processes in children* (pp. 125–159). Springer-Verlag.

Pressley, M., & Hilden, K. R. (2006). Cognitive strategies. In D. Kuhn & R. Siegler (Eds.), W. Damon & R. Lerner (Series Eds.), *Handbook of child psychology: Vol. 2. Cognition, perception, and language* (6th ed., pp. 511–556). Wiley.

Pressley, M., Wharton-McDonald, R., Hampston, J. M., & Echevarria, M. (1998). The nature of literacy instruction in ten grade-4 and -5 classrooms in upstate New York. *Scientific Studies of Reading, 2*, 159–191.

Pressley, M., Wood, E., Woloshyn, V. E., Martin, V., King, A., & Menke, D. (1992). Encouraging mindful use of prior knowledge: Attempting to construct explanatory answers facilitates learning. *Educational Psychologist, 27*, 91–110.

Pressley, M., Yokoi, L., Rankin, J., Wharton-McDonald, R., & Hampston, J. (1997). A survey of the instructional practices of grade-5 teachers nominated as effective in promoting literacy. *Scientific Studies of Reading, 1*, 145–160.

Pressley, T., Croyle, H., & Edgar, M. (2020). Different approaches to classroom environments based off teacher experience and effectiveness. *Psychology in the Schools, 57*(4), 606–626.

Pressley, T., Isom, R., Johnson, C., Barnes, A., & McAuliffe, L. (2020). Becoming a highly effective teacher and how to support teachers' development. *Journal of Educational Leadership in Action, 7*(1), Article 8.

Rayner, K., Foorman, B. R., Perfetti, C. A., Pesetsky, D., & Seidenberg, M. S. (2002). How psychological science informs the teaching of reading. *Psychological Science in the Public Interest, 2*, 31–74.

Reutzel, D. R., Jones, C. D., Fawson, P. C., & Smith, J. A. (2008). Scaffolded silent reading: A complement to guided repeated oral reading that works! *The Reading Teacher, 62*(3), 194–207.

Reynolds, P. L., & Symons, S. (2001). Motivational variables and children's text search. *Journal of Educational Psychology, 93*, 14–22.

Reznitskaya, A., Anderson, R. C., McNurlen, B., Nguyen-Jahiel, K., Archodidou, A., & Kim, S. (2001). Influence of oral discussion on written argument. *Discourse Processes, 32*(1), 155–175.

Robinson, F. P. (1946). *Effective study* (2nd ed.). Harper & Row.

Roehrig, A. D., Turner, J. E., Arrastia, M. C., Christesen, E., McElhaney, S., & Jakiel, L. M. (2012). Effective teachers and teaching: Characteristics and practices related to positive student outcomes. In K. R. Harris, S. Graham, T. Urdan, S. Graham, J. M. Royer, & M. Zeidner (Eds.), *APA educational psychology handbook: Vol. 2. Individual differences and cultural and contextual factors* (pp. 501–527). American Psychological Association.

Rosenblatt, L. M. (1938). *Literature as experience.* Progressive Education Association.

Rosenblatt, L. M. (1978). *The reader, the text, the poem: The transactional theory of the literary work.* Southern Illinois University Press.

Rosenshine, B., & Meister, C. (1994). Reciprocal teaching: A review of nineteen experimental studies. *Review of Educational Research, 64*, 479–530.

Rupley, W. H., Willson, V. L., & Nichols, W. D. (1998). Exploration of the developmental components contributing to elementary school children's reading comprehension. *Scientific Studies of Reading, 2*, 143–158.

Schwanenflugel, P. J., Stahl, S. A., & McFalls, E. L. (1997). Partial word knowledge and vocabulary growth during reading comprehension. *Journal of Literacy Research, 29*, 531–553.

Seidenberg, M. S. (2013). The science of reading and its educational implications. *Language Learning and Development, 9*, 331–360.

Sendak, M. (1963). *Where the wild things are.* Harper & Row.

Shanahan, T., Callison, K., Carriere, C., Duke, N. K., Pearson, P. D., Schatschneider, C., et al. (2010). *Improving reading comprehension in kindergarten through 3rd grade: A practice guide.* National Center for Education Evaluation and Regional Assistance.

Shankweiler, D., Lundquist, E., Katz, L., Stuebing, K. K., Fletcher, J. M., Brady, S., et al. (1999). Comprehension and decoding: Patterns of association in children with learning difficulties. *Scientific Studies of Reading, 3*, 69–94.

Short, E. J., & Ryan, E. B. (1984). Metacognitive differences between skilled and less-skilled readers: Remediating deficits through story grammar and attribution training. *Journal of Educational Psychology, 76*, 225–235.

Snow, C., & O'Connor, C. (2016). Close reading and far-reaching classroom discussion: Fostering a vital connection. *Journal of Education, 196*(1), 1–8.

Spires, H. A., & Estes, T. H. (2002). Reading in web-based learning environments. In C. C. Block & M. Pressley (Eds.), *Comprehension instruction: Research-based best practices* (pp. 115–125). Guilford Press.

Stahl, S. (2004). What do we know about fluency? In P. McCardle & V. Chhabra (Eds.), *The voice of evidence in reading research* (pp. 187–211). Brookes.

Stein, N. L., & Glenn, C. G. (1979). An analysis of story comprehension in elementary school children. In R. O. Freedle (Ed.), *New directions in discourse processing* (Vol. 2, pp. 53–120). Ablex.

Sternberg, R. J. (1987). Most vocabulary is learned from context. In M. G. McKeown & M. E. Curtis (Eds.), *The nature of vocabulary acquisition* (pp. 89–105). Erlbaum.

Swanborn, M. S. L., & De Glopper, K. (1999). Incidental word learning while reading: A meta-analysis. *Review of Educational Research, 69*(3), 261–286.

Symons, S., MacLatchy-Gaudet, H., Stone, T. D., & Reynolds, P. L. (2001). Strategy instruction for elementary students searching informational text. *Scientific Studies of Reading, 5*, 1–33.

Taylor, B. M. (1982). Text structure and children's comprehension and memory for expository material. *Journal of Educational Psychology, 74*, 323–340.

Taylor, B. M., Pearson, P. D., Peterson, D. S., & Rodriguez, M. C. (2003). Reading growth in high-poverty classrooms: The influences of teacher practices that encourage cognitive engagement in literacy learning. *Elementary School Journal, 104*(1), 4–28.

Tierney, R. J., Readence, J. E., & Dishner, E. K. (Eds.). (1980). *Reading strategies and practices: Guide for improving instruction.* Allyn & Bacon.

Torgesen, J. K., & Hudson, R. F. (2006). Reading fluency: Critical issues for struggling readers. In S. J. Samuels & A. E. Farstrup (Eds.), *What research has to say about fluency instruction* (pp. 130–158). International Reading Association.

Tovani, C. (2000). *I read it, but I don't get it: Comprehension strategies for adolescent readers.* Stenhouse.

Van den Branden, K. (2000). Does negotiation of meaning promote reading comprehension?: A study of multilingual primary school classes. *Reading Research Quarterly, 35*, 426–443.

van Dijk, T. A., & Kintsch, W. (1983). *Strategies of discourse comprehension*. Academic Press.

Vaughn, S., Klingner, J. K., Swanson, E. A., Boardman, A. G., Roberts, G., Mohammed, S. S., et al. (2011). Efficacy of collaborative strategic reading with middle school students. *American Educational Research Journal, 48*(4), 938–964.

Vygotsky, L. S. (1962). *Thought and language*. MIT Press.

Vygotsky, L. S. (1978). *Mind in society: The development of higher psychological processes*. Harvard University Press.

Watson, M. (2014). Freedom schools then and now: A transformative approach to learning. *Journal for Critical Education Policy Studies (JCEPS), 12*(1), 170–190.

Weaver, C. (1994). *Reading process and practice: From socio-psycholinguistics to whole language*. Heinemann.

Wilder, A. A., & Williams, J. P. (2001). Students with severe learning disabilities can learn higher-order comprehension skills. *Journal of Educational Psychology, 93*, 268–278.

Williams, J. P. (1993). Comprehension of students with and without learning disabilities: Identification of narrative themes and idiosyncratic text representations. *Journal of Educational Psychology, 85*, 631–641.

Williams, J. P. (2002). Using the theme scheme to improve story comprehension. In C. C. Block & M. Pressley (Eds.), *Comprehension instruction: Research-based best practices* (pp. 126–139). Guilford Press.

Williams, J. P. (2003). Teaching text structure to improve reading comprehension. In H. L. Swanson, K. R. Harris, & S. Graham (Eds.), *Handbook of learning disabilities* (pp. 293–305). Guilford Press.

Wolf, M. K., Crosson, A. C., & Resnick, L. B. (2005). Classroom talk for rigorous reading comprehension instruction. *Reading Psychology, 26*(1), 27–53.

Wood, E., Pressley, M., & Winne, P. H. (1990). Elaborative interrogation effects on children's learning of factual content. *Journal of Educational Psychology, 82*, 741–748.

Wozniak, R. (1972). Verbal regulation of motor behavior: Soviet research and non-Soviet replications. *Human Development, 15*, 13–57.

9 Reading Instruction for Emergent Bilinguals

Ana Taboada Barber

As discussed in previous chapters, reading comprehension is the ability to read fluently, understand what we read, and, most often, build meaning from text. When we think of reading comprehension, we think of skills that are linked directly to written language–word decoding, punctuation, perhaps use of reading strategies such as asking questions while we read, and knowledge of text genres–narrative or informational. As educators, we know that children need to be taught these kinds of skills and knowledge because they are not usually acquired naturally; they need some form of instruction. Some of this instruction is formal and happens at school such as when a student monitors her or his own understanding or when she or he needs to make an inference. We also know that there are other forms of literacy instruction that are more informal and take place at home, through stories read to children by their parents or caretakers or via conversations about text. However, there is much variation in children's prior experiences with literacy among our monolingual English-speaking students, and this variation is likely vaster among those students who speak English as a second language and whose home language is a language other than English. I refer to *emergent bilinguals* (EBs) as students from households in which a language other than English is spoken, regardless of whether they are designated by their school districts as *limited English*

Ana Taboada Barber, PhD, is Professor and Associate Dean for Research, Innovation and Partnerships in the College of Education at the University of Maryland.

306

proficiency (LEP; Mancilla-Martinez et al., 2020) or not. In fact, I stay away from LEP denominations because the term itself emphasizes a deficit model, a *limited* language repertoire, rather than the richness of using two or more languages. Instead, the term EB captures the language and cultural assets of those students who either by school records and/or through self- or parental report indicate that their families speak a non-English language at home. Reflective of the overall population of EBs in U.S. public schools, the majority of EBs in the United States are of Spanish-speaking backgrounds; there are almost 4 million Spanish-speaking EBs, making Spanish-speaking EBs the largest percentage (75%) among the broader population of EBs in U.S. public schools (Institute of Education Sciences [IES]: National Center for Education Statistics [NCES], 2021; U.S. Department of Education, 2021). Although the focus of this chapter will be on Spanish-speaking EBs, the instructional approaches described can support all EBs.

In this chapter, I focus on the literacy development and, more specifically, the reading comprehension instruction of EBs in the early and later elementary school years. In doing so, I draw from research in the last two and half decades and have organized the chapter by following the findings of three major reports on literacy in EBs: The *National Literacy Panel on Language-Minority Children and Youth* (August & Shanahan, 2006), the IES practice guide *Effective Literacy and English Language Instruction for English Learners in the Elementary Grades* (Gersten et al., 2007), and the IES guide *Teaching Academic Content and Literacy to English Learners in Elementary and Middle School* (Baker et al., 2014). Given that research on EB students' literacy has blossomed in the last two decades, I support findings and recommendations from each of these volumes with empirical research findings that have either not been included in the three main reports or that have emerged in the last decade after the 2014 IES guide. I conclude the chapter with recommendations on reading motivation for EBs that has emerged from our research in the last 14 years.

WHAT IS SPECIFIC ABOUT EB STUDENTS' (BI-)LITERACY DEVELOPMENT?

EB students come to US schools with varying levels of literacy in their home languages; some of these children have well-developed literacy skills, with on-grade or advanced vocabulary in their home language and limited English proficiency; others have well-developed English oral social-language but limited academic, or school, language. And yet other EB students have limited literacy skills in both English and their home language. In fact, research points out that EBs' language proficiency in their first or home language (L1) and their second or school language (L2) runs along a continuum, with some EBs having fully developed L1 across language domains and others being, for instance, strong in their L1 oral language but without having had experiences with literacy in formal contexts (Gottlieb, 2006). Most teachers are aware that these different levels of biliteracy impact their students' reading comprehension in English. This impact can be at the syllable or phoneme level (as when students learn to differentiate long and short vowels in English, versus one vowel sound in Spanish), at the word level (as when students use cognates across languages), at the sentence level (as when EBs learn to use pronoun referents in English that may differ from their use in their L1), and of course at the paragraph level (as when students have to understand the meaning of the word *nevertheless* or *therefore* at the beginning or middle of a paragraph). These are important considerations for teaching EBs in English settings. Due to space limitations and the focus of this volume, in this chapter, I focus on EBs' literacy findings that inform reading comprehension instruction in what are mostly English-only settings and research conducted in EBs' reading in English. This is because the majority of the research on EBs' literacy development has taken place in these settings. However, in writing this chapter I am fully aware that all teachers receiving EBs in their classrooms are doing their best to become aware of these children's dual languages and the role that the home language may play or take in a child's life.

Starting To Build on Empirical Research on Emergent Bilinguals' Literacy: The *National Literacy Panel on Language-Minority Children and Youth Report*

The first panel that exclusively focused on the literacy development of EBs in the United States included 13 experts in second-language development, cognition, curriculum and instruction, assessment, and methodology (August & Shanahan, 2006). The panel reviewed the available empirical evidence from 2002 to 2006 on word-level and text-level skills as well as on the complexity of the reading process and its development and individual differences among EBs, including the contexts in which they learned to read. Studies included referred to literacy processes in EBs' L1 and to their L2. Among the panel's conclusions, EBs were determined to perform at grade level as compared with their English-monolingual (EM) peers on measures of word recognition and spelling, unlike those on measures of vocabulary, reading comprehension, and writing. In addition, it was concluded that intensive and differentiated instruction in word-level skills would lead to better performance than instruction that was not systematic; however, the panel also reported that "instruction good enough to produce expected levels of second-language performance on word-level skills does not ensure expected levels of performance on text-level skills" (August & Shanahan, 2006, p. 633). Yet, at that time, there were only three experimental studies that focused on vocabulary, three that examined comprehension, and four on writing processes and instruction. As noted by the panel, these small numbers contrasted markedly with 45 experimental studies focused on vocabulary and 205 comprehension studies reported in the summary of research by the National Reading Panel (NRP & National Institute of Child Health and Human Development, 2000).

It is important to note that, despite the clear strengths in word reading or word decoding that EBs were found to have across multiple studies, the evidence at that point did not reveal how fluent EBs could become over time, nor was it known how they could perform when reading novel, multisyllabic, and technical vocabulary words. The few studies on reading comprehension available before 2006 yielded consistent results indicating that EBs' reading comprehension fell well below that of their English monolingual (EM) peers. However, because most of the studies reviewed by the panel had been limited to students in the elementary grades, the possibility was open that, although EBs might take longer, they would eventually catch up on comprehension to the levels of their EM peers. Later research would, however, provide evidence against this belief, showing that, by the time they reached early adolescence, U.S.-born children of Spanish immigrants (enrolled in U.S. schools since preschool) had achieved word-reading skills that were within the national average but had significantly lower vocabulary and oral comprehension levels as compared with their EM peers at the national level (Lesaux et al., 2010; Mancilla-Martinez & Lesaux, 2011).

Other major findings from the *National Literacy Panel on Language-Minority Children and Youth* included the following:

• Adjust instruction to meet the needs of EBs. When possible, consider the language of instruction or the language of texts. Evidence in multiple studies showed that EBs' reading comprehension improved when they read culturally familiar materials, with students performing better when they read materials in the language they knew better.

• Consider literacy knowledge in the first language: Students with native language literacy skills performed better in English literacy than those who did not have L1 literacy skills. Some of these L1 literacy skills included background knowledge, metacognitive capacity to treat those L1 language skills as resources in the L2, strategies to apply to text comprehension, and motivation to read and socially succeed in the L2.

• When possible, use cross-language features. The use of cross-language features at the word and sublexical level (syllables, phonological awareness) are a resource to be used as part of instruction. In fact, evidence shows that phonological awareness, phonological memory, and phonological recoding are strongly related across languages (Genesee & Geva, 2006).

• Relations across languages: Word reading and spelling (orthographic mappings) in an L2 relate with those in the L1, but the extent of these relations varies depending on the orthographic relations between the first and the second language (i.e., we would not expect word reading to be as strong from Chinese to English as it would be from Spanish to English).

• Vocabulary knowledge in the L2 can be enhanced by the use of vocabulary knowledge in the L1 in cases where etymological relations between the L1 and L2 exist (e.g., cognates, *anchoa/anchovy*, *armada/ armada*, *cucaracha/cockroach*).

• Reading comprehension in the L2 correlates with that in the L1, perhaps more strongly in later grades, when comprehension tasks are more complex.

• Use of reading-comprehension strategies in L1 transfers to L2, depending on whether L2 reading is developed enough such that strategies can be effectively used.

Effective Literacy and English Language Instruction for English Learners in the Elementary Grades (IES Practice Guide, 2007)

In 2007, the IES, the research and evaluation arm of the U.S. Department of Education, convened a panel of experts on effective literacy practices for EB students and produced a guide based on the available evidence-based practices. One of the goals of a practice guide is for it to be used as a tool to assist in decision making, rather than a "cookbook" (Gersten et al., 2007, p. ii). Different from previous guides, IES practice guides generate a list of discrete recommendations that are explicitly connected to the level of evidence supporting it (e.g., high, moderate or low) and that are actionable (i.e., followed by specific steps for action). The levels of evidence are determined by preestablished criteria that assess the quality of evidence supporting educational programs and practices. The IES practice guide from 2007 only focused on elementary grades, and, as such, some of its recommendations coincided with those of the 2006 Literacy Panel previously described. Also, the guide did not address the language of instruction; rather, its recommendations are relevant for all students, regardless of their language of reading instruction, and for students who are immersed in English-language settings (Gersten et al., 2007). The IES practice guide recommendations and their corresponding levels of empirical evidence are included in Table 9.1.

TABLE 9.1. Recommendations from IES Practice Guide (2007)

Recommendations	Level of evidence	
	Strong	Weak
1. Conduct formative assessments with English learners using English language measures of phonological processing, letter knowledge, and word and text reading. Use these data to identify English learners who require additional instructional support and to monitor their reading progress over time.	♦	
2. Provide focused, intensive small-group interventions for English learners determined to be at risk for reading problems. Although the amount of time in small-group instruction and the intensity of this instruction should reflect the degree of risk, determined by reading assessment data and other indicators, the interventions should include the five core reading elements (phonological awareness, phonics, reading fluency, vocabulary, and comprehension). Explicit, direct instruction should be the primary means of instructional delivery.	♦	
3. Provide high-quality vocabulary instruction throughout the day. Teach essential content words in depth. In addition, use instructional time to address the meanings of common words, phrases, and expressions not yet learned.	♦	
4. Ensure that the development of formal or academic English is a key instructional goal for English learners, beginning in the primary grades. Provide curricula and supplemental curricula to accompany core reading and mathematics series to support this goal. Accompany them with relevant training and professional development.		♦
5. Ensure that teachers of English learners devote approximately 90 minutes a week to instructional activities in which pairs of students at different ability levels or different English language proficiencies work together on academic tasks in a structured fashion. These activities should practice and extend material already taught.	♦	

Note: Adapted from Gersten et al. (2007).

Recommendation 1: Assessments with English Bilingual Students

Given the level and amount of evidence gathered at the time (e.g., 2007), these recommendations were helpful to many teachers in the elementary grades. However, some of them needed more precision due to the fact that EBs' L1 was not considered. For example, under Recommendation 1, the panel advised collecting progress-monitoring data three times a year, especially for those EBs at high risk for reading problems. However, knowing about EBs' literacy practices or language background is needed to inform their L2/English language. In this case, it can inform the language of the assessment to be used. If EBs' mastery of English is limited such that students struggle with understanding the assessment directions or even the content of it, and the focus of the assessment is English only, chances are that EBs may be overidentified as having reading challenges or a learning disability, when in fact this might be that their English proficiency is not on par with the assessment provided. The chance of misinterpretation of assessment results may become higher as children move through the grades and practitioners become increasingly confident that struggles with language and literacy might be due to an underlying challenge or disability and not to language barriers (Goodrich et al., 2022).

Conversely, consider the kindergartner who just immigrated to the United States, joins an English-only school, and has had some exposure to literacy in his home language. If there are no available assessments for early reading, nor to monitor progress over time, in the student's home language, a teacher or school psychologist might choose to wait to refer the student for further evaluation if a reading challenge or a learning disability is suspected. The thinking in this case would be that, with strong Tier 1 core literacy instruction, the student can be more accurately evaluated in English in the later grades. However, since this recommendation came out, it has been established that, although EBs entering kindergarten who are proficient in English have trajectories similar to those of their EM peers, EBs entering kindergarten with limited English have trajectories of growth different from native English-speaking students, yielding large differences in English achievement by the time they reach grade 5 (Kieffer, 2008). Thus, in this scenario, the student may either have been undiagnosed or mislabeled as not having enough language proficiency to perform in the assessment, neglecting the possibility of whether the student might have had reading challenges that might put him or her at risk, and need to be detected early, using assessments in the appropriate language. Therefore, it is important for language and literacy practitioners (i.e., speech language pathologists, school psychologists, literacy specialists, bilingual educators) to work collaboratively to identify and use culturally and linguistically appropriate evidence-based instruments and practices when screening for learning or reading challenges and/or disabilities in children who come from varied language backgrounds.

Recommendation 2: Explicit, Systematic Instruction in the Five Core Components of Reading

The five key components of reading (NRP & National Institute of Child Health and Human Development, 2000)—phonological awareness, phonics, reading fluency, vocabulary, and comprehension—taught in small groups, are indeed key to the literacy development of EBs—as much as for their EM peers. The panel made this recommendation with students at risk for reading in mind, whether they were EBs or EMs. Important to note is that, given the limitations in assessments used in schools (see above), there might be limitations to the diagnostic precision of identifying EBs who are at risk at early stages of literacy. As previously mentioned, many of these students are identified as struggling with reading comprehension in the later grades, once the cycle of reading failure is, unfortunately, established.

Various interventions for small-group explicit instruction, including some components of the NRP, have been developed for the earlier grades, including EBs, but these do not often focus on text-level skills with EBs' needs particularly in mind. As a result, small-group interventions with EBs in the early grades have focused *either* on basic literacy processes (e.g., Vadasy & Sanders, 2021; Olsen et al., 2020) or on reading comprehension or text-level dimensions of literacy. Within the former, an intervention for kindergartners focused on letter sounds, phoneme segmenting and blending, and explicit phonics instruction as compared with a second intervention with the same elements but with an emphasis on flexible thinking by changing letter names and sounds, sorting words by last sound, and semantic categories (i.e., cognitive flexibility), as well as practice for automatic naming of the phonic patterns learned (e.g., Vadasy & Sanders, 2020, 2021). Although explicit instruction on these basic processes led to small improvements in all students' spelling, no particular notable benefits were specifically found for EB students as a result of the intervention that focused on cognitive flexibility (Cartwright, 2002). These findings indicate that, although explicit instruction in phonics and phonemic awareness is crucial for all students, including EBs in the early stages of reading, EBs need targeted basic processes/word-level interventions that are suited to their bilingualism and biliteracy and, when possible, leverages their knowledge of sound–grapheme correspondences across their two languages—more so if they share similar and contrastive patterns as English and Spanish.

When we turn our attention to the second type of intervention, on text-level skills, small-group instruction for EBs often takes the form of dyad or paired interventions—matched by English proficiency level (e.g., EM and EB) or by reading levels—combined with small-group activities. For example, second-grade students met two times a week for 20 minutes in small groups with a teacher specialist in L2, in addition to regular class literacy instruction (Klvacek et al., 2019). Within small groups, students were put into dyads, matched by reading proficiency using the Developmental Reading Assessments—Second Edition (DRA2; Beaver & Carter, 2006), in which a weak reader was matched with a stronger reader, and two EBs were matched with EM peers. Children had a choice of books among nonfiction chapter books such as *If You Give a Mouse a Cookie* (Numeroff, 2015),

Enemy Pie (Munson, 2000), *Emergency Vehicles* (Arlon, 2013), *Hippos Are Huge!* (London, 2017), *Dig, Wait, Listen: A Desert Toad's Tale* (Sayre, 2001), and *The Runaway Racehorse* (Roy, 2002; part of the A–Z Mysteries series). Dyads were led to read together, underline key vocabulary words, and read fluently ("use with two voices, read at an appropriate rate, stop and share"; Klvacek et al., 2019, p. 229). The qualitative, in-depth methodology of this study allowed the researchers to learn about practices in these dyads that specifically helped EBs, including exposure to texts that proved difficult but interesting to them, and the opportunity to discuss texts with their peers, as well as higher confidence and positive attitudes toward nonfiction texts (p. 236). However, little is known from this study about the ability of EBs to decode and read text independently, which brings us back to the recommendation of focusing small-group reading on all five dimensions of literacy, including word-level skills.

In another multicomponent large intervention (i.e., NRP components) with approximately 3,500 kindergarten to second-grade students who were below the 30th percentile in vocabulary and reading-related skills and attending 55 low-performing schools in Florida, researchers aligned Tier 2, small-group intervention materials with the Tier 1 core reading instruction (Foorman et al., 2018). There were two Tier 2 small-group interventions, one embedded with the Tier 1 construction and one that was a stand-alone. Common components to both Tier 2 small groups consisted of a 25- to 30-minute daily reading component and 15-minute daily language component. As part of the latter, students received explicit and systematic instruction in phonemic awareness, phonics, spelling, and reading for 30 minutes a day. Daily lessons include decoding and encoding skills taught in isolation and through sentence and storybook reading. Kindergartners, on average, regardless of whether they were EBs or EMs, improved in phonological awareness, word reading, and listening comprehension as a result of the intervention; however, word-reading skills for students in grades 1 and 2 were not sufficiently developed to achieve reading comprehension outcomes that were above the 15th percentile. When the Tier 2 small-group intervention included comprehension activities (i.e., the embedded intervention with Tier 1), EBs' ability to segment sounds and decode was improved, emphasizing the value of explicit reading comprehension instruction when building EBs' awareness to sounds in speech, which may in turn lead to mapping of sound-spelling patterns crucial to reading (Foorman et al., 2018).

Because the majority of the multicomponent interventions with EBs in their samples have focused on English instruction, little is known about the possibilities of leveraging EBs' first-language initial literacy development for their literacy in English. Empirical studies looking at the literacy development of EBs of various language backgrounds (e.g., Farsi,

Cantonese, Spanish, and Urdu) in the elementary and middle school grades across different instructional contexts have shown that early phonological processes (i.e., phonological awareness, rapid automatized naming , verbal working memory) in the first language are highly correlated with word reading and pseudoword decoding skills in English concurrently and in later grades (Durgunoğlu et al., 1993; Gholamain & Geva, 1999; Gottardo et al., 2001; Quiroga et al., 2002). Also, EBs who had poor word-level reading skills in the second language had been found to have similar profiles in both languages (Da Fontoura & Siegel, 1995). These findings indicate that not only are first- and second-language word-level reading skills highly interrelated, but so too are phonological processes skills—across languages—which undergird the foundation for word-level skills within and across languages.

Recommendations 3-5: Small-Group Interventions; High-Quality Vocabulary; Academic English; Students Paired Across Proficiency Levels

Student Pairs. In adding evidence-driven interventions from the last decade that support the recommendation for small group instruction, this section focuses on interventions with high-quality vocabulary as part of a reading-comprehension program with EBs particularly in mind. One such example is the Reading Buddies program (Martin-Beltrán et al., 2017, 2019; Silverman et al., 2017) in which researchers led teachers to match kindergarteners (little buddies) with fourth-grade students (big buddies) during 14 lessons on STEM topics using either videos, digital, or informational printed texts. After previewing a video or text and receiving direct instruction on target vocabulary words by the teacher, cross-age buddy dyads were encouraged to read or view the video, and big buddies were encouraged to follow a checklist to guide their kindergarten buddies using the PAWS procedure (Prepare to read or watch, Ask and answer questions, and Wrap it up with a Summary). Then, big buddies led little buddies in using the PET procedure (Pronounce, Explore, and Try it out) to review target words from the text or video. Finally, big buddies guided little buddies through extension activities, typically involving writing and drawing, which encouraged discussion and review of vocabulary and content. Reading Buddies was specifically designed with EBs in mind for whom the explicit instruction of targeted vocabulary, the use of informational texts and visual tools such as videos, and the focused discussion about texts in English were helpful scaffolds for oral language development in L2. Benefits for both little and big EB buddies are shared below.

- Extended time for EBs to talk with their peers led them to use cognitive, linguistic, and social supports to elicit buddies' ideas during reading, to build word knowledge by connecting it with prior knowledge, and to make meaning from text together (Martin-Beltrán et al., 2017).

• Time for extended conversations among children during lessons was found to be crucial for language development and student engagement with text.

• All EBs, kindergarteners, and fourth graders improved their vocabulary, both content-specific to the texts and standardized measures of vocabulary; however, no improvement as a result of the program was found using standardized measures of reading comprehension (Silverman et al., 2017).

• Supplemental programs that include the combination of teacher-led instruction and cross-age peer learning may be useful for supporting kindergarten and fourth-grade vocabulary knowledge (Silverman et al., 2017).

• Fourth graders made gains in their use of reading-comprehension strategies.

• Students were found to use both their home language (Spanish) as well as English in their interactions, suggesting that students can make meaning and use their linguistic repertoire across languages (Martin-Beltrán et al., 2017). As long as discussion is text-centered and structured such that key concepts and key vocabulary words are addressed, text-based discussion can be encouraged in L1, L2, or both. If both languages are encouraged, it is most helpful to have bilingual teacher assistants or volunteers in the classroom.

Different from the cross-age pairing, in another more recent intervention, students in kindergarten to fifth grade were paired such that within the same grade EBs and EMs were in dyads (Kazakoff et al., 2018). In this case, students participated in a blended learning approach that used a digital, online component to adapt instruction based on student performance. Across grades, students received explicit phonological awareness, word identification and decoding, automaticity/fluency, vocabulary, and comprehension/higher-order thinking skills. In the early grades, they received oral comprehension first through listening-comprehension activities designed to enhance vocabulary and an understanding of story structure (e.g., main idea, sequencing) and then progressed to reading-comprehension strategies in later grades (Kazakoff et al., 2018). Students who struggled in the online program (Lexia Reading Core5) received individual or small-group instruction on specific skills that can be delivered by a trained staff member. Students were assessed in two subsequent years; in year 1, students who were at risk of failing moved up tiers at similar rates for EBs and EMs, with at least 40% moving up from Tier 3 to Tier 1, although all students made end-of-year benchmark assessments. Overall, across most grades, EBs improved more on several dimensions of reading, including reading comprehension, than their EM counterparts. In year 2, second to fifth graders both grew significantly but at similar pacing, both EBs and EMs reached end-of-year benchmarks on reading assessments, and most of the students who were at risk of reading failure—both EMs and EBs—moved to Tier 1 core instruction by the end of the year. The finding that EBs benefited to the same extent or, in one case, to a greater extent than non-EBs from a blended approach contrasts with studies showing that older, middle grade EBs generally do not fare as well as non-ELs in terms of reading performance (e.g., Kieffer, 2008). In fact, it appears that a multicomponent, highly structured blended learning approach that can efficiently differentiate instruction—especially if students need to work on skills to fill reading gaps well below their grade level—with matched groups for EBs and EMs in kindergarten through grade 5, is likely effective for EBs and EMs alike.

Small Groups. With a focus on small-group oral language and reading comprehension instruction, CLAVES, which stands for the word *keys* in Spanish, as well as the acronym for "Comprehension, Linguistic Awareness, and Vocabulary in English and Spanish" (Proctor et al., 2019, 2021) was developed with EBs in grades 3 to 5 specifically in mind. CLAVES was developed around three units that brought together four principles of multilingual literacy instruction (Table 9.2): metalinguistic awareness, meaningful dialogue among students, use of multimodal content-rich texts, and encouraging students to use their full linguistic repertoire.

CLAVES was initially developed between researchers and third- to fifth-grade teachers seeking to integrate English language arts (ELA) and social studies. CLAVES was developed in schools with approximately 75% of students were considered low income, and approximately half of all students were EBs (with Spanish and Portuguese language background in the majority). The three units were Human–Nature Interactions, Rights and Freedoms, and Immigration and Bilingualism. Rich, complex texts, and print and supplemental videos that presented varying perspectives on controversial issues (e.g., deforestation, workers' rights, bilingual education) were part of each unit. Units comprised three instructional cycles (see Figure 9.1). The first two 5-day cycles were text-based and consisted of students reading in small groups, focused on academic vocabulary, student-friendly definitions, and reading comprehension (days 1 and 2) through the use of texts and multimedia. As part of these 5-day text cycles, students also focused on morphology and syntax as they were reflected in the texts, including study of morphology as well as prefixes, suffixes, and root word meanings across English and Spanish (e.g., _reintroduce_ = to bring something back again, and in Spanish, _reintroducir_; days 3 and 4). The third

TABLE 9.2. Principles of Multilingual Literacy Instruction in CLAVES

Principle	Description
1. Focus on all dimensions of language.	Explicitly teach *semantics, syntax,* and *morphology.* Encourage reflection on, and manipulation of, language dimensions.
2. Encourage meaningful dialogue among students around meaningful text.	Encourage students to talk about target and key vocabulary words and key concepts within a topic or theme (e.g., immigrants' language use, animals in captivity). Anchor discussions around rich texts.
3. Use multimodal texts and scaffolds to support receptive and expressive language.	Expose student to different text modalities including, but not limited to, video, gesturing, acting, and movement to allow students to learn various functions of language and text.
4. Foster a multilingual perspective.	Encourage students to use their full linguistic repertoire across their languages and reflect on language use for sociopolitical uses.

Note: Based on Proctor et al. (2021).

cycle in a unit (see Figure 9.2) was 3 days of process writing in which students composed an authentic persuasive text grounded in argumentation following discussion questions and writing prompts to stimulate meaningful dialogues. Finally, across both morphology and syntax instruction, gamification techniques were employed to strengthen linguistic understanding. When controlling for pretest differences in language skills (vocabulary, morphology, and syntax), students who participated in CLAVES did much better in academic language, reading comprehension, and argumentative writing than did students who did not participate (Proctor et al., 2019, 2021). Important to note is that CLAVES intentionally provided opportunities for open-ended questioning and sense making around language and content such that all students, particularly EBs, could participate in collaboratively constructing meanings through discussion. To ensure meaningful dialogic interactions, the authors chose print texts and multimodal scaffolds (e.g., visual, audio, gestural and spatial) that encouraged these conversations about relevant topics (e.g., Should animals like wolves, who eat other animals, be reintroduced into areas where they will encounter humans and livestock?) that were also rich in language with anchor discourse around vocabulary, morphology, and syntax.

Teaching Academic Content and Literacy to English Learners in Elementary and Middle School (IES Educators Practice Guide, 2014)

As in the 2007 IES guide, the 2014 IES guide (Baker et al., 2014) focused on teaching EBs in English contexts and specifically in learning academic

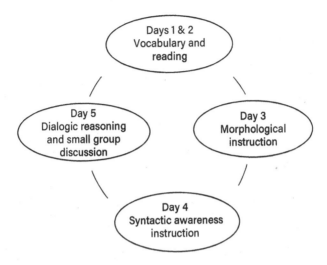

FIGURE 9.1. Five-day text cycle for units in CLAVES curriculum. Based on Proctor et al. (2021).

content in English as a second language for EBs in the United States. Different from the previous 2007 IES guide that focused on peer learning and principles of literacy instruction in the elementary grades, this 2014 guide had a major focus on academic vocabulary and writing, given that significant advances in teaching EBs had made it possible to bring new evidence-based practices up to that point.

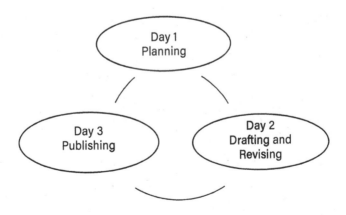

FIGURE 9.2. Three-day writing cycle for units in CLAVES curriculum. Based on Proctor et al. (2021).

Academic vocabulary is defined as words that are used primarily in the academic disciplines (sciences, geography, history, mathematics etc.). These words are much more frequently used in discussions, essays, and articles in these disciplines than in informal conversations and social settings. Typically, people define *general academic* vocabulary as terms that are used across academic disciplines, such as *environment, factor,* and *investigate.* *Domain-specific* vocabulary is defined as words that are unique to an academic discipline: Words like *photosynthesis* and *chlorophyll* are linked to biology or the natural sciences, while words like *atom* and *neutron* are linked to physics. All four recommendations from the 2014 panel revolved around the teaching of academic vocabulary words (Table 9.3). I also provide some of the studies that were either not included by the panel's review or came after the publication of the guide. For instance, regarding the significance of teaching academic vocabulary to EBs that the panel recommended almost a decade ago, a 2019 review of the literature on the topic found that, across twelve programs that included academic vocabulary in some form (e.g., academic language for all students, integrated language and science instruction, morphological problem solving, multicomponent social studies instruction, and adolescents' text comprehension), nine had a positive impact on the academic vocabulary learning of both EM and EB students, with those programs that focused on teaching academic vocabulary in the content areas of science and social studies resulting in increased content knowledge for both groups of students (Truckenmiller et al., 2019). This latter synthesis expanded previous ones by showing a demonstrable impact hat academic language instruction is also beneficial for EMs in grades 4–8.

How do you carry out the recommendation?

1. Choose a brief, engaging piece of informational text that includes academic vocabulary as a basis for intensive vocabulary instruction that:
   - Is brief, interesting, and engaging for students;
   - Contains a variety of target academic words on which to focus;
   - Connects to a given unit of study and builds students' knowledge of a topic;
   - Provides sufficient detail and examples for students to be able to comprehend the passage; and
   - Contains ideas that can be discussed from a variety of perspectives.

2. Choose a small set of academic vocabulary for in-depth instruction. The panel recommended selecting a small set of words—perhaps eight from a selected text—over the course of four to five lessons. The number of words will depend on the students' ages and grade. However, the panel observed that selecting more than 10 words for *explicit instruction* (i.e.,

TABLE 9.3. Recommendations and Corresponding Levels of Evidence in IES Practice Guide (2014)

Recommendations	Level of evidence		
	Strong	Moderate	Minimal
1. Teach a set of academic vocabulary words intensively across several days using a variety of instructional activities.	♦		
2. Integrate oral and written English language instruction into content-area teaching.	♦		
3. Provide regular, structured opportunities to develop written language skills.			♦
4. Provide small-group instructional intervention to students struggling in areas of literacy and English language development.		♦	

Note: Adapted from Baker et al. (2014).

not necessarily *exposure* to words, which will likely be more) is likely to be counterproductive, as sufficient time will not be available to teach the words in depth. Clearly, these recommendations point to the multiple criteria that needs to be attended to when selecting academic words for explicit instruction. Following these and other studies on academic vocabulary instruction, the 2014 panel followed five criteria for selecting words for instruction to EBs and their EM peers (see Table 9.4).

Most, if not all of these criteria for word selection for explicit instruction have been supported by research published after the IES guide in 2014. In particular, the two last criteria—words with multiple meanings and words with affixes—have been particularly highlighted by researchers promoting vocabulary development for EBs.

• *Teaching words with multiple meanings.* After teaching words in an explicit direct way, it is important to provide opportunities for all students, but especially EBs, to respond to questions or activities where they have to show their understanding of subtle differences in words usage and meaning. This knowledge contributes to students' vocabulary *depth*. Whereas vocabulary *breadth* refers to the number of words that a person might know some aspects of meaning, vocabulary *depth* refers to the quality of understanding, including understanding of the meaning (semantics) and how to use the word syntactically (e.g., Anderson & Freebody, 1981; Kieffer & Lesaux, 2012; Leider et al., 2013). Studies within the last decade have shown that EBs' vocabulary depth (syntax and semantics) contributed to students' reading comprehension after the word decoding skills and vocabulary breadth of elementary school Spanish–English EBs had been taken into account (Leider et al., 2013). In our own research, we have

TABLE 9.4. Choosing Words for In-Depth, Explicit Academic Vocabulary Instruction

Words central to understanding the text	Words frequently used in the text	Words that might appear in other content areas	Words with multiple meanings	Words with affixes
Choose words that are important for understanding the text (e.g., bolded words by the publisher relevant to key concepts). Note how unbolded words may relate or enhance the understanding of the bolded words.	Academic words that appear frequently in a text are particularly important to target—both discipline-specific and general academic words.	Choose words that students may encounter in multiple content areas. These are, often, general academic words (e.g., *factor, dimensions, inhibit, exhibit, parallel*).	Words that have multiple related meanings across multiple domains are useful for understanding their use in multiple contexts. For example, in science and mathematics, *volume* refers to the amount of space an object occupies, while in English language arts, *volume* refers to a book in a series.	Words that can be altered by adding prefixes and/or suffixes allow teachers and students to attend to how word parts change a root word's meaning or grammatical form (i.e., morphological awareness). For example, adding the prefix *un-* to the word *altered* changes the word's meaning, whereas adding the suffix *-ed* to *eliminate* changes it from present to past tense.

Note: Adapted from Baker et al. (2014).

recently found that ambiguous words in math (i.e., casual and academic sense, *difference* as in dissimilarity in everyday language, and *difference* as subtraction in math) contributed to third- to fifth-grade EBs' ability to understand math word problems, again indicating the role that vocabulary depth has for students' understanding of text in different content domains (Cartwright et al., 2022).

These findings, over two decades, point to the importance of emphasizing academic vocabulary depth for all students, but particularly for EBs, who are generally managing two (or more) lexicons. In doing so, EBs might manage multiple word meanings in two or more languages (vocabulary breadth) but have limited knowledge of the appropriate grammatical context for using a word, nuances of its meaning in different social circumstances, or when its use is academic or colloquial—vocabulary depth refers to knowledge of all these dimensions of a word. When teachers lead vocabulary activities that allow students to consider multiple meanings of a word, they promote the deep processing of meanings contributing to a child's vocabulary depth or to the quality of word understandings. For instance, in Figure 9.3, the instructional example depicts an activity for students in which the teacher presents two sentences that highlight two different meanings of the same word *exhibit*. Students are asked to match the word's correct definition to each sentence. Specifically, in sentence 1, *exhibit is* a noun, indicating a display, presentation, or demonstration, while in sentence 2, *exhibit* is a verb, indicating when a person shows a particular behavior. Examples such as these provide an opportunity to draw students' attention not only to different meanings carried by the same word, but also to how the syntax in the sentence provides context for a word's meaning.

- *Teaching words with affixes.* Learning about Latin roots—that is, how the meaning of <u>nov</u> meaning "new" connects to the meaning of *in<u>no</u>vative*, *re<u>nov</u>ate*, and *<u>nov</u>ice*—was taught to adolescent students of diverse language backgrounds (10.7% of the students spoke a Latinate language, such as Spanish or French). The teaching of Latin roots of general academic words took place in conjunction with instruction in morphological problem solving (e.g., Spanish friends were introduced in each lesson, such that a high-frequency root like *dic* was used to connect to target words in English [e.g., in<u>dic</u>ate], its root, and the Spanish friend). The lessons were taught over 10 weeks in the fall and over 10 weeks in the spring of the school year.

Definitions for the word *exhibit*

1. The exhibit we saw at the museum helped us understand how the tribes tried to secure their territories.

2. After coming back from the museum, some of us exhibited disappointment in how frequent wars between tribes were.

Question: Which definition goes with each sentence? Explain why.

Exhibit: to show or express feelings

Exhibit: a show or display that is meant for a lot of people to see and learn from

---

FIGURE 9.3. How to clarify multiple meanings. Adapted from Baker et al. (2014).

When comparing the teaching of Latin roots to another robust academic vocabulary instruction (without teaching Latin roots), the explicit teaching of morphological analysis with a focus on Latin roots showed students' improvement in problem solving for discerning unfamiliar words in text and enhanced vocabulary learning (Crosson et al., 2019). These findings agree with prior studies that also pointed out the benefits of teaching bound roots and their effects on word learning and morphological problem solving to derive word meanings (Bowers & Kirby, 2010; Goodwin, 2016).

3. Teach academic vocabulary in depth using multiple modalities (writing, speaking, and listening). Activities for explicit instruction (adapted from Baker et al., 2014) include the following:

- *Provide student-friendly definitions of the target academic words.* For example, if the target word is *environment*, a student-friendly definition is "a place where an animal or a plant lives. It can also mean a place where a person goes often or lives." It is important to apply these definitions to the context of the text.
- *Explicitly clarify and reinforce the definitions using examples, non-examples, and concrete representations.* Clarify the meaning of target academic words by having students complete graphic organizers such as the word map presented in Figure 9.4 (see p. 328). Word maps are very useful in supporting students as they begin to solidify their word knowledge. Teachers need to model how to complete the graphic organizer (see Figure 9.4a) and provide guided practice before asking students to complete them independently in pairs or small groups. (See word maps from an EM and EB students in Figures 9.4b and 9.4c, respectively.)

MULTICOMPONENT READING INTERVENTIONS FOR WHOLE-CLASS SETTINGS

An Academic Vocabulary and Reading Comprehension Intervention for Fourth-Grade EBs and EMs

Although research-evidence programs described up to this point have focused on explicit instruction of *academic vocabulary* (both content-specific such as *revolutionary* or *ecosystem* and general words such as *nevertheless* or *reintroduce*), some evidence-based interventions have a clear purpose of setting lessons and units with the explicit teaching of *academic vocabulary* in the context of content area reading comprehension. In this section, I focus on one particular evidence-driven program that brings several text-level skills together. Using a distributed professional development model emphasizing reading comprehension and vocabulary in social studies, Vaughn and colleagues (2021) developed a multicomponent intervention for grade 4 EMs and EBs in whole-class settings. Teachers learned to use a set of vocabulary and reading comprehension instructional practices within social studies as part of three 6-week social studies units, aligned with the state curriculum. The introduction of six vocabulary and reading comprehension instructional practices were *distributed* over time so that teachers and students incrementally built knowledge and use over the course of time. Teachers delivered two 45-minute lessons per week (36 lessons total). During Unit 1, background knowledge activation, explicit vocabulary instruction, test-based discussion and gist statements (identification of main idea) were taught. During Unit 2, teachers added summary writing, and during Unit 3, teachers added the context clue strategy (Vaughn et al., 2021). Within a given lesson under Unit 1, teachers first used illustrations within the text selection or a visual (hard-copy image, video) to prompt students to make connections between prior knowledge and new content and to build background knowledge prior to reading. Second, explicit academic vocabulary instruction included introducing the word using a student-friendly definition, leading a discussion guided by a visual representation of the word, and providing examples of the word in the appropriate context. In later units, teachers taught students a context clue strategy to derive the meaning of words rather than providing them with a student-friendly definition. An example science lesson with these literacy components is available at *https://meadowscenter.org/files/resources/PACTPlus_SampleLessons.pdf*.

This science lesson was developed across two intervention projects following the ingredients in the Vaughn et al.'s program for social studies (Wexler, 2020). The fact that these lessons are developed across both science and social studies shows that literacy in the content areas shares some common principles. Within the lesson, students were taught how to use the *Get the Gist* strategy—a method for writing main idea statements that support content comprehension—several times during passage reading (Klingner et al., 2012; Vaughn et al., 2011; Wexler, 2020). After text reading, teachers returned to explicit vocabulary instruction and asked students to assess a list of four words to identify the ones related to the target word. Students also wrote a sentence using the word to demonstrate understanding and engaged in a turn-and-talk activity to apply their understanding of words in a way that connected to their own lives (e.g., "If you could go on an expedition, where would you go and why?"). Important to note is that when teachers introduced new practices, they engaged in explicit instruction by following the *gradual release of responsibility model*: (1) telling students about the practice (e.g., we will focus on main idea), (2) modeling each step of the practice using a think aloud, (3) engaging in multiple practice opportunities with students, and (4) allowing students to practice tasks independently.

What was the impact of this multicomponent program with an emphasis on academic vocabulary? Findings with 235 grade 4 teachers with an average of 10 years teaching experience, from recruited schools, and 4,757 students—921 of whom were identified as EBs of Spanish-speaking backgrounds—revealed the following:

1. Professional development (PD) for teachers focused on evidence-based practices for content-area vocabulary and reading comprehension showed positive impact for students, though the impact may vary for ELs and non-ELs based on the proportion of ELs at their school site.
2. Specifically, all students in the intervention, regardless of language status (EBs or EMs) outperformed students who did not participate in the program on content knowledge tests of social studies in multiple-choice format.
3. There were no differences on reading comprehension between students in schools in the program and regular instruction schools.
4. The intervention seemed to have had a more positive impact on EBs' content knowledge in social studies than it did on that of non-EBs. The researchers attribute gains on content knowledge for EBs to the reading comprehension and vocabulary practices their teachers learned during PD.
5. Importantly, the EBs in the study were only of Spanish-speaking backgrounds, thus limiting generalizability of the findings to other multilingual students (Vaughn et al., 2021). The lack of assessments in literacy and language proficiency in the home language also limits individualizing benefits for specific groups of EBs students as discussed in the introduction to this chapter.

Other Academic Vocabulary and Reading Comprehension Interventions for EBs and EMs in the Elementary Grades

A multicomponent intervention combined direct, explicit instruction on phonological awareness, word reading, reading fluency and explicit vocabulary instruction for an average of 15 minutes a day, 4 days a week, for 8 weeks to first-grade students, 84% of whom were EBs of Spanish-speaking backgrounds. Interestingly, findings varied according to the time spent on the different components. Specifically, children who spent only 30% of instructional time on phonological and decoding skills and the remaining time on explicit vocabulary instruction that included focus on word meanings including use of synonyms, antonyms, picture examples, and nonexamples, and definitional sentences (as depicted, for instance, in Figure 9.4) showed gains in phonological awareness, reading, and comprehension measures as great or even greater than those of their peers who spent 100% of instructional time on phonological and decoding skills (Fillipini et al., 2012). These findings were supported by a later study that consistently observed instruction on vocabulary and comprehension for both EMs an EBs in language arts. Study participants included 274 students in third- to fifth-grade classrooms from three schools across two East Coast states (Silverman et al., 2013). Researchers found that providing explicit definition instruction was related to vocabulary growth for both EM and EB students across grades; they also found that instruction that pays "attention to word relations" (roots and meaning relations—such as in antonyms and synonyms) in classroom instruction was equally helpful to EMs and EBs (Silverman et al., 2013). Figure 9.4a shows an example provided by an elementary school teacher following the IES 2014 guide and Fillipini et al.'s principles. Note that the student uses his full language repertoire—in English and Spanish—to complete his word map. Figure 9.4b shows an example word map from Zadie, a fourth-grade EM student. Figure 9.4c shows a word map from Lucas, a second-grade EB student.

Reading Motivation and Engagement Enable Reading Achievement for EBs

Researchers over the last two decades have documented that, in addition to complex cognitive skills, reading comprehension and achievement also require reading motivation to make meaning from text (e.g., Guthrie & Wigfield, 2000; Schiefele et al., 2012). In fact, it has been broadly documented that many children and adolescents show limited motivation and engagement in reading, with 40% of student samples from 50 countries reported as "somewhat" or "less than" engaged in reading lessons (Mullis et al., 2017; OECD, 2017). However, our own research has shown that EBs in the upper elementary and middle grades who struggle with reading comprehension tend to be very responsive to instruction that pays attention to supporting their reading motivation (Taboada Barber et al., 2015, 2018), such as opportunities for small group reading and follow-up discussion (Taboada Barber et al., 2015). For example, when instruction in reading in social studies included leveled books that allowed students to delve into topics and build academic vocabulary *and* students were given choice of books or choice on how to complete a group literacy project (i.e., choice is a support for motivation), EBs grew in their self-efficacy or competence for reading (Taboada Barber et al., 2015). See Appendix 9.1 at the end of this chapter for text characteristics in choosing books for EBs. Similarly, when sixth-grade social studies teachers gave students time for sustained, focused reading (cognitive

a)

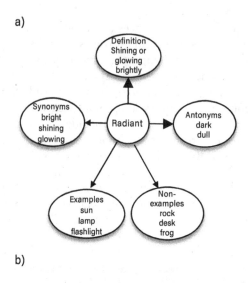

b)

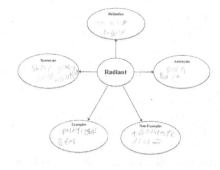

c)

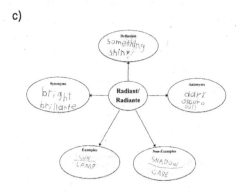

FIGURE 9.4. Word maps. (*a*) elementary school teacher example, (*b*) fourth-grade EM example, (*c*) second-grade EB example. Adapted from Baker et al. (2014).

engagement) as part of a literacy–U.S. history program. Both EBs and EMs increased their knowledge of history but also their sense of competence on using comprehension strategies such as student-led text-based questioning and comprehension monitoring (Taboada Barber et al., 2018).

Reading motivation and engagement are closely related; however, they are slightly different in how educational psychology researchers understand them. Reading motivation refers to an individual's personal goals, values, and beliefs with respect to the topics, processes, and outcomes of reading (Guthrie & Wigfield, 2000; also see Chapter 11). Even though reading motivation captures a person's thoughts, values, and feelings about reading, *reading engagement* refers to a person's actual involvement in reading, as this reflects in his or her behavior, affect, or cognition (Guthrie et al., 2012). When a child shows sustained attention in reading a mystery book or shows gratification in sharing knowledge acquired from books with his friends, both behaviors are manifestations of reading engagement.

Researchers in reading motivation have identified over the last two decades several practices that can support reading achievement and comprehension in students in classrooms settings (e.g., Guthrie et al., 2004; Guthrie & Klauda, 2014; Taboada et al., 2009; Wigfield et al., 2008). For the sake of space in this chapter, I draw on a recent article in which we summarized some of the frequently studied motivation practices that support EB reading comprehension and learning from text (Taboada Barber & Lutz Klauda, 2020). I encourage the reader to refer to the full article for further reading but also see Table 9.5 for a summary of five motivation dimensions and reading engagement, all amenable to instructional practices using the acronym SMILE to represent these dimensions (Guthrie & Wigfield, 2017; Taboada Barber & Lutz Klauda, 2020).

In sum, although in this chapter concentrated on language and cognitive dimensions of reading instruction for EBs, it is essential for teachers and practitioners to keep in mind that EBs need support through classroom practices in their motivation to read broadly and deeply on a variety of topics. Our work on the motivation and engagement of EBs shows that not only do EBs have similar reading motivation needs and profiles to their EM counterparts (Lutz Klauda et al., 2020; Taboada Barber, Lutz Klauda, Stapleton, et al., 2020) but also that teacher practices and efforts that support engaged reading make a difference in how all children, and EBs in particular, engage with texts.

LIMITATIONS AND CONCLUDING REFLECTIONS

This chapter discussed empirical studies and panel reviews from the last two decades on literacy instruction, with an emphasis on reading

TABLE 9.5. Reading Motivation and Engagement for All Learners, Including EBs

Reading motivation dimensions	Instructional practices to support that motivation
S *Sharing and social connections* Research tells us that relatedness to others motivates people to act (Ryan & Deci, 2000) and that positive social relations at school are crucial to students' academic success (Eccles & Wang, 2012; Wentzel, 2010).	Collaboration among students for meaningful literacy activities such as: • Brainstorming unfamiliar vocabulary from shared group reading • Discussing key concepts in a text and providing a team summary • Determining roles within the group for reporting back on specific assigned portions of a text • Generating student-made questions about text in a given content domain (e.g., science) and posting them in a group chart for the class to see • Having "peer discussion" or "think–pair–share" about preferred sections in a novel or favorite X in a nonfiction book
M *"Me" as a reader:* What is my sense of competence or self-efficacy as a reader? Students who have reading self-efficacy believe that they can succeed in reading tasks (Bandura, 1997; Schunk & Pajares, 2009). Self-efficacy depends on students performing well in reading and being aware of that performance.	To promote self-efficacy in reading, teachers need to ensure success in reading. Because reading development spans basic skills in the earlier grades and comprehension of complex texts as students move through the grades, self-efficacy will vary according to the cognitive dimensions of reading. A kindergarten teacher can foster self-efficacy by ensuring students feel comfortable in applying phonics rules and their knowledge of mapping sound–grapheme correspondences. A fifth grader's self-efficacy, on the other hand, will likely be tied to his ability to make local and global inferences from a content-area text or his senesce of competence to apply or use knowledge acquired from his reading.
I *Importance* Importance as a dimension of reading motivation comes from expectancy value theory (EVT; Eccles & Wigfield, 2002). EVT posits valuing, importance, and usefulness as important dimensions of motivation in school and academic contexts.	The importance of reading can be fostered through value, usefulness, and importance for learning and achievement. • One way to do so is to provide strong role models of readers (school visitors, teachers themselves, reader role models via the internet or visits to the library). • Another way is to engage students in purposeful activities for reading and ask them about the value or importance of those reading activities or experiences.
L *Liking* Intrinsically motivated readers have a true liking or enjoyment of reading, as manifested in feelings of enjoyment and involvement with reading.	Teachers can promote the liking of reading in many varied ways. One of them is through *autonomy support*. Providing support for autonomy in reading, by affording *student choice*. Choices can take multiple forms, but often they need a structure, such that students know what to choose from—for example, arranging opportunities so that EBs choose books that relate to their mores, cultural backgrounds, countries and communities. These can come from a "choice menu" elaborated by teachers and parents. *(continued)*

TABLE 9.5. (*continued*)

Reading motivation dimensions	Instructional practices to support that motivation
	Another form of student choice, can be "choice of questions to ask" about a text. Structure for this latter option can come from explicitly teaching types or levels of questions to ask from text. Appendix 9.1 offers four question levels that have provided engaged time-on text, inquisitive, motivated reading with fourth graders, both EBs and EMs (Taboada Barber, 2016; Taboada Barber & Guthrie, 2004).
E *Engagement* Engagement refers to actively involved reading. Engaged reading is the product of motivation—the values, goals and beliefs one holds about reading (Guthrie & Klauda, 2014).	Supporting and fostering engaged reading requires a plethora of strategies. Teachers who are avid readers themselves are often aware and implement many of these. Here are just a few important ones that we have found work well with struggling readers as well as on-grade readers. • Provide a plethora of interesting books that allow students to delve into topics in depth. Deep, involved reading takes place when students have access to books, articles and websites that lend themselves to sustained, in-depth reading on a topic. Isolated, disconnected text sections might serve other instructional purposes but are unlikely to lead to engaged reading. Again, refer to our recommendations for texts for EB students in Appendix 9.1. • Allow time for sustained, involved reading. Allowing time for sustained, quiet reading can be challenging in a busy school schedule, yet all teachers should strive for it. • Coordinate the motivation practices described in SMILE as a panoply for fostering engaged reading. "Students' sustained reading engagement is not driven just by their reading experience of enjoying collaboration, feeling efficacious, finding reading important, or simply liking it. Rather, children and adolescents will be the most engaged when they possess a variety of motivations" (Taboada Barber & Lutz Klauda, 2020, p. 31).

Note: Based on Taboada Barber et al. (2020).

comprehension, for students who are EBs or whose home language is a language other than English. Most of the research and recommendations offered come from English-only contexts, where most of the research has been conducted to date. Although in my introduction I highlighted that EBs' literacy development is unique to the fact that they speak, and possibly read, more than one language, I have not reviewed evidence that points to the need and importance of leveraging EBs' home language for literacy instruction neither in English-only settings nor in bilingual contexts. Also missing from this chapter is a focus on dual language instructional contexts (i.e., broadly referred to as "bilingual programs," an umbrella term for a variety of bilingual approaches that teach two languages and content in two languages). In the past few years, research has started to indicate that EB children have benefited from these programs in significant ways, including ways that go beyond standardized tests that assess their performance in each language. Due to the focus of this volume and for space reasons, I chose not to focus on this incipient body of work. However, I will be remiss if I did not state that the findings are so relevant to EBs' development of literacy that they deserve their own chapter. I look forward to contributing to such work. Despite these limitations, important conclusions can be derived from the research shared in this chapter:

1. EBs require and deserve a comprehensive approach to literacy instruction—one that encompasses the foundational role of oral language, word recognition, reading comprehension instruction and that recognizes the assets they bring as dual or multilingual learners. Such an approach needs to be considered regarding the assessments used, the language of the assessments administered, and the type of literacy instruction offered to our EBs.

2. EBs need consistent, strong scaffolds to support their reading comprehension. They tend to develop word-recognition skills (and other basic reading processes, such as phonological awareness) on par with their EM peers, but as they move up through the grades, their reading comprehension tends to lag.

3. EBs need vocabulary-rich, engaging texts that allow them to learn meaningful content from text in all content areas *from the early grades.*

4. EBs should receive explicit academic vocabulary instruction on words and terms that are thoughtfully selected by teachers, following selection criteria that situate word usage in meaningful texts and that allow for both vocabulary *breadth* and *depth.*

5. Young EBs should receive explicit phonics instruction, but this should always be accompanied by meaning making or comprehension skills—such as building and activating background knowledge, integration of language development with learning content, and opportunities for text-based discussion and oral expression, as well as metalanguage awareness. Of course, older EBs need the latter type of instruction as well, but it is just as important to build comprehension instruction *early* in literacy development as well.

6. When feasible, reading instruction (basic reading processes, oral and reading comprehension) for EBs should leverage their skills and knowledge of the home or first language. Opportunities for cross-language connections should be considered throughout and along the various dimensions of literacy development.

7. Like their EM peers, EBs need opportunities to become involved, life-long engaged readers. The more school administrators and teachers themselves understand how to support EBs' reading motivation, the higher the chances all children will become engaged readers.

APPENDIX 9.1. CONSIDERATIONS FOR CHOOSING TEXTS FOR STUDENTS WHO ARE EMERGENT BILINGUALS

WHEN DOING PARTNER/PAIR READING

Researchers found that selecting texts appropriate to the lead reader (the more experienced of the two second graders in a dyad reading pair) and of interest to the partnership was important (Klvacek et al., 2019). Sample titles included both picture books and beginning chapter books, such as *If You Give a Mouse a Cookie* (Numeroff, 2015), *Enemy Pie* (Munson, 2000), *Emergency Vehicles* (Arlon, 2013), *Hippos Are Huge!* (London, 2017), *Dig, Wait, Listen: A Desert Toad's Tale* (Sayre, 2001), *The Runaway Racehorse* (Roy, 2002; part of the A–Z Mysteries series), *Pandas* (Schreiber, 2010; part of the National Geographic Kids series), *Harriet Tubman: Leading Slaves to Freedom* (Housel, 2010; part of the Primary Source Readers: American Biographies series), and *Cam Jansen and the Scary Snake Mystery* (Adler, 2005; part of the Cam Jansen series) (Klvacek et al., 2019, p. 229).

TEXTS THAT LEAD TO USE OF COGNITIVE STRATEGIES

Instruction for bilingual students should be "choosing texts that maximize engagement, encouraging students to use the comprehension strategies they were learning in their ELA instruction, and scaffolding students in reading challenging texts" (Proctor et al., 2019, p. 114).

CULTURALLY RELEVANT TEXTS

Readings for the interventions with second- and third-grade students were a combination of culturally relevant and distant and were chosen based on "ELs' L1 background, cognitive abilities, reading level, and English proficiency, following Bishop's [1993] attention to cultural authenticity, the characters' language, picture quality, and how people of color are characterized" (Kim, 2018, p. 4). Giving students readings from different perspectives (e.g., Columbus and Native Americans) can allow students to practice intertextuality, as they make connections between the texts, can synthesize the material for a fuller understanding, and can evaluate the information presented. As Kim wrote, "Culturally relevant stories, as I defined them, included concepts, ethnicities, first language, values, beliefs, and experiences familiar in the EL's home culture, focusing on seminal experiences such as arrival in the United States and adjusting to a new language and culture" (2018, p. 4). However, teachers should also be mindful that these are often difficult to supply, mostly because there are so many language backgrounds in some geographic locations in the United States; or, when there is predominance of Spanish-speaking EBs, cultural references are quite idiosyncratic—for example, food traditions for Dia de los Muertos in Mexico is very different from arepas that are eaten in Colombia. Classroom libraries would have to be built up over time for culturally responsive books for emergent bilinguals of multiple backgrounds. Yet, unifying/overarching themes such as immigration and bilingualism might be especially helpful for selecting books that cut across national backgrounds of ELs/EBs.

EARLY-GRADES TEXTS

- Martha's True Stories Buddies Program for early readers used books available online from PBS Kids (Silverman et al., 2017).
- Fairy tales can be good early texts in English because the stories are often familiar across cultures, giving students background knowledge that is helpful for comprehension in English (Bauer & Arazi, 2011).

Informational (Science) Books

- National Geographic has a great leveled collection of informational books in science in English and Spanish. They are great for science concepts and vocabulary.
- "The focus on habitats was in alignment with the school district's science standards. There were two main reasons that we chose to use science content in our intervention. First, given the vast number of reading and math standards that must be addressed on a given school day, teachers often argue that there is not enough time for vocabulary instruction. Many teachers also feel that there is not enough time for science. Integrating vocabulary and science in the intervention allowed teachers to address both of these important instructional components at the same time. Second, a focus on content area topics in the early grades is

essential for building children's background knowledge" (Dreher, 2003; Duke, 2003; Silverman & Hines, 2009, pp. 307–308).

- Titles included *The Great Kapok Tree* (Cherry, 1990), *Life in the Rainforest* (Berger, 1996), and *Nature's Green Umbrella* (Gibbons, 1994).

MIDDLE-GRADES TEXTS

Third- and Fourth-Grade Discussion-Oriented Books

Proctor, Silverman, and Jones "chose print texts that encouraged critical conversations about relevant topics, and also included rich language with which to anchor discourse around vocabulary, morphology, and syntax" (2021, p. 262) The authors also included digital text because it is more interactive. The authors "sought to provide a wide range of opportunities for students to take in new information and express what they understood" (p. 262). To accomplish this, students first read a print-based text, next they watched videos about the same topic, and, finally, they engaged in a guided discussion in which they were asked about their own understanding of the concepts presented as well as relevant vocabulary. "The multiple (con)texts constituted the opportunity . . . to build metalinguistic awareness" (Proctor et al., 2021, p. 262).

Sixth- and Seventh-Grade Different-Level Reading Books on Topics of Interest to a Variety of Students

"We selected texts on the basis of several criteria: potential for student engagement, readability at the fourth- to sixth-grade instructional level, length, and the opportunities available for teaching academic vocabulary" (Lesaux et al., 2010, pp. 202–203). Middle school intervention readings included "topics salient to adolescent youth culture, such as single-gender classrooms and television viewing rates, while others addressed issues of diversity, such as how different ethnic groups in Africa learn to get along" (Lesaux et al., 2010, p. 203). Taboada Barber et al. (2016) chose U.S. history trade books (e.g., Scholastic or National Geographic) that were below, on, and above sixth-grade level to assess students' reading comprehension in history (Taboada Barber et al., 2016).

In a later study, Taboada Barber et al. "selected trade books to represent a variety of reading levels while addressing standards-based knowledge and concepts in the social studies curriculum" (2018, p. 84). Students in one study group read texts related to "American Indians, European exploration, and Two cultures Meet (i.e., interactions between the American Indians and European Explorers)" (Taboada Barber et al., 2018, p. 84). Students in the second study group read texts related "to colonization, people in colonial America, and events leading to the American Revolution" (Taboada Barber et al., 2018, p. 84).

Fiction/Literature Books

Medina "selected . . . books based on how they could facilitate the students' understandings of new interpretative strategies, such as making connections and questioning through multiple forms of multimodal engagements" (2010, p. 43). The books were all fiction; fiction tends to be less demanding on specific vocabulary than informational texts, so it is a good starter for young emergent bilinguals. However, several researchers and teachers encourage the use of informational/nonfiction texts from the early grades. Emergent bilinguals should be exposed to informational texts from the early grades (Taboada Barber et al., 2018) for engagement purposes and also because these books facilitate the focus on cognates in science and social studies. Titles (from Medina, 2010, p. 44) were *Tomás and the Library Lady/Tomás y la señora de la biblioteca* (Mora, 1997), *My Diary from Here to There/Mi diario de aquí hasta allá* (Pérez, 2002), and *Prietita and the Ghost Woman/Prietita y la llorona* (Anzaldúa, 1996).

Culturally Responsive Texts

Culturally responsive teaching involves "[a] wide range of content with characters, situations, and places that students can recognize from their own lives, and from which they can learn about other worlds and perspectives. Education expert Rudine Sims Bishop, often called the mother of multicultural literature, wrote the essay 'Mirrors, Windows, and Sliding Glass Doors,' which led to shifts in teaching and the inclusion of authentic, diverse voices in literature for students. As Bishop established, *mirrors* allow children to see themselves reflected in what they read; *windows* help children develop empathy and understanding for others; and *sliding glass doors* provide children with safe passageways into new worlds, so they can develop their creativity, imagination, and knowledge" (Benchmark Education).

REFERENCES

Anderson, R. C., & Freebody, P. (1981). Vocabulary knowledge. In J. T. Guthrie (Ed.), *Comprehension and teaching: Research reviews* (pp. 77–117). International Reading Association.

August, D., & Shanahan, T. (2006). *Developing literacy in second-language learners: Report of the National Literacy Panel on language-minority children and youth.* Erlbaum.

Baker, S., Lesaux, N., Jayanthi, M., Dimino, J., Proctor, C. P., Morris, J., et al. (2014). *Teaching academic content and literacy to English learners in elementary and middle school* (NCEE 2014-4012). National Center for Education Evaluation and Regional Assistance (NCEE), Institute of Education Sciences, U.S. Department of Education.

Bandura, A. (1997). *Self-efficacy: The exercise of control.* Freeman.

Bauer, E. B., & Arazi, J. (2011). Promoting literacy development for beginning English learners. *The Reading Teacher, 64*(5), 383–386.

Beaver, J., & Carter, M. A. (2006). *DRA2: Developmental reading assessment.* Celebration Press.

Benchmark Education. (n.d.) Achieve culturally responsive reading. Retrieved May 16, 2020, from *www.benchmarkeducation.com/knowledge-hub/culturally-responsive teaching.*

Bowers, P. N., & Kirby, J. R. (2010). Effects of morphological instruction on vocabulary acquisition. *Reading and Writing: An Interdisciplinary Journal, 23,* 515–537.

Cartwright, K. B. (2002). Cognitive development and reading: The relation of reading-specific multiple classification skill to reading comprehension in elementary school children. *Journal of Educational Psychology, 94*(1), 56–63.

Cartwright, K. B., Taboada Barber, A., & Archer, C. J. (2022). What's the difference? Contributions of lexical ambiguity, reading comprehension, and executive functions to math word problem solving in linguistically diverse 3rd to 5th graders. *Scientific Studies of Reading.*

Crosson, A. C., McKeown, M. G., Moore, D. W., & Ye, F. (2019). Extending the bounds of morphology instruction: Teaching Latin roots facilitates academic word learning for English learner adolescents. *Reading and Writing, 32*(3), 689–727.

Da Fontoura, H. A., & Siegel, L. S. (1995). Reading, syntactic, and working memory skills of bilingual Portuguese-English Canadian children. *Reading and Writing, 7*(1), 139–153.

Dreher, M. J. (2003). Motivating struggling reading by tapping the potential of information books. *Reading and Writing Quarterly, 19*(1), 25–38.

Duke, N. K. (2003). Reading to learn from the very beginning: Informational books in early childhood. *Young Children, 58,* 14–20.

Durgunoğlu, A. Y., Nagy, W. E., & Hancin-Bhatt, B. J. (1993). Cross-language transfer of phonological awareness. *Journal of Educational Psychology, 85*(3), 453–465.

Eccles, J. S., & Wang, M. (2012). Part I commentary: So what is student engagement anyway? In S. Christenson, A. Reschly, & C. Wylie (Eds.), *Handbook of research on student engagement* (pp. 133–149). Springer.

Eccles, J. S., & Wigfield, A. (2002). Motivational beliefs, values, and goals. *Annual Review of Psychology, 53,* 109–132.

Filippini, A. L., Gerber, M. M., & Leafstedt, J. M. (2012). A vocabulary-added reading intervention for English learners at-risk of reading difficulties. *International Journal of Special Education, 27*(3), 14–26.

Foorman, B. R., Herrera, S., & Dombek, J. (2018). The relative impact of aligning Tier 2 intervention materials with classroom core reading materials in grades K–2. *The Elementary School Journal, 118*(3), 477–504.

Genesee, F. & Geva, E. (2006) Cross-linguistic relationships in working memory, phonological processes, and oral language. In August, D. & Shanahan, T. (Eds.), *Developing literacy in second-language learners: Report of the National Literacy Panel on language-minority children and youth* (pp. 175–184). Erlbaum.

Gersten, R., Baker, S.K., Shanahan, T., Linan-Thompson, S., Collins, P., & Scarcella, R. (2007). *Effective literacy and English language instruction for English learners in the elementary grades: A practice guide* (NCEE 2007–4011). National Center for Education Evaluation and Regional Assistance, Institute of Education Sciences, U.S. Department of Education.

Gholamain, M., & Geva, E. (1999). Orthographic and cognitive factors in the concurrent development of basic reading skills in English and Persian. *Language Learning, 49*(2), 183–217.

Goodrich, J. M., Fitton, L., Chan, J., & Davis, C. J. (2022). Assessing oral language when screening multilingual children for learning disabilities in reading. *Intervention in School and Clinic, 58*(3).

Goodwin, A. P. (2016). Effectiveness of word solving: Integrating morphological problem-solving within comprehension instruction for middle school students. *Reading and Writing: An Interdisciplinary Journal, 29*, 91–116.

Gottardo, A., Yan, B., Siegel, L. S., & Wade-Woolley, L. (2001). Factors related to English reading performance in children with Chinese as a first language: More evidence of cross-language transfer of phonological processing. *Journal of Educational Psychology, 93*(3), 530–542.

Gottlieb, M. H. (2006). How should you assess the language proficiency of English language learners? In E. Hamayan & R. Freeman (Eds.) *English language learners at school: A guide for administrators.* Caslon.

Guthrie, J. T., & Klauda, S. L. (2014). Effects of classroom practices on reading comprehension, engagement, and motivations for adolescents. *Reading Research Quarterly, 49*, 387–416.

Guthrie, J. T., & Wigfield, A. (2000). Engagement and motivation in reading. In M. L. Kamil, P. B. Mosenthal, P. D. Pearson, & R. Barr (Eds.), *Reading research handbook* (Vol. 3, pp. 403–424). Erlbaum.

Guthrie, J. T., & Wigfield, A. (2017). Literacy engagement and motivation: Rationale, research, teaching, and assessment. In D. Lapp & D. Fisher (Eds.), *Handbook of research on teaching the English language arts* (pp. 57–84). Routledge.

Guthrie, J. T., Wigfield, A., Barbosa, P., Perencevich, K. C., Taboada, A., Davis, M., et al. (2004). Increasing reading comprehension and engagement through Concept-Oriented Reading Instruction. *Journal of Educational Psychology, 96*(3), 403–423.

Guthrie, J. T., Wigfield, A., & You, W. (2012). Instructional contexts for engagement and achievement in reading. In S. J. Christenson, A. L. Reschly, & C. Wylie (Eds.), *Handbook of research on student engagement* (pp. 601–634). Springer.

Institute of Education Sciences: National Center for Education Statistics. (2021). English language learners in public schools. Retrieved from *https://nces.ed.gov/programs/coe/indicator/cgf.*

Kazakoff, E. R., Macaruso, P., & Hook, P. (2018). Efficacy of a blended learning approach to elementary school reading instruction for students who are English learners. *Educational Technology Research and Development, 66*(2), 429–449.

Kieffer, M. J. (2008). Catching up or falling behind? Initial English proficiency, concentrated poverty, and the reading growth of language minority learners in the United States. *Journal of Educational Psychology, 100*(4), 851–868.

Kieffer, M. J., & Lesaux, N. K. (2012). Knowledge of words, knowledge about words: Dimensions of vocabulary in first and second language learners in sixth grade. *Reading and Writing, 25*(2), 347–373.

Kim, D. (2019). Elementary English learners' use of reading strategies with culturally relevant and culturally distant stories. *Journal of Language, Identity and Education, 18*(2), 73–91.

Klingner, J. K., Vaughn, S., & Boardman, A. (2012). *Now we get it! Boosting comprehension with collaborative strategic reading.* Wiley.

Klvacek, M. L., Monroe, E. E., Wilcox, B., Hall-Kenyon, K. M., & Morrison, T. G. (2019). How second-grade English learners experienced dyad reading with fiction and nonfiction texts. *Early Childhood Education Journal, 47*(2), 227–237.

Leider, C. M., Proctor, C. P., Silverman, R. D., & Harring, J. R. (2013). Examining the role of vocabulary depth, cross-linguistic transfer, and types of reading measures on the reading comprehension of Latino bilinguals in elementary school. *Reading and Writing, 26*(9), 1459–1485.

Lesaux, N. K., Kieffer, M. J., Faller, S. E., & Kelley, J. G. (2010). The effectiveness and ease of implementation of an academic vocabulary intervention for linguistically diverse students in urban middle schools. *Reading Research Quarterly, 45*(2), 196–228.

Logan, K. J., & Kieffer, M. J. (2017). Evaluating the role of polysemous word knowledge in reading comprehension among bilingual adolescents. *Reading and Writing, 30*(8), 1687–1704.

Lutz Klauda, S. L., Taboada Barber, A., & McAllen, E. B. (2020). Reading motivation in Spanish-speaking dual language learners: Comparing two types of student report. *Reading Psychology* (Themed issue: Affective dimensions of student literacy learning), *41*(6), 605–630.

Mancilla-Martinez, J., Hwang, J. K., Oh, M. H., & McClain, J. B. (2020). Early elementary grade dual language learners from Spanish-speaking homes struggling with English reading comprehension: The dormant role of language skills. *Journal of Educational Psychology, 112*(5), 880–894.

Mancilla-Martinez, J., & Lesaux, N. K. (2011). The gap between Spanish speakers' word reading and word knowledge: A longitudinal study. *Child Development, 82*(5), 1544–1560.

Martin-Beltrán, M., Daniel, S., Peercy, M., & Silverman, R. (2017). Developing a zone of relevance: Emergent bilinguals' use of social, linguistic, and cognitive support in peer-led literacy discussions. *International Multilingual Research Journal, 11*(3), 152–166.

Martin-Beltrán, M., Montoya-Ávila, A., García, A. A., Peercy, M. M., & Silverman, R. (2019). "Time for una pregunta": understanding Spanish use and interlocutor response among young English learners in cross-age peer interactions while reading and discussing text. *International Journal of Bilingual Education and Bilingualism, 22*(1), 17–34.

Medina, C. (2010). "Reading across communities" in biliteracy practices: Examining translocal discourses and cultural flows in literature discussions. *Reading Research Quarterly, 45*(1), 40–60.

Mullis, I. V. S., Martin, M. O., Foy, P., & Hooper, M. (2017). PIRLS 2016 international results in reading. Retrieved from *http://timssandpirls.bc.edu/pirls2016/international-results.*

National Reading Panel & National Institute of Child Health and Human Development. (2000). *Report of the National Reading Panel: Teaching children to read: an evidence-based assessment of the scientific research literature on reading and its implications for reading instruction: Reports of the subgroups.* National Institute of Child Health and Human Development, National Institutes of Health. Retrieved from *www.nichd.nih.gov/sites/default/files/publications/pubs/nrp/Documents/report.pdf.*

Olsen, L., Martinez, M., Herrera, C., & Skibbens, H. (2020). Multilingual programs and pedagogy: What teachers and administrators need to know and do. In *Improving multilingual and English learner education: From research to practice.* California Department of Education. Retrieved from *www.cde.ca.gov/sp/el/er/documents/mleleducation.pdf.*

Organisation for Economic Co-operation and Development (OECD). (2017). *PISA 2015 Results: Vol. III. Students' well-being.* OECD Publishing.

Proctor, C. P., Silverman, R. D., Harring, J. R., Jones, R. L., & Hartranft, A. M. (2019). Teaching bilingual learners: Effects of a language-based reading intervention on academic language and reading comprehension in grades 4 and 5. *Reading Research Quarterly, 55*(1), 95–122.

Proctor, C. P., Silverman, R. D., & Jones, R. L. (2021). Centering language and student voice in multilingual literacy instruction. *The Reading Teacher, 75*(3), 255–267.

Quiroga, T., Lemos-Britton, Z., Mostafapour, E., Abbott, R. D., & Berninger, V. W. (2002). Phonological awareness and beginning reading in Spanish-speaking ESL first graders. *Journal of School Psychology, 40*(1), 85–111.

Ryan, R. M., & Deci, E. L. (2000). Intrinsic and extrinsic motivations: Classic definitions and new directions. *Contemporary Educational Psychology, 25*, 54–67.

Schiefele, U., Schaffner, E., Moller, J., & Wigfield, A. (2012). Dimensions of reading motivation and their relation to reading behavior and competence. *Reading Research Quarterly, 47*, 427–463.

Schunk, D. H., & Pajares, F. (2009). Self-efficacy theory. In K. R. Wentzel & D. B. Miele (Eds.), *Handbook of motivation at school* (pp. 49–68). Routledge.

Silverman, R., & Hines, S. (2009). The effects of multimedia-enhanced instruction on the vocabulary of English-language learners and non-English-language learners in pre-kindergarten through second grade. *Journal of Educational Psychology, 101*(2), 305–314.

Silverman, R. D., Martin-Beltrán, M., Peercy, M. M., Hartranft, A. M., McNeish, D. M., Artzi, L., et al. (2017). Effects of a cross-age peer learning program on the vocabulary and comprehension of English learners and non-English learners in elementary school. *The Elementary School Journal, 117*(3), 485–512.

Silverman, R. D., Proctor, C. P., Harring, J. R., Doyle, B., Mitchell, M. A., & Meyer, A. G. (2013). Teachers' instruction and students' vocabulary and comprehension: An exploratory study with English monolingual and Spanish-English bilingual students in grades 3–5. *Reading Research Quarterly, 49*(1), 31–60.

Taboada, A., & Guthrie, J. T. (2004). Growth of cognitive strategies for reading comprehension. In J. T. Guthrie, A. Wigfield, & K. Perencevich (Eds.), *Motivating reading comprehension: Concept-Oriented Reading Instruction* (pp. 273–306). Erlbaum.

Taboada Barber, A. (2016). *Reading to learn for ELs: Motivation practices and comprehension strategies for informational texts.* Heinemann.

Taboada, A., Tonks, S. M., Wigfield, A. & Guthrie, J. T. (2009). Effects of motivational and cognitive variables on reading comprehension. *Reading and Writing: An Interdisciplinary Journal, 22*, 85–106.

Taboada Barber, A., Buehl, M. M., Beck, J. S., Ramirez, E. M., Gallagher, M., Richey Nuland, L. N., et al. (2018). Literacy in social studies: The influence of cognitive and motivational practices on the reading comprehension of English learners and non-English learners. *Reading and Writing Quarterly, 34*(1), 79–97.

Taboada Barber, A., Cartwright, K.B., Stapleton, L.M., Lutz Klauda, S., Archer, C. & Smith, P. (2020). Direct and indirect effects of executive functions, reading engagement, and higher order strategic processes in the reading comprehension of dual language learners and English monolinguals. *Contemporary Educational Psychology, 61*, 1–17.

Taboada Barber, A. T., Gallagher, M., Smith, P., Buehl, M. M., & Beck, J. S. (2016). Examining student cognitive and affective engagement and reading instructional activities: Spanish-speaking English learners' reading profiles. *Literacy Research and Instruction, 55*(3), 209–236.

Taboada Barber, A., Gallagher, M., Smith, P., Buehl, M.M., & Beck, J. S. (2015). Examining student cognitive and affective engagement and reading instructional activities: Spanish-speaking English learners' reading profiles. *Literacy Research and Instruction, 55*(3), 1-28.

Taboada Barber, A. & Lutz Klauda, S. (2020). How reading motivation and engagement enable reading achievement: Policy implications. *Policy Insights from the Behavioral and Brain Sciences, 7*(1), 27–34.

Taboada Barber, A., Lutz Klauda, S., & Stapleton, L. M. (2020). Cognition, Engagement, and Motivation as Factors in the Reading Comprehension of Dual Language Learners and English Speakers: Unified or Distinctive Models? *Reading and Writing, 33*(9), 2249 –2279.

Truckenmiller, A. J., Park, J., Dabo, A., & Wu Newton, Y. C. (2019). Academic language instruction for students in grades 4 through 8: A literature synthesis. *Journal of Research on Educational Effectiveness, 12*(1), 135–159.

U.S. Department of Education. (2021) The biennial report to Congress on the implementation of the Title III State Formula Grant Program. Retrieved from *https://ncela.ed.gov/files/biannual-reports/OELA-BiReport16–18.508.pdf*.

Vadasy, P. F., & Sanders, E. A. (2020). Introducing grapheme-phoneme correspondences (GPCs): Exploring rate and complexity in phonics instruction for kindergarteners with limited literacy skills. *Reading and Writing, 34*(1), 109–138.

Vadasy, P. F., & Sanders, E. A. (2021). Introducing phonics to learners who struggle: content and embedded cognitive elements. *Reading and Writing, 34*(8), 2059–2080.

Vaughn, S., Klingner, J. K., Swanson, E. A., Boardman, A. G., Roberts, G., Mohammed, S. S., et al. (2011). Efficacy of collaborative strategic reading with middle school students. *American Educational Research Journal, 48*(4), 938–964.

Vaughn, S., Swanson, E., Fall, A. M., Roberts, G., Capin, P., Stevens, E. A., et al. (2021). The efficacy of comprehension and vocabulary focused professional development on English learners' literacy. *Journal of Educational Psychology, 114*(2), 257–272.

Wentzel, K. R. (2010). Students' relationships with teachers. In J. L. Meece & J. S. Eccles (Eds.), *Handbook of research on schools, schooling, and human development* (pp. 75–91). Routledge.

Wexler, J. (2020). *Developing an Instructional Leader Adaptive Intervention Model (AIM) for Supporting Teachers as they Integrate Evidence-Based Adolescent Literacy Practices School-Wide (Project AIM)*. Institute of Education Sciences.

Wigfield, A., Guthrie, J. T., Perencevich, K. C., Taboada, A., Klauda, S. L., McRae, A., et al. (2008). Role of reading engagement in mediating effects of reading comprehension instruction on reading outcomes. *Psychology in the Schools, 45*(5), 432–445.

CHILDREN'S LITERATURE CITED

Adler, D. A. (2005). *Cam Jansen and the scary snake mystery* (part of the Cam Jansen series). Puffin Books.

Anzaldúa, G. (1996). *Prietita and the ghost woman/Prietita y la Llorona*. Children's Book Press.

Arlon, P. (2013). *Emergency vehicles*. Scholastic.

Berger, M. (1996). *Life in the rainforest*. Chelsea House.

Cherry, L. (1990). *The great kapok tree*. HMH Books for Young Readers.

Gibbons, G. (1994). *Nature's green umbrella*. HarperCollins.

Housel, D. J. (2010). *Harriet Tubman: Leading slaves to freedom* (part of the Primary Source Readers: American Biographies series). Teacher Created Materials.

London, J. (2017). *Hippos are huge!* Candlewick.

Mora, P. (1997). *Tomas and the Library Lady/Tomas y la señora de la biblioteca*. Dragonfly Books.

Munson, D. (2000). *Enemy pie*. Chronicle.

Numeroff, L. (2015). *If you give a mouse a cookie*. HarperCollins.

Pérez, A. I. (2002). *My diary from here to there/Mi diario de aqui hasta allá*. Children's Book Press.

Roy, R. (2002). *The runaway racehorse* (part of the A–Z Mysteries series). Turtleback Books.

Sayre, A. P. (2001). *Dig, wait, listen: A desert toad's tale*. Greenwillow Books.

Schreiber, A. (2010). *Pandas* (part of the National Geographic Kids series). National Geographic.

Expert Literacy Teaching in the Primary Grades

Ruth Wharton-McDonald

Over the last several decades, researchers have spent a great deal of time in schools and classrooms to determine the characteristics of highly effective schools and teachers. Research has undergone a shift from studies of compartmentalized skills instruction and learning environments to explorations of literacy instruction in classrooms that take into account many more of the complexities of primary-grade teaching and learning. To fully grasp what is going on in classrooms and to understand how some schools and teachers are having more success than others, researchers have had to immerse themselves into those environments.

In the 1990s, Michael Pressley and his research team spent a great deal of time exploring the instructional factors that supported early readers and writers in classrooms—as well as those factors that left a significant number of children with reading difficulties as early as grade 1. Although not all the research summarized in the previous chapters was available in the early 1990s, enough did exist to understand that the development of phonemic awareness and decoding skills was essential to success in beginning reading. We were also aware, however, that many teachers at that time (and still today) were committed to a whole-language approach to instruction, and they believed it was affecting competencies beyond the word level. The Pressley group had been in enough primary-level classrooms filled

---

Ruth Wharton-McDonald, PhD, is Associate Professor of Education in the College of Liberal Arts at the University of New Hampshire.

with literature and writing to know that there was much that was attractive about such instruction. Moreover, they had observed classrooms that seemed to be doing quite a bit of word-level skills instruction while also immersing children in literature and rich language arts experiences (a seemingly balanced approach). The question of "balanced instruction" was still wholly unresolved at the time, and the group decided that they needed to know what distinguished the most successful primary classrooms (where the vast majority of students were engaged and learning) from the less successful ones—in part to better understand the potential role of balance in literacy instruction, and in part to focus more closely on what actually went on in primary-grade classrooms. For as any serious school observer knows, a study of phonics instruction (for example) that takes place outside the classroom in small groups, with a highly trained "teacher," and none of the added challenge of 15–20 other 6-year-olds is hardly an accurate representation of the actual classroom experience.

In the decades that followed, Pressley and his colleagues spent a great deal of time in schools and classrooms in an effort to develop an informed perspective on what could and should be occurring in order to maximize the likelihood that students would learn to read and write.

EFFECTIVE SCHOOL ENVIRONMENTS

There was much research on effective elementary schools in the last quarter of the 20th century (Edmonds, 1979; Firestone, 1991), with particular attention paid to "outlier" schools—institutions that are exceptionally effective given their context (e.g., schools producing high achievement in low-socioeconomic neighborhoods). A consistent pattern emerged across case analyses of such schools. Outlier schools were found to have the following characteristics (Cole-Henderson, 2000; Firestone, 1991; Hallinger et al., 1996):

1. They have strong administrative leadership.
2. They maintain high expectations for all children.
3. They are safe and orderly environments without being overly rigid.
4. The top priority is student acquisition of basic academic skills, with willingness to divert resources from other activities to support the development of these skills.
5. They carefully monitor student progress.

In the early years of the 21st century, some researchers further narrowed the focus on outlier schools to examine schools that were particularly successful in supporting students' literacy outcomes (e.g., Cunningham,

2007; Johnson, 2002; Mosenthal et al., 2002; Pressley et al., 2007; Taylor et al., 2000). Taylor et al. (2000) studied 14 schools across the United States, each having a high proportion of students living in poverty. In each of these schools, two teachers at each grade level (K–3) were observed, with achievement in classrooms carefully analyzed. In particular, word-level measures (word recognition accuracy and fluency) and comprehension measures were taken at both the beginning and the end of the school year.

Based on improvements in reading performance over the school year, the researchers classified the schools as most, moderately, or least effective in promoting student literacy. The most effective schools included more small-group instruction, more coaching (i.e., scaffolding) by teachers, phonics instruction with an emphasis on application during real reading, more higher-order questioning, greater outreach to parents, and more independent reading than similar but less effective schools. There was a greater balance of skills and holistic instruction (i.e., reading of complete texts, composition writing) in effective schools, and greater student engagement. Thus, the correlational and observational findings from this and other studies of schools that "beat the odds" included a balance of explicit skills instruction and more holistic, authentic reading experiences; it addressed the needs of individual learners and included positive parent relationships.

As schools entered into standardized testing era, Michael Pressley and his colleagues spent time in a variety of schools that produced high levels of reading and writing achievement. These studies not only provided more evidence and detail of how effective schools ran, but focused on three different settings: Benchmark School (discussed throughout this book); Bennett Woods, a public elementary school located in suburban Michigan; and Providence St. Mel, a Catholic school in urban Chicago (Pressley et al., 2004, 2006, 2007). These three schools were selected because of their continued success in student achievement. In each school, students had success across subjects for many years. Though different, all three schools faced their own challenges and provided insight into three different school contexts, suggesting that the school location and demographics are not a sole reason for lack of success. Through interviews and observations, Pressley and colleagues provided great detail of what made each school unique and successful.

Bennett Woods Elementary

Bennett Woods elementary supported student reading and writing in the physical environment and through the policy and administrative approaches implemented in the building. Books were found throughout the school, including in every classroom, in the hallways, and in an inviting and extensive school library. The school also had several computer labs to support student learning, including one specifically set up for struggling students in grades 4 and 5. The school hosted academic focused events such as a family science night and a reading month assembly. Additionally, the school administrators emphasized language arts instruction and allowed the most knowledgeable reading and writing teachers and reading specialist to develop the language arts programs for the school . The reading program focused on teachers connecting texts to current content themes across subjects. Lastly, the administrators spent a lot of time in classrooms working with teachers, searching out relevant professional development for teachers, and providing formative feedback. This support was evident as the teachers in Bennett Woods thrived with the school having the highest test scores in the state.

Getting the highest state test scores was not the overall goal for faculty at Bennett Woods, but teachers were determined to prepare their students. However, teachers did not "teach to the test," but rather enriched the instruction. Additionally, teachers at Bennett Woods had analyzed previous tests to gather the most information about how their students would be assessed by the state. This information was used as another tool for instruction. Beyond the state tests, teachers at Bennett Woods analyzed student data regularly to inform their instruction. They targeted the lowest performing students for remediation and used every resource possible to help all students. Furthermore, teachers and administrators at Bennett Woods never stopped learning themselves. Professional development attendance was regular and information learned was then shared with others at faculty meetings. For the faculty at Bennett Woods, the overall approach was you can always get better.

At Bennett Woods, the reading and content instruction were woven together. Teachers wanted to motivate students to read and did so through read-aloud books, showing excitement for the content being taught and connecting reading and the instructional content to student lives. Bennett Woods was also an inclusive environment in which teachers ensured that all students participated in activities. This included making necessary accommodations and modifications to activities for exceptional ability students and including the cultures of international students. Other reading instruction included a focus on letter-sound, phonics, and word recognition skills. To support learning new vocabulary, teachers had students use both internal and external context clues to figure out unknown words with much of the learning occurring through discussions. Furthermore, teachers monitored student reading progress and asked many questions about readings to have ongoing data collection of student progress.

Providence St. Mel

Providence St. Mel is a K–12 Catholic school located in one of the poorest sections of Chicago and served a student population of mostly African

American students. Pressley et al. (2004) specifically selected Providence St. Mel due to its 100% college acceptance rate of graduates over the past 25 years. One reason for the success was teachers and administrators closely monitored student learning and took an active role in supporting student success. For example, the school principal would have informal interactions in the hallway or cafeteria with all students about their grades ranging from students who had slipping grades to those students who had good grades. The school administrators also invested in the teachers of the school by supporting instruction, spending time in classrooms, and listening to teacher needs. Every decision made by school administrators at Providence St. Mel was based on research from motivating students to the reading curriculum. Furthermore, administrators had high expectations for every member of the staff, which included ensuring an academic focus throughout the day, intensive instruction when and where it was needed, a safe and orderly environment, and strong classroom management of every teacher. Administrators held teachers to high accountability standards through consistent observations throughout the year. Observations focused on instruction and classroom management, with teachers being let go who did not develop effective classrooms.

Within the school, teachers took advantage of every minute with students. Though Providence St. Mel had a rigorous testing schedule, teachers worked with students to prepare for the tests and feel confident in their ability to perform well. This included providing exam reviews, detailed feedback on assignments, and praising student success. Teachers were also described as dedicated to their students because of the relationships built in the classroom and extending their time beyond school hours with activities such as school tutoring, chaperoning school clubs, and leading school fundraisers. At Providence St. Mel, the connections did not stop with students, but also included parents. It was expected that teachers were in contact with parents regularly throughout the year with parent–teacher conferences, letters to parents, and inviting parents to view assemblies and concerts at the school.

Providence St. Mel, provided an environment that promoted student success and set high standards for every member of the school community. Students felt motivated and supported within the building and received necessary feedback to grow. As readers, Providence St. Mel students took an active role in their learning by reflecting on discussions had in class about a text, including text relevant to students' backgrounds.

Summary

Bennett Woods and Providence St. Mel are just two examples of highly effective schools serving two different demographics of students. While both Bennett Woods and Providence St. Mel found success in two drastically different locations, the school environments and atmospheres shared many similar traits. Other studies of effective school have echoed findings that building leadership and the school environment play a major role in the success of the school (e.g., Cunningham, 2007; Johnson, 2002; Mosenthal et al., 2002; Taylor et al., 2000). These traits often pushed from the top down can play a major role in student success. While school administrators play a critical role in building effective schools, it goes beyond just them. Teachers, parents, and students must also invest in the overall goal of student learning. Teachers especially have a major influence on student success as teachers provide the instruction, assesses students, and establish the classroom environment. At the elementary level, classroom teachers are especially key as classroom teachers spend a majority of the day with students and have a major role in a child's development. Thus, it is important for researchers to go beyond just effective schools, but also explore the characteristics of highly effective teachers.

A SURVEY STUDY OF OUTSTANDING PRIMARY-LEVEL TEACHERS OF READING

In order to get an understanding of highly effective primary-level teaching, Pressley and his associates (1996) selected a sample of elementary language-arts supervisors throughout the United States and asked them to identify their very best kindergarten, first-grade, and second-grade teachers—teachers who were exceptional in promoting literacy achievement in students. These teachers were then simply asked to describe in an open-ended fashion the 10 most important elements of their teaching. When all the responses to this question were catalogued, the list came to more than 400 individual practices that the teachers described as being important to their teaching. These lists were the first indication to the researchers of the deep complexity of effective primary-grade literacy instruction.

For each of the elements of instruction specified in the initial open-ended query, the researchers developed a question that could be responded to on a quantitative scale and returned to the teachers with a questionnaire constructed from these questions. Example questions included:

Do you use "big books"? (Answered on a "never" to "several times a day" scale.)
After a story, do you ask students "comprehension questions"? (Answered on a "not at all" to "all stories" scale.)
What percentage of the material read by your students is outstanding

children's literature? Written at a "controlled" reading level? Written to provide practice in phonetic elements and/or patterns?

Are home/parents involved in your reading instruction for good readers? Average readers? Weaker readers?

Most of the teachers from the initial sample responded again. The teachers described their instructional practices, indicating in their responses that their classrooms involved a complex articulation of components.

Literate Classroom Environments

Virtually all the teachers reported that they identified, at least to some extent, with whole-language and language-experience approaches. The teachers reported that they attempted to create a literate environment in the classroom, including an in-class library, display of student work, and display of chart stories and poems. These classrooms were portrayed as rich with stories being told, read, and reread. Teachers reported that they overtly modeled literacy skills and strategies, as well as positive attitudes toward literacy.

The instruction reported by the teachers included daily practice of reading and writing, with limited practice of skills in isolation, such as with worksheets or workbooks. Even so, the teachers also reported that they made certain that skills not yet mastered by their students—including phonics, letter recognition, and spelling—were experienced repeatedly by students, often in the context of other reading and writing activities. The use of learning centers dedicated to the development of listening, reading, and writing were also typical of these effective primary classrooms.

The teachers reported extensive monitoring of their students, including comprehension checks (e.g., questions following a reading, student retelling of stories heard or read, student retelling with story strips or pictures), writing portfolios, and reading portfolios. The teachers also reported regular conferences with parents and frequent communications with the parents of students as part of accountability. They expressed concern with the individual literacy achievement of students, monitoring student needs, giving mini-lessons, and reteaching as needed. Reading and writing were portrayed as individually guided on a student-by-student basis.

The teachers indicated that literacy instruction was integrated with the rest of the curriculum. As part of this integration, extension experiences were reported as common, including arts and crafts, illustrating activities, and games. In short, these expert teachers presented their classrooms as places in which literacy development occurred throughout the day, connected both to formal curriculum and less formal activities.

Teaching of Reading

Teachers described a great deal of concern with the development of reading skills, not only in context, as favored by the whole-language model, but also using decontextualized approaches (e.g., games, spelling tests). The teachers reported developing many specific competencies as part of their reading instruction, including skills prerequisite to reading (e.g., auditory and visual discrimination, attending and listening skills), concepts of print, letter recognition, the alphabetic principle, letter–sound associations, punctuation, decoding strategies, sight words and vocabulary, spelling, text elements (e.g., cause–effect relations, theme/main idea, character analysis), comprehension strategies (especially prediction and visualization), and critical thinking skills (including brainstorming, categorization, and recalling details).

Many different types of reading were reported as occurring in these classrooms, including students reading along with the teacher, echo and choral reading, shared reading, students reading aloud with others, daily silent reading, student rereading of books and stories, and reading homework (e.g., teachers sending books home and asking parents to listen to their children read). Many different types of material were read, including outstanding children's literature, big books, chart poems and stories, picture books, and patterned and predictable books. Reading often included author studies, involving the reading of several books by distinguished children's authors and illustrators. The teachers reported limited reading of basal readers, and instead using leveled books, chapter books, and expository materials.

Writing

In addition to the strong emphasis on reading development, teachers described many practices related to writing. Teachers taught the writing process, including planning, drafting, revising, and publishing. They employed story and journal writing. Students in their classrooms reportedly wrote responses to pictures, wordless picture books, and books read aloud. Teachers implemented shared writing activities, such as having the class dictate stories to the teacher, who served as a scribe. For these teachers, writing was viewed as connected to reading in a number of ways, with students reading aloud to classmates and the teacher the stories they had written.

Qualitatively Similar Instruction Regardless of Ability

The teachers surveyed were emphatic that they offered the same types of materials and activities to all students, regardless of ability. However, they described their instruction as being more explicit and more extensive for weaker readers. That is, they seemed to understand—at least implicitly—that weaker students would not develop the skills needed to be literate simply through immersion in the literate environments of their classrooms. Consistent with this concern, the teachers reported providing more guidance during reading and writing instruction with weaker readers than with stronger ones. In a follow-up questionnaire study (Rankin-Erickson & Pressley, 2000), primary-level special educators also reported commitment to providing much direct instruction and support of reading and writing skills. That is, in two different studies, primary-level educators claimed that explicit instruction in skills was essential for weaker students. Even so, they thought that all readers needed to be taught the same skills and that all readers should experience good literature and composing experiences.

Grade-Level Shifts in Teaching

Not surprisingly, teachers reported changes in instructional practices when advancing from kindergarten to grade 2.

With advancing grade level, the teachers reported fewer signs and labels in their classrooms and less use of learning centers. Letter-recognition drills and singing of the alphabet song occurred less often, as did the emphasis on the alphabetic principle, letter–sound associations, and simple concepts of print (e.g., concept of a "letter," directions of print). Teachers were less likely to reread stories, conduct shared big book reading, or use chart stories and poems with advancing grade level. Picture, patterned, and controlled-reading-level books declined in frequency of use. Shared writing (e.g., students dictating stories to teachers) also declined. There were fewer parent conferences.

With increasing grade level, teachers reported more round-robin reading and more reading aloud in general by individual students. There was also more independent reading occurring within the classroom. Basal readers were reported to be used more frequently as students advanced through the primary years. Consistent with whole language, there was an increased emphasis on the use of syntactic cues to decode words. On the other hand, teachers were also more likely to describe instruction in phonics rules, sounding out, and orthographic analysis for decoding. Sight-word and spelling drills increased, as did spelling tests. There was more vocabulary instruction and the reported teaching of comprehension strategies increased with advancing grade. In writing, students produced more stories and more writing in response to reading. Punctuation was emphasized more. Writing portfolios were reported as increasing in saliency with increasing grade level.

Summary

The teachers in this early survey study described school days packed with a great deal of varied reading and writing experiences. Most critically, from the perspective of this book, great balance was reported in the instruction offered to students. Consistent with the recommendation of a number of educators and theorists (e.g., Adams, 1990; Cazden, 1992; Delpit, 1988; Duffy, 1991; Fisher & Hiebert, 1990; McCaslin, 1989; Pressley, 1994; Stahl et al., 1994), the teachers in this study depicted their classrooms as integrating the attractive features of whole language with explicit skills instruction.

Even though the teacher survey data were closer to actual teaching than the musings of a curriculum professor sitting at her or his computer, they were nonetheless still removed from actual classroom experience. Thus, Pressley and his colleagues followed up the survey with studies of grade 1 teaching that involved spending time in actual classrooms and observing.

STUDIES OF OUTSTANDING FIRST-GRADE TEACHING

A Study of Outstanding Teaching in Upstate New York

In an effort to understand in greater detail the practices that made some primary teachers extremely effective, the Pressley group followed its survey work with a series of classroom-based, observational studies (Pressley, Allington, et al., 2001; Pressley, Wharton-McDonald, et al., 2001; Wharton-McDonald et al., 1997, 1998). In the first of these studies, researchers asked language arts supervisors in the Albany, New York, area to nominate exceptionally effective grade 1 teachers, as well as a contrasting group of more typical teachers at the same grade level. Throughout the year, the researchers conducted at least 10 observations in each of nine classrooms and gathered additional data from at least two in-depth interviews.

Although they respected the supervisors' judgments of excellence, they wanted to determine more objectively which of the teachers produced exceptional student achievement. Thus, as the observations progressed, they identified three types of information used as measures of teaching effectiveness:

1. *Student engagement.* Every 10–15 minutes, the observer calculated the percentage of students attentively engaged in academic activities. The classrooms varied with respect to this dimension: Some were characterized by consistently high engagement, whereas others were much more variable in engagement.

2.   *Reading level.* This was defined not by standardized test scores, but by the difficulty levels of books that students were reading at the end of the year. There was wide variation among the classes by the end of the year, ranging from classrooms where most students seemed to be working regularly with texts that were at or above grade level to others in which many students were regularly reading books intended for early or middle first-grade reading.

3.   *Writing.* Writing was appraised by examining the stories and essays that children wrote. In some classrooms, typical end-of-the-year compositions were several pages long, reflecting knowledge of a variety of writing conventions, accurate spelling, and appropriate punctuation. The writing in these classrooms often reflected real coherence in expression, with a single topic developed over the pages of writing. At the other extreme were classrooms in which end-of-year writing was typically less than a page long and often lacked coherence. In these classrooms, topical development and mechanics were typically much less impressive.

By the conclusion of the study, the researchers identified three clusters of teachers. In three classrooms, student engagement was consistently high, reading levels were at or above grade level, and writing was relatively coherent and sophisticated. Three classrooms were at the other extreme, with much more variable, and often low engagement and more modest indications of reading and writing achievement. Three classrooms were in the middle. The researchers developed a model of each teacher's teaching. Then, they compared and contrasted the nine teachers to develop an understanding of aspects of instruction that were common across classrooms as well as aspects of instruction that distinguished the three best teachers from the other six.

Commonalities in Instruction Across Classrooms

The nine classrooms, in fact, did have much in common, with the following characteristics observed in at least seven of them:

- They were positive places, led by caring teachers.
- There was little competition.
- There were classroom routines, and thus much of the time students knew what they were supposed to be doing.
- There were a variety of teaching configurations—whole- and small-group instruction, cooperative learning, and independent work.
- Teachers mixed direct skills instruction (i.e., of decoding,

punctuation, capitalization, spelling) and meaning-emphasis activities.

- All teachers recognized the importance of parental participation in children's literacy development.

In summary—important in the context of this book—there was some balancing of the skills-emphasis and meaning-emphasis activities in all of the classrooms observed.

Unique Characteristics of the Three Outstanding Teachers

- The best teachers in the sample were masterful classroom managers. They were so good, in fact, that classroom management was hardly noticeable. In similar observations, Hamre and Pianta (2010) refer to the highly effective classroom as a "well-oiled machine" (p. 32), noting the same high level of student engagement and almost invisible management procedures.

- The top three teachers were also skillful managers of the human resources available to them. Thus, resource teachers who "pushed in" to these classrooms were always busy providing instruction and assistance to students. In contrast, resource teachers often were underused by the more typical teachers—for example, they would spend a great deal of time on the periphery of the classroom with nothing to do as the classroom teacher conducted a whole-group lesson.

- There was a high density of instruction in the best classrooms— that is, there was always something to keep the children engaged and many lessons had multiple goals, pursued simultaneously. Activities connected with one another. Reading materials connected to writing topics, and literacy instruction tied in with content instruction. For example, one of the outstanding teachers integrated her lessons on nutrition, a required part of the grade 1 science curriculum for the district, with readings of works such as Judith Barrett's *Cloudy with a Chance of Meatballs* (1978), which motivated the writing of menus in the style of the children's book.

- In the most effective classrooms, the activities were consistently academically rich in comparison to academically vacuous activities that were often observed in other classrooms. For example, in the more typical classrooms there was a great deal of copying and much of the literacy instruction was devoted to "sharing" discussions not related to what the children were reading or to other academic content. In general, there was more going on—in terms of both activities and objectives covered—in the more outstanding classrooms than in the typical classrooms.

- The classrooms with outstanding teachers were filled with the message that students can and will learn. These teachers fully expected that their students would develop as readers and writers. In the outstanding classrooms, students were reinforced for their accomplishments. Each of the three best teachers enthusiastically recognized the progress being made by struggling students in particular.

- Literacy instruction in the most successful classrooms was exceptionally well balanced with respect to both meaning emphasis and the explicit teaching of skills. Reading, writing, and skills instruction were very well integrated in these classrooms. The skills lessons were filled with reminders about how the skills related to the children's writing and reading. Moreover, the children had many opportunities to use the skills as they read and wrote. As one of the outstanding teachers described it, teaching beginning reading "is a fine balance between immersing the child in whole language and teaching through . . . sounds, going back to using skills . . . . If you don't have a balance, it's kind of like trying to fit a square through a circle. It doesn't work. You don't connect with everyone if you don't use a variety of [teaching] strategies."

- In contrast to the integrated, balanced approach displayed by teachers in the most effective group, the less effective teachers tended to present instruction that was either heavily skills based or heavily whole language, or they attempted to combine the two approaches but did so in a disjointed or inconsistent way. Thus, one teacher in the middle group whose instruction was heavily influenced by the whole-language philosophy also had a weekly spelling program based on basic decoding skills. Students learned to spell word families and practiced words each week but were not necessarily expected to be responsible for spelling words correctly when they wrote stories or compositions in their journals.

- One of the reasons for students' achievement in the three most successful classrooms was that they received help as needed. The teachers in these classrooms were exceptionally active in scaffolding students' learning (Wood et al., 1976), providing hints and prompts when students faltered, whether during whole-group instruction or one-on-one interactions. Students received assistance as they attempted to read challenging texts and as they drafted and revised what they wrote. The assistance often involved prompting students to use the skills they were learning. For example, on the day before Valentine's Day, one effective teacher managed to insert mini-lessons on shapes and phonemic awareness as she introduced an art project:

TEACHER: I think of things when I think of Valentine's Day, too, and I write them down. What shape did I write them on? (*Students are quiet.*) Is it a square? A circle? A rectangle? A triangle? What shape is it?

STUDENT 1: A heart.

TEACHER: Can anyone try to spell *heart*?

STUDENT 2: H-E-A-R-T.

TEACHER: My goodness. If I wanted to use my sounds to spell heart, what would I start with?

STUDENT 3: H.

TEACHER: And what would it end with?

STUDENT 3: T.

TEACHER: So right away, you know some of the letters in *heart*.

• Given many such opportunistic reviews, it was clear that the most effective teachers viewed skill development as they viewed all of reading and writing—as involving long-term construction of knowledge about how to read and write. At the same time, these teachers were not so committed to developmental educational models that they did not occasionally use worksheets or provide practice opportunities for some skills.

• The most effective teachers provided ongoing support for learners. But their support did not prevent students from developing independence. Rather, self-regulation was most common in the three best classrooms. Students in these classrooms often worked independently or with other children. The most effective teachers developed students who could do much of what was required of them without adult assistance. They provided instructional tasks that challenged students but did not overwhelm them. Students learned to regulate their behavior and their learning.

• The best teachers were highly aware both of their practices and of the purposes driving those practices. There was nothing haphazard about literacy instruction in these classrooms. This was in contrast to some of the other teachers, who justified some frequently observed activities as giving the children "something to do" while the teacher worked with small groups. "Busy work" was just not a concept in the thinking of the outstanding teachers.

The observers were struck by the fact that, despite the commonalities among the outstanding classrooms (summarized in Table 10.1), every classroom in this study had its own personality, including the three classes headed by the most effective teachers. Thus, it is difficult to illustrate outstanding teaching by describing the work of any one outstanding teacher. That said, the following case study provides a more detailed description of the effective teaching observed in one of the most effective classrooms.

Andy's Classroom

One of the three outstanding teachers observed by Wharton-McDonald et al. (1998) was a middle-aged male named Andy. Andy's classroom was an extremely attractive world. One student said it all when he was heard exclaiming to himself one day, "I wish I lived here!" Andy never criticized students. Rather, he always intervened positively to get students back on task or to correct behavior. For example, when classroom conversations rose above an acceptable level one day, Andy directed students, "I hear productive talk, but how about a little softer?" When a student was off-task during an observation, Andy suggested, "Kenny, why don't you read your essay with Mark?" Kenny and Mark then read together with enthusiasm, with Mark providing revision feedback to Kenny.

When other adults entered Andy's classroom, nothing stopped. He dealt with the adults efficiently and quickly, never missing a step in his teaching as he did so. Maintaining attention to students to the exclusion of visiting adults was a characteristic of all three of the most effective teachers, whereas more typical teachers were much more willing to attend to visiting adults. Student engagement was invariably high in Andy's class, with students being attentive during their whole-group and small-group lessons and working hard when on their own. The students started reading and writing on their own as soon as they arrived in the classroom. Moreover, their time was mostly spent on actual reading and writing, with very little time devoted to activities such as illustrating stories they had written. In other classrooms in this study, the observers noted much more art, often involving time-consuming, difficult-to-manage materials such as paste or silhouette tracings. Such difficult-to-manage materials rarely entered Andy's classroom. In short, time was spent well largely because the students managed themselves, with the environment set up so that their attentions were not diverted to solving low-level problems like getting enough paste.

Andy strongly encouraged self-regulation, regularly praising students for making decisions and taking responsibility for their learning. There were many comments like "Some of you already had the words in alphabetical order before I told you to do so. Good." Each group of desks had a bin of independent reading books, and students knew how to make their own choices about which ones to read. On their own, students selected books from the Reading Is Fundamental project that were related to ongoing themes in the class. Andy taught his students to read "inside your heads." He encouraged students to monitor whether what they were reading was

TABLE 10.1. Distinguishing Characteristics of the Best Teachers in the Wharton-McDonald, Pressley, and Hampston (1998) Study

- Masterful classroom management
- High density of instruction and activity
- Reading, writing, and other instruction well integrated
- Good balancing of whole-language and explicit-skills instruction
- High expectations that students would learn
- Extensive use of scaffolding
- Consistent encouragement of self-regulation

making sense and to reread a passage when it did not. During writing, Andy urged students to attend to mechanics themselves, although mechanics were, in fact, checked by the teacher as part of his monitoring of writing. The classroom included a revision and editing chart so that students could begin to check their own writing and begin revision rather than wait for the teacher. Students practiced a variety of comprehension strategies: comparing, contrasting, and summarizing. These strategies occurred in the context of other activities. For example, students were encouraged to plan, an important critical thinking skill, as part of their book projects.

Although students learned to work independently, there was also a lot of cooperation in the classroom, with students checking each other's work and helping one another work through difficult materials. Andy assigned weaker readers to work with stronger reading partners. Students worked together on important projects and helped one another, just as Andy often helped them.

One of the notable features of Andy's expert instruction was his extensive scaffolding for students when they experienced difficulties, inserting frequent mini-lessons appropriate to the problems of particular students. Students' tasks were always within their reach, at least with scaffolding. He monitored what his students were understanding during group discussions and provided helpful prompts to assist in their understanding of elusive concepts. For example, when group members were having difficulty differentiating the habitats of ducks and chickens, Andy pondered aloud to himself, "I wonder if it might have something to do with water." Andy checked on his students individually as they worked at their seats, providing help as needed, but never solving a problem for a student. For example, when a student had difficulties spelling a word during writing, Andy prompted the student to think about the sounds in the word. There were lots of comments like "Shawn, is that the way we used those letters when we did the other words? Think about it." Shawn went on to spell the word correctly.

During independent work times, Andy first sought out students most likely to be having problems. The struggling readers were never isolated, however. Rather, Andy went out of his way to maintain their participation in the class in ways that were decidedly inclusive. For example, when it was time for students to read their essays aloud to the class, the students most likely to struggle sat at a table near Andy, so he could support their reading. The table had several other seats, each of which was occupied only by bidding from other members of the class. Sitting near Andy was seen as special for the students in his class, with no stigma ever attached to any student who spent time interacting with the teacher. His relationships with his students were consistently positive and conflict-free.

Excellent literature was extremely important in Andy's class, with student writing typically involving responses to high-quality stories and trade books. If one wanted to make an edited tape of outstanding literature experiences, it could be done using footage from Andy's classroom. Consistent with whole language, there was extensive reading of trade books, with much attention to and discussion of distinguished children's authors. Students read *Weekly Reader*. There were many different types of reading, from choral reading to partner reading to independent (silent) reading.

In Andy's classroom, there was a great deal of discussion about what had been read, something rarely observed in most classrooms (Nystrand, 2006). Andy asked a lot of questions intended not simply to assess students' understanding, but to begin conversations. In these conversations, students did a lot of explaining, with Andy constantly using follow-up questions to draw out students' conceptions of things and encourage elaborated use of oral language. These efforts to elicit student language were deliberate, as he had several students that year with notable language delays. Andy's follow-up questions typically reflected consideration of previous answers, sending the message that what the students said about the reading was important. Yes, Andy often elaborated on the students' ideas, but the students' voices and ideas were always honored.

Consistent with a meaning-emphasis model, there was a great deal of writing in this classroom, with clear reading–writing connections (e.g., rewrite in your own words a story just heard). This writing instruction covered macrostructural characteristics of stories—for example, clear emphasis on having a beginning, middle, and end—and a title. It involved writing and revision as a function of conferencing with the teacher. There was also some peer conferencing, with students responding in writing to what they read by following four steps: read, think, tell a neighbor, write.

Inconsistent with whole language, however, was Andy's systematic use of a basal reader. He liberally used stories from other basal readers as well, especially when they related to content themes. That Andy was not married to meaning-emphasis philosophy comes through in many other ways as well. In this classroom, skills instruction intelligently complemented the reading of authentic literature and student writing. He provided systematic, explicit phonics instruction, both in formal lessons and opportunistically as part of mini-lessons. He taught simple phonics rules (such as the "bossy final *e*" causing the preceding vowel to say its name). This occurred in the context of spelling instruction with, for example, lists of words that exemplified particular phonic principles. During the reading of a story, there was often discussion of words with particular characteristics (e.g., a word with a "short *o*" sound). During small-group lessons, there often were word analysis activities, such as finding the little words in big words. Workbook pages sometimes complemented instruction when Andy believed the students could benefit from such work.

Andy consciously stimulated students to think critically as they did skill activities, often requiring explanations from them. There were frequent exchanges like this one during a whole-group alphabetizing activity:

ANDY: Why did you put *whale* before *woman*?

TOMMY: Both start with a *w*, but I used the second letter—*h* comes before *o*, so *whale* before *woman*.

ANDY: That's right . . . . Your group has been learning how to alphabetize using the second letter . . . . This one is tricky because one letter in it can have two different sounds.

EDDY: Huge (*pronounced correctly*).

ANDY: Why is it tricky?

EDDY: Because *g* can have a hard *g* or a soft *g* sound.

ANDY: That's right. Sometimes *g* can say (*makes hard* g *sound*) and sometimes (*makes soft* g *sound*). So that's why this word needs a little extra practice.

Andy and his students talked a lot about what was in the books they were reading, how the ideas in their readings related to other ideas being covered in the curriculum, and how to use basic reading skills. There was dialoguing all day long in this classroom.

There also was explicit attention to vocabulary development in Andy's classroom. Consistent with the thinking of meaning-emphasis advocates, Andy regularly discussed new vocabulary words with his students. These discussions were supplemented, however, with many sight words posted around the room. There were sight-word drills. Resource teachers provided more explicit and extensive instruction to weaker students.

There were strong connections across the curriculum, with a gardening theme in the spring, for example, represented in reading, writing, and science—as well as in students' self-selected independent reading books.

Students continued to read books about plants long after the unit on gardening had ended. Such integration was observed with respect to other themes as well, including the hatching of chickens in the late spring. Literature, science, and values came together dynamically as students read about chickens and discussed the biology that permitted the birth of 12 chickens in their classroom. Students wrote independently about the incubation process, but they also worked together to prepare a news story celebrating their 100% hatching success. Connections were everywhere in Andy's teaching, creating a dynamic, engaging classroom.

Finally, Andy fostered a strong *home–school* connection through homework that he carefully monitored. He encouraged students to take home challenging stories to read with a parent in the evening. When students talked about doing something literacy-related with a parent, Andy noted and praised it publicly. Before vacation breaks, Andy sent home a packet of homework and a letter to parents to encourage them to work with their students over the break, including writing in their journals.

At the end of the school year, every student in Andy's class was writing at least three sentences in response to writing assignments, and most of the students were writing a full page or more. Their ideas were well connected in most compositions and were related to content coverage in the class. Their printing was excellent, as was capitalization and punctuation. The students' writing reflected understanding of line and page conventions. There were some invented spellings, but many words were spelled correctly.

By June, all students except one were reading end-of-first-grade-level material. Most students in the class had read through all of the first-grade basal readers covered systematically in the class and seemed comfortable doing so. Quite a few students were reading second-grade trade books and middle second-grade basal readers. As the researchers observed Andy's teaching in the context of visiting the more typical classrooms in the Wharton-McDonald et al. (1998) study, they could not help but think how fortunate his students were.

It has been noted that "in the U.S. right now, a good teacher is a matter of luck" (Pianta, 2013). The students in Andy's classroom were surely lucky. What a difference it made for them to spend the year in Andy's classroom versus one of the more typical classrooms in the sample. This was particularly salient given that in soliciting classrooms for the study the researchers emphasized that they did not want *weak* grade 1 classrooms; they were specifically interested in observing outstanding classrooms and others that provided solid ("typical") grade 1 experiences. Thus, the contrast between what happened in Andy's classroom and what happened in the weakest of the classrooms in the sample probably *under*estimated the full range of experience of grade 1 students. Many children in American grade 1 classrooms do not experience what Andy's students had; many do not even get close!

Comments

The first time the authors presented the Wharton-McDonald et al. (1998) data at a professional conference, one prominent whole-language advocate stormed out of the session, and they later received reports that the individual had characterized the results of the study as "dangerous." Despite some residual extremism, however, Pressley and his colleagues were not alone in proposing a "radical middle" approach, recognizing the need for explicit skills instruction in the context of a classroom saturated with authentic reading and writing experiences—that is, a balanced approach (e.g., Adams, 1990; Cazden, 1992; Duffy, 1991; Fisher & Hiebert, 1990; McCaslin, 1989). The unique contribution of the Pressley group's classroom-based research was in demonstrating that effective teachers were *already* enacting balance in their classrooms—and it was working.

A National Follow-Up

Following the observational study in upstate New York, Pressley and a group of colleagues expanded their exploration of expert literacy instruction to a national sample of teachers, including schools in New York, New Jersey, Texas, Wisconsin, and California (Pressley, Allington, et al., 2001; Pressley, Wharton-McDonald, et al., 2001). In each locale, they identified grade 1 classrooms that were highly effective and ones that were more typical, using about the same criteria as applied in Wharton-McDonald et al. (1998). Although it took a book-length presentation to summarize those results, they were highly consistent with those of the regional study. Effective grade 1 teachers teach very differently from less effective ones. Pressley, Allington, et al. (2001) made the case that many more skills were covered during each hour of instruction in the effective classrooms. Word recognition instruction was richer, more often involving the teaching of multiple strategies (i.e., phonics, identifying word parts, looking at the whole word, using picture clues, using semantic context information, using syntactic cues). Effective teachers were more likely to teach comprehension strategies (e.g., making predictions, using mental imagery, summarizing, looking for the parts of a story). Effective teachers scaffolded much more extensively, serving as academic coaches to their students. The writing process was emphasized more in the effective classrooms, including many prompts to plan, draft, revise, and edit. Teachers had higher expectations for writing conventions, such as capitalization, punctuation, and accurate spelling of high-frequency words. The tasks that students were assigned were academic (e.g., involving a lot of writing and a little artwork, in contrast to tasks in more typical classrooms involving a lot of artwork and a little writing). In effective classrooms, students' writing was everywhere, including in big books the students wrote and displayed proudly.

The case studies described in Pressley, Allington, and associates' (2001) book made clear the conclusion that effective primary literacy instruction includes extensive teaching of skills, much reading of high-quality literature, a great deal of student composition, precise matching of task demands to student competencies, extensive encouragement of student self-regulation, and frequent, deliberate connections across the curriculum. Moreover, the classrooms described were very attractive student-centered worlds. Teachers were positive and reinforcing, with the day carefully managed. Cooperation abounded. The students loved being in these classrooms.

Comments

Effective teachers play a vital role in student learning. As seen through the case studies above, highly effective teachers immerse themselves in their student learning. Highly effective teachers build relationships, analyze student data on a regular basis, motivate their students, develop self-regulated learners, and engage students in the learning process (e.g., Pressley, Croyle, et al., 2020; Raphael et al., 2008; Roehrig et al., 2012; Stronge, 2018). It is important to remember that a teacher does not become highly effective just because they walked in the classroom, it takes time, support, and reflection (Feiman-Nemser, 2003; Howe, 2006; Pressley, Isom, et al., 2020). In the end, one must remember that effective teaching is complex. However, one revealing aspect about how the outstanding classrooms and teachers discussed in this chapter as compared with the more typical classrooms, namely: They focused on the students.

Children who enter grade 1 vary tremendously in their preparation for the instruction they will encounter there. Some enter with a history of rich emergent literacy experiences, and hence they have well-developed language and communication competencies as compared with less fortunate classmates. Some enter with advanced phonemic awareness, able to manipulate sounds in words up to and including the demands required by Pig Latin! Others, however, have much more rudimentary phonemic awareness, perhaps understanding that some words rhyme but little more. Some children have even less phonemic awareness, and cannot identify words that rhyme. The elements of instruction that occur in the grade 1 classroom must meet the needs of all of these children—no small task. Moreover, if children are, in fact, learning, then their skills and understandings are by definition changing all the time. Thus, their needs in September are quite different from their needs in October, much less those in March. In the introduction to their influential study *Preventing Reading Disabilities,* Catherine Snow and her colleagues suggest that, if we have learned anything from the study of effective teachers and classrooms, "it is that effective teachers are able to craft a special mix of instructional ingredients for every child they work with" (Snow et al., 1998, pp. 2–3).

A key mechanism for addressing students' individual learning needs— for serving up this "special mix of instructional ingredients"—is scaffolding. Sometimes the scaffolding is in the form of differentiating task demands for students. For example, it was common in the observational studies to see excellent teachers encourage the most developed writers to compose a couple of pages about a topic and in the next instant cheer on a struggling writer for composing a couple of sentences. More often the scaffolding consisted of reminding students about how skills they were learning might be applied in a particular situation. By providing more frequent and intense scaffolding for students who were struggling, the most effective teachers were able to create classrooms in which all students experienced essentially the same curriculum while receiving instruction appropriate to their individual needs and progress. The best teachers knew their students well and understood what it would take to move them forward. In contrast, scaffolding was not as prominent or as frequent in the other, more typical, classrooms observed. Indeed, the needs of the students did not seem to be as prominent in many of these classrooms, with the teachers more often focused on the demands of the curriculum than on the needs of individual students. The most effective classrooms observed were as decidedly student centered as they were balanced with respect to skills- and meaning-emphasis instruction.

NEW FRAMEWORKS FOR OBSERVATIONAL RESEARCH IN CLASSROOMS

Until recently, observational studies of the type described here were conducted primarily by educational researchers and focused primarily on instructional factors and contexts. In recent years, however, developmental psychologists have adapted methods used for observing children in home contexts to classroom settings to create new systematic measures for observing classroom environments (e.g., Hamre & Pianta, 2010; National Institute of Child Health and Human Development [NICHD], 2002, 2003). Working from this developmental perspective, Pianta and his colleagues (2008) developed an observational tool, called the Classroom Assessment Scoring System (CLASS), which is being used to assess classroom environments along three dimensions: emotional support, classroom organization, and instructional support—each of which can be understood in terms of more specific features of classrooms and teachers. For example, the emotional support dimension includes measures of classroom climate, teacher sensitivity, and regard for student perspectives. At the elementary level, the instructional support dimension includes concept development, language modeling, and quality of feedback.

In a large-scale observational study using the CLASS, Stuhlman and Pianta (2009) documented remarkable variability in the quality of educational experiences across classrooms. Their sample included 820 first-grade classrooms in over 700 schools in 32 states. All of the classrooms contained children who were being followed as part of the NICHD's longitudinal Study of Early Child Care and Youth Development (SECCYD). Based on classroom observations and teacher questionnaires, researchers identified 23% of the classrooms as "high overall quality," in which all of the positive indicators from the rating scales were above average and the two negative indicators were below average. Children in these classrooms would be expected to produce academic gains, regardless of demographic or academic risk factors. Stuhlman and Pianta also identified a set of classrooms they labeled "low overall quality" in which the positive indicators were all below average and the negative indicators were both above average. Children in these classrooms would clearly be disadvantaged in terms of expected developmental progress. In between was a group of "mediocre" classrooms that made up 28% of the sample classrooms, where the indicators were mixed. Interestingly, the largest group consisted of 31% of the classrooms that made up "positive emotional climate, low academic demand." In these classrooms, teachers created positive emotional environments but tended not to promote children's engagement in learning by giving them feedback that focused on mastery, developing understanding, or trying new strategies. The authors report that, among the 820 classrooms studied, the children who appeared to be most at risk for difficulties in the early grades due to demographic or academic factors were also the *least* likely to be enrolled in the highest-quality classrooms.

Other similar studies investigating teacher–child relationships have also found that the quality of these relationships predict both academic and socioemotional outcomes. Wu et al. (2010) studied 706 second- and third-grade students and reported strong support that the quality of teacher–student relationships predicted children's academic growth. In a study of 910 first-grade students, Hamre and Pianta (2005, 2010) found that teacher–child interactions could actually account for up to a year's progress on standardized measures of achievement, including reading. Moreover, these interactions seemed to be especially important for students considered to be at risk for school failure.

These observational measures created by developmental researchers combine emphases on cognitive and emotional learning factors and have yielded findings consistent with the earlier surveys and observations reported here—with an important focus on the teacher–child relationship.

They offer a systematic approach to measuring and evaluating the socio-emotional contributions of teachers that appear to contribute significantly to students' success in early learning.

READING RECOVERY®: INSTRUCTIONAL SUPPORT BEYOND THE CLASSROOM

Despite effective classroom instruction, some first-grade students make little progress in learning how to read and thus are at long-term risk for academic difficulties. You may have heard of Reading Recovery, which is an intervention program that was originally aimed at supporting such children (e.g., Clay, 1985). It involves daily one-teacher, one-child sessions for 10–20 weeks, with each session lasting approximately 30–40 minutes. There is a great deal of teacher monitoring throughout the Reading Recovery process to ensure that the child's particular problems are the focus of instruction, with the child's reading extensively observed and assessed before instruction even begins (Marks et al., 1994). The goal of the intervention is to help these students catch up with their peers. The starting assumption is that students may be learning too narrow a range of strategies for dealing with print and may not be flexible in their use of the strategies they have acquired. However, as you will see later, the strategies emphasized in Reading Recovery methods do not improve children's ability to decode print.

The emphasis in Reading Recovery is on helping the student build a repertoire of strategies and on providing supervised opportunities to practice those strategies in reading and writing. Much of Reading Recovery consists of teaching students strategies defined by Clay (1985; see also Pinnell, 1989) as the processes required for reading, including the following:

- Reading left to right on a page
- Using a return sweep rather than a slow return from the right-hand side of the page to the left-hand side
- Monitoring whether what is being read makes sense
- Using cross-checks on meaning-making processes (predict word with one source of information and check prediction using another source of information)
- Searching for cues to meaning from pictures, language structures, and visual cues in print
- Rereading when meaning is unclear
- Self-correcting rather than waiting for teacher correction of errors

Though Reading Recovery contains many whole language approaches, there is some daily teaching of phonics in the approach (Stahl, 2001). However, the teaching of phonics is not systematic or based on a particular scope and sequence. Instead, it is related to the patterned (i.e., non-decodable) texts that are typically used in Reading Recovery lessons.

Reading Recovery as Effective Instruction

The What Works Clearinghouse (*whatworks.ed.gov*) endorsed Reading Recovery as an intervention "found to have positive effects on general reading achievement and potentially positive effects on alphabetics, reading fluency, and comprehension for beginning readers." Previous research conducted in the 1990s and early 2000s found positive results with Reading Recovery texts and the program has been shown to be at least as effective as other one-on-one tutoring programs (Cunningham & Allington, 2007; D'Agostino & Murphy, 2004; Wasik & Slavin, 1993).

However, it is important to note that recent studies have questioned the longevity of reading recovery (e.g., May & Blakeney, 2022; May et al., 2022; Shrestha et al., 2022). These studies found that third- and fourth-grade students who received Reading Recovery in first grade had lower reading scores on state standardized tests compared to students who did not receive Reading Recovery. This shortcoming was due to students having early success with "reading" Reading Recovery texts, but eventually students struggled to read other texts beyond texts provided within the Reading Recovery instruction. Based on these studies, we caution teachers' reliance on programs like Reading Recovery due to the long-term outcomes but urge teachers to take a more evidence-based approach to teaching reading.

Despite the mixed results of the Reading Recovery intervention, it is important for teachers to understand that the program demands intense ongoing training for its tutors, and a typical load for a Reading Recovery teacher is only four or five students each half day when they work as Reading Recovery teachers. Thus, schools must make a significant investment in the program to sustain it. At the same time, schools implementing Reading Recovery have fewer students identified and served as having disabilities and fewer struggling readers needing long-term remediation services (Lyons & Beaver, 1995; Schwartz, 2005). Because of this, Reading Recovery may not be the best choice for general education teachers responsible for teaching whole classes how to read. We would encourage teachers to continue to follow the ongoing research surrounding reading recovery to have the most comprehensive understanding of the intervention.

Karyn Beach's Classroom

One study in particular explored spent 2 years documenting the classroom teaching of 10 former Reading Recovery teachers teaching reading in a general education setting (Roehrig et al., 2001). Teachers with training and experience in Reading Recovery used some of the strategies emphasized in Reading Recovery in their regular classroom instruction in addition to instruction resembling the instruction of the exemplary teachers discussed in this chapter. In particular, these teachers presented a complex balance of direct instruction, often in the form of mini-lessons and in the context of authentic reading and writing activities. Given their training and experience, they were particularly sensitive to the competencies of individual students and focused on the scaffolding necessary for the development of literacy and self-regulation. Karyn Beach was one of the teachers observed in the Roehrig et al. (2001) investigation. As described, Karyn Beach implemented some of the Reading Recovery aspects she had previously learned into her classroom along, but also included evidence based practices, such as decoding, fluency, and comprehension strategies mentioned in this book. Observations of Ms. Beach's classroom highlighted many ways in which evidence based practices are compatible with literacy instruction in an effective classroom setting.

Karyn Beach taught in a school with decidedly underprivileged children. Some students arrived at her first grade with language skills far below the 6-year-old level; others were not emotionally prepared for school, actively rejecting the teacher and participation in school activities. Despite these disadvantages, Ms. Beach's classroom was one of high student engagement with high-intensity instruction. She provided well-targeted explicit instruction, followed by a great deal of scaffolding. Ms. Beach frequently directed students to analyze words into parts, had students read and reread books for mastery, and asked students to craft written responses to books they had read.

Throughout the day, students were immersed in high-quality literature; that is, her focused-skills instruction did not come at the expense of good books. Ms. Beach was especially adept at including literature in her curriculum, consistent with her belief that excellent literature was an essential component of effective reading instruction.

Students' high level of engagement in the classroom was also due to Ms. Beach's active encouragement of their self-regulation. During an interview with the researchers, she explained that she spent a great deal of time at the beginning of the year laying the foundations for self-regulation for the rest of the year: She let the students know that she fully expected them to be working in her classroom. She made certain that students knew the choices they had when they finished their assignments. And when students exhibited self-regulation, Ms. Beach noticed—and offered positive feedback. Thus, when students who had previously come to school sleepy arrived at school alert, they heard about it ("You must have gotten more sleep. I like that."). Ms. Beach consistently reminded students to go back and reread to correct mistakes, reinforcing them when they did so ("I like how you reread there. Good readers catch mistakes and reread to correct them.").

Ms. Beach had a way of demanding excellence while simultaneously encouraging risk taking. Thus, when a student faltered when taking a risk, it was common to hear a comment like "It's no big deal when you make a mistake. Just do it over." Alternatively, when a student fooled around and came up short on a task that Ms. Beach knew he or she could do, there was a different reaction ("I only have time for the right way. Otherwise, I won't call you up to the board again."). In each instance, she was able to match the level of press and expectation to the ability and effort of the child before her. Ms. Beach consistently encouraged students to give others a chance to "get it," but she also sent the message that getting it was not as important as *trying* to get it ("I don't expect you to be perfect, but I expect you to try hard."). And encouragement of self-regulation and self-control paid off in this classroom. In general, students did know what they were expected to do and did it, perhaps most apparently during centers, when students frequently worked without much need for teacher direction. Although she engaged the class with much direct instruction and she engaged individual students with scaffolding when they needed it, students were also able to engage and direct themselves much of the time.

The students in Karyn Beach's class were successful—in no small measure because she was masterful at giving them tasks that were a little bit challenging for them but not overwhelming. This was apparent in the way she helped them to select books for independent reading; despite being first graders and having limited experience with the process, students consistently chose books that were not too easy but not too hard (using the "Goldilocks principle"). Ms. Beach knew her students well, as individual readers and writers, and she intervened with targeted activities and support that helped them progress. Moreover, she taught them to use self-regulation strategies so that, as first graders, they were already developing independence as readers and writers.

PREPARING TEACHERS FOR THE CLASSROOM

Along with us, other scholars have systematically observed outstanding and more typical teachers in their classrooms in order to develop more complex understandings of the competencies they embody. In part, this observation has been driven by the desire to better prepare new teachers to be successful and to support experienced teachers more effectively. While the current arguments about this topic are too lengthy to address here, our growing understandings do have some implications for teacher preparation. If our goal is to prepare teachers who are effective in their support of primary-grade learners, then a brief exercise in backward mapping would include (at the least) the following broad areas:

- *Highly effective teachers have deep understandings of the processes of reading and writing development.* Teacher-preparation programs must therefore develop understandings of both the skills that promote literacy development (phonemic awareness, phonics, vocabulary, fluency, comprehension, writing) and the habits, dispositions, and resources of readers and writers. Thus, the programs should present literacy instruction as being a carefully orchestrated balance of explicit instruction and authentic reading and writing experiences, featuring great literature, complex text, and thoughtful writing.

- *Highly effective teachers know their students very well.* This, combined with the content knowledge described above, enables them to scaffold their students' learning effectively. Teachers therefore need tools for observing and interacting with students in ways that yield useful (usable) information about them as learners. Standardized test scores returned to the teacher several months after testing are not helpful for guiding instruction. In classrooms where students are learning, they are changing every day; thus, even a score that accurately reflected a student's understandings in November is no longer relevant when it is returned to the teacher in February. Schools of education must provide teachers with more effective tools for knowing their students and the knowledge to use them.

- *Highly effective teachers are flexible. They adapt their instruction to meet the dynamic needs of their students.* Developing flexibility comes largely from the experience of working with actual students; new teachers tend to be less flexible (Corcoran, 1981, 1998; Pressley, Isom, et al., 2020). Thus, developing teachers need many opportunities to spend time in classrooms with real students, with highly effective teachers, and receive the feedback they need to make sense of their interactions (Ronfeldt et al., 2018). As most readers of this chapter will know, reading *about* a 6-year-old in a book and interacting with a live child are two very different experiences. New teachers need enough experience working with real students in authentic classroom environments so that they understand how to adapt what they're doing to meet the needs of a variety of learners—and eventually, they can do it on the fly.

- *The quality of the teacher–student relationship is important to students' academic growth.* Teachers must be able to forge and maintain supportive, low-conflict relationships with their students. Yet, teachers differ in their ability to accomplish this goal (Pianta et al., 2007; Pressley, Croyle, et al., 2020). For example, some teachers find it especially challenging to provide social and emotional support to children who present an overly confident sense of self (Wu et al., 2010). Developmental researchers (e.g., Pianta, 2013; Wu et al., 2010) have identified this as a high priority for preservice and inservice professional development.

SUMMARY AND CONCLUDING REFLECTIONS

1. Highly effective primary-grade literacy teachers (defined by their positive effects on the literacy achievement of their students) balance elements of a meaning-emphasis approach (e.g., immersion in authentic literature and writing experiences) and systematic, explicit skills instruction. Excellent primary-level literacy education involves the complex articulation of many specific elements, often including both use of skills in context and decontextualized skills experiences.

2. Explicit teaching of skills is the beginning of a constructivist process for young learners. It gives them a good start, but it is only that. As children attempt to use and adapt knowledge that they are taught (e.g., of letter–sound associations), their understanding of it deepens. The opportunities to apply skills during real reading and writing provide especially rich constructivist experiences, which is why balancing of meaning-emphasis and skills-emphasis teaching makes so much sense as compared with either an extreme antiskills approach or an exclusive skills-emphasis approach.

3. Expert early literacy teachers are very knowledgeable about the processes of literacy development and about their students. The integration of these two types of knowledge enables these teachers to scaffold student learning very effectively.

4. Expert teachers are flexible. They understand that each student has unique learning needs and strengths. Moreover, they expect students to change and grow, and they readily adapt their instruction to meet those evolving needs. They do this in ways that are both planned and opportunistic.

5. In addition to the instructional characteristics that predict literacy growth, there are social-emotional factors related to teacher–child interactions that also appear to be significant in predicting achievement—particularly among students considered to be at risk for school failure.

6. Many students who experience difficulties in learning to read in the grade 1 classroom can benefit from tutoring and evidence based

approaches. Even so, students whose reading improves as a function of intensive tutoring may require much more support if they are to continue to succeed in school. Teachers trained in Reading Recovery can use what they learned in their training, but should also include a balance of evidence based approaches as discussed throughout this book.

7. Given the complexities of effective instruction in a primary-level classroom, the challenges for teacher preparation are significant but not insurmountable. To date, the field still lacks a strong and reliable model for preparing teachers, and while we have learned a great deal about what *doesn't* work for inservice professional development, we still have a ways to go in determining what *does* work well.

Perhaps the relevant question now, as we approach the fifth edition of this volume, is not whether balance is appropriate—we know that it is—but where the fulcrum should be placed, and when, and for how long, and for whom. Some struggling readers benefit from more explicit, more intense instruction (Connor et al., 2007; Foorman & Torgesen, 2001; Gersten et al., 2001; Torgesen, 2000). Others need more instruction, period (Allington, 2012; Allington & McGill-Franzen, 2018). They would benefit from longer school days and/or summer programming. Students arrive in primary-grade classrooms with a wide range of background experiences. Some prefer fairy tales and fantasy; others prefer nonfiction or history. Some have strong phonemic awareness; others struggle to identify a rhyme. The challenge of teaching all of these different children is not a unitary endeavor; there can be no one-size-fits-all model that will address the needs of all learners at all times. Great instruction accounts for multiple dimensions of balance. The most effective literacy teachers balance the amount of time students spend reading and writing; they balance the amount of time students spend reading in various genres; they balance the proportion of time students spend in large groups, small groups, with peer partners, and individually; they balance the amount of time students spend reading aloud and reading silently; they balance the amount of teacher and student choice in the selection of reading materials . . . and the list goes on.

The work done by Pianta and colleagues (2007) and Connor and associates (2013) offers yet another layer of complexity to understanding the primary-level classroom. The promise of developing reliable measures of both cognitive and socioemotional variables in classrooms is great. The challenge of developing teachers who are not only knowledgeable about literacy development and instruction, but who are also sensitive to the socioemotional needs of their students—teachers who maintain positive relationships with even the most difficult among them—is also great.

Finally, we would be remiss if we did not include a note of profound caution in interpreting any of these studies of teacher quality. We must not lose sight of the goal of primary-level literacy instruction. Ultimately, the goal is not to prepare test-takers for the world. Rather, our goal is to develop learners who are able—and eager—to use written expression to communicate, to express and comprehend ideas, to solve real problems in the world, to improve their lives by relaxing with a good book (or tablet). In developing measurement tools for classroom observations, then, we cannot rely on standardized test scores as the sole outcomes of import. If we direct our efforts with laser focus on test scores, we will surely succeed in raising them. But in doing so, we miss the real target—and we risk forfeiting the enthusiasm and critical thinking of those students raising baby chicks in Andy's first-grade classroom.

REFERENCES

Adams, M. J. (1990). *Beginning to read*. Harvard University Press.

Allington, R. L. (2012). *What really matters for struggling readers: Designing research-based programs* (3rd ed.). Pearson.

Allington, R. L., & McGill-Franzen, A. (2018). *Summer reading: Closing the rich/poor reading achievement gap* (2nd ed.). Teachers College Press.

Barrett, J. (1978). *Cloudy with a chance of meatballs*. Macmillan.

Cazden, C. B. (1992). *Whole language plus: Essays on literacy in the United States and New Zealand*. Teachers College Press.

Clay, M. M. (1985). *The early detection of reading difficulties: A diagnostic survey with recovery procedure*. Heinemann.

Cole-Henderson, B. (2000). Organizational characteristics of schools that successfully serve low-income urban African American students. *Journal of Education for Students Placed at Risk, 5*, 77–91.

Connor, C. M., Morrison, F. J., Fishman, B., Crowe, E. C., Al Otaiba, S., & Schatschneider, C. (2013). A longitudinal cluster-randomized control study on the accumulating effects of individualized literacy instruction on students' reading from 1st through 3rd grade. *Psychological Science, 24*(8), 1408–1419.

Connor, C. M., Morrison, F. J., Fishman, B., Schatschneider, C., & Underwood, P. (2007). The early years: Algorithmic-guided individualized reading instruction. *Science, 315*, 464–465.

Corcoran, E. (1981). Transition shock: The beginning teacher's paradox. *Journal of Teacher Education, 32*(3), 19–23.

Corcoran, E. (1998, November 2). Personal communication.

Cunningham, P. M. (2007). High-poverty schools that beat the odds. *Reading Teacher, 60*, 382–385.

Cunningham, P. M., & Allington, R. L. (2007). *Classrooms that work: They can all read and write*. Pearson.

D'Agostino, J. V., & Murphy, J. A. (2004). A meta-analysis of Reading Recovery in United States schools. *Educational Evaluation and Policy Analysis, 26*, 23–38.

Delpit, L. D. (1988). The silenced dialogue: Power and pedagogy in educating other people's children. *Harvard Educational Review, 58*, 280–298.

Duffy, G. G. (1991). What counts in teacher education?: Dilemmas in educating empowered teachers. In J. Zutell & S. McCormick (Eds.), *Learner factors/teacher factors: Issues in literacy research and instruction—Fortieth yearbook of the National Reading Conference* (pp. 1–18). National Reading Conference.

Edmonds, R. R. (1979). Effective schools for the urban poor. *Educational Leadership, 37*, 15–24.

Feiman-Nemser, S. (2003). What new teachers need to learn. *Educational Leadership, 60*(8), 25–29.

Firestone, W. A. (1991). Educators, researchers, and the effective schools movement. In J. R. Bliss, W. A. Firestone, & C. E. Richards (Eds.), *Rethinking effective schools research and practice* (pp. 12–27). Prentice-Hall.

Fisher, C. W., & Hiebert, E. H. (1990). Characteristics of tasks in two approaches to literacy instruction. *Elementary School Journal, 91*, 3–18.

Foorman, B. R., & Torgesen, J. (2001). Critical elements of classroom and small-group instruction promote reading success in all children. *Learning Disabilities Research and Practice, 16*, 203–212.

Gersten, R., Fuchs, L. S., Williams, J. P., & Baker, S. (2001). Teaching reading comprehension strategies to students with learning disabilities: A review of the research. *Review of Educational Research, 71*, 279–320.

Hallinger, P., Bickman, L., & Davis, K. (1996). School context, principal leadership, and student reading achievement. *Elementary School Journal, 96*, 527–549.

Hamre, B. K., & Pianta, R. C. (2005). Can instructional and emotional support in the first-grade classroom make a difference for children at risk of school failure? *Child Development, 76*, 949–967.

Hamre, B. K., & Pianta, R. C. (2010). Classroom environments and developmental processes: Conceptualization and measurement. In J. Meece & J. Eccles (Eds.), *Handbook of research on schools, schooling, and human development* (pp. 25–41). Routledge.

Howe, E.R. (2006). Exemplary teacher induction: An international review. *Educational Philosophy and Theory, 38*(3), 287–297.

Johnson, F. F. (2002). High performing, high poverty, urban elementary schools. In B. M. Taylor & P. D. Pearson (Eds.), *Teaching reading: Effective schools, accomplished teachers* (pp. 89–114). Erlbaum.

Lyons, C. A., & Beaver, J. (1995). Reducing retention and learning disability placement through Reading Recovery: An educationally sound, cost-effective choice. In R. L. Allington & S. A. Walmsley (Eds.), *No quick fix: Rethinking reading programs in America's elementary schools* (pp. 116–136). Teachers College Press.

Marks, T. A., O'Flahaven, J. F., Pennington, L., Sutton, C., Leeds, S., & Steiner-O'Malley, J. (1994). *A study of two first-grade teachers "roaming around the known" with their students* (Reading Research Report No. 9). National Reading Research Center.

May, H. & Blakeney, A. (2022, April 23). *Replication of short-term experimental impacts of Reading Recovery's investing in innovation fund (i3) scale-up with regression discontinuity.* Paper presented at the annual meeting of the American Educational Research Association, San Diego, CA.

May, H., Blakeney, A., Shrestha, P., Mazal, M., & Kennedy, N. (2022, April 23). *Long-term impacts of Reading Recovery through third and fourth grade: A regression discontinuity study from 2011–12 through 2016–17.* Paper presented at the annual meeting of the American Educational Research Association, San Diego, CA.

McCaslin, M. M. (1989). Whole language: Theory, instruction, and future implementation. *Elementary School Journal, 90*, 223–229.

Mosenthal, J., Lipson, M., Sortino, S., Russ, B., & Mekkelsen, J. (2002). Literacy in rural Vermont: Lessons from schools where children succeed. In B. M. Taylor & P. D. Pearson (Eds.), *Teaching reading: Effective schools, accomplished teachers* (pp. 115–140). Erlbaum.

National Institute of Child Health and Human Development, Early Child Care Research Network. (2002). The relation of global first-grade classroom environment to structural classroom features and teacher and student behaviors. *Elementary School Journal, 102*, 367–387.

National Institute of Child Health and Human Development, Early Child Care Research Network. (2003). The NICHD study of early child care: Contexts of development and developmental outcomes over the first seven years of life. In J. Brooks-Gunn, A. S. Fuligni, & L. J. Berlin (Eds.), *Early child development in the 21st century* (pp. 181–201). Teachers College Press.

Nystrand, M. (2006). Research on the role of classroom discourse as it affects reading comprehension. *Research in the Teaching of English, 40*, 392–412.

Pianta, R. C. (2013, February). Elevating the capacity of classroom experiences for promoting children's learning and development: Observations of teacher–child interactions (Helen Kelley Symposium for Excellence in Education). Retrieved from *http://vimeo.com/61560362*.

Pianta, R. C., Belsky, J., Houts, R., Morrison, F., & the NICHD Early Child Care Research Network. (2007). Opportunities to learn in America's elementary classrooms. *Science, 315*, 1795–1796.

Pianta, R. C., La Paro, K., & Hamre, B. K. (2008). *Classroom Assessment Scoring System*. Brookes.

Pinnell, G. S. (1989). Reading Recovery: Helping at-risk children learn to read. *Elementary School Journal, 90*, 161–183.

Pressley, M. (1994). Commentary on the ERIC whole language debate. In C. B. Smith (Moderator), *Whole language: The debate* (pp. 155–178). ERIC/REC.

Pressley, M., Allington, R. L., Wharton-McDonald, R., Block, C. C., & Morrow, L. M. (2001). *Learning to read: Lessons from exemplary first-grade classrooms*. Guilford Press.

Pressley, M., Gaskins, I. W., Solic, K., & Collins, S. (2006). A portrait of Benchmark school: How a school produces high achievement in students who previously failed. *Journal of Educational Psychology, 98*(2), 282–306.

Pressley, M., Mohan, L., Raphael, L. M., & Fingeret, L. (2007). How does Bennett Woods Elementary School produce such high reading and writing achievement? *Journal of Educational Psychology, 99*(2), 221–240.

Pressley, M., Rankin, J., & Yokoi, L. (1996). A survey of instructional practices of primary teachers nominated as effective in promoting literacy. *Elementary School Journal, 96*, 363–384.

Pressley, M., Raphael, L., Gallagher, J. D., & DiBella, J. (2004). Providence-St. Mel school: How a school that works for african american students works. *Journal of Educational Psychology, 96*(2), 216–235.

Pressley, M., Wharton-McDonald, R., Allington, R., Block, C. C., Morrow, L., Tracey, D., et al. (2001). A study of effective grade-1 literacy instruction. *Scientific Studies of Reading, 5*, 35–58.

Pressley, T., Croyle, H., & Edgar, M. (2020). Different approaches to classroom environments based off teacher experience and effectiveness. *Psychology in the Schools, 57*(4), 606–626.

Pressley, T., Isom, R., Johnson, C., Barnes, A., & McAuliffe, L. (2020). Becoming a highly effective teacher and how to support teachers' development. *Journal of Educational Leadership in Action, 7*(1).

Rankin-Erickson, J. L., & Pressley, M. (2000). A survey of instructional practices of special education teachers nominated as effective teachers of literacy. *Learning Disabilities Research and Practice, 15*, 206–225.

Raphael, L. M., Pressley, M., & Mohan, L. (2008). Engaging instruction in middle school classrooms: An observational study of nine teachers. *The Elementary School Journal, 109*(1), 61–81.

Roehrig, A. D., Pressley, M., & Sloup, M. (2001). Reading strategy instruction in regular primary-level classrooms by teachers trained in Reading Recovery. *Reading and Writing Quarterly, 17*, 323–348.

Roehrig, A. D., Turner, J. E., Arrastia, M. C., Christesen, E., McElhaney, S., & Jakiel, L. M. (2012). Effective teachers and teaching: Characteristics and practices related to positive student outcomes. In K. R. Harris, S. Graham, T. Urdan, S. Graham, J. M. Royer, & M. Zeidner (Eds.), *APA educational psychology handbook: Vol. 2. Individual differences and cultural and contextual factors* (pp. 501–527). American Psychological Association.

Ronfeldt, M., Brockman, S. L., & Campbell, S. L. (2018). Does cooperating teachers' instructional effectiveness improve preservice teachers' future performance? *Educational Researcher, 47*(7), 405–418.

Schwartz, R. M. (2005). Literacy learning of at-risk first-grade students in the Reading Recovery early intervention. *Journal of Educational Psychology, 97*(2), 257–267.

Shrestha, P., Tracy, T., Mazal, M., Blakeney, A., Kennedy, N., & May, H. (2022, April 23). *A cost analysis of Reading Recovery and Alternate interventions under the i3 scale-up.* Paper presented at the annual meeting of the American Educational Research Association, San Diego, CA.

Snow, C. E., Burns, M. S., & Griffin, P. (1998). *Preventing reading disabilities in young children: A report of the National Research Council.* National Academy Press.

Stahl, S. A. (2001). Teaching phonics and phonological awareness. In S. B. Neuman & D. K. Dickinson (Eds.), *Handbook of early literacy research* (pp. 333–347). Guilford Press.

Stahl, S. A., McKenna, M. C., & Pagnucco, J. R. (1994). The effects of whole language instruction: An update and reappraisal. *Educational Psychologist, 29*, 175–186.

Stronge, J. H. (2018). *Qualities of effective teachers.* ASCD

Stuhlman, M. W., & Pianta, R. C. (2009). Profiles of educational quality in first grade. *Elementary School Journal, 109*, 323–342.

Taylor, B. M., Pearson, P. D., Clark, K., & Walpole, S. (2000). Effective schools and accomplished teachers: Lessons from primary-grade reading instruction in low-income schools. *Elementary School Journal, 101*, 121–165.

Torgesen, J. K. (2000). Individual differences in response to early interventions in reading: The lingering problem of treatment resisters. *Learning Disabilities Research and Practice, 15*, 55–64.

Wasik, B. A., & Slavin, R. E. (1993). Preventing early reading failure with one-to-one tutoring: A review of five programs. *Reading Research Quarterly, 28*, 178–200.

Wharton-McDonald, R., Pressley, M., & Hampston, J. M. (1998). Outstanding literacy instruction in first grade: Teacher practices and student achievement. *Elementary School Journal, 99*, 101–128.

Wharton-McDonald, R., Pressley, M., Rankin, J., Mistretta, J., Yokoi, L., & Ettenberger, S. (1997). Effective primary-grades literacy instruction = balanced literacy instruction. *The Reading Teacher, 50*, 518–521.

Wood, S. S., Bruner, J. S., & Ross, G. (1976). The role of tutoring in problem solving. *Journal of Child Psychology and Psychiatry, 17*, 89–100.

Wu, J., Hughes, J N., & Kwok, O. (2010). Teacher–student relationship quality type in elementary grades: Effects on trajectories for achievement and engagement. *Journal of School Psychology, 48*, 357–387.

11 Motivation and Literacy

During the early 1990s, when the National Reading Research Center was established, the organizers conducted a national survey of teachers that asked their opinions about the most pressing issues confronting education. One concern was much more prominent than any other in the responses: The teachers were emphatic that maintaining student academic motivation was a major challenge that needed to be addressed by any center concerned with promoting the reading achievement of students. In response to that input from teachers, the National Reading Research Center immediately focused on the promotion of student engagement in literacy (O'Flahavan et al., 1992).

A great deal about academic motivation was learned during the National Reading Research Center tenure, and researchers have continued to explore academic motivation, as it is still an important area of interest for teachers. For example, the center was able to establish that the main reason that teachers were concerned about motivation was that they recognized that motivation to read is connected to good grades (Sweet et al., 1998). Other important discoveries that the center found that researchers continue to study were the many facets of student motivation that can affect reading (Baker & Wigfield, 1999; Cartwright et al., 2016; Morgan & Fuchs, 2007; Schiefele et al., 2012; Wigfield & Guthrie, 1997; Wigfield, Guthrie, & McGough, 1996; Wigfield, Wilde, et al., 1996). These include the following:

- *Reading self-efficacy* Believing that one can read well affects one's commitment to reading.
- *Reading challenge* How challenging a book is for a reader at a particular competence level can affect whether the book will be read.

- *Reading curiosity* Students are more likely to read about topics that are interesting to them.
- *Aesthetically enjoyable reading topics* Some things are read because they are fun to read.
- *Importance of reading* Recognition that reading is important can affect motivation to read and to be a good reader.
- *Reader recognition* Being recognized as a good reader can affect motivation to read.
- *Reader grades* Grades earned for reading can affect motivation to read.
- *Reading competition* Being a better reader than others can motivate reading and working at becoming an even better reader.
- *Social reasons for reading* Opportunities to read with family and friends can affect motivation to read.
- *Compliance* Students sometimes read to fulfill academic obligations (e.g., assignments).
- *Reading work avoidance* There are factors that certainly reduce the likelihood of reading (e.g., difficult words in a text, too-complicated stories).

The center's work must be reported in the context of many other analyses of student motivation that have been conducted in the past three decades. This research activity permits a much more complete understanding of student motivation for reading and the determinants of that motivation than was possible in the past.

It will become clear as this chapter proceeds that academic motivation is a fragile commodity. Although kindergarten children arrive at school expecting to do well and are enthusiastic about school and academic tasks, expectations often diminish as students go through school. For academic motivation to remain high, students must be successful and perceive that they are successful. Perhaps it is not surprising that students who have a difficult time in school experience declining academic motivation. More surprising is that the policies of most elementary schools are such that most students will experience declining motivation, perceiving that they are not doing well, at least as compared with other students.

More positively, much is being learned about how to reengineer school so that high academic motivation is maintained (Johnston, 2012). Some of the most important ideas about how to maintain student motivation are taken up in the second half of this chapter. When the messages in the latter half of this chapter are combined with the messages in the first half, it will be clear that more is now known about how to keep students motivated than is being done to motivate students in contemporary schools.

THE DECLINE OF ACADEMIC MOTIVATION DURING THE ELEMENTARY YEARS

Humans are born intrinsically motivated to learn and improve their performances. Developmental psychologists have made a good case that young children have great motivation to explore their world and that such exploration is important in stimulating mental and physical development (White, 1959). Despite a motivated start on life, motivation often declines during the elementary years (e.g., Eccles, 1993; Harter, 1990; Meece & Miller, 1999, 2001; Scherrer & Preckel, 2019). Moreover, as children proceed through elementary school, they generally value school less; they are less interested in school and what is studied in school (e.g., Eccles et al., 1989; Jacobs et al., 2002; McKenna et al., 2012; Meece & Miller, 1999, 2001; Wigfield, 1994, 2000; Wigfield & Eccles, 1992; Wigfield et al., 1991; Wigfield & Guthrie, 1997).

Academically, kindergarten and grade 1 children believe they can do anything. If you ask them whether they are going to learn to read, they are certain of it (e.g., Entwisle & Hayduk, 1978; Wigfield et al., 2015). Moreover, even after failure, they remain confident that next time they will do better (e.g., Clifford, 1978, 1984; Parsons & Ruble, 1977; Pressley & Ghatala, 1989; Stipek & Hoffman, 1980). Although grade 1 students who experience difficulties learning to read generally understand that it is a difficult task, confidence in their competence to read remains high (Chapman & Tunmer, 1995). In contrast, students in grades 5 and 6 are much less confident that they will meet teacher and parent expectations with respect to academic achievement. They are much more aware of their failures than of their successes (Kloosterman, 1988). Students in grades 5 and 6 often believe they are doing worse than they are (e.g., Juvonen, 1988). The weaker the student, the more pessimistic the self-appraisal and the less enthusiastic the student is about academic activities (e.g., Hall, 2006; Renick & Harter, 1989).

McKenna and his associates (1995) most clearly documented the declines in student attitudes about reading. They surveyed more than 17,000 elementary students in grades 1–6 from across the United States. The survey contained 10 questions assessing how students felt about reading as a recreational activity (e.g., "How do you feel about spending free time reading?"; "How do you feel about going to a bookstore?"). It also included 10 questions assessing students' academic attitudes about reading (e.g., "How do you feel about reading your school books?"; "How do you feel when it is time for reading class?"). The students rated each question on a 1 (very negative) to 4 (very positive) scale.

For both boys and girls, for all ethnic and racial groups, and all ability levels, there were clear declines in students' positive attitudes toward reading, both recreational and academic. Yes, girls were more positive than boys, and the declines in attitude were not as consistent for high-ability readers as for other students. Even so, what was most striking in the data was that, no matter how the researchers looked at them, attitudes toward reading were relatively high in grade 1, with student indifference toward reading becoming the norm by grade 6. Similar findings came out of a more recent study in which Parsons et al. (2018) surveyed over 1,000 students in grades 3–6 across the United States. Findings suggested a decrease in student motivation to read as students progressed through school. Specifically, girls had significantly higher motivation than boys to read fiction texts, but there was no difference between the two genders' motivation to read nonfiction texts.

McKenna and his colleagues (2012) extended their work into middle schools. They surveyed almost 4,500 middle school students in 23 states, asking them about academic literacy, voluntary reading, and digital reading. They reported that motivation to read continues to decline across middle school, though boys' motivation declined more than girls'. Only with digital voluntary reading were boys more positive than girls. Wigfield et al. (1997) also examined reading motivation across the elementary years. They found a clear decline in interest in reading during the elementary years as well as a clear decline in student perceptions that reading was useful.

Perhaps most disturbing is that by the middle-grade-school years, some children are really "down" on reading. When Gambrell and her colleagues (Gambrell, Codling, et al., 1996; Gambrell, Palmer, et al., 1996) administered a reading motivation inventory to grade 3 and grade 5 students, they found nontrivial proportions of children who claimed that they would rather clean their rooms than read (17% of respondents), who expected to spend little time reading when they grew up (14%), and who felt that people who read are boring (10%). There is reason for concern when children are so turned off by an activity as important as reading.

Developmental and educational psychologists analyzed some of the reasons for the declines in positive academic attitudes and motivation during the elementary years. Several contributing factors were identified, each of which is reviewed in what follows. These factors coalesce so that declining academic motivation with advancing grade level is inevitable for many students, at least given the nature of contemporary schooling.

Developmental Shifts in Attributions About the Causes of Performance

Different people explain their successes and failures in different ways. When some people experience success or failure, they explain the outcome as due to personal effort. That is, a success is attributed to trying hard, while a failure is explained as reflecting lack of effort. Alternatively, successes and failures can be explained in terms of abilities: Such people might reason that "I succeeded because I am naturally smart, being born with a high IQ" or "I cannot read well because I was born with dyslexia." Sometimes people explain successes or failures in terms of task characteristics. For example, a student who did well on a test might believe it was because the test was easy, and a student who did poorly might blame the failure on the test being too difficult. Finally, some believe that what happens to them is determined by luck, with successes due to good luck and failures due to bad luck.

Of all these explanations—effort, ability, task difficulty, and luck—the only one that is under personal control is effort. Thus, if you believe that you succeeded on a task because of high effort, there is reason to exert effort in the future. If you think that your failure reflects insufficient effort, the route to future success is to do more and try harder: Indeed, effort attributions are consistently associated with high effort in the future (Weiner, 1979). In contrast, there is nothing a person can do about inherited abilities, the difficulty of tasks, or luck; thus, individuals who believe their academic outcomes depend on ability, task difficulty, or luck have little or no motivation to try hard in the future.

One of the reasons that children's motivations decline is that, as children mature during the elementary school years, the ways that they explain their performance outcomes change. Kindergarten and grade 1 students do not differentiate between effort and ability. Thus, young children typically attribute their successes to effort. Moreover, whenever they exhibit effort, they believe their effort reflects high ability. Thus, if they fail but expended high effort, they leave the task still believing they have high ability because they exerted effort! In short, 6- and 7-year-olds typically believe that they can succeed by trying hard (Folmer et al., 2008; Nicholls, 1978, 1990).

With increasing age during the elementary years, children differentiate effort and ability. Thus, by the end of the elementary years, children understand that, if two people expend the same amount of effort, the more successful one probably has a higher ability. Moreover, by the end of the elementary school years, students explain successes and failures more in terms of ability than effort. Thus, successes are considered to be indications of high ability and failures to be indications of low ability.

Of course, such attributions are much less motivating than the effort attributions of younger children. When a person believes that ability determines performance, there is no motivation for exerting effort since effort does not matter. That children increasingly believe their failures are due to low ability probably goes far in explaining their decreasing motivation to tackle academic tasks.

Developmental Differences in Making Social Comparisons

Young children tend not to compare themselves much with others, especially with respect to psychological characteristics such as intelligence, reading ability, or extent of prior knowledge. Yes, preschool children can and do compare the tangible goodies they have with the tangible goodies another child has (Ruble et al., 1980), but they do not make much of differences or similarities in performance on academic tasks. Thus, a grade 1 student who feels bad because she or he is having difficulty with two-column addition is unlikely to feel better if the teacher reminds the student that all the other kids in the class are experiencing the same difficulty. With increasing age during the elementary school years, students become concerned with their academic standing relative to others (Ruble, 1983). Again, because for most students there will be others around who are doing better, the increasing focus on comparing one's achievement with that of classmates has increasing potential for leading to negative conclusions about one's own ability (see Dijkstra et al., 2008 for full review). Such conclusions can then translate into reduced motivation to achieve.

Young Students and Their Attributions as They Try To Learn To Read

Learning to decode and recognize words is a very challenging task for some children. Children can make a lot of mistakes along the way. The grade 1 child is not as likely to be discouraged by such mistakes as a child in grade 4 who is struggling to learn decoding. After all, for the grade 1 child, trying hard is what counts. In contrast, the grade 4 child has come to believe that having to try harder on a task that others accomplish with much less effort is a sign of low ability. Thus, for the grade 4 child still struggling with decoding as classmates read with ease, there is plenty of reason to conclude that he or she does not have the ability to read. Such a conclusion would undermine the student's expenditure of effort in learning how to decode. This is one reason why the first grader struggling to read is much more likely to be influenced by teacher and parent urgings to try harder than an older child. From a motivational perspective, it makes no sense to expect that, if children do not learn to read on their own in grades 1 or 2, they will learn later, when they are ready. The motivation to exert the effort to learn to read will never be greater than it is during the primary years. The older the struggling reader, the more the struggle will be interpreted as reflecting low ability, with the child increasingly unmotivated to learn to read.

Children with Learning Disabilities

The role of attributions in motivating academic efforts has been studied, especially in children with learning disabilities. Children with learning disabilities are much more likely than their typically achieving classmates to believe that their academic performances are determined by ability and to be very pessimistic about their academic abilities (e.g., Brooks, 2001; Elbaum & Vaughn, 2003; Gans et al., 2003; Johnston & Winograd, 1985). Yes, there are exceptions: Some children with learning disabilities continue to believe that they can do better by trying hard. Continuing to believe that effort matters probably makes a difference for these children. Such low achievers who believe they can control their academic progress through effort, in fact, do achieve at higher levels than low achievers who believe that their low achievement reflects low ability (Kistner et al., 1988).

Often, we speak to groups of special educators, and when we do we always ask the audience the following question: "What if you talk with grade 5 or 6 students with learning disabilities about how they are doing in school and ask a student to explain why he or she is having problems in school. What does such a child say?" Every audience provides the same answer: "The kid says, 'It's because I'm stupid.'" Years of school failure result in students concluding that their academic achievement is not controllable, that they do not have the ability to do well academically. They have come to expect academic failure. Developmental studies show that such attributions are very different from the attributions these children made when they were younger, when they believed that effort might help them make progress.

What is going on here? How does a spirited 6-year-old who knows he can learn to read become a 10-year-old who believes that reading is something that he cannot accomplish? (No sexism implied here, for young boys are more likely than young girls to experience difficulties in learning to read.) The child's continued failures lead to negative affect (Covington & Omelich, 1979a) and decreasing expectancies for future success (Covington & Omelich, 1979b). That classmates are experiencing success following their efforts does not help; in fact, it probably intensifies the struggling student's feelings of personal incapacity (Covington, 1987). Learned helplessness—that is, the belief that nothing one does can lead to success—develops in such a situation (Dweck & Goetz, 2018). Children who struggle to learn to read quickly come to believe that they are not good readers and that reading is difficult and something they do not like (Chapman et al., 2000). Doing nothing can actually be therapeutic for such children, for at least failure following lack of effort does not lead to the conclusion that one is stupid. In that case, children with learning disabilities can more easily convince themselves that they do not do well in reading because they are not interested enough to try (Covington & Omelich, 1981, 1984). Is it any surprise that children with reading disabilities often seem passive in school? Trying gets them nowhere; not trying permits an explanation of failure that is not as damaging to their self-esteem as failure following effort (Johnston & Winograd, 1985).

Failing to make progress in decoding during grade 1 may seem less frustrating to the child because the grade 1 child is so willing to persist. Such willingness to persist wanes as the child matures and comes to understand that she or he is making little progress, eventually interpreting this lack as an indication of low ability. Not intervening when children are experiencing initial reading difficulties is setting students up for additional failure and diminishing self-esteem. School days filled with failure are school days filled with the lesson that "You are stupid." That the grade 1 child is not much ruffled by failures is no reason not to intervene, for it will not be long before that same child is interpreting failures as indications of a lack of ability. Once children come to the conclusion that they lack ability with respect to reading, there is little or no reason for them to make additional efforts to learn to read, and hence interventions at that point must also be targeted at increasing the child's academic self-esteem. Reading difficulties that might have been addressed in grade 1 through simple decoding instruction becomes much more serious now that the once vital child seems helpless. Waiting to intervene makes no sense from the perspective of attribution theory. Early difficulties in learning to read reduce subsequent efforts to learn to read, thus producing more reading problems (Onatsu-Arvilommi & Nurmi, 2000), a cycle that should be stopped as soon as there is any hint of it, if there is going to be any hope of developing a competent, motivated reader.

Other Factors Affecting Attributions

The belief that efforts pay off is affected by histories of success and failure, the former encouraging the students' continuing belief in effort and the latter causing them to doubt their abilities. Other factors play a role as well. Teachers and parents can encourage effort attributions. They can make children aware of how their successes are tied to their efforts (Schunk, 1991). Parents' and teachers' awareness of their power to be persuasive about the role of effort in success is the main reason that effective educational environments (such as the ones considered in previous chapters) and the motivating environments considered later in this chapter always include the repeated message that effort matters.

Teachers and parents can also help to develop in children an understanding of intelligence that is very different from the theory that intelligence is determined by genes and thus unmodifiable. The message can be sent to students that ability is not a fixed entity but, rather, is changeable. Carol Dweck and her colleagues (e.g., Dweck, 2010; Dweck & Leggett, 1988; Haimovitz & Dweck, 2017; Henderson & Dweck, 1990) have proposed that a critical determinant of achievement motivation is whether a person believes that intelligence is fixed biologically and hence neither malleable nor affected by environmental variables. Dweck describes people who believe that intelligence is fixed as possessing an "entity" theory of intelligence: Such people believe that intelligence is a thing that one either has in great quantity or does not. In contrast, those who think intelligence is modifiable subscribe to an "incremental" theory of intelligence.

Dweck (2010; also see Yeager & Dweck, 2012) found that the particular view of intelligence held by an individual has a powerful impact on his or her achievement behavior. Entity theorists are oriented toward seeking positive evaluations of their abilities and avoiding negative evaluations. Such a perspective can be damaging when negative feedback occurs, as it inevitably does in school. Such students are likely to interpret failures as indications of low intelligence and hence to be discouraged by their failures. Students who are entity theorists are more likely to experience negative emotion when confronted with failure, believing that failure signals low ability and allowing that belief to undermine future attempts at academic tasks. In contrast, incremental theorists are much more oriented toward increasing their abilities, believing that daily efforts lead to small gains, all of which can add up to substantially higher intelligence when effort persists over the long term. Such students keep trying when obstacles occur because they see obstacles as a natural part of the learning process.

As long as there is success, there is little difference in the behaviors of entity and incremental theorists. However, when failure occurs, the differences in their outlooks become apparent, with the entity theorists much more at risk for believing they are helpless when they experience difficulties during challenging tasks, leading to low persistence and task avoidance. In contrast, incremental theorists just keep plugging away following a failure.

It is for these reasons that effective classrooms should include the following messages:

- Trying hard fosters achievement and intelligence.
- Failure is a natural part of learning.
- Being best is not what school is about; getting better *is*.

Every teacher and parent can send the messages that people get smarter by trying hard, that part of getting smart is bouncing back from failures, and that school is about becoming better, not becoming best. Given the tendency of children to explain their performances in terms of ability, there is plenty of reason to do everything possible to encourage students to believe that effort attributions are the way to go when explaining performance.

Reading Class Is Boring

One final possibility that has to be acknowledged is that many of the tasks presented to students in the name of reading are, in fact, boring. In many states, a great deal of time labeled "reading instruction" is diverted from actual reading to preparation for the tasks on the state reading test, with such tests heavy on low-level skills (i.e., word recognition, rapid reading of simple text) rather than reading and responding to interesting texts. Additionally, many curricula integrate nontested subjects into the reading curriculum. Instead of giving students autonomy in what they read, students must read about specific topics aligned with the state standards.

By sixth grade, the boredom can be so great that the challenge is for students to put up with the test preparation without their boredom spilling over into misbehavior (Fairbanks & Broughton, 2003). Test preparation is not reading but has the potential for decreasing interest in reading as well as decreasing reading achievement.

Summary

Primary-grade children have much more faith in effort than do students in the later grades. This faith provides great motivation for accomplishing complicated tasks such as learning to read. When grade 1 children experience frustration, their effort attributions support the expenditure of additional effort. In contrast, older children are more likely to make ability attributions than effort attributions, so that failures are no longer seen as indications of insufficient effort but as indications of low ability. Failures followed by attributions of low ability lead to reduced motivation for the frustrating activity. Thus, grade 1 students are more likely to be motivated to continue with challenging tasks than are grade 3 students. The grade 3 student who has not yet learned to read interprets his or her failures to date as strong evidence of a lack of ability to read, undermining attempts to make additional efforts to learn to read.

Researchers have done a good job of establishing the value of encouraging students to continue to make attributions as they did when they were in grade 1 and to believe that academic success depends on effort. Even more generally, psychologists have determined that academic motivation is more likely to be encouraged if students come to believe that intelligence itself is the result of effort rather than the reflection of innate ability. A lot of input about the value of effort is necessary, however, because with increasing grade level the implicit message in the classroom is that effort is not what matters—that there are the smart students and the not-so-smart ones.

Classroom Environments

Academic failures kill off intrinsic academic motivation. An important reason that such failures are more devastating with increasing grade level is that competition between students accelerates during the elementary years.

Competition is a way of life in many classrooms with approaches such as grading on the curve, students "call in" their grades as the teacher marks them in the grade book, or when students retrieve their papers from the "graded bin." Thus, each student in a class knows how she or he is doing relative to others. Parents also support such competitiveness by asking how "so-and-so" did, followed by remarks about how it would be nice if their son or daughter were like "so-and-so."

One result of this obsession with identifying who is smart and, implicitly, who is not is to undermine the academic motivation of many children. Classroom competition and evaluation foster what Nicholls (1989) referred to as "ego involvement." Success in the competitive classroom (especially relative to peers) implies high intellectual capacity (i.e., that one is smart, which is ego-enhancing), while failure implies low capacity (which is ego-diminishing). Since most students will not end up doing "best" in the class, feelings of failure, self-criticism, and negative self-esteem occur often (Ames, 1984). Many students come to expect that they will not earn top grades or be reinforced as much as other students. Such a system has high potential for undermining effort when success is not certain (e.g., with new task demands), for trying and failing leads to feelings of low ability.

One likely reason that there is a clear decline in academic motivation from the early primary to the later elementary grades is that comparative evaluations are less frequent and salient in the early primary years than in the later primary and middle grades (Harter et al., 1992; Stipek & Daniels, 1988). With increasing age, children are more aware of the competitiveness in their classrooms (see Harter et al., 1992; also see Schmidt et al., 1988) and of the implications of not succeeding. What is certain, based on research (e.g., Wigfield, 1988), is that, by the middle elementary years, paying attention to how one does as compared with others affects perceptions of one's competency, expectancies about future success, and thus (potentially) school performance.

Life in Noncompetitive Classrooms

The problems produced by classroom competitiveness are especially apparent when competitive classrooms are compared with ones that are not so competitive. In some classrooms, rather than rewarding students for being better than one another, students are rewarded for personal improvement on academic tasks. Nicholls referred to such classrooms as "fostering task involvement." Nicholls and Thorkildsen (e.g., 1987) studied 30 grade 5 classrooms ranging in ego and task involvement. They found that work avoidance was much more commonly reported in ego-involved (competitive) classrooms than in task-involved (noncompetitive) classrooms. The students in the task-oriented classrooms believed that success in school depended on interest, effort, and attempting to learn, whereas the students in the ego-involved classrooms believed that success depended on being smarter than other kids and trying to beat out other students. That is, whether grade 5 students continued to believe in effort, as they had when they were younger, or in ability as a determinant of performance depended on the reward structure of the classroom.

Task-oriented classrooms are much more likely to keep students interested in and committed to school than are ego-oriented classrooms (Meece & Miller, 1999; Nicholls, 1989). The problem is that many more classrooms are of the ego-involved type than of the task-involved type. Far too often, the goal is to get better grades than the ones earned by peers rather than to learn (e.g., Ames, 1992; Blumenfeld, 1992; Corpus et al., 2009). Many other classrooms are structured so as to encourage expectations of failure (i.e., relative to other students) rather than success. This has significant consequences for students.

Johnston (2004) provides an analysis of the nature of teacher interactions with students in the classrooms of highly effective elementary teachers. He noted that all teacher talk imputes intentions, positions, and identities. For example, if a literature discussion group has ceased to function well or has broken down into a sort of chaos, consider what the students hear when the teacher says the following:

"Get back to work or you'll be staying in at lunch."
"You are interfering with the others and making me feel frustrated."
"This is not like you guys. What's the problem you've encountered? How can you solve it?"

As Johnston (2004) notes, each of these remarks says something different about student identity and agency. Each has the potential to impact future interactions in this classroom. The first remark suggests a laborer–supervisor relationship, the second suggests a cooperative relationship, and the third suggests a collaborative relationship. These different relationships indicate different sorts of agency for students as well (heed authority, be respectful of others' rights, engage in collaborative problem solving). He notes that language is both representational and constitutive. It invites identities, for better or worse. Johnston (2004) notes that saying "You're so smart" is quite different from saying "You're so thoughtful." Likewise, saying "Good job!" sends a different message than saying "You must have worked really hard on this." The ways teachers talk position them and the children in their classrooms. That positioning can situate a teacher as the giver of information as in the traditional transmission classroom. Or it can position the teacher as a co-collaborator as in the inquiry classroom. It positions students as dependent or independent as classroom resources or as classroom competitors. This is key as a teacher plays a vital role in building student competence and persistence through complex tasks, which are both critical to increasing student motivation (Bureau et al., 2021; Hattie, 2009; Levesque-Bristol et al., 2022).

Furthermore, Johnston (2004) lays out many such differences in the talk of more and less effective teachers. His analyses encourage the thought that it may be differences in teacher talk that give rise to the notion that the lack of motivation and decreasing interest in reading observed in the upper elementary grades may be a function more of the classroom interactional environment than anything unique to the students. Ultimately, the relationships teachers build with their students can play a critical role in students' motivation and must include building caring classroom communities and understanding the unique backgrounds of each student (Bondy et al., 2007). The question left unanswered is this: How do we help all teachers learn to interact with their students in ways that are as productive as was observed in highly effective classrooms?

Inclusive Classrooms

The effects of classroom competitiveness are also striking when the fate of students with learning difficulties is considered. In recent years, there has been a national movement to eliminate special classrooms for students experiencing academic difficulties and, instead, to have them receive their education in regular classrooms. By the middle elementary grades, mainstreaming means placement into a competitive classroom in which failure relative to others is virtually assured for the child with learning difficulties. A similar situation occurs with respect to the education of English-as-a-second-language students. Such students often enter competitive classrooms far behind the other students. The competitive nature of the classrooms guarantees failure relative to other students, with potentially devastating impact on the motivation of the students who were disadvantaged from the outset. Whenever a class includes a mix of abilities and preparation levels, classroom competition virtually guarantees that many students will experience failure, potentially impacting most negatively on at-risk students' academic self-esteem and motivation.

Consequences of Success

So far in this section, the concern has been with the negative effects of rewards on those who do not often receive them in classrooms. As it turns out, classroom rewards can undermine the intrinsic motivation of those who receive the rewards (Deci et al., 1999; Wigfield et al., 2004). When students receive tangible rewards for intrinsically interesting activities, their intrinsic interest in the activity can decline. Thus, when teachers begin to reward behaviors that had been intrinsically rewarding, they may undermine students' interest in those activities in the future when rewards are not available. This is known as the "overjustification effect," with students coming to believe that they are engaging in rewarded activities for the reward they are receiving rather than because of the intrinsic value of the activity (Lepper et al., 1996). Once rewarded, they begin to justify their behavior to themselves, making the case to themselves that they are carrying out the behavior because of the tangible reward. The person who does something in the absence of reward can only explain her or his behavior to her- or himself in terms of personal interest in the activity.

McLoyd (1979) provided an apt demonstration of the overjustification effect with respect to reading. Children read high-interest books, with some receiving a reward for doing so. McLoyd observed that, when students could read independently without the possibility of reward, those who had not received rewards for reading did more reading than those who previously received rewards for doing it. Thus, there is very good reason to suspect that students who are reading and writing for "points" given by a teacher or for high grades may not be as highly motivated to read in the absence of teacher rewards than they would have been had they participated in instruction in which classroom rewards for performance were not so salient.

Gambrell (2011) proposes seven rules that would promote students' intrinsic motivation to read:

1. Students are more motivated to read when the reading tasks and activities are relevant to their lives.
2. Students are more motivated to read when they have access to a wide range of reading materials.
3. Students are more motivated to read when they have ample opportunities to engage in sustained reading.
4. Students are more motivated to read when they have opportunities to make choices about what they read and how they engage in and complete literacy skills.
5. Students are more motivated to read when they have opportunities to socially interact with others about the text they are reading.
6. Students are more motivated to read when they have opportunities to be successful with challenging texts.
7. Students are more motivated to read when classroom incentives reflect the value and importance of reading. (Gambrell notes that when free books are the incentives earned for wide voluntary reading, students' intrinsic motivation is extended rather than curbed as is the case with points and prizes as incentives.)

We are often asked about the implications of the overjustification effect for reading reward programs such as the one sponsored by Pizza Hut. The answer is that it depends on the kid. For children who are already motivated to read, providing extrinsic rewards has the potential to undermine their intrinsic motivation to read. For children who are not motivated to read, such programs can motivate reading that would not otherwise occur, unless, of course, the number of books read is highly public, with competition between students to read the most books. We urge teachers to use such programs only with unmotivated students but to refrain from using tangible incentive programs with students who are already reading for the fun of it and to implement the programs to downplay competition (e.g., the reward is received without public reference to the total number of books read by individual students).

We are also often asked about Accelerated Reader® (AR), a system of providing points to students for reading texts and answering literal questions about the texts to demonstrate comprehension of the material. Based on our reading of studies that have been done, we cannot decide what impact this system has on achievement. With respect to motivation, however, it, at best, has variable impact on motivation and attitudes (Huang, 2012; Mallette et al., 2004; Vollands et al., 1999). The largest evaluation study we found was conducted by Nunnery et al. (2006). That study examined the effects of teachers randomly assigned to use the AR program for 90 minutes daily while the control teachers continued using the district core reading program. Across the nine urban schools where the study took place, a positive effect was found for AR as compared with the control program. However, the effect sizes decreased at each grade level from small to trivial (grade 3 $d = 0.36$, grade 4 $d = 0.16$, grade 5 $d = 0.09$). Additionally, and not surprisingly, classrooms rated as high in implementation fidelity produced much better outcomes than classrooms rated as exhibiting low implementation fidelity.

That the AR approach involves a great deal of public display of achievement data—for example, charts indicating how many books each student has read—certainly has to give one pause from a motivational perspective, with this approach definitely stimulating classroom competition, which is known to undermine academic motivation. If a teacher is going to use this approach, we would urge that efforts be made to keep student reading data private, with students plotting their progress to note how much they have read but not getting caught up in comparing their progress with that of other readers—the more public comparative achievement data, the greater the risk for undermining motivation. There are other technology-related reading programs used in schools, but the overall verdict on the success of these various programs in improving reading achievement is modest, at best (Cheung & Slavin, 2012; Dynarski, 2007; Ross et al., 2004). In other words, using the various technology-related reading programs improves reading achievement when compared with control students who do not engage with the program, but that improvement is negligible (e.g., raising reading achievement from the 21st to the 24th percentile). At this point, all we can advise is buyer beware.

Summary

With respect to information processing, there is an increasing tendency with increasing age during the elementary grades to make achievement comparisons with others. For many children, this means increasing recognition that their performance is not as good as that of other students. There are also developmental shifts in attributional tendencies. Although preschoolers and early-elementary-grade students do not interpret academic difficulties as indications of low ability, the tendency to do so increases with age. The greater the effort required to obtain academic success, the more likely it is to encourage an inference of low ability with increasing grade level. In short, developmental shifts in information processing lead to developmental shifts in expectations about future success and failure.

These shifts favoring student inferences about low ability occur in the context of schooling that increasingly emphasizes competition with increasing grade level. Despite the healthiness of sending the message that intelligence is incremental, school is an institution that often signals that intelligence is fixed, something a student either has or does not have (Ames, 1992). This message is very discouraging for many students who do not do well in such a competitive environment. The bad attitudes that many high school students have about school seem very justified. School has shaped them to expect academic failure or at least feelings of less-than-complete success relative to many classmates.

Competitive classrooms foster the attribution that ability is what matters, thus undermining student academic motivation. Unfortunately, this is more common than not, for the competitive classroom model thrives in contemporary America. However, it is possible to structure classrooms so that students are graded on improvement or mastery of skills rather than in comparison to other students. In such classrooms, there seems to be greater academic motivation and more sophisticated reading. A further complication is that rewards such as grades can undermine students' intrinsic motivations. Whenever the emphasis on grades is high enough that students can convince themselves that they are reading only to obtain a high grade or some other tangible reward, there is danger of undermining whatever intrinsic motivation a student might have (Sweet & Guthrie, 1996).

One of the strengths of elementary school classrooms has been that they have been more likely to be organized along cooperative principles.

The increasing shift to competitiveness during the later primary (i.e., increasingly in grades 2 and 3 as compared with kindergarten and grade 1) and middle elementary years comes at a time when students' thinking abilities mature in ways that increase the notice of their achievements relative to those of others.

Our view is that changing the motivational structure of schooling should be a major priority in education reform. In the meantime, individual teachers and parents can do their part by repeatedly sending the message to children that effort counts and that an excellent mind is built a little bit at a time through academic effort. Teachers, especially, must become more aware of how their interactions with pupils may decrease motivation for reading. School would be a better place for all children if we rewarded children for growth, not for outperforming others.

INCREASING STUDENT MOTIVATION FOR LITERACY

Research in the past three decades on student motivation has heightened awareness that students often are not motivated to read or learn to read better. This awareness has energized efforts to identify ways to increase student motivation. Admittedly, most of what is described here has not been researched so thoroughly that any recommendations can be given with great confidence. As a whole, however, the research community has identified various methods with the potential for increasing student motivation for reading, each of which is conceptually sensible, if not yet fully validated. Teachers who use the methods described in this section will be on the cutting edge of educational motivation, although we expect that edge to be sharpened somewhat in the next few years as more evaluation data on the various techniques reviewed here accumulate. (See Table 11.1 for a summary of implication strategies.)

The methods described in this section range from individual components of literacy instruction (e.g., interesting materials, attribution retraining) to entire redefinitions of the literacy program (e.g., concept-oriented instruction; self-selected reading).

Appropriately Challenging Texts and Tasks

The data are overwhelming that tasks a little bit beyond the learner's current competence level are motivating (e.g., Allington et al., 2015; Brophy, 1987). Tasks that are a bit challenging cause students to work hard and feel good about what they are doing. In addition to being boring, low-challenging tasks never provide learners with the opportunity to see what they can do and thus undermine their confidence (Miller & Meece, 1999). Teachers

TABLE 11.1. Developing a Highly Motivated Classroom

Motivation strategy	Classroom implications
Select appropriate texts	• Have each student read at a level that challenges them but is not too easy or too hard. • Teach students to select books at particular levels to avoid texts that are too easy too challenging. • If working at grade level text, support students through scaffolding to avoid frustration
Attributional interventions	• Teach students that using specific reading strategies can help them have success while reading. • Focus on effort and accomplishing short, attainable goals.
Select texts on student interests	• Conduct interest surveys and develop relationships with students to learn about their interests and hobbies. • Fill the classroom library with texts on student interests. Texts might include nontraditional books such as comic books, graphic novels, or magazines. • Allow for student autonomy in selecting books from the class or school library. • Recommend books and series on topics of interest to students. • Include student topics of interest in class read-alouds. ◦ A bonus: Read books from a series. If students enjoy the texts, they can read additional books in the series themselves.
Have class discussions about books	• Have students share books they enjoyed reading with their classmates. • Discuss books that you want to read. • Ask students questions about what they are reading and if they would recommend it to a friend.
Incorporate literature activities	• Felt-board enactments of stories • Listening to taped stories • Writing about stories • Writing original stories • Reading and telling of stories by teachers • Student retelling and rewriting of stories • Time for student choice to engage in reading, writing, listening, and enacting • For upper elementary, allow for student-led discussions

A community-of-learners approach	• For example, concept-oriented reading instruction (CORI)
	  ◦ Have students generate questions of interest about the topic the class is studying.
	  ◦ Build in time for collaborative research, reading, and writing on the topic.
	  ◦ The goal is for students to acquire strategic and conceptual knowledge on a topic.

Focus on the classroom environment and teacher behavior	• Incorporate cooperative learning activities (students work together in small groups with each member having a role in reaching the end goal) with reading. ◦ For example, jigsaw, mind mapping, pair interview, or round table discussions *(continued)*

TABLE 11.1. (*continued*)

Motivation strategy	Classroom implications
	• Scaffold student learning
	◦ For example, *I do, we do, you do*; model activity then provide support when needed, but allow the student to work through challenges
	• Support student risk-taking
	• Encourage creativity
	• Incorporate engaging activities
	• Show off student-produced work
	• Encourage curiosity
	• Provide detailed, encouraging feedback
	• Model how to problem solve
	• Limit competition between students

must walk the fine line of promoting texts that will challenge students but will not be too challenging, as more difficult texts can lead to a decrease in fluency, accuracy, and prosody (Amendum et al., 2016). Recall from previous chapters that effective teachers monitor what children are capable of doing and then nudge them to try something slightly more challenging. Such challenge is at the heart of a healthy motivational outlook.

Attribution Retraining

That the attributions of many low-achieving children are dysfunctional (i.e., the students attribute their failures to uncontrollable ability factors and hence are not motivated to exert academic effort; e.g., Carr et al., 1991; Johnston & Winograd, 1985) has inspired some researchers to attempt to retrain attributional tendencies. Both applied efforts and basic research (e.g., Foersterling, 1985; Stipek & Kowalski, 1989) have documented the reality that attribution retraining can make a substantial difference in the motivation of students who otherwise tend to attribute their poor performances to factors other than effort. Particularly relevant here, Borkowski and his colleagues (e.g., Borkowski et al., 1988, 1990; Reid & Borkowski, 1987) have provided the most compelling analyses and data about interventions aimed at shifting the attributions of low achievers in order to promote reading comprehension.

Borkowski has recognized that, for low-functioning students, attributing success to effort alone would probably be ineffective. This is consistent with the perspective emphasized throughout this book that strategies, metacognition, and conceptual knowledge also contribute to reading achievement. Thus, Borkowski's group has been teaching students to use strategies to accomplish intellectual tasks at the same time that they persuade students that their successes and failures on academic tasks are due to their efforts while using appropriate strategies (Clifford, 1984). Borkowski and his colleagues persuade students that, as they learn strategies, they are acquiring tools that will permit them to improve their academic performance, providing them with a powerful motivation to use the strategies that they are acquiring (Chapman et al., 1990).

For example, in one study (Carr & Borkowski, 1989), underachieving elementary students were assigned to one of three conditions:

1. In the *strategies + attribution training condition*, children were taught comprehension strategies. They were instructed to self-test while they read in order to determine whether they understood their reading. The students were also taught summarization, topic sentence, and questioning strategies to understand a text. The attributional part of the training emphasized to students that they could understand the text by applying the comprehension strategies—that their comprehension of the text was a function of how they approached it rather than of any inherent comprehension abilities.
2. Participants in the *strategies-only condition* were taught the same strategies but without the benefit of attributional training.
3. Students in the *control condition* were provided neither strategies instruction nor attributional training.

What a difference the strategies + attributional training made! When tested 3 weeks following the conclusion of the instruction, the strategies + attribution participants were more likely to be using the strategies than other participants in the study, and recall of text was higher in this condition than in the other conditions of the study. In addition, the strategies + attribution subjects were using comprehension strategies in the classroom much more than the students in the other conditions of the study.

Researchers have continued to test the effectiveness of attributional training with students of all ages. Specifically, elementary students have seen changes in attributions and an increase in math scores after attributional training (Horner & Gaither, 2004).

Although much more work analyzing the effects of attributional retraining needs to be done to completely understand its potential for modifying views of self as learner, many who work with students with disabilities, in particular, are already employing attributional retraining with their students. For example, as students with learning disabilities are taught comprehension, writing, and memory strategies in a well-known learning-disabilities curriculum created by Donald Deshler, Jean Schumaker, and their colleagues (e.g., Deshler et al., 1998, 2007; Deshler &

Schumaker, 1988), there is a consistent emphasis on the role of controllable factors, such as the use of strategies, as a determinant of performance. This is because the group recognizes that the attributions made by students with learning disabilities often are dysfunctional (e.g., "I am stupid"). If permitted to persist, such attributions have high potential for defeating other instruction since believing that one is stupid is also believing that there is nothing that can be done about it.

Interesting Texts To Read

Throughout the 20th century, it has been recognized that interest matters with students: High interest increases student engagement and learning from text (e.g., Hidi, 1990, 2001; Renninger & Wozniak, 1985; Schiefele, 1992). This insight has prompted many authors and materials developers to attempt to create academic materials that "grab" students' interest.

Anderson and his colleagues (e.g., Anderson et al., 1984) carried out some of the best-known work on the role of interest in children's reading of texts. Children read sentences that had been rated either as interesting or uninteresting. Interesting sentences were much more certain to be remembered later than were uninteresting sentences, producing a very large effect relative to the size of effects produced by other manipulations (e.g., readability of sentences).

Anderson's group also conducted some extremely detailed analytical studies (e.g., Anderson, 1982) to determine the mechanisms underlying the interest effect, hypothesizing that more interesting materials were more likely to be attended to by students. In fact, that seemed to be the case, with students spending more time reading interesting texts. In addition, interesting texts were so absorbing that readers failed to respond to an external signal (e.g., to press a button in response to a sound heard while they were reading) as quickly as they did when reading uninteresting texts. Even so, greater attention alone did not account for their greater learning of the interesting materials for, when differences in attention and effort were factored out of the learning data (i.e., the amount of time spent reading sentences was controlled statistically), there were still large effects for interest (e.g., Shirey & Reynolds, 1988). Thus, interest can affect directly both attention and learning, but only some of the increases in learning are due to its effect on attention to academic content.

Unfortunately, when Anderson et al. (1987) analyzed social studies and science textbooks presented to children in school, they found them to be dull. They also determined that authors often attempted to make texts interesting by adding stimulating anecdotes. Texts filled with anecdotes, however, often lack coherence (e.g., Armbruster, 1984). In addition, the reader can completely miss the point of the text, even while remembering the anecdotes in it. That is, stimulating information and seductive details can be recalled (e.g., John F. Kennedy and Robert F. Kennedy played touch football on the White House lawn with their children), although there is no learning of either abstract or general points covered in the text (e.g., the Kennedy administration proposed sweeping social reforms; Garner, 1992; Garner et al., 1991; Hidi & Baird, 1988; Wade & Adams, 1990).

While there is not much reason to be sanguine that texts can be made more interesting without also being seductive, we should not dismiss the possibility of increasing student interest in what they read. A low-cost way to increase students' interest is to permit them to choose for themselves what they will read. Self-selection of books that will be read was one of the main motivations of whole-language educators to provide students with so much choice. Of course, a problem with letting kids read what they are interested in reading is that classroom libraries and school libraries are mostly filled with books that are of little interest to youngsters (Ivey & Broaddus, 2001; Worthy et al., 1999). What grade schoolers want are scary books, comics and cartoons, graphic novels, some popular magazines, sports books, books about drawing, books about cars and trucks, animal books, and funny novels, with only funny novels in abundant supply in schools (Gabriel et al., 2012; Ives et al., 2020; Ivey & Broaddus, 2001; Worthy et al., 1999). Reading a topic of interest is important and influences upper elementary motivation to read (Ives et al., 2020; Taboada Barber et al., 2018). To support student motivation, teachers can use genre surveys to select books for class libraries or lessons.

We need to think hard about how to increase access to books and magazines that are attractive to kids as well as how to make really worthwhile readings more attractive to elementary students. We've seen enough classrooms where teachers have gotten the kids turned on to excellent literature to know that it is possible to do so. Balanced literacy teachers know what the good stuff is for kids to be reading and find ways to make certain their students are reading it.

Literature and Literature-Based Activities

A consistent claim of whole-language theorists was that literacy-rich environments are motivating to students. In fact, there is considerable support for their assertion. Barbara Palmer and colleagues (1994) asked grade 3 and grade 5 students from 16 classrooms about the factors that motivated them to read. Forty-eight children varying in their reading ability and motivation to read were interviewed in depth. In many different ways, the students reported that their motivations to read depended on rich literacy environments.

Thus, prior experiences with books were a major motivation for wanting to read, as well as for choosing to read particular books. Children reported wanting to read books after hearing a book read by a teacher or parent. Similarly, prior experience with books in a series motivated continued reading of the series (McGill-Franzen, 2009). For example, the American Girls series permits the child to learn more about characters who they have learned to like from reading previous books in the series. Series books also typically have common characters and settings as well as shared vocabulary. The evidence suggests that almost all avid adult readers were avid readers of series books in elementary school (Ross, 1995).

Social interactions revolving around books also matter. The participants in the Palmer et al. (1994) study reported wanting to read books that their friends, parents, and teachers talked about. Remarks such as the following were common:

> "My friend Kristin was reading it and told me about it and I said, 'Hmmm, that sounds pretty interesting.'"

> "I got interested in it because the other group . . . [was] reading it, so I checked it out of the library." (p. 177)

Book access was also reported as important by the children in the Palmer et al. (1994) study, who reported high motivation to read books they owned and ones available to them in their classroom. Particularly striking was the importance that the students attributed to the classroom library, consistent with the emphasis in meaning-emphasis approaches that classrooms filled with books motivate literate interactions with them (Fractor et al., 1993; Morrow, 1992).

Children's ease of access to interesting reading materials has been largely overlooked in both discussions of effective reading instruction and in the creation of policies meant to bolster reading achievement. However, that fact that almost two-thirds of America's free-lunch students own no books of their own (Binkley & Williams, 1996) indicates the scope of the access problem. Lindsay (2018) conducted a meta-analysis to determine the impact of improving children's access to books on reading development. He reports that, when examining the outcomes of rigorous experimental studies, where access was experimentally manipulated among populations of randomly assigned subjects, the impact of increasing book access on reading achievement produced an effect size of $d = 0.435$. Access also increased motivation to read with an effect size of $d = 0.967$. Ease of access to children's books varies enormously in America both in homes and in schools. Susan Neuman's work provides a compelling description of the differences based on family incomes and neighborhood wealth (1999, 2009; Neuman & Celano, 2001). Summarizing her findings, Neuman and Celano

(2001) wrote, "For every one line of print read by low-income children, middle-income children read three" (p. 19). In other words, children from low-income families have a very restricted access to books at home and at school as compared with children from middle-class families.

Evans et al. (2010) studied the longer-term effect of home access to books in 27 nations. They found that children who lived in homes where many books were present attained an additional 3 years of schooling as compared with children growing up in homes with few books. This advantage remained after controlling for fathers' occupation, parental education, and family socioeconomic status. The having-books-in-the-home advantage was twice as large as the difference between having a professional father versus having an unskilled laborer as your father. Access to many books also equaled the impact of having university-educated parents versus unschooled parents. Bradley et al. (2001) reported that children living in low-income homes owned far fewer books than more economically advantaged children. Halle et al. (1997) reported that, of all the family influences studies in their examination of the relationship between the beliefs, attitudes, and home environments of African American families, the number of books in the homes was the only measure that correlated with reading achievement of the children. In short, what we know is that home access to books varies enormously in America and this differential ease of access is related to both reading frequency and reading development.

Much like the differential access found for children from homes of differing levels of socioeconomic status, others have noted that schools that enroll many children from low-income families have smaller school library collections, smaller classroom library collections, and more restrictive policies on whether books owned by the school are allowed to leave the building (Allington et al., 1995; McGill-Franzen et al., 2002; Neuman & Celano, 2001). In sum, children from low-income families have a far more restricted access to books they want to read and can read than is the case for more economically advantaged peers.

Finally, Guthrie and Humenick (2004) report a meta-analysis of 23 studies designed to improve reading comprehension. Two huge effect sizes were found, $d = 1.64$ for improving access to interesting texts and $d = 1.20$ for allowing students to choose which books they will read. There were similar effect sizes on the same two factors for motivation to read. What all this evidence indicates is that access to books that children find interesting is an important factor in determining whether the children will read or not. Similarly, student self-selection from a wide array of different texts is also linked both to reading volume and improved reading achievement. Both factors, access and choice, seem severely restricted in too many American classrooms where a single teacher- (or district-) selected anthology is the only text available for students to read.

A hallmark of the meaning-emphasis philosophy (as well as educational motivational theorists; see Schraw et al., 2001) is that literacy instruction should include freedom of choice and will be more motivating if it does. Consistent with the perspective that choice is important in motivating literacy, the children in the Palmer et al. (1994) study reported they were more excited about reading books they chose to read than those they were required to read (Spaulding, 1992). Our predilections are to believe the children, for they are closer to their motivations than anyone else. Many social scientists are skeptical of self-reports, however, especially with respect to motivation. They prefer observations of motivated reading. What would be most believable to the social science community would be observations of greater motivation in literacy-rich environments than in more conventional classroom environments. There is in fact some evidence of this type.

Julianne Turner's (1995) dissertation at the University of Michigan was a very thorough comparison of motivation in literacy-rich whole-language grade 1 classrooms versus grade 1 classrooms that emphasized skills. She studied six grade 1 classrooms in a school district that used whole language and six grade 1 classrooms in a similar district that used a basal instructional program. Teachers in these whole-language classrooms offered quite a bit of explanation about phonics and other skills. This explanation often came in the context of group reading of texts (e.g., big books), however. The basal instructional program included stories and skill work, including worksheets as part of phonics instruction.

One of the most striking outcomes in Turner's (1995) study was that the children in the whole-language classrooms used more learning strategies than did the students in the basal classes. That is, they seemed more engaged with the content, rehearsing it more, elaborating on ideas they encountered, planning more, and monitoring whether they were understanding what they read. Thus, whole language seemed to make a difference. Even so, both types of classrooms afforded opportunities for the types of tasks and situations that Palmer et al. (1994) concluded were motivating. Consistent with Palmer and colleagues' (1994) conclusions, across both types of classrooms, students persisted most in reading when they were involved in activities like partner reading and reading of trade books, in contrast to when they were involved in activities such as worksheets. When children could select texts on their own, they read more. In short, Turner (1995) observed that when the classroom conditions matched those that the children in the Palmer et al. (1994) study claimed were motivating, students seemed more motivated.

Morrow and her colleagues (1992; Morrow & Sharkey, 1993), also explored the motivational consequences of instruction consistent with meaning-emphasis principles. She introduced a literature-based reading program into grade 2 classrooms. The program included literacy centers that stimulated a variety of literacy activities (e.g., reading, felt-board enactments of stories, listening to taped stories, writing), teacher-guided literature activities (e.g., reading and telling of stories by teachers, student retelling and rewriting of stories, writing of original stories, book sharing), and independent reading and writing periods that permitted student choice of literacy activities (i.e., reading, writing, listening, enacting). In the meaning-emphasis classrooms, there was a great deal of social, cooperative interaction between students as they engaged in literacy activities.

In contrast, students in control classrooms participated in a traditional basal program supported by workbook exercises. Control instruction included small-group lessons and seatwork. After completing workbook activities, students read library books. Although teachers occasionally read stories to children in the control classrooms, such reading was not a focus of instruction.

By the end of the intervention, there were clear advantages for the students in the meaning-emphasis classrooms. For example, students in these classrooms were better able to retell and rewrite stories that were read to them than were students in control classrooms. Students in the meaning-emphasis classrooms outperformed control participants on a listening comprehension test. They also outperformed controls when asked to compose their own stories, using more complex language and included more diverse vocabulary than the language of the control participants. Most critical in the context of this chapter on student motivation, the students in the meaning-emphasis classrooms read more books and stories outside of school. When the meaning-emphasis students talked about their literacy program, they did so with enthusiasm, emphasizing that it was fun.

Even small instructional changes by teachers can influence student motivation to read (Marinak, 2013; Wu et al., 2013). For example, Marinak (2013) reported on fifth graders' motivation to read when teachers implemented just three interventions into their classrooms. The intervention included giving students a choice in teacher read-aloud books, implementing a cooperative learning jigsaw approach when completing information text reading, and started book clubs for students along with self-selected reading. Results found that treatment teachers who implemented the three interventions reported higher student motivation than the control teachers.

Wu et al. (2013) report two studies completed with fourth- and fifth-grade students enrolled in either rural or urban elementary schools. Treatment teachers organized collaborative, peer-managed discussion groups in their classrooms while control teachers organized traditional teacher-managed discussions in their classrooms. Children in peer-managed discussion classrooms were rated as more often engaged than students in teacher-managed classrooms with student academic ability unrelated to engagement levels. Students in the collaborative, peer-managed discussion classrooms demonstrated both higher levels of engagement and higher levels of motivation for school.

In summary, there is converging evidence that when classroom life is rich in literature and authentic reading experiences students are more motivated than when instruction is more consistent with traditional skills and drills. Perhaps the most incontrovertible conclusion with respect to instruction filled with social interactions around the reading of real literature is that such experiences enliven classrooms. Meaning-emphasis classrooms can be very motivating learning environments.

A Community-of-Learners Approach: Concept-Oriented Reading Instruction

Ann L. Brown and her associates pioneered the community-of-learners approach, in which content-area instruction is integrated with literacy instruction (Brown, 1992; Brown et al., 1993; Brown & Campione, 1994; Campione et al., 1995). Rather than superficially covering many topics, communities of learners explore a few issues in great depth during an academic year. When students begin to study a new topic, they generate questions that they want to answer. Students are taught strategies for carrying out research. Much of their time is spent doing collaborative research aimed at answering the questions that they have posed. This research will include library research, field observations, carrying out experiments, or any of a variety of activities that might reveal something about the concept that is being explored. Students also learn comprehension strategies that increase their abilities to find and remember the important parts of texts they read as part of their research.

Finally, they do a great deal of writing. The overarching goal is for community-of-learners students to acquire strategic and conceptual knowledge that they can use broadly. The group generated considerable evidence that students learn skills that transfer, which are acquired as they attempt to understand concepts that they research and write about (Campione et al., 1995). Guthrie (1996) and his National Reading Research Center associates (Grant et al., 1993–1994; Guthrie et al., 1996) developed a variation of the community-of-learners approach. They studied literacy instruction that integrates reading, writing, and teaching of science, emphasizing real-world science observations, student self-direction, strategy instruction, and student collaboration and interaction during learning. Guthrie refers to this approach as "concept-oriented reading instruction" (CORI).

In a year-long evaluation of the approach, grade 3 and grade 5 students observed concrete objects in their natural world as part of an effort to develop conceptual interests that would motivate their study of the phenomena observed. Thus, to begin their study of birds and the environment, students observed bird nests in the wild. This was followed by other concrete experiences, including attempts to build birds' nests; observing and recording behaviors at bird feeding stations; and visiting a collection of stuffed birds. Such concrete experiences provided much learning, illustrated by this report from a student after attempting to build a bird's nest:

> I learned that it's hard to make a nest unless you really try to. I learned that birds have a hard time making nests but we read a book that helped us learn and I found out that if you try with a group it might be easy. And you might make a lot of friends. (Guthrie et al., 1996, p. 312)

The concrete observations led to the development of students' questions, and to collaborative brainstorming to come up with questions. These questions would motivate additional observations, reading, writing, and discussions. Questions were displayed on the walls of the classroom as a reminder of what students wanted to discover through their research, reading, and writing. This was science instruction that involved making observations, gathering and recording data, recognizing patterns, and developing explanations for these observations and patterns.

In order to answer the questions that students had posed for themselves, they needed to develop their search skills. As part of CORI, students were taught how to search for books and other materials. They learned how to use tables of contents, indexes in books, headings, and pictures in texts in order to narrow their search for relevant information. Students learned to (1) be certain of what they wanted to find out before they searched (i.e., to form a search goal); (2) identify the organization of materials they are searching; (3) extract critical information from sources, constructing summaries and paraphrases of critical material; and (4) abstract across sources, producing syntheses of important ideas and general concepts emerging from the various sources of information. These strategies were taught using teacher and peer modeling followed by teacher scaffolding of these skills as students searched. Of course, because students worked together as they searched, there was also peer scaffolding of skills.

CORI students also learned comprehension strategies, which included identifying the main ideas in texts, looking for critical details, summarizing, comparing between texts, relating illustrations in texts to verbal content, evaluating a book, and reflecting on the point of view expressed in a text. These skills were practiced with narratives and expository pieces, with students learning that topics can be addressed and explored in both fictional and factual writing. Students learned how to take notes about main ideas, details, and so on as well.

Virtually all reading was of authentic literature, with a variety of trade books read as part of units. Thus, as students studied birds, they read *Owl Moon* (Yolen, 1987), *White Bird* (Bulla, 1966), and *Wingman* (Pinkwater, 1975). Students also read poems relating to birds. As they read these texts, students were taught about the importance of imagery during reading and how the story grammar elements (i.e., setting, plot, conflict, resolution) combine as part of a story. By reading materials related to the thematic topic and searching for answers to critical questions, the students became experts about the topic. This expertise was used by students as they wrote reports relating to the concept, developed stories pertaining to focal concepts, and created visual displays (e.g., bulletin boards). As students carried out these activities, they learned how to tailor their messages to particular audiences and how to express meaning in a variety of ways.

CORI students improved in search and comprehension skills, writing, understanding of focal concepts, comprehension of texts, and interpretation skills (e.g., Guthrie et al., 1998, 1999). Particularly important to note here is that the majority of students reported greater motivation to read and participate in literacy activities as the program continued (e.g., Guthrie et al., 2000). Moreover, the majority of students reported reading more as the year proceeded.

Guthrie and his colleagues have continued to evaluate and validate the impact of CORI on student engagement, comprehension, and achievement (e.g., Guthrie, 2004; Guthrie & Cox, 2001; Guthrie et al., 2004, 2009). We are increasingly convinced that this approach is effective relative to conventional classroom instruction. At the same time, we do not feel that Guthrie's group has yet conducted rigorous comparisons with alternative methods that can be effective in promoting reading achievement. For example, Guthrie et al. (2004) compared CORI with a condition in which students were only taught comprehension strategies. CORI students did better, and, in fact, the students receiving comprehension strategies instruction were at about the level of students receiving conventional instruction. That is, CORI did better relative to an ineffective version of comprehension strategies instruction. Our guess is that the version was ineffective because the comprehension strategies–instruction teachers received very brief training in how to teach that way, which is a problem since it is known based on previous work that it takes about a year to become proficient in teaching comprehension strategies (Pressley & El-Dinary, 1997), and when comprehension strategies instruction has worked, it has been with teachers who understand the approach very well (e.g., Brown et al., 1996). Guthrie et al. (2009) compared CORI with traditional basal reader instruction (TI) over a 12-week period in grade 5 classrooms. Of particular concern were the low-achieving-student responses including students with learning disabilities. Compared with TI students, CORI students scored higher on posttest measures of word recognition speed, reading comprehension on the Gates–MacGinitie Reading Test, and ecological knowledge. CORI was equally effective for lower achievers and higher achievers.

Finally, Swan (2003) has offered a book-length summary about how to implement CORI in elementary schools. This resource is invaluable for teachers who want to attempt to do highly motivating conceptually driven instruction that also impacts literacy development, most particularly aiming to improve student comprehension and understanding of what they read.

Summary

Many researchers are studying the nature of instruction that grabs students' interest, motivating them to read and learn. Although there have been frustrations, there have been many more successes than failures. Perhaps most encouraging of all, instructional practices that motivate are enjoying dissemination. Despite justifiable reservations about meaning-emphasis with respect to the development of basic decoding skills, many meaning-emphasis practices are motivating, and they certainly are widely disseminated. Even if a school does not adopt these efforts, however, much can be gleaned from the motivational research that can be adopted and adapted in any classroom.

An important point that sometimes gets overlooked in discussions of motivation is that nothing motivates like success! To the extent that educators devise literacy interventions that cause children to succeed in literacy, there will be increased motivation to do things literate. A child's identity and commitment to reading depends greatly on getting good at it; hence, as you reflect on the many recommendations for increasing student motivation, never forget that promoting success in reading goes far in promoting motivation to read (McCarthey, 2001). Moreover, success is more likely with the types of high-quality instruction emphasized in this book.

FLOODING THE CLASSROOM WITH MOTIVATION

In our studies of effective grade 1 classrooms, we had noted that effective teachers did much to motivate their students. This observation motivated us to focus more on the motivational differences between engaging and not-so-engaging grade 1 classrooms. Bogner et al. (2002) observed seven grade 1 classrooms over the course of a school year. Two of those classrooms were very engaging in that students were working on reading and writing much of the time, raptly attentive as they did so. The other five teachers who were observed were much less successful in motivating their students to read and write. Inattention and off-task behaviors were much more common in these less engaging classrooms than in the two classrooms that were very engaging.

Teaching Behaviors Discouraging Engagement

In contrast to the truly engaging teachers, the less engaging teachers routinely undermined student motivation. Some teachers encouraged competition between students. They taught in ways that actually encouraged inattentiveness (e.g., encouraging the students to give big cheers when they did something right, which always resulted in several minutes of disruption). Some teachers provided very public grades, which made obvious which students did poorly. Some provided extrinsic rewards for behaviors that the students were intrinsically motivated to do already. In the less engaging classrooms, the *content* was often boring or so easy that students did not have to engage in order to complete it. In the less engaging classrooms, *communications* often were disturbing, with negative feedback to students common. The *self-concept development* efforts in less engaging classrooms sometimes ran counter to encouraging student effort—for example, encouraging students to believe their successes reflect high ability and failures reflect low ability. Effective *classroom management* was lacking in the less engaging classrooms: There was little monitoring of the class. Teachers often tried to control the class with threats and punishments. In short, the less effective teachers did much less that positively encouraged academic engagement and, in fact, did quite a bit to discourage academic engagement.

Teacher Behaviors Encouraging Engagement

The most important finding in this study was that the two very engaging teachers did a great deal to motivate literacy in their classrooms relative to the five teachers who were less engaging. Thus, there were many aspects of their teaching style that were motivating, including the following: There was a great deal of cooperative learning in the class, although individual students were held accountable for their work. The two engaging teachers did a lot of scaffolding. There were many connections in the classroom, including to library readings. The engaging teachers encouraged autonomy in their students and gave them choices. The engaging teachers had a gentle and caring manner, with many positive one-to-one interactions, home–school connections, and opportunistic mini-lessons. The engaging teachers connected with their students personally. They supported appropriate risk taking, made the classroom fun, and encouraged the students to be creative. The two most engaging classrooms were very positive places.

Beyond teaching style, the engaging teachers had great content in their classrooms. The material each child covered was challenging but not over-whelming. The engaging teachers used games in instruction. They worked with the students to produce products that the students were proud of, such as big books written by the class. The engaging teachers favored depth over breadth, often having several readings that connected to current social studies and science units, each of which might last several weeks. There was good literature everywhere in the engaging classrooms.

The engaging teachers also had great communications with their students. They provided concrete examples when covering abstract concepts. The engaging teachers encouraged their students to be curious and created suspense (e.g., "I wonder how Ebenezer is going to react to the ghosts"). The engaging teachers made certain the students knew the learning goals and understood assignments. They provided a lot of praise and feedback, consistently modeling interest and enthusiasm as they did so. The engaging teachers also modeled thinking and problem-solving skills (e.g., how to sound out words, figure out what a word encountered in a text context means). The engaging teachers sent the message consistently that school-work was important and deserved intense attention, often expressing confidence that the students were equal to the academic demands of school.

Self-concept development was important in the classrooms taught by the two engaging teachers. These teachers encouraged their students to make effort attributions (i.e., to believe their successes were due to their hard work, to interpret failure as a sign to work harder). The engaging teachers sent the message that people get smarter through their efforts—for example, by reading a lot.

The engaging teachers had terrific classroom management skills. In particular, they monitored student learning and engagement well. They knew what the whole class was doing all the time, and they were exceptionally aware of who needed help, moving quickly to provide assistance. Nancy Masters was one of the two very engaging teachers studied by Bogner et al. (2002).

Nancy Masters's Teaching

On a typical day, Nancy Masters used more than 40 different positive motivational mechanisms to inspire and engage her students. Her classroom was filled to overflowing with motivating activities and positive tone. Cooperation was emphasized consistently during both whole-class and small-group instruction. Thus, when students read books with partners, Ms. Masters reminded them: "The point is, you're supposed to *help* your partner." She provided reassurance and interesting scaffolding when students took on challenging activities. Thus, before a test requiring application of phonics skills, Ms. Masters reminded her students of the phonics they had been learning and emphasized that they should apply what they knew about phonics on the upcoming test.

Ms. Masters was always teaching. Teaching was what was important in Ms. Masters's classroom, teaching that was more often offered in a side-by-side format than in a whole-class lecture format. Ms. Masters emphasized depth in her teaching, covering mature and interesting ideas. For example, during Black History Month, not only did students complete detailed group book reports about five prominent African Americans, but Ms. Masters also led a discussion about the Jim Crow laws, one in which the students participated enthusiastically, demonstrating that they had learned a great deal about racial discrimination during the month. During this conversation, Ms. Masters talked about different ways that people can affect social change, covering civil disobedience, disobeying unjust laws, and working within the system to change such laws. She and the first-grade students discussed equality and inequality, with student comments reflecting their grasp of some very difficult concepts.

Nancy Masters's teaching connected across the curriculum and community, between school and home. During the first month of the school year, she took her class to visit the kindergarten room. In doing so, she became acquainted with her future students while forging connections across grade levels for the kindergarten and grade 1 students. Her students wrote in their journals about this visit. When they wrote stories a few weeks later, Ms. Masters held out as a carrot another visit to the kindergarten room. She told her grade 1 students, "Maybe we'll show the kindergarten [your stories]." Nancy also pointed out times when students' home experiences connected with school. Thus, when a student read the word *little* very quickly, Ms. Masters commented, "Have you been working at home with your mom? I'm so proud of you!" In doing so, she simultaneously emphasized the importance of effort and homework while connecting to the student's home life. Ms. Masters also hosted a career day during which parents talked about and demonstrated their professional skills. After the visits, the students wrote in journals and did an at-home art project about their favorite profession. This special home assignment complemented the regular homework, which consisted of reading 15 minutes a night, doing a short math worksheet, and practicing spelling words.

Nancy Masters gave many opportunistic mini-lessons. In-class assignments seemed appropriately challenging and engaging (i.e., students could not finish them quickly, and they seemed interested in them). Her emphasis on good literature, the writing process, and comprehension was apparent during every class visit. Also, the class constructed many products, which were tangible evidence of accomplishment, including big books that were displayed prominently in the classroom and discussed often. Ms. Masters promised the class that each student would be able to take home one class-constructed book at the end of the year. She made many across-curriculum connections for her students (e.g., having students use the internet and the library to find material about Black History Month, material then used in writing an essay). Student choice was important in her classroom. Students selected not just which books they would read, but what things they would write about and what topics they would research. Offering students choices meant that far fewer one-size-fits-all tasks were assigned, and more differentiated assignments dominated the work students engaged in.

Ms. Masters expressively communicated with students. As she read to students, she modeled her interest and enthusiasm and reflected her curiosity about what would happen next in a story, often creating a sense of suspense about the events in a reading. When the class received a new basal reader, she opened it and said, "A brand-new book! It's like a present. I know you want to open it and look inside. Go ahead and look inside. See anything interesting? Anything you've read?"

Ms. Masters provided clear learning objectives and goals. Thus, at the beginning of the school year, she had the students copy stories she had written on the board, explaining that they were copying stories so that "You can see what good writing looks like." Similarly, when she taught strategies during writing workshop, Ms. Masters emphasized that use of the strategies would help students write as they needed to write by the end of grade 1.

Nancy Masters emphasized effort attributions. Thus, on the day report cards were distributed to students, she told the students twice that their most important grade was their grade for effort. She and her students often used the term "personal best" to describe how they were doing.

Nancy Masters monitored the students well. She often said, "When I come around, I want to hear you reading or helping your partner or discussing the story." During her walk-arounds, she provided help to students who were having difficulties with their work. Probably the most interesting thing we learned was that effective grade 1 teachers teach quite differently from less effective grade 1 teachers. The first thing we noticed about Ms. Masters's teaching was how active she was! While there was a teacher's desk in her room, she was almost never sitting at the desk or even near that desk during the school day. Similarly, while it was easy to locate the front of the classroom, we rarely observed Ms. Masters in that location. In short, she was up and among her students, consistently and constantly moving about the classroom. As she moved around the classroom she was monitoring attentiveness and behavior. It seemed that her proximity to the children made it possible for her to "see" potential problems before they became problems.

Of course, Ms. Masters's efforts to motivate her students paid off. There was consistently high engagement in her class. The pace was always quick. The assignments were always interesting. She excited her students about their work. Her students were always engaged in productive work! We believe that virtually every grade 1 teacher could learn to teach the way Ms. Masters teaches. Unfortunately, few school systems and state education agencies seem to recognize that such teachers exist, much less advance policies that might result in increasing the supply of teachers who teach really effectively.

Motivational Flooding Beyond First Grade

Since Bogner et al. (2002), the Pressley group carried out comparable studies across the primary grades (Dolezal et al., 2003; Pressley et al., 2003) and in sixth-grade middle school settings (Raphael et al., 2008). Essentially, the results obtained at those levels are identical to the grade 1 outcomes. Teachers varied widely in whether they engaged students, with the most engaging teachers being the ones who motivationally flooded their classrooms. In the most engaging classrooms, the teacher was doing something every minute to motivate the whole class, small groups, or individuals. She or he used many motivational mechanisms to do so, ones making a great deal of sense based on the educational motivational research. In addition, engaging teachers did nothing that had the potential to undermine student motivation. In contrast, less engaging teachers used far fewer positive motivational mechanisms and used them less often, relying much more on tactics that can turn students off (e.g., punishment).

Going beyond individual classrooms, the Pressley group turned its attention to whole schools. One investigation, conducted at Benchmark School, is especially relevant here (Pressley et al., 2006). Students come to Benchmark after experiencing school failure for one or more years, typically failure to learn to read. Over 1–9 years (the average is 4–7 years), students learn how to read, compose, and experience conceptually focused math, social studies, and science instruction, with much of this content-area instruction consistent with the motivating CORI conception of teaching and learning considered earlier in this chapter. The most important finding here, however, is that, in every class and across the school day, there is motivational saturation. Students are consistently encouraged to believe they can determine their achievement through their efforts and by learning and using the strategies and content taught at the school. There is much praise of achievements, with praise informing the students about what they did right. Grades are downplayed, with grading for improvement the norm. The students are given appropriately challenging tasks, ones just a bit beyond their current levels, matched to individual students.

Cooperative learning occurs in every engaging class. The teachers do all that is possible to teach interesting content in interesting ways and succeed in doing so, with many connections made across the curriculum. Discipline is intelligent and reflective, with the centerpiece being reflection on the effects of misbehavior on self and others. Finally, and very importantly, the teachers show great pedagogical care (Goldstein, 1999; Noddings, 1984), with teachers' concerns for students apparent in every class. Benchmark teachers know their students very well, with this deep personal knowledge translating to great teaching commitment and real teacher determination to motivate high achievement and success in students (Worthy & Patterson, 2001). And, of course, both academic engagement and achievement are high at Benchmark, consistent with other educational settings that are perceived as pedagogically caring places—warm and supportive environments—by students (e.g., Skinner et al., 1990; Wentzel, 1998).

SUMMARY AND CONCLUDING REFLECTIONS

1. In general, academic motivation declines from the onset of schooling through high school. There are various psychological developments contributing to declining motivation, including developmental changes in how students react to failures. Younger children believe failure reflects lack of effort than ability. Older children are more likely than younger children to make comparisons with others, which undermines motivation for the child experiencing difficulties. There are also structural changes in the school setting that contribute to declining motivation with increasing grade level.

2. There are a variety of mechanisms that are being validated in research as positively affecting student motivation. One is the training of students to make effort attributions rather than ability attributions to explain both failures and successes. A variety of mechanisms favored by meaning-emphasis advocates, such as the choice and reading of excellent literature, seem to promote student motivation to read. The community-of-learners approach promises to increase depth of conceptual understanding, as it motivates students to engage academically. There has been a lot of progress in understanding academic motivation in the past three decades. It is essential that such work continue and that the results of such work be applied to school reform.

3. Some teachers, like Nancy Masters, succeed in flooding their classrooms with motivation, and it shows! Notably, Ms. Masters also does nothing that undermines her kids' efforts. What we want teachers to get from her example is inspiration—that it is possible to do much to motivate literacy engagement. We've never spent an hour in her classroom when we were not confident that every kid was getting much out of the lessons being taught. We've never spent a moment in her classroom when it was not obvious that every student just loved being there. Effective literacy teachers are

loved teachers, living in classroom worlds that make their own lives as fulfilling as the developing lives of their students.

One productive way to think about the motivational research summarized in this chapter is to think about the ideas that emerge that can be used in any elementary classroom. We think there is enough evidence available right now to recommend that every teacher do everything possible to follow these guidelines that relate to student motivation:

- Ensure student success. This can be accomplished by making certain that students are attempting tasks that are within their reach. During challenging tasks, be a teacher who scaffolds student learning so that students are able to make progress.

- Encourage students to attribute their successes to expending appropriate efforts and their failures to lack of effort or failing to deploy effort appropriately (e.g., using a wrong strategy). Encourage students to believe that intelligence is not innate and fixed, but rather ever changing. Good readers improve by reading more and by learning to use reading strategies that good readers use.

- Failures occur. Encourage students to interpret failures as a natural part of learning. Discourage students from believing that failures reflect low ability. Students are served well when you foster in them the understanding that failures indicate a need to approach a challenge in a different way or use a different strategy. Furthermore, do not permit failures to persist, believing that failure represents a lack of developmental readiness. Teachers should use student failures to diagnose when and how they can scaffold a student.

- Do not encourage student competition. Student competition undermines motivation rather than fostering it. In competitive classrooms, many more students are going to feel like losers than winners. Rather than encouraging competition between students, it is better to reward students for improving on their past performances and to send the message consistently that improvement is what matters.

- Encourage student cooperation and interaction over literacy tasks. When students talk about books, they let one another know what is worth reading and what is exciting to read. Students' conceptual knowledge develops more completely when they work together in communities of learners, especially when motivation is high in such classroom communities.

- Play down "grades as rewards" for literacy activities, especially activities that are intrinsically motivating for students. When students begin to be artificially rewarded for doing what they like to do, their intrinsic motivation for the activity can decline. In general, the more a classroom encourages working for grades, the more it discourages intrinsic motivation.

• Make certain that students have access to a wide range of interesting books. Classroom libraries are a critically important source of reading material for all students; thus, do everything possible to ensure the availability of a rich classroom library.

• As much as possible, permit student choice with respect to what they read and to what topics are the conceptual focus of instruction. Teach children how to find books on the topics that most interest them.

• Integrate literacy instruction with content learning. Such integration makes clear to students that the reading and writing skills that they are acquiring are useful for learning important ideas, which is especially likely if the conceptual ideas that are explored as part of science and social studies grab students.

• Favor depth over breadth as much as possible, as is done in communities of learners, choosing a few exceptionally motivating topics as the conceptual focus for the school year.

Not surprisingly, many of these concepts have been encountered in previous chapters. Why? Excellent teachers are very motivating, largely because they integrate many of the ideas covered in this chapter into their teaching. In reviewing what is now known about student motivation, it is clear that there is no evidence whatsoever that any one of these mechanisms is so powerful that it alone is more powerful than the others. At the same time, nothing motivates a student like successful accomplishment of personally interesting and appropriately challenging tasks. Educators should worry less about raising test scores and more about creating classrooms where all students are motivated to learn.

REFERENCES

Allington, R. L., Guice, S., Baker, K., Michelson, N., & Li, S. (1995). Access to books: Variations in schools and classrooms. *Language and Literacy Spectrum, 5*(Spring), 23–25.

Allington, R. L., McCuiston, K. F., & Billen, M. (2015). What research says about text complexity and learning to read. *The Reading Teacher, 68,* 491–501.

Amendum, S. J., Conradi, K., & Liebfreund, M. D. (2016). The push for more challenging texts: An analysis of early readers' rate, accuracy, and comprehension. *Reading Psychology, 37,* 570–600.

Ames, C. (1984). Competitive, cooperative, and individualistic goal structures: A motivational analysis. In R. Ames & C. Ames (Eds.), *Research on motivation in education* (Vol. 1, pp. 117–207). Academic Press.

Ames, C. (1992). Classrooms: Goals, structures, and student motivation. *Journal of Educational Psychology, 84,* 261–271.

Anderson, R. C. (1982). Allocation of attention during reading. In A. Flammer & W. Kintsch (Eds.), *Discourse processing* (pp. 292–305). North-Holland.

Anderson, R. C., Mason, J. M., & Shirey, L. (1984). The reading group: An experimental investigation of a labyrinth. *Reading Research Quarterly, 20, 6–38.*

Anderson, R. C., Shirey, L. L., Wilson, P. T., & Fielding, L. G. (1987). Interestingness of children's reading material. In R. E. Snow & M. J. Farr (Eds.), *Aptitude, learning, and instruction: Vol. 3. Cognitive and affective process analyses* (pp. 287–299). Erlbaum.

Armbruster, B. B. (1984). The problem of "inconsiderate text." In G. G. Duffy, L. R. Roehler, & J. Mason (Eds.), *Comprehension instruction* (pp. 202–217). Longman.

Baker, L., & Wigfield, A. (1999). Dimensions of children's motivation for reading and their relations to reading activity and reading achievement. *Reading Research Quarterly, 34,* 452–477.

Binkley, M., & Williams, T. (1996). *Reading literacy in the United States: Findings from the IEA reading literacy study* (No. NCES 96-258). U.S. Department of Education, Office of Educational Research and Improvement.

Blumenfeld, P. C. (1992). Classroom learning and motivation: Clarifying and expanding goal theory. *Journal of Educational Psychology, 84,* 272–281.

Bogner, K., Raphael, L. M., & Pressley, M. (2002). How grade-1 teachers motivate literate activity by their students. *Scientific Studies of Reading, 6,* 135–165.

Bondy, E., Ross, D. D., Gallingane, C., & Hambacher, E. (2007). Creating environments of success and resilience: Culturally responsive classroom management and more. *Urban Education, 42,* 326–348.

Borkowski, J. G., Carr, M., Rellinger, E. A., & Pressley, M. (1990). Self-regulated strategy use: Interdependence of metacognition, attributions, and self-esteem. In B. F. Jones (Ed.), *Dimensions of thinking: Review of research* (pp. 53–92). Erlbaum.

Borkowski, J. G., Weyhing, R. S., & Carr, M. (1988). Effects of attributional retraining on strategy-based reading comprehension in learning-disabled students. *Journal of Educational Psychology, 80,* 46–53.

Bradley, R. H., Corwyn, R. F., McAdoo, H. P., & Coll, C. G. (2001). The home environments of children in the United States, Part I: Variations by age, ethnicity, and poverty status. *Child Development, 72,* 1844–1867.

Brooks, R. B. (2001). Fostering motivation, hope, and resilience in children with learning disorders. *Annals of Dyslexia, 51,* 9–20.

Brophy, J. (1987). On motivating students. In D. Berliner & B. Rosenshine (Eds.), *Talks to teachers* (pp. 201–245). Random House.

Brown, A. L. (1992). Design experiments: Theoretical and methodological challenges in creating complex interventions in classroom settings. *Journal of the Learning Sciences, 2,* 141–178.

Brown, A. L., Ash, D., Rutherford, M., Nakagawa, K., Gordon, A., & Campione, J. C. (1993). Distributed expertise in the classroom. In G. Salomon (Ed.), *Distributed cognitions: Psychological and educational considerations* (pp. 188–228). Cambridge University Press.

Brown, A. L., & Campione, J. C. (1994). Guided discovery in a community of learners. In K. McGilly (Ed.), *Classroom lessons: Integrating cognitive theory and classroom practice* (pp. 229–270). MIT Press/Bradford Books.

Brown, R., Pressley, M., Van Meter, P., & Schuder, T. (1996). A quasi-experimental validation of transactional strategies instruction with low-achieving second grade readers. *Journal of Educational Psychology, 88,* 18–37.

Bulla, C. R. (1966). *White bird.* Philomel.

Bureau, J. S., Howard, J. L., Chong, J. X. Y., & Guay, F. (2021). Pathways to student motivation: A meta-analysis of antecedents of autonomous and controlled motivations. *Review of Educational Research.*

Campione, J. C., Shapiro, A. M., & Brown, A. L. (1995). Forms of transfer in a community of learners: Flexible learning and understanding. In A. McKeough, J. Lupart, & A. Marini (Eds.), *Teaching for transfer: Fostering generalization in learning* (pp. 35–68). Erlbaum.

Carr, M., & Borkowski, J. G. (1989). Attributional training and the generalization of reading strategies with underachieving children. *Learning and Individual Differences, 1,* 327–341.

Carr, M., Borkowski, J. G., & Maxwell, S. E. (1991). Motivational components of underachievement. *Developmental Psychology, 27,* 108–118.

Cartwright, K. B., Marshall, T. R., & Wray, E. (2016). A longitudinal study of the role of reading motivation in primary students' reading comprehension: Implications for a less simple view of reading. *Reading Psychology, 37,* 55–91.

Chapman, J. W., & Tunmer, W. E. (1995). Development of young children's reading self-concept: An examination of emerging subcomponents and their relationship with reading achievement. *Journal of Educational Psychology, 87,* 154–167.

Chapman, J. W., Tunmer, W. E., & Prochnow, J. E. (2000). Early reading-related skills and performance, reading self-concept, and the development of academic self-concept: A longitudinal study. *Journal of Educational Psychology, 92,* 703–708.

Chapman, M., Skinner, E. A., & Baltes, P. B. (1990). Interpreting correlations between children's perceived control and cognitive performance: Control, agency, or means–ends beliefs? *Developmental Psychology, 26,* 246–253.

Cheung, A. C. K., & Slavin, R. E. (2012). The effects of educational technology applications on reading outcomes for struggling readers: A best-evidence synthesis. *Reading Research Quarterly, 48,* 277–299.

Clifford, M. M. (1978). The effects of quantitative feedback on children's expectations of success. *Journal of Educational Psychology, 48,* 220–226.

Clifford, M. M. (1984). Thoughts on a theory of constructive failure. *Educational Psychologist, 19,* 108–120.

Corpus, J. H., McClintic-Gilbert, M. S., & Hayenga, A. O. (2009). Within-year changes in children's intrinsic and extrinsic motivational orientations: Contextual predictors and academic outcomes. *Contemporary Educational Psychology, 34,* 154–166.

Covington, M. V. (1987). Achievement motivation, self-attributions, and the exceptional learner. In J. D. Day & J. G. Borkowski (Eds.), *Intelligence and exceptionality* (pp. 355–389). Ablex.

Covington, M. V., & Omelich, C. L. (1979a). Effort: The double-edged sword in school achievement. *Journal of Educational Psychology, 71,* 169–182.

Covington, M. V., & Omelich, C. L. (1979b). It's best to be able and virtuous too: Student and teacher evaluative responses to successful effort. *Journal of Educational Psychology, 71,* 688–700.

Covington, M. V., & Omelich, C. L. (1981). As failures mount: Affective and cognitive consequences of ability demotion in the classroom. *Journal of Educational Psychology, 73,* 796–808.

Covington, M. V., & Omelich, C. L. (1984). Task-oriented versus competitive learning structures: Motivational and performance consequences. *Journal of Educational Psychology, 6,* 1038–1050.

Deci, E. L., Koestner, R., & Ryan, R. M. (1999). A meta-analytic review of experiments examining the effects of extrinsic rewards on intrinsic motivation. *Psychological Bulletin, 125,* 627–668.

Deshler, D. D., Palincsar, A. S., Biancarosa, G., & Nair, M. (2007). *Informed choices for struggling adolescent readers: A research-based guide to instructional programs and practices.* International Reading Association.

Deshler, D. D., & Schumaker, J. B. (1988). An instructional model for teaching students how to learn. In J. L. Graden, J. E. Zins, & M. J. Curtis (Eds.), *Alternative educational delivery systems: Enhancing instructional options for all students* (pp. 391–411). National Association of School Psychologists.

Deshler, D. D., Schumaker, J., Harris, K. R., & Graham, S. (1998). *Teaching every child every day: Learning in diverse schools and classrooms.* Brookline Books.

Dijkstra, P., Kuyper, H., Van der Werf, G., Buunk, A. P., & van der Zee, Y. G. (2008). Social comparison in the classroom: A review. *Review of educational research, 78,* 828–879.

Dolezal, S. E., Welsh, L. M., Pressley, M., & Vincent, M. (2003). How do grade-3 teachers motivate their students? *Elementary School Journal, 103,* 239–267.

Dweck, C. S. (2010). Even geniuses work hard. *Educational Leadership, 6*(1), 16–21.

Dweck, C. S., & Goetz, T. E. (2018). Attributions and learned helplessness. In *New directions in attribution research* (pp. 157–179). Psychology Press.

Dweck, C. S., & Leggett, E. L. (1988). A social–cognitive approach to motivation and personality. *Psychological Review, 95,* 256–273.

Dynarski, M. (2007). *Effectiveness of reading and mathematics software products: Findings from the first student cohort.* Institute of Education Sciences, U.S. Department of Education. Available at *http://ies.ed.gov/ncee/pubs/20074005.*

Eccles, J. S. (1993). School and family effects on the ontogeny of children's interests, self-perceptions, and activity choices. In J. E. Jacobs (Ed.), *Nebraska Symposium on Motivation: Vol. 40. Developmental perspectives on motivation* (pp. 145–208). University of Nebraska Press.

Eccles, J. S., Wigfield, A., Flanagan, C., Miller, C., Reuman, D., & Yee, D. (1989). Self-concepts, domain values, and self-esteem: Relationships and changes in early adolescence. *Journal of Personality, 57,* 283–310.

Elbaum, B., & Vaughn, S. (2003). Self-concept and students with learning disabilities. In H. L. Swanson, K. R. Harris, & S. Graham (Eds.), *Handbook of learning disabilities* (pp. 229–241). Guilford Press.

Entwisle, D., & Hayduk, L. (1978). *Too great expectations: The academic outlook of young children.* Johns Hopkins University Press.

Evans, M. D. R., Kelley, J., Sikora, J., & Treiman, D. J. (2010). Family scholarly culture and educational success: Books and schooling in 27 nations. *Research in Social Stratification and Mobility, 28,* 171–197.

Fairbanks, C. M., & Broughton, M. A. (2003). Literacy lessons: The convergence of expectations, practices, and classroom culture. *Journal of Literacy Research, 34,* 391–428.

Foersterling, F. (1985). Attribution retraining: A review. *Psychological Bulletin, 98,* 495–512.

Folmer, A. S., Cole, D. A., Sigal, A. B., Benbow, L. D., Satterwhite, L. F., Swygert, K. E., et al. (2008). Age-related changes in children's understanding of effort and ability: Implications for attribution theory and motivation. *Journal of Experimental Child Psychology, 99,* 114–134.

Fractor, J., Woodruff, M. C., Martinez, M. G., & Teale, W. H. (1993). Let's not miss opportunities to promote voluntary reading: Classroom libraries in the elementary school. *Reading Teacher, 46,* 476–485.

Gabriel, R., Allington, R. L., & Billen, M. (2012). Background knowledge and the magazine reading students choose. *Voices from the Middle, 20,* 52–57.

Gambrell, L. B. (2011). Seven rules of engagement: What's most important to know about motivation to read. *The Reading Teacher, 65,* 172–178.

Gambrell, L. B., Codling, R. M., & Palmer, B. M. (1996). *Elementary students' motivation to read* (Research Report). National Reading Research Center.

Gambrell, L. B., Palmer, B. M., Codling, R. M., & Mazzoni, S. A. (1996). Assessing motivation to read. *Reading Teacher, 49,* 518–533.

Gans, A. M., Kenny, M. C., & Ghany, D. L. (2003). Comparing the self-concept of students with and without learning disabilities. *Journal of Learning Disabilities, 36,* 287–295.

Garner, R. (1992). Learning from school texts. *Educational Psychologist, 27,* 53–63.

Garner, R., Alexander, P. A., Gillingham, M. G., Kulikowich, J. M., & Brown, R. (1991). Interest and learning from text. *American Educational Research Journal, 28,* 643–660.

Goldstein, L. S. (1999). The relational zone: The role of caring relationships in the co-construction of mind. *American Educational Research Journal, 36,* 647–673.

Grant, R., Guthrie, J., Bennett, L., Rice, M. E., & McGough, K. (1993–1994). Developing engaged readers through concept-oriented instruction. *The Reading Teacher, 47,* 338–340.

Guthrie, J. T. (1996). Educational contexts for engagement in literacy. *The Reading Teacher, 49,* 432–445.

Guthrie, J. T. (2004). Teaching for literacy engagement. *Journal of Literacy Research, 36,* 1–30.

Guthrie, J. T., Anderson, E., Alao, S., & Rinehart, J. (1999). Influences of concept-oriented reading instruction on strategy use and conceptual learning from text. *Elementary School Journal, 99,* 343–366.

Guthrie, J. T., & Cox, K. E. (2001). Classroom conditions for motivation and engagement in reading. *Educational Psychology Review, 13,* 283–302.

Guthrie, J. T., & Humenick, N. M. (2004). Motivating students to read: Evidence for classroom practices that increase motivation and achievement. In P. McCardle & V. Chhabra (Eds.), *The voice of evidence in reading research.* Brookes.

Guthrie, J. T., McRae, A., Coddington, C. S., Klauda, S. L., Wigfield, A., & Barbosa, P. (2009). Impacts of comprehensive reading instruction on diverse outcomes of low- and high-achieving readers. *Journal of Learning Disabilities, 42,* 195–214.

Guthrie, J. T., Van Meter, P., Hancock, G. R., Alao, S., Anderson, E., & McCann, A. (1998). Does concept-oriented reading instruction increase strategy use and conceptual learning from text? *Journal of Educational Psychology, 90,* 261–278.

Guthrie, J. T., Van Meter, P., McCann, A. D., Wigfield, A., Bennett, L., Poundstone, C. C., et al. (1996). Growth of literacy engagement: Changes in motivations and strategies during concept-oriented reading instruction. *Reading Research Quarterly, 31,* 306–332.

Guthrie, J. T., Wigfield, A., Barbosa, P., Perencevich, C., Taboada, A., Davis, M. H., et al. (2004). Increasing reading comprehension and engagement through concept-oriented reading instruction. *Journal of Educational Psychology, 96,* 403–423.

Guthrie, J. T., Wigfield, A., & VonSecker, C. (2000). Effects of integrated instruction on motivation and strategy use in reading. *Journal of Educational Psychology, 92,* 331–341.

Haimovitz, K., & Dweck, C. S. (2017). The origins of children's growth and fixed mindsets: New research and a new proposal. *Child Development, 88,* 1849–1859.

Hall, L. A. (2006). Anything but lazy: New understanding about struggling readers, teaching, and text. *Reading Research Quarterly, 41,* 424–426.

Halle, T., Kurtz-Costes, B., & Mahoney, J. (1997). Family influences on school achievement in low-income, African-American children. *Journal of Educational Psychology, 89,* 527–537.

Harter, S. (1990). Cause, correlates, and the functional role of self-worth: A life-span perspective. In R. J. Sternberg & J. Kolligian (Eds.), *Competence considered* (pp. 67–97). Yale University Press.

Harter, S., Whitesell, N. R., & Kowalski, P. (1992). Individual differences in the effects of educational transitions on young adolescents' perceptions of competence and motivational orientation. *American Educational Research Journal, 29,* 777–807.

Hattie, J. (2009). Visible learning: *A synthesis of over 800 meta-analyses relating to achievement.* Routledge.

Henderson, V. L., & Dweck, C. S. (1990). Motivation and achievement. In S. S. Feldman & G. R. Elliott (Eds.), *At the threshold: The developing adolescent* (pp. 308–329). Harvard University Press.

Hidi, S. (1990). Interest and its contribution as a mental resource for learning. *Review of Educational Research, 60,* 549–571.

Hidi, S. (2001). Interest, reading, and learning: Theoretical and practical considerations. *Educational Psychology Review, 13,* 191–209.

Hidi, S., & Baird, W. (1988). Strategies for increasing text-based interest and students' recall of expository text. *Reading Research Quarterly, 23,* 465–483.

Horner, S. L., & Gaither, S. M. (2004). Attribution retraining instruction with a second-grade class. *Early Childhood Education Journal, 31,* 165–170.

Huang, S. (2012). A mixed method study of the effectiveness of the Accelerated Reader program on middle school students' reading achievement and motivation. *Reading Horizons: A Journal of Literacy and Language Arts, 51,* 229–246.

Ives, S. T., Parsons, S. A., Parsons, A. W., Robertson, D. A., Daoud, N., Young, C., et al. (2020). Elementary students' motivation to read and genre preferences. *Reading Psychology, 41,* 660–679.

Ivey, G., & Broaddus, K. (2001). "Just plain reading": A survey of what makes students want to read in middle school classrooms. *Reading Research Quarterly, 36,* 350–377.

Jacobs, J. E., Lanza, S., Osgood, D. W., Eccles, J. S., & Wigfield, A. (2002). Changes in children's self-competence and values: Gender and domain differences across grades one through twelve. *Child Development, 73,* 509–527.

Johnston, P. H. (2004). *Choice words: How our language affects children's learning.* Stenhouse.

Johnston, P. H. (2012). *Opening minds: Using language to change lives.* Stenhouse.

Johnston, P., & Winograd, P. (1985). Passive failure in reading. *Journal of Reading Behavior, 17,* 279–301.

Juvonen, J. (1988). Outcome and attributional disagreements between students and their teachers. *Journal of Educational Psychology, 80,* 330–336.

Kistner, J. A., Osborne, M., & LeVerrier, L. (1988). Causal attributions of learning-disabled children: Developmental patterns and relation to academic progress. *Journal of Educational Psychology, 80,* 82–89.

Kloosterman, P. (1988). Self-confidence and motivation in mathematics. *Journal of Educational Psychology, 80,* 345–351.

Lepper, M. R., Keavney, M., & Drake, M. (1996). Intrinsic motivation and extrinsic rewards: A commentary on Cameron and Pierce's meta-analysis. *Review of Educational Research, 66,* 5–32.

Levesque-Bristol, C., Richards, K. A. R., Zissimopoulos, A., Wang, C., & Yu, S. (2022). An evaluation of the integrative model for learning and motivation in the college classroom. *Current Psychology, 41,* 1447–1459.

Lindsay, J. J. (2018). Interventions that increase children's access to print material and improve their reading proficiencies. In R. L. Allington & A. McGill-Franzen (Eds.), *Summer reading: Closing the rich/poor reading achievement gap* (2nd ed., pp. 20–38). Teachers College Press.

Mallette, M. H., Henk, W. A., & Melnick, S. A. (2004). The influence of Accelerated Reader on the affective literacy orientations of intermediate grade students. *Journal of Literacy Research, 36,* 73–84.

Marinak, B. A. (2013). Courageous reading instruction: The effects of an elementary motivation intervention. *Journal of Educational Research, 106,* 39–48.

McCarthey, S. J. (2001). Identity construction in elementary readers and writers. *Reading Research Quarterly, 36,* 122–151.

McGill-Franzen, A. M. (2009). Series books for young readers: Seeking pleasure and developing reading competence. In D. A. Wooten & B. E. Cullinan (Eds.), *Children's literature in the reading program: An invitation to read* (pp. 57–65). International Reading Association.

McGill-Franzen, A. M., Lanford, C., & Adams, E. (2002). Learning to be literate: A comparison of five urban early childhood programs. *Journal of Educational Psychology, 94*(3), 443–464.

McKenna, M. C., Conradi, K., Lawrence, C., Jang, B. G., & Meyer, J. P. (2012). Reading attitudes of middle school students: Results of a U.S. survey. *Reading Research Quarterly, 47*(3), 283–306.

McKenna, M. C., Ellsworth, R. A., & Kear, D. J. (1995). Children's attitudes toward reading: A national survey. *Reading Research Quarterly, 30,* 934–956.

McLoyd, V. C. (1979). The effects of extrinsic rewards of differential value on high and low intrinsic interest. *Child Development, 50,* 1010–1019.

Meece, J. L., & Miller, S. D. (1999). Changes in elementary school children's achievement goals for reading and writing: Results of a longitudinal and an intervention study. *Scientific Studies of Reading, 3,* 207–229.

Meece, J. L., & Miller, S. D. (2001). A longitudinal analysis of elementary school students' achievement goals in literacy activities. *Contemporary Educational Psychology, 26,* 454–480.

Miller, S. D., & Meece, J. L. (1999). Third graders' motivational preferences for reading and writing tasks. *Elementary School Journal, 100,* 19–35.

Morgan, P. L., & Fuchs, D. (2007). Is there a bidirectional relationship between children's reading skills and Reading Motivation? *Exceptional Children, 73,* 165–183.

Morrow, L. M. (1992). The impact of a literature-based program on literacy achievement, use of literature, and attitudes of children from minority backgrounds. *Reading Research Quarterly, 27,* 250–275.

Morrow, L. M., & Sharkey, E. A. (1993). Motivating independent reading and writing in the primary grades through social cooperative literacy experiences. *The Reading Teacher, 47,* 162–169.

Neuman, S. B. (1999). Books make a difference: A study of access to literacy. *Reading Research Quarterly, 34,* 286–311.

Neuman, S. B. (2009). *Changing the odds for children at risk.* Teachers College Press.

Neuman, S. B., & Celano, D. (2001). Access to print in low-income and middle-income communities. *Reading Research Quarterly, 36,* 8–26.

Nicholls, J. G. (1978). The development of the concepts of effort and ability, perception of academic attainment, and the understanding that difficult tasks require more than ability. *Child Development, 49,* 800–814.

Nicholls, J. G. (1989). *The competitive ethos and democratic education.* Harvard University Press.

Nicholls, J. G. (1990). What is ability and why are we mindful of it?: A developmental perspective. In R. Sternberg & J. Kolligian (Eds.), *Competence considered* (pp. 11–40). Yale University Press.

Nicholls, J. G., & Thorkildsen, T. A. (1987, October). *Achievement goals and beliefs:*

Individual and classroom differences. Paper presented at the annual meeting of the Society for Experimental Social Psychology, Charlottesville, VA.

Noddings, N. (1984). *Caring: A feminine approach to ethics and moral education.* University of California Press.

Nunnery, J. A., Ross, S. M., & McDonald, A. (2006). A randomized experimental evaluation of the impact of Accelerated Reader/Reading Renaissance implementation on reading achievement in grades 3 to 6. *Journal of Education for Students Placed At-Risk, 11,* 1–18.

O'Flahavan, J., Gambrell, L. B., Guthrie, J., Stahl, S., & Alvermann, D. (1992). Poll results guide activities of research center. *Reading Today, 10,* 12.

Onatsu-Arvilommi, T., & Nurmi, J. E. (2000). The role of task-avoidant and task-focused behaviors in the development of reading and mathematical skills during the first school year: A cross-lagged longitudinal study. *Journal of Educational Psychology, 92,* 478–491.

Palmer, B. M., Codling, R. M., & Gambrell, L. B. (1994). In their own words: What elementary students have to say about motivation to read. *Reading Teacher, 48,* 176–178.

Parsons, A. W., Parsons, S. A., Malloy, J. A., Gambrell, L. B., Marinak, B. A., Reutzel, D. R., et al. (2018). Upper elementary students' motivation to read fiction and nonfiction. *The Elementary School Journal, 118,* 505–523.

Parsons, J., & Ruble, D. N. (1977). The development of achievement-related expectancies. *Child Development, 48,* 1075–1079.

Pinkwater, D. (1975). *Wingman.* Bantam-Skylark.

Pressley, M., Dolezal, S. E., Raphael, L. M., Welsh, L. M., Bogner, K., & Roehrig, A. D. (2003). *Motivating primary-grade students.* Guilford Press.

Pressley, M., & El-Dinary, P. B. (1997). What we know about translating comprehension strategies instruction research into practice. *Journal of Learning Disabilities, 30,* 486–488.

Pressley, M., Gaskins, I. W., Solic, K., & Collins, S. (2006). A portrait of the Benchmark School: How a school produces high-achievement in students who previously failed. *Journal of Educational Psychology, 98,* 282–306.

Pressley, M., & Ghatala, E. S. (1989). Metacognitive benefits of taking a test for children and young adolescents. *Journal of Experimental Child Psychology, 47,* 430–450.

Raphael, L. M., Pressley, M., & Mohan, L. (2008). Engaging instruction in middle school classrooms: An observational study of nine teachers. *Elementary School Journal, 109,* 61–81.

Reid, M. K., & Borkowski, J. G. (1987). Causal attributions of hyperactive children: Implications for teaching strategies and self-control. *Journal of Educational Psychology, 79,* 296–307.

Renick, M. J., & Harter, S. (1989). Impact of social comparisons on the developing self-perceptions of learning disabled students. *Journal of Educational Psychology, 81,* 631–638.

Renninger, K. A., & Wozniak, R. H. (1985). Effect of interest on attentional shift, recognition, and recall in young children. *Developmental Psychology, 21,* 624–632.

Ross, C. S. (1995). "If they read Nancy Drew, so what?" Series book readers talk back. *Library and Information Science Research, 17(3),* 201–236.

Ross, S. M., Nunnery, J., & Goldfeder, E. (2004). *A randomized experiment on the effects of Accelerated Reader/Reading Renaissance in an urban school district: Final evaluation report.* Center for Research in Educational Policy, University of Memphis.

Ruble, D. N. (1983). The development of social-comparison processes and their role in achievement-related self-socialization. In E. T. Higgins, D. N. Ruble, & W. Hartup (Eds.), *Social cognition and social development* (pp. 134–157). Cambridge University Press.

Ruble, D. N., Boggiano, A. K., Feldman, N. S., & Loebl, J. H. (1980). Developmental analysis of the role of social comparison in self-evaluation. *Developmental Psychology, 16,* 105–115.

Scherrer, V., Preckel, F. (2019). Development of motivational variables and self-esteem during the school career: A meta-analysis of longitudinal studies. *Review of Educational Research, 89,* 211–258.

Schiefele, U. (1992). Topic interest and levels of text comprehension. In K. A. Renninger, S. Hidi, & A. Krapp (Eds.), *The role of interest in learning and development* (pp. 151–182). Erlbaum.

Schiefele, U., Schaffner, E., Möller, J., & Wigfield, A. (2012). Dimensions of reading motivation and their relation to reading behavior and competence. *Reading Research Quarterly, 47,* 427–463.

Schmidt, C. R., Ollendick, T. H., & Stanowicz, L. B. (1988). Developmental changes in the influence of assigned goals on cooperation and competition. *Developmental Psychology, 24,* 574–579.

Schraw, G., Flowerday, T., & Lehman, S. (2001). Increasing situational interest in the classroom. *Educational Psychology Review, 13,* 211–224.

Schunk, D. H. (1991). Self-efficacy and academic motivation. *Educational Psychologist, 26,* 207–232.

Shirey, L. L., & Reynolds, R. E. (1988). Effect of interest on attention and learning. *Journal of Educational Psychology, 80,* 159–166.

Skinner, E. A., Wellborn, J. G., & Connell, J. P. (1990). What it takes to do well in school and whether I've got it: A process model of perceived control and children's engagement and achievement in school. *Journal of Educational Psychology, 82,* 22–32.

Spaulding, C. C. (1992). The motivation to read and write. In J. W. Irwin & M. A. Doyle (Eds.), *Reading/writing connections: Learning from research* (pp. 177–201). International Reading Association.

Stipek, D. J., & Daniels, D. H. (1988). Declining perceptions of competence: A consequence of changes in the child or in the educational environment? *Journal of Educational Psychology, 80,* 352–356.

Stipek, D. J., & Hoffman, J. M. (1980). Children's achievement-related expectancies as a function of academic performance histories and sex. *Journal of Educational Psychology, 72,* 861–865.

Stipek, D., & Kowalski, P. (1989). Learned helplessness in task-orienting versus performance-orienting test conditions. *Journal of Educational Psychology, 81,* 384–391.

Swan, E. A. (2003). *Concept-oriented reading instruction: Engaging classrooms, lifelong learners.* Guilford Press.

Sweet, A. P., & Guthrie, J. T. (1996). How children's motivations relate to literacy development and instruction. *Reading Teacher, 49,* 660–662.

Sweet, A. P., Guthrie, J. T., & Ng, M. M. (1998). Teacher perceptions and students' regulation of motivation. *Journal of Educational Psychology, 90,* 210–223.

Taboada Barber, A., Levush, K. C., & Klauda, S. L. (2018). *The role of motivation theory in literacy instruction.* In D. E. Alvermann, N. J. Unrau, M. Sailors, & R. B. Ruddell (Eds.), *Theoretical models and processes of literacy* (7th ed., pp. 233–251). Routledge.

Turner, J. C. (1995). The influence of classroom contexts on young children's motivation for literacy. *Reading Research Quarterly, 30,* 410–441.

Vollands, S. R., Topping, K. J., & Evans, R. M. (1999). Computerized self-assessment of reading comprehension with the accelerated reader: Action research. *Reading and Writing Quarterly: Overcoming Learning Disabilities, 15,* 197–211.

Wade, S. E., & Adams, R. B. (1990). Effects of importance and interest on recall of biographic text. *Journal of Reading Behavior, 22,* 331–353.

Weiner, B. (1979). A theory of motivation for some classroom experiences. *Journal of Educational Psychology, 71,* 3–25.

Wentzel, K. R. (1998). Social relationships and motivation in middle school: The role of parents, teachers, and peers. *Journal of Educational Psychology, 90*, 202–209.

White, R. W. (1959). Motivation reconsidered: The concept of competence. *Psychological Review, 66*, 297–333.

Wigfield, A. (1988). Children's attributions for success and failure: Effects of age and attentional focus. *Journal of Educational Psychology, 80*, 76–81.

Wigfield, A. (1994). Expectancy-value theory of achievement motivation: A developmental perspective. *Educational Psychology Review, 6*, 49–78.

Wigfield, A. (2000). Facilitating children's reading motivation. In L. Baker, M. Dreher, & J. Guthrie (Eds.), *Engaging young readers: Promoting achievement and motivation* (pp. 140–158). Guilford Press.

Wigfield, A., & Eccles, J. S. (1992). The development of achievement task values: A theoretical analysis. *Developmental Review, 12*, 265–310.

Wigfield, A., Eccles, J. S., Fredricks, J. A., Simpkins, S., Roeser, R.W., & Schiefele, U. (2015). Development of achievement motivation and engagement. In M. E. Lamb, R. M. Lerner, M. E. Lamb, & R. M. Lerner (Eds.), *Handbook of child psychology and developmental science* (Vol. 3, 7th ed., pp. 657–700). Wiley.

Wigfield, A., Eccles, J. S., MacIver, D., Reuman, D. A., & Midgley, C. (1991). Transitions during early adolescence: Changes in children's domain-specific self-perceptions and general self-esteem across the transition to junior high school. *Developmental Psychology, 27*, 552–565.

Wigfield, A., Eccles, J. S., Yoon, K. S., Harold, R. D., Arbreton, A. J. A., Freedman-Doan, C., et al. (1997). Change in children's competence beliefs and subjective task values across the elementary school years: A 3–year study. *Journal of Educational Psychology, 89*, 451–469.

Wigfield, A., & Guthrie, J. T. (1997). Relations of children's motivation for reading to the amount and breadth of their reading. *Journal of Educational Psychology, 89*, 420–432.

Wigfield, A., Guthrie, J. T., & McGough, K. (1996). *A questionnaire measure of children's motivation for reading* (Instructional Resource No. 22). National Reading Research Center.

Wigfield, A., Guthrie, J. T., Tonks, S., & Perencevich, K. C. (2004). Children's motivation for reading: Domain specificity and instructional influences. *The Journal of Educational Research, 97*, 299–310.

Wigfield, A., Wilde, K., Baker, L., Fernandez-Fein, S., & Scher, D. (1996). *The nature of children's motivation for reading, and their relations to reading frequency and reading performance*. National Reading Research Center.

Worthy, J., Moorman, M., & Turner, M. (1999). What Johnny likes to read is hard to find in school. *Reading Research Quarterly, 34*, 12–27.

Worthy, J., & Patterson, E. (2001). "I can't wait to see Carlos!": Preservice teachers, situation learning, and personal relationships with students. *Journal of Literacy Research, 33*, 303–344.

Wu, X., Anderson, R. C., Nguyen-Jahiel, K., & Miller, B. (2013). Enhancing motivation and engagement through collaborative discussion. *Journal of Educational Psychology, 105*, 622–632.

Yeager, D. S., & Dweck, C. S. (2012). Mindsets that promote resilience: When students believe that personal characteristics can be developed. *Educational Psychologist, 47*, 302–314.

Yolen, J. (1987). *Owl moon*. Philomel Books.

12 Concluding Reflections

The overarching conclusion we reached in writing this book is that balanced elementary reading instruction—that is, a balancing of skills-emphasis and meaning-emphasis components—seems more defensible, given the available research, than instruction that is only immersion in reading and writing, on the one hand, or predominantly skills-driven, on the other. A great deal of this book is about how good reading involves the learning and use of word recognition and comprehension strategies, with the effectiveness of strategies use depending, in part, on the reader's prior knowledge about the world, including knowledge built up through reading. Of course, we are not the only people talking about these issues!

FOUR NATIONAL REPORTS

Since the publication of the first edition of this book, four important reports have come out of Washington, DC, all purporting to provide insights about reading instructional practices that are based on research. The conclusions offered in these reports complement the ideas presented in this book but were less emphatic about balancing than we have been here.

The National Research Council Report

Preventing Reading Difficulties in Young Children (Snow et al., 1998) was published by the National Research Council (NRC), reflecting the work of a committee of scholars who had previously contributed distinguished reading and allied research (e.g., work on language development, writing, and literacy). The Snow et al. (1998) volume was a consensus document, with the authors reading the literature and agreeing among themselves about reading instructional practices that are research-defensible. Given that seven members of the committee had studied sound-, letter-, and word-level reading competencies more completely than other aspects of instruction, it was not surprising that Snow et al. (1998) argued extensively in favor of sound-, letter-, and word-level skills in reading instruction. Perhaps one reason that the first edition of the book you have just read was so successful was that its appearance coincided with the publication of Snow et al. (1998), both coming out in the spring of 1998. Many who read Snow et al. (1998) complained that it was too imbalanced in favor of skills instruction, prompting some to seek alternatives.

The National Reading Panel Report

From its outset, the National Reading Panel (NRP, 2000) decided to operate differently from Snow et al. (1998), intentionally limiting its scope, with the publicly admitted motivation for doing so being the overwhelming volume of evidence pertaining to early reading instruction. The panel decided to review only the following topics of instruction: alphabetics (i.e., phonemic awareness instruction, phonics instruction), fluency, comprehension (i.e., vocabulary instruction, text comprehension instruction, teacher preparation, and comprehension-strategies instruction), teacher education and reading instruction, and computer technology and reading instruction. Members of the panel also limited their focus to true experiments and quasi-experiments, presumably in response to a congressional demand that the panel adopt rigorous research methodological standards. In order to generate conclusions using meta-analysis, the members preferred a research integration strategy; that is, a number of experimental and/or quasi-experimental comparisons on a topic had to be available. The technique generates an average effect size (i.e., a numerical average of effect sizes observed in all the comparisons conducted to date). In short, the panel circumscribed its mandate, focusing only on particular topics studied many times over in experiments and/or quasi-experiments.

In summary, the NRP argued that there is much support for skills-based instruction: instructional development of phonemic awareness, phonics competencies, knowledge of vocabulary, and comprehension strategies. Although there were some comments about teacher development and computer-based reading instruction, the conclusions offered about these topics were less complete and emphatic because there was so little research on those issues that the panel regarded as credible. The message emerging from the panel report was that there is substantial scientific evidence in favor of teaching reading skills. A meta-message was that there is much less support for anything besides teaching of isolated skills. Thus, even with respect to the higher-order competency of comprehension, the panel emphasized the many studies about the teaching of individual strategies. In discussing the teaching of the entire complicated processing that sophisticated readers employ when they read challenging texts (Pressley & Afflerbach, 1995), they emphasized that only a very few studies provided telling data.

Though the NRP report is one of the widely cited reading research reports, it has also received criticism from other researchers for the selection of research studies and the overall claims made by the report as discussed in Chapter 1 (e.g., Cunningham, 2001; Hammill & Swanson, 2006).

The RAND Report on Comprehension

The RAND Reading Study Group, commissioned by the U.S. Department of Education, consisted of a who's who of scholars in the area of comprehension. They produced *Reading for Understanding: Toward an R&D Program in Reading Comprehension* (RAND Reading Study Group, 2001). This was an exceptionally intelligent discussion of what is known about comprehension instruction and what needs to be known, what is known about preparing teachers to teach comprehension and what needs to be known, as well as what is known about assessing comprehension and what needs to be known. For example, with respect to the issue of what is known about increasing comprehension through instruction, the report contains commentary on fluency, comprehension-strategies instruction, vocabulary instruction, cross-curricular connections, representation of diverse genres in comprehension instruction, motivation as key to instructional success, and how teachers articulate a variety of instructional procedures to develop student comprehension.

An overarching point with respect to instruction was that not nearly enough time is devoted to comprehension instruction in contemporary schools (this seemed to indicate that most teachers believed that reading where the words were all correctly pronounced should result in perfect comprehension). With respect to what needs to be known about comprehension instruction, among other recommendations, the RAND group encouraged more work on comprehension instruction in the context of current curricula, especially with respect to the understanding of weaker readers. The researchers were especially concerned that there be inquiry about how to work comprehension instruction into already busy schedules, especially for low achievers. The RAND group noted the need to know more about how to use assessment to guide comprehension instruction. It was also very concerned that there be more research on promoting comprehension in English-as-a-second-language learners. In short, the RAND group provided a wide-ranging discussion of the many issues surrounding comprehension instruction. This document is must reading in its complete form for all K–12 educators in our view and all concerned with the development of reading competence in K–12 education.

The National Early Literacy Panel Report

Because the earlier National Reading Panel report had focused on research involving school-age children, the National Early Literacy Panel (NELP; Lonigan & Shanahan, 2009) was created to report on the research conducted with younger children in homes, preschools, and kindergartens. The NELP completed meta-analyses on both correlational studies and experimental studies.

The NELP report noted that five early literacy skills were moderately correlated to at least one aspect of reading development (knowledge of print conventions and print concepts, alphabet knowledge, vocabulary, oral language, and visual discrimination among visually presented symbols). In addition six other variables including alphabet naming, phonological awareness, phonological memory, rapid automatized naming of letters and digits, rapid automatized naming of objects and colors, and ability to write letters on request were moderately correlated with at least one measure of later literacy achievement. The NELP notes that code-emphasis interventions, book-sharing interventions, and home and parent interventions all produced moderately large effects, but often on different aspects of emergent literacy development.

Pearson and Hiebert (2010) were quite critical of the NELP report, noting that it "does not provide insights or recommendations that can move the field of early literacy instruction ahead. To the contrary, it simply reinforces practices that have already been widely implemented without resounding success" (p. 287). They also argue that the NELP is wrong in its assertion that children begin school with few relevant prereading skills, noting that two-thirds of kindergartners enter school knowing the letters of the alphabet and one-third enter knowing the consonant sounds. They conclude that knowing the letter names seems not to have produced any substantial effect on later reading development and ask, So what else do kindergartners need to know to be on track as readers when they enter grade 4?

Summary Evaluations

Our first reactions to the NRC (Snow et al., 1998), NRP (2000), and the NELP (Lonigan & Shanahan, 2009) reports were that they were very credible, as far as they went. For example, most of the conclusions in these three reports were included in the first edition of this book, and most of the findings were well known to those who had spent time studying the scientific literature on reading instruction. Even though the conclusions of these reports were believable, it also seemed to us (Allington, 2002; Pearson & Hiebert, 2010; Pressley et al., 2004) that both the NRP and the NELP were unacceptably narrow in their consideration of reading instruction.

Although the coverage by Snow et al. (1998) was broader, that report never got beyond commenting on the efficacy of particular components. As the descriptions of the teaching of "Andy," Karyn Beach and Nancy Masters made clear earlier in this volume, balanced teaching is the orchestration of many components. The reports coming out of Washington have little to say about such orchestration. Twenty-four years after writing the first edition of this book, and hundreds of observations of balanced teaching later, we are convinced that balanced teaching is best understood by reflecting both on the individual components and about how masterful teachers like Andy, Karyn Beach, and Nancy Masters weave those components together to create their teaching methods. The voices and teaching of such teachers were excluded from the reports, and that is regrettable from our point of view.

Even if the NRP's willingness only to consider experimental and quasi-experimental data is respected, there was plenty covered in the present book that would have made sense to include in the NRP report. For example, we are impressed by the comparative data establishing that families can be taught to interact productively with their children over literacy tasks (Jordan et al., 2000; Morrow & Young, 1997). There are very good evaluations establishing that volunteer tutors can make a difference (Baker et al., 2000; Elbaum et al., 2000; Fitzgerald, 2001; Invernizzi et al., 1997; Wasik, 1998). Given the substantial body of experimental and quasi-experimental data confirming that meaning emphasis practices do have positive impacts on literacy (e.g., Dahl & Freppon, 1995; Dahl et al., 1999; Freppon & McIntyre, 1999; McIntyre & Freppon, 1994), and given the prevalence of meaning-emphasis practices in many classrooms, it would have made sense to offer some analyses of the research on meaning-emphasis approaches. In short, many of the elements of balanced instruction that enjoy empirical support were ignored by the NRP (2000).

That is not to say that the NRP had no impact on teaching. In fact, its view of reading went far in informing the Reading First provisions of the No Child Left Behind Act (2002). That legislation went far in stimulating much more skills instruction at the kindergarten through grade 3 levels, emphasizing phonemic awareness, phonics, fluency, vocabulary development, and comprehension strategies (Pressley et al., 2004). However, the legislation might have had a more beneficial impact on instruction and benefited more children (Gamse et al., 2009) had it been more broadly informed by a panel more committed to covering completely the evidence that can inform elementary reading instruction.

The RAND Reading Study Group (2001) document is without a doubt the most impressive of the national reports from the perspective of balanced scholarship and its forward look. The other two reports are mostly about what is known; the RAND report is as much about what needs to be known. It is stimulating and informative reading for educators and researchers. That said, a decade after its release, we have seen little evidence that the document has had much of an impact. With the endorsement here, we are urging all teachers and teachers-in-training to read the RAND document and to act on it.

Though these four reports have provided extensive reviews of research based reading practices, it is important to note that it has now been 10–20 years since these reports were put together. In the past several decades, there has been significant findings in the many different areas of reading that teachers should bring into their instruction. As discussed in Chapter 1, the special issues of *Reading Research Quarterly* (Goodwin & Jiménez, 2020, 2021) is an example of more recent summaries of critical aspects of reading. Additionally, the Institute of Educational Sciences (IES) held a virtual reading summit in 2021 (IES, 2021). The reading summit included over 40 speakers and panels of researchers and teachers discussing the current research and areas that more research is needed in the field of reading. Some of the topics covered in the special summit included the current state of reading research, developing instruction for emergent bilinguals, ways to involve parents in the reading process, equitable reading instruction for all, and policy and practice on dyslexia. A key feature of special issues and reading summits that differs from the past major four reports is the addition of topics that have become more prevalent in the field of reading in the past two decades, such as supporting emerging bilingual students and students with dyslexia.[1]

Special journal issues and summits can shed light on more recent research, but we believe more comprehensive reports such as the NRP, RAND, NRC, and NELP should be updated since it has been over two decades since these reports were put together. We have done our best to update the literature within this book, but would encourage teachers to continue seeking out research based practices.

THREE MODELS OF BEGINNING READING AND EARLY READING INSTRUCTION

Three instructional models were considered in this book. Each continues to be present in contemporary classrooms.

The Skills-Emphasis Model

According to the skills-emphasis approach, reading depends on the development of a number of particular competencies. Because some competencies

---

[1]We encourage all readers to visit the Reading Summit YouTube page to learn more: *www.youtube.com/playlist?list=PLkEhwZQdyNEEdolnYmOX2YhX1EhlFpC4k.*

are logical prerequisites to others, different competencies are the focus of development and instruction at different grade/age levels.

During the preschool years, or at the latest kindergarten, children should be able to differentiate letters from one another as well as know the names of letters and letter–sound associations. Children also need to learn that words are blendings of sounds. Such phonemic awareness depends critically on experiences that emphasize the sounds in words and how those sounds can be manipulated. Without phonemic awareness, instruction to sound out words by mapping the letters to their sounds and blending the letters would make little sense (i.e., the purpose of decoding instruction would not be clear).

At first, letter–sound mapping and blending require much effort and need a great deal of support. With practice, associating component letters to their sounds and blending them become more automatic. In addition, frequently encountered letter combinations come to be perceived automatically as chunks. When familiar chunks are part of unfamiliar words, they serve as foundations for sounding out and blending. As initially unfamiliar words are reencountered, recognition of the word as a whole is increasingly automatic. Such automatic recognition requires little if any effort.

The decreasing effort needed for word recognition frees up cognitive capacity for comprehension of the words being read. That is, decoding and comprehension compete for the limited attentional capacity that is available, the 5 ± 2 slots of short-term memory. One reason that comprehension often is low when students are struggling decoders is that all their capacity is being devoted to identifying the words, with little left over for understanding them (LaBerge & Samuels, 1974).

Once words are recognized automatically, their meanings are also accessed automatically. One of the ways that psychologists have demonstrated this fact is with research on the Stroop effect. Tim, Mike Pressley's then 9-year-old son, was so taken with this effect that his grade 4 science project was dedicated to it. Tim presented his friends and some younger children with lists of color words—blue, red, green, yellow, black, purple, orange, and brown. On one list, each word was printed in the color ink that corresponded to it (i.e., "blue" was printed in blue ink, "red" printed in red ink). On the other list, each word was printed in an ink not corresponding to its color (e.g., "blue" was printed in red ink, "red" was printed in blue ink). His friends' task was not to read the words, but simply to name the ink colors in the order of presentation. Consistent with classic Stroop results, Tim found that, when his grade 4 and 5 friends attempted this task, it was really difficult for them when the color words were printed in an ink other than the color for which the word stands. In contrast, kindergarten and grade 1 students had no difficulty reading off the sequence of colored inks, regardless of the meaning of the word. What was happening? The grade 4 and 5 students' reading of words was so automatic that they accessed the meaning of the words, even when they were not trying to read them, and this accessing of meaning produced interference when they attempted to say the name of the different-colored ink in which the word was printed. Becoming adept at reading words definitely affects comprehension. With the exception of situations like the Stroop task, automaticity of comprehension typically improves performance.

Word-level processes certainly are not all there is to comprehension, however. Good readers process the details in a text, as specified by word-by-word reading of that text, but do not get bogged down in those details as they construct an understanding of the main ideas in the text (e.g., Kintsch & van Dijk, 1978). Good readers are very active in this construction process, selectively attending to informative aspects of the text, explicitly attempting to elaborate upon and remember points in the text that seem particularly relevant to the reader's reason for reading, and responding affectively to ideas encoded in the text.

As previously discussed, skills-development approaches have fared reasonably well in experimental evaluations. In particular, instruction aimed at fostering emergent literacy and phonemic awareness skills has proven to affect reading in the long term. Early and explicit decoding instruction intended to develop sounding-out and blending skills has proven potent. Comprehension instruction that encourages more active strategic processing of a text really does make a difference in student understanding (e.g., Pressley, El-Dinary, et al., 1992).

As positive as the evaluations have been of instructional development of particular reading competencies, the skills-emphasis approach often does not appeal to educators. It seems mechanistic and reductionistic, especially to educators who are confronting children who seem ready to try to write, even though they cannot spell, who are enthralled by stories long before they can read many words well, and who use language that seems quite complex. The skills-emphasis approach especially seems mechanistic and unattractive when presented in publisher products that overemphasize skills, such as published decoding programs that are nothing more than daily worksheets, or when "phonics fanatics," as we think of them, literally scream that phonics should be first in grade 1 reading and continually present as a segment of reading lessons for as long as the teacher is still working to develop literate proficiencies. Such educational hawkers often show little understanding of how literature can be used to develop literacy competencies and enthusiasm for reading, and little knowledge about the important links between writing and the development of reading. Moreover, the phonics-first crowd often seems to assume that, if the child learns to decode with phonics, everything else will fall into place. According to them, the only bottleneck in learning to read is learning to decode.

The skills-emphasis model does not fail because skills are not critical; it fails because the skills that are the focus of skills-emphasis enthusiasts, especially decoding skills, are not all there is to literacy. The skills-emphasis model is an incomplete model of literacy development, one that does not even acknowledge as important many defensible meaning-emphasis practices that are embraced by those who control the American elementary classrooms—elementary school teachers.

The Meaning-Emphasis Model

The other end of the reading continuum is the meaning-emphasis approach, which takes the position that instruction focusing on the development of specific skills is essentially wrongheaded. Literate people read whole texts and sometimes write them, too. The message from meaning-emphasis proponents is that, if you want children to become readers of texts, have them read texts; if you want them to be writers, have them write. Holistic reading and writing will foster a deep understanding of the nature and purposes of reading; it will make obvious to the child why letter- and word-level processes, developing as a natural consequence of doing real reading and writing, are important.

Meaning-emphasis advocates concede that skills should be taught, but in the context of reading and writing. In other words, the child should be taught the skills that she or he in particular needs for meaning-emphasis reading and writing. Thus, if a teacher notices that a student is having difficulties with writing plurals (e.g., an English language–learning student is required to write in English, which uses very different approaches to pluralization than is the case should the child's native language be Spanish), it makes sense to do some explicit teaching of plurals at that point. The reason for such teaching will be obvious to the student in such a context, and the improvements in reading and writing gained from such instruction will also make clear the importance of learning about plurals.

The meaning-emphasis model is premised on a belief that children have powerful language-learning capabilities. The proof of this is that children learn oral language without explicit teaching, simply from immersion in a speaking world. Analogously, it is presumed that children should be able to learn to read and write from immersion in print and print experiences. The flaw in this thinking, however, is that learning to read and write is not much like learning to speak; humans have not evolved to be able to discover how to read and write simply from immersion in print experiences.

Meaning-emphasis approaches have not enjoyed as much experimental validation as alternative approaches, such as the skills-emphasis model. There are several reasons for this situation:

1. There is a great deal of data that seem inconsistent with the fundamental assumptions of the approach, such as demonstrations that only weak readers rely on semantic–contextual cues to decode words.
2. The data that do document the positive effects of meaning-emphasis approaches are not abundant, but there are such data, though those reports are often ignored.
3. Even though there are data documenting positive effects of meaning-emphasis approaches on many aspects of literacy development, it does not seem as certain to result in adequate decoding competency as other approaches. This is a point of emphasis since decoding increasingly seems like a critical literacy competency.

If the meaning-emphasis versus skills-emphasis debate has done nothing else, it has inspired a lot of analyses substantiating how critical being able to decode is for the development of mature literacy. Meaning-emphasis approaches are attractive in many ways, however. It is extremely child-centered, and educational models that focus on the natural development of children in authentic contexts have a long history of appeal. Nonetheless, effective meaning-emphasis environments demand much of teachers: excellent meaning-emphasis teachers must know literature well, understand the writing process, and be committed to monitoring their students intensively in order to identify the competencies that should be developed, the ones students most need to master in order to read and write. Unfortunately, most teachers in today's classrooms do not have the time to complete all these aspects well.

Because of the limited experimental support for meaning-emphasis approaches and inattention to the supportive studies that exist, it is being questioned by policymakers and researchers, so that the teacher who uses it often will do so in the face and wake of substantial administrative resistance. Because students in meaning-emphasis classrooms often do not make rapid progress in word-level decoding, parents are often very concerned about their students. For many parents, reading is being able to recognize the words!

Basically, the meaning-emphasis approach has the same flaw as the skills-emphasis approach: It is an incomplete model of the literacy development process. It seems especially incomplete with respect to its specification of a realistic conception of sound-, letter-, and word-level learning.

The Balanced Teaching Model

Between the skills emphasis approach and meaning emphasis, there is an intermediate position, which includes both in constructing meaning from a text. In our own work and that of our closest colleagues, the classrooms where reading and writing seem to be developing best are ones in which there is a lot of coverage of skills and a great deal of teacher support as children apply the skills they are learning to the reading of excellent literature and to writing. We do not see reading as skill emphasis versus meaning emphasis, but rather believe teachers should use research-based practices that support all aspects of reading. As we have discussed throughout this book, we believe the most effective reading instruction is at the center of the continuum. A balanced approach takes the research evidence on the potential of early and explicit decoding instruction and the evidence on explicit comprehension strategies instruction and blends it with the research evidence on the potential of meaning emphasis instruction for developing vocabulary, comprehension, and motivation to read.

BALANCED LITERACY TEACHING COMPARED WITH PRACTICE

In 1995, Mike Pressley participated in a symposium at the National Reading Conference, an organization composed of literacy researchers of various persuasions. His task that day was to be the discussant for a session on balanced reading instruction. As is typical in discussions about beginning reading, there were strong reactions to the presentations. The panelists wanted to emphasize to the audience that it makes sense to forget both the extremes in favor of balance.

Mike Pressley simply could not say directly what he wanted to say without potentially setting off a shouting match, but he was determined to get the message out anyway. Several who were attending that evening subsequently urged him to write up his remarks. Presented here is the gist of his remarks.

Commentary for a Symposium on Balanced Literacy Instruction

"I come here today not as a literacy researcher but as a candidate for Little League commissioner in my hometown. The reason I am running for the position is because I disagree with the two opposing models of our minor league program in Little League baseball. Some of the parents and managers believe that our minor league program should focus more than anything on the development of baseball skills. They are so adamant that some even believe that the minor leagues should not schedule regular games. The other side of the argument is that our 6- to 9-year-olds should be playing baseball as a game most of the time, for such immersion is how a person learns to play the game. At present, our minor league program is much more this second model than the first, and thus I will talk about my perceptions of that approach first.

"Our 6- to 9-year-olds are playing a lot of baseball games. For some of the kids, this is working just great. Unfortunately, however, many others are not making progress. If their understanding of the overall game is developing, however, their understanding of many fundamental details is lacking. I know the argument that, by playing the game, the kids will come to like the game. I have to be honest, however, that I see too many youngsters who are bored stiff because they do not understand the game. I see too many children in tears because they do not even know what they are doing wrong when they make an error. They know only that they are not playing well. And, lastly, I am struck that so many children have dropped out of baseball and will never play in the regular Little League because of what they felt was a bad experience. That is not to say that I favor the other side of this debate. Practice all has its place, but practice after practice without ever playing a game would be a drag. Unless the kids actually use the skills in games, they will never understand they are practicing particular skills.

"My memory of success was that there was some practice of skills, typically more early in the season than later, and typically more at the start of practice than at the end of it. After the skills practice, however, came the scrimmage game, with the team divided into two squads that played each other. During the scrimmage, the coaches did a lot of teaching, reminding players especially about how the skills they had been practicing transferred to the scrimmage. What the coach was doing is called scaffolding. The coach knew the kids did not 'get it' completely during the skill instruction and practice. 'Getting it' depends on using the skill in context, and the player is much more likely to 'get it' if given a hint at an appropriate moment than if the moment passes without the coach offering a mini-lesson.

"My position is for a balanced approach to our minor league program, one in which practices involve skills instruction plus scrimmages. The practices would be interwoven with some real games, but real games that are structured so that a lot of scaffolding and mini-lessons can take place. Our games should not be about winning and losing but about learning in the exciting and motivating environment. There should be a score book, but one that is a running record of player accomplishments and weaknesses that the coach can review later to reflect on what needs to be emphasized in future practice sessions. The center of attention has to be the improvement of the players, with every kid getting the help she or he needs and getting stroked for making improvements."

Balanced Instruction and Student Construction of Knowledge in General

Mike was well aware of the many suggestions made by constructivists that boil down to "Don't teach—let the child discover." There is a long history of such thinking in education, going back to Dewey (1933) and continuing with the Piagetians (Inhelder et al., 1974; Kohlberg & Mayer, 1972) to the present generation of so-called radical constructivists, including the whole-language theorists. There is also a long history of student discovery that does not result in rapid and certain cognitive development (e.g., Schauble, 1990), certainly not as rapid and certain as can occur with instruction (Brainerd, 1978; Mayer, 2004; Shulman & Keislar, 1966; Wittrock, 1966).

In Chapter 11, we made the case that academic achievement is most likely when instruction is matched to student competence. Whatever instruction the teacher provides should be matched to the level of the student's competence—in the student's zone of proximal development, to use the Vygotskian term (Vygotsky, 1978). There should be no illusion, however, that the student will really understand the lesson from the teacher's presentation. Mike and Karen Harris (Harris & Pressley, 1991; Pressley, Harris, et al., 1992) have made the case that, when a teacher explains a strategy to a student, the student does not really understand it well, but the instruction is a start. If the teacher then places the student in a situation where the strategy can be applied and scaffolds the student's use of the strategy in the situation, more learning will occur. With additional scaffolded practice opportunities, there is more learning still, as the student comes to understand how and when the strategy can be applied and adapted. With increasing experience, there is less need for the teacher to assist the student or even provide a hint that the strategy might be applied. Eventually, the student uses the strategy flexibly and appropriately, coordinating its use with the other strategies and knowledge.

If there is anything that can be learned from Vygotsky, it is that cognitive skills and strategies are passed from one generation to the next. Adults guide cognitive development by leading children to think in ways that many children would not discover on their own. There is some explaining in such cross-generational transmissions, but there is much more scaffolding, which is necessary because people do not learn by listening alone but also by doing, which should occur in a realistic context. Adults who are effective in promoting development do not leave development to the child's discovery. Discovery learning is the wrong approach to reading instruction; the case in favor of teaching as scaffolding is much more conceptually compelling.

DEVELOPMENT OF LITERACY COMPETENCE

Appendix 12.1, at the end of this chapter, summarizes much that was covered in this book, laid out along the lines of the ages and stages of development. Much must develop for a person to become a highly skilled reader, which involves efficient processing of individual words during active and selective processing of a text.

Literacy development begins long before the child passes through the school doors for the first time. Understanding has increased greatly in the past several decades about how literacy development proceeds early in life. With respect to elementary instruction, plenty has been learned about the value of explicit decoding and comprehension strategies instruction but also about the value of real reading opportunities and daily composition. The most important findings are summarized in Appendix 12.1, which concludes with a summary of what is known about literacy development beyond the elementary years, as a reminder that literacy development is not a childhood thing, but rather a life-span development.

The complexities reflected in the developmental progression detailed in Appendix 12.1 make clear that simplistic notions regarding development and instruction of literacy are not adequate—whether from the meaning-emphasis camp or from the skills-emphasis enthusiasts. Many simplistic claims about reading instruction continue to be made, however, that are simply wrong. Ten of the most offensive ones are taken up later in this chapter.

The Research That Is Needed

Much more research is needed on effective elementary literacy instruction. The great progress to date gives good reason to believe that even greater progress can be made by researchers who are informed by what has been discovered so far. As new technology and resources become available for teachers, researchers must continue to explore the best approaches to learning to read at the elementary level. Additionally, researchers need to continue to communicate research in terms of classroom practices to improve reading instruction. In this section, we take up some of the big and broad research efforts that are needed with respect to reading education and the development of skilled reading.

More Descriptive Studies of Effective Balanced Teaching

Much can be learned in laboratory-like experiments about how skills can be developed, and the skills-instruction enthusiasts have provided such work. Much can be learned about the types of literature and writing experiences that are possible by reading the mostly testimonial writing of meaning-emphasis teachers, and the meaning-emphasis enthusiasts have provided many testimonials. To understand the complex articulation of skills instruction and meaning-emphasis instruction that represents balanced instruction, however, one must begin with observation of excellent balanced instruction.

Descriptive studies are not as valued in the social sciences as are studies aimed at evaluating predetermined hypotheses about causes and effects. More positively, however, shifts in educational research toward more qualitative methodologies have led to more enthusiasm for descriptive work. As scholars who have done a great deal of descriptive research, we see this as a good sign, especially because this work has produced great insights about what really good elementary literacy instruction looks like. Still, much more is needed if sure conclusions are to be drawn from such work and if the generalizability of existing conclusions is to be tested. Then, there is a need for comparative studies informed by the observational work—that is, in situ evaluations of balanced classrooms as compared with other types of instructional environments.

What seems especially important to further study is the nature of teacher–child interactions in effective balanced literacy classrooms. Several characteristics of the effective balanced literacy teachers observed so far seem underused in less effective classrooms. Engaging students in actual discussions of what has been read tops our list. We are learning more about the potential power of discussion in fostering both improved comprehension (Nystrand, 2006) and improved motivation for reading (Wu et al., 2013). However, only a few studies experimentally contrast the outcomes from classrooms where more and less discussion is available (e.g., Applebee et al., 2003), and more such studies will be beneficial. Our second characteristic of effective balanced classrooms is the high level of motivational support provided by these teachers. Pressley et al. (2003) describe many of the classroom characteristics of these high-motivation environments and contrast them with less effective and less motivating classrooms. Johnston (2004) analyzes the teacher talk in classrooms of differing levels of effectiveness and notes that the effective teachers engage in much more talk that affirms effort and collaborative work. How we might better develop such teachers is of immediate interest. Our third characteristic of effective balanced classrooms, individual attention, can be found described in the reports by Carol Conner (Connor & Morrison, 2016; Connor et al., 2004). In these studies, individual needs are the focus with a balance between skills instruction and opportunities to read and write. As has often been noted by literacy scholars, no two effective teachers teach the same way. Nevertheless, all effective teachers teach every child what they need when they need it.

Balanced instruction is complex and calls for more complex methodologies to evaluate and elucidate it. That is, scientific work does more than inform scientists: at its best, it also informs practitioners; to achieve that, detailed descriptions are absolutely necessary. People often can learn better from specific concrete examples (i.e., cases) than from abstract descriptions. And we must also note that teachers can develop many of the proficiencies observed in effective teachers (McGill-Franzen et al., 1999; Scanlon & Anderson, 2020; Scanlon et al., 2010). In both efforts, the reading achievement of at-risk children was raised such that for most students the risk factor was eliminated. These studies also suggest that almost all students benefit more from high-quality classroom reading lessons than benefit from pull-out intervention programs.

Teacher Education Research

Substantial resources need to be devoted to research on teacher education that helps teachers develop into effective literacy educators who can deliver effective balanced instruction. Logically, it seems that such teachers must have in-depth understanding of children's literature, a sophisticated understanding of the linguistic structure of the American language and vocabulary, and a good understanding of the cognitive–instructional models that underlie scaffolded instruction and the most effective approaches to process writing. Teachers must learn how to mix explanations with students' scaffolded participation in reading and writing. Such teaching requires consistent detailed monitoring of students as they read and write, as well as detailed understanding of the reading and writing tasks themselves, in order to envision how students can be encouraged as they attempt those tasks.

Pamela El-Dinary and Mike Pressley (e.g., Pressley & El-Dinary, 1997; see also Deshler & Schumaker, 1993; Klingner et al., 1999, 2004) found that it was very challenging for teachers to become balanced comprehension instruction teachers. Complex articulations of components must occur if students are going to learn the decoding and comprehension skills so that they can apply them in real reading and writing. As work on balanced teaching proceeds, it is imperative that the research community be sensitive to the challenging nature of such teaching, making it a priority to conduct research that reveals how teachers can overcome the challenges to becoming maximally effective teachers.

In our view, those education faculty members in colleges and universities who wish to inform young adults about how to be teachers must immerse themselves in elementary schooling. As scholars who have done so, we have become adept at spotting those faculty colleagues who are so grounded and those who are not. There is no need for more books by individuals who have not spent extensive time in the school settings they wish to affect. There now exist powerful observational approaches that can inform scholars about complex settings, such as classrooms. It is the scholars who choose to wrap themselves in those methods and devote their days to on-site classroom analyses who deserve the attention of the educator community. We would have never come to the insights about teaching reflected in this volume without those hundreds of mornings and days spent in elementary classrooms during the past four decades.

Longitudinal Research

It is part of our being to believe in the longitudinal study of development—to believe that much can be learned by following individual children for a number of years. To some extent, there has been longitudinal study of literacy development, but unfortunately such study has often failed to provide the types of comprehensive descriptions of development and explanations of developmental differences that are needed to make one feel confident that much is really known about the children being studied. Thus, there are now a number of studies examining quantitative indicators of phonemic awareness in 4- and 5-year-olds as predictors of standardized test achievement in the elementary grades. We have never felt that we knew much about these children after reading such studies, however. But when more detailed descriptions have been provided (e.g., Snow et al., 1991), important insights have emerged on such issues as why schooling becomes more important with increasing age as students' progress through it. (Homes of at-risk students are more certain to be able to provide support of primary-level skills than skills developed in later grades.) Snow and colleagues' (1991) work also made clear in vividly concrete ways the discontinuities in the quality of teaching as children progress through school, as well as the consequences of such discontinuities.

Such work is really critical because American students do experience discontinuities in their schooling. The assumption that students receive either meaning-emphasis or skills-emphasis instruction exclusively fails many times because a student can have a meaning-emphasis teacher one year and a skills-emphasis teacher the next. Is it not possible that, were balanced instruction to become the majority view, instruction might become more continuous from one grade to the next for many more children? We think this possibility is worth exploring. Moreover, the effects of such year-to-year continuity on literacy development should also be evaluated.

Extending Elementary Reading Principles Into the Middle School and High School Years

No one could come away from reading this book without appreciating the enormous amount that has been learned during the past three decades about literacy development in the preschool and elementary years. It is striking how much attention has been given to young children's literacy development, however, as compared with students in the upper elementary, middle, and high school years. That really needs to change because many middle school and high school students need reading instruction.

As researchers who have principally focused on elementary school, we are proud of the many reforms in American elementary education that are linked to research. In contrast, there has been much less reform in the secondary schools, and often the reform that has occurred is not inspired so much by research as by inspiring visions of high school education, such as Theodore R. Sizer's (e.g., 1996) essential schools. The excitement of change in the local elementary school often is not mirrored by exciting changes in the district's middle school or high school.

Amid the backdrop of little or no research-based change in secondary schools—although, see Jetton and Dole (2004)—there is one important exception. Some special educators have made enormous progress in developing, validating, and disseminating effective literacy instruction to students with learning disabilities (e.g., Deshler & Schumaker, 1993). We cannot tell you how many times we have heard secondary literacy educators react to descriptions of the work of Deshler and Shumaker with the appraisal that "all high school students need to learn the comprehension and writing strategies that students with learning disabilities are being taught." There is enough research on literacy-strategies instruction at the secondary level for us to respond confidently that such claims are on target (see Deshler & Hock, 2007; Deshler et al., 2001, 2007; Ivey & Johnston, 2013; Wood et al., 1995).

TEN DANGEROUS CLAIMS ABOUT READING INSTRUCTION

There are many strong claims being made about reading instruction, many of which fly in the face of considerable data. In this section, we offer what we consider to be 10 dangerous claims about reading instruction that are commonplace in contemporary conversations about education. Of course, we are aware that others might order these claims differently, or even have alternative claims that they feel should be on the list. Nonetheless, we think by providing such a list—and briefly reminding readers of the evidence that counters each of these claims—we can provide an effective review of some of the most disturbing beliefs about reading instruction that are not in synchrony with scientific evidence.

1. *When otherwise normal students have difficulties learning to read, there is a neurological basis for the problem, and thus instruction will do little good.* In fact, dyslexia is incredibly rare as compared with reading failures due to lack of appropriate instruction. Almost all children who experience difficulties in learning to decode, given normal classroom instruction, benefit from more expert and more intensive instruction, such as is provided by small group instruction or one-on-one tutoring.

2. *Students learn to read in the first three grades and read to learn after that.* Even learning to decode is far from complete by the end of grade 3, so there is much learning to read yet to be accomplished. There is also much left to accomplish with respect to comprehension—good reason to continue teaching students to read long after the primary years are completed. In addition, it should be emphasized that even during the height of learning to read—in grades 1 to 3—children are learning while they read if they are reading worthwhile texts.

3. *Teachers who use published reading materials or teach skills are being de-skilled themselves.* These claims, which are embraced by some meaning-emphasis enthusiasts, are not true. In fact, when effective teachers use published programs, they typically do not follow the prescriptions in the programs blindly; rather, they pick and choose, using the components and activities of the published programs that make sense in their own reading programs. We hope commercial reading materials will soon evidence the substantial research that is available because it is evident the current materials do not. We also urge teachers to do their own research rather than just blindly following a reading curriculum or professional development handed to them by their district.

4. *Meaning-emphasis models, such as whole language, do not promote literacy.* Immersion in reading and writing experiences increases understanding of the elements of reading and writing, such as the structural characteristics of stories and other types of writing. Hearing and reading stories increases vocabulary and world knowledge. Invented spelling experiences promote understanding of the sound structure of words. What many meaning-emphasis primary grade classrooms do not promote sufficiently for many students, however, are letter-level, letter–sound, and word recognition skills.

5. *Children will come to phonemic awareness and discover the letter and sound facts through immersion in reading and writing alone. Teaching these competencies rather than allowing them to emerge naturally might do some harm; for example, it could decrease children's motivation to read.* Yes, meaning-emphasis immersion results in some learning of phonemic awareness and phonics, but much more can be accomplished through more explicit teaching of skills than occurs in meaning-emphasis environments. The idea that teaching interferes with natural development is an old one with no credible evidence in support of it. Indeed, with respect to motivation, leaving a child to struggle and experience failures and frustrations has very high potential to undermine motivation to read.

6. *If a child experiences difficulties in learning to decode, simply wait and the child will learn to read when ready.* Children who are behind at the

end of grade 3 typically remain behind throughout their schooling. Rather than waiting and hoping that the child catches on to reading, real progress can be made with early, expert teaching that promotes reading development in children experiencing difficulties in early reading. Unfortunately, not all American schools have the resources to provide expert and intensive reading interventions in kindergarten through grade 3. Thus, while we have accumulated research demonstrating that virtually all children could be reading grade level by the end of grade 3 (Mathes et al., 2005; Phillips & Smith, 2010; Scanlon & Anderson, 2020; Vellutino et al., 1996), most schools continue to flunk or classify these low-achieving pupils as students with learning disabilities. Classification as a pupil with a learning disability rarely results in more expert and more intensive interventions so reading development falters and such children rarely become proficient readers (Judge & Bell, 2011).

7. *Short-term tutoring for students experiencing reading difficulties can get them on par with other students, and those students will stay on par once tutoring has concluded.* For students experiencing difficulties in school, sustained, long-term excellent instruction is more likely to be successful than short-term instruction. Vellutino et al. (2007) noted, however, that in four of the schools that enrolled students from their kindergarten and grade 1 intervention study, 100% of the at-risk students who participated in their tutorial intervention were reading on grade level at the end of grade 3, while fewer than 60% of similar students enrolled in four other schools had attained that level of proficiency. In other words, schools with at-risk children who attended had an impact on their continued reading development. It seems that, when at-risk students are brought to grade-level reading achievement through expert and early intensive interventions, many will continue to develop on-level reading skills but only if the ongoing quality of classroom reading lessons is consistently high.

8. *Students become good comprehenders if they just read, read, and read.* There is substantial evidence that children improve their reading comprehension with extensive reading practice. However, these same students become much better comprehenders if they are taught to use the active comprehension processes that skilled readers use. As is true for phonemic awareness and word recognition skills proficiency, both improve with wide reading activity, but all students do not seem to discover sophisticated comprehension strategies through immersion in reading alone. Research suggests (Almasi & Garas-York, 2009; Malloy & Gambrell, 2011) a powerful potential role for developing higher-order comprehension proficiencies through engaging readers in conversations, or discussions, of what they have been reading.

9. *Students should be taught to give priority to meaning (i.e., seman-tic–contextual) cues in word recognition.* This is a very dated idea that just has not died because of some meaning-emphasis theorists' embrace of it, despite analyses making it clear that good readers give priority to phono-logical, letter-combination, and word-chunk cues in word recognition. In addition, instruction that emphasizes sounding out and decoding by anal-ogy promotes word recognition more than does instruction emphasizing semantic contexts. That does not mean that semantic–contextual cues play no role. Such cues permit evaluation of whether an attempted decoding based on phonological or orthographic cues is accurate. However, the role that semantic–contextual cues play comes after the word is pronounced. It is the use of these cues that allow readers to self-correct their misreading of a word because the word pronounced made no sense in the sentence. Such self-correction was identified as a potent predictor of which children became proficient readers (Clay, 1969).

10. *Skills-emphasis instruction and meaning-emphasis instruction are incompatible.* Systematic skills instruction has a reasonable track record, and there are plenty of effective balanced-literacy teachers who carry out systematic instruction of skills, scaffolding student use of skills into real reading and writing. Such teachers are proof that systematic skills instruc-tion can occur in the context of extensive reading of literature and student writing. The case for balanced teaching as detailed in this book is a case for optimism that many children can learn to read better than they would if the 10 ideas just reviewed were to prevail in determining who is taught and how.

We hope that this book permits many more teachers, parents, and policymakers to realize that the thinking reviewed in this top-10 list should not continue to affect educational decision making.

FINAL COMMENTS

Much has been learned about what makes sense in elementary reading instruction. Still, the meaning-emphasis and skills-emphasis proponents continue to try and shout one another down. This is a debate that has endured for at least 100 years!

Analogously, reading involves the development of skills but also practice in their application during reading and writing tasks that are appropriately challenging to students. That is why the balanced model of instruction is a better model than either the skills-emphasis approach or the meaning-emphasis approach. Balanced instruction involves much more systematic instruction of skills than do most meaning-emphasis models, with its emphasis on teaching only when there is demonstrated need. But balance also suggests much more involvement with literature and writing than occurs in many skills-emphasis classrooms.

When students are skilled in reading and writing and their motivation is maintained through appropriately challenging literacy experiences, they read and write more. Lack of skills, which is a danger of meaning-emphasis approaches, has a high potential to undermine long-term motivation for literacy. Lack of exposure to interesting reading and writing experiences, which can characterize skills-emphasis classrooms, also can undermine motivation for literacy experiences since children, like everyone else, thrive on interesting experiences and are turned off by boredom. Balanced literacy instruction is the best bet for maintaining and even enhancing student motivation to do literate things, providing students with the skills they need to be successful in reading and writing and having them practice those skills by reading interesting books and writing about topics that are important to them.

Before we end the fifth edition of this book, we feel obligated to address a question often posed to us: Why did we not say more about assessment, a topic so much on the minds of many present-day educational policymakers? One answer is that this is a book about instruction. The other is that assessment has just not been that visible in the excellent classrooms that we have studied, with one exception: Excellent teachers are always informally assessing their students, monitoring where each student is and what each student needs. The excellent teacher acts on that monitoring, providing appropriate instruction or direction to each and every student in the room.

Although excellent teachers give curriculum-based tests—for example, spelling tests and sight-word fluency assessments—there is very little concern with standardized tests among these teachers. Yes, they may give their students short-term practice in filling in bubble sheets just before the children take such tests, but they do not obsess nor do they massively change their curriculum in advance of school- or state-mandated tests. That said, we have heard many of the best teachers we have studied express great reservations about the validity of the standardized assessments forced on them. In short, the excellent balanced teachers we have encountered seem to think like the assessment scholars we most admire (Johnston, 2005; Johnston & Rogers, 2001; Murphy et al., 1998; Paris, 2005; Paris & Paris, 2003; Paris & Urdan, 2001). They see great value in informal assessment and do it constantly, but they are not convinced of the validity of many standardized tests (see especially Johnston & Rogers, 2001). They do not view standardized assessments as doing much good for the kids they teach, and they feel that every school day should be filled only with activities that are good for their students' heads and hearts.

That said, we know that the national obsession with assessment is going to continue. As it does, we hope there is some better thinking brought to the enterprise about what should be measured. Jill Fitzgerald (Fitzgerald & Noblit, 2000), a distinguished literacy scholar, decided to teach grade 1 for a year and committed to do it in a balanced fashion, as described in this book. As Jill did so, she came to a number of insights about how the children in her class were growing:

1. Phonological awareness increased.
2. Sight-word knowledge increased.
3. Children's matching of letters and sounds improved, as did their knowledge of orthographic patterns in words.
4. Children's word recognition strategies increased and improved, with children using visual–letter cues, syntactic cues, and contextual meaning cues.
5. Their vocabularies expanded.
6. Students came to understand that reading was about understanding and communicating, and as they did so, they communicated more about what they learned from reading.
7. They developed a love of reading and wanted to do more reading.
8. They learned to respond to literature emotionally (e.g., loving a story, being scared).
9. One of those emotions was joy in becoming better readers, being able to do something they could not do previously.

These are huge accomplishments, with contemporary standardized assessments only tapping some of them. As this assessment animal matures, we hope new measures are developed that better capture all of these dimensions.

In recent years, much of what has been said about beginning literacy instruction has been nothing more than rancorous and partisan bickering. Alternatively, discussions about beginning literacy can be healthy and lead to additional research on elementary reading instruction that can inform practice. We hope it is the latter—but even if it is not, we are confident that much revealing reading instructional research is yet to come. Thus, the conclusions offered in this fifth edition are only for the time being, subject to revision in light of new evidence.

APPENDIX 12.1. LANDMARKS IN DEVELOPMENT OF LITERACY COMPETENCE (OR, WHAT HAPPENS WHEN)

0–2 YEARS OF AGE (INFANCY)

- Emergent literacy experiences begin; infants who have rich verbal interactions during infancy are advantaged over those who do not, with language development beginning from birth. For example, vocabulary development is more extensive with rich language interactions.

- A secure parent–child attachment sets the stage for healthier emergent literacy experiences than if attachment is insecure.

- Prior knowledge development is schematic from infancy onward, with the children's schematic knowledge reflective of the experiences they have had (e.g., children have schemata for what happens at fast-food restaurants when they pay many visits to McDonald's and Burger King).

2–5 YEARS OF AGE (PRESCHOOL YEARS)

- Many and diverse emergent literacy experiences are possible; readiness for school-based literacy instruction is determined in part by the quality and quantity of emergent literacy experiences.

- Over the long term, rich verbal and cognitive interactions with adults result in internalization of verbal and cognitive skills that are critically relevant to reading. Thus, egocentric speech is more prevalent in the early preschool years than in later years, when inner speech predominates.

- When parents are not naturally adept at emergent literacy interactions, they can often be taught to be so, with improvements in children's language being the result.

- Learning the names of the alphabetic letters is an important acquisition, as is learning the letter–sound associations. Such learning is acquired in a variety of ways, from interactions with parents to viewing of such programs as *Sesame Street*.

- Word recognition skills begin to develop, with preschoolers, for example, able to read logographs (e.g., McDonald's, as long as the name is on the famous golden arches logo). Four-year-olds can use analogies based on word chunks to some extent to read new words (e.g., if a child is shown the word *bee*, she or he can recognize that *see* is like *bee* in that both include the *-ee* part).

- The beginnings of phonemic awareness sometimes are stimulated through such parent–child activities as reading of rhymes and playing of rhyming games.

- Children can begin to write, with the first invented spellings often only the first consonant of a word, and one- or two-word stories that the child can expand to many words and sentences as she or he "reads" the story back to another child or an adult.

5–7 YEARS OF AGE (LAST YEAR OF PRESCHOOL AND EARLY PRIMARY GRADES)

- Academic motivation is at its highest during the primary years. Students tend to believe they can succeed if they try.

- Complete phonemic awareness typically does not develop through emergent literacy experiences alone but can be activated through instruction during kindergarten, which can have a positive impact on later learning. The instruction typically involves a variety of activities aimed at students listening for sounds in words and manipulating the various sounds in words. When such phonemic-awareness instruction is added to meaning-emphasis preschool and kindergarten experiences, there are positive effects on later literacy development.

- Alphabetic reading begins for many children, including approximations to it at first (e.g., reading a word based on only a few salient letters).

- Formal schooling now includes daily reading and composing from the first days of kindergarten. As students gain proficiency in reading and writing words, the diversity of reading and writing activities expands.

- Children can learn to decode through phonics instruction. They can also learn to decode through analogy-based approaches. There is no logical reason that phonics and analogy-based approaches cannot be combined, as children learning via phonics can acquire knowledge of word parts as they experience them and children learning by initial focus on word parts can also learn to blend the sounds produced by word chunks with individual sounds (e.g., blending the sounds of s and -ee to pronounce see). There is a lot of evidence that effective decoding instruction involves teaching students how to analyze words with respect to component sounds and how to blend those sounds. As students learn to decode, their automatic sight-word skills improve (i.e., words decoded frequently become sight words).

- Excellent classrooms involve a balancing of meaning-emphasis experiences (i.e., reading of real texts, composition) and skills instruction. Teachers scaffold student use of skills during realistic reading and writing. There also is integration of literacy and content-area instruction. There is good reason to suspect that classrooms that are either extremely skills oriented or extremely anti-skills oriented are not as effective as more balanced classrooms.

- Some 20–30% of normally intelligent grade 1 students experience difficulties learning to decode. Most of these students can learn to decode with more expert and intensive instruction.

- Children can begin to learn writing strategies, specifically, strategies for planning, drafting, and revising, with possibly multiple-page stories by the end of the first grade.

- Vocabulary acquisition continues, with explicit teaching of vocabulary having an impact over and above the incidental learning of vocabulary from immersion in a rich language environment.

7-11 YEARS OF AGE (LATER-PRIMARY AND UPPER-ELEMENTARY GRADES)

- Academic motivation tends to decline. This is especially likely the more a student experiences academic failures and frustrations. Students' faith in success with effort declines during the elementary years. Students increasingly view academic frustrations as indications of low ability.

- Classroom competition increases with increasing grade level, with the potential to undermine the motivation of many students, who increasingly notice how they do as compared with others and interpret their relative failures as signaling low ability. Good grades given to good readers are not unambiguously beneficial for them either, having the potential to undermine the intrinsic motivation to read that many good readers bring to the task. That is, good readers can come to justify the reading they are doing as motivated by good grades; in situations where there are no grades for reading, there is no longer an incentive to read.

- Effective classrooms emphasize that effort matters, sending the message that trying hard fosters achievement and intelligence, failure is a natural part of learning, and school is more about getting better than being the best. Rewarding students for improvement rather than performance relative to others promotes academic motivation.

- With increasing grade level, there is greater variability in the core emphases in classrooms. That is, first-grade classes across the country typically are more similar to each other than to fifth-grade classes in the same school. Some core emphases (e.g., encouragement of comprehension-strategies use) can make a significant positive difference in the development of literacy competence in grades 2 through 5.

- Comprehension strategies can be taught, typically resulting in improved understanding of texts, especially if strategies instruction is long term and thoroughly integrated across the school day. Many times, however, such skills are not taught as explicitly or extensively as they could be taught. Consequently, students are not as active in their reading.

- Excellent classrooms report a balancing of meaning-emphasis and skills-emphasis instruction. Teachers scaffold use of skills during realistic reading and writing. There also is integration of literary and content-area instruction.

- Reading of novels becomes an important language arts activity.

- With greater reading, automatic word recognition increases, as does the extent of vocabulary and other knowledge. Those who do a lot of reading become better readers than those who do little reading.

- Teaching of vocabulary continues to make sense, with many words for the student to learn.

- Writing emphasizes even more planning, drafting, and revising processes. Conventions and spelling are emphasized increasingly with advancing grade levels.

- Students begin to experience content-area texts, many of which are not interesting. When students have some choice in what they read, motivation is higher.

BEYOND THE ELEMENTARY YEARS

- Skilled reading is both top-down (e.g., predictions about the upcoming text based on prior knowledge) and bottom-up (e.g., individual letters and words are processed).

- Skilled readers can read at 200–300 words per minute, processing most words, and indeed most letters within words, as they read. Eye movement is from left to right within each line of text, with fixations on informative words.

- Skilled readers rely more on letter- and word-level graphemic–phonological cues (including recognition of common word parts) for word recognition than do unskilled readers. Unskilled readers attend more to semantic–contextual cues than do skilled readers in attempting to recognize (i.e., decode) a word. Once a word is recognized, however, good readers use semantic–contextual cues to determine the exact meaning of the decoded word in the present context and do so with greater certainty and success than less skilled readers.

- Skilled readers effortlessly recognize many words (i.e., they have large sight vocabularies). Such effortful recognition of sight words frees up short-term cognitive capacity, permitting it to be used for comprehension.

- Skilled readers probably continue to benefit from vocabulary instruction over and above the vocabulary learning that occurs incidentally.

- Good readers remember the gist of what they read, to some extent as an automatic consequence of reading the text. Comprehension and memory of text, however, are also enhanced through the use of a variety of active comprehension strategies, which are enabled, in part, by extensive prior knowledge, permitting construction of bridging inferences.

- For those who did not make progress in learning to write in the elementary grades, planning, drafting, and revising strategies can still be taught with great benefit.

- Reading skills continue to develop well into adulthood.

- Many adults remain unskilled readers, from those who cannot decode at all to many others who cannot do things commonly attributed to skilled readers.

REFERENCES

Allington, R. L. (2002). *Big brother and the national reading curriculum: How ideology trumped evidence.* Heinemann.

Almasi, J. F., & Garas-York, K. (2009). Comprehension and peer discussion. In S. Israel & G. G. Duffy (Eds.), *Handbook of research on reading comprehension* (pp. 470–493). Erlbaum.

Applebee, A. N., Langer, J. A., Nystrand, M., & Gamoran, A. (2003). Discussion-based approaches to developing understanding: Classroom instruction and student performance in middle and high school English. *American Educational Research Journal*, *40*(3), 685–730.

Baker, S., Gersten, R., & Keating, T. (2000). When less may be more: A 2-year longitudinal evaluation of a volunteer tutoring program requiring minimal training. *Reading Research Quarterly*, *35*, 494–519.

Brainerd, C. J. (1978). Learning research and Piagetian theory. In L. S. Siegel & C. J. Brainerd (Eds.), *Alternatives to Piaget: Critical essays on the theory* (pp. 69–109). Academic Press.

Clay, M. M. (1969). Reading errors and self-correction behaviour. *British Journal of Educational Psychology*, *37*, 47–56.

Connor, C. M., & Morrison, F. J. (2016). Individualizing student instruction in reading: Implications for policy and practice. *Policy Insights from the Behavioral and Brain Sciences*, *3*(1), 54–61.

Connor, C. M., Morrison, F. J., & Petrella, J. N. (2004). Effective reading comprehension instruction: Examining child x instruction interactions. *Journal of Educational Psychology*, *96*(4), 682–698.

Cunningham, J. W. (2001). The National Reading Panel report. *Reading Research Quarterly*, *30*(3), 326–335.

Dahl, K. L., & Freppon, P. A. (1995). A comparison of inner-city children's interpretations of reading and writing instruction in the early grades in skills-based and whole language classrooms. *Reading Research Quarterly*, *30*, 50–74.

Dahl, K. L., Scharer, P. L., & Lawson, L. L. (1999). Phonics instruction and student achievement in whole language first-grade classrooms. *Reading Research Quarterly*, *34*(3), 312–341.

Deshler, D. D., & Hock, M. F. (2007). Adolescent literacy: Where we are, where we need to go. In M. P. Pressley, A. K. Billman, K. H. Perry, K. E. Reffitt, & J. M. Reynolds (Eds.), *Shaping literacy achievement: Research we need* (pp. 98–128). Guilford Press.

Deshler, D. D., Palinscar, A. S., Biancarosa, G., & Nair, M. (2007). *Informed choices for struggling adolescent readers: A research-based guide to instructional programs and practices*. International Reading Association.

Deshler, D. D., & Schumaker, J. B. (1993). Strategy mastery by at-risk students: Not a simple matter. *Elementary School Journal*, *94*, 153–167.

Deshler, D. D., Schumaker, J. B., Lenz, B. K., Bulgren, J. A., Hock, M. F., Knight, J., & Ehren, B. J. (2001). Ensuring content-area learning by secondary students with learning disabilities. *Learning Disabilities Research & Practice*, *16*(2), 96–108.

Dewey, J. (1933). *How we think: A restatement of the relation of reflective thinking in the education process*. Heath.

Elbaum, B., Vaughn, S., Hughes, M. T., & Moody, S. W. (2000). How effective are one-to-one tutoring programs in reading for elementary students at risk for reading failure? A meta-analysis of the intervention research. *Journal of Educational Psychology*, *92*, 605–619.

Fitzgerald, J. (2001). Can minimally trained college student volunteers help young at-risk children to read better? *Reading Research Quarterly*, *36*, 28–47.

Fitzgerald, J., & Noblit, G. (2000). Balance in the making: Learning to read in an ethnically diverse first-grade classroom. *Journal of Educational Psychology*, *92*, 3–22.

Freppon, P. A., & McIntyre, E. (1999). A comparison of young children learning to read in different instructional settings. *Journal of Educational Research*, *92*(4), 206–217.

Gamse, B. C., Jacob, R. T., Horst, M., Boulay, B., & Unlu, F. (2009). *Reading First Impact Study: Final report* (NCEE 2009–4038). National Center for Education Evaluation and Regional Assistance, Institute of Education Sciences, U.S. Department of Education.

Goodwin, A. P., & Jiménez, R. T. (2020). The science of reading: Supports, critiques, and questions. *Reading Research Quarterly, 55*, S7–S22.

Goodwin, A. P., & Jiménez, R. T. (2021). The science of reading: Supports, critiques, and questions. *Reading Research Quarterly, 56*, S7–S22.

Hammill, D. D., & Swanson, H. L. (2006). The National Reading Panel's meta-analysis of phonics instruction: Another point of view. *The Elementary School Journal, 107*(1), 17–26.

Harris, K. R., & Pressley, M. (1991). The nature of cognitive strategy instruction: Interactive strategy construction. *Exceptional Children, 57*, 392–404.

Inhelder, B., Sinclair, H., & Bovet, M. (1974). *Learning and the development of cognition.* Harvard University Press.

Institute of Educational Sciences. (2021, December 12). IES Reading Summit [Video]. Viewed at *www.youtube.com/playlist?list=PLkEhwZQdyNEEdolnYmOX2YhX1EhlFpC4k.*

Invernizzi, M., Juel, C., & Rosemary, C. A. (1997). A community tutorial that works. *The Reading Teacher, 50*, 304–311.

Ivey, G., & Johnston, P. H. (2013). Engagement with young adult literature: Outcomes and processes. *Reading Research Quarterly, 48*(3), 255–275.

Jetton, T. L., & Dole, J. A. (Eds.). (2004). *Adolescent literacy research and practice.* Guilford Press.

Johnston, P. H. (2004). *Choice words: How our language affects children's learning.* Stenhouse.

Johnston, P. H. (2005). Literacy assessment and the future. *The Reading Teacher, 58*(7), 684–686.

Johnston, P. H., & Rogers, R. (2001). Early literacy development: The case for "informed assessment." In S. B. Neuman & D. K. Dickinson (Eds.), *Handbook of early literacy research* (pp. 377–389). Guilford Press.

Jordan, G. E., Snow, C. E., & Porche, M. V. (2000). Project EASE: The effect of a family literacy project on kindergarten students' early literacy skills. *Reading Research Quarterly, 35*, 524–546.

Judge, S., & Bell, S. M. (2011). Reading achievement trajectories for students with learning disabilities during the elementary school years. *Reading and Writing Quarterly, 27*(1), 153–178.

Kintsch, W., & van Dijk, T. A. (1978). Toward a model of discourse comprehension and production. *Psychological Review, 85*, 363–394.

Klingner, J. K., Vaughn, S., Arguelles, M. E., Hughes, M. T., & Leftwich, S. A. (2004). Collaborative strategic reading: "Real-world" lessons from classroom teachers. *Remedial and Special Education, 25*, 291–302.

Klingner, J. K., Vaughn, S., Hughes, M. T., & Arguelles, M. E. (1999). Sustaining research-based practices in reading: A 3-year follow-up. *Remedial and Special Education, 20*, 263–274.

Kohlberg, L., & Mayer, R. (1972). Development as the aim of education: The Dewey view. *Harvard Educational Review, 42*, 449–496.

LaBerge, D., & Samuels, S. J. (1974). Toward a theory of automatic information processing in reading. *Cognitive Psychology, 6*, 293–323.

Lonigan, C. J., & Shanahan, T. (2009). *Executive summary: Developing early literacy: Report of the National Early Literacy Panel.* National Institute for Literacy.

Malloy, J. A., & Gambrell, L. B. (2011). The contribution of discussion to reading comprehension and critical thinking. In A. McGill-Franzen & R. L. Allington (Eds.), *Handbook of reading disability research* (pp. 253–261). Routledge.

Mathes, P. G., Denton, C. A., Fletcher, J. M., Anthony, J. L., Francis, D. J., & Schatschneider, C. (2005). The effects of theoretically different instruction and student characteristics on the skills of struggling readers. *Reading Research Quarterly, 40*(2), 148–182.

Mayer, R. E. (2004). Should there be a three-strikes rule against pure discovery learning? *American Psychologist, 59*, 14–19.

McGill-Franzen, A., Allington, R. L., Yokoi, L., & Brooks, G. (1999). Putting books in the classroom seems necessary but not sufficient. *Journal of Educational Research, 93*(2), 67–74.

McIntyre, E., & Freppon, P. A. (1994). A comparison of children's development of alphabetic knowledge in a skills-based and a whole-language classroom. *Research in Teaching of English, 28*(4), 391–417.

Morrow, L. M., & Young, J. (1997). Parent, teacher, and child participation in a collaborative family literacy program: The effects of attitude, motivation, and literacy achievement. *Journal of Educational Psychology, 89*, 736–742.

Murphy, S., with Shannon, P., Johnston, P., & Hansen, J. (1998). *Fragile evidence: A critique of reading assessment.* Erlbaum.

National Reading Panel. (2000). *Teaching children to read: An evidence-based assessment of the scientific research literature on reading and its implications for reading instruction—reports of the subgroups.* National Institute of Child Health and Human Development.

No Child Left Behind Act of 2001. (2002). Public Law 107-110.

Nystrand, M. (2006). Research on the role of classroom discourse as it affects reading comprehension. *Research in the Teaching of English, 40*, 392–412.

Paris, A. H., & Paris, S. G. (2003). Assessing narrative competence in young children. *Reading Research Quarterly, 38*(1), 36–76.

Paris, S. G. (2005). Reinterpreting the development of reading skills. *Reading Research Quarterly, 40*(2), 184–202.

Paris, S. G., & Urdan, T. (2001). Policies and practices of high-stakes testing that influence teachers and schools. *Issues in Education, 6*, 83–107.

Pearson, P. D., & Hiebert, E. H. (2010). National reports in literacy: Building a scientific base for practice and policy. *Educational Researcher, 39*(4), 286–294.

Phillips, G., & Smith, P. (2010). Closing the gaps: Literacy for the hardest to teach. In P. Johnston (Ed.), *RTI in literacy: Responsive and comprehensive* (pp. 219–246). International Reading Association.

Pressley, M., & Afflerbach, P. (1995). *Verbal protocols of reading.* Erlbaum.

Pressley, M., Dolezal, S. E., Raphael, L. M., Mohan, L., Roehrig, A. D. & Bogner, K. (2003). *Motivating primary grade children.* Guilford Press.

Pressley, M., Duke, N. K., & Boling, E. C. (2004). The educational science and scientifically-based instruction we need: Lessons from reading research and policy making. *Harvard Educational Review, 74*, 30–61.

Pressley, M., & El-Dinary, P. B. (1997). What we know about translating comprehension strategies instruction research into practice. *Journal of Learning Disabilities, 30*, 486–488.

Pressley, M., El-Dinary, P. B., Gaskins, I., Schuder, T., Bergman, J. L., Almasi, J., et al. (1992). Beyond direct explanation: Transactional instruction of reading comprehension strategies. *Elementary School Journal, 92*, 511–554.

Pressley, M., Harris, K. R., & Marks, M. B. (1992). But good strategy instructors are constructivists! *Educational Psychology Review, 4*, 1–32.

RAND Reading Study Group. (2001). *Reading for understanding: Toward an R&D program in reading comprehension.*

Scanlon, D. M., & Anderson, K. L. (2020). Using context as an assist in word solving: The contributions of 25 years of research on the Interactive Strategies Approach. *Reading Research Quarterly, 55*, S19–S34.

Scanlon, D. M., Gelzheiser, L. M., Vellutino, F. R., Schatschneider, C., & Sweeney, J. M. (2010). Reducing the incidence of early reading difficulties: Professional development for classroom teachers versus direct interventions for children. In P. H. Johnston (Ed.), *RTI in literacy: Responsive and comprehensive* (pp. 257–295). International Reading Association.

Schauble, L. (1990). Belief revision in children: The role of prior knowledge and strategies for generating evidence. *Journal of Experimental Child Psychology, 49,* 31–57.

Shulman, L. S., & Keislar, E. R. (Eds.). (1966). *Learning by discovery: A critical appraisal.* Rand McNally.

Sizer, T. R. (1996). *Horace's hope: What works for the American high school.* Houghton Mifflin.

Snow, C. E., Barnes, W. S., Chandler, J., Goodman, I. F., & Hemphill, L. (1991). *Unfulfilled expectations: Home and school influences on literacy.* Harvard University Press.

Snow, C. E., Burns, M. S., & Griffin, P. (1998). *Preventing reading difficulties in young children.* National Academy Press.

Vellutino, F. R., Scanlon, D. M., Sipay, E. R., Small, S. G., Pratt, A., Chen, R., et al. (1996). Cognitive profiles of difficult-to-remediate and readily remediated poor readers: Early intervention as a vehicle for distinguishing between cognitive and experiential deficits as basic causes of specific reading disability. *Journal of Educational Psychology, 88*(4), 601–638.

Vellutino, F. R., Scanlon, D. M., Small, S. G., Fanuele, D. P., & Sweeney, J. M. (2007). Preventing early reading difficulties through intervention in kindergarten and first grade: A variant on the three tier model. In D. Haager, J. Klingner, & S. Vaughn (Eds.), *Evidence-based reading practices for Response to Intervention* (pp. 185–219). Brookes.

Vygotsky, L. S. (1978). *Mind in society: The development of higher psychological processes.* Harvard University Press.

Wasik, B. A. (1998). Volunteer tutoring programs in reading: A review. *Reading Research Quarterly, 33,* 266–292.

Wittrock, M. C. (1966). The learning by discovery hypothesis. In L. S. Shulman & E. R. Keislar (Eds.), *Learning by discovery: A critical appraisal* (pp. 33–75). Rand McNally.

Wood, E., Woloshyn, V. E., & Willoughby, T. (Eds.). (1995). *Cognitive strategy instruction for middle and high schools.* Brookline Books.

Wu, X., Anderson, R. C., Nguyen-Jahiel, K., & Miller, B. (2013). Enhancing motivation and engagement through collaborative discussion. *Journal of Educational Psychology, 105*(3), 622–632.

Author Index

Subject Index

Note. *f* or *t* following a page number indicates a figure or table.

research reports regarding reading
    instruction and, 27
struggling readers and, 53–54, 55–59, 69–72
through analogy to known words, 152–160,
    154t
through letter sounds, 151–152
Word ID approach and, 153–158, 154t
Word recognition skills. *See also* Word reading
    balanced approach to literacy instruction
        and, 446
    blending letter–sound correspondences and,
        139–150, 142t
    brain imagery research and, 188–189
    claims about reading instruction and, 444
    comprehension instruction and, 277, 284
    decline of motivation during the elementary
        years and, 382
    decontextualized word recognition, 39–41
    development of, 128–135, 169
    emergent bilingual (EB) students and, 316
    fluency and, 196–197
    instructional practices and, 430
    letter–sound relationships and, 136–138, 138f
    literacy development and, 447, 449, 450
    overview, 127–128, 162–171
    phonics instruction and, 135–150, 138f,
        142t, 167–169
    research reports regarding reading
        instruction and, 25

skilled reading and, 49
struggling readers and, 53–55, 59–60,
    62
Word ID approach and, 153–158, 154t
Word-level processes. *See also* Word reading;
    Word recognition skills
    instructional practices and, 247, 431
    literacy development and, 450
    skilled reading and, 37–41, 49–50
    word-part clues, 226
Working memory, 59, 60, 191–192. *See also*
    Executive function skills; Memory
World knowledge, 97–98, 279–282, 442. *See
    also* Background knowledge
Writing
    emergent bilingual (EB) students and, 319,
        319f, 321t
    increasing motivation and, 403
    literacy development and, 446–450
    literacy instruction in fourth and fifth grades
        and, 247
    science of reading (SOR) and, 30
    teaching quality and, 349, 350, 351,
        352–353, 358, 359, 360–361, 371,
        372

Z
Zone of proximal development, 84–85,
    257–259, 436